BASIC
ECONOMICS

BASIC ECONOMICS

A Common Sense Guide to the Economy

THOMAS SOWELL

Third Edition

BASIC
BOOKS
A Member of the Perseus Books Group
New York

Books published by Basic Books are available at special discounts for bulk purchases in the United States by corporations, institutions, and other organizations. For more information, please contact the Special Markets Department at the Perseus Books Group, 11 Cambridge Center, Cambridge, MA 02142, or call (617) 252-5298 or (800) 255-1514, or e-mail special.markets@perseusbooks.com.

Library of Congress Cataloging-in-Publication Data

Sowell, Thomas, 1930-
  Basic economics : a common sense guide to the economy / Thomas Sowell.
—3rd ed.
    p. cm.
  Includes index.
  ISBN-13: 978-0-465-00260-3 (hardcover : alk. paper)
  ISBN-10: 0-465-00260-9 (hardcover : alk. paper) 1. Economics. I. Title.

HB171.S713 2007
330--dc22

                                                2006039835

10 9 8 7 6 5 4

A few lines of reasoning can change the way we see the world.

Steven E. Landsburg

CONTENTS

PREFACE

This is a book for the general public or for beginning students in economics. Its sales at home and its translations overseas[1] suggest that there is a widespread desire for *readable* information on economics, as distinguished from the jargon, graphs, and equations that are all too common in writings on the subject. *Basic Economics* has been updated and upgraded from previous editions and a new chapter has been added, but the changes that have been made have not been made just for the sake of change, and the benefits of the basic organization and presentation of the book have been retained in this expanded third edition. *Basic Economics* is written to be read—and even enjoyed.

Most of us are necessarily ignorant of many complex fields, from botany to brain surgery. As a result, we simply do not attempt to operate in, or comment on, those fields. However, every voter and every politician that they vote for affects economic policies. We cannot opt out of economic issues. Our only options are to be informed or not informed when making our choices. *Basic Economics* is intended to make it easier to be informed. The fundamental principles of economics are not hard to understand but they are easy to forget, especially amid the heady rhetoric of politics and the media. The vivid real-life examples used throughout this book make these principles indelible, in a way that graphs and equations might not.

In keeping with the nature of *Basic Economics* as an introduction to economics for the general public, the usual footnotes or end-notes are left out. However, those who wish to check up on some of the surprising facts they will learn about here can find the sources listed at the end of the book.[2]

---

[1] *Basic Economics* has been translated into Japanese, Swedish, Korean, and Polish, and is currently being translated into Hebrew and Chinese.
[2] Collecting all this material has been the work primarily of my extraordinary research assistants, Na Liu and Elizabeth Costa. Ms. Costa also did the copy-editing and Na Liu created the computer files from which this book was printed.

For instructors who are using *Basic Economics* as a textbook in their courses, or for parents who are homeschooling their children, there are more than a hundred questions in the back of the book, along with a list of pages after each question, showing where the answer can be found in the text.

Whether you are reading *Basic Economics* for a course or just for your own understanding of the economy, it has been written with the thought that it should be not only a relaxed experience, but also an enjoyable one.

THOMAS SOWELL
The Hoover Institution
Stanford University

BASIC ECONOMICS

Chapter 1

WHAT IS ECONOMICS?

> *None of us can have as much as we want of all the things we want.*
>
> *Justice Oliver Wendell Holmes*

Some basic principles of economics apply in many different kinds of economies—capitalist, socialist, feudal, or whatever—and among a wide variety of peoples, cultures, and governments. Policies which led to rising price levels under Alexander the Great have led to rising price levels in America, thousands of years later. Rent control laws have led to a very similar set of consequences in Hong Kong, Stockholm, Melbourne, and New York. So have similar agricultural policies in India and the European Union countries.

Differences in economic practices from one country to another are also revealing. There were economic reasons why manufacturing enterprises in the days of the Soviet Union kept almost enough inventory on hand to last a year, while inventories of supplies in some Japanese companies like Toyota are only enough to last a matter of hours, with new parts and equipment arriving at the factory at various times during the day, to be installed immediately on cars as they are being assembled.

Economics is more than a way to see patterns or to unravel puzzling anomalies. Its fundamental concern is with the material standard of living of society as a whole and how that is affected by particular decisions made by individuals and institutions. One of the ways of doing this is to look at economic policies and economic systems in terms of the incentives they create, rather than simply the goals they pursue. This means that

1

consequences matter more than intentions—and not just the immediate consequences, but also the longer run repercussions of decisions, policies, and institutions.

Virtually everyone agrees on the importance of economics, but there is far less agreement on just what economics is. Among the many misconceptions of economics is that it is something that tells you how to make money or run a business or predict the ups and downs of the stock market. But economics is not personal finance or business administration, and predicting the ups and downs of the stock market has yet to be reduced to a set of dependable principles.

To know what economics is, we must first know what an economy is. Perhaps most of us think of an economy as a system for the production and distribution of the goods and services we use in everyday life. That is true as far as it goes, but it does not go far enough. The Garden of Eden was a system for the production and distribution of goods and services, but it was not an economy, because everything was available in unlimited abundance. Without scarcity, there is no need to economize—and therefore no economics. A distinguished British economist named Lionel Robbins gave the classic definition of economics:

> *Economics is the study of the use of scarce resources*
> *which have alternative uses.*

In other words, economics studies the consequences of the decisions that are made about the use of land, labor, capital and other resources that go into producing the volume of output which determines a country's standard of living. Those decisions and their consequences can be more important than the resources themselves, for there are poor countries with rich natural resources and countries like Japan and Switzerland with relatively few natural resources but high standards of living. The values of natural resources per capita in Uruguay and Venezuela are several times what they are in Japan and Switzerland but income per capita in Japan and Switzerland is about double that of Uruguay and several times that of Venezuela.

The decisions that influence such outcomes are not only the decisions of individuals, or industrial or agricultural enterprises, or the policies of governments. Among the major decisions affecting economic outcomes are decisions about what kinds of enduring institutions a society has for making those decisions—what kind of economic system, operating in what kind of legal system, and controlled by what kind of political system. In analyzing all these decisions and examining the evidence of their consequences, it is crucial to keep in mind at all times that the resources being used are both scarce and have alternative uses.

What does "scarce" mean? It means that what everybody wants adds up to more than there is. This may seem like a simple thing, but its implications are often grossly misunderstood, even by highly educated people. For example, a feature article in the *New York Times* laid out the economic woes and worries of middle-class Americans—one of the most affluent groups of human beings ever to inhabit this planet. Although this story included a picture of a middle-class American family in their own swimming pool, the main headline read: "The American Middle, Just Getting By." Other headings in the article included:

Wishes Deferred and Plans Unmet

Goals That Remain Just Out of Sight

Dogged Saving and Some Luxuries

In short, middle-class Americans' desires exceed what they can comfortably afford, even though what they already have would be considered unbelievable prosperity by people in many other countries around the world—or even by earlier generations of Americans. Yet both they and the reporter regarded them as "just getting by" and a Harvard sociologist was quoted as saying "how budget-constrained these people really are." But it is not something as man-made as a budget which constrains them: Reality constrains them. There has never been enough to satisfy everyone completely. That is the real constraint. That is what scarcity means.

Although per capita real income in the United States increased 50 percent in just one generation, these middle-class families "have had to work hard for their modest gains," according to a Fordham University professor quoted in the same article. However, it is doubtful whether most other people in the world would regard Americans' work in air-conditioned offices with coffee breaks as "hard" or their standard of living as "just getting by." Still, the situation seemed to be viewed as not wholly satisfactory, and perhaps even puzzling, by the people themselves.

The *New York Times* reported that one of these middle-class families "got in over their heads in credit card spending" but then "got their finances in order."

> "But if we make a wrong move," Geraldine Frazier said, "the pressure we had from the bills will come back, and that is painful."

To all these people—from academia and journalism, as well as the middle-class people themselves—it apparently seemed strange somehow that there should be such a thing as scarcity and that this should imply a need for both productive efforts on their part and personal responsibility in spending. Yet nothing has been more pervasive in the history of the human race than scarcity and all the requirements for economizing that go with scarcity.

Regardless of our policies, practices, or institutions—whether they are wise or unwise, noble or ignoble—there is simply not enough to go around to satisfy all our desires to the fullest. "Unmet needs" are inherent in these circumstances, whether we have a capitalist, socialist, feudal, or other kind of economy. These various kinds of economies are just different institutional ways of making trade-offs that are inescapable in any economy.

Economics is not just about dealing with the existing output of goods and services as consumers. It is also about *producing* that output from scarce resources—turning inputs into output. Not only scarcity but also "alternative uses" are at the heart of economics. If each resource had only one use, economics would be much simpler. But water can be used to produce ice or steam by itself or innumerable mixtures and compounds in combination with other things. Similarly, from petroleum comes not only gasoline, kerosene, and fuel oil, but also plastics and Vaseline. Iron ore can be used to produce steel products ranging from paper clips to automobiles to the frameworks of skyscrapers.

How much of each resource should be allocated to each of its many uses? Every economy has to answer that question, and each one does, in one way or another, efficiently or inefficiently. Doing so efficiently is what economics is all about. Different kinds of economies are essentially different ways of making decisions about the allocation of scarce resources—and those decisions have repercussions on the life of the whole society. During the days of the Soviet Union, for example, that country's industries used more electricity than American industries to produce a smaller amount of output than American industries produced. More steel, cement, and other resources used in production likewise resulted in less output in the Soviet Union than in countries like the United States, Japan or Germany. Such inefficiencies in turning inputs into outputs translated into a lower standard of living, in a country richly endowed with natural resources—perhaps more richly endowed than any other country in the world.

It was much the same story in early twenty-first century China, which used seven times as much energy to produce a given value of output as Japan used to produce that same value of output. Here again, huge differences in efficiency meant huge differences in standards of living for millions of human beings. Efficiency in production—the rate at which inputs are turned into output—is not just some technicality that economists talk about. It affects the life of whole societies. When visualizing this process, it helps to think of the real things—the iron ore, petroleum, wood and other inputs that go into the production process and the food, furniture, and automobiles that come out the other end, rather than think of economic decisions as being simply decisions about money.

Although the word "economics" suggests money to some people, for a society as a whole money is just a device to get real things done. Otherwise, the government could make us all rich by simply printing more money. It is not money but the volume of goods and services which determines whether a country is poverty stricken or prosperous.

Economics is not about the financial fate of particular individuals or particular enterprises. It is about the material well-being of society as a whole. When economists analyze prices, wages, profits, or the international balance of trade, for example, it is from the standpoint of how decisions in various parts of the economy affect the allocation of scarce resources in a way that raises or lowers the material standard of living of the people as a whole.

Economics is not simply a topic on which to express opinions or vent emotions. It is a systematic study of what happens when you do specific things in specific ways. In economic analysis, the methods used by a Marxist economist like Oskar Lange did not differ in any fundamental way from the methods used by a conservative economist like Milton Friedman. It is these basic economic principles that this book is about.

While there are controversies in economics, as there are in science, this does not mean that the basic principles of economics are just a matter of opinion, any more than the basic principles of chemistry or physics are just a matter of opinion. Economics is a tool of analysis and a body of tested knowledge—and of principles derived from that knowledge.

Money doesn't even have to be involved to make a decision be economic. When a military medical team arrives on a battlefield where soldiers have a variety of wounds, they are confronted with the classic economic problem of allocating scarce resources which have alternative uses. Almost never are there enough doctors, nurses, or paramedics to go around, nor enough medications. Some of the wounded are near death and have little chance of being saved, while others have a fighting chance if they get immediate care, and still others are only slightly wounded and will probably recover whether they get immediate medical attention or not.

If the medical team does not allocate its time and medications efficiently, some wounded soldiers will die needlessly, while time is being spent attending to others not as urgently in need of care or still others whose wounds are so devastating that they will probably die in spite of anything that can be done for them. It is an economic problem, though not a dime changes hands.

Most of us hate even to think of having to make such choices. Indeed, as we have already seen, some middle-class Americans are distressed at having to make much milder choices and trade-offs. But life does not ask what we want. It presents us with options. Economics is one of the ways of trying to make the most of those options.

When India and China—historically, two of the poorest countries in the world—began in the late twentieth century to make fundamental changes in their economic policies, their economies began growing dramatically. It has been estimated that 20 million people in India rose out of destitution in a decade and more than a million Chinese *per month* rose out of poverty.

Things like this are what make the study of economics important.

PART I: PRICES AND MARKETS

Chapter 2

THE ROLE OF PRICES

We couldn't live a day without depending on everybody.
Will Rogers

There are some relatively simple, but important, principles of economics which together help explain how a complex society of millions of human beings supply one another with the countless goods and services that sustain, enhance, and prolong their lives. Since we know that the key task facing any economy is the allocation of scarce resources which have alternative uses, the next question is: How does an economy do that?

Different kinds of economies obviously do it differently. In a feudal economy, the lord of the manor simply told the people under him what to do and where he wanted resources put: Grow less barley and more wheat, put fertilizer here, more hay there, drain the swamps. It was much the same story in twentieth century Communist societies, such as the Soviet Union, which organized a far more complex modern economy in much the same way, with the government issuing orders for a hydroelectric dam to be built on the Volga River, for so many tons of steel to be produced in Siberia, so much wheat to be grown in the Ukraine. By contrast, in a market economy coordinated by prices, there is no one at the top to issue orders to control or coordinate activities throughout the economy.

How an incredibly complex, high-tech economy can operate without any central direction is baffling to many. The last President of the Soviet Union, Mikhail Gorbachev, is said to have asked British Prime Minister Margaret Thatcher: How do you see to it that people get food? The answer was that she didn't. Prices did that. Moreover, the British people were better fed than those in the Soviet Union, even though the British have not produced enough food to feed themselves in more than a century. Prices bring them food from other countries.

Without the role of prices, imagine what a monumental bureaucracy it would take to see to it that the city of London alone is supplied with the tons of food, of every variety, which it consumes every day. Yet such an army of bureaucrats can be dispensed with—and the people that would be needed in such a bureaucracy can do productive work elsewhere in the economy— because the simple mechanism of prices does the same job faster, cheaper, and better.

This is also true in China, where the Communists still run the government but, by the early twenty-first century, were allowing free markets to operate in much of that country's economy. Although China has one-fourth of the total population of the world, it has only 10 percent of the world's arable land, so feeding its people could continue to be the serious problem that it once was, back in the days when recurring famines took millions of lives in China. Today prices attract food to China from other countries:

> China's food supplement is coming from abroad—from South America, the U.S. and Australia. This means prosperity for agricultural traders and processors like Archer Daniels Midland. They're moving into China in all of the ways you'd expect in a $100 billion national market for processed food that's growing more than 10% annually. It means a windfall for farmers in the American Midwest, who are enjoying soybean prices that have risen about two-thirds from what they were a year ago. It means a better diet for the Chinese, who have raised their caloric intake by a third in the past quarter-century.

Given the attractive power of prices, the American fried-chicken company KFC was by the early twenty-first century making more sales in China than in the United States.

The fact that no given individual or set of individuals controls or coordinates all the innumerable economic activities in a market economy does not mean that these things just happen randomly or chaotically. Each consumer, producer, retailer, landlord, or worker makes individual transactions with other individuals on whatever terms are mutually agreeable. Prices convey those terms, not just to the particular individuals immediately involved but throughout the whole economic system—and indeed, throughout the world. If someone else somewhere else has a better product or a lower price for the same product, that fact gets conveyed and acted upon through prices, without any elected official or planning commission having to issue orders to consumers or producers—indeed, faster than any planners could assemble the information on which to base their orders.

You may not be able to locate Fiji on a map, or even be conscious of its existence, but if someone in Fiji figures out how to manufacture better shoes at lower costs, it will not be long before you are likely to see those shoes on sale at attractive prices in the United States—or India, or anywhere in between. After the Second World War ended, Americans could begin buying cameras from Japan, whether or not officials in Washington were even aware at that time that the Japanese made cameras. Given that any modern economy has millions of products, it is too much to expect the leaders of any country to even know what all those products are, much less know how much of each resource should be allocated to the production of each of those millions of products.

Prices play a crucial role in determining how much of each resource gets used where and how the resulting products get transferred to millions of people. Yet this role is seldom understood by the public and it is often disregarded entirely by politicians. Prime Minister Margaret Thatcher in her memoirs said that Mikhail Gorbachev "had little understanding of economics," even though he was at that time the leader of the largest nation on earth. Unfortunately, he was not unique in that regard. The same could be said of many other national leaders around the world, in countries large and small, democratic or undemocratic. In countries where prices coordinate economic activities automatically, that lack of knowledge of economics does not matter nearly as much as in countries where political leaders try to direct and coordinate economic activities.

Misconceptions of the role of prices are common. Many people see prices as simply obstacles to their getting the things they want. Those who would like to live in a beach-front home, for example, may abandon such plans when they discover how expensive beach-front property is. But high prices are not the reason we cannot all live on the beach front. On the contrary, the inherent reality is that there are not nearly enough beach-front homes to go around and prices simply convey that underlying reality. When many people bid for a relatively few homes, those homes become very expensive because of supply and demand. But it is not the prices that cause the scarcity, which would exist under whatever other kind of economic system or social arrangements might be used instead of prices. There would be the same scarcity under feudalism or socialism or in a tribal society.

If the government today were to come up with a "plan" for "universal access" to beach-front homes and put "caps" on the prices that could be charged for such property, that would not change the underlying reality of the high ratio of people to beach-front land. With a given population and a given amount of beach-front property, rationing without prices would have to take place by bureaucratic fiat, political favoritism or random chance—but the rationing would still have to take place. Even if the government were to decree that beach-front homes were a "basic right" of all members of society, that would still not change the underlying scarcity in the slightest.

Prices are like messengers conveying news—sometimes bad news, in the case of beach-front property desired by far more people than can possibly live at the beach, but often also good news. For example, computers have been getting both cheaper and better at a very rapid rate, as a result of technological advances. Yet the vast majority of beneficiaries of those high-tech advances have not the foggiest idea of just what specifically those technological changes are. But prices convey to them the end results—which are all that matter for their own decision-making and their own enhanced productivity and general well-being from using computers.

Similarly, if vast new rich iron ore deposits were suddenly discovered somewhere, perhaps no more than one percent of the population would be likely to be aware of it, but everyone would discover that things made of steel were becoming cheaper. People thinking of buying desks, for example, would discover that steel desks had become more of a bargain compared to wooden desks and some would undoubtedly change their minds as to which kind of desk to purchase because of that. The same would be true when comparing various other products made of steel to competing products made of aluminum, copper, plastic, wood, or other materials. In short, price changes would enable a whole society—indeed, consumers around the world—to adjust automatically to a greater abundance of iron ore, even if 99 percent of those consumers were wholly unaware of the new discovery.

Prices are not just ways of transferring money. Their primary role is to provide incentives to affect behavior in the use of resources and their resulting products. Prices not only guide consumers, they guide producers as well. When all is said and done, producers cannot possibly know what millions of different consumers want. All that automobile manufacturers, for example, know is that when they produce cars with a certain combination of features they can sell those cars for a price that covers their production costs and leaves them a profit, but when they manufacture cars with a different combination of features, these don't sell as well. In order to get rid of the unsold cars, the sellers must cut the prices to whatever level is necessary to get them off the dealers' lots, even if that means taking a loss. The alternative would be to take a bigger loss by not selling them at all.

While markets coordinated by price movements—"capitalism" as it is called—may seem like a simple thing, markets are misunderstood more often than some other things that are considered more complex. Although a free market economic system is sometimes called a profit system, it is in reality a profit-and-loss system—and the losses are equally important for the efficiency of the economy, because losses tell producers what to stop producing. Without really knowing why consumers like one set of features rather than another, producers automatically produce more of what earns a profit and less of what is losing money. That amounts to producing what the consumers want and stopping the production of what they don't want. Although the producers are only looking out for themselves and their companies' bottom line, nevertheless from the standpoint of the economy as a whole the society is using its scarce resources more efficiently because decisions are guided by prices.

Prices formed a worldwide web of communication long before there was an Internet. Prices connect you with anyone, anywhere in the world where markets are allowed to operate freely, so that places with the lowest prices for particular goods can sell those goods around the world and you can end up wearing shirts made in Malaysia, shoes produced in Italy, and slacks made in Canada, while driving a car manufactured in Japan with tires produced in France. Price-coordinated markets enable people to signal to other people how much they want and how much they are willing to offer for it, while others signal what they are willing to supply at what price. Prices responding to supply and demand cause natural resources to move from places where they are abundant, like Australia, to places where they are almost non-existent, like Japan, because the Japanese are willing to pay higher prices than Australians for those resources—and these higher prices will cover shipping costs and still leave a larger profit than selling the same resources within Australia, where their abundance makes their prices lower. A discovery of large bauxite deposits in India would reduce the cost of aluminum baseball bats in America. A disastrous failure of the wheat crop in Argentina would raise the incomes of farmers in Ukraine, who would now find more demand for their wheat in the world market and therefore higher prices.

The staggering number of economic transactions, on ever-changing terms as supply and demand vary, is beyond the knowledge and capacity of any individual or any manageable-sized group of planners to direct in any economy, much less in the world market. But all that each of the billions of people involved around the world need concern themselves with are their own relatively few individual transactions, leaving the broader coordination of the national or world economy to the fluctuations of prices in response to changing supply and demand. When more of some item is supplied than demanded, competition among sellers trying to get rid of the excess will force the price down, discouraging future production, with the resources used for that item being set free for use in producing something else that is in greater demand. Conversely, when the demand for a particular item exceeds the existing supply, rising prices due to competition among consumers encourages more production, drawing resources away from other parts of the economy to accomplish that.

The significance of free market prices in the allocation of resources can be seen more clearly by looking at situations where prices are *not* allowed to perform this function. During the era of the government-directed economy of the Soviet Union, for example, prices were not set by supply and demand but by central planners who sent resources to their various uses by direct commands, supplemented by prices that the planners raised or lowered as they saw fit. Two Soviet economists, Nikolai Shmelev and Vladimir Popov, described a situation in which their government raised the price it would pay for moleskins, leading hunters to get and sell more of them:

> State purchases increased, and now all the distribution centers are filled with these pelts. Industry is unable to use them all, and they often rot in warehouses before they can be processed. The Ministry of Light Industry has already requested Goskomsten twice to lower purchasing prices, but the "question has not been decided" yet. And this is not surprising. Its members are too busy to decide. They have no time: besides setting prices on these pelts, they have to keep track of another 24 *million* prices.

However overwhelming it might be for a government agency to try to keep track of 24 million prices, a country with more than a hundred million people can far more easily keep track of those prices individually, because no given individual or business enterprise has to keep track of more than the relatively few prices that are relevant to their own decision-making. The over-all coordination of these innumerable isolated decisions takes place through the effect of supply and demand on prices and the effect of prices on the behavior of consumers and producers. Money talks—and people listen. Their reactions are usually faster than central planners could get their reports together.

While telling people what to do might seem to be a more rational or orderly way of coordinating an economy, it has turned out to be far less effective in practice. The situation as regards pelts was common for many other goods during the days of the Soviet Union's centrally planned economy, where a recurrent problem was a piling up of unsold goods in warehouses at the very time when there were painful shortages of other things that could have been produced with the same resources. In a market economy, the prices of surplus goods would fall automatically by supply and demand, while the prices of goods in short supply would rise automatically for the same reason—the net result being a shifting of resources from the former to the latter, again automatically, as producers seek to gain profits and avoid losses.

The problem was not that particular planners made particular mistakes in the Soviet Union or in other planned economies. Whatever the mistakes made by central planners, there are mistakes made in all kinds of economic systems—capitalist, socialist, or whatever. The more fundamental problem with central planning has been that the task taken on has repeatedly proven to be too much for human beings, in whatever country that task has been taken on. As Soviet economists Shmelev and Popov put it:

> No matter how much we wish to organize everything rationally, without waste, no matter how passionately we wish to lay all the bricks of the economic structure tightly, with no chinks in the mortar, it is not yet within our power.

This lesson proved hard for many others who lived in a centrally planned economy to accept. Mikhail Gorbachev was not the only leader raised in the Soviet Union who found the market's operations and results in the West baffling.   Boris Yeltsin, later destined to become Russia's first post-Communist leader, was equally struck by what he saw in a capitalist economy:

> A turning point in Yeltsin's intellectual development occurred during his first visit to the United States in September 1989, more specifically his first visit to an American supermarket, in Houston, Texas. The sight of aisle after aisle of shelves neatly stacked with every conceivable type of foodstuff and household item, each in a dozen varieties, both amazed and depressed him. For Yeltsin, like many other first-time Russian visitors to America, this was infinitely more impressive than tourist attractions like the Statue of Liberty and the Lincoln Memorial. It was impressive precisely because of its ordinariness. A cornucopia of consumer goods beyond the imagination of most Soviets was within the reach of ordinary citizens without standing in line for hours. And it was all so attractively

displayed. For someone brought up in the drab conditions of communism, even a member of the relatively privileged elite, a visit to a Western supermarket involved a full-scale assault on the senses.

When he returned to Moscow, Yeltsin spoke of the pain he felt after seeing in Houston the contrast between American and Soviet living standards. He told of what he had seen in America to what was described as "a stunned Moscow audience." Yeltsin's aide said that the Houston supermarket experience destroyed the last vestiges of Yeltsin's belief in the Communist system, setting the stage for his becoming the first leader of post-Communist Russia.

It should not be surprising that people in market economies have succeeded better at a more manageable task.[1] What we need to understand is how all the millions of individual economic decisions in a complex society are coordinated by prices in such a way as to allocate scarce resources which have alternative uses. Let us now look at that process more closely.

PRICES AND COSTS

Prices in a market economy are not simply numbers plucked out of the air. While you may put whatever price you wish on the goods or services that you provide, those prices will become economic realities only if others are willing to pay them—and that depends not on whatever prices you have chosen but on what prices other producers charge for the same goods and services, and what prices the customers are willing to pay. Even if you produce something that would be worth $100 to a customer and offer it for sale at $90, that customer will still not buy it from you if another producer offers the same thing for $80. Obvious as all this may seem, its implications

---

[1] It might seem as if the central planners' task could be made more manageable by hiring more people to work as central planners. But the problem of setting millions of prices could not be solved by sharing out the work more widely, assigning some individuals or groups the task of setting some prices and assigning others to set other prices. The whole point is that these prices must be set and adjusted *relative to one another* if resources are to be allocated efficiently. If the prices of pelts have been set too high relative to the prices of undershirts,

are not at all obvious to some people—those who blame high prices on "greed," for example, for that implies that a seller can set prices at will and make sales at those arbitrary prices. A front-page article in *The Arizona Republic*, for example, began:

> Greed drove metropolitan Phoenix's home prices and sales to new records in 2005. Fear is driving the market this year.

This implies that lower prices meant less greed, rather than *changed circumstances* that reduced the sellers' ability to charge the same prices as before and still make sales. These circumstances in this case included the fact that homes for sale in Phoenix remained on the market for an average of just 43 days in 2005 but took 61 days before being sold a year later, and the fact that home builders were "struggling to sell even deeply discounted new homes." There was not the slightest indication that sellers were any less interested in getting as much money as they could for the houses they sold. Competition in the market is what limits how much anyone can charge and still make sales, so what is at issue is not anyone's disposition, whether greedy or not, but what the circumstances of the market cause to happen. What was happening in Phoenix was happening across the country, as the inventory of existing homes on the market rose and the rising housing prices of previous years gave way to declining prices, due to supply and demand. It had nothing to do with less "greed," any more than the previous rises in housing prices were due to more "greed."

Resource Allocation by Prices

We now need to look more closely at the process by which prices allocate scarce resources that have alternative uses. The situation where the

---

then both prices need to be adjusted, in order to provide incentives to transfer resources from one to the other. In fact, since thousands of other things use some of the same resources used in producing both pelts and undershirts, all these prices needed to be adjusted to one another simultaneously—something that happens automatically through price competition in the marketplace but which is an overwhelming task for a given set of human beings trying to plan a whole economy.

consumers want product *A* and don't want product *B* is the simplest example of how prices lead to efficiency in the use of scarce resources. But prices are at least equally important in more common and more complex situations, where consumers want both *A* and *B*, as well as many other things, some of which require the same ingredients in their production. For example, consumers not only want cheese, they want ice cream and yogurt, as well as other products made from milk. How do prices help the economy to determine how much milk should go to each of these products?

In bidding for cheese, ice cream, and yogurt, consumers are in effect bidding indirectly for the milk from which these products are produced. In other words, money that comes in from the sales of these products is what enables the producers to again buy milk to use to continue making their respective products. When the demand for cheese goes up, cheese-makers bid away some of the milk that before went into making ice cream or yogurt, in order to increase the output of their own product to meet the rising demand. When the cheese-makers demand more milk, this increased demand forces up the price of milk—to everyone, including the producers of ice cream and yogurt. As the producers of these products raise the prices of ice cream and yogurt to cover the higher cost of the milk that goes into them, consumers are likely to buy less of these other dairy products at these higher prices.

How will each producer know just how much milk to buy? Obviously they will buy only as much milk as will repay its higher costs from the higher prices of these dairy products. If consumers who buy ice cream are not as discouraged by rising prices as consumers of yogurt are, then very little of the additional milk that goes into making more cheese will come from a reduced production of ice cream and more will come from a reduced production of yogurt.

What this all means as a general principle is that the price which one producer is willing to pay for any ingredient becomes the price that other producers are forced to pay for that same ingredient. This applies whether we are talking about the milk that goes into making cheese, ice cream, and yogurt or we are talking about the wood that goes into making baseball bats, furniture, and paper. If the amount of paper demanded doubles, this means that the demand for wood pulp to make paper goes up. As the price of wood rises in response to this increased demand, that in turn means that the prices of baseball bats and furniture will have to go up, in order to cover the higher costs of the wood from which they are made.

Incremental Substitution

Since scarce resources have alternative uses, the value placed on one of these uses by one individual or company sets the cost that has to be paid by others who want to bid some of these resources away for their own use. From the standpoint of the economy as a whole, this means that *resources tend to flow to their most valued uses* when there is price competition in the marketplace. This does not mean that one use categorically precludes all other uses. On the contrary, adjustments are incremental. Only that amount of milk which is as valuable to ice cream consumers or consumers of yogurt as it is to cheese purchasers will be used to make ice cream or yogurt. Only that amount of wood which is as valuable to the makers of baseball bats or furniture as it is to the producers of paper will be used to make bats and furniture.

Now look at the demand from the consumers' standpoint: Whether considering consumers of cheese, ice cream, or yogurt, some will be anxious to have a certain amount, less anxious to have additional amounts, and finally—beyond some point—indifferent to having any more, or even unwilling to consume any more after becoming satiated. The same principle applies when more wood pulp is used to make paper and the producers and consumers of furniture and baseball bats have to make their incremental adjustments accordingly. In short, prices coordinate the use of resources, so that only that amount is used for one thing which is equal in value to what it is worth to others in other uses. That way, a price-coordinated economy does not flood people with cheese to the point where they are sick of it, while others are crying out in vain for more ice cream or yogurt.

· Absurd as such a situation would be, it has happened many times in economies where prices are *not* used to allocate scarce resources. Pelts were not the only unsalable goods that were piling up in Soviet warehouses while people were waiting in long lines trying to get other things that were in short supply.[2] The efficient allocation of scarce resources which have alternative uses is not just an abstract notion of economists. It determines how well or how badly millions of people live.

Again, as in the example of beach-front property, prices convey an underlying reality: *From the standpoint of society as a whole, the "cost" of anything is the value that it has in alternative uses.* That cost is reflected in the market when the price that one individual is willing to pay becomes a cost that others are forced to pay, in order to get a share of the same scarce resource or the products made from it. But, no matter whether a particular society has a capitalist price system or a socialist economy or a feudal or other system, the real cost of anything is still its value in alternative uses. The real costs of building a bridge are the other things that could have been built with that same labor and material. This is also true at the level of a given individual, even when no money is involved. The cost of watching a television sitcom or soap opera is the value of the other things that could have been done with that same time.

Economic Systems

Different economic systems deal with this underlying reality in different ways and with different degrees of efficiency, but the underlying reality exists independently of whatever particular kind of economic system happens to exist in a given society. Once we recognize that, we can then compare how economic systems which use prices to force people to share scarce resources among themselves differ in efficiency from economic systems which determine such things by having kings, politicians, or bureaucrats issue orders saying who can get how much of what.

---

[2] A visitor to the Soviet Union in 1987 reported "long lines of people still stood patiently for hours to buy things: on one street corner people were waiting to buy tomatoes from a cardboard box, one to a customer, and outside a shop next to our hotel there was a line for three days, about which we learned that on the day of our arrival that shop had received a new shipment of men's undershirts." Midge Decter, *An Old Wife's Tale*, p. 169.

During a brief era of greater openness in the last years of the Soviet Union, when people became more free to speak their minds, the two Soviet economists already mentioned wrote a book giving a very candid account of how their economy worked and this book was later translated into English.[3] As Shmelev and Popov put it, production enterprises in the Soviet Union "always ask for more than they need" in the way of raw materials, equipment, and other resources used in production. "They take everything they can get, regardless of how much they actually need, and they don't worry about economizing on materials," according to these economists. "After all, nobody 'at the top' knows exactly what the real requirements are," so "squandering" makes sense—from the standpoint of the manager of a Soviet enterprise. Among the resources that were squandered were workers. These economists estimated that "from 5 to 15 percent of the workers in the majority of enterprises are surplus and are kept 'just in case.'"

The consequence was that far more resources were used to produce a given amount of output in the Soviet economy as compared to a price-coordinated economic system, such as that in Japan, Germany, and other market economies. Citing official statistics, Shmelev and Popov lamented:

> To make one ton of copper we use about 1,000 kilowatt hours of electrical energy, as against 300 in West Germany. To produce one ton of cement we use twice the amount of energy that Japan does.

The Soviet Union did not lack for resources, but was in fact one of the most richly endowed nations on earth—if not *the* most richly endowed in natural resources. Nor was it lacking in highly educated and well-trained people. What it lacked was an economic system that made efficient use of its resources. Because Soviet enterprises were not under the same financial constraints as capitalist enterprises, they acquired more machines than they needed, "which then gather dust in warehouses or rust out of doors," as the Soviet economists put it. In short, Soviet enterprises were not forced to economize—that is, to treat their resources as both scarce and valuable in alternative uses, for the alternative users were not bidding for those

---

[3] *The Turning Point: Revitalizing the Soviet Economy* (New York: Doubleday, 1989).

resources, as they would in a market economy. While such waste cost individual Soviet enterprises little or nothing, they cost the Soviet people dearly, in the form of a lower standard of living than their resources and technology were capable of producing.

Such a waste of inputs as these economists described could not of course continue in the kind of economy where these inputs would have to be purchased in competition with alternative users, and where the enterprise itself could survive only by keeping its costs lower than its sales receipts. In such a price-coordinated capitalist system, the amount of inputs ordered would be based on the enterprise's most accurate estimate of what was really required, not on how much its managers could persuade higher government officials to let them have. These higher officials could not possibly be experts on all the wide range of industries and products under their control, so those with the power in the central planning agencies were to some extent dependent on those with knowledge of their own particular industries and enterprises. Central planners could be skeptical of what the enterprise managers told them but skepticism is not knowledge. If resources were denied, production could suffer—and heads could roll in the central planning agencies. The net result was the excessive use of resources described by the Soviet economists. The contrast between the Soviet economy and the economies of Japan and Germany is just one of many that can be made between economic systems which use prices to allocate resources and those which have relied on political or bureaucratic control. In other regions of the world as well, and in other political systems, there have been similar contrasts between places that used prices to ration goods and allocate resources versus places that have relied on hereditary rulers, elected officials or appointed planning commissions.

When many African colonies achieved national independence in the 1960s, a famous bet was made between the president of Ghana and the president of the neighboring Ivory Coast as to which country would be more prosperous in the years ahead. At that time, Ghana was not only more prosperous than the Ivory Coast, it had more natural resources, so the bet might have seemed reckless on the part of the president of the Ivory Coast.

However, he knew that Ghana was committed to a government-run economy and the Ivory Coast to a freer market. By 1982, the Ivory Coast had so surpassed Ghana economically that the poorest 20 percent of its people had a higher real income per capita than most of the people in Ghana.

This could not be attributed to any superiority of the country or its people. In fact, in later years, when a new generation of Ivory Coast politicians eventually succumbed to the temptation to have the government control more of their country's economy, while Ghana finally learned from its mistakes and began to loosen government controls, these two countries' roles reversed—and now Ghana's economy began to grow, while that of the Ivory Coast declined.

Similar comparisons could be made between Burma and Thailand, the former having had the higher standard of living before instituting socialism and the latter a much higher standard of living afterwards. Other countries—India, Germany, China, New Zealand, South Korea, Sri Lanka—have experienced sharp upturns in their economies when they freed those economies from many government controls and relied more on prices to allocate resources. As of 1960, India and South Korea were at comparable economic levels but, by the late 1980s, South Korea's per capita income was ten times that in India.

India remained committed to a government-controlled economy for many years after achieving independence in 1947. However, in the 1990s, India "jettisoned four decades of economic isolation and planning, and freed the country's entrepreneurs for the first time since independence," in the words of the distinguished London magazine *The Economist*. There followed a new growth rate of 6 percent a year, making it "one of the world's fastest-growing big economies." From 1950 to 1990, India's average growth rate had been 2 percent.

In China, government controls were relaxed on an experimental basis in particular economic sectors and in particular geographic regions earlier, during the reforms of the 1980s, leading to stunning economic contrasts within the same country, as well as rapid economic growth overall. Before, back in 1978, less than 10 percent of China's agricultural output was sold in open markets, instead of being turned over to the government for distribution. But, by 1990, 80 percent was sold directly to the market. The net result was more food and a greater variety of food available to city dwellers in China and a rise in farmers' income by more than 50 percent within a few years. In contrast to China's severe economic problems when there was heavy-handed government control under Mao, who died in 1976, the subsequent freeing up of prices in the marketplace led to an astonishing economic growth rate of 9 percent per year between 1978 and 1995.

While history can tell us that such things happened, economics helps explain *why* they happened—what there is about prices that allows them to accomplish what political control of an economy can seldom match. There is more to economics than prices, but understanding how prices function is the foundation for understanding much of the rest of economics. A rationally planned economy sounds more plausible than an economy coordinated only by prices linking millions of separate decisions by individuals and organizations. Yet Soviet economists who saw the actual consequences of a centrally planned economy reached very different conclusions—namely, "there are far too many economic relationships, and it is impossible to take them all into account and coordinate them sensibly."

In a society of millions of producers and consumers, no given individual or set of government decision-makers sitting around a table can possibly know just how much these millions of consumers prefer one product to another or how much of the ingredients that go into producing millions of products would produce if applied to millions of other products instead. In an economy coordinated by prices, no one has to know. Each producer is simply guided by what price that producer's product can sell for and by how much must be paid for the ingredients that go into making that particular product, while each consumer has to consider only those relatively few prices which are relevant to his or her own purchases.

Knowledge is one of the most scarce of all resources and a pricing system economizes on its use by forcing those with the most knowledge of their own particular situation to make bids for goods and resources based on that knowledge, rather than on their ability to influence other people in planning commissions, legislatures, or royal palaces. However much articulation may be valued by intellectuals, it is not nearly as efficient a way of conveying accurate information as confronting people with a need to "put your money where your mouth is." That forces them to summon up their most accurate information, rather than their most plausible words.

Human beings are going to make mistakes in any kind of economic system. The key question is: What kinds of incentives and constraints will force them to correct their own mistakes? In a price-coordinated economy, any producer who uses ingredients which are more valuable elsewhere in the economy is likely to discover that the costs of those ingredients cannot be repaid from what the consumers are willing to pay for the product. After all, the producer has had to bid those resources away from alternative users, paying more than the resources are worth to some of those alternative users. If it turns out that these resources are not more valuable in the uses to which this producer puts them, then he is going to lose money. There will be no choice but to discontinue making that product with those ingredients. For those producers who are too blind or too stubborn to change, continuing losses will force their businesses into bankruptcy, so that the waste of the resources available to the society will be stopped that way. That is why losses are just as important as profits, from the standpoint of the economy, even though losses are not nearly as popular with businesses.

In a price-coordinated economy, employees and creditors insist on being paid, regardless of whether the managers and owners have made mistakes. This means that capitalist businesses can make only so many mistakes for so long before they have to either stop or get stopped—whether by an inability to get the labor and supplies they need or by bankruptcy. In a feudal economy or a socialist economy, leaders can continue to make the same mistakes indefinitely. The consequences are paid by others in the form of a standard of living lower than it would be if there were greater efficiency in the use of scarce resources.

The many products which remained unsold in stores or in warehouses in the Soviet Union, while there were desperate shortages of other things, were a sign of the fatal weakness of central planning. But, in a price-coordinated economy, the labor, management, and physical resources that went into producing unwanted products would have had to go into producing something that could pay its own way from sales revenues. That means producing something that the consumers wanted more than they wanted what was actually produced. In the absence of compelling price signals and the threat of financial losses to the producers that they convey, inefficiency and waste in the Soviet Union could continue until such time as each particular instance of waste reached proportions big enough and blatant enough to attract the attention of central planners in Moscow, who were preoccupied with thousands of other decisions.

Ironically, the problems caused by trying to run an economy by direct orders or by arbitrarily-imposed prices created by government fiat were foreseen a century earlier by Karl Marx and Friedrich Engels, whose ideas the Soviet Union claimed to be following. Engels pointed out that price fluctuations have "forcibly brought home to the commodity producers what things and what quantity of them society requires or does not require." Without such a mechanism, he demanded to know "what guarantee we have that necessary quantity and not more of each product will be produced, that we shall not go hungry in regard to corn and meat while we are choked in beet sugar and drowned in potato spirit, that we shall not lack trousers to cover our nakedness while trouser buttons flood us in millions." Marx and Engels apparently understood economics much better than their latter-day followers. Or perhaps Marx and Engels were more concerned with economic efficiency than with maintaining political control from the top.

There were also Soviet economists who understood the role of price fluctuations in coordinating any economy. Near the end of the Soviet Union, two of these economists, Shmelev and Popov, whom we have already quoted, said: "Everything is interconnected in the world of prices, so that the smallest change in one element is passed along the chain to millions of others." Adam Smith, the most famous of all free market economists, could not have said it better. The Soviet economists were especially aware of the role of prices from having seen what happened when prices were not allowed to perform that role. But economists were not in charge of the Soviet economy. Under Stalin, a number of economists were shot for saying things he did not want to hear.

SUPPLY, DEMAND AND "NEED"

There is perhaps no more basic or more obvious principle of economics than the fact that people tend to buy more at a lower price and less at a higher price. By the same token, people who produce goods or supply services tend to supply more at a higher price and less at a lower price. Yet the implications of these two simple principles, singly or in combination, cover a remarkable range of economic activities and issues—and contradict an equally remarkable range of misconceptions and fallacies.

When people try to quantify a country's "need" for this or that product or service, they are ignoring the fact that there is no fixed or objective "need." The fact that people demand more at a lower price and less at a higher price may be easy to understand, but it is also easy to forget. Seldom, if ever, is there a fixed quantity demanded. For example, communal living in an Israeli kibbutz was based on its members' collectively producing and supplying each other goods and services without resort to money or prices. However, supplying electricity and food without charging prices led to a situation where people often did not bother to turn off electric lights during the day and members would bring friends from outside the kibbutz to join them for meals. But, after the kibbutz began to charge prices for electricity and food, there was a sharp drop in the consumption of both. In short, there was no fixed quantity of "need" or demand.

Likewise, there is no fixed supply. Statistics on the amount of petroleum, iron ore, or other natural resources seem to indicate that this is just a simple matter of how much physical stuff there is in the ground. In reality, most natural resources are available at varying costs of discovery, extraction, and processing from one place to another. There is some oil that can be extracted and processed from some places for $20 a barrel and other oil that cannot repay all its production costs at $40 a barrel, but which can at $60 a barrel. With goods in general, *the quantity supplied varies directly with the price,* just as the quantity demanded varies inversely with the price.

When the price of oil falls, certain low-yield oil wells are shut down because the cost of extracting and processing the oil from those wells would exceed the price that the oil would sell for in the market. If the price later rises—or if the cost of extraction or processing is lowered by some new technology—then such oil wells will be put back into operation again. Certain sands containing oil in Venezuela and in Canada had such low yields that they were not even counted in the world's oil reserves until oil prices hit new highs in the early twenty-first century. That changed things, as the *Wall Street Journal* reported:

> These deposits were once dismissed as "unconventional" oil that couldn't be recovered economically. But now, thanks to rising global oil prices and improved technology, most oil-industry experts count oil sands as recoverable reserves. That recalculation has vaulted Venezuela and Canada to first and third in global reserves rankings. . .

In short, there is no fixed supply of oil—or of most other things. In some ultimate sense, the earth has a finite amount of each resource but, even when that amount may be enough to last for centuries or millennia, at any given time the amount that is economically feasible to extract and process varies directly with the price for which it can be sold. Many false predictions over the past century or more that we were "running out" of various natural resources in a few years were based on confusing the economically available current supply at current prices with the ultimate physical supply in the earth, which is vastly greater.[4]

Natural resources are not the only things that will be supplied in greater quantities when their prices rise. That is true of many commodities and even workers. When people project that there will be a shortage of engineers or teachers or food in the years ahead, they usually either ignore prices or implicitly assume that there will be a shortage at today's prices. But shortages are precisely what cause prices to rise. At higher prices, it may be no harder to fill vacancies for engineers or teachers than today and no harder to find food, as rising prices cause more crops to be grown and more livestock to be raised. In short, a larger quantity is usually supplied at higher prices than at lower prices, whether what is being sold is oil or apples, lobsters or labor.

---

[4] This confusion is explained in Chapter 12 under "Natural Resources."

Price fluctuations are a way of letting a little knowledge go a long way. Price changes guide people's decisions through trial and error adjustments to what other people can and will pay as consumers, as well as what others can and will supply as producers. The producer whose product turns out to have the combination of features that are closest to what the consumers really want may be no wiser than his competitors. Yet he can grow rich while his competitors who guessed wrong go bankrupt. But the larger result is that society as a whole gets more benefits from its limited resources by having them directed toward where those resources produce the kind of output that millions of people want, instead of producing things that they don't want.

Rationing by Prices

There are all kinds of prices. The prices of consumer goods are the most obvious examples but labor also has prices called wages or salaries, and borrowed money has a price called interest. In addition to prices for tangible things, there are prices for services ranging from haircuts to brain surgery and from astrology to advice on speculating in gold or soybeans. Prices provide incentives to conserve. That is why the Israeli kibbutz used less electricity and less food after it began to charge its members for these things, and why German and Japanese enterprises used less input for a given output than their Soviet counterparts whose managers did not have to worry about prices or profits—or losses.

In so far as prices—whether of soybeans or surgery—result from supply and demand in a free market, they effectively allocate scarce resources which have alternative uses. So long as people are free to spend their money for what they see fit, price changes in response to supply and demand direct resources to where they are most in demand and direct people to where their desires can be satisfied most fully and cheaply by the existing supply. Simple as all this may seem, it contradicts many widely held ideas. For example, not only are high prices often blamed on "greed," people often speak of something being sold for more than its "real" value, or of workers being paid less than they are "really" worth—or of corporate executives, athletes, and entertainers being paid more than they are "really" worth.

To treat prices as resulting from greed implies that sellers can set prices where they wish, that prices are not determined by supply and demand. It may well be true that some—or all—sellers prefer to get the highest price that they can. But it is equally true that buyers usually wish to pay the lowest price they can for goods of a given quality. More important, the competition of numerous buyers and numerous sellers results in prices that leave each individual buyer and seller with very little leeway. Any deal depends on both parties agreeing to the same terms. Anyone who doesn't offer as good a deal as a competitor is likely to find nobody willing to make a deal at all. Obvious as all this may seem, it was literally front-page news in the *New York Times* when rising apartment vacancy rates in cities across the United States led to lower rents, both directly and in the form of gifts to prospective tenants:

> Waiting for the tenants in some building lobbies around Memphis every morning are free cups of Starbucks coffee. In the Atlanta suburbs, people who move into one garden-style apartment building receive $500 gift certificates to Best Buy, the electronics chain. In Cleveland, Denver and many other cities, landlords have been giving new tenants gifts worth $1,000 or more: one, two, or even three months of rent-free living.

The reason for all this apparent generosity? "The portion of apartments sitting vacant this summer rose to 9.9 percent, the highest level since the Census Bureau began keeping statistics in 1956." Blaming high prices on "greed" or crediting low prices to generosity would be assuming that sellers can set and maintain prices by an act of will. But supply and demand explain most price changes far better than any assumption of volitional pricing. Where there are monopolies or cartels, higher prices are often possible compared to prices in a competitive market but, fortunately, monopolies and cartels are the exception rather than the rule. Competition is the crucial factor in explaining why prices usually cannot be maintained at arbitrarily set levels. But even people who would not deny this may nevertheless forget it when asking such questions as: "Will lower production costs be passed on to the consumers in lower prices?" Those producers who do not pass on these cost savings in lower prices can find themselves losing customers to those who do.[5]

Competition is the key to the operation of a price-coordinated economy. It not only forces prices toward equality, it likewise causes capital, labor, and other resources to flow toward where their rates of return are highest until the returns are evened out through competition, much like water seeking its own level. However, the fact that water seeks its own level does not mean that the Atlantic Ocean has a glassy smooth surface. Waves and tides are among the ways in which water seeks its own level, without being frozen at that level. Similarly, in an economy, the fact that prices and rates of return on investments tend to equalize means only that their fluctuations, relative to one another, are what move resources from places where their earnings are lower to where their earnings are higher.

"Real" Value

The fact that prices fluctuate over time, and occasionally have a sharp rise or a steep drop, misleads some people into concluding that prices are deviating from their "real" values. But their usual level under usual conditions is no more real or valid than their much higher or much lower levels under different conditions.

When a large employer goes bankrupt in a small community, or simply moves away to another region or country, many of the business' former employees may decide to move away themselves—and when their numerous homes go on sale in the same small area at the same time, the prices of those houses are likely to be driven down by competition. But this does not mean that people are selling their homes for less than their "real" value. The value of living in that particular community has simply declined with the decline

---

[5] This is not a matter of faith in free market capitalism. Karl Marx, who could certainly not be accused of having faith in free market capitalism, was nevertheless an economist who pointed out that cost-lowering new technology not only *enables* the capitalist to charge lower prices but also *compels* him to charge lower prices. See Karl Marx, *Wage Labor and Capital*, Part V. See also Karl Marx, *Capital*, Vol. III, pp. 310-311 (Kerr edition).

of job opportunities, and housing prices reflect this underlying fact. The new and lower prices reflect the new reality just as well as the previous prices reflected the previous reality. A survey of home prices in a number of upstate New York cities that were losing population in the 1990s found that home prices were falling in those particular communities, while home prices were rising elsewhere in the same state and around the country. This is exactly what one should expect on the basis of elementary economic principles. The rising prices were no more "real" than the falling prices.

The most fundamental reason why there is no such thing as an objective or "real" value is that there would be no rational basis for economic transactions if there were. When you pay 50 cents for a newspaper, obviously the only reason you do so is that the newspaper is more valuable to you than the 50 cents is. At the same time, the only reason people are willing to sell the newspaper is that 50 cents is more valuable to them than the newspaper is. If there were any such thing as a "real" or objective value of a newspaper—or anything else—neither the buyer nor the seller would benefit from making a transaction at a price equal to that objective value, since what would be acquired would be of no greater value than what was given up. Why bother to make the transaction then?

On the other hand, if either the buyer or the seller was getting more than the objective value from the transaction, then the other one must be losing—in which case, why continue to get cheated? Continuing transactions between buyer and seller make sense only if value is subjective, each getting what is worth more subjectively.

Prices and Supplies

Prices not only ration existing supplies, they also act as powerful incentives to cause supplies to rise or fall in response to changing demand. When a crop failure in a given region creates a sudden increase in demand for imports of food into that region, food suppliers elsewhere rush to be the first to get there, in order to capitalize on the high prices that will prevail until more supplies arrive and drive food prices back down again through competition. What this means, from the standpoint of the hungry people in that region, is that food is being rushed to them at maximum speed by "greedy" suppliers, probably much faster than if the same food were being transported to them by salaried government employees sent on a humanitarian mission.

Those spurred on by greed may well drive throughout the night or take short cuts over rough terrain, while those operating "in the public interest" are more likely to proceed at a less hectic pace and by safer or more comfortable routes. In short, people tend to do more for their own benefit than for the benefit of others. Freely fluctuating prices can make that turn out to be beneficial to others. In the case of food supplies, earlier arrival can be the difference between temporary hunger and death by starvation or by diseases to which people are more susceptible when they are undernourished. Where there are local famines in Third World countries, it is not at all uncommon for food supplied by international agencies to the national government to sit spoiling on the docks while people are dying of hunger inland.[6] However unattractive greed may be, it is likely to move food much faster, saving more lives.

In other situations, the consumers may not want more, but less. Prices also convey this. When automobiles began to displace horses and buggies in the early twentieth century, the demand for saddles, horseshoes, carriages and other such paraphernalia declined. As the manufacturers of such products faced losses instead of profits, many began to abandon their businesses or were forced to shut down by bankruptcy. In a sense, it is unfair when some people are unable to earn as much as others with similar skills and diligence, because of innovations which were as unforeseen by most of the people who benefited as by most of the people who were made worse off. Yet this unfairness to particular individuals is what makes the economy as a whole operate more efficiently for the benefit of vastly larger numbers of others. Would creating

---

[6] The same thing can happen when the food arrives by land. See "Death by Bureaucracy," on page 40 of the December 8, 2001 issue of *The Economist*, for examples of Afghan refugees dying of starvation while waiting for paperwork to be completed by aid workers.

more fairness among producers, at the cost of reduced efficiency and a resulting lower standard of living, be fair to consumers?

The gains and losses are not isolated or independent events. The crucial role of prices is in tying together a vast constellation of economic activities among people too widely scattered to all know each other. A poignant line by a woman in the play and movie *A Streetcar Named Desire* says, "I have always depended on the kindness of strangers." We all have to depend, for the things that sustain our lives and our standard of living, if not on the kindness of strangers, then at least on the cooperation of innumerable strangers, most of whom we will never see. Among free people in a market economy, prices are what help secure that cooperation.

Chapter 3

PRICE CONTROLS

> *The record of price controls goes as far back as human history. They were imposed by the Pharaohs of ancient Egypt. They were decreed by Hammurabi, king of Babylon, in the eighteenth century B.C. They were tried in ancient Athens.*
>
> Henry Hazlitt

Just as nothing makes us appreciate the role of electricity like a power failure, nothing shows more vividly the role and importance of price fluctuations in a market economy than the *absence* of such price fluctuations when the market is controlled. What happens when prices are not allowed to fluctuate freely according to supply and demand, but instead their fluctuations are fixed within limits set by law under various kinds of price controls?

Typically, price controls are imposed in order to keep prices from rising to the levels that they would reach in response to supply and demand. The political rationales for such laws have varied from place to place and from time to time, but there is seldom a lack of rationales whenever it becomes politically expedient to hold down some people's prices in the interest of other people whose political support seems more important. However, in addition to laws putting a "ceiling" on how high prices will be allowed to rise, there are also laws establishing a "floor" below which prices will not be allowed to fall.

Many countries have set limits to how low certain agricultural prices will be allowed to fall, sometimes with the government being legally obligated to buy up the farmer's output whenever free market prices go below the officially specified levels. Equally widespread are minimum wage laws, which set a limit to how low a worker's wage rate may be. Here the government seldom offers to buy up the surplus labor which the free market does not employ, though it usually offers unemployment compensation, covering some proportion of the wages that might otherwise have been earned.

To understand the effects of price control, it is first necessary to understand how prices rise and fall in a free market. There is nothing esoteric about it, but it is important to be very clear about what happens. Prices rise because the amount demanded exceeds the amount supplied *at existing prices*. Prices fall because the amount supplied exceeds the amount demanded *at existing prices*. The first case is called a "shortage" and the second is called a "surplus"—but both depend on *existing prices*. Simple as this might seem, it is often misunderstood, sometimes with disastrous consequences.

PRICE CEILINGS AND SHORTAGES

When there is a "shortage" of a product, there is not necessarily any less of it, either absolutely or relative to the number of consumers. During and immediately after the Second World War, for example, there was a very serious housing shortage in the United States, even though the country's population and its housing supply had both increased by about 10 percent from their prewar levels—and there was no shortage when the war began. In other words, even though the ratio between housing and people had not changed, nevertheless many Americans looking for an apartment during this period had to spend weeks or months in an often futile search for a place to live, or else resorted to bribes to get landlords to move them to the top of waiting lists. Meanwhile, they doubled up with relatives, slept in garages or used other makeshift living arrangements.

Although there was no less housing space per person than before the war, the shortage was very real and very painful *at existing prices,* which were kept artificially lower than they would have been because of rent control laws that had been passed during the war. At these artificially low prices, more people had a demand for more housing space than before rent control laws were enacted. This is a practical consequence of the simple economic principle already noted in Chapter 2, that the quantity demanded varies according to how high or how low the price is. When some people used more housing than usual, other people found less housing available. The same thing happens under other forms of price control: Some people use the price-controlled goods or services more generously than usual because of the artificially lower price, while other people find that less than usual is left for them. There are other consequences to price controls in general, and rent control provides examples of these as well.

Demand under Rent Control

Some people who would normally not be renting their own apartments, such as young adults still living with their parents or some single or widowed elderly people living with relatives, were enabled by the artificially low prices created by rent control to move out and into their own apartments. These artificially low prices also caused others to seek larger apartments than they would ordinarily be living in or to live alone when they would otherwise have to share an apartment with a room-mate, in order to be able to afford the rent. More tenants seeking both more apartments and larger apartments created a shortage, even though there was not any greater physical scarcity of housing relative to the total population.[1]

---

[1] My own family, which occupied a two-bedroom apartment in 1939, before the war, occupied two apartments with a total of four bedrooms in 1944, and of course two kitchens and two bathrooms. Yet we were as baffled as everyone else as to why there was suddenly a housing shortage.

When rent control ended after the war, the housing shortage quickly disappeared. As rents rose in a free market, some childless couples living in four-bedroom apartments decided that they could live in two-bedroom apartments and save the difference in rent. Some late teenagers decided that they could continue living with mom and dad a little longer, until their pay rose enough for them to be able to afford their own apartment, now that rent was no longer artificially cheap. The net result was that families looking for a place to stay found more places available, now that rent-control laws were no longer keeping such places occupied by people with less urgent requirements.

Just as price fluctuations allocate scarce resources which have alternative uses, price controls which limit those fluctuations reduce the incentives for individuals to limit their own use of scarce resources desired by others. Rent control, for example, tends to lead to many apartments being occupied by just one person. Before rent control was imposed in Sweden, less than one-fourth of all unmarried adults there lived in their own separate housing units in 1940, but that proportion rose over the years until just over half did by 1975. In San Francisco, a study in 2001 showed that 49 percent of that city's rent-controlled apartments had only a single occupant, while a severe housing shortage in the city had thousands of people living considerable distances away and making long commutes to their jobs in San Francisco. Meanwhile, a Census report showed likewise that 48 percent of all households in Manhattan, where most apartments are under some form of rent control, are occupied by only one person.

In the normal course of events, people's demand for housing space changes over a lifetime. Their demand for space usually increases when they get married and have children. But, years later, after the children have grown up and moved away, the parents' demand for space may decline, and it often declines yet again after a spouse dies and the widow or widower moves into smaller quarters or goes to live with relatives or in an institution for the elderly. In this way, a society's total stock of housing is shared and circulated among people according to their changing individual demands at different stages of their lives. This sharing takes place, not because the individuals themselves have a sense of cooperation, but because of the prices—rents in this case—which confront them. In a free market, these prices are based on the value that other tenants put on housing. Young couples with a growing family are often willing to bid more for housing, even if that means buying fewer consumer goods and services, in order to have enough money to pay for additional housing space. A couple who begin to have children may cut back on how often they go out to restaurants or movies, or wait longer to buy new clothes or new cars, in order that each child may have his or her own bedroom. But, once the children are grown and gone, such sacrifices may no longer make sense, when additional other amenities can now be enjoyed by reducing the amount of housing space being rented.

Given the crucial role of prices in this process, suppression of that process by rent control laws leaves elderly people with little incentive to vacate apartments that they would normally vacate, if that would result in a significant reduction in rent, leaving them more money with which to improve their living standards in other respects. Moreover, the chronic housing shortages which accompany rent control greatly increase the time and effort required to search for a new and smaller apartment, while reducing the financial reward for finding one. In short, rent control reduces the rate of housing turnover.

New York City has had rent control longer and more stringently than any other major American city. One consequence has been that the annual rate of turnover of apartments in New York is less than half the national average and the proportion of tenants who have lived in the same apartment for 20 years or more is more than double the national average. As the *New York Times* summarized the situation:

> New York used to be like other cities, a place where tenants moved frequently and landlords competed to rent empty apartments to newcomers, but today the motto may as well be: No Immigrants Need Apply. While immigrants are crowded into bunks in illegal boarding houses in the slums, upper-middle-class locals pay low rents to live in good neighborhoods, often in large apartments they no longer need after their children move out.

Supply under Rent Control

Rent control has effects on supply as well as on demand. Nine years after the end of World War II, not a single new building had been built in Melbourne, Australia, because of rent control laws there which made buildings unprofitable. Declines in building construction have likewise followed in the wake of rent control laws elsewhere. After rent control was instituted in Santa Monica, California in 1979, building permits declined to less than one-tenth of what they were just five years earlier. A housing study in San Francisco in 2001 found that three quarters of its rent-controlled housing was more than half a century old and 44 percent of it was more than 70 years old.

Although the construction of office buildings, factories, warehouses, and other commercial and industrial buildings requires much of the same kind of labor and materials used to construct apartment buildings, it is not uncommon for many new office buildings to be constructed in cities where few new apartment buildings are built. Rent control laws often do not apply to industrial or commercial buildings. Thus, even in cities with severe housing shortages, there may be much vacant space in such buildings. Despite a severe housing shortage in New York, San Francisco, and other cities with rent control, a nationwide survey in 2003 found the vacancy rates in buildings used by business and industry to be nearly 12 percent, the highest in more than two decades. This is just one more piece of evidence that housing shortages are a price phenomenon. High vacancy rates show that there are obviously ample resources available to construct buildings but rent control keeps those resources from being used to construct apartments and thereby diverts these resources into constructing office buildings and other commercial properties. Not only is the supply of new apartment construction less after rent control, even the supply of existing housing tends to decline, as landlords provide less maintenance and repair under rent control, since the housing shortage makes it unnecessary for them to maintain the appearance of their premises in order to attract tenants. Thus housing tends to deteriorate faster under rent control and to have fewer replacements when it wears out.

Studies of rent control in the United States, England, and France have found rent-controlled housing to be deteriorated far more often than non-rent-controlled housing.

Typically, the rental housing stock is relatively fixed in the short run, so that a shortage occurs first because more people want more housing at the artificially low price. Later, there may be a real increase in scarcity as well, as rental units deteriorate more rapidly with reduced maintenance, while not enough new units are being built to replace them as they wear out, because new privately built housing would be unprofitable under rent control. Under rent control in England and Wales, for example, privately-built rental housing fell from being 61 percent of all housing in 1947 to being just 14 percent by 1977. A study of rent control in various countries concluded: "New investment in unsubsidized rented housing is essentially nonexistent in all the European countries surveyed, except for luxury housing."

In short, a policy intended to make housing affordable for the poor has had the net effect of shifting resources toward the building of housing that is affordable only by the affluent or the rich, since luxury housing is often exempt from rent control, just as office buildings and other commercial properties are. Among other things, this illustrates the crucial importance of making a distinction between intentions and consequences. Economic policies need to be analyzed in terms of the incentives they create, rather than the hopes that inspired them.

The incentives towards a reduced supply of housing under rent control are especially pronounced when people who have been renting out rooms or apartments in their own homes, or bungalows in their back yards, decide that it is no longer worth the bother, when rents are kept artificially low under rent control laws. In addition, there are often conversions of apartments to condominiums. During 8 years of rent control in Washington during the 1970s, that city's available rental housing stock declined absolutely, from just over 199,000 units on the market to just under 176,000 units. After rent control was introduced in Berkeley, California, the number of private rental housing units available to students at the university there declined by 31 percent in five years.

None of this should be surprising, given the incentives created by rent control laws. In terms of incentives, it is likewise easy to understand what happened in England when rent control was extended in 1975 to cover furnished rental units. According to *The Times* of London:

> Advertisements for furnished rented accommodation in the London *Evening Standard* plummeted dramatically in the first week after the Act came into force and are now running at about 75 percent below last year's levels.

Since furnished rooms are often in people's homes, these represent housing units that are easily withdrawn from the market when the rents no longer compensate for the inconveniences of having renters living with you. The same principle applies where there are small apartment buildings like duplexes, where the owner is also one of the tenants. Within three years after rent control was imposed in Toronto in 1976, 23 percent of all rental units in owner-occupied dwellings were withdrawn from the housing market.

Even when rent control applies to apartment buildings where the landlord does not live, eventually the point may be reached where the whole building becomes sufficiently unprofitable that it is simply abandoned. In New York City, for example, many buildings have been abandoned after their owners found it impossible to collect enough rent to cover the costs of services that they are required by law to provide, such as heat and hot water. Such owners have simply disappeared, in order to escape the legal consequences of their abandonment, and such buildings often end up vacant and boarded up, though still physically sound enough to house people, if they continued to be maintained and repaired.

The number of abandoned buildings taken over by the New York City government over the years runs into the thousands. It has been estimated that there are at least four times as many abandoned housing units in New York City as there are homeless people living on the streets there. Homelessness is not due to a physical scarcity of housing, but to a price-related shortage, which is painfully real nonetheless. Such inefficiency in the allocation of resources means that people are sleeping outdoors on the pavement on cold winter nights—some dying of exposure—while the means of housing them already exist, but are not being used because of laws designed to make housing "affordable." Once again, this demonstrates that the efficient or inefficient allocation of scarce resources is not just some abstract notion of economists, but has very real consequences, which can even include matters of life and death. It also illustrates that the goal of a law—"affordable housing," in this case—tells us nothing about its actual consequences.

Just as rent control reduces the housing stock, so the end of rent control often marks the beginning of renewed private building. In Massachusetts, a statewide ban on local rent control laws in 1994 led to the construction of new apartment buildings in some formerly rent-controlled Massachusetts cities for the first time in 25 years. In short, with housing as with other things, less is supplied at a lower price than at a higher price—less both quantitatively and qualitatively. Polls of economists have found virtually unanimous agreement that declines in product quantity and quality are the usual effects of price controls in general. Of course, there are not enough economists in the entire country for their votes to matter very much to politicians.

The Politics of Rent Control

Politically, rent control is often a big success, however many serious economic and social problems it creates. Politicians know that there are always more tenants than landlords and more people who do not understand economics than people who do.

Often it is politically effective to represent rent control as a way to keep greedy rich landlords from "gouging" the poor with "unconscionable" rents. In reality, rates of return on investments in housing are seldom higher than on alternative investments and landlords are often people of very modest means. This is especially so for owners of small, low-end apartment buildings that are in constant need of repair, the kinds of places where tenants are likely to be low-income people. Many of the landlords with buildings like this are handymen who use their own skills and labor as carpenters or electricians to repair and maintain the premises, while trying to pay off the mortgage with the rents they collect. In short, the kind of housing likely to be rented by the poor often has owners who are by no means rich.

Where rent control laws apply on a blanket basis to all housing in existence as of the time the law goes into effect, even luxurious housing becomes low-rent housing. Then, after the passage of time makes clear that no new housing is likely to be built unless it is exempted from rent control, such exemptions or relaxations of rent control for new housing mean that even new apartments that are very modest in size and quality may rent for far more than older, more spacious and more luxurious apartments that are still under rent control. This non-comparability of rents has been common in European cities under rent control, as well as in New York and other American cities. Similar incentives produce similar results in many different settings. A news story in the *Wall Street Journal* pointed up this non-comparability of rents under New York's rent control laws:

> Les Katz, a 27-year-old acting student and doorman, rents a small studio apartment on Manhattan's Upper West Side for $1,200—with two roommates. Two sleep in separate beds in a loft built atop the kitchen, the third on a mattress in the main room.
> Across town on Park Avenue, Paul Haberman, a private investor, and his wife live in a spacious, two-bedroom apartment with a solarium and two terraces. The apartment in an elegant building on the prestigious avenue is worth at least $5,000 a month, real-estate professionals say. The couple pay around $350, according to rent records.

This example of cheap rent for the affluent or the wealthy under rent control was by no means unique. The chairman of the American Stock Exchange likewise paid only a few hundred dollars a month for a rent-controlled apartment on fashionable Central Park South. New York mayor Edward Koch kept his rent-controlled apartment during the entire 12 years when he lived in Gracie Mansion, the official residence of mayors. Hollywood actress Shelley Winters, who owned a home in Beverly Hills, also rented a two-bedroom apartment in Manhattan for a rent-controlled price of a few hundred dollars a month. Ironically, a statistical study indicated that the biggest difference between prices under New York's rent control law and free-market prices is in luxury apartments. In other words, the affluent and the wealthy get more benefit from rent control than do the poor who are invoked to justify such laws.

In New York, city welfare agencies have paid much higher rents than those just mentioned when they housed poverty-stricken families in cramped and roach-infested apartments in run-down hotels. The image that rent control protects poor tenants from rich landlords may be politically effective, but often it bears little resemblance to the reality. The people who actually benefit from rent control can be at any income level and so can those who lose out. It depends on who happens to be on the inside looking out, and who happens to be on the outside looking in, when such laws are passed.

San Francisco's rent control laws are not as old as those in New York City but they are similarly severe—and have produced very similar results. A study published in 2001 showed that more than one-fourth of the occupants of rent-controlled apartments in San Francisco had household incomes of more than $100,000 a year. It should also be noted that this was the first empirical study of rent control commissioned by the city of San Francisco. Since rent control began there in 1979, this means that for more than two decades these laws were enforced and extended, with no serious attempt being made to gauge their actual economic and social consequences, as distinguished from their political popularity.

Cities with strong rent control laws, such as New York and San Francisco, tend to end up with *higher* average rents than cities without rent control. Where such laws apply only to rents below some specified level, presumably to protect the poor, builders then have incentives to build only apartments luxurious enough to be above the rent-control level. Thereafter, rich and poor alike who move into a city where rent control has created a housing shortage typically cannot find a rent-controlled apartment vacant, and so have available only housing that costs more than it would in a free market, because of the housing shortage and the shift to the building of luxury housing. Not surprisingly, homelessness tends to be greater in cities with rent control—New York and San Francisco again being classic examples.

Scarcity versus Shortage

One of the crucial distinctions to keep in mind is that between an increased scarcity—where fewer goods are available relative to the population—and a "shortage" as a *price* phenomenon. There can be a growing shortage without an increased scarcity or a growing scarcity without a shortage.

As already noted, there was a severe housing shortage in the United States during and immediately after the Second World War, even though the ratio of housing to people was the same as it had been before the war, when there was no housing shortage. It is also possible to have the opposite situation, where the actual amount of housing suddenly declines in a given area without any price control—and without any shortage. This happened in the wake of the great San Francisco earthquake and fire of 1906. More than half the city's housing supply was destroyed during that catastrophe in just three days. Yet there was no housing shortage. When the *San Francisco Chronicle* resumed publication a month after the earthquake, its first issue contained 64 advertisements of apartments or homes for rent, compared to only 5 ads from people seeking apartments to live in.

Of the 200,000 people suddenly made homeless by the earthquake and fire, temporary shelters housed 30,000 and an estimated 75,000 left the city. Still, that left nearly 100,000 people to be absorbed into the local housing market. Yet the newspapers of that time mention no housing shortage. Rising prices not only allocate existing housing, they provide incentives for rebuilding. In short, just as there can be a shortage without any greater physical scarcity, so there can be a greater physical scarcity without any shortage. People made homeless by the huge 1906 San Francisco earthquake found housing more readily than people made homeless by New York's rent control laws that took thousands of buildings off the market.

Similar economic principles apply in other markets. During the American gasoline "crisis" of 1973-74, when oil prices were kept artificially low by the federal government, there were long lines of automobiles waiting at filling stations in cities across the United States, but there was in fact more gasoline sold in 1973 and 1974 than there was in any of the previous years, when there were no gasoline lines at filling stations, no shortage and no crisis atmosphere. Similarly, during the gasoline crisis of 1979, the amount of gasoline sold that year was only 3.5 percent less than in the record-breaking year of gasoline sales in 1978. Moreover, when the gasoline shortages ended after price controls were ended in 1981, there was less gasoline sold than there was during the "crisis" year with its long lines at filling stations. As with housing and other price-controlled goods, shortages and physical scarcities are two different things.[2]

The usual function of prices in directing goods and resources to where they are most in demand no longer operates under price controls, so that gasoline remained in short supply in many cities, even though it was more available in various communities to which people were driving less, such as rural or recreational areas. With prices being frozen in both places, there was little or no incentive to move the gasoline from one area to another, as would normally happen automatically with free market prices responding to supply and demand. Commenting on the unusual 1979 gasoline shortages in the United States, two Soviet economists pointed out an analogy with what happened regularly in the government-controlled economy of the Soviet Union:

> In an economy with rigidly planned proportions, such situations are not the exception but the rule—an everyday reality, a governing law. The absolute majority of goods is either in short supply or in surplus. Quite often the same product is in both categories—there is a shortage in one region and a surplus in another.

In a free market, supply and demand would cause prices to rise where goods are in short supply and fall where they are abundant, providing incentives to move things from regions where there is a surplus to regions where there is a shortage. But where prices are fixed by law, no such price movements occur and there is no incentive to move goods between the two regions. Theoretically, a government planning commission could either

_____

[2] Many have blamed the gasoline shortages and long lines at filling stations in 1973 on the Arab oil embargo of that year. However, the shortages and long lines began months *before* the Arab oil embargo, right after price controls were imposed. See Thomas Hazlett, *TV Coverage of the Oil Crises*, page 15.

issue orders to move these goods or change the prices in order to provide incentives for others to move them. In reality, Soviet planning commissions were overwhelmed by having to set more than 20 million prices and could hardly respond as quickly as a market where prices fluctuate freely and quickly in response to supply and demand. The U.S. government, with much less experience than the Soviets in trying to manage an economy, was even less able to micro-manage the gasoline market.

Just as price controls on apartments cause a cutback in painting, maintenance, and other auxiliary services that go with apartments, so price controls on gasoline led to a cutback on the hours that filling stations remained open for their customers' convenience. Because of the long lines of automobiles waiting to buy gasoline during the shortage, filling stations could sell gas continuously for a relatively few hours and then shut down for the day, instead of having to stay open around the clock to dispense the same amount of gasoline at a normal pace, with cars stopping in at whatever times were convenient to the motorists. In New York City, for example, the average filling station was open 110 hours a week in September 1978, before the shortage, but only 27 hours a week in June 1979, during the shortage. Yet the total amount of gasoline pumped differed by only a few percentage points between these two periods.

In short, the problem was not a substantially greater physical scarcity, but a shortage at artificially low prices. Shortages mean that the seller no longer has to please the buyer. That is why landlords can let maintenance and other services deteriorate under rent control. In this case, the filling station owners could save on the time during which they had to pay for electricity and other costs of remaining open long hours. No doubt many or most of the motorists whose daily lives and work were disrupted by having to spend hours driving around looking for a filling station with gas, or waiting in line behind other cars when they found one, would gladly have paid a few cents more per gallon of gasoline, in order to avoid such problems and stresses. But price control prevents buyers and sellers from making mutually advantageous transactions on terms different from those specified in the law.

Black Markets

Bolder and less scrupulous buyers and sellers make mutually advantageous transactions outside the law. Price controls almost invariably produce black markets, where prices are not only higher than the legally permitted prices, but also higher than they would be in a free market, since the legal risks must also be compensated. While small-scale black markets may function in secrecy, large-scale black markets usually require bribes to officials to look the other way. In Russia, for example, a local embargo on the shipment of price-controlled food beyond regional boundaries was dubbed the "150-ruble decree," since this was the cost of bribing police to let the shipments pass through checkpoints. Even during the early Soviet period, when operating a black market in food was punishable by death, black markets still existed. As two Soviet economists of a later era put it: "Even at the height of War Communism, speculators and food smugglers at the risk of their lives brought as much grain into the cities as all the state purchases made under *prodrazverstka*."

Statistics on black market activity are by nature elusive, since no one wants to let the whole world know that they are violating the law. However, sometimes there are indirect indications. Under American wartime price controls during and immediately after the Second World War, employment in meat-packing plants declined as meat was diverted from legitimate packing houses into black markets. This often translated into empty meat counters in butcher shops and grocery stores.[3]

As in other cases, however, this was not due simply to an actual physical scarcity of meat but to its diversion into illegal channels. Within one month after price controls were ended, employment in meat-packing plants rose from 93,000 to 163,000 and then rose again to 180,000 over the next two months. This nearly doubling of employment in meat-packing plants in just

---

[3] In many cases, goods in short supply were kept in the back of the store for sale to those people who were willing to offer more than the legal price. Black markets were not always separate operations, but were also a sideline of some otherwise legitimate businesses.

three months indicated that meat was clearly no longer being diverted from the packing houses after price controls were ended.

In the Soviet Union, where price controls were more pervasive and longer lasting, two Soviet economists wrote of a "gray market" where people paid "additional money for goods and services." Although these illegal transactions "are not taken into account by official statistics," the Soviet economists estimated that 83 percent of the population used these forbidden economic channels. These illegal markets covered a wide range of transactions, including "almost half of the repair of apartments," 40 percent of automobile repairs and more video sales than in the legal markets: "The black market trades almost 10,000 video titles, while the state market offers fewer than 1,000."

Quality Deterioration

One of the reasons for the political success of price controls is that part of their costs are concealed. Even the visible shortages do not tell the whole story. *Quality* deterioration, such as already noted in the case of housing, has been common with many other products and services whose prices have been kept artificially low by government fiat.

One of the fundamental problems of price control is defining just what it is whose price is being controlled. Even something as simple as an apple is not easy to define because apples differ in size, freshness, and appearance, quite aside from the different varieties of apples. Produce stores and supermarkets spend time (and hence money) sorting out different kinds and qualities of apples, throwing away those that fall below a certain quality that their respective customers expect. Under price control, however, the amount of apples demanded at an artificially low price exceeds the amount supplied, so there is no need to spend so much time and money sorting out apples, as they will all be sold anyway. Some apples that would ordinarily be thrown away under free market conditions may, under price control, be kept for sale to those people who arrive after all the good apples have been sold.

As with apartments under rent control, there is less incentive to maintain high quality when everything will sell anyway during a shortage.

Some of the most painful examples of quality deterioration have occurred in countries where there are price controls on medical care. At artificially low prices, more people go to doctors' offices with minor ailments like sniffles or skin rash that they might otherwise ignore, or else might treat with over-the-counter medications, perhaps with a pharmacist's advice. But all this changes when price controls reduce the cost of visits to the doctor's office, and especially when these visits are paid for by the government and are therefore free to the patient.

In short, more people make more claims on doctors' time under price control, leaving less time for other people with more serious, or even urgent, medical problems. Thus, under Britain's government-controlled medical system, a twelve-year-old girl was given a breast implant while 10,000 people waited 15 months or more for surgery, including a woman with cancer who had her operation postponed so many times that the malignancy eventually became inoperable. The priorities which prices automatically cause individuals to consider are among the first casualties of price controls.

A study conducted by the international agency Organization for Economic Co-operation and Development found that, among five English-speaking countries surveyed, only in the United States was the percentage of patients waiting for elective surgery for more than four months in single digits. All the other English-speaking countries—Australia, Canada, New Zealand, and the United Kingdom—had more than 20 percent of their patients waiting more than four months, with 38 percent of those in the United Kingdom waiting at least that long. In this group, the United States was the only country without government-set prices for medical treatment. Incidentally "elective surgery" is not confined to cosmetic surgery or other medically unnecessary procedures, but in this study included cataract surgery, hip replacement and coronary bypass surgery.

Delayed medical treatment is one aspect of quality deterioration when prices are set below the levels that would prevail under supply and demand. The quality of the treatment received is also affected when doctors spend less time per patient. In countries around the world, the amount of time that physicians spend per patient visit has been shorter under government-controlled medical care prices, compared to the time spent by physicians where prices are not controlled. Black markets are another common feature of price control that apply to medical care as to other things. In China and Japan, black markets have taken the form of bribes to doctors to get expedited treatment. In short, whether the product or service has been housing, apples, or medical care, quality deterioration under price control has been common in the most disparate settings.

PRICE FLOORS AND SURPLUSES

Just as a price set below the level that would prevail by supply and demand in a free market tends to cause more to be demanded and less to be supplied, creating a shortage at the imposed price, so a price set *above* the free market level tends to cause more to be supplied than demanded, creating a surplus. Simple as this principle seems, it is often lost sight of in the swirl of more complex events and more politically popular beliefs.

Agricultural price-support programs are one of the classic examples of a lower limit to prices imposed by government. As often happens, a real but transient problem led to the establishment of enduring government programs, which long outlived the conditions that initially caused these programs to be created.

Among the many tragedies of the Great Depression of the 1930s was the fact that many American farmers simply could not make enough money from the sale of their crops to pay their bills. The prices of farm products fell much more drastically than the prices of the things that farmers bought. As many farmers lost their farms because they could no longer pay the mortgages, and as other farm families suffered privations as they struggled to hang on to their farms and their traditional way of life, the federal government sought to restore what was called "parity" between agriculture and other sectors of the economy by intervening to keep farm prices from falling so sharply.

This intervention took various forms. One approach was to reduce by law the amount of various crops that could be grown and sold, so as to prevent the supply from driving the price below the level that government officials had decided upon. Thus, supplies of peanuts and cotton were restricted by law. Supplies of citrus fruit, nuts and various other farm products were regulated by local cartels of farmers, backed up by the authority of the Secretary of Agriculture to issue "marketing orders" and prosecute those who violated these orders by producing and selling more than they were authorized to produce and sell. Such arrangements continued for decades after the poverty of the Great Depression was replaced by the prosperity of the boom following World War II.

These indirect methods of keeping prices artificially high were only part of the story. The key factor in keeping farm prices artificially higher than they would have been under free market supply and demand was the government's willingness to buy up the surpluses created by its control of prices. This they did for such farm products as corn, rice, tobacco, and wheat, among others.

Price control in the form of a "floor" under prices, preventing these prices from falling further, produced surpluses as dramatic as the shortages produced by price control in the form of a "ceiling" preventing prices from rising higher. In some years, the federal government bought more than one-fourth of all the wheat grown in the United States and took it off the market, in order to maintain prices at a pre-determined level.

During the Great Depression of the 1930s, agricultural price support programs led to vast amounts of food being deliberately destroyed at a time when malnutrition was a serious problem in the United States and hunger marches were taking place in cities across the country. For example, the federal government bought 6 million hogs in 1933 alone and destroyed them. Huge amounts of farm produce were plowed under, in order to keep it off the market and maintain prices at the officially fixed level, and vast amounts of milk were poured down the sewers for the same reason. Meanwhile, many American children were suffering from diseases caused by malnutrition.

Still, there was a food surplus. A surplus, like a shortage, is a *price* phenomenon. A surplus does not mean that there is some excess relative to the people. There was not "too much" food relative to the population during the Great Depression. The people simply did not have enough money to buy everything that was produced at the artificially high prices set by the government. A very similar situation existed in poverty-stricken India at the beginning of the twenty-first century, where there was a surplus of wheat and rice under government price supports. The *Far Eastern Economic Review* reported:

> India's public stock of food grains is at an all-time high, and next spring, it will grow still further to a whopping 80 million tonnes, or four times the amount necessary in case of a national emergency. Yet while that wheat and rice sits idle—in some cases for years, to the point of rotting— millions of Indians don't have enough to eat.

A report from India in the *New York Times* told a very similar story under the headline, "Poor in India Starve as Surplus Wheat Rots":

> Surplus from this year's wheat harvest, bought by the government from farmers, sits moldering in muddy fields here in Punjab State. Some of the previous year's wheat surplus sits untouched, too, and the year's before that, and the year's before that.
>
> To the south, in the neighboring state of Rajasthan, villagers ate boiled leaves or discs of bread made from grass seeds in late summer and autumn because they could not afford to buy wheat. One by one, children and adults—as many as 47 in all—wilted away from hunger-related causes, often clutching pained stomachs.

A surplus or "glut" of food in India, where malnutrition is still a serious problem, may seem like a contradiction in terms. But food surpluses under "floor" prices are just as real as the housing shortages under "ceiling" prices. In the United States, the vast amount of storage space required to keep surplus crops off the market once led to such desperate expedients as storing these farm products in unused warships, when all the storage facilities on land had been filled to capacity. Otherwise, American wheat would have had to be left outside to rot, as in India. A series of bumper crops in the United States could lead to the federal government's having more wheat in storage than was grown by American farmers all year. In India, it was reported in 2002 that the Indian government was spending more on storage of its surplus produce than on agriculture, rural development, irrigation and flood control combined.

None of this is peculiar to the United States or to India.

The countries of the European Union spent $39 billion in direct subsidies in 2002 and their consumers spent twice as much as that in the inflated food prices created by these agricultural programs. Meanwhile, the surplus food was sold below cost on the world market, driving down the prices that Third World farmers could get for their produce. In all these countries, not only the government but also the consumers are paying for agricultural price-support programs—the government directly in payments to farmers and storage companies and the consumers in inflated food prices. As of 2001, American consumers were paying $1.9 billion a year in artificially higher prices, just for products containing sugar, while the government was paying $1.4 million per *month* just to store the surplus sugar. Meanwhile, the *New York Times* reported that sugar producers were "big donors to both Republicans and Democrats" and that the costly sugar price support program had "bipartisan support."

In 2002, the U.S. Congress passed a farm subsidy bill that was estimated to cost the average American family more than $4,000 over the next decade in taxes and inflated food prices. Nor was this a new development. During the mid-1980s, when the price of sugar on the world market was four cents a pound, the wholesale price within the United States was 20 cents a pound. The government was subsidizing the production of something that Americans could have gotten cheaper by not producing it at all and buying it in the world market. This has been true of sugar for decades. Moreover, sugar is not unique in this respect, nor is the United States. In the nations of the European Union, the prices of lamb, butter, and sugar are all more than twice as high as their world market prices. As a writer for the *Wall Street Journal* put it, every cow in the European Union gets more subsidies per day than most Africans have to live on.

Although the original rationale for the American price-support programs was to save family farms, in practice more of the money went to big agricultural corporations, some of which received millions of dollars each, while the average farm received only a few hundred dollars. Most of the money from the 2002 bipartisan farm bill will likewise go to the wealthiest 10 percent of farmers—including David Rockefeller, Ted Turner, and a dozen companies on the *Fortune* 500 list. In Mexico as well, 85 percent of agricultural subsides go to the largest 15 percent of farmers.

What is crucial from the standpoint of understanding the role of prices in the economy is that persistent surpluses are as much a result of keeping prices artificially high as persistent shortages are of keeping prices artificially low. Nor were the losses simply the sums of money extracted from the taxpayers or the consumers for the benefit of agricultural corporations and farmers. These are internal transfers within a nation, which do not directly reduce the total wealth of the country. The real losses to the country as a whole come from the misallocation of scarce resources which have alternative uses.

Scarce resources such as land, labor, fertilizer, and machinery are needlessly used to produce more food than the consumers are willing to consume at the artificially high prices decreed by the government. All the vast resources used to produce sugar in the United States are wasted when sugar can be imported from countries in the tropics, where it is produced much more cheaply. Poor people, who spend an especially high percentage of their income on food, are forced to pay far more than necessary to get the amount of food they receive, leaving them with less money for other things. Those on food stamps are able to buy less food with those stamps when food prices are artificially inflated. From a purely economic standpoint, it is working at cross purposes to subsidize farmers by forcing food prices up and then subsidize some consumers by bringing down their particular costs of food with subsidies—as is done in both India and the United States. However, from a political standpoint, it makes perfect sense to gain the support of two different sets of voters, especially since most of them do not understand the full economic implications of the policies.

Even when agricultural subsidies and price controls originated during hard times as a humanitarian measure, they have persisted long past those times because they developed an organized constituency which threatened to create political trouble if these subsidies and controls were removed or even reduced. Farmers have blocked the streets of Paris with their farm machinery when the French government showed signs of scaling back its agricultural programs or allowing more foreign farm produce to be imported. In Canada, farmers protesting low wheat prices blocked highways and formed a motorcade of tractors to the capital city of Ottawa.

While roughly one-fifth of farming income in the United States comes from government subsidies, more than 40 percent of farming income in countries of the European Union comes from such subsidies, as does an absolute majority of the farming income in Japan.

THE POLITICS OF PRICE CONTROLS

Simple as basic economic principles may be, their ramifications can be quite complex, as we have seen with the various effects of rent control laws and agricultural price support laws. However, even this basic level of economics is seldom understood by the public, which often demands political "solutions" that turn out to make matters worse. Nor is this a new phenomenon of modern times in democratic countries.

When a Spanish blockade in the sixteenth century tried to starve Spain's rebellious subjects in Antwerp into surrender, the resulting high prices of food within Antwerp caused others to smuggle food into the city, even through the blockade, enabling the inhabitants to continue to hold out. However, the authorities within Antwerp decided to solve the problem of high food prices by laws fixing the maximum price to be allowed to be charged for given food items and providing severe penalties for anyone violating those laws. There followed the classic consequences of price control—a larger consumption of the artificially lower-priced goods and a reduction in the supply of such goods, since suppliers were less willing to run the risk of sending food through the Spanish blockade without the additional incentive of higher prices. Therefore, the net effect of price control was that "the city lived in high spirits until all at once provisions gave out" and Antwerp had no choice but to surrender to the Spaniards.

Halfway around the world, in eighteenth-century India, a local famine in Bengal brought a government crackdown on food dealers and speculators, imposing price controls on rice. Here the resulting shortages led to widespread deaths by starvation. However, when another famine struck India in the nineteenth century, under the colonial rule of British officials and during the heyday of free market economics, opposite policies were followed, with opposite results:

> In the earlier famine one could hardly engage in the grain trade without becoming amenable to the law. In 1866 respectable men in vast numbers went into the trade; for the Government, by publishing weekly returns of the rates in every district, rendered the traffic both easy and safe. Everyone knew where to buy grain cheapest and where to sell it dearest and food was accordingly bought from the districts which could best spare it and carried to those which most urgently needed it.

As elementary as all this may seem, in terms of economic principles, it was made possible politically only because the British colonial government was not accountable to local public opinion. In an era of democratic politics, the same actions would require either a public familiar with basic economics or political leaders willing to risk their careers to do what needed to be done. It is hard to know which is less likely.

Chapter 4

AN OVERVIEW

We need education in the obvious more than investigation of the obscure.

Justice Oliver Wendell Holmes

Many of the basic principles of economics may seem obvious but the implications to be drawn from them are not. Someone once pointed out that Newton was not the first man who saw an apple fall. His fame was based on his being the first to understand its implications. Economists have understood for centuries that when prices are higher, people tend to buy less than when prices are lower. But, even today, many people do not understand the many implications of that simple fact.[1]

Understanding any subject requires that it first be defined, so that you are clear in your own mind as to what you are talking about—and what you are not talking about. It is not merely the subject matter which defines economics, but also its methods and its purposes. Just as a poetic discussion of the weather is not meteorology, so an issuance of moral pronouncements or political creeds about the economy is not economics. Economics is a study of *cause-and-effect* relationships in an economy. Its purpose is to discern the consequences of various ways of allocating scarce resources

---

[1] One consequence of not thinking through the implications of this simple fact is that government-provided medical care has repeatedly cost far more than initially estimated, in countries around the world. These estimates have usually been based on current usage of doctors, hospitals, and pharmaceutical drugs. But the introduction of free or subsidized medical care leads to vastly greater usage, entailing vastly greater costs than initially estimated.

which have alternative uses. It has nothing to say about social philosophy or moral values, any more than it has anything to say about music, literature, or medical science.

These other things are not necessarily any less important, they are simply not what economics is about. No one expects mathematics to explain love and no one should expect economics to be something other than what it is or to do something other than what it can. But both mathematics and economics can be very important where they apply. Careful and complex mathematical calculations can be the difference between having an astronaut who is returning to earth from orbit end up crashing in the Himalayas or landing safely in Florida. We have also seen similar social disasters from misunderstanding the basic principles of economics.

CAUSE AND EFFECT

Analyzing economic actions in cause-and-effect terms means examining the logic of the incentives being created, rather than simply the goals being sought. It also means examining the empirical evidence of what actually happens under such incentives.

The kind of causation at work in an economy is often *systemic interactions*, rather than the kind of simple one-way causation involved when one billiard ball hits another billiard ball and knocks it into a pocket. Systemic causation involves more complex reciprocal interactions, such as adding lye to hydrochloric acid and ending up with salty water,[2] because both chemicals are transformed by their effects on one another, going from being two deadly substances to becoming one harmless one.

In an economy as well, the plans of buyers and sellers are transformed as they discover each other's reactions to supply and demand conditions and the resulting price changes that force them to reassess their plans. For

---

[2] Do *not* try this at home. Professional chemists can handle these dangerous chemicals, with appropriate safeguards, in a laboratory but either can be fatal in other hands.

example, those who start out planning to buy a villa at the beach may end up settling for a bungalow farther inland, after they discover the high prices of villas at the beach. Likewise, suppliers sometimes end up selling their goods for less than they paid to buy them or produce them, when the demand is inadequate to get any higher price from the consuming public and the alternative is to get nothing at all for an item that is unsalable at the price originally planned.

Systemic Causation

Because systemic causation involves reciprocal interactions, rather than one-way causation, that in turn reduces the role of individual intentions. As Friedrich Engels put it, "what each individual wills is obstructed by everyone else, and what emerges is something that no one willed." Economics is concerned with what *emerges*, not what anyone intended. Similar reasoning had appeared even earlier in the writings of Adam Smith, where the benefits of competitive capitalism were said to be "no part" of the capitalist's intention. (That is why Adam Smith had a high opinion of capitalism, despite his low opinion of capitalists.) If the stock market closes at 10,463 on a given day, that is the end result of a process of complex interactions among innumerable buyers and sellers of stocks, none of whom may have intended for the market to close at 10,463, even though it was their own actions in pursuit of other intentions which caused it to do so.

While causation can sometimes be explained by intentional actions and sometimes by systemic interactions, too often the results of systemic interactions are falsely explained by individual intentions. Just as primitive peoples tended to attribute such things as the swaying of trees in the wind to some intentional action by an invisible spirit, rather than to such systemic causes as variations in atmospheric pressure, so there is a tendency toward intentional explanations of systemic events in the economy, when people are unaware of basic economic principles. For example, while rising prices are likely to reflect changes in supply and demand, people ignorant of economics may attribute the rises to "greed."

Such an intentional explanation raises more questions than it answers. For example, if greed is the explanation, why do prices vary so much from one time to another or from one place to another? Does greed vary that much and in the same pattern? In the Los Angeles basin, homes near the ocean sell for much higher prices than similar homes located in the smoggy interior. Does this mean that fresh air promotes greed, while smog makes home sellers more reasonable? To say that prices are due to greed is to imply that sellers can set prices by an act of will. If so, no company would ever go bankrupt, since it could simply raise its prices to cover whatever its costs happened to be. But the systemic interactions of the marketplace through supply and demand force the high-cost company to keep its prices down to where their competitors' prices are, thereby leading to losses and bankruptcy. Charging higher prices would simply mean more losses of sales and faster bankruptcy.

Free markets with millions of buyers and sellers are governed by systemic interactions, since the intentions of any of these individual buyers and sellers has so small an effect. The implications of this simple fact are many. Not only can prices not be set and sustained by an act of will, neither can businesses that compete with other businesses make other important decisions on the whim of the owner and expect to survive. When Henry Ford headed the largest automobile manufacturing company in the world, he thought that he could offer his car in just one color (black) and just one style from year to year. But that is the very reason General Motors overtook the Ford Motor Company to become number one in the automobile industry, by offering cars in a variety of colors and changing the style from year to year. The Ford Motor Company survived only by eventually following the new pattern set by General Motors. But it never regained its position as the leading seller of automobiles.

People shocked by the high prices charged in stores in low-income neighborhoods have often been quick to blame greed or exploitation on the part of the people who run such businesses. Similar conclusions about intentions have often been reached when they noticed the much higher interest rates charged by pawnbrokers and small finance companies that operate in low-income neighborhoods, as compared to the interest rates charged by banks in middle-class communities. Yet studies show that profit rates are generally no higher in inner city businesses than elsewhere, and the fact that many businesses are leaving such neighborhoods—and others, such as supermarket chains, are staying away—reinforces that conclusion.

The painful fact that poor people end up paying more than affluent people for many goods and services has a very plain—and systemic— explanation. It often costs more to deliver goods and services in low-income neighborhoods. Higher insurance costs and higher costs for various security precautions, due to higher rates of crime and vandalism, are just some of the systemic reasons that get ignored by those seeking an explanation in terms of personal intentions. For example, an inner city shopping center in one midwestern city had to spend 15 percent more on security guards and lighting than a comparable suburban shopping complex. All these costs get passed along to the local customers in higher prices.

In addition, the cost of doing business tends to be higher per dollar of business in low-income neighborhoods. Lending $100 each to fifty low-income borrowers at pawn shops or local finance companies takes more time and costs more money to process the transactions than lending $5,000 at a bank to one middle-class customer, even though the same total sum of money is involved in both cases.[3] An armored car delivering money in small denominations to a small check-cashing agency in a ghetto costs just as much as an armored car delivering a hundred times as much value of money, in larger bills, to a bank in a suburban shopping mall. With the cost of business being higher per dollar of business in the low-income community, it is hardly surprising that these higher costs get passed on in higher prices and higher interest rates. Higher prices for people who can least afford them is a tragic end-result, but its causes are systemic.

---

[3] In many cases, the middle-class borrower who already has a checking account at the bank from which he wishes to borrow also has an automatic line of credit available with that checking account. When the need for a $5,000 loan arises, there may be no need even to file an application. The borrower simply writes $5,000 more in checks than there is money in the account, and the automatic line of credit covers it, with minimum time and trouble to both the borrower and the bank, since the potential borrower's credit rating was already established when the account was first opened and the size of the line of credit was established on the basis of that credit rating.

This is not merely a philosophical distinction. There are major practical consequences to the way causation is understood. Treating the causes of higher prices and higher interest rates in low-income neighborhoods as being personal greed or exploitation, and trying to remedy it by imposing price controls and interest rate ceilings only ensures that even less will be supplied to people living in low-income neighborhoods thereafter. Just as rent control reduces the supply of housing, so price controls and interest rate controls can reduce the number of stores, pawn shops, and local finance companies willing to operate in neighborhoods with higher costs, when those costs cannot be recovered by legally permissible prices and interest rates. The alternative, for many residents of low-income neighborhoods, may be to go outside the legal money-lending organizations and borrow from loan sharks, who charge even higher rates of interest and have their own methods of collecting.

When stores and financial institutions close down in low-income neighborhoods, more people in such neighborhoods are then forced to travel to other neighborhoods to shop for groceries or other goods, paying money for bus fare or taxi fare, in addition to the costs of their purchases. Such business closings have already occurred for a variety of reasons, including riots and higher rates of shoplifting and vandalism, with the net result that many people in low-income neighborhoods already have to go elsewhere for shopping or banking.

An old adage says: "First, do no harm." Understanding the distinction between systemic causation and intentional causation is one way to do less harm with economic policies. It is especially important to do no harm to people who are already in painful economic circumstances. It is also worth noting that most people are not criminals, even in high-crime neighborhoods. The fraction of dishonest people in such neighborhoods are the real source of many of the higher costs behind the higher prices charged by businesses operating in those neighborhoods. But it is both intellectually and emotionally easier to blame high prices on those who collect them, rather than on those who cause them. It is also more politically popular to blame outsiders, especially if those outsiders are of a different ethnic background.

Systemic causes, such as are often found in economics, provide no such emotional release for the public or moral melodrama for the media and politicians as such intentional causes as "greed," "exploitation," "gouging," "discrimination," and the like. Intentional explanations of cause and effect may also be more natural, in the sense that less sophisticated individuals and less sophisticated societies tend to turn first to such explanations. In some cases, it has taken centuries for intentional explanations embodied in superstitions about nature to give way to systemic explanations based on science. It is not yet clear whether it will take that long for the basic principles of economics to replace many people's natural tendency to try to explain systemic results by intentional causes.

Complexity and Causation

Although the basic principles of economics are not very complicated, the very ease with which they can be learned also makes them easy to dismiss as "simplistic" by those who do not want to accept analyses which contradict some of their cherished beliefs. Evasions of the obvious are often far more complicated than the plain facts. Nor is it automatically true that complex effects must have complex causes. The ramifications of something very simple can become enormously complex. For example, the simple fact that the earth is tilted on its axis causes innumerable very complex reactions in plants, animals, and people, as well as in such non-living things as ocean currents, weather changes and changes in the length of night and day.

If the earth stood straight up on its axis,[4] night and day would be the same length all year around and in all parts of the world at the same time. Climate would still differ between the equator and the poles but, at any given place, the weather would be the same in winter as in summer. The fact

---

[4] Purists can say that there is no up or down in space, but that simply requires rephrasing the same facts by saying that the axis on which the earth rotates is not perpendicular to the plane of the planet's orbit around the sun.

that the earth is tilted on its axis means that sunlight is striking the same country at different angles at different points during the planet's annual orbit around the sun, leading to changing warmth and changing lengths of night and day. In turn, such changes trigger complex biological reactions in plant growth, animal hibernations and migrations, as well as psychological changes in human beings and many seasonal changes in their economies. Changing weather patterns affect ocean currents and the frequency of hurricanes, among many other phenomena. Yet all of these complications are due to the one simple fact that the earth is tilted on its axis, instead of being straight up.

In short, complex effects may be a result of either simple causes or complex causes. The specific facts can tell us which. *A priori* pronouncements about what is "simplistic" cannot.

Few things are more simple than the fact that people tend to buy more at lower prices and buy less at higher prices. But, when putting that together with the fact that producers tend to supply more at higher prices and less at lower prices, that is enough to predict many sorts of complex reactions to price controls, whether in the housing market or in the market for food, electricity, or medical care. Moreover, these reactions have been found on all inhabited continents and over thousands of years of recorded history. Simple causes and complex effects have been common among wide varieties of peoples and cultures.

Individual versus Systemic Rationality

The tendency to personalize causation leads not only to charges that "greed" causes high prices in market economies, but also to charges that "stupidity" among bureaucrats is responsible for many things that go wrong in government economic activities. In reality, many of the things that go wrong in these activities are due to perfectly rational actions, *given the incentives* faced by government officials who run such activities and given the constraints on the amount of knowledge available to any given decision-maker or set of decision-makers.

Where a policy or institution has been established by top political leaders, officials subject to their authority may well hesitate to contradict their beliefs, much less point out the counterproductive consequences that later follow from these policies and institutions. Messengers carrying bad news could be risking their careers or—under Stalin or Mao—their lives.

Officials carrying out particular policies may be quite rational, however negative the impact of these policies may prove to be for society at large. During the Stalin era in the Soviet Union, for example, there was at one time a severe shortage of mining equipment, but the manager of a factory producing such machines kept them in storage after they were built, rather than sending them out to the mines, where they were sorely needed. The reason was that the official orders called for these machines to be painted with red, oil-resistant paint and the manufacturer had on hand only green, oil-resistant paint and red varnish that was not oil-resistant. Disobeying official orders in any respect was a serious offense under Stalin and "I don't want to get eight years," the manager said.

When he explained the situation to a higher official and asked for permission to use the green, oil-resistant paint, this official's response was: "Well, I don't want to get eight years either." However, the higher official cabled to his ministry for their permission to give his permission. After a long delay, the ministry eventually granted his request and the mining machinery was finally shipped to the mines. None of these people was behaving stupidly or irrationally. They were responding quite rationally to the incentives and constraints of the system in which they worked. Under any economic or political system, people can make their choices only among the alternatives actually available—and different systems present different alternatives.

INCENTIVES VERSUS GOALS

Because economics is a study of cause and effect among human beings, it deals with incentives and their consequences. That often leads to radically different conclusions from those reached by people who think primarily or solely in terms of goals and their desirability. As already noted in Chapter 3, the goal of providing "affordable housing" for the poor through rent control can lead to diverting resources toward the building of luxury housing or office buildings, when these latter are exempted from rent control and therefore offer a rate of return on investment that is higher than what is available by building housing for the poor. In short, the consequences are the exact opposite of the goal.

It must be emphasized that these are *empirical* consequences, because some people seem to think that the role of prices in the economy is simply a theory by those with "faith in the market." However, it was a Swedish socialist—presumably lacking such "faith" in the capitalist market—who said that rent control "appears to be the most efficient technique presently known to destroy a city—except for bombing." He was an economist familiar with the empirical evidence. Another comparison between bombing and rent control was made by an official of the Communist government of Vietnam, some years after the Vietnam war. "The Americans couldn't destroy Hanoi" by bombing it during the war, he said, "but we have destroyed our city by very low rents." As a Communist with no bias toward the free market, he had learned the hard way that artificially low rents encouraged demand while discouraging supply—a very simple principle, indeed, but one with major impacts on those who fail to heed it.

While bombing does more immediate damage to a city, wars end and many cities have been rapidly rebuilt in the postwar world. Rent control does more long-lasting damage because most people do not understand the basic economics of it and that allows it to continue reducing the housing supply for decades.

Economics was christened "the dismal science" precisely because its analysis frustrated so many hopes and desires. On the other hand, knowing what is not possible can spare us many disappointments and avoid many disasters. Because human beings can be as wrong in their pessimism as in their optimism, economics has also served to expose the fallacies of many doom-and-gloom prophets. This will become especially apparent in Chapter 12, which includes an analysis of the economic reasons why so many predictions of natural resource exhaustion have repeatedly turned out to be so wrong, by such huge margins, for so many years or even generations.

Incentives matter because most people will usually do more for their own benefit than for the benefit of others. Incentives link the two concerns together. A waitress brings food to your table, not because of your hunger, but because her salary and tips depend on it. In the absence of such incentives, service in restaurants in the Soviet Union was notoriously bad. Unsold goods piling up in warehouses were not the only consequences of a lack of the incentives that come with a free market price system. Prices not only help determine which particular things are produced, they are also one of the ways of rationing the inherent scarcity of all goods and services. However, prices do not create that scarcity, which will require some form of rationing under any other economic system.

Simple as all this may seem, it goes counter to many programs and policies designed to make various goods and services "affordable" or to keep them from becoming "prohibitively expensive." Being prohibitive is precisely how prices limit how much each person uses. If everything were made affordable by government decree, there would still not be any more to go around than when things were prohibitively expensive. There would simply have to be some alternative rationing method. Whether that method was through ration coupons, political influence, black markets, or just fighting over things when they go on sale, the rationing would still have to be done, since artificially making things affordable does not create any more total output. On the contrary, price "ceilings" tend to cause less output to be produced.

While scarcity is inherent, shortages are not. Scarcity simply means that there is not enough to satisfy everyone's desires completely. Only in the Garden of Eden was there enough to do that. A shortage, however, means that there are people who are willing to pay the price of the product but are unable to find it. Price is an integral part of what a shortage is all about, even though many people mistakenly believe that there is a greater physical scarcity of goods during a shortage.

Many apparently humanitarian policies have backfired throughout history because of a failure to understand the role of prices. Attempts to keep food prices down by imposing price controls have led to hunger and even starvation, whether in seventeenth-century Italy, eighteenth-century India, France after the French Revolution, Russia after the Bolshevik revolution, or in a number of African countries after they obtained independence during the 1960s. Some of these African countries, like some of the countries in Eastern Europe, once had such an abundance of food that they were food exporters before the era of price control and government planning turned them into countries unable to feed themselves.

None of this is new or peculiar to a modern capitalist economy. Back in the days of the Roman Empire, the emperor Diocletian issued imperial decrees which set the prices of many goods—and, as a contemporary account put it, "people brought provisions no more to markets." It would be much the same story nearly two thousand years later in America, when price controls during the Nixon administration led to declining supplies of the goods subject to those controls. In Ghana, the country lost its long-standing position as the world's number one producer of cocoa when the government limited how much money would be paid to farmers growing cocoa—and Ghana regained that position after the disastrous decline in the cocoa crop that followed forced the government to change its policy.

Failure to supply goods, as a result of political restrictions on the economy, must be sharply distinguished from an inability to produce them. Food can be in short supply in a country with extraordinarily fertile soil, as in post-Communist Russia that had not yet achieved a free-market economy:

> Undulating gently through pastoral hills 150 miles south of Moscow, the Plava River Valley is a farmer's dream come true. This is the gateway to what Russians call "Chernozym"—"Black Earth country"—which boasts some of the most fertile soil in Europe, within three hours' drive of a giant, hungry metropolis. . . Black Earth country has the natural wealth to feed an entire nation. But it can barely feed itself.

It is hard even to imagine, in a free market economy, a hungry city, dependent on imports of foreign food, when there is extraordinarily fertile farmland not far away. Yet the people on that very fertile farmland were as poor as the city dwellers were hungry. The workers harvesting that land earned the equivalent of about $10 a week, with even this small amount being paid in kind—sacks of potatoes or cucumbers—because of a lack of money. As the mayor of a town in this region said:

> We ought to be rich. We have wonderful soil. We have the scientific know-how. We have qualified people. But what does it add up to?

If nothing else, it adds up to a reason for understanding economics as a means of achieving an efficient allocation of scarce resources which have alternative uses. All that was lacking in Russia was a market to connect the hungry city with the products of the fertile land and a government that would allow such a market to function freely. In some places, local Russian officials forbad the movement of food across local boundary lines, in order to assure low food prices within their own jurisdictions, and therefore local political support for themselves. Again, it is necessary to emphasize that this was not a stupid policy, from the standpoint of officials trying to gain local popularity with consumers by maintaining low food prices. This protected their political careers, however disastrous such policies were for the country as a whole.

While systemic causation is in one sense impersonal, in the sense that its outcomes are not specifically predetermined by any given person, "the market" is ultimately a way by which many people's individual personal desires are reconciled with those of others. Too often a false contrast is made between the impersonal marketplace and the compassionate policies of various government programs. But both systems face the same scarcity of resources and both systems make choices within the constraints of that scarcity. The difference is that one system involves each individual making choices for himself or herself, while the other system involves a smaller number of people making choices for millions of others. The mechanisms of the market are impersonal but the choices made by individuals are as personal as choices made anywhere else.

It may be fashionable for journalists to refer to "the whim of the marketplace," as if that were something different from the desires of people, just as it was once fashionable to refer to "production for use, rather than profit"—as if profits could be made by producing things that people cannot use or do not want to use. The real contrast is between choices made by individuals for themselves and choices made for them by others who presume to define what these individuals "really" need.

SCARCITY AND COMPETITION

Scarcity means that everyone's desires cannot be satisfied completely, regardless of which particular economic system or government policy we choose—and regardless of whether an individual or a society is poor or prosperous. Therefore competition among people for these resources is inherent. It is not a question whether we like or dislike competition. Scarcity means that we do not have the option to *choose* whether or not to have an economy in which people compete. That is the only kind of economy that is possible—and our only choice is among the particular methods that can be used for this competition.

Economic Institutions

One way in which competition for scarce resources might take place would be for those who hold political power to decide how resources should be allocated to different uses and the resulting products shared among different people. This has happened in ancient despotisms and under modern communism. Conceivably, the people themselves might decide voluntarily how to share things, as in some tribal societies or in an Israeli kibbutz, though it is hard to imagine how that could happen in societies consisting of millions of people.

Yet another method of sharing resources among competing uses and competing individuals is by having them bid for these resources and the products resulting from them. In this system—a price-coordinated economy—those who want to use wood to produce furniture must bid against those who want to use it to produce paper, houses, or baseball bats. Those who want to use milk to produce cheese must bid against those who want to use it to produce yogurt or ice cream. Most people may be unaware that they are competing and simply see themselves as deciding how much of various things to buy at whatever prices they find, but scarcity ensures that they are competing with others, even if they are conscious only of weighing their own purchasing decisions against the amount of money they have available.

One of the incidental benefits of competing and sharing through prices is that different people are not as likely to think of themselves as rivals, nor to develop the kinds of hostility that rivalry can breed. For example, much the same labor and construction material needed to build a Protestant church could be used to build a Catholic church. But, if a Protestant congregation is raising money to build a church for themselves, they are likely to be preoccupied with how much money they can raise and how much is needed for the kind of church they want. Construction prices may cause them to scale back some of their more elaborate plans, in order to fit within the limits of what they can afford. But they are unlikely to blame Catholics, even though the competition of Catholics for the same construction materials makes their prices higher than otherwise.

If, instead, the government were in the business of building churches and giving them to different religious groups, Protestants and Catholics would be explicit rivals for this largess and neither would have any financial incentive to cut back on their building plans to accommodate the other. Instead, each would have an incentive to make the case, as strongly as possible, for the full extent of their desires, to mobilize their followers politically to insist on getting what they want, and to resent any suggestion that they scale back their plans. The inherent scarcity of materials and labor would still limit what could be built, but that limit would now be imposed politically and would be seen by each as due to the rivalry of the other. The Constitution of the United States of course prevents the American government from building churches for religious groups, no doubt in order to prevent just such political rivalries and the bitterness, and sometimes bloodshed, to which such rivalries have led in other countries.

The same economic principle, however, applies to groups that are not based on religion but on ethnicity, geographical regions, or age brackets. All are inherently competing for the same resources, simply because these resources are scarce. However, competing indirectly by having to keep your demands within the limits of your own pocketbook is very different from seeing your desires for government benefits thwarted directly by the rival claims of some other group. Self-rationing not only tends to mean less social and political friction but also more economic efficiency, since each individual knows his or her own preferences better than any third party can, and can therefore make incremental trade-offs that are more personally satisfying within the limits of the available resources.

Because of the inescapable reality of scarcity, rationing must take place under any form of economic system, ranging from capitalism to the kibbutz or other communal arrangements, and regardless of whether the particular economy is prosperous or poor, large or small. Under a price system, people ration themselves. Price rationing limits the amount of each individual's claims on the output of others to what that individual's own productivity has created for others and thereby earned as income. What price controls, subsidies, or other substitutes for price allocation do is reduce the incentives for self-rationing. That is why people with minor ailments go to doctors when medical care is either free or heavily subsidized by the government and why farmers receiving government-subsidized water from irrigation projects grow crops requiring huge amounts of water that they would never grow if they had to pay the full costs of that water themselves.

Society as a whole always has to pay the full costs, regardless of what prices are or are not charged to individuals. Greater self-indulgence by some when there are fewer price restraints means that less is left for others. Thus many apartments occupied by just one person under rent control mean that others have trouble finding a place to stay, even when they are perfectly willing and able to pay the rent-controlled price.

Moreover, since rationing must take place with or without prices, this simply means that some form of non-price rationing becomes a substitute.

Simply waiting until what you want becomes available has been a common form of non-price rationing. This can mean waiting in line at stores, as was common in the Soviet economy, or being put on a waiting list for surgery, as patients often are in countries where government-provided medical care is either free or heavily subsidized. Luck and corruption are other substitutes for price rationing. Whoever happens to be in a store when a new shipment of some product in short supply arrives can get the first opportunity to buy it, while people who happen to learn about it much later can find the coveted product all gone by the time they get there. In other cases, personal or political favoritism or bribery takes the place of luck in gaining preferential access, or formal rationing systems may replace favoritism with some one-size-fits-all policy administered by government agencies. However it is done, the rationing that is done by prices in some economies cannot be gotten rid of by getting rid of prices or reducing their role.

Incremental Substitution

Because economic resources are not only scarce but have alternative uses, the efficient use of these resources requires both consumers and producers to make trade-offs and substitutions. Prices provide the incentives for doing so. When the price of oranges goes up, some consumers switch to tangerines. When bacon becomes more expensive, some consumers switch to ham. When the cost of a vacation at the beach rises, some people decide to go on a cruise instead. Note that what is happening here is not just substitution—it is *incremental* substitution. Not everyone stops eating oranges when they become more pricey. Some people continue to eat the same number of oranges they always ate, some cut back a little, some cut back a lot, and others forget about oranges completely and go on to some other fruit.

When the price of oranges rises, it is very likely because the number of oranges demanded at the existing price exceeds the number of oranges actually available. Something has to give. Incremental substitution, because of price increases, causes the loss to be minimized by being borne more by those who are relatively indifferent as between oranges and other substitutes, rather than by those who are so devoted to oranges that they will simply pay the higher prices and continue to eat the same number of oranges as before, cutting back somewhere else in their budget to offset the additional money spent on oranges.

Incremental substitutions take place in production as well as consumption. Petroleum, for example, can be used to make heating oil or gasoline, among many other things. More petroleum is turned into heating oil during the winter, when the demand for heating oil is greatest, and more into gasoline during the summer, when many people are doing more driving to recreational areas. This is not a total substitution, since some petroleum is turned into both products (and many others) throughout the year. It is *incremental* substitution—somewhat more of *A* at the cost of somewhat less of *B*. Prices facilitate this kind of substitution, as they reflect incrementally changing amounts demanded, leading to incremental changes in the amount supplied.

Trade-offs and substitution can take place either intentionally or systemically. For example, automobiles have intentionally substituted technology for gasoline by becoming more fuel-efficient as a result of adding high-tech equipment to their engines. Thus, the average American car drove 2,000 miles more in 1998 than in 1973, but used about 200 gallons less gasoline than a quarter of a century earlier. The equipment added to engines obviously has a cost, but the cost of this technology substitutes incrementally for the cost of gasoline.

A *systemic* trade-off occurs when the economy as a whole uses less oil because the composition of its output changes. As a higher proportion of the output of the American economy has over the years come to consist of services, rather than material goods, less fuel is required in their production. It takes less fuel to create more advanced software than to manufacture steel or automobiles. Over all, the amount of fuel used per dollar of national output in the American economy has declined steadily since the early 1970s, when oil prices were raised dramatically by the international petroleum cartel. Because different kinds of economic activities were affected differently by the rising price of oil, investors and entrepreneurs found the relative profitability of various industries changing and changed their own decisions accordingly, whether or not they considered the role of oil prices in all this.

As important as it is to understand the role of substitutions, it is also important to keep in mind that the efficient allocation of resources requires that these substitutions be *incremental*, not total. For example, one may believe that health is more important than amusements but, however reasonable that may sound as a general principle, no one really believes that having a twenty-year's supply of band-aids in the closet is more important than having to give up all music in order to pay for it. A price-coordinated economy facilitates incremental substitution, but political decision-making tends toward categorical *priorities*—that is, declaring one thing absolutely more important than another and creating laws and policies accordingly.

When a political figure says that we need to "set national priorities" about one thing or another, what that amounts to is making *A* categorically more important than *B*. That is the opposite of incremental substitution, in which the value of each depends on how much of each we already have at the moment, and therefore on the changing amount of *A* that we are willing to give up in order to get more *B*. This variation in value can be so great as to convert something that is beneficial into something that is detrimental, and vice versa. For example, human beings cannot live without salt, fat, and cholesterol, but most Americans get so much of all three that their lifespan is reduced. Conversely, despite the many problems caused by alcohol, from fatal automobile accidents to deaths from cirrhosis of the liver, studies show that very modest amounts of alcohol have health benefits that can be life-saving.[5] It is not categorically good or bad.

Whenever there are two things which each have some value, one cannot be categorically more valuable than another. A diamond may be worth much more than a penny but enough pennies will be worth more than any diamond. That is why incremental trade-offs tend to produce better results than categorical priorities.

Chronic complaints about government red tape in countries around the world are understandable in view of the incentives facing those who create

---

[5] Men who drank either nothing alcoholic or just one drink per week had a reduction in cardiovascular disease when they increased their alcohol intake by from one to six drinks per week. However, among men who already averaged seven or more alcoholic drinks per week, an increase in their drinking led to more

government forms, rules, and requirements for innumerable activities that need official approval. Nothing is easier than thinking of additional requirements that might be useful in some way, and nothing is harder than remembering to ask the crucial incremental question: *At what cost?* People who are spending their own money are confronted with those costs at every turn, whether they remember or not, but people who are spending the taxpayers' money—or who are simply imposing uncounted costs on businesses, homeowners, and others—have no real incentives to even find out how much the additional costs are, much less to hold off on adding requirements when the incremental costs threaten to become larger than the incremental benefits. Red tape grows as a result.

Any attempt to get rid of some of this red tape is likely to be countered by officials who point out what useful purpose it may serve in some circumstances. But they are unlikely even to pose the question whether its incremental value exceeds its incremental costs. There are no incentives for them to look at things that way.

Subsidies and Taxes

Ideally, prices allow alternative users to compete for scarce resources in the marketplace. However, this competition is distorted to the extent that special taxes are put on some products or resources but not on others, or when some products or resources are subsidized by the government but others are not. Prices charged to the consumers of such specially taxed or specially subsidized goods and services do not convey the real costs of producing them and therefore do not produce the same trade-offs as if they did. Yet there is always a political temptation to subsidize "good" things and tax "bad" things. However, when neither good things nor bad things are good or bad categorically, this prevents our finding out just how good or

---

cardiovascular disease, according to the *Archives of Internal Medicine*, September 25, 2000 issue. The medical publication *The Lancet* reported that "light-to-moderate alcohol consumption is associated with a reduced risk of dementia in individuals aged 55 years or older" in its January 26, 2002 issue.

how bad any of these things is by letting people choose freely, uninfluenced by politically changed prices. People who want special taxes or subsidies for particular things seem not to understand that what they are really asking for is for the prices to *misstate* the relative scarcities of things and the relative values that the users of these things put on them.

One of the factors in California's periodic water crises, for example, is that California farmers' use of water is subsidized so heavily that its price to farmers is less than one percent of what the same amount of water costs people living in Los Angeles or San Francisco. The net result is that agriculture, which accounts for about 10 percent of the state's output, consumes three-quarters of its water. Another consequence of subsidized water is that farmers grow crops requiring great amounts of water, such as rice and cotton, in California's very dry climate, where such crops would never be grown if farmers had to pay the real costs of the water they use. Inspiring as it may be to some that California's arid lands have been enabled to produce vast amounts of fruits and vegetables with the aid of subsidized water, those same fruits and vegetables could be produced more cheaply elsewhere with water supplied free of charge from the clouds.

The way to tell whether the California produce is worth what it costs to grow is to allow all those costs to be paid by California farmers who compete with farmers in other states that have higher rainfall levels. There is no need for government officials to decide arbitrarily—and categorically—whether it is a good thing or a bad thing for particular crops to be grown in California with water artificially supplied below cost from federal irrigation projects. Such questions can be decided incrementally, by those directly confronting the alternatives, through price competition in a free market.

California is, unfortunately, not unique in this respect. In fact, this is not a peculiarly American problem. Halfway around the world, the government of India provides "almost free electricity and water" to farmers, according to *The Economist* magazine, encouraging farmers to plant too much "water-guzzling rice," with the result that water tables in the Punjab "are dropping fast." Making anything artificially cheap usually means that it will be wasted, whatever that thing might be and wherever it might be located.

From the standpoint of the allocation of resources, government should either not tax resources, goods, and services or else tax them all equally, so as to minimize the distortions of choices made by consumers and producers. For similar reasons, particular resources, goods, and services should not be subsidized, even if particular people are subsidized out of humanitarian concern over their being the victims of natural disasters, birth defects, or other misfortunes beyond their control. Giving poor people money would accomplish the same humanitarian purpose without the same distortion in the allocation of resources.

From a political standpoint, however, politicians win votes by doing special favors for special interests or putting special taxes on whomever or whatever might be unpopular at the moment. The free market may work best when there is a level playing field but politicians win more votes by tilting the playing field to favor particular groups.

The Meaning of "Costs"

In light of the role of trade-offs and substitutions, it is easier to understand the real meaning of costs as the foregone opportunities to use the same resources elsewhere. Because an economy deals with scarce resources which have alternative uses, every benefit has a cost in the alternative uses that could have been made of the same resources that created a particular benefit. We do not simply "put" a price on things. Things have inherent costs and our political choice is only between trying to suppress the conveying of those costs to the users in prices or allowing these inherent costs to be expressed in the marketplace.

Free-market prices are not mere arbitrary obstacles to getting what people want. Prices are symptoms of an underlying reality that is not nearly as susceptible to political manipulation as the prices are. Prices are like thermometer readings—and a patient with a fever is not going to be helped by plunging the thermometer into ice water to lower the reading. On the contrary, if we were to take the new readings seriously and imagine that the patient's fever was over, the dangers would be even greater, now that the underlying reality was being ignored.

Despite how obvious all this might seem, there are never-ending streams of political schemes designed to escape the realities being conveyed by prices—whether through direct price controls or by making this or that "affordable" with subsidies or by having the government itself supply various goods and services free, as a "right." There are probably more ill-conceived economic policies based on treating prices as just nuisances to get around than on any other single fallacy. What all these schemes have in common is that they exempt some things from the process of weighing costs and benefits against one another.

Sometimes the rationale for removing particular things from the process of weighing costs against benefits is expressed in some such question as: "How can you put a price on art?"—or education, health, music, etc. The fundamental fallacy underlying this question is the belief that prices are simply "put" on things. So long as art, education, health, music, and thousands of other things all require time, effort, and raw material, the costs of these inputs are inherent. These costs do not go away because a law prevents them from being conveyed through prices in the marketplace. Ultimately, to society as a whole, costs are the other things that could have been produced with the same resources. Money flows and price movements are symptoms of that fact—and suppressing those symptoms will not change the underlying fact.

One reason for the popularity of price controls is a confusion between prices and costs. For example, politicians who say that they will "bring down the cost of medical care" almost invariably mean that they will bring down the *prices* paid for medical care. The actual costs of medical care—the years of training for doctors, the resources used in building and equipping hospitals, the hundreds of millions of dollars for years of research to develop a single new medication—are unlikely to decline in the slightest. Nor are these things even likely to be addressed by politicians. What they mean by bringing down the cost of medical care is reducing the price of medicines and reducing the fees charged by doctors or hospitals.

Once the distinction between prices and costs is recognized, then it is not very surprising that price controls have the negative consequences that they do, because price ceilings mean a refusal to pay the costs. Those who supply housing, food, medications or innumerable other goods and services are unlikely to keep on supplying them in the same quantities and qualities when they cannot recover the costs that such quantities and qualities require. This may not become apparent immediately, which is why price controls are often popular, but the consequences are lasting and often become worse over time. Housing does not disappear immediately when there is rent control but it deteriorates over time without being replaced by sufficient new housing as it wears out. Existing medicines do not vanish under price controls but new medicines to deal with cancer, AIDS, Alzheimer's and numerous other afflictions are unlikely to continue to be developed at the same pace when the money to pay for it is just not there any more. But all this takes time to unfold and memories may be too short for most people to connect the bad consequences they see to the popular policies they supported some years back.

PART II: INDUSTRY AND COMMERCE

Chapter 5

THE RISE AND FALL
OF BUSINESSES

Failure is part of the natural cycle of business. Companies
are born, companies die, capitalism moves forward.
Fortune *magazine*

Ordinarily, we tend to think of businesses as simply money-making enterprises, but that can be very misleading, in at least two ways. First of all, most businesses go out of business within a very few years after getting started, so it is likely that at least as many businesses are losing money as are making money. More important, from the standpoint of economics, is not what money the business owner hopes to make or whether he succeeds, but how all this affects the use of scarce resources which have alternative uses—and therefore how it affects the economic well-being of millions of other people in the society at large.

ADJUSTING TO CHANGES

The businesses we hear about, in the media and elsewhere, are usually those which have succeeded, and especially those which have succeeded on a grand scale—Microsoft, Toyota, Sony, Lloyd's of London, Credit Suisse. In an earlier era, Americans would have heard about the A & P grocery chain, once the largest retail chain in any field, anywhere in the world. Its 15,000 stores in 1929 were more than any other retailer ever had in

America, before or since. The fact that A & P has now shrunk to a minute fraction of its former size, and is virtually unknown, suggests that industry and commerce are not static things, but dynamic processes, in which individual companies and whole industries rise and fall, as a result of relentless competition under changing conditions.

In just one year—between 2001 and 2002—36 businesses dropped off the list of the *Fortune* 500 largest companies, including Enron, which had been the fifth largest company in America the previous year. F.A.O. Schwarz, once the grand toy store chain of them all, succumbed to competition from Wal-Mart. As the *New York Times* reported:

> The corporate owner of F.A.O. Schwarz stores said last week that it would file for bankruptcy. Bemoaning the news, analysts explained that the F.A.O. Schwarz formula of selling premium-priced toys in sumptuous surroundings could not withstand the steady advance of Wal-Mart into the toy business.

Such falls from the financial peaks are by no means confined to the United States. At one time the largest bank in the world, Japan's Mizuho had a $20 billion loss in its fiscal year ending in 2003 and the value of its stock fell by 93 percent. The amount by which its total stock value fell was greater than the Gross Domestic Product of New Zealand.

At the heart of all of this is the role of profits—and of *losses*. Each is equally important from the standpoint of forcing companies and industries to use scarce resources efficiently. Industry and commerce are not just a matter of routine management, with profits rolling in more or less automatically. Masses of ever-changing details, within an ever-changing surrounding economic and social environment, mean that the threat of losses hangs over even the biggest and most successful businesses. There is a reason why business executives usually work far longer hours than their employees, and why so many businesses fail within a few years after getting started. Only from the outside does it look easy.

Just as companies rise and fall over time, so do profit rates—even more quickly. When compact discs began rapidly replacing vinyl records in the late 1980s, Japanese manufacturers of CD players "thrived" according to the *Far Eastern Economic Review*. But "within a few years, CD-players only offered manufacturers razor-thin margins." This has been a common experience with many products in many industries. The companies which first introduce a product that consumers like may make large profits, but those very profits attract more investments into existing companies and encourage new companies to form, both of which add to output, driving down prices and profit margins through competition as prices decline in response to supply and demand. Sometimes prices fall so low that profits turn to losses, forcing some firms into bankruptcy until the industry's supply and demand balance at levels that are financially sustainable.

Even the largest corporations can see profits turn to losses and vice versa. Sony lost $354 million in a six-month period and then, about a year later, had profits that topped one billion dollars. Lloyd's of London had losses of $4 billion in 1990, profits of $2 billion in 1994 and 1995, losses in excess of $4 billion in 2001 and profits of just over a billion dollars in 2002. General Motors lost $30 billion during a three-year period in the early 1990s but rebounded under new management to earn nearly $4 billion in profits in 2002.

Over longer periods of time, relative rankings in an industry also change. United States Steel was founded in 1901 as the largest steel producer in the world. It made the steel for the Panama Canal, the Empire State Building, and more than 150 million automobiles. Yet, by 2003, U.S. Steel had fallen to 10th place in the industry and, more important, was losing $218 million a year. Boeing, producer of the famous B-17 "flying fortress" bombers in World War II and since then the largest producer of commercial airliners such as the 747, was in 1998 selling more than twice as many such aircraft as its nearest rival, the French firm Airbus. But, in 2003, Airbus passed Boeing as the number one producer of commercial aircraft in the world and had a far larger number of back orders for planes to be delivered in the future. Yet Airbus too faltered and in 2006 its top managers were fired for falling behind schedule in the development of new aircraft, while Boeing regained the lead in sales of planes.

In short, although corporations may be thought of as big, impersonal and inscrutable institutions, they are ultimately run by human beings who all differ from one another and who all have shortcomings and make mistakes in every kind of economic system in countries around the world. Companies superbly adapted to a given set of conditions can be left behind when those conditions change suddenly and their competitors are quicker to respond. Sometimes the changes are technological, as in the computer industry, and sometimes these changes are social or economic.

Social Changes

The A & P grocery chain was for decades a company superbly adapted to social and economic conditions in the United States. It was by far the leading grocery chain in the country, renowned for its high quality and low prices. During the 1920s the A & P chain was making a phenomenal rate of profit on its investment—never less than 20 percent per year, about double the national average—and it continued to prosper on through the decades of the 1930s, 1940s and 1950s. But all this began to change drastically in the 1970s, when A & P lost more than $50 million in one 52-week period. A few years later, it lost $157 million over the same span of time. Its decline had begun and, in the years ahead, many thousands of A & P stores were forced to close, as the chain shrank to become a shadow of its former self.

A & P's fate, both when it prospered and when it lost out to rival grocery chains, illustrates the dynamic nature of a price-coordinated economy and the role of profits and losses. When A & P was prospering up through the 1950s, it did so by charging *lower* prices than competing grocery stores. It could do this because its exceptional efficiency kept its costs lower than those of other grocery stores and chains, and the resulting lower prices attracted vast numbers of customers. Later, when A & P began to lose customers to other grocery chains, this was because these other chains now had lower costs than A & P and could therefore sell for lower prices. Changing conditions in the surrounding society brought this about—together with differences in the speed with which different companies spotted these changes, realized their implications, and adjusted accordingly.

What were these changes? In the years following the end of World War II, suburbanization and the American public's rising prosperity gave huge supermarkets in shopping malls with vast parking lots decisive advantages over neighborhood stores—such as those of A & P—located along the streets in the central cities. As the ownership of automobiles, refrigerators and freezers became far more widespread, this completely changed the economics of the grocery industry. The automobile, which made suburbanization possible, also made possible greater economies of scale for both customers and supermarkets. Shoppers could now buy far more groceries at one time than they could have carried home in their arms from an urban neighborhood store before the war. That was the crucial role of the automobile. Moreover, refrigerators and freezers now made it possible to stock up on perishable items like meat and dairy products. This led to fewer trips to grocery stores, with larger purchases each time.

What this meant to the supermarket itself was a larger volume of sales at a given location, which could now draw customers in automobiles from miles around, whereas a neighborhood store in the central city was unlikely to draw customers on foot from ten blocks away. High volume meant savings in delivery costs from the producers to the supermarket, as compared to delivering the same total amount of groceries in smaller individual lots to many scattered neighborhood stores, whose total sales would add up to what one supermarket sold. This also meant savings in the cost of selling within the supermarket, because it did not take as long to check out one customer buying $50 worth of groceries at a supermarket as it did to check out ten customers buying $5 worth of groceries each at a neighborhood store. Because of these and other differences in the costs of doing business, supermarkets could be very profitable while charging prices lower than those in neighborhood stores that were struggling to survive.

All this not only lowered the costs of delivering groceries to the consumer, it changed the relative economic advantages and disadvantages of different locations for stores. Some supermarket chains, such as Safeway, responded to these radically new conditions faster and better than A & P did. The A & P stores lingered in the central cities longer and also did not follow the shifts of population to California and other sunbelt regions.

A & P was also reluctant to sign long leases or pay high prices for new locations where the customers and their money were now moving. As a result, after years of being the lowest-price major grocery chain, A & P suddenly found itself being undersold by rivals with even lower costs of doing business.[1]

Lower costs reflected in lower prices is what made A & P the world's leading retail chain in the first half of the twentieth century. Similarly, lower costs reflected in lower prices is what enabled other supermarket chains to take A & P's customers away in the second half of the twentieth century. While A & P succeeded in one era and failed in another, what is far more important is that the economy as a whole succeeded in both eras in getting its groceries at the lowest prices possible at the time—from whichever company happened to have the lowest prices. Such displacements of industry leaders continued in the early twenty-first century, when general merchandiser Wal-Mart moved to the top of the grocery industry, with nearly double the number of stores selling groceries as Safeway had.

Many corporations that once dominated their fields have likewise fallen behind in the face of changes or have even gone bankrupt. Pan American Airways, which pioneered in commercial flights across the Atlantic and the Pacific in the first half of the twentieth century, went out of business in the late twentieth century, as a result of increased competition among airlines in the wake of the deregulation of the airline industry. Famous newspapers like the *New York Herald-Tribune*, with a pedigree going back more than a century, stopped publishing in a new environment, after television became a major source of news and newspaper unions made publishing more costly. Between 1949 and 1989, the total number of copies of all the newspapers

---

[1] Why did A & P not adjust to the new conditions as fast as Safeway? Partly, the answer may be that there are always differences among individuals in how fast they notice changes, realize their implications, and respond. Another factor in the case of A & P was that the company was owned and operated for nearly a century by the same family, and the death of the last brother to run it in 1951 brought to leadership a man who had served faithfully under the old system. Was such a man at such a time, in the wake of his leader's death, likely to radically change the company's policies and throw away the managerial legacy he had inherited?

sold daily in New York City fell from more than 6 million copies to less than 3 million.

The *Herald-Tribune* was one of many local newspapers across the country to go out of business with the rise of television. The *New York Daily Mirror*, with a circulation of more than a million readers in 1949, went out of business in 1963. By 2004, the only American newspapers with daily circulations of a million or more were newspapers sold nationwide—*USA Today*, the *Wall Street Journal* and the *New York Times*. Back in 1949, New York City alone had two local newspapers that each sold more than a million copies daily—the *Daily Mirror* at 1,020,879 and the *Daily News* at 2,254,644.

Other great industrial and commercial firms that have declined or become extinct are likewise a monument to the unrelenting pressures of competition. So is the rising prosperity of the consuming public. The fate of particular companies or industries is not what is most important. Consumers are the principal beneficiaries of lower prices made possible by the more efficient allocation of scarce resources which have alternative uses. The key roles in all of this are played not only by prices and profits, but also by losses. These losses force businesses to change with changing conditions or find themselves losing out to competitors who spot the new trends sooner or who understand their implications better and respond faster. Knowledge is one of the scarcest of all resources in any economy, and the insight distilled from knowledge is scarcer still. An economy based on prices, profits, and losses gives decisive advantages to those with greater knowledge and insight.

Put differently, knowledge and insight can guide the allocation of resources, even if most people, including the country's political leaders, do not share that knowledge or do not have the insight to understand what is happening. Clearly this is not true in the kind of economic system where political leaders control economic decisions, for then the limited knowledge and insights of those leaders become decisive barriers to the progress of the whole economy. Even when leaders have more knowledge and insight than the average member of the society, they are unlikely to have nearly as much knowledge and insight as exists scattered among the millions of people subject to their governance.

Knowledge and insight need not be technological or scientific for it to be economically valuable and decisive for the material well-being of the society as a whole. Something as mundane as retailing changed radically during the course of the twentieth century, revolutionizing both department stores and grocery stores—and raising the standard of living of millions of people by lowering the costs of delivering goods to them.

Names like Sears and Ward's came to mean department store chains to most Americans by the late twentieth century. However, neither of these enterprises began as department store chains. Montgomery Ward—the original name of Ward's department stores—began as a mail-order house in the nineteenth century. Under the conditions of that time, before there were automobiles or trucks, and with most Americans living in small rural communities, the high costs of delivering consumer goods to widely-scattered local stores was reflected in the prices that were charged. These prices, in turn, meant that ordinary people could seldom afford many of the things that we today regard as basic.

Montgomery Ward cut delivery costs by operating as a mail-order house, selling directly to consumers all over the country from its huge warehouse in Chicago, and using the government's already existing mail delivery system to deliver its products to customers. Montgomery Ward's high volume of sales also reduced its cost per sale and allowed it to cut its prices below those charged by local stores in small communities. Under these conditions, it became the world's largest retailer in the late nineteenth century, at a time when Richard Sears was just a young railroad agent who sold watches on the side. Yet the small company that Sears founded grew over the years to eventually become several times the size of Montgomery Ward—and it outlasted the demise of its rival in 2001, when the latter closed its doors for the last time under its more recent name, Ward's department stores.

Differences in management had much to do with the different fates of these two companies, long after both Aaron Montgomery Ward and Richard Warren Sears were gone. One indication of the size of these two retail giants in their heyday as mail-order houses was that each had railroad tracks running through its Chicago warehouse. That was one of the ways it cut delivery costs, in addition to relying on mailmen to distribute its products in the course of their normal mail deliveries, instead of distributing those products through local retail outlets.

More important than the fates of these two businesses was the fact that millions of people were able to afford a higher standard of living than if they had to be supplied with goods through costlier channels. Meanwhile, there were changes in American society, with more and more people beginning to live in urban communities. This was not a secret, but not everyone noticed such gradual changes and even fewer had the insight to understand their implications for retail selling. It was 1920 before the census showed that, for the first time in the country's history, there were more Americans living in urban areas than in rural areas.

One man who liked to pore over such statistics was Robert Wood, an executive at Montgomery Ward. Now, he realized, selling merchandise through a chain of urban department stores would be more efficient and more profitable than selling exclusively by mail order. Not only were his insights not shared by the head of Montgomery Ward, Wood was fired for trying to change company policy.

Meanwhile, a man named James Cash Penney had the same insight and was already setting up his own chain of department stores. From very modest beginnings, the J. C. Penney chain grew to almost 300 stores by 1920 and more than a thousand by the end of the decade. Their greater efficiency in delivering goods to urban consumers was a boon to consumers—and Penney's competition became a big economic problem for the mail order giants Sears and Montgomery Ward, both of which began losing money as department stores began taking customers away from mail-order houses. The fired Robert Wood went to work for Sears and was more successful there in convincing their top management to begin building department stores of their own. After they did, Montgomery Ward had no choice but to do the same belatedly, though it was never able to catch up to Sears again.

Rather than get lost in the details of the histories of particular businesses, we need to look at this from the standpoint of the economy as a whole and the standard of living of the people as a whole. One of the biggest advantages of an economy coordinated by prices and operating under the incentives created by profit and loss is that it can tap scarce knowledge and insights, even when most of the people—or even their intellectual and political elites—do not have such knowledge or insights. The competitive advantages of those who are right can overwhelm the numerical, or even financial, advantages of those who are wrong.

James Cash Penney did not start with a lot of money. He was in fact raised in poverty and began his retail career as just a one-third partner in a store in a little town in Wyoming, at a time when Sears and Montgomery Ward were unchallenged giants of nationwide retailing. Yet his insights into the changing conditions of retailing eventually forced these giants into doing things his way, on pain of extinction. While Robert Wood failed to convince Montgomery Ward to change, competition and red ink on the bottom line finally convinced them. In a later era, a clerk in a J.C. Penney store named Sam Walton would learn retailing from the ground up and then put his knowledge and insights to work in his own store, which would eventually expand to become the Wal-Mart chain, with sales larger than those of Sears and J. C. Penney combined.

One of the great handicaps of economies run by political authorities, whether under medieval mercantilism or modern communism, is that insights which arise among the masses have no such powerful leverage as to force those in authority to change the way they do things. Under any form of economic or political system, those at the top tend to become complacent, if not arrogant. Convincing them of anything is not easy, especially when it is some new way of doing things that is very different from what they are used to. The big advantage of a free market is that you don't have to convince anybody of anything. You simply compete with them in the marketplace and let that be the test of what works best.

Imagine a system in which J. C. Penney had to verbally convince the heads of Sears and Montgomery Ward to expand beyond mail-order retailing and build a nationwide chain of stores. Their response might well have been: "Who is this guy Penney—a part-owner of some little store in a hick town nobody ever heard of—to tell us how to run the largest retail companies in the world?"

In a market economy, Penney did not have to convince anybody of anything. All he had to do was deliver the merchandise to the consumers at a lower price. His success, and the millions of dollars in losses suffered by Sears and Montgomery Ward as a result, left these corporate giants no choice but to imitate this upstart, in order to become profitable again and regain their leadership of the retail merchandise industry. Although J.C. Penney grew up in worse poverty than most people who are on welfare today, his ideas and insights prevailed against some of the richest men of his time, who eventually realized that they would not have remained rich for long if Penney and others had kept taking away their customers, leaving their companies with millions of dollars in losses each year.

Economic Changes

Economic changes include not only changes in the economy but also changes within the managements of firms, especially in their responses to external economic changes. Many things that we take for granted today, as features of a modern economy, were resisted when first proposed and had to fight uphill to establish themselves by the power of the marketplace. Even something as widely used today as credit cards were initially resisted. When MasterCard and BankAmericard first appeared in the 1960s, leading New York department stores such as Macy's and Bloomingdale's said that they had no intention of accepting credit cards as payments for purchases in their stores, even though there were already millions of people with such cards in the New York metropolitan area.

Only after the success of credit cards in smaller stores did the big department stores finally relent and begin accepting credit cards—and eventually issuing their own. In 2003, for the first time, more purchases were made by credit cards or debit cards than by cash. That same year, *Fortune* magazine reported that a number of companies made more money from their own credit card business, with its interest charges, than from selling goods and services. Sears made more than half its profits from its credit cards and Circuit City made all of its profits from its credit cards, while losing $17 million on its sales of electronic merchandise. Neither individuals nor companies are successful forever. Death alone guarantees turnover in management. Given the importance of the human factor and the variability among people—or even with the same person at different stages of life—it can hardly be surprising that dramatic changes in the relative positions of businesses have been the norm.

An A & P executive during its declining years summarized its predicament by saying: "The simple fact is that A & P had only one major management problem—the company was unable to replace Mr. John," the name long used inside the company for John Hartford, the last member of the founding family to run A & P. The decline of A & P began with his death. His successors could not simply continue his policies, for the whole retail grocery industry and the society around it were changing rapidly. "You cannot run a retail business from memory," John Hartford himself once remarked. What was needed after his death were not the particular policies and practices that were geared to his day. What was needed was the same kind of foresight, dedication, and imagination that had raised A & P to its pinnacle in the first place—and such talents are not always readily available, certainly not continuously and indefinitely in one company.

Some executives are very successful during one era in the country's evolution, or during one period in their own lives, and very ineffective at a later time. Sewell Avery, for example, was for many years a highly successful and widely praised leader of U.S. Gypsum and later of Montgomery Ward. Yet his last years were marked by public criticism and controversy over the way he ran Montgomery Ward, and by a bitter fight for control of the company that he was regarded as mismanaging. When Avery resigned as chief executive officer, the value of Montgomery Ward's stock rose immediately. Under his leadership, Montgomery Ward had put aside so many millions of dollars as a cushion against an economic downturn that *Forbes* magazine called it "a bank with a store front." Meanwhile, rivals like Sears were using their money to expand into new markets.

What is important is not the success or failure of particular individuals or companies, but the success of particular knowledge and insights in prevailing despite the blindness or resistance of particular business owners and managers. Given the scarcity of mental resources, an economy in which knowledge and insights have such decisive advantages in the competition of the marketplace is an economy which itself has great advantages in creating a higher standard of living for the population at large. A society in which only members of a hereditary aristocracy, a military junta, or a ruling political party can make major decisions is a society which has thrown away much of the knowledge, insights, and talents of most of its own people. A society in which such decisions can only be made by males has thrown away half of its knowledge, talents, and insights.

Contrast societies with such restricted sources of ability with a society in which a farm boy who walked eight miles to Detroit to look for a job could end up creating the Ford Motor Company and changing the face of America with mass-produced automobiles—or a society in which a couple of young bicycle mechanics could create the airplane and change the whole world. Neither a lack of pedigree nor a lack of academic degrees nor even a lack of money could stop ideas that worked, for investment money is always looking for a winner to back and cash in on. A society which can tap all kinds of talents from all segments of its population has obvious advantages over societies in which only the talents of a preselected few are allowed to determine its destiny.

No economic system can depend on the continuing wisdom of its current leaders. A price-coordinated economy with competition in the marketplace does not have to, because those leaders can be forced to change course—or be replaced—whether because of red ink, irate stockholders, outside investors ready to take over, or because of bankruptcy. Given such economic pressures, it is hardly surprising that economies under the thumbs of kings or commissars have seldom matched the track record of economies based on competition and prices.

Technological Changes

For more than a century, Eastman Kodak was the largest photographic company in the world. But new technology created new competitors. At the end of the twentieth century and the beginning of the twenty-first century, digital cameras began to be produced not only by such traditional producers of cameras for film as Nikon, Canon, and Minolta, but also by producers of other computerized products such as Sony and Samsung. Film sales began falling for the first time after 2000 and digital camera sales surpassed the sales of film cameras for the first time three years later. The sudden change dropped Eastman Kodak out of first place, leaving it scrambling to convert from film photography to digital photography.

Such technological revolutions were by no means confined to the photographic industry. Smith Corona dominated the typewriter industry for decades, but then laptop computers appeared on the scene and displaced portable typewriters, while desktop computers began displacing other typewriters. Like A & P before it, Smith Corona began losing millions of dollars under changed conditions. It went five years in a row without making a profit during the 1980s. Only by beginning to produce word processors, a sort of half-way house between typewriters and computers, was Smith Corona able to survive and begin making money again. Yet the relentless spread of personal computers continued to shrink the market for these alternatives. Although Smith Corona manufactured over half the typewriters and word processors sold in North America as late as 1989, six years later it filed for bankruptcy.

THE COORDINATION OF KNOWLEDGE

In medieval times, when craftsmen produced everything from swords to plowshares on a direct order from the customer, there was no problem of knowing what was wanted by whom. But a modern economy—whether capitalist or socialist—faces an entirely different situation. Today's supermarket or department store stocks an incredible variety of goods without knowing who will buy how much of what. Automobile dealers, bookstores, florists, and other businesses likewise keep a stock on hand to sell, without really knowing what the consumers will turn out to want. In a capitalist economy, wrong guesses can lead to anything from clearance sales to bankruptcy.

Under both capitalism and socialism, the scarcity of knowledge is the same, but the way these different economies deal with it can be quite different. The problem is not simply with the over-all scarcity of knowledge, but also with the fact that this knowledge is often fragmented into tiny bits and pieces, the totality of which is not known to anybody.

Imagine the difficulties of an oil company headquartered in Texas trying to decide how much gasoline—and what kinds—will be needed in a filling station at the corner of Market and Castro Streets in San Francisco during the various seasons of the year, as well as in thousands of other locations across the country. The people who actually own and operate the filling stations at all these locations have far better knowledge of what their particular customers are likely to buy at different times of the year than anybody in a corporate headquarters in Texas can hope to have.

Variations can be great, even within a single city at a single time. If people who live in the vicinity of Market and Castro Streets in San Francisco own more sports cars than people who live near the filling station at 19th Avenue and Irving Street, then the filling station owner at Market and Castro is likely to order more premium gasoline than the filling station owner who sells to people with cheaper cars that use cheaper gasoline or to truckers who want diesel fuel. No single person at any given location—whether at a filling station or in corporate headquarters—can possibly have all this information for the whole country at his fingertips, much less keep updating it for thousands of filling stations from coast to coast as the seasons and the neighborhoods change. But that is wholly unnecessary in an economy where each kind of fuel simply goes wherever the money directs it to go.

The amount of such highly localized information, known to thousands of individual filling station owners scattered across the United States, is too enormous to be transmitted to some central point and then be digested in time to lead to government allocations of fuel with the same efficiency as a price-coordinated market can achieve. No oil company knows or cares about all this detailed information. All they know is that orders are pouring in for diesel fuel in North Dakota this month, while Massachusetts is buying lots of premium gasoline and Ohio is buying mostly regular unleaded. Next month it may be a totally different pattern and the oil company may not have any more clue about the reasons for the new pattern than about the reasons for the old. But all that the oil company has to do is to supply the demand, wherever it is and for whatever reason. Their job is infinitely easier than the task facing central planners in a socialist economy.

Like oil company executives in the United States, the executives who ran Soviet enterprises had no way to keep track of all the thousands of local conditions and millions of individual desires in a country that stretched all the way across the Eurasian land mass from Eastern Europe to the Pacific Ocean. Unlike American executives, however, their Soviet counterparts did not have the same guidance from fluctuating prices or the same incentives from profits and losses. The net result was that many Soviet enterprises kept producing things in quantities beyond what anybody wanted, unless and until the problems became so huge and so blatant as to attract the attention of central planners in Moscow, who would then change the orders they sent out to manufacturers. But this could be years later and enormous amounts of resources would be wasted in the meantime.

The problems faced by the Soviet economy were not due to deficiencies peculiar to Russians or the other peoples of the Soviet Union. Americans faced very similar problems when the U. S. government was controlling the price of gasoline and its allocation during the 1970s. Under these conditions, both individuals and businesses had to drastically curtail their use of gasoline in some locations, such as New York and Washington, while in some other places—mostly rural areas—there was a surplus of unsold gasoline.

This was not due to stupidity on the part of government allocators, but to the fact that a process which is relatively simple, when prices direct resources and products where millions of individuals want them to go, is enormously complex when a set of central planners seeks to substitute their necessarily very limited knowledge for the knowledge scattered among all those vast numbers of people in highly varying circumstances. The federal government issued 3,000 pages of regulations, supplemented by various official "clarifications," but none of this allocated gasoline as smoothly and automatically as the ordinary operations of a free market price system.

To know how much gasoline should be sent where and when requires an enormous amount of knowledge of when and where it is most in demand at any given moment—and that changes throughout the year, as well as varying from place to place. People drive more to particular vacation spots during the summer and more diesel-powered trucks carry agricultural produce to and from other places at harvest time, in addition to other changing uses of motor vehicles for all sorts of other reasons. Nobody in any kind of economic or political system can possibly know the specifics of all these things. The advantage of a price-coordinated economy is that nobody has to. The efficiency of such an economy comes from the fact that vast amounts of knowledge do not ever have to be brought together, but are coordinated automatically by prices that convey in summary and compelling form what innumerable people want.

The difference between the limited knowledge of a business executive and the similarly limited knowledge of a government official is that the business executive is *receiving* instructions from others via the marketplace on what to do—whom to supply, and when, with what kinds of fuel, in this case—while the government official is *giving* instructions to others and compelling them to obey. In short, economic decisions are ultimately being directed or controlled by those who have specific knowledge in a price-coordinated economy, while those decisions move in the opposite direction—from those with less knowledge, who are giving orders to those with more knowledge—in a centrally planned economy. The difference is fundamental and profound in its implications for the material well-being of the population at large.

During the episodic gasoline shortages of the 1970s, Americans experienced in one industry for a limited period of time the severe economic problems that were common across the board in the Soviet Union for more than half a century. Because such an experience was so rare and shocking to Americans, they were receptive to all sorts of false political explanations and conspiracy theories for such an extraordinary situation, when in fact such situations were common in other countries using government allocation. What was uncommon was for such methods to be used in the United States.

The rationale for government control at the time was that reduced oil supplies from the Middle East required government intervention to prevent chaos in American oil markets. Needless to say, politicians were not about to admit that it was precisely their intervention which brought chaos, since the reduction in the total amount of gasoline in the country was just a few percentage points—the kind of reduction in supplies that is routinely handled in all sorts of industries by a small price increase in a free market. Indeed, a previous Arab oil embargo in 1967 had caused no such dislocations because it was not accompanied by the kinds of price controls instituted by the Nixon administration and continued by the Ford and Carter administrations. Nor were there long lines of cars waiting for hours at filling stations in other Western industrial nations or Japan, even though most of these other nations produced a far smaller percentage of their own petroleum than the United States did. These other countries did not have price controls on gasoline, so they did not have the shortages that go with price controls.

When government control of gasoline prices was ended in 1981—amid widespread warnings from politicians and the media that this would lead to drastically higher prices—what followed was virtually a lesson in elementary economics. Higher prices led to a greater quantity of gasoline being supplied and a smaller amount demanded. Oil exploration shot up and existing wells whose costs could not have been covered at the controlled prices began pumping oil again. Then gasoline prices began falling. Eventually these prices fell below what they had been under complex government controls and this fall continued over the years until gasoline prices reached an all-time low in real terms in the late twentieth century. Additional taxes were then piled onto the prices at the pump, but the gas itself was cheaper than ever—and there were no waiting lines.

Often the knowledge that is economically crucial is highly specific to a particular location or a particular group of people—and is therefore unlikely to be widely known. One of the reasons for the success of the A & P grocery chain in the first half of the twentieth century and of the McDonald's chain in the second half was the great amount of time and attention they devoted to acquiring detailed knowledge of specific locations being considered for their respective outlets, so as to have their outlets be accessible to the maximum number of customers. Real estate agents often say that the three most important factors in the value of real estate are "location, location, and location." The same is also true of many businesses serving the public. There is a reason why filling stations are often located on corners and some other businesses are usually located in the middle of the block, why stationery stores seldom locate near each other but automobile dealers often do.

Highly specific knowledge of particular groups of people can prove to be just as economically decisive as knowledge of particular places. At the beginning of the twentieth century, an Italian immigrant in San Francisco, well aware that other Italian immigrants regularly saved money, even out of small incomes, and were reliable in repaying loans, established a bank that he called the Bank of Italy, so as to attract Italian immigrant depositors and borrowers whom the other banks overlooked. His bank began in a little office with three wooden desks, some chairs, an adding machine, a safe, and one teller's window. But, capitalizing on its owner's understanding of the particular community this bank served, and his general business astuteness, the bank became so successful that it grew and eventually spread its branches across the state. Once firmly established, it began attracting so many depositors from beyond the Italian American community that it became at one time the largest bank in the world under its new name, the Bank of America.

Chapter 6

THE ROLE OF PROFITS
—AND LOSSES

*Rockefeller got rich selling oil. . . He found cheaper ways
to get oil from the ground to the gas pump.*

John Stossel

To those who run businesses, profits are obviously desirable and losses deplorable. But economics is not business administration. From the standpoint of the economy as a whole, and from the standpoint of the central concern of economics—the allocation of scarce resources which have alternative uses—profits and losses play equally important roles in maintaining and advancing the standards of living of the population as a whole.

Part of the efficiency of a price-coordinated economy comes from the fact that goods can simply "follow the money," without the producers really knowing just why people are buying one thing here and something else there and yet another thing during a different season. However, it is necessary for those who run businesses to keep track not only of the money coming in from the customers, it is equally necessary to keep track of how much money is going out to those who supply raw materials, labor, parts, electricity, and other inputs. Keeping careful track of these numerous flows of money in and out can make the difference between profit and loss. Therefore electricity, machines or cement cannot be used in the same careless way that caused far more of such inputs to be used per unit of output in the Soviet economy than in the German or Japanese economy. From the standpoint of the economy as a whole, and the well-being of the consuming public, the threat of losses is just as important as the prospect of profits.

When one business enterprise in a market economy finds ways to lower its costs, competing enterprises have no choice but to scramble to try to do the same. After the general merchandising chain Wal-Mart began selling groceries in 1988, it moved up over the years to become the nation's largest grocery seller by the early twenty-first century. Its lower costs benefitted not only its own customers, but those of other grocers as well. As the *Wall Street Journal* reported:

> When two Wal-Mart Supercenters and a rival regional grocery opened near a Kroger Co. supermarket in Houston last year, the Kroger's sales dropped 10%. Store manager Ben Bustos moved quickly to slash some prices and cut labor costs, for example, by buying ready-made cakes instead of baking them in-house, and ordering precut salad-bar items from suppliers. His employees used to stack displays by hand: Now, fruit and vegetables arrive stacked and gleaming for display.
> Such moves have helped Mr. Bustos cut worker-hours by 30% to 40% from when the store opened four years ago, and lower the prices of staples such as cereal, bread, milk, eggs and disposable diapers. Earlier this year, sales at the Kroger finally edged up over the year before.

In short, the economy operated more efficiently, to the benefit of the consumers, not only because of Wal-Mart's ability to cut costs and lower prices, but also because this forced Kroger's to do the same. This is a microcosm of what happens throughout a free market economy. It is no accident that people in such economies tend to have higher standards of living.

PROFITS

Profits may be the most misconceived subject in economics. Socialists have long regarded profits as simply "overcharge," as Fabian socialist George Bernard Shaw called it, or a "surplus value" as Karl Marx called it. "Never talk to me about profit," India's first prime minister, Jawaharlal Nehru, warned his country's leading industrialist. "It is a dirty word."

From all these men's perspectives, profits were simply unnecessary charges added on to the inherent costs of producing goods and services, driving up the cost to the customer. One of the great appeals of socialism, especially back when it was simply an idealistic theory without any concrete examples in the real world, was that it sought to eliminate these supposedly unnecessary charges, making things generally more affordable, especially for people with lower incomes. Only after socialism went from being a theory to being an actual economic system in various countries around the world did the fact become painfully apparent that people in socialist countries had a harder time trying to afford things that most people in capitalist countries could afford with ease and took for granted.

With profits eliminated, prices should have been lower in socialist countries, according to theory, and the standard of living of the masses correspondingly higher. Why then was it not that way in practice?

Profits as Incentives

Let us go back to square one. The hope for profits and the threat of losses is what forces a business owner in a capitalist economy to produce at the lowest cost and sell what the customers are most willing to pay for. In the absence of these pressures, those who manage enterprises under socialism have far less incentive to be as efficient as possible under given conditions, much less to keep up with changing conditions and respond to them quickly, as capitalist enterprises must do if they expect to survive.

It was a Soviet premier, Leonid Brezhnev, who said that his country's enterprise managers shied away from innovation "as the devil shies away from incense." But, given the incentives of government-owned and government-controlled enterprises, why should those managers have stuck their necks out by trying new methods or new products, when they stood to gain little or nothing if it succeeded and might have lost their jobs (or worse) if it failed? Under Stalin, failure was often equated with sabotage, and was punished accordingly. Even under the milder conditions of democratic socialism, as in India for decades after its independence, innovation was by no means necessary for protected enterprises, such as automobile manufacturing.

Until the freeing up of markets that began in India in 1991, the country's most popular car was the Hindustan Ambassador—an unabashed copy of the British Morris Oxford. Moreover, even in the 1990s, *The Economist* referred to the Ambassador as "a barely upgraded version of a 1950s Morris Oxford." A London newspaper, *The Independent*, reported: "Ambassadors have for years been notorious in India for their poor finish, heavy handling and proneness to alarming accidents." Nevertheless, there was a waiting list for the Ambassador—with waits lasting for months and sometimes years — as foreign cars were not allowed to be imported to compete with it.

Under free market capitalism, the incentives work in the opposite direction. Even the most profitable business can lose its market if it doesn't keep innovating, in order to avoid being overtaken by its competitors. For example, IBM pioneered in creating computers but, in the 1970s, IBM computers measuring 3,000 cubic feet became obsolete when Intel created a chip smaller than a fingernail that could do the same things. Yet Intel itself was then constantly forced to improve that chip at an exponential rate, as rivals like Advanced Micro Devices (AMD), Cyrix, and others began catching up with them technologically. More than once, Intel poured such huge sums of money into the development of improved chips as to risk the financial survival of the company itself. But the alternative was to allow itself to be overtaken by rivals, which would have been an even bigger risk to Intel's survival.

Later, Advanced Micro Devices made equally strenuous attempts to overtake Intel with a more advanced chip—and in the process had losses of more than a billion dollars in 2002, while AMD stock lost four-fifths of its value. But then, when Intel came out with a more powerful chip that generated much unwanted heat and ran up the users' electric bills, *Forbes* magazine reported, "AMD leaped at the opening Intel created by rolling out Opteron in 2003, a low-power, high-performance chip for servers now sold by IBM, Hewlett-Packard and Sun Microsystems." Dell computers, which had for years used Intel chips exclusively, began in 2006 to use AMD chips as well, and AMD chips were reported to be in just over half of all personal computers sold in March 2006. Meanwhile, the price of Intel stock fell by 20 percent in just three months and Intel announced that it would lay off 1,000 managers as its profits fell by 57 percent while the profits of AMD rose by 53 percent.

All this desperate competition took place in an industry where Intel sold 90 percent of the computer chips in the world at the beginning of 2004 and, even after the upsurge of AMD, still sold 83 percent two years later. In short, even among corporate giants, competition in innovation can become desperate in a free market. The dean of the Yale School of Management described the computer chip industry as "an industry in constant turmoil" and the Chief Executive Officer of Intel wrote a book titled *Only the Paranoid Survive*. The fate of AMD and Intel is not the issue. The issue is how the consumers benefit from both technological advances and lower prices as a result of these companies' fierce competition to gain profits and avoid losses.

Nor is this industry unique. In 2002, 120 of the *Fortune* 500 companies reported losses, totaling in the aggregate more than $295 billion. Such losses play a vital role in the economy, forcing corporate giants to change what they are doing, under penalty of extinction, since no one can sustain losses of that magnitude indefinitely. Inertia may be a common tendency among human beings around the world, but businesses operating in a free market are forced by red ink on the bottom line to realize that they cannot keep drifting along like the Hindustan Motor Corporation, protected from competition by the Indian government. Even in India, however, the freeing of markets toward the end of the twentieth century created competition in cars, forcing Hindustan Motors to invest in improvements, producing new Ambassadors that were now "much more reliable than their predecessors," according to *The Independent* newspaper.

While capitalism has a visible cost—profit—that does not exist under socialism, socialism has an invisible cost—inefficiency—that gets weeded out by losses and bankruptcy under capitalism. The fact that most goods are more widely affordable in a capitalist economy implies that profit is less costly than inefficiency. Put differently, profit is a price paid for efficiency. Clearly the greater efficiency must outweigh the profit or else socialism would in fact have had the more affordable prices and greater prosperity that its theorists expected, but which failed to materialize in the real world. If in fact the cost of profits exceeded the value of the efficiency they promote, then non-profit organizations or government agencies could get the same work done cheaper or better than profit-making enterprises and could displace them in the competition of the marketplace. Yet that seldom, if ever, happens, while the opposite happens increasingly—that is, private profit-making companies taking over various functions formerly performed by government agencies or by non-profit organizations like colleges and universities.[1]

While capitalists have been conceived of as people who make profits, what a business owner really gets is legal ownership of whatever residual is left over after the costs have been paid out of the money received from customers. That residual can turn out to be positive, negative, or zero. Workers must be paid and creditors must be paid—or else they can take legal action to seize the company's assets. Even before that happens, they can simply stop supplying their inputs when the company stops paying them. The only person whose payment is contingent on how well the business is doing is the owner of that business. This is what puts unrelenting pressure on the owner to monitor everything that is happening in the business and everything that is happening in the market for the business' products.

In contrast to the layers of authorities monitoring the actions of those under them in a government-run enterprise, the business owner is essentially an *unmonitored monitor* as far as the economic efficiency of the business is concerned. Self-interest takes the place of external monitors, and forces far closer attention to details and far more expenditure of time and energy at work than any set of rules or authorities is likely to be able to do. That simple fact gives capitalism an enormous advantage. More important, it gives the people living in price-coordinated market economies visibly higher standards of living.

---

[1] Further discussion of this phenomenon can be found in Chapter 23 in a section titled "Non-Profit Organizations."

It is not just ignorant people, but also highly educated and highly intellectual people like George Bernard Shaw, Karl Marx, and Pandit Nehru, who have misconceived profits as arbitrary charges added on to the costs of producing goods and services. To many people, even today, high profits are often attributed to high prices charged by those motivated by "greed." In reality, most of the great fortunes in American history have resulted from someone's figuring out how to reduce costs, so as to be able to charge *lower* prices and therefore gain a mass market for the product. Henry Ford did this with automobiles, Rockefeller with oil, Carnegie with steel, and Sears, Penney, Walton and other department store chain founders with a variety of products.

A supermarket chain in a capitalist economy can be very successful charging prices that allow about a penny of clear profit on each dollar of sales. Because several cash registers are usually bringing in money simultaneously all day long in a big supermarket, those pennies can add up to a very substantial annual rate of return on the supermarket chain's investment, while adding very little to what the customer pays. If the entire contents of a store get sold out in about two weeks, then that penny on a dollar becomes more like a quarter on the dollar over the course of a year, when that same dollar comes back to be re-used 25 more times. Under socialism, that penny on each dollar would be eliminated, but so too would be all the economic pressures on the management to keep costs down. Instead of prices falling to 99 cents, they might well rise, after losing the incentives to keep production costs down.

Put differently, when a company makes a million dollars in profits, that does not mean that its output would cost a million dollars less if produced by a non-profit organization or by a government-run enterprise. Without the incentives and constraints created by the prospect of profit and the threat of losses, the same output might well cost millions of dollars more. There is a reason why various traditional government functions, such as collecting garbage or running prisons, have increasingly been contracted out to private, profit-seeking companies. Such companies often get the job done more cheaply or better, or both. When most people are asked how high they think the average rate of profit is, they usually suggest some number much higher than the actual rate of profit. Over the entire period from 1960 through 2005, the rate of return on corporate assets in the United States ranged from a high of 12.4 percent to a low of 4.1 percent, before taxes. After taxes, the rate of profit ranged from a high of 7.8 percent to a low of 2.2 percent. However, it is not just the numerical rate of profit that most people misconceive. Many misconceive its whole role in a price-coordinated economy, which is to serve as incentives—and it plays that role wherever its fluctuations take it. Moreover, some people have no idea that there are vast differences between profits on sales and profits on investments.

Profit Rates

Profits on sales are very different from profits on investment. If a store buys widgets for $10 each and sells them for $15 each, some might say that it makes $5 in profits on each widget. But, of course, the store has to pay the people who work there, the utility company which supplies electricity to the store, as well as other suppliers of other goods and services needed to keep the business running. What is left over after all these people have been paid is the net profit, usually a lot less than the gross profit. But that is still not the same as profit on investment. It is simply net profits on sales, which still ignores the cost of the investments which built the store in the first place.

It is the profit on the whole investment that matters to the investor. When someone invests $10,000, what that person wants to know is what annual rate of return it will bring, whether it is invested in stores, real estate, or stocks and bonds. Profits on particular sales are not what matter most. It is the profit on the total capital that has been invested in the business that matters. That profit matters not just to those who receive it, but to the economy as a whole, for differences in profit rates in different sectors of the economy are what cause investments to flow into and out of these sectors, until profit rates are equalized, like water seeking its own level. Changing rates of profit allocate resources in a market economy—when these are rates of profit on investment.

Profits on sales are a different story. Things can be sold at prices that are much higher than what the seller paid for them and yet, if those items sit on a shelf in the store for months before being sold, the profit on investment may be less than with other items that have less of a mark-up in price but which sell out within a week. A store that sells pianos undoubtedly makes a higher percentage profit on each sale than a supermarket makes selling bread. But a piano sits in the store for a much longer time waiting to be sold than a loaf of bread does. Bread would go stale and moldy waiting for as long as a piano to be sold. When a supermarket chain buys $10,000 worth of bread, it gets its money back much faster than when a piano dealer buys $10,000 worth of pianos. Therefore the piano dealer must charge a higher percentage mark-up on the sale of each piano than a supermarket charges on each loaf of bread, if the piano dealer is to make the same annual percentage rate of return on a $10,000 investment.

Competition among those seeking money from investors makes profit rates tend to equalize, even when that requires different mark-ups to compensate for different turnover rates among different products. Piano stores can continue to exist only when their higher markups in prices compensate for slower turnover in sales. Otherwise investors would put their money elsewhere and piano stores would start disappearing.

When the supermarket gets its money back in a shorter period of time, it can turn right around and re-invest it, buying more bread or other grocery items. In the course of a year, the same money turns over many times in a supermarket, earning a profit each time, so that a penny of profit on the dollar can produce a total profit for the year on the initial investment equal to what a piano dealer makes charging a much higher percentage markup on an investment that turns over much more slowly. While supermarkets tend to have especially low rates of profit on sales, other business' profit rates on sales are also usually lower than what many people imagine. Companies that made the *Fortune* magazine list of the 500 largest companies in America averaged "a return on revenues of a penny on the dollar" in 2002, compared to "6 cents in 2000, the peak profit year."

Profits on sales and profits on investment are not merely different concepts. They can move in opposite directions. One of the keys to the rise to dominance of the A & P grocery chain in the 1920s was a conscious decision by the company management to cut profit margins on sales, in order to increase the profit rate on investment. With the new and lower prices made possible by selling with lower profits per item, A & P was able to attract greatly increased numbers of customers, making far more total profit because of the increased volume of sales. Making a profit of only a few cents on the dollar on sales, but with the inventory turning over nearly 30 times a year, A & P's profit rate on investment soared. This low price and high volume strategy set a pattern that spread to other grocery chains and to other kinds of enterprises as well. In a later era, huge supermarkets were able to shave the profit margin on sales still thinner, because of even higher volumes, enabling them to displace A & P from industry leadership by charging still lower prices.

Conversely, a study of prices in low-income neighborhoods found that there were larger than usual markups in prices charged their customers but, at the same time, there were lower than usual rates of profit on investment. Higher profits on sales helped compensate for the higher costs of doing business in low-income neighborhoods but apparently not completely, as indicated by the lower rates of profit on investments and the avoidance of such neighborhoods by many businesses. A limiting factor in how high prices can be raised to compensate for higher costs is that many low-income residents shop in stores in higher-income neighborhoods, where the prices are lower, even though this may entail paying bus fare or taxi fare. The higher the prices rise in low-income neighborhoods, the more people are likely to shop elsewhere. Thus stores in such neighborhoods are limited in the extent to which they can offset higher costs and slower turnover with higher prices, often leaving them in a precarious financial position, even while they are being denounced for "exploiting" their customers.

COSTS OF PRODUCTION

The crucial factor in prices and profits are the costs of producing whatever goods or services are being sold. Not everyone is equally efficient in production and not everyone's circumstances offer equal opportunities to achieve lower costs. Unfortunately, costs are misconceived almost as much as profits.

Economies of Scale

First of all, there is no such thing as "the" cost of producing a given product or service. Henry Ford proved long ago that the cost of producing an automobile was very different when you produced 100 cars a year than when you produced 100,000. He became the leading automobile manufacturer in the early twentieth century by pioneering mass production methods in his factories, revolutionizing not only his own company but businesses throughout the economy, who followed the mass production principles that he introduced. The time required to produce a Model T chassis shrank from 12 man-hours to an hour and a half. With a mass market for automobiles, it paid to invest in expensive but labor-saving mass production machinery, whose cost per car would turn out to be modest when spread out over a huge number of automobiles. But, if you sold only half as many cars as you expected, then the cost of that machinery per car would be twice as much. Large fixed costs are among the reasons for lower costs of production per unit of output—what economists call "economies of scale."

It has been estimated that the minimum amount of automobile production required to achieve efficient production levels today runs into the hundreds of thousands. Back at the beginning of the twentieth century the largest automobile manufacturer in the United States produced just six cars a day. At that level of output, only the truly rich could afford to buy a car. But Henry Ford's mass production methods brought the cost of producing cars down within the price range of ordinary Americans. The price of a Model T Ford was cut in half between 1910 and 1916.

Similar principles apply in other industries. It does not cost as much to deliver a hundred cartons of milk to one supermarket as it does to deliver ten cartons of milk to each of ten different neighborhood stores scattered around town. Economies in beer production include advertising. Although Anheuser-Busch spends millions of dollars a year advertising Budweiser and its other beers, its huge volume of sales means that its advertising costs per barrel of beer are about two dollars less than that of its competitors Coors and Miller. Such savings add up, permitting larger enterprises to have either lower prices or larger profits, or both. Small retail stores have long had difficulty surviving in competition with large chain stores charging lower prices, whether A & P in the first half of the twentieth century, Safeway in the second half, or Wal-Mart in the twenty-first century. The higher costs per unit in the smaller stores will not permit them to charge prices as low as the big chain stores' prices.

Advertising has sometimes been depicted as simply another cost added on to the cost of producing goods and services. However, in so far as advertising causes more of the advertised product to be sold, economies of scale can reduce production costs, so that the same product may cost less when it is advertised, rather than more. Advertising itself of course has costs, both in the financial sense and in the sense of using resources. But it is an empirical question, rather than a foregone conclusion, whether the costs of advertising are greater or less than the reductions of production costs made possible by the economies of scale which it promotes. This can obviously vary from one firm or industry to another.

Diseconomies of Scale

Economies of scale are only half the story. If economies of scale were the whole story, the question would then have to be asked: Why not produce cars in even more gigantic enterprises? If General Motors, Ford, and DaimlerChrysler all merged together, would they not be able to produce cars even more cheaply and thereby make more profit than when they produce separately?

Probably not. There comes a point, in every business, beyond which the cost of producing a unit of output no longer declines as the amount of production increases. In fact, costs per unit actually rise after an enterprise becomes so huge that it is difficult to monitor and coordinate, when the right hand may not always know what the left hand is doing. Back in the 1960s, when the American Telephone & Telegraph Company was the largest corporation in the world, its own chief executive officer put it this way: "A.T.&T. is so big that, if you gave it a kick in the behind today, it would be two years before the head said 'ouch.'"[2] In a survey of banks around the world in 2006, *The Economist* magazine reported their tendency to keep growing larger and the implications of this for diseconomies of scale:

> Management will find it harder and harder to aggregate and summarise everything that is going on in the bank, opening the way to the duplication of expense, the neglect of concealed risks and the failure of internal controls.

In other words, the risks inherent in banking may be well under control, as far as the top management is aware, but somewhere in their sprawling financial empire there may be transactions being made that expose the bank to risks that the top management is unaware of. Unknown to the top management at an international bank's New York headquarters, some bank official at a branch in Singapore may be making transactions that create not only financial risks but risks of criminal prosecution.

During General Motors' long tenure as the largest manufacturer of motor vehicles in the world, its cost of production per car has been estimated to be hundreds of dollars more than the costs of Ford, DaimlerChrysler, or leading Japanese manufacturers. A small airline in the United States, JetBlue, has more than 30 percent lower cost per seat per mile than giants like United Airlines or American Airlines. Problems associated with size can affect quality as well as price. When frequent flyers and travel professionals were asked by *BusinessWeek* magazine to rank the quality of

---

[2] I was an economist at A.T.&T. at the time and heard him say it.

airlines, the five top-rated in quality were all smaller airlines. The small McClatchy newspaper chain, with papers in a dozen small to medium-sized communities, had 20 consecutive years of circulation growth while the newspaper industry as a whole was having circulation declines—and the papers in its chain won various awards for excellence in journalism as well.

In short, while there are economies of scale, there are also what economists call "diseconomies of scale." Economies and diseconomies can exist simultaneously at many different levels of output. That is, there may be some things that a given business enterprise could do better if it were larger and other things that it could do better if it were smaller. As an entrepreneur in India put it, "What small companies give up in terms of financial clout, technological resources, and staying power, they gain in flexibility, lack of bureaucracy, and speed of decision making." With increasing size, eventually the diseconomies begin to outweigh the economies, so it does not pay a firm to expand beyond that point. That is why industries usually consist of a number of firms, instead of one giant, super-efficient monopoly.

In the Soviet Union, where there was a fascination with economies of scale and a disregard of diseconomies of scale, both its industrial and agricultural enterprises were the largest in the world. The average Soviet farm, for example, was ten times the size of the average American farm and employed more than ten times as many workers. But Soviet farms were notoriously inefficient. Among the reasons for this inefficiency cited by Soviet economists was "deficient coordination." One example may illustrate a general problem:

> In the vast common fields, fleets of tractors fanned out to begin the plowing. Plan fulfillment was calculated on the basis of hectares worked, and so it was to the drivers' advantage to cover as much territory as quickly as possible. The drivers started by cutting deep furrows around the edge of the fields. As they moved deeper into the fields, however, they began to lift the blade of the plow and race the tractor, and the furrows became progressively shallower. The first furrows were nine to ten inches deep. A little farther from the road, they were five to six inches deep, and in the center of the field, where the tractor drivers were certain that no one would check on them, the furrows were as little as two inches deep. Usually, no one discovered that the furrows were so

shallow in the middle of the field until it became obvious that something was wrong from the stunted nature of the crop.

Once again, counterproductive behavior from the standpoint of the economy was not irrational behavior from the standpoint of the person engaging in it. Clearly, the tractor drivers understood that their work could be more easily monitored at the edge of a field than in the center, and they adjusted the kind and quality of work they did accordingly, so as to maximize their own pay, based on how much land they plowed. By not plowing as deeply into the ground where they could not be easily monitored by farm officials, tractor drivers were able to go faster and cover more ground in a given amount of time, even if they covered it less effectively. No such behavior would be likely by a farmer plowing his own land because his actions would be controlled by the incentive of profit, rather than by external monitors.

The point at which the disadvantages of size begin to outweigh the advantages differs from one industry to another. That is why restaurants are smaller than steel mills. A well-run restaurant usually requires the presence of an owner with sufficient incentives to continuously monitor all the things necessary for successful operation, in a field where failures are all too common. Not only must the food be prepared to suit the tastes of the restaurant's clientele, the waiters and waitresses must do their jobs in a way that encourages people to come back for another pleasant experience, and the furnishings of the restaurant must also be such as to meet the desires of the particular clientele that it serves.

These are not problems that can be solved once and for all. Food suppliers must be continuously monitored to see that they are still sending the kind and quality of produce, fish, meats, and other ingredients needed to satisfy the customers. Cooks and chefs must also be monitored to see that they are continuing to meet existing standards—as well as adding to their repertoires, as new foods and drinks become popular and old ones are ordered less often by the customers. The normal turnover of employees also requires the owner to be able to select, train, and monitor new people on an on-going basis. Moreover, changes outside the restaurant—in the kind of neighborhood around it, for example—can make or break its business. All these factors, and more, must be kept in mind and weighed by the owner, and continuously adjusted to, if the business is to survive, much less be profitable.

Such a spectrum of details, requiring direct personal knowledge and control by someone on the scene and with incentives going beyond a fixed salary, limits the size of restaurants, as compared to the size of steel mills, automobile factories, or mining companies. Even where there are nationwide restaurant chains, often these are run by separate owners operating franchises from some national organization that supplies such things as advertising and general guidance and standards, leaving the numerous on-site monitoring tasks to local owners. Howard Johnson pioneered in restaurant franchising in the 1930s, supplying half the capital, with the local manager supplying the other half. This gave the local franchisee a vested interest in the restaurant's profitability, rather than simply a fixed salary.

Costs and Capacity

Costs vary not only with the volume of output, and to varying degrees from one industry to another, they also vary according to the extent to which existing capacity is being used. When an airplane with 200 seats is about to take off with 180 passengers on board, the cost of letting 20 "standby" passengers get on the flight is negligible. That is one reason for radically different prices being charged to people flying on the same plane. Some passengers bought guaranteed reservations and others essentially bought a chance of getting on board as standbys. Different levels of probability have different costs in airline tickets, as elsewhere. The passengers themselves also differ in how important it is for them to be at a particular place at a particular time. Those on urgent business may want a guaranteed reservation, even at a higher price, while others may be in a position where saving money is more important than being on one particular flight rather than another.

Unutilized capacity can cause price anomalies in many sectors of the economy. In Cancun, Mexico, the cheapest room available at the modest Best Western hotel there was $180 a night in mid-2001, while the fancy Ritz-Carlton nearby was renting rooms for $169 a night. The Best Western happened to be filled up and the Ritz-Carlton happened to have vacancies. Nor was this peculiar to Mexico. A four-star hotel in Manhattan was renting rooms for less than a two-star hotel nearby and the posh Phoenician in Phoenix was renting rooms for less than the Holiday Inn in the same city. Why were normally very expensive hotels renting rooms for less than hotels that were usually much lower in price? Again, the key was the utilization of capacity.

Tourists going to popular resorts on limited budgets had made reservations at the low-cost hotels well in advance, in order to be sure of finding something affordable. This meant that fluctuations in the number of tourists would be absorbed by the higher-priced hotels. A general decline in tourism in 2001 thus led to vacancies at the luxury hotels, which had no choice but to cut prices in order to attract more people to fill their rooms. Thus the luxurious Boca Raton Club & Spa in Florida gave guests their third night free and tourists were able to get last-minute bargains on beachfront villas at Hilton Head, South Carolina, where reservations usually must be made six months in advance.

Conversely, a rise in tourism would also be absorbed by the luxury hotels, which could raise their prices even more than usual. After three consecutive years of declining profits, hotels in 2004 began "yanking the discounts," as the *Wall Street Journal* put it, when increased travel brought more guests. The luxury hotels' reactions took the form of both price increases—$545 a night for the smallest and cheapest room at the Four Seasons Hotel in New York—and elimination of various free extras:

> It's already tougher this year for families to find the offers of free breakfasts and other perks that business hotels have been freely distributing for the past three years in an effort to fill empty beds.

In many industries and enterprises, capacity must be built to handle the peak volume—which means that there is excess capacity at other times. The cost of accommodating more users of the product or service during the times when there is excess capacity is much less than the cost of handling those who are served at peak times. A cruise ship, for example, must receive enough money from its passengers to cover not only such current costs as paying the crew, buying food, and using fuel, it must also be able to pay such overhead costs as the purchase price of the ship and the expenses at the headquarters of the cruise line.

To handle twice as many passengers on a given cruise at the peak season may require buying another ship, as well as hiring another crew and buying twice as much food and fuel. However, if the number of passengers in the off season is only one-third of what it is at the peak, then a doubling of the number of off-season passengers need not require buying another ship. Existing ships can simply sail with fewer empty cabins. Therefore, it pays the cruise line to try to attract economy-minded passengers by offering much reduced fares during the off season. Groups of retired people, for example, can usually schedule their cruises at any time of the year, not being tied down to the vacation schedules of jobs and usually not having young children whose school schedules would limit their flexibility. It is common for seniors to get large discounts in off-season travel, both on land and at sea. Businesses in general can afford to do this because their costs are lower—and each particular business is forced to do it because their competition will take customers away from them if they don't.

Excess capacity can also result from over-optimistic building. Because of what the *Wall Street Journal* called "an ill-timed building frenzy in luxury ships," luxury cruise lines added more than 4,000 new berths in a little over a year during the early twenty-first century. When they found that there was no such demand as to fill all the additional cabins at their existing prices, the net result was that Crystal Cruises, for example, offered their usual $2,995 cruise through the Panama Canal for $1,695 and Seabourn Cruise Line cut the price of its Caribbean cruise from $4,495 to $1,999. They would hardly have done this unless the pressures of competition left them no choice—and unless their incremental costs, when they had excess capacity, were even lower than their reduced prices.

Since all these responses to excess capacity are due to incentives created by the prospect of profits and the threat of losses in a market economy, the same principles do *not* apply where the government provides a good or service and charges for it. There are few incentives for government officials to match prices with costs—and sometimes they charge more to those who create the least cost. When a bridge, for example, is built or its capacity expanded, the costs created are essentially the cost of building the capacity to handle rush-hour traffic. The cars that drive across the bridge during off-peak hours cost almost nothing because the bridge has idle capacity during those hours. Yet, when tolls are charged, often there are books of tickets or electronic passes available at lower prices per trip than the prices charged to those who drive across the bridge only occasionally during off-peak hours.

Although it is the regular rush-hour users who create the huge cost of building or expanding a bridge's capacity, they pay less because it is they who are more numerous voters and whose greater stake in toll policies makes them more likely to react politically to toll charges. What may seem like economic folly can be political prudence on the part of politically appointed officials operating the bridges and trying to protect their own jobs.

"Passing On" Costs and Savings

It is often said that businesses pass on whatever additional costs are placed on them, whether these costs are placed on them by higher taxes, rising fuel costs, raises for their employees under a new union contract, or a variety of other sources of higher costs. By the same token, whenever costs come down for some reason, whether because of a tax cut or a technological improvement, for example, the question is often raised as to whether these lower costs will be passed on in lower prices to the consumer.

The idea that sellers can charge whatever price they want is seldom expressed explicitly but the implication that they can often lurks in the background of such questions as what they will pass on to their customers. But the passing on of either higher costs or savings is not an automatic process and, in both cases, it depends on the kind of competition faced by each business and how many of the competing companies have the same cost increases or decreases. If you are running a gold mining company in South Africa and the government there increases the tax on gold by $10 an ounce, you cannot pass that on to buyers of gold in the world market because gold producers in other countries do not have to pay that extra $10—and to buyers around the world, gold is gold, wherever it is produced. There is no way that buyers are going to pay $10 an ounce more for your gold than for somebody else's gold, so that means that your profits on gold sales in the world market will simply decline by $10 an ounce.

The same principle applies when there are rising costs of transportation. If you ship your product to market by railroad and the railroads raise their freight charges, you can pass that on to the buyers only to the extent that your competitors also ship their product by rail. But, if your competitors are shipping by truck or by barge, while your location will not allow you to do the same, then raising your prices to cover the additional rail charges will simply allow your competitors to charge a lower price and take away some of your customers. On the other hand, if all your competitors ship by rail and for similar distances, then all of you can pass on the higher railroad freight charges to all your customers. But if you ship your output an average of 100 miles and your competitors ship their output an average of only 10 miles, then you can only raise your prices to cover the additional cost of rail charges for 10 miles and take a reduction in profit by the cost of the other 90 miles.

Similar principles apply when it comes to passing on savings to customers. If you alone introduce a new technology that cuts your production costs in half, then you can keep all the additional profits resulting from these cost savings by continuing to charge what your higher-cost competitors are charging. Alternatively—and this is what has often happened—you can cut your prices and take customers away from your competitors, which often leads to even larger total profits, despite lower profits per unit sold.

Many of the great American fortunes—by Rockefeller, Carnegie, and others—came from finding lower cost ways of producing and delivering the product to the customer, and then charging lower prices than their higher-cost competitors could meet and taking away their customers.

Over a period of time, competitors usually begin to use similar technological or organizational advances to cut costs and reduce prices, but fortunes can be made by pioneering innovators in the meantime. That provides incentives for enterprises in profit-seeking market economies to be on the lookout for new ways of doing things, in contrast to enterprises in either government-run economies like those in the days of the Soviet Union or in economies where laws protect private businesses from domestic or international competition, as in India before they began to open their economy to competition in the world market.

SPECIALIZATION AND DISTRIBUTION

A business firm is limited, not only in its over-all size, but also in the range of functions that it can perform efficiently. General Motors makes millions of automobiles, but not a single tire. Instead, it buys its tires from Goodyear, Michelin and other tire manufacturers, who can produce this part of the car more efficiently than General Motors can. Nor do automobile manufacturers own their own automobile dealerships across the country. Typically, automobile producers sell cars to local people who in turn sell to the public. There is no way that General Motors can keep track of all the local conditions across the length and breadth of the United States, which determine how much it will cost to buy or lease land on which to locate an automobile dealership, or which locations are best in a given community, much less evaluate the condition of local customers' used cars that are being traded in on new ones.

No one can sit in Detroit and decide how much trade-in value to allow on a particular Chevrolet in Seattle with some dents and scratches or a particular Honda in mint condition in Miami. And if the kind of salesmanship that works in Los Angeles does not work in Boston, those on the scene are likely to know that better than anyone in Detroit can. In short, the automobile manufacturer specializes in manufacturing automobiles, leaving other functions to people who develop different knowledge and different skills needed to specialize in those particular functions.

Middlemen

The perennial desire to "eliminate the middleman" is perennially thwarted by economic reality. The range of human knowledge and expertise is limited for any given person or for any manageably-sized collection of administrators. Only a certain number of links in the great chain of production and distribution can be mastered and operated efficiently by the same set of people. Beyond some point, there are other people who can perform the next step in the sequence more cheaply or more effectively— and, therefore, at that point it pays a firm to sell its output to some other businesses that can carry on the next part of the operation more efficiently. That is because, as we have noted in earlier chapters, *goods tend to flow to their most valued uses* in a free market, and goods are more valuable to those who can handle them more efficiently at a given stage. Furniture manufacturers usually do not own or operate furniture stores and most authors do not do their own publishing, much less own their own bookstores.

Prices play a crucial role in all of this, as in other aspects of a market economy. Any economy must not only allocate scarce resources which have alternative uses, it must determine how long the resulting products remain in whose hands before being passed along to others who can handle the next stage more efficiently. Profit-seeking businesses are guided by their own bottom line, but this bottom line is itself determined by what others can do and at what cost.

What connects the self-interest of a company with the efficiency of the economy as a whole are prices. When a product becomes more valuable in the hands of somebody else, that somebody else will bid more for the product than it is worth to its current owner. The owner then sells, not for the sake of the economy, but for his own sake. However, the end result is a more efficient economy, where goods move to those who value them most.

Despite superficially appealing phrases about "eliminating the middleman," middlemen continue to exist because they can do their phase of the operation more efficiently than others can. It should hardly be surprising that people who specialize in one phase can do that phase better than others can.

Third World countries have tended to have more middlemen than more industrialized nations, a fact much lamented by observers who have not considered the economics of the situation. Farm produce tends to pass through more hands between the African farmer who grows peanuts, for example, to the company that processes it into peanut butter than would be the case in the United States. A similar pattern was found with consumer goods moving in the opposite direction. Boxes of matches may pass through more hands between the manufacturer of matches and the African consumer who buys them. A British economist in mid-twentieth century West Africa described and explained such situations there:

> West African agricultural exports are produced by tens of thousands of Africans operating on a very small scale and often widely dispersed. They almost entirely lack suitable storage facilities, and they have no, or only very small, cash reserves. . . The large number and the long line of intermediaries in the purchase of export produce essentially derive from the economies to be obtained from bulking very large numbers of small parcels. . . In produce marketing the first link in the chain may be the purchase, hundreds of miles from Kano, of a few pounds of groundnuts, which after several stages of bulking arrive there as part of a wagon or lorry load of several tons.

Instead of ten farmers in a given area all taking time off from their farming to carry their individually small amounts of produce to a distant town for sale, one middleman can collect the produce of the ten farmers and drive it all to a produce buyer at one time, allowing ten farmers to apply their scarce resources—time and labor—to the alternative uses of those resources for growing more produce. Society as a whole thus saves on the amount of resources required to move produce from the farm to the next buyer, as well as on the number of individual negotiations required at the points of sale. This saving of time is especially important during the harvest season, when some of the crop may become over-ripe before it is picked or spoil afterwards if it is not picked promptly and gotten into a storage or processing facility.

In a wealthier country, each farm would have more produce, and motorized transport on modern highways would reduce the time required to get it to the next point of sale, so that the time lost per ton of crop would be less and fewer middlemen would be required to move it. Moreover, modern farmers in prosperous countries would be more likely to have their own storage facilities, harvesting machinery, and other aids. What is and is not efficient—either from the standpoint of the individual farmer or of society as a whole—depends on the circumstances. Since these circumstances can differ radically between rich and poor countries, very different methods may be efficient in each country and no given method need be right for both.

For similar reasons, there are often more intermediaries between the industrial manufacturer and the ultimate consumer in poor countries. However, the profits earned by each of these intermediaries is not just so much waste, as often assumed by third-party observers, especially observers from a different society. Here the limiting factor is the poverty of the consumer, which restricts how much can be bought at one time. Again, West Africa in the mid-twentieth century provided especially clear examples:

> Imported merchandise arrives in very large consignments and needs to be distributed over large areas to the final consumer who, in West Africa, has to buy in extremely small quantities because of his poverty. . . The organization of retail selling in Ibadan (and elsewhere) exemplifies the services rendered by petty traders both to suppliers and to consumers. Here there is no convenient central market, and it is usual to see petty traders sitting with their wares at the entrances to the stores of the European merchant firms. The petty traders sell largely the same commodities as the stores, but in much smaller quantities.

This might seem to be the ideal situation in which to "eliminate the middleman," since the petty traders were camped right outside stores selling the same merchandise, and the consumers could simply walk right past them to buy the same goods inside at lower prices per unit. But these traders would sell in such tiny quantities as ten matches or half a cigarette, while it would be wasteful for the stores behind them to spend their time reaking down their packaged goods that much, in view of the better alternative uses of their labor and capital. The alternatives available to the African petty traders were seldom as remunerative, so it made sense for these traders to do what it would not make sense for the European merchant to do. Moreover, it made sense for the very poor African consumer to buy from the local traders, even if the latter's additional profit raised the price of the commodity, because the consumer often could not afford to buy the commodity in the quantities sold by the European merchants.

Obvious as all this may seem, it has been misunderstood by renowned writers[3] and—worse yet—by both colonial and post-colonial governments hostile to middlemen and prone to creating laws and policies expressing that hostility.

Socialist Economies

As in other cases, one of the best ways of understanding the role of prices, profits, and losses is to see what happens in their absence. Socialist economies not only lack the kinds of incentives which force individual enterprises toward efficiency and innovation, they also lack the kinds of financial incentives that lead each given producer in a capitalist economy to limit its work to those stages of production and distribution at which it has lower costs than alternative enterprises. Capitalist enterprises buy components from others who have lower costs in producing those particular components, and sell their own output to whatever middlemen can most efficiently carry out its distribution. But a socialist economy may forego these advantages of specialization—and for perfectly rational reasons, given the very different circumstances in which they operate.

---

[3] Gunnar Myrdal, for example, in his *Asian Drama* referred to a "proliferation of retail outlets and petty traders" in Third World countries in South Asia as being "clearly underutilization of labor." But he provided neither evidence nor analysis to show that the middlemen had alternative uses of their time that were more remunerative to them or more valuable to society.

In the Soviet Union, for example, many enterprises produced their own components, even though specialized producers of such components existed and could manufacture them at lower cost. Two Soviet economists estimated that the costs of components needed for a machine-building enterprise in the U.S.S.R. were two to three times as great as the costs of producing those same components in specialized enterprises. But why would cost matter to the individual enterprise making these decisions in a system where profits and losses were not decisive?

This was not peculiar to machine-building enterprises. According to the same Soviet economists, "the idea of self-sufficiency in supply penetrates all the tiers of the economic administrative pyramid, from top to bottom." Just over half the bricks in the U.S.S.R. were produced by enterprises that were *not* set up for that purpose, but which made their own bricks in order to build whatever needed building to house their main economic activity. That was because these Soviet enterprises could not rely on deliveries from the Ministry of Construction Materials, which had no financial incentives to be reliable in delivering bricks on time or of the quality required.

For similar reasons, far more Soviet enterprises were producing machine tools than were specifically set up to do so. Meanwhile, specialized plants set up for that purpose worked below their capacity—which is to say, at higher production costs per unit than if their overhead had been spread out over more units of output—because so many other enterprises were producing these machine tools for themselves. Capitalist producers of bricks or machine tools have no choice but to produce what is wanted by the customer, and to be reliable in delivering it, if they intend to keep those customers in competition with other producers of bricks or machine tools. That, however, is not the case when there is one nationwide monopoly of a particular product under government control, as was the situation in the Soviet Union.

In China's government-planned economy as well, many enterprises supplied their own transportation for the goods they produced, unlike most companies in the United States that pay trucking firms or rail or air freight carriers to transport their products. As the *Far Eastern Economic Review* put it: "Through decades of state-planned development, nearly all big

Chinese firms transported their own goods, however inefficiently."
Although theoretically firms specializing in transportation might operate
more efficiently, the absence of financial incentives to satisfy their customers
made specialized transport firms too unreliable, both as to times of delivery
and as to the care—or lack of care—when handling goods in transit. A
company manufacturing television sets in China might not be as efficient in
transporting those sets as a specialized transport company would be, but at
least they were less likely to damage their own TV sets by handling them
roughly in transit.

One of the other side effects of unreliable deliveries has been that
Chinese firms have had to keep more goods in inventory, foregoing the
advantages of "just in time" delivery practices in Japan, which reduce the
Japanese firms' costs of maintaining inventories. Dell Computers in the
United States likewise operates with very small inventories, relative to their
sales, but this is possible only because there are shipping firms like Federal
Express or UPS that Dell can rely on to get components to them and
computers to their customers quickly and safely. The net result is that China
spends about twice as high a share of its national income on transportation
as the United States does, even though the U.S. has a larger territory,
including two states separated by more than a thousand miles from the other
states.

Contrasts in the size—and therefore costs—of inventories can be extreme
from one country to another. Japan carries the smallest inventories, while
the Soviet Union carried the largest, with the United States in between. As
two Soviet economists pointed out:

> Spare parts are literally used right "off the truck": in Japan producers
> commonly deliver supplies to their ordering companies three to four
> times a day. At Toyota the volume of warehoused inventories is
> calculated for only an hour of work, while at Ford the inventories are for
> up to three weeks.

In the Soviet Union these economists said, "we have in inventories almost
as much as we create in a year." In other words, most of the people who work
in Soviet industry "could take a year's paid vacation" and the economy could
live on its inventories. This is not an advantage but a handicap because

inventories cost money—and don't earn any. From the standpoint of the economy as a whole, the production of inventory uses up resources without adding anything to either the standard of living of the public or the productivity of industry. As the Soviet economists put it, "our economy is always burdened by the heavy weight of inventories, much heavier than those that weigh on a capitalist economy during the most destructive recessions." Yet the decisions to maintain huge inventories were not irrational decisions, given the circumstances of the Soviet economy and the incentives and constraints inherent in those circumstances. Soviet enterprises had no real choice but to maintain these costly inventories. The less reliable the suppliers, the more inventory it pays to keep, so as not to run out of vital components.[4] Nevertheless, inventories add to the costs of production, which add to the price, which in turn reduces the public's purchasing power and therefore its standard of living.

Geography can also increase the amount of inventory required. As a result of severe geographical handicaps that limit land transportation in parts of sub-Saharan Africa,[5] large inventories of both agricultural produce and industrial output have had to be maintained there because regions heavily dependent on rivers and streams for transportation can be cut off if those rivers and streams fall too low to be navigable because the rainy season is either delayed or ends prematurely.

American businesses have inventory practices closer to those of the Japanese than to those which existed in the Soviet Union. The Chrysler division of DaimlerChrysler unloads about 8,000 truckloads of materials at its various plants each day. Closely following the pattern in Japan, DaimlerChrysler keeps only two hours' supply of materials on hand. It can do this only because it can rely on the deliveries of parts needed to keep their production lines operating.

---

[4] Far from being excessive under the circumstances, inventories in the Soviet Union often proved to be inadequate, as manufacturing enterprises still ran out of components. According to Soviet economists, "a third of all cars come off the assembly line with parts missing." Shmelev and Popov, *The Turning Point*, p. 136.
[5] See my *Conquests and Cultures*, pages 101-108.

The reason General Motors can produce automobiles, without producing any tires to go on them, is because it can rely on Goodyear, Michelin, and whoever else supplies their tires to have those tires waiting to go on the cars when they come off the production lines. If these suppliers failed to deliver, it would of course be a disaster for General Motors. But it would be even more catastrophic for the tire companies themselves. To leave General Motors high and dry, with no tires to go on its Cadillacs or Chevrolets, would be financially suicidal to a tire company, since it would lose a customer for millions of tires each year, quite aside from the billions of dollars in damages from lawsuits over breach of contract. Under these circumstances, it is hardly surprising that General Motors does not have to produce all its own components, as many Soviet enterprises did.

Absurd as it might seem to imagine Cadillacs rolling off the assembly lines and finding no tires to go on them, back in the days of the Soviet Union one of that country's own high officials complained that "hundreds of thousands of motor vehicles stand idle without tires." The fact that complex coordination takes place so seemingly automatically in one economic system that people hardly even think about it does not mean that coordination will be similarly automatic in another economic system operating on different principles. Ironically, it is precisely where there is no one controlling the whole economy that it is automatically coordinated by price movements, while in deliberately planned economies such coordination has repeatedly turned out to be difficult or impossible to achieve.

Reliability is an inherent accompaniment of the physical product when keeping customers is a matter of economic life and death under capitalism, whether at the manufacturing level or the retail level. Back in the early 1930s, when refrigerators were just beginning to become widely used in the United States, there were many technological and production problems with the first mass-produced refrigerators sold by Sears. The company had no choice but to honor its money-back guarantee by taking back 30,000 refrigerators, at a time when Sears could ill afford to do so, in the depths of the Great Depression, when businesses were as short of money as their customers were. This situation put enormous financial pressure on Sears to either stop selling refrigerators (which is what some of its executives and many of its store managers wanted) or else greatly improve their reliability, which is what they eventually did, thereby becoming one of the leading sellers of refrigerators in the country.

None of this was painless. Nor is it likely that a socialist monopoly would have been forced to undergo such economic trauma to please its customers. There was a reason why Soviet enterprises could not rely on their suppliers and chose instead to make many things for themselves, and why large Chinese companies often transported their own products, even though neither the Soviet nor the Chinese enterprises were specialists in these auxiliary activities. The suppliers did not have to please their customers. All they had to do was follow general orders from the central planners, who were in no position to monitor the specific details for thousands of enterprises spread out across a vast nation. But orders from central planners were not an adequate substitute for the incentives of the marketplace, where customers individually monitored their own specific details. In both countries, the population at large paid the price in a standard of living much below what their country's resources and technology were capable of producing.

Chapter 7

BIG BUSINESS AND GOVERNMENT

Competition always has been and always will be troublesome to those who have to meet it.

Frederic Bastiat

Competitive free markets are not the only kinds of markets, nor are government-imposed price controls or central planning the only interferences with the operations of such markets. Monopolies, oligopolies, and cartels also produce economic results very different from those of a free market.

MONOPOLIES AND CARTELS

A monopoly means literally one seller. However, a small number of sellers—an "oligopoly," as economists call it—may cooperate with one another, either explicitly or tacitly, in setting prices and so produce results similar to those of a monopoly. Where there is a formal organization in an industry to set prices and output—a cartel—its results can be like those of a monopoly, even though there may be numerous sellers in the cartel. Although these various kinds of non-competitive industries differ among themselves, their generally detrimental effects have led to laws and government policies designed to prevent or counter these negative effects. Sometimes this government intervention takes the form of direct regulation of the prices and policies of monopolistic industries. In other cases, government prohibits particular practices without attempting to micro-manage the companies involved. The first and most fundamental question, however, is: How are monopolistic firms detrimental to the economy?

Sometimes one company produces the total output of a given good or service in a region or a country. For many years, each local telephone company in the United States was a monopoly in its region of the country and that remains true in some other countries. For about half a century before World War II, the Aluminum Company of America (Alcoa) produced all the virgin ingot aluminum in the United States. Such situations are unusual, but they are important enough to deserve some serious attention.

Most big businesses are not monopolies and not all monopolies are big business. In the days before the automobile and the railroad, a general store in an isolated rural community could easily be the only store for miles around, and was as much of a monopoly as any corporation on the *Fortune* 500 list, even though the general store was usually an enterprise of very modest size. Conversely, today even multi-billion-dollar nationwide grocery chains like Safeway or Kroeger have too many competitors to be able to price the goods they sell the way a monopolist would price those goods.

Monopoly Prices vs. Competitive Prices

Just as we can understand the function of prices better after we have seen what happens when they are not allowed to function, so we can understand the role of competition in the economy better after we contrast what happens in competitive markets with what happens in markets that are not competitive. In earlier chapters, we considered prices as they emerged in a free market with many competing enterprises. Such markets tend to cause goods and services to be produced at the lowest costs possible under existing technology and with existing resources.

Take something as simple as apple juice. How do consumers know that the price they are being charged for apple juice is not far above the cost of producing it and distributing it, including a return on investment sufficient to keep those investments being made? After all, most people do not grow apples, much less process them into juice and then bottle the juice, transport and store it, so they have no idea how much any or all of this costs. Competition in the marketplace makes it unnecessary to know. Those few people who do know such things, and who are in the business of making investments, have every incentive to invest wherever there are higher rates of return and to reduce their investments where the rates of return are lower or negative. If the price of apple juice is higher than necessary to compensate for the costs incurred in producing it, then higher rates of profit will be made—and will attract ever more investment into this industry until the competition of additional producers drives prices down to a level that just compensates the costs with the same average rate of return on similar investments available elsewhere in the economy. Only then will the in-flow of investments from other sectors of the economy stop, with the incentives for these in-flows now being gone. If, however, there were a monopoly in producing apple juice, the situation would be very different. Chances are that monopoly prices would remain at levels higher than necessary to compensate for the costs and efforts that go into producing apple juice, including paying a rate of return on capital sufficient to attract the capital required. The monopolist would earn a rate of return higher than necessary to attract the capital required.

Many people object to the fact that a monopolist can charge higher prices than a competitive business could. But the ability to transfer money from other members of the society to itself is not the sole harm done by a monopoly. From the standpoint of the economy as a whole, these internal transfers do not change the total wealth of the society, even though such transfers redistribute wealth in a manner that may be considered objectionable. What adversely affects the total wealth in the economy as a whole is the effect of a monopoly on the allocation of scarce resources which have alternative uses.

When a monopoly charges a higher price than it could charge if it had competition, consumers tend to buy less of the product than they would at a lower competitive price. In short, a monopolist produces less output than a competitive industry would produce with the same available resources, technology and cost conditions. The monopolist stops short at a point where consumers are still willing to pay enough to cover the cost of production (including a normal rate of profit) of more output because the monopolist is charging more than the usual cost of production and making more than the usual profit. In terms of the allocation of resources which have alternative uses, the net result is that some resources which could have been used to produce more apple juice instead go into producing other things elsewhere in the economy, even if those other things are not as valuable as the apple juice that could and would have been produced in a free competitive market. In short, the economy's resources are used inefficiently when there is monopoly, because these resources would be transferred from more valued uses to less valued uses.

Fortunately, monopolies are very hard to maintain without laws to protect the monopolistic firms from competition. The ceaseless search of investors for the highest rates of return virtually ensures that such investments will flood into whatever segment of the economy is earning higher profits, until the rate of profit in that segment is driven down by the increased competition caused by that flood of investment. It is like water seeking its own level. But, just as dams can prevent water from finding its own level, so government intervention can prevent a monopoly's profit rate from being reduced by competition.

In centuries past, government permission was required to open businesses in many parts of the economy, especially in Europe and Asia, and monopoly rights were granted to various business owners, who either paid the government directly for these rights or bribed officials who had the power to grant such rights, or both. However, by the end of the eighteenth century, the development of economics had reached the point where increasingly large numbers of people understood how this was detrimental to society as a whole and counter-pressures developed toward freeing the economy from monopolies and government control. Monopolies have therefore become much rarer, at least at the national level, though restrictions on competition remain common in many cities where restrictive licensing laws limit how many taxis are allowed to operate, causing fares to be artificially higher than necessary and cabs less available than they would be in a free market.

Again, the loss is not simply that of the individual consumers. The economy as a whole loses when people who are perfectly willing to drive taxis at fares that consumers are willing to pay are nevertheless prevented from doing so by artificial restrictions on the number of taxi licenses issued, and thus either do some other work of lesser value or remain unemployed. If the alternative work were of greater value, and were compensated accordingly, then such people would never have been potential taxi drivers in the first place.

From the standpoint of the economy as a whole, monopolistic pricing means that consumers of a monopolist's product are foregoing the use of scarce resources which would have a higher value to them than in alternative uses. That is the inefficiency which causes the economy as a whole to have less wealth under monopoly than it would have under free competition. It is sometimes said that a monopolist "restricts output," but this is not the intent, nor is the monopolist the one who restricts output. The monopolist would love to have the consumers buy more at its inflated price, but the consumers stop short of the amount that they would buy at a lower price under free competition. It is the monopolist's higher price which causes the consumers to restrict their own purchases and therefore causes the monopolist to restrict production to what can be sold. But the monopolist may be advertising heavily to try to persuade consumers to buy more.

Similar principles apply to a cartel—that is, a group of businesses which agree among themselves to charge higher prices or otherwise avoid competing with one another. In theory, a cartel could operate collectively the same as a monopoly. In practice, however, individual members of cartels tend to cheat on one another secretly—lowering the cartel price to some customers, in order to take business away from other members of the cartel. When this practice becomes widespread, the cartel becomes irrelevant, whether or not it formally ceases to exist.

Governmental and Market Responses

Because some kinds of huge business organizations were once known as "trusts," legislation designed to outlaw monopolies and cartels became known as "anti-trust laws." However, such laws are not the only way of fighting monopolies and cartels. Private businesses that are not part of the cartel have incentives to fight them in the marketplace. Moreover, private businesses can take action much faster than the years required for the government to bring a major anti-trust case to a successful conclusion.

Back in the heyday of American trusts, Montgomery Ward was one of their biggest opponents. Whether the trust involved agricultural machinery, bicycles, sugar, nails or twine, Montgomery Ward would seek out manufacturers that were not part of the trust and buy from them below the cartel price, reselling to the general public below the retail price of the goods produced by members of the cartel. Since Montgomery Ward was the number one retailer in the country at that time, it was also big enough to set up its own factories and make the product itself if need be. The later rise of other huge retailers like Sears and the A & P grocery chain likewise confronted the big producers with corporate giants able to either produce their own competing products to sell in their own stores or to buy enough from some small enterprise outside the cartel, enabling that enterprise to grow into a big competitor.

Sears did both. It produced stoves, shoes, guns, and wallpaper, among other things, in addition to subcontracting the production of other products. A & P imported and roasted its own coffee, canned its own salmon, and baked half a billion loaves of bread a year for sale in its stores. While giant firms like Sears, Montgomery Ward and A & P were unique in being able to compete against a number of cartels simultaneously, smaller companies could also take away sales from cartels in their respective industries. Their incentive was the same as that of the cartel—profit. Where a monopoly or cartel maintains prices that produce higher than normal profits, other businesses are attracted to the industry. This additional competition then tends to force prices and profits down. In order for a monopoly or cartel to succeed in maintaining profits above the competitive level, it must find ways to prevent others from entering the industry. That is easier said than done.

One way to keep out potential competitors is to have the government make it illegal for others to operate in particular industries. Kings granted or sold monopoly rights for centuries, and modern governments have restricted the issuance of licenses for various industries and occupations, ranging from airlines to trucking to the braiding of hair. Political rationales are never lacking for these restrictions, but their net economic effect is to protect existing enterprises from additional potential competitors and therefore to maintain prices at artificially high levels. For much of the late twentieth century, the government of India not only decided which companies it would license to produce which products, it imposed limits on how much each company could produce. Thus an Indian manufacturer of scooters was hauled before a government commission because he had produced more scooters than he was allowed to and a producer of medicine for colds was fearful that the public had bought "too much" of his product during a flu epidemic in India. Lawyers for the cold medicine manufacturer spent months preparing a legal defense for having produced and sold more than they were allowed to, in case they were called before the same commission. All this costly legal work had to be paid for by someone and that someone was ultimately the consumer.

In the absence of government prohibition against entry into particular industries, various clever schemes can be used privately to try to erect barriers to keep out competitors and protect monopoly profits. But other businesses have incentives to be just as clever at evading these barriers. Accordingly, the effectiveness of barriers to entry has varied from industry to industry and from one era to another in the same industry. The computer industry was once difficult to enter, back in the days when a computer was a huge machine taking thousands of cubic feet of space, and the cost of manufacturing such machines was likewise huge. But the development of microchips meant that smaller computers could do the same work and chips were now inexpensive enough to produce that they could be manufactured by smaller companies. These include companies located around the world, so that even a nationwide monopoly does not preclude competition in an industry. Although the United States pioneered in the creation of computers, the actual manufacturing of computers spread quickly to East Asia, which supplied much of the American market with computers.

In addition to private responses to monopolies and cartels which arise more or less spontaneously in the marketplace, there are government responses. In the late nineteenth century, the American government began to respond to monopolies and cartels by both directly regulating the prices which monopolies and cartels were allowed to charge and by taking legal punitive action against these monopolies and cartels under the Sherman Anti-Trust Act of 1890 and other later anti-trust legislation. When railroads were first built in the nineteenth century, there were many places where only one rail line existed, leaving these railroads free to charge whatever prices would maximize their profits where they had a monopoly. Complaints about this situation led to the creation of the Interstate Commerce Commission in 1887, the first of many federal regulatory commissions to control the prices charged by monopolists. During the era when local telephone companies were monopolies in their respective regions and their parent company—A.T.&T.—had a monopoly of long-distance service, the Federal Communications Commission controlled the prices charged by A.T.&T., while state regulatory agencies controlled the price of local phone service.

Another approach has been to pass laws against the creation or maintenance of a monopoly or against various practices, such as price discrimination, growing out of monopolistic behavior. These anti-trust laws were intended to allow businesses to operate without the kinds of detailed government supervision which exist under regulatory commissions, but with a sort of general surveillance, like that of traffic police, with intervention occurring only when there are specific violations of laws.

REGULATORY COMMISSIONS

Although the functions of a regulatory commission are fairly straightforward in theory, in practice its task is far more complex and, in some respects, impossible. Moreover, the political climate in which regulatory commissions operate often lead to policies and results directly the opposite of what was expected by those who created such commissions.

Ideally, a regulatory commission would set prices where they would have been if there were a competitive marketplace. In practice, there is no way to know what those prices would be. Only the actual functioning of a market itself could reveal such prices, with the less efficient firms being eliminated by bankruptcy and only the most efficient surviving, with their lower prices now being the market prices. No outside observers can know what the most efficient ways of operating a given firm or industry are. Indeed, many managements within an industry discover the hard way that what they thought was the most efficient way to do things was not efficient enough to meet the competition, and end up losing customers as a result. The most that a regulatory agency can do is accept what appear to be reasonable production costs and allow the monopoly to make what seems to be a reasonable profit over and above such costs.

Determining the cost of production is by no means always easy. As noted in Chapter 6, there may be no such thing as "the" cost of production. The cost of generating electricity, for example, can vary enormously, depending on when and where it is generated. When you wake up in the middle of the night and turn on a light, that electricity costs practically nothing to supply, because the electricity-generating system has much unused capacity in the middle of the night, when most people are asleep. But, when you turn on your air conditioner on a hot summer afternoon, when millions of other homes and offices already have their air conditioners on, that may help strain the system to its limit and necessitate turning on costly standby generators, in order to avoid blackouts. It has been estimated that the cost of supplying the electricity required to run a dishwasher, at a time of peak electricity usage, can be 100 times greater than the cost of running that same dishwasher at a time when there is a low demand for electricity.

There are many reasons why additional electricity, beyond the usual capacity of the system, may be many times more costly per kilowatt hour than the usual costs when the system is functioning within its usual capacity. The main system that supplies vast numbers of consumers can make use of economies of scale to produce electricity at its lowest cost, while standby generators typically produce less electricity and therefore cannot take full advantage of economies of scale, but must produce at higher costs per kilowatt hour. Sometimes technological progress gives the main system lower costs, while obsolete equipment is kept as standby equipment, rather than being junked, and the costs of producing additional electricity with this obsolete equipment is of course higher. Where additional electricity has to be purchased from outside sources when the local generating capacity is at its limit, the additional cost of transmitting that electricity from greater distances raises the cost of the additional electricity to much higher levels than the cost of electricity generated closer to the consumers.

More variations in "the" cost of producing electricity come from fluctuations in the costs of the various fuels—oil, gas, coal, nuclear—used to run the generators. Since all these fuels are used for other things besides generating electricity, the demand for these fuels from other industries, or for use in homes or automobiles, makes their prices unpredictable. Hydroelectric dams likewise vary in how much electricity they can produce when rainfall varies, increasing or reducing the amount of water that flows through the generators. When the fixed costs of the dam are spread over differing amounts of electricity, the cost per kilowatt varies accordingly.

How is a regulatory commission to set the rates to be charged consumers of electricity, given that the cost of generating electricity can vary so widely and unpredictably? If state regulatory commissions set electricity rates based on "average" costs of generating electricity, then when there is a higher demand or a shorter supply within the state, out-of-state suppliers may be unwilling to sell electricity at prices lower than their own costs of generating the additional electricity from standby units. This was part of the reason for the much-publicized blackouts in California in 2001. "Average" costs are irrelevant when the costs of generation are far above average at a particular time or far below average at other times.

Because the public is unlikely to be familiar with all the economic complications involved, they are likely to be outraged at having to pay electricity rates far higher than they are used to. In turn, this means that politicians are tempted to step in and impose price controls based on the old rates. And, as already noted in other contexts, price controls create shortages—in this case, shortages of electricity that result in blackouts. A larger quantity demanded and a smaller quantity supplied has been a very familiar response to price controls, going back in history long before electricity came into use. However, politicians' success does not depend on their learning the lessons of history or of economics. It depends far more on their going along with what is widely believed by the public and the media, which may include conspiracy theories or belief that higher prices are due to "gouging" or "greed."

Halfway around the world attempts to raise electricity rates in India were met by street demonstrations, as they were in California. In the Indian state of Karnataka, controlled politically by India's Congress Party at the time, efforts to change electricity rates were opposed in the streets by one of the opposition parties. However, in the neighboring state of Andhra Pradesh, where the Congress Party was in the opposition, it led similar street demonstrations against electricity rate increases. In short, what was involved in these demonstrations was neither ideology nor party but an opportunistic playing to the gallery of public misconceptions.

The economic complexities involved when regulatory agencies set prices are compounded by political complexities. Regulatory agencies are often set up after some political crusaders have successfully launched investigations or publicity campaigns that convince the authorities to establish a permanent commission to oversee and control a monopoly or some group of firms few enough in number to be a threat to behave in collusion as if they were one monopoly. However, after a commission has been set up and its powers established, crusaders and the media tend to lose interest over the years and turn their attention to other things. Meanwhile, the firms being regulated continue to take a keen interest in the activities of the commission and to lobby the government for favorable regulations and favorable appointments of individuals to these commissions.

The net result of these asymmetrical outside interests on these agencies is that commissions set up to keep a given firm or industry within bounds, for the benefit of the consumers, often metamorphose into agencies seeking to protect the existing regulated firms from threats arising from new firms with new technology or new organizational methods. Thus, in the United States, the Interstate Commerce Commission responded to the rise of the trucking industry, whose competition in carrying freight threatened the economic viability of the railroads, by extending the commission's control to include trucking.

The original rationale for regulating railroads was that these railroads were often monopolies in particular areas of the country, where there was only one rail line. But now that trucking undermined that monopoly, by being able to go wherever there were roads, the response of the I.C.C. was not to say that the need for regulating transportation was now less urgent or perhaps even unnecessary. Instead, it sought—and received from Congress—broader authority under the Motor Carrier Act of 1935, in order to restrict the activities of truckers. This allowed railroads to survive under new economic conditions, despite truck competition that was more efficient for various kinds of freight hauling. Trucks were now permitted to operate across state lines only if they had a certificate from the Interstate Commerce Commission declaring that the trucks' activities served "public necessity and convenience" as defined by the I.C.C. This kept truckers from driving railroads into bankruptcy by taking away their customers.

In short, freight was no longer hauled in whatever way required the use of the least resources, as it would be under open competition, but only by whatever way met the arbitrary requirements of the Interstate Commerce Commission. The I.C.C. might, for example, authorize a particular trucking company to haul freight from New York to Washington, but not from Philadelphia to Baltimore, even though these cities are on the way. If the certificate did not authorize freight to be carried back from Washington to New York, then the trucks would have to return empty, while other trucks carried freight from D.C. to New York. From the standpoint of the economy as a whole, enormously greater costs were incurred than were necessary to get the work done. But what this arrangement accomplished politically was to allow far more companies—both truckers and railroads—to survive and make a profit than if there were an unrestricted competitive market, where the transportation companies would have no choice but to use the most efficient ways of hauling freight, even if lower costs and lower prices led to the bankruptcy of some railroads whose costs were too high to survive in competition with trucks. The use of more resources than necessary entailed the survival of more companies than were necessary.

While open and unfettered competition would have been economically beneficial to the society as a whole, such competition would have been politically threatening to the regulatory commission. Firms facing economic extinction because of competition would be sure to resort to political agitation and intrigue against the survival in office of the commissioners and against the survival of the commission and its powers. Labor unions also had a vested interest in keeping the status quo safe from the competition of technologies and methods that might require fewer workers to get the job done.

After the I.C.C.'s powers to control the trucking industry were eventually reduced by Congress in 1980, freight charges declined substantially and customers reported a rise in the quality of the service. This was made possible by greater efficiency in the industry, as there were now fewer trucks driving around empty and more truckers hired workers whose pay was determined by supply and demand, rather than by union contracts. Because truck deliveries were now more dependable in a competitive industry, businesses using their services were able to carry smaller inventories, saving in the aggregate tens of billions of dollars.

The inefficiencies created by regulation were indicated not only by such savings after federal deregulation, but also by the difference between the costs of interstate shipments and the costs of *intrastate* shipments, where strict state regulation continued after federal regulation was cut back. For example, shipping blue jeans within the state of Texas from El Paso to Dallas cost about 40 percent more than shipping the same jeans internationally from Taiwan to Dallas.

Gross inefficiencies under regulation were not peculiar to the Interstate Commerce Commission. The same was true of the Civil Aeronautics Board, which kept out potentially competitive airlines and kept the prices of air fares in the United States high enough to ensure the survival of existing airlines, rather than force them to face the competition of other airlines that could carry passengers cheaper or with better service. Once the CAB was abolished, airline fares came down, some airlines went bankrupt, but new airlines arose and in the end there were far more passengers being carried than at any time under the constraints of regulation. Savings to airline passengers ran into the billions of dollars.

These were not just zero-sum changes, with airlines losing what passengers gained. The country as a whole benefitted from deregulation, for the industry became more efficient. Just as there were fewer trucks driving around empty after trucking deregulation, so airplanes began to fly with a higher percentage of their seats filled with passengers after airline deregulation, and passengers usually had more choices of carriers on a given route than before. Much the same thing happened after European airlines were deregulated in 1997, as competition from new discount airlines like Ryanair forced British Airways, Air France and Lufthansa to lower their fares.

In these and other industries, the original rationale for regulation was to keep prices from rising excessively but, over the years, this turned into regulatory restrictions against letting prices *fall* to a level that would threaten the survival of existing firms. Political crusades are based on plausible rationales but, even when those rationales are sincerely believed and honestly applied, their actual consequences may be completely different from their initial goals. People make mistakes in all fields of human endeavor but, when major mistakes are made in a competitive economy, those who were mistaken can be forced from the marketplace by the losses that follow. In politics, however, those who were mistaken can often continue to survive by doing things that were never contemplated when their positions and their powers were created.

ANTI-TRUST LAWS

With anti-trust laws, as with regulatory commissions, a sharp distinction must be made between their original rationales and what they actually do. The basic rationale for anti-trust laws is to prevent monopoly and other conditions which allow prices to rise above where they would be in a free and competitive marketplace. In practice, most of the famous anti-trust cases in the United States have involved some business that charged *lower* prices than its competitors. Often it has been complaints from these competitors which caused the government to act.

The basis of many government prosecutions under the anti-trust laws is that some company's actions threaten competition. However, the most important thing about competition is that it is a *condition* in the marketplace. This condition cannot be measured by the number of competitors existing in a given industry at a given time, though politicians, lawyers and assorted others have confused the existence of competition with the number of surviving competitors. But competition as a condition is precisely what eliminates many competitors.

Obviously, if it eliminates all competitors, then the surviving firm would be a monopoly, at least until new competitors arose, and could then charge far higher prices than in a competitive market. But that is extremely rare. However, the specter of monopoly is often used to justify government policies of intervention where there is no serious danger of a monopoly. For example, back when the A & P grocery chain was the largest retail chain in the world, it still sold less than one-fifth of the groceries in the United States. Yet the Justice Department brought an anti-trust action against it, using the company's low prices, and the methods by which it achieved those low prices, as evidence of "unfair" competition against rival grocers and grocery chains. Throughout the history of anti-trust prosecutions, there has been an unresolved confusion between what is detrimental to competition and what is detrimental to competitors. In the midst of this confusion, the question of what is beneficial to the consumer has often been lost sight of.

What has often also been lost sight of is the question of the efficiency of the economy as a whole, which is another way of looking at the benefits to the consuming public. Fewer scarce resources are used when products are bought and sold in carload lots, as large chain stores are often able to do, than when the shipments are sold and delivered in much smaller quantities to numerous smaller stores. Both delivery costs and selling costs are less per unit of product when the product is bought and sold in large enough amounts to fill a railroad boxcar. Production costs are also lower when the producer receives a large enough order to be able to schedule production far ahead, instead of finding it necessary to pay overtime to fill many small and unexpected orders that happen to arrive at the same time.

Unpredictable orders also increase the likelihood of slow periods when there is not enough work to keep all the workers employed. Workers who have to be laid off at such times may find other jobs and not return when the first employer has more orders to fill, thus making it necessary for that employer to hire new workers, which entails training costs and lower productivity until the new workers gain enough experience to reach peak efficiency. Moreover, employers unable to offer steady employment may find recruiting workers to be more difficult, unless they offer higher pay to offset the uncertainties of the job. In all these ways, production costs are higher when there are unpredictable orders than when a large purchaser, such as a major department store chain, can contract for a large amount of the supplier's output, enabling cost savings to be made in production, part of which go to the chain in lower prices as well as to the producer as lower production costs that create more profit.

Despite such economies of scale, the government took action against the Morton Salt Company in the 1940s for giving discounts to buyers who bought carload lots of their product. Businesses that bought less than a carload lot of salt were charged $1.60 a case, those who bought carload lots were charged $1.50 a case, and those who bought 50,000 cases or more in a year's time were charged $1.35. Because there were relatively few companies that could afford to buy so much salt and many more that could not, "the competitive opportunities of certain merchants were injured," according to the Supreme Court, which upheld the Federal Trade Commission's actions against Morton Salt. The government likewise took action against the Standard Oil Company in the 1950s for allowing discounts to those dealers who bought oil by the tank car. The Borden Company was similarly brought into court in the 1960s for having charged less for milk to big chain stores than to smaller grocers. In all these cases, the key point was that such price differences were considered "discriminatory" and "unfair" to those competing firms unable to make such large purchases.

While the sellers were allowed to defend themselves in court by referring to cost differences in selling to different classes of buyers, the apparently simple concept of "cost" is by no means simple when argued over by rival lawyers, accountants and economists. Where neither side could prove anything conclusively about the costs—which was common—the accused lost the case. In a fundamental departure from the centuries-old traditions of Anglo-American law, the government need only make a superficial or *prima facie* case, based on gross numbers, to shift the burden of proof to the accused. This same principle and procedure were to reappear, years later, in employment discrimination cases under the civil rights laws. As with anti-trust cases, these employment discrimination cases likewise produced many consent decrees and large out-of-court settlements by companies well aware of the virtual impossibility of proving their innocence, regardless of what the facts might be.

The rarity of genuine monopolies in the American economy has led to much legalistic creativity, in order to define various companies as monopolistic or as potential or "incipient" monopolies. How far this could go was illustrated when the Supreme Court in 1962 broke up a merger between two shoe companies that would have given the new combined company less than 7 percent of the shoe sales in the United States. It likewise in 1966 broke up a merger of two local supermarket chains which, put together, sold less than 8 percent of the groceries in the Los Angeles area. Similarly arbitrary categorizations of businesses as "monopolies" were imposed in India under the Monopolies and Restrictive Trade Practices Act of 1969, where any enterprises with assets in excess of a given amount (about $27 million) were declared to be monopolies and restricted from expanding their business.

A standard practice in American courts and in the literature on anti-trust laws is to describe the percentage of sales made by a given company as the share of the market which it "controls." By this standard, such now defunct companies as Pan American Airways "controlled" a substantial share of their respective markets, when in fact the passage of time showed that they controlled nothing, or else they would never have allowed themselves to be forced out of business. The severe shrinkage in size of such former giants as A & P likewise suggests that the rhetoric of "control" bears little relationship to reality. But such rhetoric remains effective in courts of law and in the court of public opinion.

Even in the rare case where a genuine monopoly exists on its own—that is, has not been created or sustained by government policy—the consequences in practice have tended to be much less dire than in theory. During the decades when the Aluminum Company of America (Alcoa) was the only producer of virgin ingot aluminum in the United States, its annual profit rate on its investment was about 10 percent after taxes. Moreover, the price of aluminum went down over the years to a fraction of what it had been before Alcoa was formed. Yet Alcoa was prosecuted under the anti-trust laws and lost.

Why were aluminum prices going down under a monopoly, when in theory they should have been going up? Despite its "control" of the market for aluminum, Alcoa was well aware that it could not jack up prices at will, without risking the substitution of other materials—steel, tin, wood, plastics—for aluminum by many users.

This raises a question which applies far beyond the aluminum industry. Percentages of the market "controlled" by this or that company ignore the role of substitutes that may be officially classified as products of other industries, but which can nevertheless be used as substitutes by many buyers, if the price of the monopolized product rises significantly. Whether in a monopolized or a competitive market, a technologically very different product may serve as a substitute, as laptop computers did when they replaced portable typewriters, or as television did when it replaced many newspapers as sources of information and entertainment.

In Spain, when a high-speed train began to operate between Madrid and Seville, the division of passenger traffic between rail and air travel went from 33 percent rail and 67 percent air to 82 percent rail and 18 percent air. Clearly many people treated air and rail traffic as substitute ways of traveling between these two cities. No matter how high a percentage of the air traffic between Madrid and Seville might be carried ("controlled") by one airline, and no matter how high a percentage of the rail traffic might be carried by one railroad, each would still face the competition of all air lines and all rail lines operating between these cities.

Similarly, in earlier years, ocean liners carried a million passengers across the Atlantic in 1954 while planes carried 600,000. But, by 1965, the liners were carrying just 650,000 passengers while planes now carried four million. The fact that these were technologically very different things did not mean that they could not serve as economic substitutes.

Advertising is clearly a market that encompasses technologically very different media, ranging from billboards to brochures, sky-writing, the Internet, newspaper and magazine ads, and commercials on television and radio. Different businesses spend differing proportions of their respective advertising budgets in these various media and change those proportions over time. Any particular advertising firm's "control" of any given percentage of the advertising in its own particular medium—say, billboards—would mean little if jacking up its prices on billboard ads would lead advertisers to switch their advertising to newspaper ads, radio commercials, or some other medium.

Those bringing anti-trust lawsuits generally seek to define the relevant market narrowly, so as to produce high percentages of the market "controlled" by the enterprise being prosecuted. In the famous anti-trust case against Microsoft at the turn of the century, for example, the market was defined as that for computer operating systems for stand-alone personal computers using microchips of the kind manufactured by Intel. This left out not only the operating systems running Apple computers but also other operating systems such as those produced by Sun Microsystems for multiple computers or the Linux system for stand-alone computers. In its narrowly defined market, Microsoft clearly had a "dominant" share. The anti-trust lawsuit, however, did not accuse Microsoft of jacking up prices unconscionably, in the classic manner of monopoly theory. Rather, Microsoft had added an Internet browser to its Windows operating system free of charge, undermining rival browser producer Netscape. The existence of all the various sources of potential competition from outside the narrowly defined market may well have had something to do with the fact that Microsoft did not raise prices, as it could have gotten away with in the short run—but at the cost of jeopardizing its long-run sales and profits, since other operating systems could have been adaptable as substitutes if their prices were right. In 2003, the city government of Munich in fact switched from using Microsoft Windows in 14,000 computers to using Linux—one of the systems excluded from the definition of the market that Microsoft "controlled" but which was nevertheless obviously a substitute.

The spread of international free trade means that even a genuine monopoly of a particular product in a particular country may mean little if that same product can be imported from other countries. If there is only one producer of widgets in Brazil, that producer is not a monopoly in any economically meaningful sense if there are a dozen widget manufacturers in neighboring Argentina and hundreds of widget makers in countries around the world. Only if the Brazilian government prevents widgets from being imported does the lone manufacturer in the country become a monopoly in a sense that would allow higher prices to be charged than would be charged in a competitive market.

If it seems silly to arbitrarily define a market and "control" of that market by a given firm's sales of domestically produced products, it was not too silly to form the basis of a landmark U.S. Supreme Court decision in 1962, which defined the market for shoes in terms of "domestic production of nonrubber shoes." By eliminating sneakers, deck shoes, and imported shoes of all kinds, this definition increased the defined market share of the firms being charged with violating the anti-trust laws—who in this case were convicted.

Thus far, whether discussing widgets, shoes, or computer operating systems, we have been considering markets defined by a given product performing a given function. But often the same function can be performed by technologically different products. Corn and petroleum may not seem to be similar products belonging in the same industry but producers of plastics can use the oil from either one to manufacture goods made of plastic. When petroleum prices soared in 2004, Cargill Dow's sales of a resin made from corn oil rose 60 percent over the previous year, as plastics manufacturers switched from the more expensive petroleum oil. Whether or not two things are substitutes economically does not depend on whether they look alike or are conventionally defined as being in the same industry. No one considers corn as being in the petroleum industry or considers either of these products when calculating what percentage of the market is "controlled" by a given producer of the other product. But that simply highlights the inadequacy of "control" statistics.

Even products that have no functional similarity may nevertheless be substitutes in economic terms. If golf courses were to double their fees, many casual golfers might play the game less often or give it up entirely, and in either case seek recreation by taking more trips or cruises or by pursuing a hobby like photography or skiing, using money that might otherwise have been used for playing golf. The fact that these other activities are functionally very different from golf does not matter. In economic terms, when higher prices for *A* cause people to buy more of *B*, then *A* and *B* are substitutes, whether or not they look alike or operate alike. But laws and government policies seldom look at things this way, especially when defining how much of a given market a given firm "controls."

Domestically, as well as internationally, as the area that can be served by given producers expands, the degree of statistical dominance or "control" by local producers in any given area means less and less. For example, as the number of newspapers published in given American communities declined substantially after the middle of the twentieth century with the rise of television, much concern was expressed over the growing share of local markets "controlled" by the surviving papers. In many communities, only one local newspaper survived, making it a monopoly as defined by the share of the market it "controlled." Yet the fact that newspapers published elsewhere became available over wider and wider areas made such statistical "control" economically less and less meaningful.

For example, someone living in the small community of Palo Alto, California, 30 miles south of San Francisco, need not buy a Palo Alto newspaper to find out what movies are playing in town, since that information is readily available from the *San Francisco Chronicle*, which is widely sold in Palo Alto, with home delivery being easy to arrange. Still less does a Palo Alto resident have to rely on a local paper for national or international news. Technological advances have enabled the *New York Times* or the *Wall Street Journal* to be printed in California as readily as in New York, and at the same time, so that these became national newspapers, available in communities large and small across America. *USA Today* achieved the largest circulation in the country with no local origin at all, being printed in numerous communities across the country. The net result was that many local "monopoly" newspapers had difficulties even surviving financially, much less making any extra profits associated with monopoly. Yet anti-trust policies based on market shares continued to impose restrictions on mergers of local newspapers, lest such mergers leave the surviving newspapers with too much "control" of their local market. But the market as defined by the location of the newspaper's headquarters had become largely irrelevant economically.

An extreme example of how misleading market share statistics can be was the case of a local movie chain that showed 100 percent of all the first-run movies in Las Vegas. It was prosecuted as a monopoly but, by the time the case reached the 9th Circuit Court of Appeals, another movie chain was showing more first-run movies in Las Vegas than the "monopolist" that was being prosecuted. Fortunately, sanity prevailed in this instance. Judge Alex Kozinski of the 9th Circuit Court of Appeals pointed out that the key to monopoly is not market share—even when it is 100 percent—but the ability to keep others out. A company which cannot keep competitors out is not a monopoly, no matter what percentage of the market it may have at a given moment. That is why the *Palo Alto Daily News* is not a monopoly in any economically meaningful sense, even though it is the only local daily newspaper published in town.

Focusing on market shares at a given moment has also led to a pattern in which the U. S. government has prosecuted leading firms in an industry just when they were about to lose that leadership. In a world where it is common for particular companies to rise and fall over time, anti-trust lawyers can take years to build a case against a company that is at its peak—and about to head over the hill. A major anti-trust case can take a decade or more to be brought to a final conclusion. Markets often react much more quickly than that against monopolies and cartels, as early twentieth century trusts found when giant retailers like Sears, Montgomery Ward and A & P outflanked them long before the government could make a legal case against them.

Perhaps the most clearly positive benefit of American anti-trust laws has been a blanket prohibition against collusion to fix prices. This is an automatic violation, subject to heavy penalties, regardless of any justification that might be attempted. Whether this outweighs the various negative effects of other anti-trust laws on competition in the marketplace is another question. The more stringent anti-monopoly laws in India produced many clearly counterproductive results before these laws were eventually repealed in 1991. Some of India's leading industrialists were prevented from expanding their highly successful enterprises, lest they exceed an arbitrary financial limit used to define a "monopoly"—regardless of how many competitors that "monopolist" might have. As a result, Indian entrepreneurs often applied their efforts and capital outside of India, providing goods, employment, and taxes in other countries where they were not so restricted. One such Indian entrepreneur, for example, produced fiber in Thailand from pulp bought in Canada and sent this fiber to his factory in Indonesia to be exported to Belgium, where it would be made into carpets.

It is impossible to know how many other Indian businesses invested outside of India because of the restrictions against "monopoly." What is known is that the repeal of the Monopolies and Restrictive Trade Practices Act in 1991 was followed by an expansion of large-scale enterprises in India, both by Indian entrepreneurs and by foreign entrepreneurs who now found India a better place to establish or expand businesses. What also increased dramatically was the country's economic growth rate, reducing the number of people in poverty and increasing the Indian government's ability to help them, because tax revenues rose with the rising economic activity in the country.

Although India's Monopolies and Restrictive Trade Practices Act was intended to rein in big business, its actual effect was to cushion businesses from the pressures of competition, domestic and international—and the effect of that was to reduce incentives toward efficiency. Looking back on that era, India's leading industrialist, Ratan Tata of Tata Industries, said of his own huge conglomerate:

> The group operated in a protected environment. The less-sensitive companies didn't worry about their competition, didn't worry about their costs and had not looked at newer technology. Many of them didn't even look at market shares.

In short, cushioned capitalism produced results similar to those under socialism. When India's economy was later opened up to competition, at home and abroad, it was a shock. Some of the directors of Tata Steel "held their heads in their hands" when they learned that the company now faced an annual loss of $26 million because freight rates had gone up. In the past, they could simply have raised the price of steel accordingly but now, with other steel producers free to compete, local freight charges could not simply be passed on in higher prices to the consumers, without risking bigger losses through a loss of customers to global competitors. Tata Steel had no choice but to either go out of business or change the way they did business. According to *Forbes* magazine:

> Tata Steel has spent $2.3 billion closing decrepit factories and modernizing mines, collieries and steelworks as well as building a new blast furnace. . .From 1993 to 2004 productivity skyrocketed from 78 tons of steel per worker per year to 264 tons, thanks to plant upgrades and fewer defects.

But none of these adjustments would have been necessary if this and other companies in India had continued to be sheltered from competition under the guise of preventing "monopoly."

Chapter 8

AN OVERVIEW

In general, "the market" is smarter than the smartest of its individual participants.

Robert L. Bartley

In a society where most people are employees and consumers, it is easy to think of businesses as "them"—as impersonal organizations, whose internal operations are largely unknown and whose sums of money may sometimes be so huge as to be unfathomable. Perhaps the most overlooked fact about industry and commerce is that they are run by people who differ greatly from one another in insight, foresight, leadership, organizational ability, and dedication—just as people do in every other walk of life. Therefore the companies they lead likewise differ in the efficiency with which they perform their work.

The automobile industry is just one example. According to *Forbes* business magazine, "other automakers can't come close to Toyota on how much it costs to build cars" and this shows up on the bottom line. "Toyota earned $1,800 for every vehicle sold, GM made $300 and Ford lost $240," *Forbes* reported. "It makes a net profit far bigger than the combined total for Detroit's Big three," according to *The Economist* magazine. Although Toyota spent fewer hours manufacturing each automobile, according to *BusinessWeek* magazine, its cars had fewer defects than those of any of the American big three automakers and less than those of its rivals Honda and Nissan.

What matters far more than the fate of any given business is how much money their efficiency can save consumers. As *BusinessWeek* said of the Wal-Mart retail chain:

> At Wal-Mart, "everyday low prices" is more than a slogan; it is the fundamental tenet of a cult masquerading as a company. . . New England Consulting estimates that Wal-Mart saved its U.S. customers $20 billion last year alone.

Business leadership is a factor, not only in the relative success of various enterprises but more fundamentally in the advance of the economy as a whole through the spread of the impact of new and better business methods to competing companies and other industries. An overlapping factor is the role of knowledge in the economy.

LEADERSHIP

Some business leaders are very good at some aspects of management and very weak in other aspects. The success of the business then depends on which aspects happen to be crucial at the particular time. Sometimes two executives with very different skills and weaknesses combine to produce a very successful management team, whereas either one of them might have failed completely if operating alone. Ray Kroc, founder of the McDonald's chain, was a genius at operating details and may well have known more about hamburgers, milk shakes, and French fries than any other human being—and there is a lot to know—but he was out of his depth in complex financial operations. These matters were handled by Harry Sonneborn, who was a financial genius whose improvisations rescued the company from the brink of bankruptcy more than once during its rocky early years. But Sonneborn didn't even eat hamburgers, much less have any interest in how they were made or marketed. However, as a team, Kroc and Sonneborn made McDonald's one of the leading corporations in the world.

When an industry or a sector of the economy is undergoing rapid change through new ways of doing business, sometimes the leaders of the past find it hardest to break the mold of their previous experience. For example, when the fast food revolution burst forth in the 1950s, existing leaders in restaurant franchises such as Howard Johnson were very unsuccessful in trying to compete with upstarts like McDonald's in the fast food segment of the market. Even when Howard Johnson set up imitations of the new fast food restaurants under the name Howard Johnson Jr., these imitations were unable to compete successfully, because they carried over into the fast food business approaches and practices that were successful in conventional restaurants, but which slowed down operations too much to be successful in the new fast food sector, where rapid turnover with inexpensive food was the key to profits.

Selecting managers can be as chancy as any other aspects of a business. Only by trial and error did the new McDonald's discover back in the 1950s what kinds of people were most successful at running their restaurants. The first few franchisees were people with business experience who nevertheless did very poorly. The first two really successful McDonald's franchisees—who were *very* successful—were a working class married couple who drained their life's savings in order to go into business for themselves. They were so financially strained at the beginning that they even had trouble coming up with the $100 needed to put into the cash register on their opening day, so as to be able to make change. But they ended up millionaires.

Other working class people who put everything they owned on the line to open a McDonald's restaurant also succeeded on a grand scale, even when they had no experience in running a restaurant or managing a business. When McDonald's set up its own company-owned restaurants, these restaurants did not succeed nearly as well as restaurants owned by people whose life's savings were at stake. But there was no way to know this in advance.

Market economies must rely not only on price competition between various producers to allow the most successful to continue and expand, they must also find some way to weed out those business owners or managers who do not get the most from the nation's resources. Losses accomplish that. Bankruptcy shuts down the entire enterprise that is consistently failing to come up to the standards of its competitors or is producing a product that has been superseded by some other product.

Before reaching that point, however, losses can force a firm to make internal reassessments of its policies and personnel. These include the chief executive, who can be replaced by irate stockholders who are not receiving the dividends they expected.

A poorly managed company is more valuable to outside investors than to its existing owners, when these outside investors are convinced that they can improve its performance. Outside investors can therefore offer existing stockholders more for their stock than it is currently worth and still make a profit, if that stock's value later rises to the level expected when existing management is replaced by better managers. For example, if the stock is selling in the market for $50 a share under inefficient management, outside investors can start buying it up at $75 a share until they own a controlling interest in the corporation.

After using that control to fire existing managers and replace them with a more efficient management team, the value of the stock may then rise to $100 a share. While this profit is what motivates the investors, from the standpoint of the economy as a whole what matters is that such a rise in stock prices usually means that either the business is now serving more customers, or offering them better quality or lower prices, or is operating at lower cost—or some combination of these things.

Like so many other things, running a business looks easy from the outside. On the eve of the Bolshevik revolution, V. I. Lenin declared that "accounting and control" were the key factors in running an enterprise and that capitalism had already "reduced" the administration of businesses to "extraordinarily simple operations" that "any literate person can perform"—that is, "supervising and recording, knowledge of the four rules of arithmetic, and issuing appropriate receipts." Such "exceedingly simple operations of registration, filing and checking" could, according to Lenin, "easily be performed" by people receiving ordinary workmen's wages.

After just a few years in power, however, Lenin confronted a very different—and very bitter—reality. He himself wrote of a "fuel crisis" which "threatens to disrupt all Soviet work," of economic "ruin, starvation, and devastation" in the country and even admitted that peasant uprisings had become "a common occurrence" under Communist rule. In short, the economic functions which had seemed so easy and simple before having to perform them now loomed menacingly difficult.

Belatedly, Lenin saw a need for people "who are versed in the art of administration" and admitted that "there is nowhere we can turn to for such people except the old class"—that is, the capitalist businessmen. In his address to the 1920 Communist Party Congress, Lenin warned his comrades: "Opinions on corporate management are all too frequently imbued with a spirit of sheer ignorance, an anti-expert bias." The apparent simplicities of just three years earlier now required experts. Thus began Lenin's New Economic Policy, which allowed more market activity, and under which the economy began to revive.

KNOWLEDGE AND DECISIONS

Knowledge is one of the scarcest of all resources. Glib generalities abound, but specific hard facts about particular places and particular things at particular times that are relevant to economic decisions are something entirely different. In some respects, governments are better able to assemble vast amounts of knowledge, but the kind of knowledge involved is often in the form of statistical generalities or verbal generalities known as "expertise," which are no substitute for the kind of concrete knowledge that someone in the middle of a particular economic situation has. Just picking the right location for a particular business in a particular community can be the difference between profits and bankruptcy, even though that kind of knowledge may not be exciting from an intellectual standpoint. Experts may indeed have far more knowledge than the *average* amount of knowledge among individuals in the general population but the *total* amount of knowledge among millions of people in the general population vastly exceeds the total knowledge that any group of experts can assemble. The economic pressures to keep abreast of changes in an industry, the economy and the society force business owners and managers to seek a wide range of knowledge, going beyond the internal management of their own enterprises. Among the responses to this imperative have been trade associations, which provide highly detailed data on what is happening in their respective industries. A trade association for hotels, for example, provides detailed statistics on such things as what percentages of what kinds of hotels provide king-size, queen-size, and twin beds, cable television, voice mail, video games in the rooms, ironing boards, written material in foreign languages, and even what percentage of what kinds of hotels provide liquid soap in their bathrooms.

An individual hotel needs this kind of information because it competes with other hotels, and cannot afford to fall behind in what it provides to the public. Small economy motels do not need to match everything provided by large luxury resorts, but a given small motel cannot afford to fall too far behind other small motels and still expect to survive. Such details may be uninteresting to many who consider themselves knowledgeable people but those details are a matter of economic life and death to those who run businesses that will prosper or fail according to how well they meet the needs of other people. Knowledge cannot be narrowly defined to include only those things of interest to the educated classes when major economic consequences for the society as a whole depend on a vastly broader range of knowledge.

Lenin was just one of many highly educated people who assumed that running a business must be easy because it was done by people with little of the special kind of knowledge taught in schools and universities. Yet many of those who revolutionized the technologies and economies of the modern world—Thomas Edison, the Wright Brothers, Henry Ford—had relatively little of the academic training that some wish to consider synonymous with knowledge. Conversely, many with impressive academic and intellectual credentials have failed disastrously in business. In short, there is no simple hierarchy of knowledge with those higher up being able to do whatever those further down can do. Moreover, much of the coordination of scattered fragments of knowledge is done through systemic interactions in the marketplace, rather than by given experts overseeing the economy. As the late *Wall Street Journal* editor Robert L. Bartley, put it: "In general, 'the market' is smarter than the smartest of its individual participants."

When economic decisions are taken out of the hands of individuals operating in a market and put into the hands of experts on planning commissions and the like, this may be thought of as a transfer of decision-making power from those with less knowledge to those with more knowledge but it is far more likely to be a transfer of decision-making power to experts with less knowledge and more presumptions. The poor track record of central planning, which caused many nations to abandon it by the late twentieth century, is understandable in terms of the inherent difficulty of amassing the kind of knowledge that would have been required to make it work.

Agriculture is especially difficult for a government agency to plan because of the large amount of highly specific knowledge required. The qualities of the soil can vary significantly on a single acre, much less on a whole farm or on all the farms spread out across a nation. Someone sitting on a central planning commission in a distant capital city cannot know where on a given farm it would be better to grow carrots and where wheat would better suit local conditions of weather, soil, and insects. Without having a minutely detailed map of the country—which would itself probably cover several square miles—they would have little chance of deciding which farms would have land best suited for which crops.

Moreover, the products of agriculture are more perishable than the products of industry. Central planners may be able to look at official documents that tell them how many tons of what kind of steel exist in which warehouses around the country, but strawberries would have spoiled before any such nationwide data could be collected. Specific knowledge is one of the scarcest of all resources, regardless of how many people there may be who can talk in glib generalities. The net result of all this is that even countries which have long been food exporters often begin to have difficulty feeding themselves after the government has taken control of agriculture. This has happened repeatedly over the centuries and in many countries, among people of every race, and under governments ranging from democracies to totalitarian dictatorships.

Even the centrally planned economies of the Soviet Union and the Soviet bloc in Eastern Europe ended up having to allow a larger role for individual farming decisions, made by farmers guided by prices and sales, than they would permit in industry. Nevertheless, they did not permit a fully free market in agriculture and so ended up repeatedly being forced to import large amounts of food to feed their populations. While central planning has an unimpressive record in industry as well, the fact that its agricultural failures are usually far worse, and more often catastrophic, suggests the crucial role of knowledge. Industrial products and industrial production processes have a far greater degree of uniformity than is found in agriculture. Orders from Moscow on how to make steel in Vladivostok had more chances of achieving their goal than orders from Moscow on how to grow carrots or strawberries in Vladivostok. There are too many variables of soil, climate, plant diseases, and insect infestations, for example, that vary from one locality to another for anyone to successfully operate farms from thousands of miles away.

What was lacking in the Soviet Union was not expertise but highly specific knowledge. There were Soviet economists who were as much aware of general economic principles as Western economists were, in addition to highly trained experts on various aspects of agriculture. What the U.S.S.R. did not have were decision-making individuals with the same range of highly specific hard facts about each particular farm as an individual farm owner would have at his disposal. Power and knowledge were separated in their central planning system, as in all centrally planned economies.

Commercial and industrial enterprise managers knew what the specific equipment, personnel, and supplies at their disposal could and could not do, but central planners in Moscow did not—and it was the central planners who held the power to make the ultimate decisions. Nor could the central planners possibly be sufficiently knowledgeable about all the industries, technologies, and products under their command to be able to determine what would be best for each, independently of what the respective enterprise managers told them. Central planners could be skeptical of the self-serving statements and demands of the enterprise managers, but skepticism is not knowledge. Moreover, changing circumstances would almost inevitably be known first to the local managers on the scene and often much later, if at all, to the central planners, who had far too many industries and products to oversee to be able keep up with day-to-day changes for them all.

A price-coordinated economy may have no more total knowledge than a centrally-planned economy, but that knowledge is distributed very differently, as is decision-making power. When the owner of a gas station located on a highway in a capitalist country sees that the highway is being torn up for repairs, he knows to order less gasoline than usual from his supplier, because there will not be nearly as much traffic going past his station as before, at least until the repairs are completed.

This local gas station owner does not need the permission of anybody to change how much gasoline he orders or what hours he will stay open. The knowledge and the power are combined in the same person. Moreover, that person is operating under the incentives and constraints inherent in the *prospect* of profits and the threat of losses, rather than under orders from distant bureaucrats. Nor is this peculiar to gas stations. The same instant and local decision-making power by those with the facts before their eyes is common throughout a price-coordinated market economy. That is one of its key advantages over a centrally-planned economy and one of the factors behind the enormous differences in results between the two kinds of economies.

Agents

As a scarce resource, knowledge can be bought and sold in various ways in a market economy. The hiring of agents is essentially the purchase of the agent's knowledge to guide one's own decisions. Real estate agents commonly charge 6 percent of the sale price of a home and literary agents typically charge 15 percent of a writer's royalties. Why would a writer surrender 15 percent of his royalties, unless 85 percent of what the agent can get for him is worth more than 100 percent of what he can get for himself? And why would a publisher be willing to pay more to an agent than to a writer for the same manuscript? Similarly, why would a home-owner accept 6 percent less for his house when sold through a real estate agent, unless the agent could either get a higher price or a quicker sale, both of which amount to the same thing, since delay and its accompanying stresses are both costs to the home-owner?

Let's go back to a basic principle of economics: The same physical object does not necessarily have the same value to different people. This applies to an author's manuscript as well as to a house, a painting or an autograph from a rock star. What a literary agent knows is where a particular manuscript is likely to have its greatest value. If it is a cookbook, the agent knows which publishers and which editors have the knowledge and the connections to promote such a book in places that are very interested in such things— gourmet magazines, cooking programs on television, and the like. A cookbook would be far more valuable to such editors and publishers than to others who specialize in technology, social issues, or other subjects, or to editors whose knowledge of food does not extend much beyond hamburgers and fried chicken. Even if an agent is not able to get any more money out of a given publisher than a writer could have gotten, the agent knows which publishers are most likely to pay top dollar for a given kind of book, because that particular publisher can probably sell more copies.

A real estate agent is similarly more knowledgeable than the average home-owner as to the channels through which a given home can be marketed most quickly and for the highest sale price. Often there are little defects in the home that need to be corrected, or cosmetic changes that need to be made, before the house goes on the market. An agent who keeps up with changing fashions in homes and their furnishings is not only more likely to know what these things are but also whether or to what extent money spent upgrading the house will be recouped in a higher sale price, or whether it is better to sell the house "as is" as a bargain "fixer-upper." The agent is also more likely to be knowledgeable as to which particular contractors are more reliable or more reasonable in price for doing whatever repairs or remodelling are called for, as well as which financial institutions are best to deal with for the buyer and seller to arrange a mortgage for this particular house. Therefore, the same house is likely to bring in more money when sold through a real estate agent, just as a writer's manuscript is likely to sell for more through a literary agent.

It is not just in complex modern economies that the knowledge provided by agents of various sorts is necessary. Under primitive pioneering conditions in the American west, agents were at least equally important. Wagon trains heading west needed to be led by someone who already knew the west—its routes, its people, the requirements, the dangers, and the trading posts that the newcomers would encounter on their journey. Such wagon train leaders were signed up to contracts by the pioneers in the east before they set out into the unknown wilderness. Just as, in modern industry, a given firm may process its product only through a certain number of steps and then turn it over to some middleman to continue its journey to the ultimate consumer, so a particular guide might take the wagon train only a certain distance—perhaps taking a California-bound wagon train as far as the Rocky Mountains, after which some other guide would lead the pioneers through the Sierra Nevada Mountains and into the valleys beyond.

Franchises

Knowledge is shared in both directions when hotels, restaurants and other businesses are franchised. The knowledge offered by the chain that does the franchising is based on its experience with similar businesses in various locations around the country or around the world. The franchise chain is also likely to be more knowledgeable than the individual franchise owner about where and how to advertise and how to deal with suppliers. However, the local franchisee is likely to be more knowledgeable about things that only someone on the scene can know—the local labor market, changes in the surrounding community and of course all the details that have to be monitored on the premises day to day.

Chains and franchises are not synonymous. The first great hamburger chain—the chain that put the hamburger on the map in the 1920s—was the White Castle chain, which owned all of its hundreds of restaurants. Its top management, however, had much local experience before going regional and then national—and they made many visits to their local outlets to keep in touch. The era of the franchised restaurant chain began with Howard Johnson in the 1930s and the heyday of franchised hamburger stands began with McDonald's in the 1950s. By and large, franchises have been more successful in these fields. By 1990, more than one-third of all revenues from retail sales of goods and services in the United States went to franchise outlets. Nearly three-quarters of all revenues from hotels and motels were earned by those affiliated with chains.

MARKET VERSUS NON-MARKET ECONOMIES

The fact that profits are contingent on efficiency in producing what consumers want, at a price that consumers are willing to pay—and that losses are an ever-present threat if a business fails to provide that—explains much of the economic prosperity found in economies that operate under free market competition. Profits as a realized end-result are crucial to the individual business, but it is the *prospect* of profits—and the threat of losses—that is crucial to the functioning of the economy as a whole. For the economy as a whole, profits are a minor item, about 10 percent of what the American economy produces, for example. But it is a major item as an incentive to efficiency in producing the other 90 percent.

There are many other possible ways of allocating resources, and many of these alternatives are particularly attractive to those with political power. However, none of these alternative ways of organizing an economy has matched the track record of economies where prices direct what resources go where and in what quantities.

Anyone who saw East Berlin and West Berlin, during the years when communism prevailed in the eastern part of the city and a market economy in the rest of it, could not help noticing the drastic contrast between the prosperity of West Berlin and the poverty in East Berlin. Indeed, it was hard to avoid being shocked by it, especially since people of the same race, language, culture and history lived in both parts of the same city.

Monopoly is the enemy of efficiency, whether under capitalism or socialism. The difference between the two systems is that monopoly is the norm under socialism. Even in a mixed economy, with some economic activities being carried out by government and others being carried out by private industry, the government's activities are typically monopolies, while those in the private marketplace are typically activities carried out by rival enterprises.

Thus, when a hurricane, flood, or other natural disaster strikes some part of the United States, emergency aid usually comes both from the Federal Emergency Management Agency (FEMA) and from private insurance companies whose customers' homes and property have been damaged or destroyed. FEMA has been notoriously slower and less efficient than the private insurance companies. Allstate Insurance cannot afford to be slower in getting money into the hands of its policy-holders than State Farm Insurance is in getting money to the people who hold its policies. Not only would existing customers in the disaster area be likely to switch insurance companies if one dragged its feet in getting money to them, while their neighbors received substantial advances from a different insurance company to tide them over, word of any such difference would spread like wildfire across the country, causing millions of people elsewhere to switch billions of dollars worth of insurance business from the less efficient company to the more efficient one. A government agency, however, faces no such pressure. No matter how much FEMA may be criticized or ridiculed for its failure to get aid to disaster victims in a timely fashion, there is no rival government agency that these people can turn to for the same service. Moreover, the people who run these agencies are paid according to fixed salary schedules, not by how quickly or how well they serve people hit by disaster.

Inertia is common to people under both capitalism and socialism. In the early twentieth century, both Sears and Montgomery Ward were reluctant to begin operating out of stores, after decades of great success selling exclusively from their mail order catalogs. It was only when the 1920s brought competition from chain stores that cut into their profits and caused red ink to start appearing on the bottom line that they had no choice but to become chain stores themselves. In 1920, Montgomery Ward lost nearly $10 million and Sears was $44 million in debt—all this in dollars many times more valuable than today. Under socialism, Sears and Montgomery Ward could have remained mail order retailers and there would have been little incentive for the government to pay to set up rival chain stores to complicate everyone's life.

Socialist and capitalist economies differ not only in the quantity of output they produce but also in the quality. Everything from cars and cameras to restaurant service and airline service were of notoriously low quality in the Soviet Union. Nor was this a happenstance. The incentives are radically different when the producer has to satisfy the consumer, in order to survive financially, than when the test of survivability is carrying out production quotas set by central planners. The consumer is going to look not only at quantity but quality. But a central planning commission is too overwhelmed with the millions of products they oversee to be able to monitor much more than gross output.

That this low quality is a result of incentives, rather than being due to traits peculiar to Russians or other Eastern Europeans, is shown by the quality deterioration that has taken place in the United States or in Western Europe when free market prices have been replaced by rent control or by other forms of price controls and government allocation. Both excellent service and terrible service can occur in the same country, when there are different incentives, as a salesman in India found:

> Every time I ate in a roadside cafe or dhaba, my rice plate would arrive in three minutes flat. If I wanted an extra roti, it would arrive in thirty seconds. In a saree shop, the shopkeeper showed me a hundred sarees even if I did not buy a single one. After I left, he would go through the laborious and thankless job of folding back each saree, one at a time, and placing it back on the shelf. In contrast, when I went to buy a railway ticket, pay my telephone bill, or withdraw money from my nationalized bank, I was mistreated or regarded as a nuisance, and made to wait in a long queue. The bazaar offered outstanding service because the shopkeeper knew that his existence depended on his customer. If he was courteous and offered quality products at a competitive price, his customer rewarded him. If not, his customers deserted him for the shop next door. There was no competition in the railways, telephones, or banks, and their employees could never place the customer in the center.

London's *The Economist* magazine likewise pointed out that in India one can "watch the tellers in a state-owned bank chat amongst themselves while the line of customers stretches on to the street." Comparisons of government-run institutions with privately-run institutions often overlook the fact that ownership and control are not the only differences between them. Government-run institutions are almost always monopolies, while privately-run institutions usually have competitors. Competing government institutions performing the same function are referred to negatively as "needless duplication." Whether the frustrated customers waiting in line at a government-run bank would consider an alternative bank to be needless duplication is another question.

While some businesses can and do give poor service or cut corners on quality in a free market, they do so at the risk of their survival. The great financial success stories in American industry have often involved companies almost fanatical about maintaining the reputation of their products, even when these products have been quite mundane and inexpensive.

McDonald's built its reputation on a standardized hamburger and maintained quality by having its own inspectors make unannounced visits to its meat suppliers in the middle of the night, to see what was being put into the meat it was buying. Colonel Sanders was notorious for showing up unexpectedly at Kentucky Fried Chicken restaurants. If he didn't like the way the chickens were being cooked, he would dump them all into a garbage can, put on an apron, and proceed to cook some chickens himself, to demonstrate how he wanted it done. His protegé Dave Thomas later followed similar practices when he created his own chain of Wendy's hamburger stands. Although Colonel Sanders and Dave Thomas could not be everywhere in a nationwide chain, no local franchise owner could take a chance on seeing his profits being thrown into a garbage can by the head honcho of the chain.

When the processed food industry first began in nineteenth century America, it was common for producers to adulterate food items with less expensive fillers. Horseradish, for example, was often sold in colored bottles, to conceal the adulteration. But when Henry J. Heinz began selling unadulterated horseradish in clear bottles, this gave him a decisive advantage over his competitors, who fell by the wayside while the Heinz company went on to become one of the enduring giants of American industry, still in business in the twenty-first century. Similarly with the British food processing company Crosse & Blackwell, which sold quality foods not only in Britain but in the United States as well. It too remained one of the giants of the industry through the twentieth century and into the twenty first.

Quality control is of course even more important to financial success with more expensive products and services. The producers of Linhof cameras—made in Germany and costing thousands of dollars each—not only buy their lenses from the world's leading optical companies, they also subject each individual lens put on one of their cameras to their own tests and standards, even though these lenses have already passed tests performed by the manufacturers. Linhof's standards are sufficiently more stringent that an identical make and model of lens on a Linhof camera sells for a higher price, both new and used, than the same lens sells for when bought independently. Even if the lens is being bought to be put on another camera, the fact that it came off a Linhof brings a higher price than the identical model of lens by the identical manufacturer that did not come from a Linhof.

Behind all of this is the basic fact that a business is selling not only a physical product, but also the reputation which surrounds that product. Motorists traveling in an unfamiliar part of the country are more likely to turn into a hamburger stand that has a McDonald's or Wendy's sign on it than one that does not. That reputation translates into dollars and cents— or, in this case, millions and billions of dollars. People with that kind of money at stake are unlikely to be very tolerant of anyone who would compromise their reputation. Ray Kroc, the founder of the McDonald's chain, would explode in anger if he found a McDonald's parking lot littered. His franchisees were expected to keep not only their own premises free of litter, but also to see that there was no McDonald's litter on the streets within a radius of two blocks of their restaurants.

When speaking of quality in this context, what matters is the kind of quality that is relevant to the particular clientele being served. Hamburgers and fried chicken may not be regarded by others as either gourmet food or health food, nor can a nationwide chain mass-producing such meals reach quality levels achievable by more distinctive, fancier, and pricier restaurants. What the chain can do is assure quality within the limits expected by their particular customers.

While a market economy is essentially an impersonal mechanism for allocating resources, some of the most successful businesses have prospered by their attention to the personal element. One of the reasons for the success of the F. W. Woolworth retail chain was Woolworth's insistence on the importance of courtesy to the customers. This came from his own painful memories of store clerks treating him like dirt when he was a poverty-stricken farm boy who went into stores to buy or look. Ray Kroc's zealous insistence on maintaining McDonald's reputation for cleanliness paid off at a crucial juncture when he desperately needed a loan to stay in business, for the financier who toured McDonald's restaurants said later: "If the parking lots had been dirty, if the help had grease stains on their aprons, and if the food wasn't good, McDonald's never would have gotten the loan." Similarly, Kroc's good relations with his suppliers—people who sold paper cups, milk, napkins, etc., to McDonald's—had saved him before when these suppliers agreed to lend him money to bail him out of an earlier financial crisis.

What is called "capitalism" might more accurately be called consumerism. It is the consumers who call the tune, and those capitalists who want to remain capitalists have to learn to dance to it. The twentieth century began with high hopes for replacing the competition of the marketplace by a more efficient and more humane economy, planned and controlled by government in the interests of the people. However, by the end of the century, all such efforts were so thoroughly discredited by their actual results in countries around the world that even communist nations abandoned central planning, while socialist governments in democratic countries began selling off government-run enterprises, whose chronic losses had been a heavy burden to the taxpayers.

Privatization was embraced as a principle by such conservative governments as those of Prime Minister Margaret Thatcher in Britain and President Ronald Reagan in the United States. But the most decisive evidence for the efficiency of the marketplace was that even socialist and communist government leaders who were philosophically opposed to capitalism turned back towards the free market after seeing what happens when industry and commerce operate without the guidance of prices, profits and losses.

WINNERS AND LOSERS

Many people who appreciate the prosperity created by market economies may nevertheless lament the fact that particular individuals, groups, industries, or regions of the country do not share fully in the general economic advances, and some may even be worse off than before. Political leaders or candidates are especially likely to deplore the inequity of it all and to propose various government actions to "correct" the situation.

Whatever the merits or demerits of various political proposals, what must be kept in mind when evaluating them is that the good fortunes and misfortunes of different sectors of the economy may be closely related as cause and effect—and that preventing bad effects may prevent good effects. It was not accidental that Smith Corona was losing millions of dollars a year on its typewriters while Dell was making millions on its computers. Computers were replacing typewriters. It was not accidental that coal-mining regions suffered economic declines with the rise of alternative fuel sources, that the number of pay telephones declined as more people acquired their own cellular phones, or that sales of film began declining with the rise of digital cameras.

The efficient allocation of scarce resources which have alternative uses means that some must lose their ability to use those resources, in order that others can gain the ability to use them. Smith Corona had to be *prevented* from using scarce resources, including both materials and labor, to make typewriters, when those resources could be used to produce computers that the public wanted more. Nor was this a matter of anyone's fault. No matter how fine the typewriters made by Smith Corona were or how skilled and conscientious its employees, typewriters were no longer what the public wanted after they had the option to achieve the same end result—and more—with computers.

Scarcity implies that resources must be taken from some places, in order to go to other places. After Pan American Airways went out of business, its gates at Kennedy Airport in New York were taken over by JetBlue, which quickly became one of the most successful airlines, highly rated by travelers. It is hard to know how industry in general could have gotten the millions of workers that they added during the twentieth century, whose output contributed to a dramatically rising standard of living for the public at large, without the much-lamented decline in the number of farms and farm workers. Few individuals or businesses are going to want to give up what they have been used to doing, especially if they have been successful at it, for the greater good of society as a whole. But, in one way or another—under any economic or political system—they are going to have to be forced to relinquish resources and change what they themselves are doing, if rising standards of living are to be achieved and sustained.

The financial pressures of the free market are just one of the ways in which this can be done. Kings or commissars could instead simply order individuals and enterprises to change from doing *A* to doing *B*. No doubt other ways of pursuing the same goals are possible, with varying degrees of effectiveness and efficiency. What is crucial, however, is that it must be done. Put differently, the fact that some people, regions, or industries are being "left behind" or are not getting their "fair share" of the general prosperity is not necessarily a problem with a political solution, as abundant as such proposed solutions may be, especially during election years. However more pleasant and uncomplicated life might be if all sectors of the economy grew simultaneously at the same lockstep pace, that has never been the reality in any dynamic economy.

PART III: WORK AND PAY

Chapter 9

PRODUCTIVITY AND PAY

"The Distribution of Income". . .implies to many people that income is first produced, and then "distributed"— according to some arbitrary and probably unjust arrangement.

Henry Hazlitt

In discussing the allocation of resources, we have so far been concerned largely with inanimate resources. But people are a key part of the inputs which produce output. Since most people do not volunteer their labor free of charge, they must be either paid to work or forced to work, since the work has to be done in any case, if we are to live at all, much less enjoy the various amenities that go into our modern standard of living. In many societies of the past, people were forced to work, whether as serfs or slaves. In a free society, people are paid to work. But pay is not just income to individuals. It is also a set of incentives facing everyone working or potentially working, and a set of constraints on employers, so that they do not use the scarce resource of labor as was done in the days of the Soviet Union, keeping extra workers on hand "just in case" when those workers could be doing something productive somewhere else.

In short, the payment of wages and salaries has an economic role that goes beyond the provision of income to individuals. From the standpoint of the economy as a whole, it is a way of allocating scarce resources which have alternative uses. Let the pay of truck drivers double and some taxi drivers will decide that they would rather drive a truck. Let the income of engineers double and some students who were thinking of majoring in math or physics may decide to major in engineering instead. Let pay for all jobs double and some people who are retired may decide to go back to work, at least part-time, while others who were thinking of retirement may decide to postpone that for a while.

How much people are paid depends on many things. Stories about the astronomical pay of professional athletes, movie stars, or chief executives of big corporations often cause journalists and others to question how much this or that person is "really" worth.

Fortunately, since we know from Chapter 2 that there is no such thing as "real" worth, we can save all the time and energy that others put into such unanswerable questions. Instead, we can ask a more down-to-earth question: What determines how much people get paid for their work? To this question there is a very down-to-earth answer: Supply and Demand. However, that is just the beginning. Why does supply and demand cause one individual to earn more than another?

Workers would obviously like to get the highest pay possible and employers would like to pay the least possible. Only where there is overlap between what is offered and what is acceptable can anyone be hired. But why does that overlap take place at a pay rate that is several times as high for an engineer as for a messenger?

Messengers would of course like to be paid what engineers are paid, but there is too large a supply of people capable of being messengers to force the employer to raise his offer to that level. Because it takes a long time to train an engineer and not everyone is capable of mastering such training, there is no such abundance of engineers relative to the demand. That is the supply side of the story. But what determines the demand for labor? What determines the limit of what an employer is willing to pay?

It is not merely the fact that engineers are scarce that makes them valuable. It is what an engineer can add to a company's earnings that makes an employer willing to bid for his services—and sets the limit to how high the bids can go. An engineer who added $100,000 to a company's earnings and asked for a $200,000 salary would not be hired. On the other hand, if the engineer added a quarter of a million dollars to a company's earnings, it would obviously pay to hire him at $200,000—provided there were no other engineers who would do the same thing for a lower salary.

PRODUCTIVITY

The term "productivity" is sometimes used loosely to describe an employee's contribution to a company's earnings. The problem is that this word is also defined in other ways and sometimes the implication is left that each worker has a certain productivity that is inherent in that particular worker, rather than being dependent on surrounding circumstances as well. A worker using the latest modern equipment can produce more output per hour than the very same worker employed in another firm whose equipment is not quite as up-to-date or whose management does not have things organized as efficiently. For example, Japanese-owned cotton mills in China during the 1930s paid higher wages than Chinese-owned cotton mills there, but the Japanese-run mills had lower labor costs per unit of output because they had higher output per worker. This was not due to different equipment—they both used the same machines—but to more efficient management brought over from Japan.

Similarly, in the early twenty-first century, an international consulting firm found that American-owned manufacturing enterprises in Britain had far higher productivity than British-owned manufacturing enterprises. According to the British magazine *The Economist*, "British industrial companies have underperformed their American counterparts startlingly badly," so that when it comes to "economy in the use of time and materials," fewer than 40 percent of British manufacturers "have paid any attention to this" and that "Britain's top engineering graduates prefer to work for foreign-owned companies." In short, lower productivity in British-owned companies reflected management practices, even when productivity was measured in terms of labor.

In general, the productivity of any input in the production process depends on the quantity and quality of other inputs, as well as its own. Thus workers in South Africa have higher productivity than workers in Brazil, Poland, Malaysia, or China because, as *The Economist* points out, South African firms "rely more on capital than labour." In other words, South African workers are not necessarily working any harder or any more skillfully than workers in these other countries. They just have more or better equipment to work with.

The same principle applies outside what we normally think of as economic activities. In baseball, a slugger gets more chances to hit home runs if he is batting ahead of another slugger. But, if the batter hitting after him is not much of a home run threat, pitchers are more likely to walk the slugger in a tight situation, so that he may get significantly fewer opportunities to hit home runs over the course of a season.

During Ted Williams' career, for example, he had one of the highest percentages of home runs—in proportion to his times at bat—in the history of baseball. Yet he had only one season in which he hit as many as 40 homers, because he was walked as often as 162 times a season—averaging more than one walk per game during the era of the 154-game season. By contrast, when Roger Maris hit 61 home runs in 1961, breaking the record at that time, he was walked less than a hundred times because Mickey Mantle was batting right after him, and Mantle hit 54 home runs that season. There was no percentage in walking Maris to pitch to Mantle with one more man on base. Maris' productivity as a home-run hitter was greater because he batted with Mickey Mantle in the on-deck circle.

In virtually all jobs, the quality of the equipment, management and other workers goes into determining a given worker's productivity. Movie stars like to have good supporting actors, good make-up artists and good directors, all of whom enhance the star's performance. Scholars depend heavily on their research assistants, and generals rely on their staffs, as well as their troops, to win battles. Whatever the source of a given individual's productivity, that productivity determines the upper limit of how far an employer will go in bidding for that person's services.

Just as any worker's value can be enhanced by complementary factors—whether fellow workers, machinery, or more efficient management—so the worker's value can also be reduced by other factors over which the individual worker has no control. For example, the era of mass immigration to the United States from Europe in the nineteenth century not only brought millions of workers across the Atlantic, it brought language differences and animosities between some of these groups over from Europe as well. Sometimes the mere fact that different groups of immigrants spoke different languages risked communications problems that could impede work or cost lives in dangerous tasks like making steel or using explosives. American employers also discovered from experience that having members of these different groups working together often meant that fights broke out on the job, especially when the work required men to live together for extended periods of time while they travelled in order to complete such projects as digging canals or building railroads.

Even workers whose output per hour remains the same can be of very different value if the transportation costs in one place are higher than in another, so that the employer's net revenue from sales is lower where these higher costs must be recovered from the revenue received. Where the same product is produced by businesses with different transportation costs and sold in a competitive market, those firms with higher transportation costs cannot pass all those costs along to their customers because competing firms whose costs are not as high are able to charge a lower price and take their customers away. Businesses in Third World countries without modern highways or efficient trains and airlines may have to absorb higher transportation costs, so that even when they sell the same product for the same price as businesses in more advanced economies, the revenue from that product will be less and therefore the value of the labor that went into producing that product will also be worth correspondingly less.

In countries with high levels of corruption, the bribes necessary to get bureaucrats to permit the business to operate likewise have to be deducted from sales revenues and likewise reduce the value of the product and of the workers who produce it, even if these workers have the same output per hour as workers in more modern and less corrupt economies. In reality, Third World workers more typically have lower output per hour and the higher costs of transportation and corruption which must be deducted from sales revenues can leave such workers earning a fraction of what workers earn for doing similar work in other countries.

In short, productivity is not just a result solely of what the individual worker does but is a result of numerous other factors as well. To say that the demand for labor is based on the value of the worker's productivity is not to say that pay is based on merit. Merit and productivity are two different things, just as morality and causation are two different things.

PAY DIFFERENCES

Thus far the discussion has been about things affecting the demand for labor. What about supply? Employers seldom bid as much as they would if they had to, because there are other individuals willing and able to supply the same services for less. By the same token, consumers would pay a lot more for their food than they do, if there were no competing sellers and their only choice was to pay what a monopolist charged or starve. In short, it is the *combination* of supply and demand which determines pay, as it determines the prices of goods and services in general.

Wages and salaries serve the same economic purposes as other prices—that is, they guide the utilization of scarce resources which have alternative uses, so that each resource gets used where it is most valued. Yet because these scarce resources are human beings, we tend to look on wages and salaries differently. Often we ask questions that are quite emotionally powerful, even if they are logically meaningless and wholly undefined. For example: Are the wages "fair"? Are the workers "exploited"? Is this "a living wage"?

No one likes to see fellow human beings living in poverty and squalor, and many are prepared to do something about it, as shown by the vast billions of dollars that are donated to a wide range of charities every year, on top of the additional billions spent by governments in an attempt to better the condition of poor people. These socially important activities occur alongside an economy coordinated by prices, but the two things serve different purposes. Attempts to make prices, including the prices of people's labor and talents, be something other than signals to guide resources to their most valued uses, make those prices less effective for their basic purpose, on which the prosperity of the whole society depends. Ultimately, it is economic prosperity which makes it possible for billions of dollars to be devoted to helping the less fortunate.

Income "Distribution"

Nothing is more straightforward and easy to understand than the fact that some people earn more than others, for a variety of reasons. Some people are simply older than others, for example, and their additional years have given them opportunities to acquire more experience, skills, formal education and on-the-job-training—all of which allows them to do a given job more efficiently or to take on more complicated jobs that would be overwhelming for a beginner or for someone with only limited experience or training. With the passing years, older individuals may also become more knowledgeable about job opportunities, while increasing numbers of other people become more aware of them and their individual abilities, leading to offers of new jobs or promotions. These and other commonsense reasons for income differences among individuals are often lost sight of in abstract discussions of the ambiguous term "income distribution."

Although people in the top income brackets and the bottom income brackets—"the rich" and "the poor," as they are often called—may be discussed as if they were different classes of people, often they are the very same people at different stages of their lives. Three-quarters of those Americans who were in the bottom 20 percent in income in 1975 were also in the top 40 percent at some point over the next 16 years. This is not surprising. After 16 years, people usually have had 16 years more experience, perhaps including on-the-job training or formal education. Those in business or the professions have had 16 years in which to build up a clientele. It would be surprising if they were not able to earn more money as a result. It is not uncommon for most of the people in the top 5 percent of income-earners to be 45 years old and up.

None of this is unique to the United States. A study of eleven European countries found similar patterns. One-half of the people in Greece and two-thirds of the people in Holland who were below the poverty line in a given year had risen above that line within two years. A study in Britain found similar patterns when following thousands of individuals over a six-year period. At the end of six years, nearly two-thirds of the individuals who were initially in the bottom 10 percent in income had risen out of that bracket. Studies in New Zealand likewise showed significant rises of individuals out of the bottom 20 percent of income earners in just one year and of course larger numbers rising out of this bracket over a period of several years. There are similar patterns in Canada.

When some people are born, live, and die in poverty, while others are born, live, and die in luxury, that is a very different situation from one in which young people have not yet reached the income level of older people, such as their parents. But the kind of statistics often cited in the media, and even in academia, typically do not distinguish these very different situations. Moreover, those who publicize such statistics usually proceed as if they are talking about income differences between classes rather than differences between age brackets. Because of the movement of people from one income bracket to another over the years, the degree of income inequality over a lifetime is not the same as the degree of income inequality in a given year. A study in New Zealand found that the degree of income inequality over a working lifetime was less than the degree of inequality in *any* given year during those lifetimes.

Much discussion of "the rich" and "the poor"—or of the top or bottom 10 or 20 percent—fail to say just what kinds of incomes qualify to be in those categories. As of 2001, a household income of $84,000 was enough to put those who earned it in the top 20 percent of Americans. Even to make the top 5 percent required a household income of just over $150,000—that is, about $75,000 apiece for a working couple. That is a nice income, but rising to that level after working for decades is hardly a sign of being rich. Even among the truly rich, there is turnover. When *Forbes* magazine ran its first list of the 400 richest Americans in 1982, that list included 14 Rockefellers, 28 du Ponts and 11 Hunts. Twenty years later, the list included 3 Rockefellers, one Hunt and no du Ponts. Incidentally, the nation's 400 richest people lost a total of $283 billion in net worth in one year, which may be one reason for such turnover, in addition to new people like Bill Gates arriving on the scene.

Describing people in certain income brackets as "rich" is false for a more fundamental reason: Income and wealth are different things. No matter how much income passes through your hands in a given year, your wealth depends on how much you have accumulated over the years. If you receive a million dollars in a year and spend a million and a half, you are not getting rich. But many frugal people on modest incomes have been found, after their deaths, to have left surprisingly large amounts of wealth to their heirs.

Although there is much talk about "income distribution," most income is of course *not* distributed at all, in the sense in which newspapers or Social Security checks are distributed from some central place. Most income is distributed only in the figurative statistical sense in which there is a distribution of heights in a population—some people being 5 foot 4 inches tall, others 6 foot 2 inches, etc.—but none of these heights was sent out from some central location. Yet it is all too common to read journalists and others discussing how "society" *distributes* its income, rather than saying in plain English that some people make more money than others. There is no collective decision by "society" as to how much each individual's work is worth. In a market economy, those who get the direct benefit of an individual's work decide how much they are prepared to pay for what they receive. People who would prefer collective decision-making on such things can argue their case for that particular method of decision-making. But it is misleading to suggest that today "society" *distributes* its income with one set of results and should simply change to distributing its income with different results in the future.

More is involved than a misleading metaphor. Often the very units in which income differences are discussed are as misleading as the metaphor. Family income or household income statistics can be especially misleading as compared to individual income statistics. An individual always means the same thing—one person—but the sizes of families and households differ substantially from one time period to another, from one racial or ethnic group to another, and from one income bracket to another. For example, a detailed analysis of U.S. Census data showed that there were 39 million people in the bottom 20 percent of households but 64 million people in the top 20 percent of households. Although the unwary might assume that these quintiles represent dividing the country into "five equal layers," as two well-known economists have misstated it in a popular book, there is nothing equal about those layers. They represent grossly different numbers of people.

Not only do the numbers of people differ considerably between low-income households and high-income households, the proportions of people who work also differ by very substantial amounts between these households.

In the year 2000, the top 20 percent of households contained 19 million heads of households who worked, compared to fewer than 8 million heads of households who worked in the bottom 20 percent of households. These striking disparities do not even take into account whether they are working full time or part time. When it comes to working full-time the year around, even the top 5 percent of households contained more heads of household who worked full-time for 50 or more weeks than did the bottom 20 percent. That is, there were more heads of household *in absolute numbers*—3.9 million versus 3.3 million—working full-time and year-around in the top 5 percent of households compared to the bottom 20 percent.

At one time, back in the 1890s, people in the top 10 percent in income worked fewer hours than people in the bottom 10 percent, but that situation has long since reversed. We are no longer talking about the idle rich versus the toiling poor. Today we are usually talking about those who work regularly and those who, for the most part, do not work regularly. Under these conditions, the more that pay for work increases the more income inequality increases.

The sizes of families and households have differed not only from one income bracket to another at a given time, but also have differed over time. These differences are not incidental. They radically change the implications of "income distribution" statistics. For example, real income per American household rose only 6 percent over the entire period from 1969 to 1996, but real per capita income rose 51 percent over the same period. The discrepancy is due to the fact that the average size of families and households was declining during those years, so that smaller households were now earning about the same as larger households had earned a generation earlier.

Rising prosperity was one reason why more people were able to go set up their own individual households, instead of continuing to live with parents or as roomers elsewhere, or by sharing an apartment with a roommate. Yet these consequences of rising prosperity generate household income statistics that are widely used to suggest that there has been no real economic progress. A *Washington Post* writer, for example, declared that "the incomes of most American households have remained stubbornly flat over the past three decades." It might be more accurate to say that some writers have remained stubbornly blind to economic facts. When two working people in one household today earn the same total amount of money that three working people were earning in one household in the past, that is a 50 percent increase in income per person—even when household income remains the same.

Despite some confused or misleading discussions of "the rich" and "the poor," based on people's transient positions in the income stream, genuinely rich and genuinely poor people exist—people who are going to be living in luxury or in poverty all their lives—but they are much rarer than gross income statistics would suggest. Just as most American "poor" do not stay poor, so most rich Americans were not born rich. Four-fifths of American millionaires earned their fortunes within their own lifetimes, having inherited nothing. Moreover, the genuinely rich are rare, like the genuinely poor. Even if we take a million dollars in net worth as our criterion for being rich, only about 3.5 percent of American households are at that level. This is in fact a fairly modest level, given that net worth counts everything from household goods and clothing to the total amount of money in an individual's pension fund. If we count as genuinely poor that 3 percent of the population which remains in the bottom 20 percent over a period of years, then the genuinely rich and the genuinely poor—put together—add up to less than 10 percent of the American population. Nevertheless, some political rhetoric might suggest that most people are either "haves" or "have nots."

It is a common but misleading practice to try to determine whether inequality is increasing or decreasing by comparing the incomes of those in the top 20 percent with the incomes of those in the bottom 20 percent. If our concern is the well-being of flesh-and-blood human beings, rather than with statistical categories, then we need to consider not only those who are in given income brackets in a given year but also the vast majority of people who are constantly moving in and out of those brackets over the years. When an large majority of those in the bottom 20 percent in income in 1975 were also in the top 40 percent at some point by 1991, you cannot determine the degree of income inequality between *people* by looking at inequality between income brackets at a given time.

If our concern is with the economic well-being of flesh-and-blood human beings, as distinguished from statistical comparisons between income brackets, then we need to look at real income per capita, because people do not live on percentage shares. They live on real income. Among those individuals who were in the bottom 20 percent in 1975, 98 percent had higher real incomes by 1991 and two-thirds had higher real incomes in 1991 than the average American had back in 1975, when they were in the bottom 20 percent. Moreover, even when narrowly focusing on income brackets, the fact that the share of the bottom 20 percent of households declined from 4 percent of all income in 1985 to 3.5 percent in 2001 did not prevent the real income of the households in these brackets from rising by thousands of dollars in absolute terms—quite aside from the movement of actual people out of the bottom 20 percent between the two years.

Being concerned about the well-being of flesh-and-blood people has another dimension. Money earned is not the only source of the goods and services that people consume. Children living in the homes of affluent parents are not poor, even if the children's earnings are low. Nor are the wives of affluent husbands or the husbands of affluent wives poor. In a welfare state with progressive taxation, differences in consumption are seldom as large as differences in income. One study of Americans showed that, while the average American earned more than four times the average income of Americans in the bottom 20 percent, the consumption of the average American was only about one-third more.

While, in some senses, those who are called "the poor" are not as badly off as instantaneous statistics might suggest, in other respects they are worse off. Those who are poor on a long-term basis and live in poverty-stricken neighborhoods must often pay higher prices for inferior goods and services, because of the higher costs of delivering those goods and services to such neighborhoods. As already noted in Chapters 4 and 6, a suburban supermarket has lower costs of delivering groceries to its customers than does a typical neighborhood store in the inner city, and that translates into higher prices charged to low-income customers than to high-income customers. Being poor is expensive. Fortunately, most people in most modern Western countries do not remain poor very long.

Differences in Skills

Among the many reasons for differences in productivity and pay is that some people have more skills than others. No one is surprised that engineers earn more than messengers or that experienced shipping clerks tend to earn higher pay than inexperienced shipping clerks—and experienced pilots tend to earn more than either. Although workers may be thought of as people who simply supply labor, what most people supply is not just their ability to engage in physical exertions, but their ability to apply mental proficiency to their tasks. The time when "a strong back and a weak mind" were sufficient for many jobs is long past in most modern economies. Obvious as this may seem, its implications are not equally obvious nor always widely understood.

In those times and places where physical strength and stamina have been the principal work requirements, productivity and pay have tended to reach their peak in the youthful prime of life, with middle-aged laborers receiving less pay or less frequent employment, or both. A premium on physical strength likewise favored male workers over female workers. In some desperately poor countries living close to the edge of subsistence, such as China in times past, the sex differential in performing physical labor was such that it was not uncommon for the poorest people to kill female infants. While a mother was necessary for the family, an additional woman's productivity in arduous farm labor on small plots of land with only primitive tools might not produce enough food to keep her alive—and her drain on the food produced by others would thus threaten the survival of the whole family, at a time when malnutrition and death by starvation were ever-present dangers. One of the many benefits of economic development has been making such desperate and brutal choices unnecessary.

The rising importance of skills and experience relative to physical strength has changed the relative productivities of youth compared to age and of women compared to men. This has been especially so in more recent times, as the power of machines has replaced human strength in industrial societies and as skills have become crucial in high-tech economies. Even within a relatively short span of time, the age at which most people receive their peak earnings has shifted upward. In 1951, most Americans reached their peak earnings between 35 and 44 years of age, and people in those age brackets earned about half again as much as workers in their early twenties. By 1973, however, people in the 35 to 44-year-old brackets earned more than double the income of the younger workers. Twenty years later, the peak earnings bracket had moved up to people aged 45 to 54 years, and people in those brackets earned more than three times what workers in their early twenties earned.

Meanwhile, the dwindling importance of physical strength also reduced or eliminated the premium for male workers in an ever-widening range of occupations. This did not require all employers to have enlightened self-interest. Those who persisted in paying more for male workers who were not correspondingly more productive were at a competitive disadvantage compared to rival firms that got their work done at lower costs by eliminating the male premium, equalizing the pay of women and men to match their productivities. The most unenlightened or prejudiced employers had higher labor costs, which risked the elimination of their businesses by the ruthlessness of market competition. Thus the pay of women began to equal that of men of similar qualifications even before there were laws mandating equal pay.

While the growing importance of skills tended to reduce economic inequalities between the sexes, it tended to increase the inequality between those with and without skills. Moreover, rising earnings in general, growing out of a more productive economy with more skilled people, tended to increase the inequality between those who worked regularly and those who did not. As already noted, there are striking differences between the number and proportions of people who work and those who don't work as between the top income brackets and the bottom income brackets.

Job Discrimination

While pay differences often reflect differences in skills, experience, or willingness to do hard or dangerous work, these differences may also reflect discrimination against particular segments of society, such as ethnic minorities, women, lower castes, or other groups. However, in order to determine whether there is discrimination or how severe it is, we first need to define what we mean.

Sometimes discrimination is defined as judging individuals from different groups by different standards when hiring, paying or promoting. In its severest form, this can mean refusal to hire at all. "No Irish Need Apply" was a stock phrase in advertisements for many desirable jobs in nineteenth-century and early twentieth-century America. Before World War II, many hospitals in the United States would not hire black doctors or Jewish doctors, and some prestigious law firms would not hire anyone who was not a white Protestant male from the upper classes. In other cases, people might be hired from a number of groups, but individuals from different groups were channeled into different kinds of jobs. None of this has been peculiar to the United States or to the modern era. On the contrary, members of different groups have been treated differently in laws and practices all around the world and for thousands of years of recorded history. It is the idea of treating individuals the same, regardless of what group they come from, that is relatively recent as history is measured.

Overlapping with discrimination, and often confused with it, are employment differences based on very substantial differences in skills, experience, and work habits from one group to another. Mohawk Indians, for example, have long been sought after to work on the construction of skyscrapers in the United States, for they walk around high up on the steel frameworks with no apparent fear or distraction from their work. Chinese laborers on rubber plantations in colonial Malaya were found to collect twice as much sap from rubber trees in a given amount of time as Malay workers did. During the industrialization of the Soviet Union in the 1920s and 1930s, large numbers of German, American, and other foreign workers, technicians, and engineers were imported at attractive salaries. More than

10,000 Americans alone went to work in the U.S.S.R. during a one-year period beginning in September 1920.

While preferences for some groups and reluctance or unwillingness to hire others have often been described as due to "bias," "prejudice," or "stereotypes" third-party observers cannot so easily dismiss the first-hand knowledge of those who are backing their beliefs by risking their own money. Even in the absence of different beliefs about different groups, application of the same employment criteria to different groups can result in very different proportions of these groups being hired, fired, or promoted. Distinguishing discrimination from differences in qualifications and performances is not easy in practice, though the distinction is fundamental in principle. Seldom do statistical data contain sufficiently detailed information on skills, experience, performance, or absenteeism, much less work habits and attitudes, to make possible comparisons between truly comparable individuals from different groups.

Women, for example, have long had lower incomes than men, but most women give birth to children at some point in their lives and many stay out of the labor force until their children reach an age where they can be put into some form of day care while their mothers return to work. These interruptions of their careers cost women workplace experience and seniority, which in turn inhibit the rise of their incomes over the years relative to that of men who have been working continuously in the meantime. However, as far back as 1971, American women who worked continuously from high school through their thirties earned slightly *more* than men of the same description, even though women as a group earned substantially less than men as a group.

This suggests that employers were willing to pay women of the same experience the same as men, if only because they are forced to by competition in the labor market, and that women with the same experience may even outperform men and therefore earn more, but that differences in domestic responsibilities prevent the sexes from having identical workplace experience or identical incomes based on that experience. None of this should be surprising. If, for example, women were paid only 75 percent of what men *of the same level of experience and performance* were paid, then any employer could hire four women instead of three men for the same money and gain a decisive advantage in production costs over competing firms. Put differently, any employer who discriminated against women in this situation would be incurring unnecessarily higher costs, risking profits, sales, and survival in a competitive industry.

Substantial pay differentials between women and men are not the same across the board, but vary between those women who become mothers and those who do not. In 1991, women without children earned 95 percent of what men earned, while women with children earned just 75 percent of what men earned. Moreover, even those women without children need not be in the same occupations as men. The very possibility of having children makes different occupations have different attractions to women, even before they become mothers. Occupations like librarians or teachers, which one can resume after a few years off to take care of small children, are more attractive to women who anticipate becoming mothers than occupations such as computer engineers, where just a few years off from work can leave you far behind in this rapidly changing field. In short, women and men make different occupational choices and prepare for many of these occupations by specializing in a very different mix of subjects while being educated.

The question as to whether or how much discrimination women encounter in the labor market is a question about whether there are substantial differences in pay between women and men in the same fields with the same qualifications. The question as to whether there is or is not income parity between the sexes is very different, since differences in occupational choices, educational choices, and continuous employment all affect incomes. Men also tend to work in more hazardous occupations, which usually pay more than similar occupations that are safer. As one study noted, "although 54 percent of the workplace is male, men account for 92 percent of all job-related deaths."

Similar problems in trying to compare truly comparable individuals make it difficult to determine the presence and magnitude of discrimination between groups that differ by race or ethnicity. It is not uncommon, both in the United States and in other countries, for one racial or ethnic group to differ in age from another by a decade or more—and we have already seen how age makes a big difference in income. While gross statistics show large income differences among American racial and ethnic groups, finer breakdowns usually show much smaller differences. For example, black, white, and Hispanic males of the same age (29) and IQ (100) have all had average annual incomes within a thousand dollars of one another. In New Zealand, while there are substantial income differences between the Maori population and the white population, these differences likewise shrink drastically when comparing Maoris with other New Zealanders of the same age and with the same skills and literacy levels.

Much discussion of discrimination proceeds as if employers are free to make whatever arbitrary decisions they wish as to hiring or pay. This ignores the fact that employers do not operate in isolation but in markets. Businesses compete against each other for employees as well as customers. Mistaken decisions incur costs in both product markets and labor markets and, as we have seen in earlier chapters, the costs of being wrong can have serious consequences. Moreover, these costs vary with conditions in the market.

While it is obvious that discrimination imposes a cost on those being discriminated against, in the form of lost opportunities for higher incomes, it is also true that discrimination can impose costs on those who do the discriminating, where they too lose opportunities for higher incomes. For example, when a landlord refuses to rent an apartment to people from the "wrong" group, that can mean leaving the apartment vacant longer. Clearly, that represents a loss of rent—if this is a free market. However, if there is rent control, with a surplus of applicants for vacant apartments, then such discrimination costs the landlord nothing.

Similar principles apply in job markets. An employer who refuses to hire qualified individuals from the "wrong" groups risks leaving his jobs unfilled longer in a free market. This means that he must either leave some work undone and some orders from customers unfilled—or else pay overtime to existing employees to get the job done, which costs more money either way. However, in a market where wages are set artificially above the level that would exist through supply and demand, the resulting surplus of applicants can mean that discrimination costs the employer nothing. Whether these artificially higher wages are set by a labor union or by a minimum wage law does not change the principle. Empirical evidence strongly indicates that racial discrimination tends to be greater when the costs are lower and lower when the costs are greater.

Even in South Africa during the era of apartheid, where racial discrimination against blacks was required by law, white employers in competitive industries often hired more blacks and in higher occupations than they were permitted to do by the government, and were often fined when caught doing so. This was because it was in the employers' economic self-interest to hire blacks. Similarly, whites who wanted homes built in Johannesburg typically hired illegal black construction crews, often with a token white nominally in charge to meet the requirements of the apartheid laws, rather than pay the higher price of hiring a white construction crew as the government wanted them to do. White South African landlords likewise often rented to blacks in areas where only whites were legally allowed to live.

The cost of discrimination to the discriminators is crucial for understanding such behavior. Employers who are spending other people's money—government agencies or non-profit organizations, for example— are much less affected by the cost of discrimination. In countries around the world, discrimination by government has been greater than discrimination by businesses operating in private, competitive markets. Understanding the basic economics of discrimination makes it easier to understand why blacks were starring on Broadway in the 1920s, at a time when they were not permitted to enlist in the U. S. Navy and were kept out of many civilian government jobs as well. Broadway producers were not about to lose big money that they could make by hiring black entertainers who could attract big audiences, but the costs of government discrimination were paid by the taxpayers, whether they realized it or not.

Just as minimum wage laws reduce the cost of discrimination to the employer, *maximum* wage laws increase the employer's cost of discrimination. Among the few examples of maximum wage laws in recent centuries were the wage and price controls imposed in the United States during World War II. Because wages were not allowed to rise to the level that they would reach under supply and demand, there was a shortage of workers, just as there is a shortage of housing under rent control. Many employers who had not hired blacks or women, or who had not hired them for desirable jobs before the war, now began to do so. The "Rosy the Riveter" image that came out of World War II was in part a result of wage and price controls.

CAPITAL, LABOR, AND EFFICIENCY

While everything requires some labor for its production, practically nothing can be produced by labor alone. Farmers need land, taxi drivers need cars, artists need something to draw on and something to draw with. Even a stand-up comedian needs an inventory of jokes, which is his capital, just as hydroelectric dams are the capital of companies that generate electricity.

Capital complements labor in the production process, but it also competes with labor for employment. In other words, many goods and services can be produced either with much labor and little capital or much capital and little labor. When transit workers' unions force bus drivers' pay rates much above what they would be in a competitive labor market, transit companies tend to add more capital, in order to save on the use of the more expensive labor. Buses grow longer, sometimes becoming essentially two buses with a flexible connection between them, so that one driver is using twice as much capital as before and is capable of moving twice as many passengers.

Some might think that this is more "efficient" but efficiency is not so easily defined. If we arbitrarily define efficiency as output per unit of labor, as the U.S. Department of Labor sometimes does, then it is merely circular reasoning to say that having one bus driver moving more passengers is more efficient. It may in fact cost more money per passenger to move them, as a result of the additional capital needed for the expanded buses and the more expensive labor of the drivers.

If bus drivers were not unionized and were paid no more than was necessary to attract qualified people, then undoubtedly their wage rates would be lower and it would then be profitable for the transit companies to hire more of them and use shorter buses. Not only would the total cost of moving passengers be less, passengers would have less time to wait at bus stops because of the shorter and more numerous buses. This is not a small concern to people waiting on street corners on cold winter days or in high-crime neighborhoods at night.

"Efficiency" cannot be meaningfully defined without regard to human desires and preferences. Even the efficiency of an automobile engine is not simply a matter of physics. All the energy generated by the engine will be used in some way—either in moving the car forward, overcoming internal friction among the moving parts, or shaking the automobile body in various ways. It is only when we define our goal—moving the car forward—that we can regard the percentage of the engine's power that is used for that task as indicating its efficiency and the other power dissipated in various other ways as being "wasted."

Europeans long regarded American agriculture as "inefficient" because output per acre was much lower in the United States than in much of Europe. On the other hand, output per agricultural worker was much higher in the United States than in Europe. The reason was that land was far more plentiful in the U.S. and labor was more scarce. An American farmer would spread himself thinner over far more land and would have correspondingly less time to devote to each acre. In Europe, where land was more scarce, and therefore more expensive because of supply and demand, the European farmer concentrated on the more intensive cultivation of what land he could get, spending more time clearing away weeds and rocks, or otherwise devoting more attention to ensuring the maximum output per acre.

Similarly, Third World countries often get more use out of given capital equipment than do wealthier and more industrialized countries. Such tools as hammers and screw-drivers may be plentiful enough for each worker in an American factory or shop to have his own, but that is much less likely to be the case in a much poorer country, where such tools are more likely to be shared, or shared more widely, than among Americans making the same products. Looked at from another angle, each hammer in a poor country is likely to drive more nails per year, since it is shared among more people and has less idle time. That does not make the poorer country more "efficient." It is just that the relative scarcities are different. Capital tends to be scarcer and more expensive in poorer countries, while labor is more abundant and cheaper. Such countries tend to economize on the more expensive factor, just as richer countries economize on a different factor that is more expensive and scarce there, namely labor. It is just that, in richer countries, capital is more plentiful and cheaper, while labor is more scarce and more expensive.

When a freight train comes into a railroad yard or onto a siding, workers are needed to unload it. When a freight train arrives in the middle of the night, it can either be unloaded then and there, so that the train can proceed on its way intact, or some boxcars can be detached and left on a siding until the workers come to work the next morning. In a country where such capital as railroad box cars are very scarce and labor is plentiful, it makes sense to have the workers available around the clock, so that they can immediately unload box cars and this very scarce resource does not remain idle. But, in a country that is rich in capital, it may often be better to let box cars sit idle on a siding, waiting to be unloaded the next day, rather than to have expensive workers sitting around idle waiting for the next train to arrive.

It is not just a question about these particular workers' paychecks or this particular railroad company's monetary expenses. From the standpoint of the economy as a whole, the more fundamental question is: What are the alternative uses of these workers' time and the alternative uses of the railroad boxcars? In other words, it is not just a question of money. The money only reflects underlying realities that would be the same in a socialist, feudal or other non-market economy. Whether it makes sense to leave the boxcars idle waiting for the workers to arrive or to leave the workers idle waiting for trains to arrive depends on the relative scarcities of labor and capital and their relative productivity in alternative uses.

During the era of the Soviet Union and Cold War competition, the Soviets used to boast of the fact that an average Soviet box car moved more freight per year than an average American box car. But, far from indicating that their economy was more efficient, this showed that Soviet railroads lacked the abundant capital of the American railroad industry, and that Soviet labor had less valuable alternative uses of its time than did American labor. Similarly, a study of West African economies in the mid-twentieth century noted that trucks there "are in service twenty-four hours a day for seven days a week and are generally tightly packed with passengers and freight."

For similar reasons, automobiles tend to have longer lives in poor countries than in richer countries. Not only does it pay many poorer countries to keep their own automobiles in use longer, it pays them to buy used cars from richer countries. In just one year, 90,000 used cars from Japan were sold to the United Arab Emirates. Dubai, one of these emirates, has become a center for the sale of these vehicles to other Middle Eastern and African countries. The *Wall Street Journal* reported: "Many African cities are already teeming with Toyotas, even though very few new cars have been sold there." In Cameroon, the taxis "are beaten-up old Toyotas, carrying four in the back and three in the front." Even cars needing repairs are sold internationally:

> Japan's exporters also ship out thousands of cars that have been dented or damaged. Mechanics in Dubai can repair vehicles for a fraction of the price in Japan, where high labor costs make it one of the world's most expensive places to fix a car.

By and large, it pays richer countries to junk their cars, refrigerators, sewing machines, and other capital equipment in a shorter time than it would pay people in poorer countries to do so. Nor is this a matter of being able to afford "waste." It would be a waste to keep repairing this equipment, when the same efforts elsewhere in the Japanese economy—or the American economy or German economy—would produce more than enough wealth to buy replacements. But it would not make sense for poorer countries, whose alternative uses of time are not as productive, to junk their equipment at the same times when richer countries junk theirs. The fact that labor is cheaper in Dubai than in Japan is not a happenstance. Labor is more productive in richer countries. That is one of the reasons why these countries are more prosperous in the first place. The sale of used equipment from rich countries to poor countries can be an efficient way of handling the situation for both kinds of countries.

In a modern industrial economy, many goods are mass produced, thereby lowering their costs because of economies of scale, but repairs on those products are still typically done individually by hand, without the benefit of economies of scale and therefore relatively expensively. In such a mass production economy, repeated repairs can in many cases quickly reach the point where it would be cheaper to get a new, mass-produced replacement. The number of television repair shops in the United States has not kept pace with the growing number of television sets, as mass production has reduced prices to the point where many malfunctioning sets can be more cheaply replaced than repaired.

A book by two Soviet economists pointed out that in the U.S.S.R. "equipment is endlessly repaired and patched up," so that the "average service life of capital stock in the U.S.S.R. is forty-seven years, as against seventeen in the United States." They were not bragging. They were complaining.

Chapter 10

CONTROLLED LABOR MARKETS

*The attempt to protect workers from all risk has
turned out to be very risky indeed.*
                                                Michael Barone

Just as inanimate resources and their resulting products can have their prices set either by free competition or by monopolies or government, so people's pay and employment conditions may or may not be a result of free market competition. Pay or working conditions may be controlled by law, custom, or organizations of employers or employees, as well as by government officials. Among the major factors behind such controls have been desires for job security and for collectively-set limits on how high or how low pay scales will be allowed to go in particular occupations or industries, as well as desires for safer or more pleasant working conditions.

Here as elsewhere, we are concerned not so much with the goals or rationales of such policies, but with the incentives created by these arrangements and the consequences to which such incentives lead. These consequences extend beyond the workers themselves to the economy as a whole, where labor is one of the scarce resources which have alternative uses. The degree of efficiency with which this scarce resource is allocated among those alternative uses affects the total output on which the standard of living of the whole society depends.

JOB SECURITY

Virtually every modern industrial nation has faced issues of job security, whether they have faced these issues realistically or unrealistically, successfully or unsuccessfully. In some countries—France, Germany, India, and South Africa, for example—job security laws make it difficult and costly for a private employer to fire anyone. Labor unions try to do this in many industries and in many countries around the world. Teachers' unions in the United States are so successful at this that it can easily cost a school district tens of thousands of dollars—or more than a hundred thousand in some places—to fire just one teacher, even if that teacher is grossly incompetent.

The obvious purpose of job security laws is to reduce unemployment but that is very different from saying that this is their actual effect. Countries with such laws typically do not have lower unemployment rates, but instead have higher unemployment rates, than countries without widespread job protection laws. In France, which has some of Europe's strongest job security laws, double-digit unemployment rates are not uncommon, while in the United States, where there are no such national laws mandating job security in the private sector, Americans become alarmed when the unemployment rate rises to 6 percent.[1] In South Africa, the government itself has admitted that its rigid job protection laws have had "unintended consequences," among them an unemployment rate that has remained above 25 percent for years, peaking at 31 percent in 2002. As the British magazine *The Economist* put it: "Firing is such a costly headache that many prefer not to hire in the first place." This consequence is by no means unique to South Africa.

The very thing that makes a modern industrial society so efficient and so effective in raising living standards—the constant quest for newer and better ways of getting work done and more goods produced—makes it impossible to keep on having the same workers doing the same jobs in the same way.

[1] Even with an unemployment rate below 6 percent, an article in the *New York Times* deplored the lack of "full employment" or full employment policies: Louis Uchitelle, "Chasing Full Employment," *New York Times*, February 12, 2006, section 3, page 4.

For example, back at the beginning of the twentieth century, the United States had about 10 million farmers and farm laborers to feed a population of 76 million people. By the end of the twentieth century, there were fewer than one-fifth this many farmers and farm laborers, feeding a population more than three times as large. Yet, far from having less food, Americans' biggest problems now included obesity and trying to find export markets for their surplus agricultural produce. All this was made possible because farming became a radically different enterprise, using machinery, chemicals and methods unheard of when the century began—and requiring the labor of far fewer people.

There were no job security laws to keep workers in agriculture, where they were now superfluous, so they went by the millions into industry, where they added greatly to the national output. Farming is of course not the only sector of the economy to be revolutionized during the twentieth century. Whole new industries sprang up, such as aviation and computers, and even old industries like retailing have seen radical changes in which companies and which business methods have survived. More than 17 million workers throughout the American economy lost their jobs between 1990 and 1995. But there were never 17 million Americans unemployed during this period, nor anything close to that. In fact, the unemployment rate in the United States fell to its lowest point in years during the 1990s. Americans were moving from one job to another, rather than relying on job security in one place. The average American has nine jobs between the ages of 18 and 34.

In Europe, where job security laws and practices are much stronger than in the United States, jobs have in fact been harder to come by. During the decade of the 1990s, the United States created jobs at triple the rate of industrial nations in Europe. In the private sector, Europe actually lost jobs, and only its increased government employment led to any net gain at all. This should not be surprising. Job security laws make it more expensive to hire workers—and, like anything else that is made more expensive, labor is less in demand at a higher price than at a lower price. Job security policies save the jobs of existing workers, but at the cost of reducing the flexibility and efficiency of the economy as a whole, thereby inhibiting production of the wealth needed for the creation of new jobs for other workers. Because job security laws make it risky for private enterprises to hire new workers, during periods of rising demand for their products existing employees may be worked overtime instead or capital may be substituted for labor, such as using huge buses instead of hiring more drivers for regular-sized buses. However it is done, increased substitution of capital for labor leaves other workers unemployed. For the working population as a whole, there may be no net increase in job security but instead a concentration of the insecurity on those who happen to be on the outside looking in, especially younger workers entering the labor force or women seeking to re-enter the labor force after taking time out to raise children.

The connection between job security laws and unemployment has been understood by some officials but apparently not by much of the public, including the educated public. When France tried to deal with its high youth unemployment rate of 23 percent by easing its stringent job security laws for people on their first job, students at the Sorbonne and other French universities rioted in Paris and other cities across the country in 2006.

MINIMUM WAGE LAWS

Just as we can better understand the economic role of prices in general when we see what happens when prices are not allowed to function, so we can better understand the economic role of workers' pay by seeing what happens when that pay is not allowed to vary with the supply and demand for labor. Historically, political authorities set maximum wage levels centuries before they set minimum wage levels. Today, however, only the latter are widespread.

Minimum wage laws make it illegal to pay less than the government-specified price for labor. By the simplest and most basic economics, a price artificially raised tends to cause more to be supplied and less to be demanded than when prices are left to be determined by supply and demand in a free market. The result is a surplus, whether the price that is set artificially high is that of farm produce or labor. Minimum wage laws are almost always discussed politically in terms of the benefits they confer on workers receiving those wages. Unfortunately, the real minimum wage is always zero, regardless of the laws, and that is the wage that many workers receive in the wake of the creation or escalation of a government-mandated minimum wage, because they lose their jobs or fail to find jobs when they enter the labor force. Making it illegal to pay less than a given amount does not make a worker's productivity worth that amount—and, if it is not, that worker is unlikely to be employed.

Unemployment

Because the government does not hire surplus labor the way it buys surplus agricultural output, a labor surplus takes the form of unemployment, which tends to be higher under minimum wage laws than in a free market.

Unemployed workers are not surplus in the sense of being useless or in the sense that there is no work around that needs doing. Most of these workers are perfectly capable of producing goods and services, even if not to the same extent as more skilled or more experienced workers. The unemployed are made idle by wage rates artificially set above the level of their productivity. Those who are idled in their youth are of course prevented from acquiring the job skills and experience which could make them more productive—and therefore higher earners—later on. That is, they not only lose the low pay that they could have earned in an entry-level job, they lose the higher pay that they could have begun earning after gaining experience on that job. Younger workers are disproportionately represented among people with low rates of pay. Only about two percent of American workers age 25 and over earn the minimum wage.

Although most modern industrial societies have minimum wage laws, not all do. Switzerland and Hong Kong have been among the exceptions—and both have had very low unemployment rates. In 2003, *The Economist* magazine reported: "Switzerland's unemployment neared a five-year high of 3.9% in February." Back in 1991, when Hong Kong was still a British colony, its unemployment rate was below 2 percent. Although Hong Kong still did not have a minimum wage law at the end of the twentieth century, in 1997 new amendments to its labor law under China's rule mandated many new benefits for workers, to be paid for by their employers. This imposed increase in labor costs was followed, predictably, by a higher unemployment rate that reached 7.3 percent in 2002—not high by European standards but a multiple of what it had been for years. In 2003, Hong Kong's unemployment rate hit a new high—8.3 percent.

Higher costs for a given quantity and quality of labor tends to produce less employment, just as higher prices for other things tend to produce fewer sales. Moreover, higher costs in the form of mandated benefits have the same economic effect as higher costs in the form of minimum wage laws. The explicit minimum wage rate understates the labor costs imposed by European governments, which also mandate various employer contributions to pension plans and health benefits, among other things. Europe's unemployment rates shot up when such government-mandated benefits to be paid for by employers grew sharply during the 1980s and 1990s. In Germany, such benefits accounted for half of the average labor cost per hour. By comparison, such benefits accounted for less than one-fourth the average labor costs per hour in Japan and the United States.

Comparisons of Canada with the United States show similar patterns. Over a five-year period, Canadian provinces had minimum wage rates that were a higher percentage of output per capita than in American states and unemployment rates were correspondingly higher in Canada, as was the average duration of unemployment, and the Canadian rate of job creation lagged behind that in the United States. Over this five-year period, three Canadian provinces had unemployment rates in excess of 10 percent, with a high of 16.9 percent in Newfoundland, but none of the 50 American states averaged unemployment rates in double digits over that same five-year period.

A belated recognition of the connection between minimum wage laws and unemployment by government officials has caused some countries to allow their real minimum wage levels to be eroded by inflation, avoiding the political risks of trying to repeal these laws explicitly, when so many voters think of such laws as being beneficial to workers. These laws are in fact beneficial to those workers who continue to be employed—those who are on the inside looking out, but at the expense of the unemployed who are on the outside looking in.

Labor unions also benefit from minimum wage laws, and are among the strongest proponents of such laws, even though their own members typically make more than the minimum wage rate. There is a reason for this. Just as most goods and services can be produced with either much labor and little capital or vice versa, so can most things be produced using varying proportions of low-skilled labor and high-skilled labor, depending on their relative costs. Thus experienced unionized workers are competing for employment against younger, inexperienced, and less skilled workers, whose pay is likely to be at or near the minimum wage. The higher the minimum wage goes, the more the unskilled and inexperienced workers are likely to be displaced by more experienced and higher skilled unionized workers. Just as businesses seek to impose tariffs on imported goods, in order to force up the prices of competing products, so labor unions use minimum wage laws as tariffs to force up the price of non-union labor that competes with their members for jobs.

Among two million Americans earning at or near the minimum wage in the early twenty-first century, just over half were from 16 to 24 years of age. Just over half worked part time. Yet political campaigns to increase the minimum wage often talk in terms of providing "a living wage" sufficient to support a family of four—such families as most minimum wage workers do not have and would be ill-advised to have before they reach the point where they can feed and clothe their children. Nevertheless, a number of American cities have passed "living wage" laws, which are essentially local minimum wage laws specifying a higher minimum than the national minimum wage law. Their effects have been similar to the effects of national minimum wage laws in the United States and other countries—that is, the poorest people have been the ones who have most often lost jobs.

The huge financial, political, emotional, and ideological investment of various groups in issues revolving around minimum wage laws means that dispassionate analysis is not always the norm. Moreover, the statistical complexities of separating out the effects of minimum wage rates on employment from all the other ever-changing variables which also affect employment mean that honest differences of opinion are possible. However, when all is said and done, most empirical studies indicate that minimum wage laws reduce employment in general, and especially the employment of younger, less skilled, and minority workers. A majority of professional economists surveyed in Britain, Germany, Canada, Switzerland, and the United States agreed that minimum wage laws increase unemployment among low-skilled workers. Economists in France and Austria did not. However, the majority among Canadian economists was 85 percent and among American economists 90 percent.

Those officially responsible for administering minimum wage laws, such as the U. S. Department of Labor and various local agencies, prefer to claim that these laws do not create unemployment. So do labor unions, which have a vested interest in such laws as protection for their own members' jobs. In South Africa, for example, *The Economist* reported:

> The main union body, the Congress of South African Trade Unions (Cosatu) says joblessness has nothing to do with labour laws. The problem, it says, is that businesses are not trying hard enough to create jobs.

Even though most studies show that unemployment tends to increase as minimum wages are imposed or increased, those few studies that seem to indicate otherwise are hailed as having "refuted" this "myth." One common problem with some research on the employment effects of minimum wage laws is that surveys of employers before and after a minimum wage increase can survey only those particular businesses which survived in both periods. Given the high rates of business failures in many industries, the results for the surviving businesses may be completely different from the results for the industry as a whole.[2] Using such research methods, you could interview

---

[2] Imagine that an industry consists of ten firms, each hiring 1,000 workers before a minimum wage increase, for an industry total of 10,000 employees. If three of these firms go out of business between the first and the second surveys, and only one new firm enters the industry, then only the seven firms that were in existence both "before" and "after" can be surveyed and their results reported. With fewer firms, employment per firm may increase, even if employment in the industry as a whole decreases. If, for example, the seven surviving firms and the new firm all increase their employment to 1,100 employees each, this means that the industry as a whole

people who have played Russian roulette and "prove" from their experiences that it is a harmless activity, since those for whom it was not harmless are unlikely to be around to be interviewed. Thus you would have "refuted" the "myth" that Russian roulette is dangerous.

It would be comforting to believe that the government can simply decree higher pay for low-wage workers, without having to worry about unfortunate repercussions, but the preponderance of evidence indicates that labor is not exempt from the basic economic principle that artificially high prices cause surpluses. In the case of surplus human beings, that can be a special tragedy when they are already from low-income, unskilled, or minority backgrounds and urgently need to get on the job ladder if they are ever to move up the ladder by acquiring experience and skills.

Informal Minimum Wages

Sometimes a minimum wage is imposed not by law, but by custom, informal government pressures, labor unions or—especially in the case of Third World countries—by international public opinion pressuring multinational companies to pay Third World workers the kinds of wages usually found in more industrially developed countries. Although organized public pressures for higher pay for Third World workers in Southeast Asia and Latin America have made news in the United States in recent years, such pressures are not new nor confined to Americans. Similar pressures were put on companies operating in colonial West Africa in the middle of the twentieth century.

Informal minimum wages imposed in these ways have had effects very similar to those of explicit minimum wage laws. An economist studying

---

will have 8,800 employees—fewer than before the minimum wage increase—and yet a study of the seven surviving firms would show a 10 percent *increase* in employment in the firms surveyed, rather than the 12 percent *decrease* for the industry as a whole. Since minimum wages can cause unemployment by (1) reducing employment among all the firms, (2) by pushing marginal firms into bankruptcy, or (3) discouraging the entry of replacement firms, reports based on surveying only survivors can create as false a conclusion as interviewing people who have played Russian roulette.

colonial West Africa in the mid-twentieth century found signs telling job applicants that there were "no vacancies" almost everywhere. Nor was this peculiar to West Africa. The same economist—P. T. Bauer of the London School of Economics—noted that it was "a striking feature of many under-developed countries that money wages are maintained at high levels" while "large numbers are seeking but unable to find work." These were of course not high levels of wages compared to what was earned by workers in more industrialized economies, but high wages relative to Third World workers' productivity and high relative to their alternative earning opportunities, such as in agriculture, domestic service, or self-employment as street vendors and the like—that is, in sectors of the economy not subject to external pressures to maintain an artificially inflated wage rate.

The magnitude of the unemployment created by artificially high wages that multinational companies felt pressured to pay in West Africa was indicated by Professor Bauer's first-hand investigations:

> I asked the manager of the tobacco factory of the Nigerian Tobacco Company (a subsidiary of the British-American Tobacco Company) in Ibadan whether he could expand his labour force without raising wages if he wished to do so. He replied that his only problem would be to control the mob of applicants. Very much the same opinion was expressed by the Kano district agent of the firm of John Holt and Company in respect of their tannery. In December 1949 a firm of produce buyers in Kano dismissed two clerks and within two days received between fifty and sixty applications for the posts without having publicized the vacancies. The same firm proposed to erect a groundnut crushing plant. By June 1950 machinery had not yet been installed; but without having advertised a vacancy it had already received about seven hundred letters asking for employment. . . I learnt that the European-owned brewery and the recently established manufacturers of stationery constantly receive shoals of applications for employment.

Nothing had changed fundamentally more than half a century later, when twenty-first century job seekers in South Africa were lined up far in excess of the number of jobs available, as reported in the *New York Times*:

> When Tiger Wheels opened a wheel plant six years ago in this faded industrial town, the crush of job seekers was so enormous that the chief executive, Eddie Keizan, ordered a corrugated iron roof to shield them from the midday heat.

"There were hundreds and hundreds of people outside our gate, just sitting there, in the sun, for days and days," Mr. Keizan recalled in an interview. "We had no more jobs, but they refused to believe us."

Why then did wage rates not come down in response to supply and demand, leading to more employment at a lower wage level, as basic economic principles might lead us to expect? According to the same report:

> In other developing countries, legions of unskilled workers have kept down labor costs. But South Africa's leaders, vowing not to let their nation become the West's sweatshop, heeded the demands of politically powerful labor unions for new protections and benefits.

The net result was that when this company, which had made aluminum wheels solely in South Africa for two decades, expanded its production, it expanded by hiring more workers in Poland, where it earned a profit, rather than in South Africa, where it could only break even or sustain a loss. The misfortunes of eager but frustrated African job applicants were only part of the story. The output that they could have produced, if employed, would have made a particularly important contribution to the economic well-being of the consuming public in a very poor region, lacking many things that others take for granted in more prosperous societies.

It is not at all clear that workers as a whole are benefitted by artificially high wage rates in the Third World. Employed workers—those on the inside looking out—obviously benefit, while those on the outside looking in lose. For the population as a whole, including consumers, it would be hard to make a case that there is a net benefit, since there are fewer consumer goods when people willing to work cannot find jobs producing those consumer goods. The only category of clear beneficiaries are people living in richer countries who enjoy the feeling that they are helping people in poorer countries, or Third World leaders too proud to let their workers be hired at wage rates commensurate with their productivity. While South African workers' productivity is twice that of workers in Indonesia, they are paid five times as much—when they can find jobs at all. In short, these productive South African workers are not "surplus" or "unemployable" in any sense other than being priced out of the market by politicians.

As already noted in Chapter 9, South African firms use much capital per worker. This is more efficient for the firms but only because South African labor laws make labor artificially more expensive, both with minimum wage laws and with laws that make laying off workers costly. "Labour costs are more than three-and-a-half times higher than in the most productive areas of China and a good 75% higher than in Malaysia or Poland," according to *The Economist*. With such artificially high costs of South African labor, it pays employers to use more capital but this is not greater efficiency for the economy as a whole, which is worse off for having so many people unemployed, which is to say, with so many resources idled instead of being allocated.

Just as a price set by government below the free market level tends to cause quality deterioration in the product that is being sold, because a shortage means that buyers will be forced to accept things of lower quality than they would have otherwise, so a price set above the free market level tends to cause a rise in average quality, as the surplus allows the buyers to cherry-pick and purchase only the better quality items. What that means in the labor market is that job qualification requirements are likely to rise and that some workers who would ordinarily be hired in a free market may become "unemployable" when there are minimum wage laws. Unemployability, like shortages and surpluses, is not independent of price.

In a free market, low-productivity workers are just as employable at a low wage rate as high-productivity workers are at a high wage rate. During the long era from the late nineteenth century to the mid-twentieth century, when black Americans received lower quantities and lower qualities of education than whites in the South where most lived, the labor force participation rates of black workers were nevertheless slightly higher than those of white workers. For most of that era, there were no minimum wage laws to price them out of jobs and, even after a federal minimum wage law was passed in 1938, the wartime inflation of the 1940s raised wages in the free market above the minimum wage level, making the law largely irrelevant until it was amended in 1950, beginning a series of minimum wage escalations.

Differential Impact

Because people differ in many ways, those who are unemployed are not likely to be a random sample of the labor force. In country after country around the world, those whose employment prospects are reduced most by minimum wage laws are those who are younger, less experienced or less skilled. This pattern has been found in New Zealand, France, Canada, the Netherlands, and the United States, for example.

In early twenty-first century France, the national unemployment rate was 10 percent but, among workers under the age of twenty six, the unemployment rate was 23 percent. In Belgium, the unemployment rate for workers under the age of twenty five was 22 percent and in Italy 27 percent. In Australia, the *lowest* unemployment rate for workers under the age of 25, during the entire period from 1978 to 2002, remained higher than the *highest* unemployment rate for the population in general at any point during that same period. Australia has an unusually high minimum wage, relatively speaking, since its level is more than half the country's average wage, while the minimum wage in the United States is just over one-third of the American average wage.

Some countries in Europe have lower minimum wage rates for teenagers than for adults and New Zealand simply exempted teenagers from the coverage of its minimum wage law until 1994. This was tacit recognition of the fact that those workers less in demand were likely to be hardest hit by unemployment created by minimum wage laws.

Another group disproportionately affected by minimum wage laws are members of unpopular racial or ethnic minority groups. Indeed, minimum wage laws were once advocated explicitly because of the likelihood that such laws would reduce or eliminate the competition of particular minorities, whether they were Japanese in Canada during the 1920s or blacks in the United States and South Africa during the same era. Such expressions of overt racial discrimination were both legal and socially accepted in all three countries at that time.

Again, it is necessary to note how price is a factor even in racial discrimination. That is, surplus labor resulting from minimum wage laws makes it cheaper to discriminate against minority workers than it would be in a free market, where there is no chronic excess supply of labor. Passing up qualified minority workers in a free market means having to hire more other workers to take the jobs they were denied, and that in turn usually means either having to raise the pay to attract the additional workers or lowering the job qualifications at the existing pay level—both of which amount to the same thing economically, higher labor costs for getting a given amount of work done.

The history of black workers in the United States illustrates the point. As already noted, from the late nineteenth-century on through the middle of the twentieth century, the labor force participation rate of American blacks was slightly higher than that of American whites. In other words, blacks were just as employable at the wages they received as whites were at their very different wages. The minimum wage law changed that. Before federal minimum wage laws were instituted in the 1930s, the black unemployment rate was slightly *lower* than the white unemployment rate in 1930. But then followed the Davis-Bacon Act of 1931, the National Industrial Recovery Act of 1933 and the Fair Labor Standards Act of 1938—all of which imposed government-mandated minimum wages. The National Labor Relations Act of 1935, which promoted unionization, also tended to price black workers out of jobs, in addition to union rules that kept blacks from jobs by barring them from union membership. The National Industrial Recovery Act raised wage rates in the Southern textile industry by 70 percent in just five months and its impact nationwide was estimated to have cost blacks half a million jobs. While this Act was later declared unconstitutional by the Supreme Court, the Fair Labor Standards Act of 1938 was upheld and became the major force establishing a national minimum wage. As already noted, the inflation of the 1940s largely nullified the minimum wage law until it was amended in 1950. By 1954, black unemployment rates were double those of whites and have continued to be at that level or higher. Those particularly hard hit by the resulting unemployment have been black teenage males.

Even though 1949—the year before a series of minimum wage escalations began—was a recession year, black male teenage unemployment that year was lower than it was to be at any time during the later boom years of the 1960s. The usual explanations of high unemployment among black teenagers—inexperience, lack of skills, racism—cannot explain their rising unemployment, since all these things were worse during the earlier period when black teenage unemployment was much lower. Taking the more normal year of 1948 as a basis for comparison, black male teenage unemployment then was less than half of what it would be at any time during the decade of the 1960s and less than one-third of what it would be in the 1970s. Moreover, unemployment among 16 and 17-year-old black males was no higher than among white males of the same age in 1948. It was only after a series of minimum wage escalations began that black male teenage unemployment not only skyrocketed itself but became more than double the unemployment rates among white male teenagers. In the early twenty-first century, the unemployment rate for black teenagers exceeded 30 percent.

COLLECTIVE BARGAINING

So far we have been considering labor markets in which both workers and employers are numerous and compete individually and independently. However, these are not the only kinds of markets for labor. Some workers are members of labor unions which negotiate pay and working conditions with employers, whether employers are acting individually or in concert as members of an employers' association.

Employer Organizations

In earlier centuries, it was the employers who were more likely to be organized and setting pay and working conditions as a group. In medieval guilds, the master craftsmen collectively made the rules determining the conditions under which apprentices and journeymen would be hired and how much customers would be charged for the products. Today, major league baseball owners collectively make the rules as to what is the maximum amount of total salaries that any given team can pay to its players without incurring penalties.

Clearly, pay and working conditions tend to be different when determined collectively than in a labor market where employers compete against one another individually for workers and workers compete against one another individually for jobs. It would obviously not be worth the trouble of organizing employers if they were not able to gain by keeping the salaries they pay lower than they would be in a free market. Much has been said about the fairness or unfairness of the actions of medieval guilds, modern labor unions or other forms of collective bargaining. Here we are studying their economic consequences—and especially their effects on the allocation of scarce resources which have alternative uses. Almost by definition, all these organizations exist to keep the price of labor from being what it would be otherwise in free and open competition in the market. Just as the tendency of market competition is to base rates of pay on the productivity of the worker, thereby bidding labor away from where it is less productive to where it is more productive, so organized efforts to make wages artificially low or artificially high defeat this process and thereby make the allocation of resources less efficient in the economy as a whole.

For example, if an employers' association keeps wages in the widget industry below the level that workers of similar skills receive elsewhere, fewer workers are likely to apply for jobs producing widgets than if the pay rate were higher. If widget manufacturers are paying $10 an hour for labor that would get $15 an hour if employers had to compete with each other for workers in a free market, then some workers will go to other industries that pay $12 an hour. From the standpoint of the economy as a whole, this means that people capable of producing $15 an hour's worth of output are instead producing only $12 an hour's worth of output somewhere else. This is a clear loss to the consumers—that is, to society as a whole, since everyone is a consumer.

The fact that it is a more immediate and more visible loss to the workers in the widget industry does not make that the most important fact from an economic standpoint. Losses and gains between employers and employees are social or moral issues, but they do not change the key *economic* issue, which is how the allocation of resources affects the total wealth available to society as a whole. What makes the total wealth produced by the economy less than it would be in a free market is that wages set below the market level cause workers to work where they are not as productive, but where they are paid more because of a competitive labor market in the less productive occupation.

The same principle applies where wages are set above the market level. If a labor union is successful in raising the wage rate for the same workers in the widget industry to $20 an hour, then employers will employ fewer workers at this higher rate than they would at the $15 an hour that would have prevailed in free market competition. In fact, the only workers it will pay the employers to hire are workers whose productivity is $20 an hour or more. This higher productivity can be reached in a number of ways, whether by retaining only the most skilled and experienced employees, by adding more capital to enable the labor to turn out more products per hour, or by other means—none of them free.

Those workers displaced from the widget industry must go to their second-best alternative. As before, those worth $15 an hour producing widgets may end up working in another industry at $12 an hour. Again, this is not simply a loss to those particular workers who cannot find employment at the higher wage rate, but a loss to the economy as a whole, because scarce resources are not being allocated where their productivity is highest.

Where unions set wages above the level that would prevail under supply and demand in a free market, widget manufacturers are not only paying more money for labor, they are also paying for additional capital or other complementary resources to raise the productivity of labor above the $20 an hour level. Higher labor productivity may seem on the surface to be greater "efficiency," but producing fewer widgets at higher cost per widget does not benefit the economy, even though less labor is being used. Other industries receiving more labor than they normally would, because of the workers displaced from the widget industry, can expand their output. But that expanding output is not the most productive use of the additional labor. It is only the artificially-imposed union wage rate which causes the shift from a more productive use to a less productive use.

Note that either artificially low wage rates caused by an employer association or artificially high wage rates caused by a labor union reduces employment in the widget industry. Another way of saying the same thing is that the maximum employment in any industry is achieved under free and open market competition, without organized collusion among either employers or employees. Looked at more generally, the only individual bargains that can be made anywhere in a free market, whether a market for products or resources, are those bargains whose terms are acceptable to both sides—that is, buyers and sellers of labor, computers, shoes, or whatever. Any other terms, whether set higher or lower, and whether set by collective actions of employers or unions or imposed by government decree, favors one side or the other and therefore causes the disfavored side to make fewer transactions.

From the standpoint of the economy as a whole, the real loss is that things that both sides wanted to do cannot be done now, because the range of mutually acceptable terms has been artificially narrowed by adding restrictions on their choices imposed by third parties. One side or the other must now go to their second-best option—which is also second-best from the standpoint of the economy as a whole, because scarce resources have not been allocated to their most valued uses. The parties engaged in collective bargaining are of course preoccupied with their own interests, but those judging the process as a whole need to focus on how such a process affects the economic interests of the entire society, rather than the internal division of economic benefits among contending members of the society.

Even in situations where it might seem that employers could do pretty much whatever they wanted to do, history often shows that they could not—because of the effects of competition in the market. Few workers have been more vulnerable than newly freed blacks in the United States after the Civil War. They were very poor, most completely uneducated, unorganized, and unfamiliar with the operation of a market economy. Yet organized attempts by white employers and landowners in the South to hold down their wages and limit their decision-making as sharecroppers all eroded away in the market, amid bitter mutual recriminations among white employers and landowners.

When the pay scale set by the organized white employers was below the actual productivity of black workers, that made it profitable for any given employer to offer more than the others were paying, in order to lure more workers away, so long as his higher offer was still not above the level of the black workers' productivity. With agricultural labor especially, the pressure on each employer mounted as the planting season approached and the landowner knew that the size of the crop for the whole year depended on having enough workers to do the spring planting. That inescapable reality often over-rode any sense of loyalty to fellow landowners or employers.

One of the general problems of cartels is that, no matter what conditions they set collectively, it is to the advantage of individual cartel members to violate those conditions, if they can get away with it, often leading to the disintegration of the cartel. That was the situation of white employer cartels in the postbellum South, where the percentage rate of increase of black wages was higher than the percentage rate of increase in the wages of white workers in the decades after the Civil War, even though the latter had higher pay in absolute terms.

It was much the same story out in California in the late nineteenth century and early twentieth century, when white landowners there organized to try to hold down the pay of Japanese immigrant farmers and farm laborers. These cartels too collapsed amid bitter mutual recriminations among whites, as competition among landowners led to widespread violations of the agreements which they had made in collusion with one another.

In general, employers cannot simply make whatever arbitrary decisions they wish when there is a competitive market for labor and for the products they sell. The costs of discrimination cannot automatically be passed on to consumers when there are other sellers of the same product, for the least discriminatory employers would acquire cost advantages. For example, if women of the same productivity as men were paid only 75 percent of what the men were paid, then a non-discriminatory employer could hire four workers for what his competitor pays for three workers who were no more productive. All employers would have incentives to replace men with women and the resulting competition for women would erode the sex differential. Only where employers are protected from competition, or are spending someone else's money—as in government or non-profit organizations—is discrimination free of costs to those who are discriminating.

Labor Unions

Labor unions often boast of the pay rate and other benefits they have gotten for their members, and of course that is what enables unions to continue to attract members. The wage rate per hour is typically a key indicator of a union's success, but the further ramifications of that wage rate seldom receive as much attention. Legendary American labor leader John L. Lewis, head of the United Mine Workers from 1920 to 1960, was enormously successful in winning higher pay for his union's members. However, an economist also called him "the world's greatest oil salesman," because the resulting higher price of coal and the disruptions in its production due to numerous strikes caused many users of coal to switch to using oil instead. This of course reduced employment in the coal industry.

By the 1960s, declining employment in the coal industry left many mining communities economically stricken and some became virtual ghost towns. Media stories of their plight seldom connected their current woes with the former glory days of John L. Lewis. In fairness to Lewis, he made a conscious decision that it was better to have fewer miners doing dangerous work underground and more heavy machinery down there, since machinery could not be killed by cave-ins, explosions and the other hazards of mining.

To the public at large, however, these and other trade-offs were largely unknown. Many simply cheered at what Lewis had done to improve the wages of miners and, years later, were compassionate toward the decline of mining communities—but made little or no connection between the two things. Yet what was involved was one of the simplest and most basic principles of economics, that less is demanded at a higher price than at a lower price. That principle applies whether considering the price of coal, of the labor of mine workers, or anything else.

Very similar trends emerged in the automobile industry, where the danger factor was not what it was in mining. Here the United Automobile Workers' union was also very successful in getting higher pay, more job security and more favorable work rules for its members. In the long run, however, all these additional costs raised the price of automobiles and made American cars less competitive with Japanese and other imports, not only in the United States but around the world.

As of 1950, the United States produced three-quarters of all the cars in the world and Japan produced less than one percent of what Americans produced. Twenty years later, Japan was producing nearly half as many automobiles as the United States and, a decade later, more automobiles than the Americans. By 1990, one-third of the cars sold in the United States were Japanese. In a number of years since then, the Honda Accord or the Toyota Camry each sold more cars in the United States than any car made by General Motors. All this of course had its effect on employment. By 1990, the number of jobs in the American automobile industry was 200,000 less than it had been in 1979.

Political pressures on Japan to "voluntarily" limit its export of cars to the U.S. led to the creation of Japanese automobile manufacturing plants in the United States, hiring American workers. By 1990, these transplanted Japanese factories were producing nearly as many cars as were being exported to the United States from Japan. Many of these transplanted Japanese car companies had workforces that were non-union—and which rejected unionization when votes were taken among the employees in secret ballot elections conducted by the government. The net result, by the early twenty-first century, was that Detroit automakers were laying off workers by the thousands, while Toyota was hiring American workers by the thousands.

The decline of unionized workers in the automobile industry was part of a more general trend among industrial workers in the United States. The United Steelworkers of America was another large and highly successful union in getting high pay and other benefits for its members. But here too the number of jobs in the industry declined by more than 200,000 in a decade, while the steel companies invested $35 billion in machinery that replaced these workers, and while the towns where steel production was concentrated were economically devastated.

The once common belief that unions were a blessing and a necessity for workers was now increasingly mixed with skepticism and apprehension about the unions' role in the economic declines and reduced employment in many industries. Faced with the prospect of seeing some employers going out of business or having to drastically reduce employment, some unions were forced into "give-backs"—that is, relinquishing various wages and benefits they had obtained for their members in previous years. Painful as this was, many unions concluded that it was the only way to save members' jobs. A front page news story in the *New York Times* summarized the situation in the early twenty-first century:

> In reaching a settlement with General Motors on Thursday and in recent agreements with several other industrial behemoths—Ford, DaimlerChrysler, Goodyear and Verizon—unions have shown a new willingness to rein in their demands. Keeping their employers competitive, they have concluded, is essential to keeping unionized jobs from being lost to nonunion, often lower-wage companies elsewhere in this country or overseas.

Unions and their members had, over the years, learned the hard way what is usually taught early on in introductory economics courses—that people buy less at higher prices than at lower prices. It is not a complicated principle, but it often gets lost sight of in the swirl of events and the headiness of rhetoric.

The proportion of the American labor force that is unionized has declined over the years, as skepticism about unions' economic effects spread among workers who increasingly voted against being represented by unions. Unionized workers were 32 percent of all workers in the middle of the twentieth century, but only 14 percent by the end of the century. Moreover, there was a major change in the composition of unionized workers.

In the first half of the twentieth century, the great unions in the U.S. economy were in mining, automobiles, steel, and trucking. But, by the end of that century, the largest and most rapidly growing unions were those of government employees. The largest union in the country by far was the union of teachers—the National Education Association. The economic pressures of the marketplace, which had created such problems for unionized workers in industry and commerce, did not apply to government workers. Government employees could continue to get pay raises, larger benefits, and job security without worrying that they would suffer the fate of miners, automobile workers, and other unionized industrial workers. Those who hired government workers were not spending their own money but the taxpayers' money, and so had little reason to resist union demands. Moreover, they seldom faced such competitive forces in the market as would force them to lose business to imports or to substitute products.[3]

In private industry, many companies remained non-union by a policy of paying their workers at least as much as unionized workers received. Such a policy implies that the cost to an employer of having a union exceeds the wages and benefits paid to workers. The hidden costs of union rules on seniority and many other details of operations are for some companies worth being rid of for the sake of greater efficiency, even if that means paying their employees more than they would have to pay to unionized workers. The unionized big three American automobile makers, for example, required from 26 hours to 31 hours of labor per car, while the largely non-unionized Japanese auto makers required from 17 to 22 hours.

Western European labor unions have been especially powerful and the many benefits that they have gotten for their members have had their repercussions on the employment of workers and the growth rates of whole economies. Western European countries have for years lagged behind the United States both in economic growth and in the creation of jobs. A belated recognition of such facts has led some European unions and European governments to relax some of their demands and restrictions on

---

[3] This was not always true: Some state and local governments have paid private businesses to carry out some functions traditionally done by government employees, such as garbage collection and running prisons, and the federal government has also outsourced some of its functions to private companies, both in the United States and overseas. The extent to which these things can be done is, however, limited by political reactions.

employers in the wake of an economic slump. The *Wall Street Journal* reported:

> Europe's economic slump has given companies new muscle in their negotiations with workers. Governments in Europe have been slow to overhaul worker-friendly labor laws for fear of incurring voters' wrath. That slowed job growth as companies transferred operations overseas where labor costs were lower. High unemployment in Europe depressed consumer spending, helping limit economic growth in the past five years to a meager 1.4% average in the 12 countries that use the euro.

In the wake of a relaxation of labor union and government restrictions in the labor market, the growth rate in these countries has risen from 1.4 percent to 2.2 percent and the unemployment rate fell from 9.3 percent to 8.3 percent. Neither of these statistics is as good as those in the United States but they are an improvement over what existed under previous policies and practices in the European Union countries.

WORKING CONDITIONS

Both governments and labor unions have regulated working conditions, such as the maximum hours of work per week, safety rules, and various amenities to make the job less stressful or more pleasant.

The economic effects of regulating working conditions are very similar to the effects of regulating wages because better working conditions, like higher wage rates, tend to make a given job both more attractive to the workers and more costly to the employers. Moreover, employers take these costs into account thereafter, when deciding how many workers they can afford to hire when there are higher costs per worker, as well as how high they can afford to bid for workers, since money paid for creating better working conditions is the same as money spent for higher wage rates per hour.

Other things being equal, better working conditions mean lower pay than otherwise, so that workers are in effect buying improved conditions on the job. Employers may not cut pay every time working conditions are improved but, when rising productivity leads to rising pay scales through competition among employers for workers, those pay scales are unlikely to rise as much as they would have if the costs of better working conditions did not have to be taken into account. That is, employers' bids are limited not only by the productivity of the workers but also by all the other costs besides the rate of pay.[4] In some countries, these non-wage costs of labor are much higher than in others—about twice as high in Germany, for example, as in the United States, making German labor more expensive than American labor that is paid the same wage rate.

Empirical evidence on the consequences of better working conditions is not as readily obtained as evidence on the consequences of higher wage rates, since "better" working conditions consist of things too heterogeneous to be added together. You cannot add up safety goggles and coffee breaks, longer vacations and more comfortable chairs. Nor is it easy to put a price tag on a union contract clause that forbids work usually done by workers in category *A* from being assigned to workers in category *B* when workers in the first category are all busy and workers in the second category happen to be idle. What is clear, however, is that such clauses add to the costs of production, even if the exact amount cannot be known in advance, because it is impossible to predict how often such situations will arise. Nevertheless, such things are among the considerations which cause some employers to pay their workers more than the union scale, in order to keep their own workers from voting to join a union, since pay is not the only cost of labor.

Because working conditions were often much worse in the past—fewer safety precautions, longer hours, more unpleasant and unhealthy surroundings—some advocates of externally regulated working conditions, whether regulated by government or unions, argue as if working conditions would never have improved otherwise. But wage rates were also much lower

---

[4] As noted in Chapter 9, if a worker's output adds $50,000 to an employer's revenue, then $50,000 becomes the upper limit to how much the employer will pay to hire that worker. However, if the costs of better working conditions (including health insurance or other benefits) are $10,000 per worker, then the upper limit is $40,000 for the same worker.

in the past and yet they have risen in both unionized and non-unionized occupations, and in occupations covered and those not covered by minimum wage laws. Growth in per capita output permits both higher pay and better working conditions, while competition for workers forces individual employers to make improvements in both, just as they are forced to improve the products they sell to the consuming public for the same reason.

Child Labor Laws

Government control of working conditions takes many forms, including child labor laws. In most countries, laws to protect children in the workplace began before there were laws controlling working conditions for adults. Such laws reflected public concerns because of the special vulnerability of children, due to their inexperience, weaker bodies, and general helplessness against the power of adults. At one time, children were used for hard and dangerous work in coal mines, as well as working around factory machinery that could maim or kill a child who was not alert. However, laws passed under one set of conditions often remain on the books long after the circumstances that gave rise to those laws have changed. As a twenty-first century observer noted:

> Child labor laws passed to protect children from dangerous factories now keep strapping teenagers out of air-conditioned offices.

Such results are not mere examples of irrationality. Like other laws, child labor laws were not only passed in response to a given constituency— humanitarian individuals and groups, in this case—but also developed new constituencies among those who found such laws useful to their own interests. Labor unions, for example, have sought to keep children and adolescents out of the work force, where they would compete for jobs with the unions' own members. Educators in general and teachers' unions in particular likewise have a vested interest in keeping young people in school longer, where their attendance increases the demand for teachers and can be used politically to justify larger expenditures on the school system. While keeping strapping teenagers from working in air-conditioned offices might seem irrational in terms of the original reasons for child labor laws advanced by the original humanitarian constituency, it is quite rational from the standpoint of the interests of these new constituencies.

Hours of Work

One of the working conditions that can be quantified is the length of the work week. Most modern industrial countries specify the maximum number of hours per week that can be worked, either absolutely or before being forced by law to pay higher rates for overtime work beyond those specified hours. This imposed work week varies from country to country. France, for example, specified 35 hours as the standard workweek, with employers being mandated to continue to pay the same amount for this shorter work week as they had paid in weekly wages before. In addition, French law requires employees to be given 25 days of paid vacation per year, plus paid holidays—neither of which is required under American laws. Given these facts, it is hardly surprising that the average number of hours worked annually in France is less than 1,500 compared to more than 1,800 in the United States and Japan. Obviously this has an effect on annual output and therefore on the standard of living. Nor are all these costs financial. According to *BusinessWeek* magazine:

> Doctors work 20% less, on average. Staff shortages in hospitals and nursing homes due to the 35-hour week was a key reason August's heat wave killed 14,000 in France.

The French tradition of long summer vacations would have made the under-staffing problem worse during an August heat wave.

Sometimes, especially during periods of high unemployment, a government-mandated shorter work week is advocated on grounds that this would share the work among more workers, reducing unemployment. In other words, instead of hiring 35 workers working 40 hours each, an employer would hire 40 workers working 35 hours each. Plausible as this might seem, the problem is that shorter work weeks, whether imposed by government or by labor unions, often involve maintaining the same weekly pay as before, as it did in France. What this amounts to is a higher wage rate per hour, which tends to reduce the number of workers hired, instead of increasing employment as planned.

Third World Countries

Some of the worst working conditions exist in some of the poorest countries—that is, countries where the workers could least afford to accept lower pay as the price of better surroundings or circumstances on the job. Multinational companies with factories in the Third World often come under severe criticism for having working conditions in those factories that would not be tolerated in their own countries. What this means is that more prosperous workers in Europe or America in effect buy better working conditions, just as they are likely to buy better housing and better clothing than people in the Third World can afford. If employers in the Third World are forced by law or public pressures to provide better working conditions, the additional expense reduces the number of workers hired, just as wage rates higher than would be required by supply and demand left many Africans frustrated in their attempts to get jobs with multinational companies.

However much the jobs provided by multinational companies to Third World workers might be disdained for their low pay or poor working conditions by critics in Europe or the United States, the real question for workers in poor countries is how these jobs compare with their own alternatives. A *New York Times* writer in Cambodia, for example, noted: "Here in Cambodia factory jobs are in such demand that workers usually have to bribe a factory insider with a month's salary just to get hired." Clearly these are jobs highly sought after. Nor is Cambodia unique. Multinational companies typically pay about double the local wage rate in Third World countries.

It is much the same story with working conditions. Third World workers compare conditions in multinational companies with their own local alternatives. The same *New York Times* writer reporting from Cambodia described one of these alternatives—working as a scavenger picking through garbage dumps where "the stench clogs the nostrils" and where burning produces "acrid smoke that blinds the eyes," while "scavengers are chased by swarms of flies and biting insects." Speaking of one of these scavengers, the *Times* writer said:

> Nhep Chanda averages 75 cents a day for her efforts. For her, the idea of being exploited in a garment factory—working only six days a week, inside instead of in the broiling sun, for up to $2 a day—is a dream.

Would it not be still better if this young woman could be paid what workers in Europe or America are paid and work under the same kinds of conditions found on their jobs? Of course it would. The real question is how her productivity can be raised to the same level as that of workers in Europe or the United States—and what is likely to happen if productivity issues are waved aside and better working conditions are simply imposed by law or public pressures. There is little reason to doubt that the results would be similar to what happens when minimum wage rates are prescribed in disregard of productivity.

This does not mean that workers in poorer countries are doomed forever to low wages and bad working conditions. On the contrary, to the extent that more and more multinational companies locate in poor countries, working conditions as well as productivity and pay are affected when increasing numbers of multinationals compete for labor. In 2006, *BusinessWeek* magazine reported that a Chinese manufacturer of air-conditioner compressors "has seen turnover for some jobs hit 20% annually," with the general manager observing that "it's all he can do to keep his 800 employees from jumping ship to Samsung, Siemens, Nokia and other multinationals" operating in his area. Under such pressures, in just one year wages rose 9 percent in Beijing and Shanghai, and 12 percent in Nanjing. Competitive pressures have affected working conditions as well as wages:

> That means managers can no longer simply provide eight-to-a-room dorms and expect laborers to toil 12 hours a day, seven days a week. . . In addition to boosting salaries, Yongjin has upgraded its dormitories and improved the food in the company cafeteria. Despite those efforts, its five factories remain about 10% shy of the 6,000 employees they need.

The difference between having such improvements in working conditions emerge as a result of market competition and having them imposed by government is that markets bring about such improvements only as a result of more options for the workers while government impositions tend to reduce existing options.

Chapter 11

AN OVERVIEW

The promotion of economic equality and the alleviation of
poverty are distinct and often conflicting.

Peter Bauer

Although the basic economic principles underlying the allocation of labor are not fundamentally different from the principles underlying the allocation of inanimate resources, it is not equally easy to look at labor and its pay rates in the same way one looks at the prices of iron ore or bushels of wheat. Because wages and salaries are so important in the lives of most individuals, there is a tendency to look at earnings from work solely from the standpoint of the individuals receiving those earnings. However, this overlooks the important role of the price of labor in allocating resources in ways which promote economic efficiency and thereby raise the standard of living in the society as a whole.

ALLOCATION AND INEQUALITIES

In an economy that never changed, it would be possible to establish some permanent allocation of labor to its various uses and to establish some payment system—whether based on equal pay or some other principle— that would also be permanent. But no such permanent arrangements are possible in an economy that is growing in size and developing technologically. Ideas for improvements in technology and in the ways that work is organized occur to people unpredictably from time to time and from industry to industry, requiring shifts in labor and other resources from one industry or sector of the economy to another, if the new potentialities are to lead to greater output and the higher standards of living which depend on greater output.

Unless workers are to be ordered to move from one industry, region, or occupation to another, as under totalitarianism, economic incentives and constraints must accomplish these transfers in a market economy. Higher pay may attract workers to the newer and more productive sectors or unemployment may force them out of sectors whose products or technologies are becoming obsolete. Simple and obvious as this may seem, it is often misunderstood by those who are shocked to see some sectors of the economy prospering at the same time when others are being "left behind" or are even suffering losses of jobs. Too often there is no sense that these events are all part of the same process, rather than separate happenstances that are good for some and bad for others.

There were, for example, many laments in nineteenth century Britain for the plight of the handloom weavers, increasingly displaced by power looms that produced cloth more cheaply and thereby made clothing more affordable to millions. Today, in an affluent age, when physically adequate clothing is so widely available that only issues of style and brand name concern most people in modern industrial societies, it is difficult to imagine the hardships endured by many people in centuries past who were unable to afford enough clothing to provide adequate protection against the elements[1]—or what a blessing it was to them to have the prices of clothes brought down to a level where they could finally afford them, because of advances in the mechanization of production. Their good fortune and the misfortunes of the handloom weavers were inseparably part of the same process.

Often those who are concerned about the alleviation of poverty are also concerned about inequalities of income. Seldom is there any recognition that reducing poverty can sometimes conflict with reducing inequalities.

---

[1] At one time, centuries ago, hospitals in parts of Europe had to take precautions to see that clothing was not stolen from the bodies of people who had died, when there were so many people desperate for adequate clothing.

Ultimately the only thing that can cure poverty is wealth. While existing wealth can be transferred to the poor, there are limits to how far that can go and how much good it will do, especially in countries where there are many who are poor and few who are wealthy. What has greatly reduced poverty over time has been a dramatic increase in the total wealth available. This has been due not only to advances in technology but also to a better allocation of scarce resources which have alternative uses. It would be hard to explain the rapid economic growth in countries like India and China in the last decade of the twentieth century by any corresponding dramatic change in technology. Both countries simply began to make more use of free markets to allocate their resources—and free markets often result in higher standards of living, along with unequal rewards to individuals, industries, and regions.

When China's leader Deng Xiaoping said "Let some people get rich first," he was recognizing a trade-off between reducing poverty and reducing inequalities. India remained faithful to the egalitarianism of its early leaders for a longer time—and more of India's poor remained poor longer. However, eventually both countries ended up taking advantage of free markets internally and in international trade. So did other countries, rich and poor. As a result, *The Economist* magazine reported "rapid—indeed historically unprecedented—falls in poverty during the 1980s and 1990s, the new golden age of global capitalism." The number of poverty-stricken people in the world living on a dollar a day or less declined absolutely, despite the fact that the total population of the world was rising. When the United Nations announced in 2000 a goal to reduce the number of people living in such poverty by 2015 to one-half the level that had existed in 1990, it turned out that this goal had already been achieved—apparently unknown to the U.N. officials. The effectiveness of the market does not depend on officials understanding it.

Occupational Pay Differentials

Pay differentials are typically reflections of productivity differences and are part of the process of allocating scarce labor resources which have alternative uses. Again, a fairly obvious economic fact can become very confused when intertwined with very different moral questions about whether one group of people merit so much more than others. *Productivity and merit are wholly different things.* Someone born and raised in highly favorable circumstances may find it easier to become a brain surgeon than someone born and raised in dire circumstances may find it to become a carpenter. But that is very different from saying that brain surgeons are paid "too much" or carpenters "too little."

In policy terms, making it easier for people born in less fortunate circumstances to acquire the knowledge and skills to become brain surgeons is very different from simply decreeing that pay differentials between brain surgeons and carpenters be reduced or eliminated. The latter policy affects the allocation of resources, affecting not only how hard existing brain surgeons will work or how early they will retire, but also how many replacements they will have, as young people decide whether or not it is worth all the years and effort required to become a brain surgeon.

Those who have the biggest stake in all this are people suffering from medical conditions which require brain surgery. Despite a tendency in some quarters to see economic choices as a zero-sum activity involving a trade-off between the interests of two competing groups, very often the third parties who are ignored are affected most of all.

Unmerited misfortunes and windfall gains leave many observers uneasy, especially when these undeserved happenstances have large effects on someone's whole way of life. The desire to help the less fortunate may be especially strong, but whether a particular policy will in fact have that effect is not an easy question to answer—except for those who simply want to "do something" to express their sympathy or solidarity, without regard to the actual consequences that follow.

Promotions Ladders

Some employers have pre-arranged patterns of promotions which allow individuals to begin working at the bottom and rise up the career ladder over time. This has long been common in military forces around the world, where soldiers begin as privates and advance through the enlisted ranks as far as master sergeant, or where young officers begin as lieutenants and are later promoted to captains, majors, colonels, and—a few—to generals. Civil service offers similar promotions ladders and so do some private corporations, especially those which prefer to "promote from within" rather than bring in outsiders for their top posts.

Other enterprises without such pre-arranged promotions ladders may of course promote whatever individuals they choose to whatever higher posts they deem them qualified for, without any particular sequence being specified in advance. Jobs which are not part of any promotions ladder are often referred to as "dead-end jobs," though there is nothing to prevent any individual from going on from one "dead-end" job to a higher job, either with the same employer or a different employer, often on the basis of a good performance in the lower-level job.

What are the economic consequences of the presence or absence of promotions ladders? From the standpoint of the businesses choosing between these options, the question becomes one of weighing the benefits of retaining given employees longer, by holding out the prospect of promotion, versus the costs of passing up outsiders who might be available with higher skills or lower costs, as well as avoiding the sometimes even greater costs of creating an inbred corporate culture, wedded to particular ways of doing business. In an ever-changing economy, where rival businesses have a wider range of ways of thinking about and adjusting to changing conditions, an inbred corporate culture can put a company at a serious competitive disadvantage.

These are essentially questions about business administration. From the standpoint of economics, however, the question is how all this affects the allocation of scarce resources which have alternative uses. One consequence of pre-arranged job promotions ladders is that many people who are perfectly qualified to perform the tasks of the job that needs to be filled at the bottom of the ladder may be made artificially "unemployable" when applicants for that job are evaluated for their potential to perform more complex jobs higher up on the job ladder. For example, if a hotel were to make it a practice to recruit its desk clerks from the ranks of its bellmen, and its managers from the ranks of experienced desk clerks, then many people who were perfectly capable of doing a good job of handling luggage for hotel guests would not be hired if they showed little or no aptitude for the very different tasks of a desk clerk, much less the more complex tasks of those entering management.

Where pre-arranged promotions ladders are accompanied by egalitarian pay policies for those working at given levels, there may be no way to adequately compensate an outstanding bellman, desk clerk, or junior management official, except by promoting such individuals to higher positions. This is even more apparent in American public schools, where teachers with given seniority and credentials are usually paid the same, regardless of whether they are good, bad or indifferent in the classroom— but where much higher pay is available if they become principals or administrators in local or national education agencies. In these and other cases where promotions to jobs with very different duties are the main reward for superior performance of a given set of duties, such promotions may cost the organization—and, ultimately, the economy—the loss of an outstanding performer in a given position who becomes a mediocre (or worse) performer in a higher position with very different duties. Sometimes this is called "rising to the level of your incompetence."

Both equal pay for those in given jobs and pre-arranged promotions ladders have an appearance of orderliness and a certain plausibility on the surface, in addition to whatever real benefits they may have. In practice, however, they may not lead to the most efficient allocation of scarce resources which have alternative uses, especially when workers who are perfectly capable of performing given tasks are made "unemployable" by pre-arranged job promotions ladders which evaluate them on the basis of their aptitude for promotion to jobs dealing with very different tasks.

"Income Distribution"

In a market economy, the allocation of resources is closely related to income differences as between individuals, industries, and regions. As noted in Chapter 9, the phrase "income distribution" is misleading when income is not distributed from some central place but is instead earned individually by selling one's labor, talents, products, or property to whoever is willing to pay for them. In short, allocating resources affects income differences, as well as how high a country's average income will be. When China, for example, went from a government-controlled system of guaranteed incomes to a system of allowing markets to allocate resources, this affected both the absolute level of income in the country and differences in the amounts of income received by people in different industries and regions. Here was the situation before the reforms took effect, as described by *The Economist* magazine:

> When the economic reform era began in the late 1970s, urban residents enjoyed guaranteed jobs for life, free housing and health care. Unemployment was virtually non-existent and rural residents were banned from moving into urban areas. There was no private enterprise. Most people's lives were spartan.

This government-guaranteed subsidence for all at a poverty level was referred to as "the iron rice bowl" and it was egalitarian. This changed radically after the death of Mao Zedong in 1976. Private market activity was tried out experimentally at first in some geographic regions and some economic sectors of China. The rising prosperity in those regions and sectors where market incentives allocated resources meant a growing income inequality nationwide, since the state-run industries and sectors remained inefficient and poor. The reasons for growing inequalities, were not just that those left out of these experimental reforms did not experience the same prosperity, but also that to some extent enterprises in the state-owned and state-run sectors suffered from competition with more efficient private enterprises that produced the same products more efficiently and sold them more cheaply.

While about 9 percent of the people in China's cities lived below that country's official poverty level, the percentage was much higher in particular cities. For example, the poverty rate was 30 percent in the city of Xian, with 2.7 million people and was even more widespread "in some north-eastern cities that are home to many of the country's worst-performing state-owned industries," according to *The Economist*. Here 60 percent of the 1.8 million people in the city of Shuangyashan lived below the official poverty level. In short, the rising prosperity of China was accompanied by growing internal inequalities, as has happened in other countries at various times in history.

It would be a mistake to regard a given level of inequality at a particular time in this on-going process as a permanent inequality. That is not necessarily so for a nation any more than it is for individuals or families. As market reforms spread through China, more regions, sectors, and populations began to share in the resulting prosperity by becoming more productive in response to changing incentives. Similarly in India, which began allowing more free market activity in the 1990s, leading to higher economic growth rates nationally and differing levels of economic development in different regions, which in turn led to differences in income in general and different levels of poverty in particular. At the end of the twentieth century, the percentage of the population of India that lived below that country's official poverty level was 47 percent in the state of Orissa but only 6 percent in the Punjab.

The alternative to uneven economic development, and the income inequalities this often entails, can be egalitarian stagnation in poverty. In an ever-changing economy with new and more productive technologies emerging unpredictably and more efficient methods of organization being devised here and there at various times, to keep workers employed where they are already working is to force society to forego the economic benefits of such new developments. However, one of the problems of a transition from a system where people are paid according to government-decreed pay scales to one where people earn whatever other people are willing to pay for their labor, goods, or services is that different kinds of people gain and lose from the transition. Moreover, the initial introduction of uncertainty into a formerly controlled economic system apparently takes its toll, as a survey of European nations, including those making a transition from communism to market economies, reported:

> Over time, the first decade of reform brought declining happiness everywhere; initial euphoria rapidly gave way to frustration, insecurity and disillusion. But the good news is that happiness scores are now rising.

The rising happiness was especially pronounced among three groups—the well-educated, the self-employed, and women. Apparently all three did better when paid according to their productivity than when paid according to government-determined pay scales.

So-called "income distribution" issues within a given nation often include concern about the rich and the disproportionate share of the national income which they receive. Where the term "rich" simply refers to the top 10 percent or 20 percent of income earners as of a given time, then these are more likely to be people who have simply reached their peak earnings years—usually in their forties or fifties—rather than people who are genuinely rich in the sense of having enough wealth to live on without continuing to work. However, even considering the genuinely rich, how much do they cost the rest of society?

The total wealth of the rich—however defined—is not simply subtracted from the total output of the country, leaving less for the remainder of society. That would be true only if economic activity were a zero-sum game, with the winners gaining only what the losers lost. But Americans are not poorer by the amount of Bill Gates' fortune. On the contrary, they have gained economically by using the computer operating systems from which Gates earned his fortune. Indeed, Gates would never have amassed his fortune in the first place if individuals and enterprises had not valued what they received from his operating system more than they valued the money they paid for it.

By 1994, most American households *living below the official poverty line* had a microwave oven and a videocassette recorder, things that less than one percent of all American households had in 1971. For the population at large, homes were much bigger, automobiles were much better, and more Americans were connected to the Internet at the end of the twentieth century than were connected to a water supply at the beginning of that century. The economy was clearly not a zero-sum activity, in which what was gained by some was lost by others, despite many who think and talk as if it is. Other countries show similar patterns. In New Zealand, for example, most people whose incomes were in the lowest quarter owned a videocassette recorder, a freezer, a washing machine, and a vehicle. A country like China has not reached that level, and yet it was estimated in the early twenty-first century that a million Chinese a month were rising out of poverty. It is hard to imagine how anything could make something of that magnitude possible other than an increase in the total wealth being produced.

Media and even academic preoccupation with instant snapshot statistics create major distortions of economic reality. "The rich" and "the poor" have become staples of income discussions, even though, as noted in Chapter 9, most people in the top and bottom income categories tend to be the same people at different stages of their lives, at least in Western countries, rather than fixed classes of people who remain at the top and bottom throughout their lives. The great historic American fortunes—Carnegie, Ford, Vanderbilt, etc.—were often created by people who began in modest or even humble circumstances. Richard Warren Sears and James Cash Penney both began working to support themselves in lowly jobs at ages too young to be allowed to work under today's child labor laws, though each eventually rose to become fabulously wealthy as creators of the retail store chains that bore their respective names.

While such stories have long been part of what has been called the American Dream, dramatic social mobility has not been confined to the United States. Despite India's reputation as a rigid, caste-ridden society, it has likewise had its rags-to-riches stories, especially after more free markets began to emerge toward the end of the twentieth century. Such stories in various countries around the world have often been seen as simply examples of individual good fortune for exceptional people. But the more fundamental point is the great advantage for any society that can tap the talents of people from all across the social spectrum to develop its economy and thereby raise the living standards of the population as a whole. That is what Carnegie, Ford, Sears, and Penney did in America and what people from modest or even poverty-stricken backgrounds have begun to do in India after it moved in the direction of freer markets at the end of the twentieth century.

Infosys was started by six Indian computer engineers with a total capital of $600 among them, and it grew until the company was worth $15 billion.

Another Indian entrepreneur, Sam Pitroda, rose from poverty, having been born in a village where there were no telephones, no electricity, and no running water. He somehow made his way to the United States, where he became a millionaire in telecommunications. Then he returned to India and proceeded to revolutionize their antiquated and bureaucratically dominated telephone system. From a country with only 2.5 million phones for 700 million people in 1980, India had, by 1998, become a country with nearly 20 million phones—and the years-long waiting lists of the past had virtually disappeared. That Pitroda made a fortune during this process is a footnote to history. It is what he did for millions of other people in India that was historic. There, as in the United States, they would never have paid him the money that made up his fortune unless they valued what they received from him more than they valued the money they paid. His fortune measured the lower limit of the value he created for society as a whole.

In short, the more market-oriented economy of late twentieth-century India opened new avenues of social mobility for those at the bottom, and in the process raised the standard of living for millions of others who benefited from their contributions. Neither poverty nor caste discrimination has been ended in India but the effect of a free market has been to reduce the influence of both, as the talents of people from even lowly backgrounds have proved valuable to others. By contrast, the previous decades of socialist policies in India put an emphasis on helping "the poor" while they remained poor.

Fights over which individuals and groups get how big a slice of the national pie generate the kinds of emotions and controversies on which the media, politicians, and intellectuals thrive. But the economic reality is that the main reason most Americans or Chinese have prospered is that the pie itself has gotten much bigger, not because this group or that group changed a few percentage points in its share of the national income.

The changing allocation of scarce resources which makes continuing prosperity possible may change income percentages back and forth over time, as changing pay and employment prospects direct individuals to where their productivity would be higher and away from where it is lower. But it is changes in productivity and allocation which are crucial to the economic well-being of the population as a whole, not the few percentage point changes in relative shares which attract so much media, political, and other attention.

Employment and Unemployment

In our focus on the allocation of resources to alternative uses, we need not overlook the fact that some resources seem to have no alternative uses but simply remain idle. This happens not only during such catastrophes as the Great Depression of the 1930s, when unemployment among Americans peaked at 25 percent, but it happens on a much reduced scale all the time.

People who graduate from high school or college do not always have jobs waiting for them or find jobs the first day they start looking. Meanwhile, job vacancies remain unfilled while there are unemployed people looking for work because it takes time for the right employers and the right workers to find one another. Economists call this "frictional" unemployment. If you think of the economy as a big, complex machine, then there is always going to be some loss of efficiency by social versions of internal friction. That is why the unemployment rate is never literally zero, even in boom years when employers are having a hard time trying to find enough people to fill their job vacancies.

Transient unemployment must be distinguished from long-term unemployment. Countries differ in how long unemployment lasts. A study by the Organization for Economic Cooperation and Development showed that, among the unemployed, those who were unemployed for a year or more constituted 9 percent of all unemployed in the United States, 23 percent in Britain, and 48 percent in Germany. In short, even the difference between American and European rates of unemployment as a whole understates the difference in a worker's likelihood of finding a job. Ironically, it is in countries with strong job security laws, like Germany, where it is harder to find a new job.

All the people who are not employed are not classified as unemployed. Some are doing other things. They may be students, housewives, or retired people, for example. No one expects all children to be working and, children below some legally specified age are not allowed to be gainfully employed at all. Those officially counted as unemployed are people who are seeking employment but not finding it. This is all easy enough to understand when considering a particular country at a particular time. However, things become more complicated when looking at changing rates of employment for a given country over time or when comparing different countries at the same time. For example, *The Economist* magazine found that more than 80 percent of the male population between the ages of 15 and 64 were employed in Iceland but less than 70 percent were in France.

Any number of things could account for such differences. Not only are there variations from country to country in the number of people going to college but there are also variations in the ease or difficulty with which people qualify for government benefits that make it unnecessary for them to work, or to look for work, or to accept jobs that do not meet their hopes or expectations. High as the unemployment rate is in France by American standards, French unemployment statistics tend to **understate** how many adults are not working. That is because the French welfare state makes it easier for senior citizens to withdraw from the labor force altogether—and unemployment percentages are based on the labor force. Thus, while more than 70 percent of people who are from 55 to 64 years of age are working in Switzerland, only 37 percent of the people in those same age brackets are working in France.

The point here is that, while people who choose not to look for work are not employed, they are also not automatically classified as unemployed. Therefore statistics on employment rates and unemployment rates do not necessarily move in opposite directions. Both rates can rise at the same time or fall at the same time, depending on how easy or how difficult it is for people to live without working. One form of unemployment that has long stirred political emotions and led to economic fallacies is technological unemployment. Virtually every advance in technological efficiency puts somebody out of work. This is nothing new:

By 1830 Barthélemy Thimonnier, a French tailor who had been obsessed with the idea, had patented and perfected an effective sewing machine. When eighty of his machines were making uniforms for the French army, Paris tailors, alarmed at the threat to their jobs, smashed the machines and drove Thimonnier out of the city.

Such reactions were not peculiar to France. In early nineteenth century Britain, people called Luddites smashed machinery when they realized that the industrial revolution threatened their jobs. Opposition to technological efficiency—as well as other kinds of efficiency, from new organizational methods to international trade—has often focused on the effects of efficiency on jobs. These are almost invariably the short run effects on particular workers, in disregard of the effects on consumers or on workers in other fields. The rise of the automobile industry no doubt caused huge losses of employment among those raising and caring for horses, as well as among the makers of saddles, horseshoes, whips, horse-drawn carriages and other paraphernalia associated with this mode of transportation. But these were not *net* losses of jobs, as the automobile industry required vast numbers of workers, as did industries producing gasoline, batteries, and car repair services, as well as other sectors of the economy catering to motorists, such as motels, fast food restaurants, and suburban shopping malls.

THE MYSTIQUE OF "LABOR"

In various forms, the idea has persisted for centuries that labor is what "really" creates the output that we all live on and enjoy. In this view, it is the farmers who feed us and the factory workers who clothe us and provide us with furniture and television sets, while a variety of other workers build the homes we live in. Karl Marx took this vision to its logical conclusion by depicting capitalists, landlords and investors as people who, in one way or another, were enabled by the institutions of capitalism to take away much of what labor had created—that is, to "exploit" labor. Echoes of this vision can still be found today, not only among a relative handful of Marxists but also among non-Marxists or even anti-Marxists, who use such terms as "unearned income" to describe profits, interest, rent and dividends.

This view that there is something special about labor as a source of output, and of the value of individual commodities, existed before Marx was born—and not only among radicals, but even among such orthodox economists as Adam Smith, the father of *laissez-faire* economics. The first sentence of Smith's 1776 classic *The Wealth of Nations* says: "The annual labour of every nation is the fund which originally supplies it with all the necessaries and conveniences of life which it annually consumes, and which consist always either in the immediate produce of that labour, or in what is purchased with that produce from other nations."

By the late nineteenth century, however, economists had given up the notion that it is primarily labor which determines the value of goods, since capital, management and natural resources all contribute to output and must be paid for from the price of that output, if these inputs into the production process are to continue to be supplied. More fundamentally, labor, like all other sources of production costs, was no longer seen as a source of value. On the contrary, it was the value of the goods to the consumers which made it worthwhile to incur the costs required to produce those goods—provided that the consumer was willing to pay enough to cover these production costs.

This new understanding marked a revolution in the development of economics. It is also a sobering reminder of how long it can take for even highly intelligent people to get rid of a misconception whose fallacy then seems obvious in retrospect. It is not costs which create value; it is value which causes purchasers to be willing to pay for the costs incurred in the production of what they want. Where costs have been incurred in excess of what the consumers are willing to pay, the business simply loses money, because those costs do not create value, whether they are labor costs or other costs.

Despite the work of those who plan, manage and coordinate the activities of those who directly lay their hands on the things that are being manufactured or built, the term "labor" or "worker" is usually reserved for those who are employed by others. Thus, someone who works 35 or 40 hours a week in a factory or office is called a worker, while someone who works 50 or 60 hours a week managing the enterprise is not. Clearly, the amount of work you do is not what makes you a worker, as that term is popularly used.

What can be seen physically is always more vivid than what cannot be seen. Those who watch a factory in operation can see the workers creating a product before their eyes. They cannot see the investment which made that factory possible in the first place, much less the analysis and trial-and-error experience which made possible the technology and organization with which the workers are working or the vast amounts of knowledge and insights required to deal with ever-changing markets in an ever-changing economy and society. Ignoring or disregarding such things makes it possible to believe that only those currently handling tangible objects before our eyes are creating wealth and that any of this wealth which goes to others represents "exploitation" of its real producers.

The growth and development of such non-labor inputs as science, engineering and sophisticated investment and management policies, as well as the institutional benefits of a price-coordinated economy, have given hundreds of millions of people around the world higher standards of living. If labor were in fact the crucial source of output and prosperity, then we should expect to see countries where great masses of people toil long hours end up richer than countries where most people work shorter hours, in a more leisurely fashion, and under more pleasant conditions, often including air-conditioning, for example. In reality, we find just the opposite. Third World farmers may toil away under a hot sun and in difficult working conditions which were once common in Western nations that have long since gotten soft and prosperous under modern capitalism. It is precisely in the poorer countries of the world that the labor of adults is supplemented by the labor of children. More than half the children from ages 5 to 14 are working in Sierra Leone and more than 60 percent in Niger.

If those who are not laborers derive their wealth from exploiting labor, then we should expect to see countries with many wealthy people having ordinary working people who are especially poor. The United States, for example, not only leads the world in the number of billionaires, but has nearly as many billionaires as the rest of the world combined, so ordinary Americans should be especially poverty-stricken, if the exploitation theory is correct. But in fact ordinary Americans' standard of living has long been the envy of most of the world. Conversely, vast regions of poverty-stricken Africa have not a single billionaire. V.I. Lenin attempted to salvage the exploitation theory by claiming in his book *Imperialism* that whole rich countries exploited poor countries, thereby obtaining vast wealth, from which they could share a portion with their own working classes to keep them quiet. But the hard fact, then and now, is that rich countries primarily trade with and invest in each other, not with poor countries. Prosperous countries like the United States, Japan, and the countries of the European Union have only a minute fraction of their international economic transactions with Third World countries in sub-Saharan Africa or in the poorer parts of Asia or Latin America. If exploiting poor countries is the road to wealth, it is hard to understand why so many international investors and multinational corporations concentrate their efforts in rich countries instead of poor countries.

If inequalities of income and wealth were as repellent to most people as they are to some intellectuals, it would be hard to explain how the United States attracts more immigrants than any other country. Wage inequality has long been greater among Americans than among people working in Australia, Sweden, Britain, Germany and other countries. Yet, to the extent that people migrate for economic reasons, the absolute level of economic well-being seems to carry more weight than its distribution. The same was true back in 1982 when Ghana had a more equal distribution of income than the neighboring Ivory Coast but the latter had a higher average income. Net migration was from Ghana to the Ivory Coast.

As is so often the case, the economic realities are not very complicated, but there is nevertheless a great difficulty in extricating ourselves from tangled misconceptions and myths. This is especially so when it comes to labor, for people's work has been sufficiently central to their lives to help define who they are, as reflected in the great number of family names which are based on occupations—Shepherd, Weaver, Carpenter, Mason, Miller, Brewer, Cook, and Butler, for example. But, however emotionally powerful the role of labor may be, it is still part of the general economic pattern of the allocation of scarce resources which have alternative uses.

PART IV: TIME AND RISK

Chapter 12

INVESTMENT AND
SPECULATION

> *A tourist in New York's Greenwich Village decided to
> have his portrait sketched by a sidewalk artist. He
> received a very fine sketch, for which he was charged $100.*
> *"That's expensive," he said to the artist, "but I'll pay it,
> because it is a great sketch. But, really, it took you only five
> minutes."*
> *"Twenty years and five minutes," the artist replied.*

Artistic ability is only one of many things which are accumulated over time for use later on. *The Economist* magazine defines investment as "simply spending today that yields a stream of income in the future." More broadly, it is not simply the spending of money but, as in the case of the Greenwich Village artist, the investment of time. If the earlier costs, sacrifices and risks are ignored, then the reward for what was done within the present time period may often seen exorbitant. Oil wells can repay their costs many times over—but they must also cover the costs of all the dry holes that were drilled in the ground while searching in vain for petroleum deposits before finally striking oil.

Add to this the cost of keeping people alive while waiting for their artistic talent to develop, their oil exploration to pay off, or their academic credits to finally add up to enough to earn their degree, and there may be a considerable investment to be repaid. The repaying of the investment is not a matter of morality, but of economics. If the return on the investment is not enough to make it worthwhile, fewer people will make that particular investment in the future, and consumers will therefore be denied the use of

257

the goods and services that would otherwise have been produced. No one is under any obligation to make all investments pay off, but how many need to pay off, and to what extent, is determined by how many consumers value the benefits of other people's investments.

Where the consumers do not value what is being produced, the investment should *not* pay off. When people insist on specializing in a field for which there is little demand, their investment has been a waste of scarce resources that could have produced something else that others wanted. The low pay and sparse employment opportunities in that field are a compelling signal to them—and to others coming after them—to stop making such investments.

The principles of investment are involved in activities that do not pass through the marketplace, and are not normally thought of as economic. Putting things away after you use them is an investment of time in the present to reduce the time required to find them in the future. Explaining yourself to others can be a time-consuming, and even unpleasant, activity but it is engaged in as an investment to prevent greater unhappiness in the future from misunderstandings.

Investments take many forms, whether the investment is in human beings, steel mills, or transmission lines for electricity. Risk is an inseparable part of these investments and others. Among the ways of dealing with risk are speculation, insurance and the issuance of stocks and bonds. Among the kinds of investments to be considered here are investments in human beings, as well as investments in machinery, farm crops and hydroelectric dams.

While human capital can take many forms, there is a tendency of some to equate it with formal education. However, not only may many other valuable forms of human capital be overlooked this way, the value of formal schooling may be exaggerated and its counterproductive consequences in some cases not understood.

The industrial revolution was not created by highly educated people but by people with practical industrial experience. The airplane was invented by a couple of bicycle mechanics who had never gone to college. Electricity and many inventions run by electricity became central parts of the modern world because of a man with only three months of formal schooling,

Thomas Edison. Yet all these people had enormously valuable knowledge and insights—human capital—acquired from experience rather than in classrooms.

Education has of course also made major contributions to economic development. But this is not to say that all kinds of education have. From an economic standpoint, some education has great value, some has no value and some can even have a negative value. While it is easy to understand the great value of specific skills in medical science or engineering, for example, or the more general foundation for a number of professions provided by mathematics or a command of the English language, other subjects such as literature make no pretense of producing marketable skills but are available for whatever they may contribute in other ways. In a country where education or higher levels of education are new, those who have obtained diplomas or degrees may feel that many kinds of work are now beneath them. In such societies, even engineers may prefer the desk to standing in the mud in hip boots at a construction site. Depending on what they have studied, the newly educated may have higher levels of expectations than they have higher levels of ability to create the wealth from which their expectations can be met. In the Third World especially, those who are the first members of their respective families to reach higher education typically do not study difficult and demanding subjects like science, medicine, or engineering, but instead tend toward easier and fuzzier subjects which provide them with little in the way of marketable skills, which is to say, skills that can create prosperity for themselves or their country.

Large numbers of young people with schooling, but without economically meaningful skills, have produced much unemployment in Third World nations. Since the marketplace has little to offer such people that would be commensurate with their expectations, governments have created swollen bureaucracies to hire them, in order to neutralize their potential for political disaffection, civil unrest or insurrection. In turn, these bureaucracies and the voluminous and time-consuming red tape they generate can become obstacles to others who do have the skills and entrepreneurship needed to contribute to the country's economic advancement. In India, for example, two of its leading entrepreneurial families, the Tatas and the Birlas, were repeatedly frustrated in their efforts to obtain the necessary government permission to expand their enterprises:

> The Tatas made 119 proposals between 1960 and 1989 to start new businesses or expand old ones, and all of them ended in the wastebaskets of the bureaucrats. Aditya Birla, the young and dynamic inheritor of the Birla empire, who had trained at MIT, was so disillusioned with Indian policy that he decided to expand Birla enterprises outside India, and eventually set up dynamic companies in Thailand, Malaysia, Indonesia, and the Philippines, away from the hostile atmosphere of his home.

The vast array of government rules in India, micro-managing businesses, "ensured that every businessman would break some law or the other every month," according to an Indian executive. Large businesses in India set up their own bureaucracies in Delhi, parallel to those of the government, in order to try to keep track of the progress of their applications for the innumerable government permissions required to do things that businesses did on their own in free market economies, and to pay bribes as necessary to secure these permissions. The consequences of suffocating bureaucratic controls in India have been shown not only by such experiences while they were in full force but also by the country's dramatic economic improvements after many of these controls were relaxed or eliminated. The economy's growth rate increased dramatically after reforms in 1991 freed many of its entrepreneurs from some of the worst controls, and foreign investment in India rose from $150 million to $3 billion—in other words, by twenty times.

Hostility to entrepreneurial minorities like the Chinese in Southeast Asia or the Lebanese in West Africa has been especially fierce among the newly educated indigenous people, who see their own diplomas and degrees bringing them much less economic reward than the earnings of minority business owners who may have less formal schooling than themselves.

In short, more schooling is not automatically more human capital. It can in some cases reduce a country's ability to use the human capital that it already possesses. Moreover, to the extent that some social groups specialize in different kinds of education, or have different levels of performance as students, or attend educational institutions of differing quality, the same number of years of schooling do not mean the same education in any economically meaningful sense. Such qualitative differences have in fact been common in countries around the world, whether comparing the Chinese and the Malays in Malaysia, Sephardic and Ashkenazic Jews in Israel, Tamils and Sinhalese in Sri Lanka or comparing various ethnic groups with one another in the United States.

SPECULATION

Most market transactions involve buying things that exist, based on whatever value they have to the buyer and whatever price is charged by the seller. Some transactions, however, involve buying things that do not yet exist or whose value has yet to be determined—or both. For example, the price of stock in the Internet company Amazon.com rose for years before the company made its first dollar of profits. People were obviously speculating that the company would eventually make profits or that others would keep bidding up the price of its stock, so that the initial stockholder could sell the stock for a profit, whether or not Amazon.com itself ever made a profit. After years of operating at a loss, Amazon.com finally made its first profit in 2001. Exploring for oil is a costly speculation, since millions of dollars may be spent before discovering whether there is in fact any oil at all where the exploration is taking place, much less whether it is enough oil to repay the money spent.

Many other things are bought in hopes of future earnings which may or may not materialize—scripts for movies that may never be made, pictures painted by artists who may or may not become famous some day, and foreign currencies that may go up in value over time, but which could just as easily go down. Speculation as an economic activity may be engaged in by people in all walks of life but there are also professional speculators for whom this is their whole career. One of the professional speculator's main roles is in relieving other people from having to speculate as part of their regular economic activity. Put differently, risk is inherent in all aspects of human life. Speculation is one way of having some people specialize in bearing these risks, for a price. For such transactions to take place, the cost of the risk being transferred from its initial bearer must be greater than the price charged for the transfer—and, at the same time, the cost to the recipient of the risk must be less than the price charged. The cost to the speculator may be lower either because of more sophisticated methods of assessing risk or because the variety of the speculator's risks lowers his over-all risks.

When an American wheat farmer in Idaho or Nebraska is getting ready to plant his crop, he has no way of knowing what the price of wheat will be when the crop is harvested. That depends on innumerable other wheat farmers, not only in the United States but as far away as Russia or Argentina. If the wheat crop fails in Russia or Argentina, the world price of wheat will shoot up, causing American wheat farmers to get very high prices for their crop. But if there are bumper crops of wheat in Russia or Argentina, there may be more wheat on the world market than anybody can use, with the excess having to go into expensive storage facilities. That will cause the world price of wheat to plummet, so that the American farmer may have nothing to show for all his work and may be lucky to avoid taking a loss on the year. Meanwhile, he and his family will have to live on their savings or borrow from whatever sources will lend to them. In order to avoid having to speculate like this, the farmer may in effect pay a professional speculator to carry the risk, while the farmers stick to farming.

The speculator signs contracts to buy or sell at prices fixed today for goods to be delivered at some future date. This shifts the risk of the activity from the person engaging in it—such as the wheat farmer, in this case—to someone who is, in effect, betting that he can guess the future prices better than the other person and has the financial resources to ride out the inevitable wrong bets, in order to make a profit on the bets that turn out better.

Speculation is often misunderstood as being the same as gambling, when in fact it is the opposite of gambling. What gambling involves, whether in games of chance or in actions like playing Russian roulette, is creating a risk that would otherwise not exist, in order either to profit or to exhibit one's skill or lack of fear. What economic speculation involves is coping with an *inherent* risk in such a way as to minimize it and to leave it to be borne by whoever is best equipped to bear it.

When a commodity speculator offers to buy wheat that has not yet been planted, that makes it easier for a farmer to plant wheat, without having to wonder what the market price will be like later, at harvest time. A futures contract guarantees the seller a specified price in advance, regardless of what the market price may turn out to be at the time of delivery. This separates farming from economic speculation, allowing each to be done by different people, in each case by the person best able to do it. The speculator uses his knowledge of the market, and of economic and statistical analysis, to try to arrive at a better guess than the farmer may be able to make, and thus is able to offer a price that the farmer will consider an attractive alternative to waiting to sell at whatever price happens to prevail in the market at harvest time.

Although speculators seldom make a profit on every transaction, they must come out ahead in the long run, in order to stay in business. Their profit depends on paying the farmer a price that is lower on average than the price which actually emerges at harvest time. The farmer also knows this, of course. In effect, the farmer is paying the speculator for carrying the risk, just as one pays an insurance company. As with other goods and services, the question may be raised as to whether the service rendered is worth the price charged. At the individual level, each farmer can decide for himself whether the deal is worth it. Each speculator must of course bid against other speculators, as each farmer must compete with other farmers, whether in making futures contracts or in selling at harvest time. From the standpoint of the economy as a whole, competition determines what the price will be and therefore what the speculator's profit will be. If that profit exceeds what it takes to entice investors to risk their money in this volatile field, more investments will flow into this segment of the market until competition drives profits down to a level that just compensates the expenses, efforts, and risks.

Competition is visibly frantic among speculators who shout their offers and bids in commodity exchanges. Prices fluctuate from moment to moment and a five-minute delay in making a deal can mean the difference between profits and losses. Even a modest-sized firm engaging in commodity speculation can gain or lose hundreds of thousands of dollars in a day, and huge corporations can gain or lose millions in a few hours.

Commodity markets are not just for big businesses or even for farmers in technologically advanced countries. A *New York Times* dispatch from India reported:

> At least once a day in this village of 2,500 people, Ravi Sham Choudhry turns on the computer in his front room and logs in to the Web site of the Chicago Board of Trade.
>
> He has the dirt of a farmer under his fingernails and pecks slowly at the keys. But he knows what he wants: the prices for soybean commodity futures.

This was not an isolated case. As of 2003, there were 3,000 organizations in India putting as many as 1.8 million Indian farmers in touch with the world's commodity markets. The farmer just mentioned served as an agent for fellow farmers in surrounding villages. As one sign of how fast such Internet commodity information is spreading, Mr. Choudhry earned $300 the previous year but now earned that much in one month.

Agricultural commodities are not the only ones in which commodity traders speculate. One of the most dramatic examples of what can happen with commodity speculation involved the rise and fall of silver prices in 1980. Silver was selling at $6.00 an ounce in early 1979 but skyrocketed to a high of $50.05 an ounce by early 1980. However, this price began a decline that reached $21.62 on March 26th. Then, in just one day, that price was cut in half to $10.80. In the process, the billionaire Hunt brothers, who were speculating heavily in silver, lost more than a billion dollars *within a few weeks*. Speculation is one of the financially riskiest activities for the individual speculator, though it reduces risks for the economy as a whole.

Speculation may be engaged in by people who are not normally thought of as speculators. As far back as the 1870s, a food-processing company headed by Henry Heinz signed contracts to buy cucumbers from farmers at pre-arranged prices, regardless of what the market prices might be when the cucumbers were harvested. Then as now, those farmers who did *not* sign futures contracts with anyone were necessarily engaging in speculation about prices at harvest time, whether or not they thought of themselves as speculators. Incidentally, the deal proved to be disastrous for Heinz when there was a bumper crop of cucumbers, well beyond what he expected or could afford to buy, forcing him into bankruptcy. It took him years to recover financially and start over, eventually founding the H. J. Heinz Company that continues to exist today.

Because risk is the whole reason for speculation in the first place, being wrong is a common experience, though being wrong too often means facing financial extinction. Predictions, even by very knowledgeable people, can be wrong by vast amounts. The distinguished British magazine *The Economist* predicted in March 1999 that the price of a barrel of oil "may be heading for $5," but in fact the price of oil *rose* to $25 a barrel by December. Anyone speculating in oil on the basis of *The Economist's* statement could have been ruined financially. Had they signed a contract in March to sell oil at $10 a barrel in December, they might have expected a profit of $5 a barrel, but they would have ended up with losses of $15 a barrel, which can get very expensive for anyone selling an oil tanker's cargo. Futures contracts are made for delivery of gold, oil, soybeans, foreign currencies and many other things at some price fixed in advance for delivery on a future date. Commodity speculation is only one kind of speculation. People also speculate in real estate, corporate stocks, or other things.

The full cost of risk is not only the amount of money involved, it is also the worry that hangs over the individual while waiting to see what happens. A farmer may expect to get $100 a ton for his crop but also knows that it could turn out to be $50 a ton or $150. If a speculator offers to guarantee to buy his crop at $90 a ton, that price may look good if it spares the farmer months of sleepless nights wondering how he is going to support his family if the harvest price leaves him nothing to cover his costs. Not only may the speculator be better equipped financially to deal with being wrong, he may be better equipped psychologically, since the kind of people who worry a lot do not usually go into commodity speculation. A commodity speculator I know had one year when his business was operating at a loss going into December, but things changed so much in December that he still ended up with a profit for the year—to his surprise, as much as anyone else's. This is not an occupation for the faint of heart.

Economic speculation is another way of allocating scarce resources—in this case, knowledge. Neither the speculator nor the farmer knows what the prices will be when the crop is harvested. But the speculator happens to have more knowledge of markets and of economic and statistical analysis than the farmer, just as the farmer has more knowledge of how to grow the crop. My commodity speculator friend admitted that he had never actually seen a soybean and had no idea what they looked like, even though he had probably bought and sold millions of dollars worth of them over the years. He simply transferred ownership of his soybeans on paper to soybean buyers at harvest time, without ever taking physical possession of them from the farmer. He was not really in the soybean business, he was in the risk management business.

Speculation means that complementary knowledge is thus coordinated, creating greater efficiency in the production of products which have inherent risks associated with their production. These risks can never be eliminated, but they can be minimized by having them borne by those best able to bear them, both from the standpoint of specialized knowledge and skills and from the standpoint of having sufficient financial accumulations to ride out losing speculations while waiting for them to be offset by winning speculations in the long run.

INVENTORIES

Inherent risks must be dealt with by the economy not only through economic speculation but also by maintaining inventories.

Put differently, *inventory is a substitute for knowledge.* No food would ever be thrown out after a meal, if the cook knew beforehand exactly how much each person would eat and could therefore cook just that amount. Since inventory costs money, a business enterprise must try to limit how much inventory it has on hand, while at the same time not risking running out of their product and thereby missing sales. Having either too large or too small an inventory means losing money. One of the factors in the success of Dell computers has been its ability to operate with only enough inventory to last for five days, while its competitors' inventories are some multiple of that.

Clearly, those businesses which come closest to the optimal size of inventory will have their profit prospects enhanced. More important, the total resources of the economy will be allocated more efficiently, not only because each enterprise has an incentive to be efficient, but also because those firms which turn out to be right more often are more likely to survive and continue making such decisions, while those who repeatedly carry far too large an inventory, or far too small, are likely to disappear from the market through bankruptcy. Too large an inventory means excess costs of doing business, compared to the costs of their competitors, who are therefore in a position to sell at lower prices and take away customers. Too small an inventory means running out of what the customers want, not only missing out on immediate sales but also risking having those customers look elsewhere for more dependable suppliers in the future. As noted in Chapter 6, in an economy where deliveries of goods and parts were always uncertain, such as that of the Soviet Union, huge inventories were the norm.

Some of the same economic principles involving risk apply to activities far removed from the marketplace. A soldier going into battle does not take just the number of bullets he will fire or just the amount of first aid supplies he will need if wounded in a particular way, because neither he nor anyone else has the kind of foresight required to do that. The soldier carries an inventory of both ammunition and medical supplies to cover various contingencies. At the same time, he cannot go into battle loaded down with huge amounts of everything that he might possibly need in every conceivable circumstance. That would slow him down and reduce his maneuverability, making him an easier target for the enemy. In other words, beyond some point, attempts to increase his safety can make his situation more dangerous.

Inventory is related to knowledge and risk in another way. In normal times, each business tends to keep a certain ratio of inventory to its sales. However, when times are more uncertain, such as during a recession or depression, sales may be made from existing inventories without producing replacements. During the third quarter of 2003, for example, as the United

States was recovering from a recession, sales, exports, and profits were rising but, *BusinessWeek* magazine reported that manufacturers, wholesalers, and retailers were "selling goods off their shelves" and "the ratio of inventories to sales hit a record low."

The net result was that far fewer jobs were created than in periods of similar business prosperity in the past. This was due to a "lack of confidence" as to how long this prosperity would last. In short, for sellers the selling of inventory was a way of coping with economic risks. Only after inventories had hit bottom did the hiring of more people to produce more goods increase on such a large scale as to make the phrase "a jobless recovery" no longer applicable.

RETURN ON INVESTMENT

Delayed rewards for costs incurred earlier are a return on investment, whether these rewards take the form of dividends paid on corporate stock or increases in incomes resulting from having gone to college or medical school. One of the largest investments in many people's lives consists of the time and energy expended over a period of years in raising their children. At one time, the return on that investment included having the children take care of the parents in old age, but today the return on this investment often consists only of the parents' satisfaction in seeing their children's well-being and progress. From the standpoint of society as a whole, each generation that makes this investment in its offspring is repaying the investment that was made by the previous generation in raising those who are parents today.

"Unearned Income"

Although making investments and receiving the delayed return on those investments takes many forms and has been going on all over the world throughout the history of the human race, misunderstandings of this process have also been long standing and widespread. Sometimes these delayed benefits are called "unearned" income, simply because they do not represent rewards for contributions made during the current time period. Investments that build a factory may not be repaid until years later, after workers and managers have been hired and products manufactured and sold. During the particular year when dividends finally begin to be paid, investors may not have contributed anything, but this does not mean that the reward they receive is "unearned," simply because it was not earned during that particular year.

As noted in Chapter 11, the activities taking place in a factory before our eyes are not the only source of the business' success. Risks are invisible, even when they are present risks, and the past risks surrounding the initial creation of the business are readily forgotten by observers who see only a successful enterprise after the fact. Also easily overlooked are the many management decisions that had to be made in determining where to locate, what kind of equipment to acquire, and what policies to follow in dealing with suppliers, consumers, and employees—any one of which decisions could spell the difference between success and failure. And of course what also cannot be seen are all the similar businesses that went out of business because they did not do all the things done by the surviving business before our eyes, or did not do them equally well.

Because what is immediately visible to the naked eye makes a more lasting impression than past or present factors invisible inside other people's heads, it is easy to regard the visible factors as the sole or most important factors, even when other businesses with those same visible factors went bankrupt, while an expertly managed enterprise in the same industry flourished and grew. Nor are such misunderstandings inconsequential. Elaborate ideologies and mass movements have been based on the notion that only the workers really create wealth, while others merely skim off profits, without having contributed anything to producing the wealth in which they unjustly share.

Similar misconceptions have had fateful consequences for money-lenders around the world. For many centuries, money-lenders have been widely condemned in many cultures for receiving back more money than they lent—that is, for getting an "unearned" income for waiting and taking risks. Often the social stigma attached to money lending has been so great that only minorities who lived outside the existing social system anyway have been willing to take on such stigmatized activities. Thus, for centuries, Jews predominated in such occupations in Europe, as the Chinese did in Southeast Asia, the Chettiars and Marwaris in India, and other minority groups in other parts of the world. At various times and places, the hostility to such groups has reached the point where these minorities have been expelled by governments or have been forced to flee from mob violence. Although often depicted as useless parasites, the contribution of money-lending minorities has been demonstrated after their departure by shortages of credit and general economic declines in the countries that forced them out.

Misconceptions about money-lending often take the form of laws attempting to help borrowers by giving them more leeway in repaying loans. But anything that makes it difficult to collect a debt makes it less likely that loans will be made in the first place. In some societies, people are not expected to charge interest on loans to relatives or fellow members of the local community, nor to be insistent on prompt payment according to the letter of the loan agreement. These kinds of preconditions discourage loans from being made and sometimes they discourage individuals from letting it be known that they have enough money to be able to lend. In societies where such social pressures are particularly strong, incentives for acquiring wealth are reduced. This is not only a loss to the individual who might otherwise have made wealth by going all out, it is a loss to the whole society when people who are capable of producing things that many others are willing to pay for may not choose to go all out in doing so.

Investment and Allocation

Just as prices in general affect the allocation of resources from one place to another at a given time, so returns on investment affect the allocation of resources from one time period to another. A high rate of return provides incentives for people to save and invest more than they would at a lower rate of return. To say the same thing differently, a higher rate of return encourages people to consume less in the present, in order to consume more in the future. It allocates resources over time. The individual saver need not invest directly. Money saved in a bank, for example, may be lent out to someone else and invested in establishing or enlarging a business.

Investment plays another very important role in the economy. When teenage Henry Ford walked from the farm where he worked all the way into Detroit, in order to look for a job, he clearly did not have the kind of money needed to manufacture millions of automobiles. Where did he get that money, then? Obviously, someone else thought enough of his ideas and abilities to risk some money backing him to get started. As he proved himself at one step after another, more and more people were willing to put their money behind him, in order to cash in on the product and the mass-production industry that he was creating. Investment is a way of transferring resources to where they have alternative uses that are more valuable than where they are.

Nor was Henry Ford unique. The Hewlett-Packard hi-tech corporate empire began in a garage rented with borrowed money. Numerous other entrepreneurs, starting with little more than an idea and determination, have found investors willing to take a chance on them, just as investors take chances on oil wells or soybean futures. Although willing to take risks, these investors cannot be reckless or they will end up with nothing to invest. In this way, entrepreneurial talent gets a chance to prove itself in the marketplace, even if that talent originates in someone with no money of his own and utterly unknown to the general public or to the political powers that be. It is yet another way in which a free market system taps knowledge and abilities that have no avenues to emerge in more restrictive societies. This is often looked at in terms of a benefit to a fortunate few who are allowed to rise in the economic system but its more consequential impact is in allowing whole populations to rise in prosperity by tapping the talents and insights of people scattered across a vast social spectrum.

Interest, as the price paid for investment funds, plays the same allocational role as other prices in bringing supply and demand into balance. When interest rates are low, it is more profitable to borrow money to invest in building houses or modernizing a factory or other economic ventures. On the other hand, low interest rates make saving money less attractive. Higher interest rates lead more people to save more money but lead fewer investors to borrow that money. As with supply and demand for products in general, imbalances between supply and demand for money lead to rises or falls in the price—in this case, the interest rate. When the supply of savings exceeds the demand to invest those savings, the interest rate goes down as lenders discover that they can no longer find borrowers for all the money they want to lend at the existing interest rate. But, when investors are demanding more loans than the lenders can supply at the existing interest rate, that interest rate rises, making investors less eager to borrow and savers more willing to save. As *The Economist* magazine put it:

> Most of the time, mismatches between the desired levels of saving and investment are brought into line fairly easily through the interest-rate mechanism. If people's desire to save exceeds their desire to invest, interest rates will fall so that the incentive to save goes down and the willingness to invest goes up.

PRESENT VALUE

Although many goods and services are bought for immediate use, many other benefits come in a stream over time, whether as a season's ticket to baseball games or an annuity that will make monthly pension payments to you after you retire. That whole stream of benefits may be purchased at a given moment for what economists call its "present value." However, more is involved than simply determining the price to be paid, important as that is. The implications of present value affect economic decisions and their consequences, even in areas that are not normally thought of as economic, such as determining the amount of natural resources available for future generations.

Prices and Present Values

Whether a home, business, or farm is maintained, repaired or improved today determines how long it will last and how well it will operate in the future. However, the owner who has put in these improvements does not have to wait to see the future effects on the property's value. These future benefits are immediately reflected in the property's *present value*. The "present value" of an asset is in fact nothing more than its anticipated future benefits, added up and discounted for the fact that they are delayed. Your home, business, or farm may be functioning no better than your neighbor's today, but if the prospective toll of wear and tear on your property over time is reduced by installing heavier pipes, stronger woods, or other more durable building materials, then your property's market value will *immediately* be worth more than that of your neighbor, even if there is no visible difference in the way they are functioning today.

Conversely, if the city announces that it is going to begin building a sewage treatment plant next year, on a piece of land next to your home, the value of your home will decline *immediately*, before the adjoining land has been touched. The present value of an asset reflects its future benefits or detriments, so that anything which is expected to enhance or reduce those benefits or detriments will immediately affect the price at which the asset can be sold today.

Present value links the future to the present. It makes sense for a ninety-year-old man to begin planting fruit trees that will take 20 years before they reach their maturity because his land will *immediately* be worth more as a result of those trees. He can sell the land a month later and go live in the Bahamas if he wishes, because he will be receiving additional value from the fruit that is expected to grow on those trees, years after he is no longer alive. Part of the value of his wealth today consists of the value of food that has not yet been grown—and which will be eaten by children who have not yet been born.

One of the big differences between economics and politics is that politicians are not forced to pay attention to future consequences that lie beyond the next election. An elected official whose policies keep the public happy up through election day stands a good chance of being voted another term in office, even if those policies will have ruinous consequences in later years. There is no "present value" to make political decision-makers today take future consequences into account, when those consequences will come after election day.

Although the general public may not have sufficient knowledge or training to realize the long-run implications of today's policies, financial specialists who deal in government bonds do. Thus the Standard & Poor's bond-rating service downgraded California's state bonds in the midst of that state's electricity crisis in 2001, even though there had been no defaults on those bonds, nor any lesser payments made to those who had bought California bonds, and there were billions of dollars of surplus in the state's treasury. What Standard & Poor's understood was that the heavy financial responsibilities taken on by the California government to meet the electricity crisis meant that heavy taxes or heavy debt were waiting over the horizon. That increased the risk of future defaults or delay in payments to bondholders—thereby reducing the present value of those bonds.

Any series of future payments can be reduced to a present value that can be paid immediately in a lump sum. Winners of lotteries who are paid in installments over a period of years can sell those payments to a financial institution that will give them a fixed sum immediately. So can accident victims who have been awarded installment payments from insurance companies. Because the present value of a series of payments due over a period of decades may be considerably less than the sum total of all those payments, due to discounting for delays, the lump sums paid may be less than half of those totals, causing some people who sold to relieve immediate financial problems to later resent the deal they made. Others, however, are pleased and return to make similar deals in the future.

Conversely, some individuals wish to convert a fixed sum of money into a stream of future payments. Elderly people who are retiring with what seems like an adequate amount to live on must be concerned with whether they will live longer than expected—"outlive their money" as the expression goes—and end up in poverty. In order to avoid this, they may use a portion of their money to purchase an annuity from an insurance company. For example, in the early twenty-first century, a seventy year old man could purchase an annuity for $100,000 and thereafter receive $772 a month for life—whether that life was three more years or thirty more years. In other words, the risk would be shifted to the insurance company, for a price. As in other cases, the risk is not only shifted but reduced, since the insurance company can more accurately predict the average lifespan of millions of people to whom it has sold annuities than any given individual can predict his own lifespan. Incidentally, a woman aged 70 would get somewhat smaller monthly payments—$725—for the same price, given that women usually live longer than men.

The key point is that the reduced risk comes from the greater predictability of large numbers. A news story some years ago told of a speculator who made a deal with an elderly woman who needed money. In exchange for her making him the heir to her house, he agreed to pay her a fixed sum every month as long as she lived. However, this one-to-one deal did not work out as planned because she lived far longer than anyone expected and the speculator died before she did. An insurance company not only has the advantage of large numbers, it has the further advantage that its existence is not limited to the human lifespan.

Natural Resources

Present value profoundly affects the discovery and use of natural resources. There may be enough oil underground to last for centuries, but its present value determines how much oil will repay what it costs anyone to discover it at any given time—and that may be no more than enough oil to last for a dozen or so years. A failure to understand this basic economic reality has, for many years, led to numerous and widely publicized false predictions that we were "running out" of petroleum, coal, or some other natural resource.

In 1960, for example, a best-selling book said that the United States had only a 13-year supply of domestic petroleum at the existing rate of usage. At that time, the known petroleum reserves of the United States were not quite 32 billion barrels. At the end of the 13 years, the known petroleum reserves of the United States were more than 36 billion barrels. Yet the original statistics and the arithmetic based on them were both accurate. Why then did the United States not run out of oil by 1973? Was it just dumb luck that more oil was discovered—or were there more fundamental economic reasons?

Just as shortages and surpluses are not simply a matter of how much physical stuff there is, either absolutely or relative to the population, so known reserves of natural resources are not simply a matter of how much physical stuff there is underground. For natural resources as well, prices are crucial. So are present values.

How much of any given natural resource is known to exist depends on how much it costs to know. Oil exploration, for example, is very costly. This includes not only the costs of geological exploration but also the costs of drilling expensive dry holes before finally striking oil. As these costs mount up while more and more oil is being discovered, the growing abundance of known supplies of oil reduces its price through supply and demand. Eventually the point is reached where the cost per barrel of finding more oil in a given place and processing it exceeds the present value per barrel of the oil that you are likely to find there. At that point, it no longer pays to keep exploring. Depending on a number of circumstances, the total amount of oil discovered at that point may well be no more than the 13 years' supply which led to dire predictions that we were running out. Only as the existing supplies of oil are being used up will rising prices lead to more huge investments in oil exploration.

As one example of the kinds of costs that can be involved, a major oil exploration venture in the Gulf of Mexico spent $80 million on the initial exploration and leases, and another $120 million for exploratory drilling, just to see if it looked like there was enough oil to justify continuing further. Then there were $530 million spent for building drilling platforms, pipelines, and other infrastructure, and—finally—$370 million for drilling for oil where there were proven reserves. This adds up to a total of $1.1 billion.

Imagine if the interest rate had been twice as high on this much money borrowed from banks or investors, making the total cost of exploration even higher. Or imagine that the oil companies had this much money of their own and could put it in a bank to earn twice the usual interest in safety. Would they have sunk as much money as they did into the more risky investment of looking for oil? Would you? Probably not. A higher interest rate would probably have meant less oil exploration and therefore smaller amounts of known reserves of petroleum. But that would not mean that we were any closer to running out of oil than if the interest rate were lower and the known reserves were correspondingly higher.

As more and more of the known reserves of oil get used up, the present value of the remaining oil begins to rise and once more exploration for additional oil becomes profitable. But, as of any given time, it never pays to discover all the oil that exists in the ground or under the sea. In fact, it does not pay to discover more than a minute fraction of that oil. What does pay is for people to write hysterical predictions that we are running out of natural resources. It pays not only in book sales and television ratings, but also in political power and in personal notoriety. Even the huge usages of energy resources in the twentieth century have not reduced the known reserves of the natural resources used to generate that energy. Given the enormous drain on energy resources created historically by such things as the spread of railroad networks, factory machinery, and the electrification of cities, it has been estimated that more energy was consumed in the first two decades of the twentieth century than in all the previously recorded history of the human race. Moreover, energy usage has continued to escalate since then. Yet known petroleum reserves have risen. At the end of the twentieth century, the known reserves of petroleum were more than ten times as large as they were in the middle of the twentieth century. Improvements in technology have made oil discovery and its extraction more efficient. In the 1970s, only about one-sixth of all wells drilled in search of oil turned out to actually produce oil. But, by the early twenty-first century, two-thirds of these exploratory wells produced oil.

The economic considerations which apply to petroleum apply to other natural resources as well. No matter how much iron ore there is in the ground, it will never pay to discover more of it when its present value per ton is less than the cost per ton of exploration and processing. Yet, despite the fact that the twentieth century saw vast expansions in the use of iron and steel, the proven reserves of iron ore increased several fold. So have the known reserves of copper, aluminum, and lead, among other natural resources. As of 1945, the known reserves of copper were 100 million metric tons. After a quarter of a century of unprecedented use of copper, the known reserves of copper were *three times* what they were at the outset and, by 1999, copper reserves had doubled again.

Even after a pool of petroleum has been discovered underground or under the sea and the oil is being extracted and processed, economic considerations prevent that pool of oil from being drained dry. As *The Economist* magazine put it:

> A few decades ago, the average oil recovery rate from reservoirs was 20%; thanks to remarkable advances in technology, this has risen to about 35% today.

In other words, about two-thirds of the oil in an underground pool is left in the pool because it would be too costly to drain all of it—or even most of it—with today's technology and today's oil prices. But the oil is still there and its location is known. If and when we are genuinely "running out" of oil that is available at today's costs of extraction and processing, then the next step would be to begin extracting and processing oil that costs a little more and, later, oil that costs a little more than that. But we are clearly not at that point when most of the oil that has been discovered is still left underground or under the sea. Nor is this situation unique to petroleum. When coal was readily available above ground, it did not pay to dig into the ground and build coal mines, since the coal extracted at higher costs underground could not compete in price with coal that could be gathered at lower cost on the surface. Only after the coal available at the lowest cost was exhausted did it pay to begin digging in the ground for more.

The difference between the economic approach and the hysterical approach to natural resource usage was shown by a bet between the late economist Julian Simon and environmentalist Paul Ehrlich. Professor Simon offered to bet anyone that any set of five natural resources they chose would not have risen in real cost over any time period they chose. A group led by Professor Ehrlich took the bet and chose five natural resources. They also chose ten years as the time period for measuring how the real costs of these natural resources had changed. At the end of that decade, not only had the real cost of that set of five resources declined, so had the cost of every single resource which they had expected to rise in cost! Obviously, if we had been anywhere close to running out of those resources, their costs would have risen because the present value of these potentially more scarce resources would have risen.

In some ultimate sense, the total quantity of resources must of course be declining. However, a resource that is going to run out centuries after it becomes obsolete, or a thousand years after the sun grows cold, is not a serious practical problem. If it is going to run out within some time period that is a matter of practical relevance, then the rising present value of the resource whose exhaustion looms ahead will automatically force conservation, without either public hysteria or political exhortation.

Just as prices cause us to share scarce resources and their products with others at a given time, present value causes us to share those resources over time with future generations—without even being aware that we are sharing. It is of course also possible to share politically, by having the government assume control of natural resources, as it can assume control of other assets, or in fact of the whole economy.

The efficiency of political control versus impersonal control by prices in the marketplace depends in part on which method conveys the underlying realities more accurately. As already noted in earlier chapters, price controls and direct allocation of resources by political institutions require far more explicit knowledge by a relatively small number of planners than is required for a market economy to be coordinated by prices to which millions of people respond according to their own first-hand knowledge of their own individual circumstances and preferences—and the relative handful of prices that each individual has to deal with. Planners can easily make false projections, either from ignorance or from various political motives, such as seeking more power, re-election, or other goals. For example, during the 1970s, a government scientist was asked to estimate the size of the American reserves of natural gas and how long it would last at the current rate of usage. His estimate was that the United States had enough natural gas to last for 4,000 years! While some might consider this good news, politically it was bad news at a time when the President of the United States was trying to arouse public support for more government programs to deal with the energy "crisis." This estimate was repudiated by the Carter administration and a new study begun, which reached more politically acceptable results.

Sometimes the known reserves of a natural resource seem especially small because the amount available at currently feasible costs is in fact nearing exhaustion within a few years. There may be vast amounts available at a slightly higher cost of extraction and processing, but these additional amounts will of course not be touched until the amount available at a lower cost is exhausted. For example, back when there were large coal deposits available on top of the ground, someone could sound an alarm that we are "running out" of coal that is "economically feasible" to use, coal that can be gotten without "prohibitive costs." But again, the whole purpose of prices is to be prohibitive. In this case, that prohibition prevented more costly resources from being used needlessly, so long as there were less costly sources of the same resource available. A similar situation exists today, when two-thirds of the petroleum found in an oil pool is left there because the costs of extracting more than the most easily accessible oil cannot be repaid by the current market price.

During the oil crisis of 2005, when the price of gasoline in the United States shot up to double what it had been less than two years earlier, and people worried that the world was running out of petroleum, the *Wall Street Journal* reported:

> The Athabasca region in Alberta, Canada, for instance, theoretically could produce about 1.7 trillion to 2.5 trillion barrels of oil from its 54,000 square miles of oil-sands deposits—making it second to Saudi Arabia in oil reserves. The Athabasca reserves remain largely untapped because getting the oil out of the sand is expensive and complicated. It takes about two tons of sand to extract one barrel of oil. But if oil prices remain near current levels—indeed, if prices stay above $30 a barrel, as they have since late 2003—oil-sands production would be profitable. Limited investment and production have been under way in Athabasca.

If technology never improved, then all resources would become more costly over time, as the most easily obtained and most easily processed deposits were used up first and the less accessible, or less rich, or more difficult to process deposits were then resorted to. However, with improving technology, it can actually cost less to acquire future resources when their time comes, as happened with the resources that Julian Simon and Paul Ehrlich bet on. For example, the average cost of finding a barrel of oil fell from $15 in 1977 to $5 by 1998. It is hardly surprising that there were larger known oil reserves after the cost of knowing fell.

Although the reserves of natural resources in a nation are often discussed in terms of physical quantities, economic concepts of cost, prices, and present values must be considered if practical conclusions are to be reached. In addition to needless alarms about natural resources running out, there have also been, conversely, unjustifiably optimistic statements that some poor country has so many billions of dollars' worth of "natural wealth" in the form of iron ore or bauxite deposits or some other natural resource. Such statements mean very little without considering how much it would cost to extract and process those resources. A country with $10 billion worth of some natural resource might as well not have it if the costs of exploration, extraction and processing add up to $11 billion. Only if the demand for that resource rises enough in the future to raise its price above the costs of using it, or if future technological improvements lower the costs of producing it, would this resource become economically relevant.

Chapter 13

RISKS AND INSURANCE

Even in ancient times the risks of merchants and mariners, the dangers from disaster at sea and fire on land induced people who had large stakes to lose to pay others to share their risks.

Daniel J. Boorstin

Risks inherent in economic activities can be dealt with in a wide variety of ways. In addition to the commodity speculation and inventory management discussed in the previous chapter, other ways of dealing with risk include stocks, bonds, and insurance. There are also other economic activities analogous to stocks, bonds, and insurance which deal with risks in ways that are legally different, though similar economically. Conversely, there are sources of income which seem similar to ordinary wages, salaries and profits but which are in fact quite different. These include capital gains. There are also systems that call themselves "social insurance" which are not insurance at all. Here, as in so many other places, we cannot go by words but must examine the underlying reality.

Whenever a home, a business, or any other asset increases in value over time, that increase is called a "capital gain." While it is another form of income, it differs from wages and salaries in not being paid right after it is earned, but usually only after an interval of some years. A thirty-year bond, for example, can be cashed in only after thirty years. If you never sell your home, then whatever increase in value it has will be called an "unrealized capital gain." The same is true for someone who opens a grocery store that grows more valuable as its location becomes known throughout the neighborhood, and as it develops a set of customers who get into the habit of shopping at that particular store. Perhaps after the owner dies, his widow or children may decide to sell the store—and only then will the capital gain be realized.

Sometimes a capital gain comes from a purely financial transaction, where you simply pay someone a certain amount of money today in order to get back a somewhat larger amount of money later on. This happens when you put money into a savings account that pays interest, or when a pawnbroker lends money, or when you buy a $10,000 U. S. Treasury bond for somewhat less than $10,000.

However it is done, this is a trade-off of money today for money in the future. The fact that interest is paid implies that money today is worth more than the same amount of money in the future. How much more depends on many things, and varies from time to time, as well as from country to country at the same time.

BONDS

In the heyday of 19th-century British industrialization, railroad companies could raise the huge sums of money required to build miles of tracks and buy trains, by selling bonds that paid about 3 percent per year. This was possible only because the public had great confidence in both the railroads and the stability of the money. If inflation had been 4 percent a year, those who bought the bonds would have lost real value instead of gaining it. But the value of the British pound sterling was very stable and reliable during that era.

Since those times, inflation has become more common, so the interest rate would now have to cover whatever level of inflation was expected and still leave a prospect of a real gain in terms of an increase in purchasing power. The risk of inflation varies from country to country and from one era to another, so the rate of return on investments must include an allowance for the risk of inflation, which also varies. At the beginning of the twenty-first century, Mexico's government bonds paid a quarter of a point higher interest than those of the United States, while those of Brazil paid half a point higher than those of Mexico. Brazil's interest rate then shot up another percentage point after the emergence of a left-wing candidate for president of the country. Varying risks are reflected in varying risk premiums added to interest rates. As of April 2003, short-term interest rates ranged from less than 2 percent in Hong Kong to 18 percent in Russia and 39 percent in Turkey.

Leaving inflation aside, however, how much would a $10,000 bond that matures a year from now be worth to you today? That is, how much would you bid today for a bond that can be cashed in for $10,000 next year? Clearly it would not be worth $10,000, because future money is not as valuable as the same amount of present money. Even if you felt certain that you would still be alive a year from now, and even if there were no inflation expected, you would still prefer to have the same amount of money right now rather than later. If nothing else, money that you have today can be put in a bank and earn a year's interest on it. For the same reason, if you had a choice between buying a bond that matures a year from now and another bond of the same face value that matures ten years from now, you would not be willing to bid as much for the one that matures a decade later. What this says is that the same nominal amount of money has different values, depending on how long you must wait to get a return on it.

At a sufficiently high interest rate, you might be willing to wait a long time to get your money back. People buy 30-year bonds regularly, though usually at a higher rate of return than what is paid on financial securities that mature in a year or a decade. On the other hand, at a sufficiently low interest rate, you would not be willing to wait any time at all to get your money back. Somewhere in between is an interest rate at which you would be indifferent between lending money or keeping it. At that interest rate, the present value of a given amount of future money is equal to some smaller amount of present money. For example if you are indifferent at 4 percent, then a hundred dollars today is worth $104 a year from now to you. Any business or government agency that wants to borrow $100 from you today with a promise to pay you back a year from now will have to make that repayment at least $104. If everyone else has the same preferences that you do, then the interest rate in the economy as a whole will be 4 percent.

What if everyone does not have the same preferences that you do? Suppose that others will lend only when they get back 5 percent more at the end of the year? In that case, the interest rate in the economy as a whole will be 5 percent, simply because businesses and government cannot borrow the money they want for any less and they do not have to offer any more. Faced with a national interest rate of 5 percent, you would have no reason to accept less, even though you would take 4 percent if you had to.

In this situation, let us return to the question of how much you would be willing to bid for a $10,000 bond that matures a year from now. With an interest rate of 5 percent being available in the economy as a whole, it would not pay you to bid more than $9,523.81 for a $10,000 bond that matures a year from now. By investing that same amount of money somewhere else today at 5 percent, you could get back $10,000 in a year. Therefore, there is no reason for you to bid more than $9,523.81 for the $10,000 bond. What if the interest rate in the economy as a whole had been 12 percent, rather than 5 percent? Then it would not pay you to bid more than $8,928.57 for a $10,000 bond that matures a year from now. In short, what people will bid for bonds depends on how much they could get for the same money by putting it somewhere else. That is why bond prices go down when the interest rate goes up, and vice-versa.

What this also says is that, when the interest rate is 5 percent, $9,523.81 in the year 2000 is the same as $10,000 in the year 2001. This raises questions about the taxation of capital gains. If someone buys a bond for the former price and sells it a year later for the latter price, the government will of course want to tax the $476.19 difference. But is that really the same as an increase in value, if the two sums of money are just equivalent to one another? What if there has been a one percent inflation, so that the $10,000 received back would not have been enough to compensate for waiting, if the investor had expected inflation to reduce the real value of the bond? What if there had been a 5 percent inflation, so that the amount received back was worth no more than the amount originally lent, with no reward at all for waiting? Clearly, the investor would be worse off than if he or she had never bought the bond. How then can this "capital gain" really be said to be a gain?

These are just some of the considerations that make the taxation of capital gains more complicated than the taxation of such other forms of income as wages and salaries. Some governments in some countries do not tax capital gains at all, while the rate at which such gains are taxed in the United States remains a matter of political controversy.

VARIABLE RETURNS VERSUS FIXED RETURNS

There are many ways of confronting the fact that the real value of a given sum of money varies with when it is received and with the varying likelihood that it will be received at all. Stocks and bonds are among the many ways of dealing with differing risks. But people who have no interest in buying these financial securities must also confront the same principles in other ways, when choosing a career for themselves or when considering public policy issues for the country as a whole.

Stocks versus Bonds

Bonds differ from stocks because bonds are legal commitments to pay fixed amounts of money on a fixed date. Stocks are simply shares of the business that issues them, and there is no guarantee that the business will make a profit in the first place, much less pay out dividends instead of re-investing these profits in the business itself. Bond-holders have a legal right to be paid what they were promised, whether the business is making money or losing money. In that respect, they are like the business' employees, to whom fixed commitments have been made as to how much they would be paid per hour or per week or per month. They are legally entitled to those amounts, regardless of whether the business is profitable or unprofitable. The owners of a business—whether that is a single individual or millions of stockholders—are not legally entitled to anything, except whatever happens to be left over after a business has paid its employees, bond-holders and other creditors. Considering the fact that most new businesses fail within a few years, what is left over can just as easily be negative as positive. In other words, people who set up businesses may not only fail to make a profit but may even lose part or all of what they originally invested. In short, stocks and bonds have different amounts of risk. Moreover, the mixture of stocks and bonds sold by different kinds of businesses may reflect the inherent risks of those businesses themselves.

Imagine that someone is raising money to go into a business where (1) the chances are 50-50 that he will go bankrupt and (2) if the business does survive financially, the value of the initial investment will increase ten-fold. Perhaps the entrepreneur is drilling for oil or speculating in foreign currencies. What if he wants you to contribute $5,000 to this venture? If you can afford the risk, would you be better off buying $5,000 worth of stock in this enterprise or $5,000 worth of this company's bonds?

If you buy bonds, your chances are still only 50-50 of getting all your money back. And if this enterprise prospers, you are only entitled to whatever rate of return was specified in the bond at the outset, no matter how many millions of dollars the entrepreneur makes with your money. Buying bonds in such a venture does not seem like a good deal. Buying stocks, on the other hand, might make sense. If the business goes bankrupt, your stock could be worthless, while a bond would have some residual value, based on whatever assets might remain to be sold, even if that only pays the bondholders and other creditors pennies on the dollar. On the other hand, if the business succeeds and its assets increase ten-fold, then the value of your stock likewise increases ten-fold.

This is the kind of investment often called "venture capital," as distinguished from buying the stocks or bonds of some long-established corporation that is unlikely to either go bankrupt or to have a spectacular rate of return on its investments. As a rule of thumb, it has been estimated that a venture capitalist needs at least a 50 percent rate of return on successful investments, in order to cover the losses on the many unsuccessful investments and come out ahead over all. In real life, rates of return on venture capital can vary greatly from year to year. For the 12 months ending September 30, 2001, venture capital funds lost 32.4 percent. That is, not only did these venture capitalists as a whole not make any net profit, they lost nearly one-third of the money they had invested. But, just a couple of years earlier, venture capitalists averaged a rate of return of 163 percent in 1999.

The question of whether this kind of activity is worthwhile from the standpoint of the venture capitalist can be left to the venture capitalist to worry about. From the standpoint of the economy as a whole, the question is whether this kind of financial activity represents an efficient allocation of scarce resources which have alternative uses. Although individual venture capitalists can go bankrupt, just like the companies they invest in, the venture capital industry as a whole usually does not lose money—that is, it does not waste the available resources of the economy. From the time when data began to be kept on venture capital in 1970, there was not a single year over the next 30 years in which venture capitalists as a whole lost money. However, the fact that they lost money in the 31st year means that nothing is a sure thing. It is in fact remarkable that something which looks as risky as venture capital usually works out from the standpoint of the economy as a whole, even if not from the standpoint of each venture capitalist.

Now look at stocks and bonds from the standpoint of the entrepreneur who is trying to raise money for a risky undertaking. Knowing that bonds would be unattractive to investors and that a bank would likewise be reluctant to lend to him because of the high risks, he would almost certainly try to raise money by selling stocks instead. At the other end of the risk spectrum, consider a public utility that supplies something the public always needs, such as water or electricity. There is usually very little risk involved in putting money into such an enterprise, so the utility can issue and sell bonds, without having to pay the higher amounts that investors would earn on stocks.[1]

---

[1] There are exceptions to virtually every rule. People who bought bonds in California's electric utility companies, as a safe investment for their retirement years, saw most of the value of those investments vanish into thin air during that state's electricity crisis of 2001. The state forced these utilities to sell electricity to their customers for less than they were paying their suppliers. As these utilities went billions of dollars into debt, their bonds were downgraded to the level of junk bonds.

In short, risks vary among businesses and their financial arrangements vary accordingly. At one extreme, a commodity speculator can go from profits to losses and back again, not only from year to year but even from hour to hour on a given day. That is why there are television pictures of frantic shouting and waving in commodity exchanges, where prices are changing so rapidly that the difference between making a deal right now and making it five minutes from now can be vast sums of money.

A more common pattern among those businesses that succeed is one of low income or no income at the beginning, followed by higher earnings after the enterprise develops a clientele and establishes a reputation. For example, a dentist first starting out in his profession after graduating from dental school and buying the costly equipment needed, may have little or no net income the first year, before becoming known widely enough in the community to attract a large clientele. During that interim, the dentist's secretary may be making more money than the dentist. Later on, of course, the situation will reverse and some observers may then think it unfair that the dentist makes several times the income of the secretary.

Even when variable sums of money add up to the same total as fixed sums of money, they are unlikely to be equally attractive. Would you be equally as likely to enter two occupations with the same average income—say, $50,000 a year—over the next decade if one occupation paid $50,000 every year while the income in the other occupation might vary from $10,000 one year to $90,000 the next year and back again, in an unpredictable pattern? Chances are you would require a somewhat higher average income in the occupation with variable pay, to make it equally attractive with the occupation with a reliably fixed income. Accordingly, stocks usually yield a higher average rate of return than bonds, since stocks have a variable rate of return (including, sometimes, no return at all), while bonds have a guaranteed fixed rate of return. It is not some moral principle that makes this happen. It happens because people will not take the risk of buying stocks unless they can expect a higher average rate of return than they get from bonds.

The degree of risk varies not only with the kind of investment but also with the period of time. For a period of one year, bonds are likely to be much safer than stocks. But for a period of 20 or 30 years, the risk of inflation threatens the value of bonds or other assets with fixed-dollar amounts, such as bank accounts, while stock prices tend to rise with inflation like real estate, factories, or other real assets. Being shares of real assets, stocks rise in price as the assets themselves rise in price during inflation. Therefore the relative safety of the two kinds of assets can be quite different in the long run than in the short run.

Someone planning for retirement many years in the future may find a suitable mixture of stocks a much safer investment than someone who will need the money in a year or two. "Like money in the bank" is a popular phrase used to indicate something that is a very safe bet, but money in the bank is not particularly safe over a period of decades, when inflation can steal much of its value. The same is true of bonds. Eventually, after reaching an age when the remaining life expectancy is no longer measured in decades, it may be prudent to begin transferring money out of stocks and into bonds, bank accounts, and other assets with greater short-run safety.

Risk and Time

As an extreme example of how risk can vary over time, a dollar invested in bonds in 1801 would be worth nearly a thousand dollars by 1998, while a dollar invested in stocks that same year would be worth more than half a million dollars. All this is in real terms, taking inflation into account. Meanwhile, a dollar invested in gold in 1801 would in 1998 be worth just 78 cents. The phrase "as good as gold" can be as misleading as the phrase "money in the bank," when talking about the long run. While there have been many short-run periods when bonds and gold held their values as stock prices plummeted, the relative safety of these different kinds of investments varies greatly with how long a time period you have in mind. Moreover, the pattern is not the same in all eras.

The real rate of return on American stocks was just 3.6 percent during the Depression decade from 1931 to 1940, while bonds paid 6.4 percent. However, bonds had a negative rate of return in real terms during the succeeding decades of the 1940s, 1950s, 1960s and 1970s, while stocks had positive rates of return during that era. In other words, money invested in bonds during those inflationary decades would not buy as much when these bonds were cashed in as when the bonds were bought, even though larger sums of money were received in the end. With the restoration of price stability in the last two decades of the twentieth century, both stocks and bonds had positive rates of real returns.

Risk is always specific to the time at which a decision is made. "Hindsight is twenty-twenty," but risk always involves looking forward, not backward. During the early, financially shaky years of McDonald's, the company was so desperate for cash at one point that its founder, Ray Kroc, offered to sell half interest in McDonald's for $25,000—and no one accepted his offer. If anyone had, that person would have become a billionaire over the years. But, at the time, it was neither foolish for Ray Kroc to make that offer nor for others to turn it down.

The relative safety and profitability of various kinds of investments depends on your own knowledge. An experienced expert in financial transactions may grow rich speculating in gold, while people of more modest knowledge are losing big. However, with gold you are unlikely to be completely wiped out, since gold always has a value for jewelry and industrial uses, while any given stock can end up not worth the paper it is written on. Nor is it only novices who lose money in the stock market. In 2001 the 400 richest Americans lost a total of $283 billion.

Risk and Diversification

The various degrees and varieties of risk can be dealt with by having a variety of investments—a "portfolio," as they say—so that when one kind of investment is not doing well, other kinds may be flourishing, thereby reducing the over-all risk to your total assets. For example, as already noted, bonds may not be doing well during a period when stocks are very profitable, or vice versa. A portfolio that includes a combination of stocks and bonds may be much less risky than investing exclusively in either. Even adding an individually risky investment like gold, whose price is very volatile, to a portfolio can reduce the risk of the portfolio as a whole, since gold prices tend to move in the opposite direction from stock prices.

A portfolio consisting mostly—or even solely—of stocks can have its risks reduced by having a mixture of stocks from different companies. These may be a group of stocks selected by a professional investor who charges others for selecting and managing their money in what is called a "mutual fund." Where the selection of stocks bought by the mutual fund is simply a mixture based on whatever stocks make up the Dow Jones industrial average or the Standard & Poor's index, then there is less management required and less may be charged for the service. Mutual funds manage vast sums of investors' money: More than fifty of them have assets of at least $10 billion.

Theoretically, those mutual funds where the managers actively follow the various markets and then pick and choose which stocks to buy and sell should average a higher rate of return than those mutual funds which simply buy whatever stocks happen to make up the Dow Jones average or Standard & Poor's index. Some actively managed mutual funds do in fact do better than index mutual funds, but in many years the index funds have had higher rates of return than most of the actively managed funds, much to the embarrassment of the latter. In 2005, for example, of 1,137 actively managed mutual funds dealing in large corporate stocks, just 55.5 percent did better than the Standard & Poor's index.

On the other hand, the index funds offer little chance of a big killing, such as a highly successful actively managed fund might. A reporter for the *Wall Street Journal* who recommended index funds for people who don't have the time or the confidence to buy their own stocks individually said: "True, you might not laugh all the way to the bank. But you will probably smile smugly." However, index mutual funds lost 9 percent of their value in the year 2000, so there is no complete freedom from risk anywhere. For mutual funds as a whole—both managed funds and index funds—a $10,000 investment in early 1998 would by early 2003 be worth less than $9,000. Out of a thousand established mutual funds, just one made money every year of the decade ending in 2003. What matters, however, is whether they usually make money.

While mutual funds made their first appearance in the last quarter of the twentieth century, the economic principles of risk-spreading have long been understood by those investing their own money. In centuries past, shipowners often found it more prudent to own 10 percent of ten different ships, rather than own one ship outright. The dangers of a ship sinking were much greater in the days of wooden ships and sails than in the modern era of metal, mechanically powered ships. Owning 10 percent shares in ten different ships increased the danger of a loss through sinking but greatly reduced how catastrophic that loss would be.

Investing in Human Capital

Investing in human capital is in some ways similar to investing in other kinds of capital and in some ways different. People who accept jobs with no pay, or with pay much less than they could have gotten elsewhere, are in effect investing their working time, rather than money, in hopes of a larger future return than they would get by accepting a job that pays a higher salary initially. But, where someone invests in another person's human capital, the return on this investment is not as readily recovered by the investor. Typically, those who use other people's money to pay for their education, for example, either receive that money as a gift—from parents or philanthropic individuals or organizations—or else borrow the money.

While students can, in effect, issue bonds, they seldom issue stocks. That is, many students go into debt to pay for their education but rarely sell percentage shares of their future earnings. In the few cases where students have done that, they have often felt resentful in later years at having to continue contributing a share of their income after their payments have already covered all of the initial investment made in them. But dividends from corporations that issue stock likewise continue to be paid in disregard of whether the initial investment has already been repaid. That is the difference between stocks and bonds.

It is misleading to look at this situation only after an investment in human capital has paid off. Stocks are issued precisely because of risks that the investment will not pay off. Given that a substantial number of college students will never graduate, and that even some of those who do may have meager incomes, the pooling of risks enables more private financing to be made available to college students in general. Ideally, if prospective students could and did issue both stocks and bonds in themselves, it would be unnecessary for parents or taxpayers to subsidize their education, and even poverty-stricken students could go to the most expensive colleges without financial aid. However, legal problems, institutional inertia, and social attitudes have kept such arrangements from becoming widespread in colleges and universities. When Yale University in the 1970s offered loans whose future repayment amounts varied with the students' future earnings, those students who were going into law, business, and medicine usually would not borrow from the university.

In some endeavors, however, it is feasible to have human beings in effect issue both stocks and bonds in themselves. Boxing managers have often owned percentage shares of their fighters' earnings. Thus many poor youngsters have received years of instruction in boxing that they would have been unable to pay for. Nor would simply going into debt to pay for this instruction be feasible because the risks are too high for lenders to lend in exchange for a fixed repayment. Some boxers never make it to the point where their earnings from fighting would enable them to repay the costs of their instruction and management. Nor are such boxers likely to have alternative occupations from which they could repay large loans to cover the costs of their failed boxing careers. Boxers are more likely to have been in prison or on welfare than to have a college degree.

Given the low-income backgrounds from which most boxers have come and the high risk that they will never make any substantial amount of money, financing their early training in effect by stocks makes more sense than financing it by bonds. A fight manager can collect a dozen young men from tough neighborhoods as boxing prospects, knowing that most will never repay his investment of time and money, but calculating that a couple probably will, if he has made wise choices. Since there is no way to know in advance which ones these will be, the point is to have enough financial gains from shares in the winning fighters to offset the losses on the fighters who never make enough money to repay the investment.

For similar reasons, Hollywood agents have acquired percentage shares in the future earnings of young unknown actors and actresses who looked promising, thus making it worthwhile to invest time and money in the development and marketing of their talent. The alternative of having these would-be movie stars pay for this service by borrowing the money would be far less feasible, given the high risk that the majority who fail would never be able to repay the loans and might well disappear after it was clear that they were going nowhere in Hollywood.

At various times and places, it has been common for labor contractors to supply teams of immigrant laborers to work on farms, factories, or construction sites, in exchange for a percentage share of their earnings. In effect, the contractor owns stock in the workers, rather than bonds. Such workers have often been both very poor and unfamiliar with the language and customs of the country, so that their prospects of finding their own jobs individually have been very unpromising. In the nineteenth and early twentieth centuries, vast numbers of contract laborers from Italy went to countries in the Western Hemisphere and contract laborers from China went to countries in Southeast Asia, while contract laborers from India spread around the world to British Empire countries from Malaysia to Fiji to British Guiana.

In short, investment in human capital, as in other capital, has been made in the form of stocks as well as bonds. Although these terms have not been used legally, that is what they have amounted to economically. These are just some of the ways in which risks can be spread, thereby reducing the total risk. Insurance is another example.

INSURANCE

Like commodity speculators, insurance companies deal with inherent and inescapable risks. Insurance both transfers and reduces those risks. In exchange for the premium paid by its policy-holder, the insurance company assumes the risk of compensating for losses caused by automobile accidents, houses catching fire, earthquakes, hurricanes, and numerous other misfortunes which befall human beings. There are more than 41,000 insurance carriers in the United States alone. That includes more than 11,000 life insurance companies, whose total assets exceed 3 trillion dollars.

In addition to transferring risks, an insurance company seeks to reduce them. For example, it charges lower prices to safe drivers and refuses to insure some homes until brush and other flammable materials near a house are removed. People working in hazardous occupations are charged higher premiums. In a variety of ways, it segments the population and charges different prices to people with different risks. That way it reduces its own over-all risks and, in the process, sends a signal to people working in dangerous jobs or living in dangerous neighborhoods, conveying to them the costs created by their chosen behavior or location.

The most common kind of insurance—life insurance—compensates for a misfortune that cannot be prevented. Everyone must die but the risk involved is in the time of death. If everyone were known in advance to die at age 70, there would be no point in life insurance, because there would be no risk involved. Each individual's financial affairs could be arranged in advance to take that predictable death into account. Paying premiums to an insurance company would make no sense, because the total amount to which those premiums grew over the years would have to add up to an amount no less than the compensation to be received by one's surviving beneficiaries. A life insurance company would, in effect, become an issuer of bonds redeemable on fixed dates. Buying life insurance at age 30 would be the same as buying a 40-year bond and buying life insurance at age 40 would be the same as buying a 30-year bond.

What makes life insurance different from a bond is that neither the individual insured nor the insurance company knows when that particular individual will die. The financial risks to others that accompany the death of a family breadwinner or business partner are transferred to the insurance company, for a price. Those risks are also reduced because the average death rate among millions of policy-holders is far more predictable than the death of any given individual. As with other forms of insurance, risks are not simply transferred from one party to another, but reduced in the process. That is what makes buying and selling an insurance policy a mutually beneficial transaction. The insurance policy is worth more to the buyer than it costs the seller because the seller's risk is less than the risk that the buyer would face without insurance.

Where a given party has a large enough sample of risks, there may be no benefit from buying an insurance policy. The Hertz car rental agency, for example, owns so many automobiles that its risks are sufficiently spread that it need not pay an insurance company to assume those risks. It can use the same statistical methods used by insurance companies to determine the financial costs of its risk and incorporate that cost into what it charges people who rent their cars. There is no point transferring a risk that is not reduced in the process, because the insurer must charge as much as the risk would cost the insured—plus enough more to pay the administrative costs of doing business and still leave a profit to the insurer. Self-insurance is therefore a viable option for those with a large enough sample of risks.

Insurance companies do not simply save the premiums they receive and later pay them out when the time comes. More than half of current premiums are paid out in current claims—61 percent for Allstate Insurance Company and 83 percent for State Farm Mutual Insurance, for example. Insurance companies can then invest what is left over after paying claims and other costs of doing business. Because of these investments, the insurance companies will have more money available than if they had let the money gather dust in a vault. About two-thirds of life insurance companies' income comes from the premiums paid by their policy-holders and about one-fourth from earnings on their investments. Obviously, the money invested has to be put into relatively safe investments—government securities and conservative real estate loans, for example, rather than commodity speculation.

If, over a period of ten years, you pay a total of $9,000 in premiums for insurance to cover some property and then suffer $10,000 in property damages that the insurance company must pay for, it might seem that the insurance company has lost money. If, however, your $9,000 in premium payments have been invested and have grown to $12,000 by the time you require reimbursement for property damage, then the insurance company has come out $2,000 ahead. According to *The Economist* magazine, "premiums alone are rarely enough to cover claims and expenses," and in the United States "this has been true of property/casualty insurers for the past 25 years." In 2004, automobile and property insurers in the United States made a profit from the actual insurance underwriting itself for the first time since 1978.

While it might seem that an insurance company could just keep the profit from its investments for itself, in reality competition forces the price of insurance down, as it forces other prices down, to a level that will cover costs and provide a rate of return sufficient to compensate investors without attracting additional competing investment. In an economy where investors are always on the lookout for higher profits, an inflated rate of profit in the insurance industry would tend to cause new insurance companies to be created, in order to share in this bonanza. The role of competition in forcing prices and profits into line can be seen in the decline of the price of term life insurance after an Internet website began to list all the insurance companies providing this service and their respective prices. Other changes in circumstances are also reflected in changing prices, as a result of competition. For example, when the large baby boomer generation became middle-aged, their declining automobile accident rates as they moved into the safest age brackets were reflected in the end of sharply rising automobile insurance rates in previous years. Crackdowns on automobile insurance frauds also helped.

"Moral Hazard" and "Adverse Selection"

While insurance generally reduces risks as it transfers them, there are also risks created by the insurance itself. Someone who is insured may then take more risks than if he or she were not insured. An insured motorist may park a car in a neighborhood where the risk of theft or vandalism would be too great to risk parking an uninsured automobile. Jewelry that is insured may not be as carefully kept under lock and key as if it were uninsured. Such increased risk as a result of having insurance is known as "moral hazard."

Such changes in behavior, as a result of having insurance, make it more difficult to calculate the right premium to charge. If one out of every 10,000 automobiles suffers $10,000 worth of damage from vandalism annually, then it might seem as if charging each motorist $1 to cover damage from vandalism would be sufficient. However, if *insured* motorists become sufficiently careless that one out of every 5,000 cars suffers the same damage from vandalism, then the premium would need to be twice as large to cover the costs. In other words, statistics showing how motorists currently behave and what damages they currently incur may under-estimate what damages they will incur after they are insured. That is what makes "moral hazard" a hazard to the insurance companies and a source of higher premiums to those who buy insurance.

Knowing what percentage of the population comes down with a given illness can also be misleading as to how much it would cost to sell insurance for that illness. If one out of every million people comes down with disease X and the average cost of treating that disease is $100,000, it might seem that adding insurance coverage for disease X to a policy would cost the insurance company only an additional ten cents per policy. But what if some people are more likely to get that disease than others—and those people know it?

What if people who work in and around water are more likely to come down with this disease than people who work in dry, air-conditioned offices? Then fishermen, lifeguards and sailors are more likely to buy this insurance coverage than are secretaries, executives, or computer programmers. This is known as "adverse selection" because statistics on the incidence of disease X in the population at large may seriously under-estimate its incidence among the kinds of people who are likely to buy insurance coverage for the disease.

Although determining costs and probabilities for various kinds of insurance involve complex statistical calculations of risk, this can never be reduced to a pure science because of such unpredictable things as changes in behavior caused by the insurance itself and differences among people who choose or do not choose to be insured against a given risk.

Government Regulation

Government regulation can either increase or decrease the risks faced by insurance companies and their customers. The power of government can be used to forbid some dangerous behavior, such as storing flammable liquids in schools or driving on tires with thin treads. This limits "moral hazard"—that is, how much additional risky behavior and its consequent damage may occur among people who are insured. Forcing everyone to have a given kind of insurance coverage, such as automobile insurance for all drivers, likewise eliminates the "adverse selection" problem. These are not always net benefits, however, because there are other kinds of government regulation which increase risks and costs.

During the Great Depression of the 1930s, for example, the federal government forced all banks to buy insurance that would reimburse depositors if their bank went bankrupt. There was no reason why banks could not have bought such insurance voluntarily before, but those banks which followed sufficiently cautious policies, and which had a sufficient diversification of their assets that setbacks in some particular sector of the economy would not ruin them, found such insurance not worth paying for. Despite the thousands of banks that went out of business during the Great Depression, the vast majority of these were small banks with no branch offices. That is, their loans and their depositors were typically from a given geographic location, so that their risks were concentrated, rather than diversified. None of the largest and most diversified banks failed.

Forcing all banks and savings & loan associations to have deposit insurance eliminated the problem of adverse selection—but it increased the problem of moral hazard. That is, insured financial institutions could attract depositors who no longer worried about whether those institutions' policies were prudent or reckless, because deposits were insured up to a given amount, even if the bank or savings & loan association went bankrupt. In other words, those who managed these institutions no longer had to worry about depositors pulling their money out when the managements made risky investments. The net result was more risky behavior—"moral hazard"—which led to losses of more than half a trillion dollars by savings & loan associations during the 1980s.

Government regulation can also adversely affect insurance companies and their customers when insurance principles conflict with political principles. For example, arguments are often made—and laws passed accordingly—that it is "unfair" that a safe young driver is charged a higher premium because other young drivers have higher accident rates,[2] or that young male drivers are charged more than female drivers the same age for similar reasons, or that people with similar driving records are charged different premiums according to where they live. A City Attorney in Oakland, California, called a press conference in which he asked: "Why should a young man in the Fruitvale pay 30 percent more for insurance" than someone living in another community. "How can this be fair?" he demanded.

Running through such political arguments is the notion that it is wrong for people to be penalized for things that are not their fault. But insurance is about risk—and risks are greater when you live where your car is more likely to be stolen, vandalized, or wrecked in a collision with local drag racers. Fraudulent insurance claims also differ from one location to another, with insurance premiums being higher in places where such fraud is more prevalent. Thus the same insurance coverage for the same car can vary from city to city and even from one part of the same city to another.

The same automobile insurance coverage that costs $5,162 in Detroit costs $3,225 in Los Angeles and $948 in Green Bay. The same insurance coverage for the same car costs more in Brooklyn than in Manhattan because Brooklyn has been one of the hotspots for insurance fraud.

These are all risks that differ from one place to another with a given driver. Forcing insurance companies to charge the same premiums to groups of people with different risks means that premiums must rise over all, with safer groups subsidizing those who are either more dangerous in themselves or who live where they are vulnerable to more dangerous other people or where insurance fraud rings operate. In the case of automobile insurance,

---

[2] Although fatality rates from motor vehicle deaths are highest for drivers age 16 to 19, the declining fatality rates with age end at around age 50 and then rise again, with drivers aged 80 to 84 having nearly as high a fatality rate from motor vehicle deaths as teenagers.

this also means that more unsafe drivers can afford to be on the road, so that their victims pay the highest and most unnecessary price of all in injuries and deaths.

Concern for politically defined "fairness" over risk also led to a 95-to-nothing vote in the United States Senate in 2003 for a bill banning insurance companies from "discriminating" against people whose genetic tests show them to have a higher risk of certain diseases. It is certainly not these people's fault that their genes happen to be what they are but insurance premiums are based on risk, not fault. Laws forbidding risks to be reflected in insurance premiums and coverage means that premiums in general must rise, not only to cover higher uncertainties when knowledge of certain risks is banned, but also to cover the cost of increased litigation from policy-holders who claim discrimination, whether or not such claims turn out to be true.

Such political thinking is not peculiar to the United States.

Charging different premiums by sex is banned in France and efforts have been made to extend this ban to other countries in the European Union. In a free market, premiums paid for insurance or annuities would reflect the fact that men have more car accidents and women live longer. Therefore men would pay more for car insurance and life insurance in general, while women would pay more for an annuity providing the same annual income as an annuity for men, since that amount would usually have to be paid for more years for a woman.

Unisex insurance and annuities would cost more total money than insuring the sexes separately and charging them different amounts for given insurance or annuities. That is because, with one sex subsidizing the other, an insurance company's profit-and-loss situation would be very different if more women than expected bought annuities or more men than expected bought life insurance. Since those who buy insurance or annuities choose which companies to buy from, no given company can know in advance how many women or men will buy their insurance or annuities, even though their own profit or loss depends on which sex buys what. In other words, there would be more financial risk to selling unisex insurance policies and annuities, and this additional risk would have to be covered by charging higher prices for both products.

Government Programs

Government programs that deal with risk are often analogized to insurance, or may even be officially called "insurance" without in fact being insurance. For example, the National Flood Insurance Program in the United States insures homes in places too risky for a real insurance company and charges premiums far below what would be necessary to cover the costs. In addition, the Federal Emergency Management Agency (FEMA) helps victims of floods, hurricanes and other natural disasters to recover and rebuild. Far from being confined to helping people struck by unpredictable disasters, FEMA also helps affluent resort communities built in areas known to face high levels of danger.

As the former mayor of one such community, Emerald Isle, North Carolina, put it: "Emerald Isle basically uses FEMA as an insurance policy." Shielded by heavily subsidized financial protection, many vulnerable coastal communities have been built along the North Carolina shore. As the *Washington Post* reported:

> In the past two decades, beach towns have undergone an unprecedented building boom, transforming sleepy fishing villages into modern resorts. Land values have doubled and tripled, with oceanfront lots selling for $1 million or more. Quaint shore cottages have been replaced by hulking rentals with 10 bedrooms, game rooms, elevators, whirlpool bathtubs and pools.

All this has been made possible by the availability of government money to replace all this vulnerable and expensive real estate built on a shore often struck by hurricanes. After one such hurricane, FEMA bought "an estimated $15 million worth of sand" to replace sand washed away in the storm, according to the *Washington Post*.

Unlike real insurance, such programs as FEMA and the National Flood Insurance Program do not reduce the over-all risks. Often people rebuild homes and businesses in the well-known paths of hurricanes and floods, often to the applause of the media for their "courage." But the financial risks created are not paid by those who create them, as with insurance, but are instead paid by the taxpayers. What this means is that the government makes it less expensive for people to live in risky places—and more costly to society as a whole, when people distribute themselves in more risky patterns than they would do if they had to bear the costs themselves, either in higher insurance premiums or in financial losses and anxieties. Television reporter John Stossel's experience was typical:

> In 1980, I built a beach house. A wonderful one. Four bedrooms—every room with a view of the Atlantic Ocean.
> It was an absurd place to build. It was on *the edge of the ocean*. All that stood between my house and ruin was a hundred feet of sand. My father told me, "Don't do it, it's too risky. No one should build so close to an ocean."
> But I built anyway.
> Why? As my eager-for-the-business architect said, "Why not? If the ocean destroys your house, the government will pay for a new one."

Four years later, the ocean surged in and wiped out Mr. Stossel's first floor—and the government replaced it. Then, a decade after that, the ocean came in again and wiped out the whole house. The government then paid for the entire house and its contents. John Stossel described the premiums he paid for coverage under the National Flood Insurance Program as "dirt cheap," while the same coverage from a private insurance company would undoubtedly have been "prohibitively expensive." But this is not a program for low-income people. It covers mansions in Malibu and vacation homes owned by wealthy families in Hyannis and Kennebunkport. The National Flood Insurance Program is in fact the largest insurer in the country.

More than 25,000 properties have received flood insurance payments from the federal government on more than four different occasions. One property in Houston was flooded 16 times, requiring more than $800,000 worth of repairs—several times the value of the property itself. It was one of more than 4,500 properties whose insurance reimbursements exceeded the value of the property during the period from 1978 to 2006. There is an almost politically irresistible inclination to provide disaster relief to people struck by earthquakes, wildfires, tornadoes and other natural disasters. The tragic pictures on television over-ride any consideration of what the situation was when they decided to live where they did.

Disaster relief from the government differs from private payments from insurance companies in another way. Competition among insurance companies involves not only price but service. When floods, hurricanes or other disasters strike an area, insurance company *A* cannot afford to be slower than insurance company *B* in getting money to their policy-holders. Imagine a policy-holder whose home has been destroyed by a flood or hurricane, and who is still waiting for his insurance agent to show up, while his neighbor's insurance agent arrives on the scene within hours to advance a few thousand dollars immediately, so that the family can afford to go find shelter somewhere. Not only will the customer of the tardy insurance company be likely to change companies afterward, so will people all across the country, if word gets out as to who provides prompt service and who drags their feet. For the tardy insurance company, that can translate into losing billions of dollars' worth of business nationwide. The lengths to which some insurance companies go to avoid being later than competing insurance companies was indicated by a *New York Times* story:

> Prepared for the worst, some insurers had cars equipped with global positioning systems to help navigate neighborhoods with downed street signs and missing landmarks, and many claims adjusters carried computer-produced maps identifying the precise location of every customer.

After the catastrophic hurricane Katrina struck New Orleans in 2005, the difference between private and governmental responses was reported in the *Wall Street Journal*:

> The private-sector planning began *before* Katrina hit. Home Depot's "war room" had transferred high-demand items—generators, flashlights, batteries and lumber—to distribution areas surrounding the strike area. Phone companies readied mobile cell towers and sent in generators and fuel. Insurers flew in special teams and set up hotlines to process claims.

The kind of market competition which forces such extraordinary efforts is of course lacking in government emergency programs, which have no competitors. They may be analogized to insurance but do not have the same incentives or results. Political incentives can even delay getting aid to victims of natural disasters. When there were thousands of deaths in the wake of a huge cyclone that struck India in 1999, it was reported in that country's press that the government was unwilling to call on international agencies for help, for fear that this would be seen as admitting the inadequacies of India's own government. The net result was that many villages remained without either aid or information, two weeks after the disaster.

Chapter 14

AN OVERVIEW

> *The purpose of capital markets is to direct scarce
> capital to its highest uses.*
>
> > Robert L. Bartley

Economic systems that depend on individual rewards to get all the innumerable things done that have to be done—whether labor, investment, invention, research, or managerial organization—must then confront the fact that time must elapse between the performance of these vital tasks and receiving the rewards that flow from completing them. Moreover, the amount of time varies enormously. Someone who shines shoes is paid immediately after the shoes are shined, but a decade or more can elapse between the time an oil company begins exploring for petroleum deposits and the time when gasoline from those deposits finally comes out of a pump at a filling station and earns money to begin repaying the costs incurred.

Different people are willing to wait different amounts of time. One labor contractor created a profitable business by hiring men who normally worked only intermittently for money to meet their immediate needs. Such men were unwilling to work on Monday morning for wages that they would not receive until Friday afternoon, so the labor contractor paid them all at the end of each day, waiting until Friday to be reimbursed by the employer for whom the work was being done. On the other hand, some people buy thirty-year bonds and wait for them to mature during their retirement years. Most of us are somewhere in between.

Somehow, all these different time spans between contribution and reward must be coordinated with innumerable individual differences in patience and risk-taking. But, for this to happen, there must be some over-all assurance that the reward will be there when it is due. That is, there must be property rights which specify who has exclusive access to particular things and to whatever financial benefits flow from those things. Moreover, the protection of these property rights of individuals is a precondition for the economic benefits to be reaped by society at large.

FINANCIAL INSTITUTIONS

Unless the law protects contracts and property rights, huge sums of money are unlikely to be forthcoming for economic development, especially since huge sums of money are often a result of aggregating individually modest sums of money from millions of people, such as stockholders in giant corporations or depositors in savings banks. Financial institutions allow vast numbers of individuals who cannot possibly know each other personally to nevertheless use one another's money by going through some intermediary institution which assumes the responsibility of assessing risks, taking precautions to reduce those risks, and making transfers through loans to individuals or institutions, or investments in businesses, real estate or other ventures. These financial institutions include not only banks but also pension funds, savings & loan associations, and mutual funds, among others. Financial intermediaries not only allow the pooling of money from innumerable individuals to finance gigantic economic undertakings by businesses, they also allow individuals to redistribute their own consumption over time, borrowers in effect drawing on future income to pay for current purchases or, alternatively, savers postponing purchases till a later time, when the interest received for the delay will enable larger purchases to be made.

Everything depends on the changing circumstances of each individual's life, with many—if not most—people being both debtors and creditors at different stages of their lives. People who are middle-aged, for example, tend to save more than young people, not only because their incomes are higher but also because of a need to prepare financially for retirement in the years ahead and for the higher medical expenses that old age can be expected to bring. In the United States, Canada, Britain, Italy, and Japan, the highest rates of saving have been in the 55 to 59 year old bracket and the lowest in the under 30 year old bracket—the whole under 30 cohort having zero net savings in Canada and negative net savings in the United States. While those who are saving may not think of themselves as creditors, the money they put into banks is then lent out by those banks, acting as intermediaries between those who are saving and those who are borrowing.

What makes such activities something more than matters of personal finance is that these financial transactions are for the economy as a whole another way of allocating scarce resources which have alternative uses—allocating them over time, as well as among individuals and enterprises at a given time. To build a factory, a railroad, or a hydroelectric dam requires that labor, natural resources, and other factors of production that would otherwise go into producing consumer goods in the present be diverted to creating something that may take years before it begins to produce any output that can be used by the consuming public.

In short, from the standpoint of society as a whole, present goods and services are sacrificed for the sake of future goods and services. Only where those future goods and services are more valuable than the present goods and services that are sacrificed will financial institutions be able to receive a rate of return on their investments that will allow them to offer a high enough rate of return to innumerable individuals to induce those individuals to sacrifice their current consumption by supplying the savings required.

With financial intermediaries as with other economic institutions, nothing shows their function more clearly than seeing what happens when they are not able to function. A society without well-functioning financial institutions has fewer opportunities to generate greater wealth over time. Poor countries may remain poor, despite having an abundance of natural resources, when they have not yet developed the financial institutions required to mobilize the scattered savings of innumerable individuals, so as to be able to make the large investments required to turn natural resources into usable output. Sometimes foreign investors from countries which do have such institutions are the only ones able to come in to perform this function. At other times, however, there is not the legal framework of dependable laws and secure property rights required for either domestic or foreign investors to function.

Financial institutions not only transfer resources from one set of consumers to another and transfer resources from one use to another, they also create wealth by joining the entrepreneurial talents of people who lack money to the savings of many others, in order to finance new firms and new industries. Many, if not most, great American industries and individual fortunes began with entrepreneurs who had very limited financial resources at the outset. The Hewlett-Packard Corporation, for example, began in a garage rented with borrowed money and many other famous entrepreneurs—Henry Ford, Thomas Edison, and Andrew Carnegie, for example—had similarly modest beginnings. That these individuals and the enterprises they founded later became wealthy was an incidental by-product of the fact that they created vast amounts of wealth for the country as a whole. But the ability of poorer societies to follow similar paths is thwarted when they lack the financial institutions to allocate resources to those with great entrepreneurial ability but little or no money.

Such institutions took centuries to develop in the West. Nineteenth-century London was the greatest financial capital in the world, but there were earlier centuries when the British were so little versed in the complexities of finance that they were dependent on foreigners to run their financial institutions—notably Lombards and Jews. That is why there is a Lombard Street in London's financial district today and another street there named Old Jewry. Not only Third World countries, but also some countries in the former Communist bloc of nations in Eastern Europe, have yet to develop the kinds of sophisticated financial institutions which promote economic development. They may now have capitalism, but they have not yet developed the financial institutions that would mobilize capital on a scale that Western countries can. It is not that the wealth is not there. Rather, this wealth cannot be collected from innumerable small sources, concentrated, and then allocated in large amounts to particular entrepreneurs, without financial institutions equal to the complex task of evaluating risks, markets, and rates of return.

In recent years, American banks and banks from Western Europe have gone into Eastern Europe to fill the vacuum. As of 2005, 70 percent of the assets in Poland's banking system were controlled by foreign banks, as were more than 80 percent of the banking assets in Bulgaria. Still, these countries lagged behind other Western nations in the use of such things as credit cards or even bank accounts. Only one-third of Poles had a bank account and only two percent of purchases in Poland were made with credit cards.

The complexity of financial institutions means that relatively few people are likely to understand them, which makes them vulnerable politically. Where those who have the expertise to operate such institutions are either foreigners or domestic minorities, they are especially vulnerable. Money-lenders have seldom been popular and terms like "Shylock" or even "speculator" are not terms of endearment. Many unthinking people in many countries and many periods of history have regarded financial activities as not "really" contributing anything to the economy and have regarded the people who engage in such financial activities as mere parasites.

This was especially so at a time when most people engaged in hard physical labor in agriculture or industry, and were both suspicious and resentful of people who simply sat around handling pieces of paper, while producing nothing that could be seen or felt. Centuries-old hostilities have arisen—and have been acted upon—against minority groups who played such roles, whether they were Jews in Europe, overseas Chinese minorities in Southeast Asia, or Chettiars in their native India or in Burma, East Africa, or Fiji. Often such groups have been expelled or harassed into leaving the country—sometimes by mob violence—because of popular beliefs that they were parasitic. Those with such misconceptions have then often been surprised to discover economic activity and the standard of living declining in the wake of their departure. An understanding of basic economics could have prevented many human tragedies, as well as many economic inefficiencies.

TIME AND MONEY

The old adage, "time is money" is not only true but has many serious implications. Among other things, it means that whoever has the ability to delay has the ability to impose costs on others—sometimes devastating costs.

People who are planning to build housing, for example, often borrow millions of dollars to finance the construction of homes or apartment buildings, and must pay the interest on these millions, whether or not their construction is proceeding on schedule or is being delayed by some legal challenge or by some political decision or indecision by officials who are in no hurry to decide. Huge interest payments can be added to the cost of the construction itself while claims of environmental damage are investigated or while local planning commissioners wrangle among themselves or with the builders over whether the builder should be required to add various amenities such as gardens, ponds, or bicycle paths, including amenities for the benefit of the general public, as well as those to whom homes will be sold or apartments rented.

Weighing the costs of these amenities against the costs of delay, the builder may well decide to build things that neither he nor his customers want enough to pay for otherwise. But pay they will, in higher home prices and higher apartment rents. The largest cost of all may be hidden—fewer homes and apartments built when extra costs are imposed by third parties through the power of delay. In general, wherever A pays a low cost to impose high costs on B through delay, then A can either extort money from B or thwart B's activities that A does not like, or some combination of the two.

Slow-moving government bureaucracies are a common complaint around the world, not only because bureaucrats usually receive the same pay whether they move slowly or quickly, but also because in some countries corrupt bureaucrats can add substantially to their incomes by accepting bribes to speed things up. The greater the scope of the government's power and the more red tape is required, the greater the costs that can be imposed by delay and the more lucrative the bribes that can be extorted.

In less corrupt countries, bribes may be taken in the form of things extorted indirectly for political purposes, such as forcing builders to build things that third parties want—or not build at all, where either local home owners or environmental movements prefer leaving the status quo unchanged. The costs of demanding an environmental impact report may be quite low, compared to the costs of the delay which preparing this report will impose in the form of mounting interest charges on millions of dollars of borrowed money that is left idle while this time-consuming process goes on. Even if the report ends up finding no environmental damage whatever, the report itself may nevertheless have imposed considerable economic damage, sometimes enough to force the builder to abandon plans to build in that community.

Similar principles apply when it comes to health regulations applied to imported fruits, vegetables, flowers, or other perishable things. While some health regulations have legitimate functions, just as some environmental regulations do, it is also true that either or both can be used as ways of preventing people from doing what third parties object to, by the simple process of imposing high costs through delay.

Time is money in yet another way. Merely by changing the age of retirement, governments can help stave off the day of reckoning when the pensions they have promised exceed the money available to pay those pensions. Hundreds of billions of dollars may be saved by raising the retirement age by a few years. This violation of a contract amounts to a default on a financial obligation on which millions of people were depending. But, to those who do not stop to think that time is money, it may all be explained away politically in wholly different terms. Where the retirement age is not simply that of government employees but involves that of people employed by private businesses as well, the government not only violates its own commitments but violates prior agreements made between private employees and employers. In the United States, the government is explicitly forbidden by the Constitution from changing the terms of private contracts, but judges have over the years "interpreted" this Constitutional provision more or less out of existence.

Where the government has changed the terms of private employment agreements, the issue has often been phrased politically as putting an end to "mandatory retirement" for older workers. In reality, there has seldom, if ever, been any requirement for mandatory retirement. What did exist was simply an age beyond which a given business was no longer committed to employing those who worked for it. These people remained free to work wherever others wished to employ them, usually while continuing to receive their pensions. Thus a professor who retired from Harvard might go teach at one of the campuses of the University of California, military officers could go to work for companies producing military equipment, engineers or economists could work for consulting firms, while people in innumerable other occupations could market their skills to whoever wanted to hire them.

There was no mandatory retirement. Yet those skilled in political rhetoric were able to depict the government's partial default on its own obligations to pay pensions at a given age as a virtuous rescue of older workers, rather than as a self-serving transfer of billions of dollars in financial liabilities from the government itself to private employers.[1]

Remembering that time is money is, among other things, a defense against political rhetoric, as well as an important economic principle in itself.

ECONOMIC ADJUSTMENTS

Time is important in another sense, in that most economic adjustments take time, which is to say, the consequences of decisions unfold over time— and markets adjust at different rates for different decisions.

---

[1] Elimination of the ability of private employers to cease employing people at a given age had further economic repercussions, the most obvious being that it now became harder for younger workers to move up the occupational ladder, with older employees at the top blocking their rise by staying on. From the standpoint of the economy as a whole, that was a loss of efficiency. The elimination of a "mandatory retirement" age meant that, instead of automatically phasing out employees when they reached the age at which productivity usually begins to decline, employers

The fact that economic consequences take time has enabled many people to have successful political careers by creating current benefits at future costs. Government-financed pension plans are perhaps a classic example, since great numbers of voters are pleased to be covered by government-provided pension plans, while only a few economists and actuaries point out that there is not enough wealth set aside to cover the promised benefits—and it will be decades before the economists and actuaries are proved right.

With time comes risk, given the limitations of human foresight. This *inherent* risk must be sharply distinguished from the kinds of risk that are created by such activities as gambling or playing Russian roulette. Economic activities for dealing with inescapable risks seek both to minimize these risks and shift them to those best able to carry them. Those who accept these risks typically have not only the financial resources to ride out short-run losses but also have lower risks from a given situation than the person who transferred the risk. A commodity speculator can reduce risks overall by engaging in a wider variety of risky activities than a farmer does, for example. While a wheat farmer can be wiped out if bumper crops of wheat around the world force the price far below what was expected when the crop was planted, a similar disaster would be unlikely to strike wheat, gold, cattle, and foreign currencies simultaneously, so that a professional speculator who speculated in all these things would be in less danger than someone who speculated in any one of them, as a wheat farmer does.

Whatever statistical or other expertise the speculator has further reduces the risks below what they would be for the farmer or other producer. More fundamentally, from the standpoint of the efficient use of scarce resources, speculation reduces the costs associated with risks for the economy as a whole. One of the important consequences, in addition to more people

---

faced the prospect of having to prove that decline in each individual case to the satisfaction of third parties in government, in order to avoid an "age discrimination" lawsuit. The costs and risks of this meant that many older people would be kept employed when there were younger people who could perform their duties more efficiently. As for those older individuals whose productivity did not decline at the usual age, employers had always had an option to waive retirements on an individual basis. Neither for the employer nor the employee was there in fact a mandatory retirement age.

being able to sleep well at night because of having a guaranteed market for their output, is that more people find it worthwhile to produce things under risky conditions than would have otherwise. In other words, the economy can produce more soybeans because of soybean speculators, even if the speculators themselves know nothing about growing soybeans.

It is especially important to understand the interlocking mutual interests of different economic groups—the farmer and the speculator being just one example—and, above all, the effects on the economy as a whole, because these are things often neglected or distorted in the zest of the media for emphasizing conflicts, which is what sells newspapers and gets larger audiences for television news programs. Politicians likewise benefit from portraying different groups as enemies of one another and themselves as the saviors of the group they claim to represent.

When wheat prices soar, for example, nothing is easier for a demagogue than to cry out against the injustice of a situation where speculators sitting comfortably in their air-conditioned offices grow rich on the sweat of farmers toiling in the fields for months under a hot sun. The years when the speculators took a financial beating at harvest time, while the farmers lived comfortably on the guaranteed wheat prices paid by speculators, are of course forgotten.

Similarly, when an impending or expected shortage drives up prices, much indignation is often expressed in politics and the media about the higher retail prices being charged for things that the sellers bought from their suppliers when prices were lower. What things cost under earlier conditions is history; what the supply and demand are today is economics. During the early stages of the 1991 Persian Gulf War, for example, oil prices rose sharply around the world, in anticipation of a disruption of Middle East oil exports because of impending military action in the region. At this point, a speculator rented an oil tanker and filled it with oil purchased in Venezuela to be shipped to the United States. However, before the tanker arrived at an American port, the Gulf War was over sooner than anyone expected and oil prices fell, leaving the speculator unable to sell his oil for enough to recover his costs. Here too, what he paid in the past was history and what he could get now was economics.

From the standpoint of the economy as a whole, different batches of oil purchased at different times, under different sets of expectations, are the same when they enter the market today. There is no reason why they should be priced differently, if the goal is to allocate scarce resources in the most efficient way.

Time and Politics

Politics and economics differ radically in the way they deal with time. For example, when it becomes clear that the fares being charged on municipal buses are too low to permit those buses to be replaced as they wear out, the logical economic conclusion for the long run is to raise the fares. However, a politician who opposes the fare increase as "unjustified" may gain the votes of bus riders at the next election. Moreover, since all the buses are not going to wear out immediately, or even simultaneously at some future time, the consequences of holding down the fare will not appear all at once but will be spread out over time. It may be some years before enough buses start breaking down and wearing out, without adequate replacements, for the bus riders to notice that there now seem to be longer waits between buses and buses do not arrive on schedule as often as they used to.

By the time the municipal transit system gets so bad that many people begin moving out of the city, taking the taxes they pay with them, so many years may have elapsed since the political bus fare controversy that few people remember it or see any connection between that controversy and their current problems. Meanwhile, the politician who won a municipal election by assuming the role of champion of the bus riders may now have moved on up to statewide office, or even national office, on the basis of that popularity. As a declining tax base causes deteriorating city services and neglected infrastructure, the erstwhile hero of the bus riders may even be able to boast that things were never this bad when he was a city official, and blame the current problems on the failings of his successors.

In economics, however, future consequences are anticipated in the concept of "present value." If, instead of fares being regulated by a municipal government, these fares were set by a private bus company operating in a free market, any neglect of financial provisions for replacing buses as they wear out would begin *immediately* to reduce the value of the bus company's stock. In other words, the present value of the bus company would decline as a result of the long-run consequences that were anticipated by investors concerned about the safety and profitability of their own money.

If a private bus company's management decided to keep fares too low to maintain and replace its buses as they wore out, perhaps deciding to pay themselves higher executive salaries instead of setting aside funds for the maintenance of their bus fleet, 99 percent of the public might still be unaware of this or its long-run consequences. But among the other one percent who would be far more likely to be aware would be those in charge of financial institutions that owned stock in the bus company, or were considering buying that stock or lending money to the bus company. For these investors, potential investors, or lenders examining financial records, the company's present value would be seen as reduced, long before the first bus wore out.

As in other situations, a market economy allows accurate knowledge to be effective in influencing decision-making, even if 99 percent of the population do not have that knowledge. In politics, however, the 99 percent who do not understand can create immediate political success for elected officials and policies that will turn out in the end to be harmful to society as a whole. It would of course be unreasonable to expect the general public to become financial experts or any other kind of experts. What may be more reasonable is to expect enough voters to see the dangers in letting many economic decisions be made through political processes.

Time can turn economies of scale from an economic advantage to a political liability. After a business has made a huge investment in a fixed installation—a gigantic automobile factory, a hydroelectric dam, a skyscraper—the fact that this asset cannot be moved makes it a tempting target for high local taxation or for the unionization of employees who can shut it down with a strike and impose huge losses unless their demands are met. Where labor costs are a small fraction of the total costs of an enterprise with a huge capital investment, even a doubling of wages may be a price worth paying to keep a multi-billion dollar operation going. By contrast, an office—even the headquarters office of a national or international corporation—can much more readily be moved elsewhere, as New York discovered after its high taxes caused many of its big corporations to move their headquarters out of the city. With enough time, even many industries with huge fixed installations can change their regional distribution—not by physically moving existing dams, buildings, or other structures, but by not building any new ones in the unpromising locations where the old ones are, and by placing new and more modern structures and installations in states and localities with a better track record of treating businesses as economic assets, rather than economic prey.

A hotel cannot move across state lines, but a hotel chain can build their new hotels somewhere else. New steel mills with the latest technology can likewise be built elsewhere, while the old obsolete steel mill is closed down or phased out. As in the case of bus fares kept too low to sustain the same level and quality of service in the long run, here too the passage of time may be so long that few people connect the political policies and practices of the past with the current deterioration of the region into "rustbelt" communities with declining employment opportunities for its young people and a declining tax base to support local services.

Time and Foresight

Even though many government officials may not look ahead beyond the next election, individual citizens who are subjected to the laws and policies that officials impose nevertheless have foresight that causes many of these laws and policies to have very different consequences from those that were intended. For example, the foresight of people subjected to various government policies can cause results to differ from intentions. When money was appropriated by the U.S. government to help children with learning disabilities and psychological problems, the implicit assumption was that there was a more or less given number of such children. But the availability of the money created incentives for more children to be classified into these categories. Organizations running programs for such children had incentives to diagnose problem children as having the particular problem for which government money was available. Some low-income mothers on welfare have even told their children to do badly on tests and act up in school, so as to add more money to their meager household incomes.

Where Third World governments have contemplated confiscation of land for redistribution to poor farmers, many years can elapse between the political campaign for redistribution of land and the time when the land is actually transferred. During those years, the foresight of existing landowners is likely to lead them to neglect to maintain the property as well as they did when they expected to reap the long-term benefits of investing time and money in weeding, draining, fencing and otherwise caring for the land. By the time the land actually reaches the poor, it may be much poorer land. As one development economist put it, land reform can be "a bad joke played on those who can least afford to laugh."

The political popularity of threatening to confiscate the property of rich foreigners—whether land, factories, railroads or whatever—has led many Third World leaders to make such threats, even when they were too fearful of the economic consequences to actually carry out these threats. Such was the case in Sri Lanka in the middle of the twentieth century:

> Despite the ideological consensus that the foreign estates should be nationalized, the decision to do so was regularly postponed. But it remained a potent political threat, and not only kept the value of the shares of the tea companies on the London exchange low in relation to their dividends, but also tended to scare away foreign capital and enterprise.

Even very general threats or irresponsible statements can affect investment, as in Malaysia, during an economic crisis:

> Malaysia's prime minister, Mahathir Mohamad, tried to blame Jews and whites who "still have the desire to rule the world," but each time he denounced some foreign scapegoat, his currency and stock market fell another 5 percent. He grew quieter.

In short, people have foresight, whether they are landowners, welfare mothers, investors, taxpayers or whatever. A government which proceeds as if the planned effect of its policies is the only effect often finds itself surprised or shocked because those subject to its policies react in ways that benefit or protect themselves, often with the side effect of causing the polices to produce very different results from what was planned.

Foresight takes many forms in many different kinds of economies. During periods of inflation, when people spend money faster, they also tend to hoard consumer goods and other physical assets, accentuating the imbalance between the reduced amount of real goods available in the market and the increased amount of money available to purchase these goods. In other words, they anticipate future difficulties in finding goods that they will need or in having assets set aside for a rainy day, when money is losing its value too rapidly to fulfill that role as well. During the runaway inflation in the Soviet Union in 1991, both consumers and businesses hoarded:

> Hoarding reached unprecedented proportions, as Russians stashed huge supplies of macaroni, flour, preserved vegetables, and potatoes on their balconies and filled their freezers with meat and other perishable goods.

Business enterprises likewise sought to deal in real goods, rather than money:

> By 1991, enterprises preferred to pay each other in goods rather than rubles. (Indeed, the cleverest factory managers struck domestic and international barter deals that enabled them to pay their employees, not with rubles, but with food, clothing, consumer goods, even Cuban rum.)

Both social and economic policies are often discussed in terms of the goals they proclaim, rather than the incentives they create. For many, this may be due simply to shortsightedness. For professional politicians, however, the fact that their time horizon is often bounded by the next election means that any goal that is widely accepted can gain them votes, while the long-run consequences come too late to be politically relevant, and the lapse of time can make the connection between cause and effect too difficult to prove without complicated analysis that most voters cannot or will not engage in.

In the private marketplace, however, experts can be paid to engage in such analysis and exercise such foresight. Thus the bond-rating services Moody's and Standard & Poor's downgraded California's state bonds in 2001, even though there had been no default and the state budget still had a surplus in its treasury. What Moody's and Standard & Poor's realized was that the huge costs of dealing with California's electricity crisis were likely to strain the state's finances for years to come, raising the possibility of a default on state bonds or a delay in payment, which amounts to a partial default. A year after these agencies had downgraded the state's bonds, it became public knowledge that the state's large budget surplus had suddenly turned into an even larger budget deficit—and many people were shocked by the news.

PART V: THE NATIONAL ECONOMY

Chapter 15

NATIONAL OUTPUT

*Commonsense observation as well as statistics are
necessary for assessing the success of an economy.*
                                        Theodore Dalrymple

Just as there are basic economic principles which apply in particular
markets for particular goods and services, so there are principles which
apply to the economy as a whole. For example, just as there is a demand for
particular goods and services, so there is an aggregate demand for the total
output of the whole nation. Moreover, aggregate demand can fluctuate, just
as demand for individual products can fluctuate. In the four years following
the great stock market crash of 1929, the money supply in the United States
declined by a staggering one-third. This meant that it was now impossible
to continue to sell as many goods and hire as many people *at the old price
levels*, including the old wage levels. If prices and wage rates had also
declined immediately by one-third, then of course the reduced money
supply could still have bought as much as before, and the same real output
and employment could have continued. There would have been the same
amount of real things produced, just with smaller numbers on their price
tags, so that paychecks with smaller numbers on them could have bought
just as much as before. In reality, however, a complex national economy can
never adjust that fast or that perfectly, so there was a massive decline in total
sales, with corresponding declines in production and employment. The
nation's real output in 1933 was one-fourth lower than it was in 1929.

Stock prices plummeted to a fraction of what they had been and
American corporations as a whole operated at a loss for two years in a row.
Unemployment, which had been 3 percent in 1929, rose to 9 percent in

1930 and 16 percent in 1931. Before the decade was out, the
unemployment rate hit a staggering 25 percent. It was the greatest
economic catastrophe in the history of the United States. Moreover, the
depression was not confined to the United States but was worldwide. In
Germany, unemployment hit 34 percent in 1931, setting the stage for the
Nazi's electoral triumph in 1932 that brought Hitler to power in 1933.
Around the world, the fears, policies and institutions generated by the Great
Depression of the 1930s are still evident in the twenty-first century.

THE FALLACY OF COMPOSITION

While some of the same principles which apply when discussing markets
for particular goods, industries, or occupations may also apply when
discussing the national economy, it cannot be assumed in advance that this
is always the case. When thinking about the national economy, a special
challenge will be to avoid what philosophers call "the fallacy of
composition"—the mistaken assumption that what applies to a part applies
automatically to the whole. For example, the 1990s were dominated by
news stories about massive reductions in employment in particular
American firms and industries, with tens of thousands of workers being laid
off by some large companies and hundreds of thousands in some industries.
Yet the rate of unemployment in the U.S. economy as a whole was the
lowest in years during the 1990s, while the number of jobs nationwide rose
to record high levels. What was true of the various sectors of the economy
that made news in the media was the opposite of what was true of the
economy as a whole.

The fallacy of composition threatens confusion in many aspects of the
study of the national economy, because what is true of an individual or even
an industry is not necessarily true for the economy. For example, any given
individual who doubles the amount of money he or she has will be richer,
but a nation cannot be made richer by printing twice as much money. That
is because the price level will rise in the economy as a whole if there is twice
as much money in circulation, bidding for a given supply of goods.

Another example of the fallacy of composition would be adding up all individual investments to get the total investments of the country. When individuals buy government bonds, for example, that is an investment for those individuals. But, for the country as a whole, there are no more investment goods—factories, office buildings, hydroelectric dams, etc.— than if those bonds had never been purchased. What the individuals have purchased is a right to sums of money to be collected from future taxpayers. These individuals' additional assets are the taxpayers' additional liabilities, which cancel out for the country as a whole.

The fallacy of composition is not peculiar to economics. In a sports stadium, any given individual can see the game better by standing up but, if everybody stands up, everybody will not see better. In a burning building, any given individual can get out faster by running than by walking. But, if everybody runs, the stampede is likely to create bottlenecks at doors, preventing escapes by people struggling against one another to get out, causing some of these people to lose their lives needlessly in the fire. That is why there are fire drills, so that people will get in the habit of leaving during an emergency in an orderly way, so that more lives can be saved.

What is at the heart of the fallacy of composition is that it ignores *interactions* among individuals, which can prevent what is true for one of them from being true for them all.

Among the common economic examples of the fallacy of composition are attempts to "save jobs" in some industry threatened with higher unemployment for one reason or another. Any given firm or industry can always be rescued by a sufficiently large government intervention, whether in the form of subsidies, purchases of the firm's or industry's products by government agencies, or by other such means. The interaction that is ignored by those advocating such policies is that everything the government spends is taken from somebody else. The 10,000 jobs saved in the widget industry may be at the expense of 15,000 jobs lost elsewhere in the economy by the government's taxing away the resources needed to keep those other people employed. The fallacy is not in believing that jobs can be saved in given industries or given sectors of the economy. The fallacy is in believing that these are net savings of jobs for the economy as a whole.

OUTPUT AND DEMAND

One of the most basic things to understand about the national economy is how much its total output adds up to. We also need to understand the important role of money in the national economy, which was so painfully demonstrated in the Great Depression of the 1930s. The government is almost always another major factor in the national economy, even though it may or may not be in particular industries. As in many other areas, the facts are relatively straightforward and not difficult to understand. What gets complicated are the misconceptions that have to be unravelled.

One of the oldest confusions about national economies is reflected in fears that the growing abundance of output threatens to reach the point where it exceeds what the economy is capable of absorbing. If this were true, then masses of unsold goods would lead to permanent cutbacks in production, leading in turn to massive and permanent unemployment. Such an idea has appeared from time to time over more than two centuries, though usually not among economists. However, a Harvard economist of the mid-twentieth century named Seymour Harris seemed to express such views when he said: "Our private economy is faced with the tough problem of selling what it can produce." A popular best-selling author of the 1950s and 1960s named Vance Packard expressed similar worries about "a threatened overabundance of the staples and amenities and frills of life" which have become "a major national problem" for the United States.

Yet today's output is several times what it was when Professor Harris and Mr. Packard expressed their worries, and many times what it was in the eighteenth and nineteenth centuries, when others expressed similar worries. Why has this not created the problem that so many have feared for so long, the problem of insufficient income to buy the ever-growing output that has been produced?

First of all, while income is usually measured in money, real income is measured by what that money can buy, how much real goods and services. The national output likewise consists of real goods and services. The total real income of everyone in the national economy and the total national output are one and the same thing. They do not simply happen to be equal at a given time or place. They are necessarily equal always because they are the same thing looked at from different angles—that is, from the standpoint of income and from the standpoint of output. The fear of a permanent barrier to economic growth, based on output exceeding income, is as inherently groundless today as it was in past centuries when output was a small fraction of what it is today.

What has lent an appearance of plausibility to the idea that total output can exceed total income is the fact that both output and income fluctuate over time, sometimes disastrously, as in the Great Depression of the 1930s. At any given time, for any of a number of reasons, either consumers or businesses—or both—may hesitate to spend their income. Since everyone's income depends on someone else's spending, such hesitations can reduce aggregate income and with it aggregate demand. So can mismanagement of the money supply by government officials, such as happened during the Great Depression of the 1930s. Moreover, when various government policies generate uncertainty and apprehensions, this can lead individuals and businesses to want to hold on to their money until they see how things are going to turn out.

When millions of people do this at the same time, that in itself can make things turn out badly. An economy cannot continue operating at full capacity if people are no longer spending and investing at full capacity, so cutbacks in production and employment may follow until things sort themselves out. How such situations come about, how long it will take for things to sort themselves out, and what policies are best for coping with these problems are all things on which different schools of economists may disagree. However, what economists in general agree on is that this situation is very different from the situation feared by those who foresaw a national economy simply glutted by its own growing abundance because people lack the income to buy it all.

MEASURING NATIONAL OUTPUT

The distinction between income and wealth that was made when discussing individuals in Chapter 9 applies also when discussing the income and wealth of the nation as a whole. A country's total wealth includes everything it has accumulated from the past. Its income or national output, however, is what is produced during the current year. Accumulated wealth and current output are both important, in different ways, for indicating how much is available for different purposes, such as maintaining or improving the people's standard of living or for carrying out the functions of government, business, or other institutions.

National output during a year can be measured in a number of ways. The most common measure today is the Gross Domestic Product (GDP), which is the sum total of everything produced within a nation's borders. An older and related measure, the Gross National Product (GNP) is the sum total of all the goods and services produced by the country's people, wherever they or their resources may be located. These two measures of national output are sufficiently similar that people who are not economists need not bother about the differences. For the United States, the difference between GDP and GNP has been less than one percent.

The real distinction that must be made is between both these measures of national output during a given year—a *flow* of real income—versus the accumulated *stock* of wealth as of a given time. For example, at any given time, a country can live beyond its current production by using up part of its accumulated stock of wealth from the past. During World War II, for example, American production of automobiles stopped, so that factories which normally produced cars could instead produce tanks, planes and other military equipment. This meant that existing cars simply deteriorated with age, without being replaced. So did most refrigerators, apartment buildings and other parts of the national stock of wealth. Wartime government posters said:

> Use it up,
> Wear it out,
> Make it do,
> Or do without.

After the war was over, there was a tremendous increase in the production of cars, refrigerators, housing, and other parts of the nation's accumulated stock of wealth which had been allowed to wear down or wear out while production was being devoted to urgent wartime purposes. The durable equipment of consumers declined in real value between 1944 and 1945, the last year of the war—and then more than doubled in real value over the next five years, as the nation's stock of durable assets that had been depleted during the war was replenished. This was an unprecedented rate of growth. Businesses as well had an accelerated growth of durable equipment after the war.

Just as national income does not refer to money or other paper assets, so national wealth does not consist of these pieces of paper either, but of the real goods and services that such things can buy. Otherwise, any country could get rich immediately just by printing more money. Sometimes national output or national wealth is added up by using the money prices of the moment, but most serious long-run studies measure output and wealth in real terms, taking into account price changes over time. This is necessarily an inexact process because the prices of different things change differently over time. In the century between 1900 and 2000, for example, the real cost of electricity, eggs, bicycles, and clothing all declined in the United States, while the real cost of bread, beer, potatoes, and cigarettes all rose.

The Composition of Output

Prices are not the only things that change over time. The real goods and services which make up the national output also change. The cars of 1950 were not the same as the cars of 2000. The older cars did not have air-conditioning, seat belts, anti-lock brakes, or many other features that have been added over the years. So when we try to measure how much the production of automobiles has increased in real terms, a mere count of how many such vehicles there were in both time periods misses a huge qualitative difference in what we are defining as being the same thing—cars. A J. D. Power survey in 1997 found both cars and trucks to be the best they had ever tested.   Similarly, a 2003 report on sports utility vehicles by *Consumer Reports* magazine began:

> All five of the sport-utilities we tested for this report performed better overall than the best SUV of five years ago.[1]

Housing has likewise changed qualitatively over time. The average American house at the end of the twentieth century was much larger, had more bathrooms, and was far more likely to have air conditioning and other amenities than houses which existed in the United States in the middle of that century. Merely counting how many houses there were at both times does not tell us how much the production of housing had increased. Just between 1983 and 2000, the median square feet in a new single-family house in the United States increased from 1,585 to 2,076.

While these are problems which can be left for professional economists and statisticians to try to wrestle with, it is important for others to at least be aware of such problems, so as not to be misled by politicians or media pundits who throw statistics around for one purpose or another.

Comparisons over Time

Over a period of generations, the goods and services which constitute national output change so much that statistical comparisons can become practically meaningless, because they are comparing apples and oranges. At the beginning of the twentieth century, the national output of the United States did not include any airplanes, television sets, computers or nuclear power plants. At the end of that century, American national output did not include many typewriters, slide rules (once essential for engineers, before there were pocket calculators), or a host of equipment and supplies once widely used in connection with horses that formerly provided the basic transportation of many societies around the world.

------

[1] "Luxury Lineup," *Consumer Reports*, September 2003, p. 52. An earlier report by J.D. Power found both cars and trucks to be the best they had ever tested. See *Myths of Rich and Poor* by Cox and Alm, p. 32.

What then, does it mean to say that the Gross Domestic Product was X percent larger in the year 2000 than in 1900, when it consisted of very different things? It may mean something to say that output this year was 5 percent higher or 3 percent lower than it was last year because it consists of much the same things in both years. But the longer the time span involved, the more such statistics approach meaninglessness.

A further complication in comparisons over time is that attempts to measure real income depend on statistical adjustments with a built-in inflationary bias. Money income is adjusted by taking into account the cost of living, which is measured by the cost of some collection of items commonly bought by most people. The problem with that approach is that what people buy is affected by price. When videocassette recorders were first produced, they sold for $30,000 each and were sold at luxury-oriented Neiman Marcus stores. Only many years later, after their price had fallen below $200, were videocassette recorders so widely used that they were now included in the collection of items used to determine the cost of living, as measured by the consumer price index. But all the previous years of dramatically declining prices of videocassette recorders had no effect on the statistics used to compile the consumer price index. The same general pattern has occurred with innumerable other goods that went from being rare luxuries of the rich to common items used by most consumers, since it was only after becoming commonly purchased items that they began to be included in the collection of goods and services whose prices determine the consumer price index.

While many goods that are declining in price are not counted when measuring the cost of living, common goods that are increasing in price are measured. A further inflationary bias in the consumer price index or other measures of the cost of living is that many goods which are increasing in price are also increasing in quality, so that the higher prices do not necessarily reflect inflation, as they would if the prices of the same identical goods were rising. The practical—and political—effects of these biases can be seen in such assertions as the claim that the real wages of Americans have been declining for years. Real wages are simply money wages adjusted for the cost of living, as measured by the consumer price index. But if that index is biased upward, then that means that real wage statistics are biased downward.

Various economists' estimates of the upward bias of the consumer price index range about one percentage point or more. That means that when the consumer price index shows 3 percent inflation per year, it is really more like 2 percent inflation per year. That might seem like a small difference but the consequences are not small. A difference of one percentage point, over a period of 25 years, means that the average American income per person is under-estimated by almost $9,000 a year. In other words an American family of three has a real income of more than $25,000 a year higher than the official statistics on real wages would indicate. Alarms in the media and in politics about statistics showing declining real wages over time are describing a statistical artifact rather than an actual fact of life. It was during this period of "declining real wages" that the average American's consumption has increased dramatically while the average American's net worth more than doubled.

A further complication in measuring changes in the standard of living is that more of the increase in compensation for work takes the form of fringe benefits, rather than direct wages. Thus, in the United States, total compensation has been rising over the same span of years during which real wages have been declining.

International Comparisons

The same problems which apply when comparing a given country's output over time can also apply when comparing the output of two very different countries at the same time. If some Caribbean nation's output consists largely of bananas and other tropical crops, while some Scandinavian country's output consists more of industrial products and crops more typical of cold climates, how is it possible to compare totals made up of such differing items? This is not just comparing apples and oranges, it may be comparing cars and sugar.

Statistical comparisons of incomes in Western and non-Western nations are affected by the same age differences that exist within nations. For example, the median ages in Nigeria, Afghanistan, and Tanzania are all below twenty, while the median ages in Japan, Italy, and Germany are all over forty. Such huge age gaps mean that the real significance of some international differences in income may be seriously overstated. Just as nature provides—free of charge—the heat required to grow pineapples or bananas in tropical countries, while other countries would run up huge heating bills growing these same fruits in greenhouses, so nature provides free for the young many things that can be very costly to provide for older people.

Enormously expensive medications and treatments for dealing with the many physical problems that come with aging are all counted in statistics about a country's output, but fewer such things are necessary in a country with a younger population. Thus statistics on real income per capita overstate the difference in economic well-being between older Western nations and younger non-Western nations. If it were feasible to remove from national statistics all the additional wheelchairs, nursing homes, pacemakers, and medications ranging from Geritol to Viagra—all of which are ways of providing for an older population things which nature provides free to the young—then international comparisons of real income would more accurately reflect actual levels of economic well-being. After all, an elderly person in a wheelchair would gladly change places with a young person who does not need a wheelchair, so the older person cannot be said to be economically better off than the younger person by the value of the wheelchair—even though that is what gross international statistical comparisons would imply.

One of the usual ways of making international comparisons is to compare the total money value of outputs in one country versus another. However, this gets us into other complications created by official exchange rates between their respective currencies, which may or may not reflect the actual purchasing power of those currencies. Governments may set their official exchange rates anywhere they wish, but that does not mean that the actual purchasing power of the money will be whatever they say it is. Country *A* may have more output per capita than Country *B* if we measure by official exchange rates, while it may be just the reverse if we measure by the purchasing power of the money. Surely we would say that Country *B* has the larger total value of output if it could purchase everything produced in country *A* and still have something left over. As in other cases, the problem is not with understanding the basic economics involved. The problem is with verbal confusion spread by politicians, the media and others trying to prove some point with statistics.

Some have claimed, for example, that Japan has had a higher per capita income than the United States, using statistics based on official exchange rates of the dollar and the yen. But, in fact, the United States has consistently had significantly higher per capita income than Japan when measured by the purchasing power of the two countries' national outputs. The average American's annual income could buy everything the average Japanese annual income buys and still have thousands of dollars left over. Therefore the average American has a higher standard of living than the average Japanese. Yet statistics based on official exchange rates may show the average Japanese earning thousands of dollars more than the average American in some years, leaving the false impression that the Japanese are more prosperous than Americans. In reality, output per person in Japan is about three-quarters of that in the United States, and it is this wealth that is generated which determines how much either Americans or Japanese can consume. Even when part of what they consume is produced in some other country, it is their own production which provides the goods which they are able to trade for imported goods.

Another complication in comparisons of output between nations is that more of one nation's output may have been sold through the marketplace, while more of the other nation's output may have been produced by government and either given away or sold at less than its cost of production. When too many automobiles have been produced in a market economy to be sold profitably, the excess cars have to be sold for whatever price they can get, even if that is less than what they cost to produce. When the value of national output is added up, these cars are counted according to what they sold for. But, in an economy where the government provides many free or subsidized goods, these goods are valued at what it cost the government to produce them. These ways of counting exaggerate the value of government-provided goods and services, many of which are provided by government precisely because they would never cover their costs of production if sold in a free market economy.

Given this tendency to overvalue the output of socialist economies relative to capitalist economies when adding up their respective Gross Domestic Products, it is all the more striking that capitalist economies still generally show higher per capita output. Despite all the problems with comparisons of national output between very different countries or between time periods far removed from one another, Gross Domestic Product statistics provide a reasonable, though rough, basis for comparing similar countries at the same time—especially when population size differences are taken into account by comparing Gross Domestic Product per capita. Thus, when the data show that the Gross Domestic Product per capita in Norway in 2002 was double what it was in Portugal the same year, we can reasonably conclude that the Norwegians had a significantly higher standard of living. We need not pretend to precision. As John Maynard Keynes said, "It is better to be roughly right than precisely wrong."

Ideally, we would like to be able to measure people's personal sense of well-being but that is impossible. The old saying that money cannot buy happiness is no doubt true. However, an opinion survey in various European countries did find a rough correlation between national prosperity and personal satisfaction.

If the purpose of an international comparison is to determine which countries have the largest total output—things that can be used for military, humanitarian, or other purposes—then that is very different from determining which countries have the highest standard of living. For example, the countries with the five highest Gross Domestic Products in 2003 were:

1. United States
2. China
3. Japan
4. India
5. Germany

Although China had the second highest Gross Domestic Product in the world, it was by no means among the leaders in Gross Domestic Product *per capita*, since its output is divided among the largest population in the world. The Gross Domestic Product per capita in China was in fact less than one-fifth that of Japan. The countries with the five highest Gross Domestic Products per capita are:

1. Luxembourg
2. Norway
3. United States
4. Bermuda
5. Switzerland

Neither China nor India is among even the top 70 countries in Gross Domestic Product per capita.

Statistical Trends

One of the problems with comparisons of national output over some span of time is the arbitrary choice of the year to use as the beginning of the time span. For example, one of the big political campaign issues of 1960 was the rate of growth of the American economy under the existing administration. Presidential candidate John F. Kennedy promised to "get America moving again" economically if he were elected, implying that the national economic growth rate had stagnated under the party of his opponent. The validity of this charge depended entirely on which year you chose as the year from which to begin counting.

The long-term average annual rate of growth of the Gross National Product of the United States had been about 3 percent per year. As of 1960, this growth rate was as low as 1.9 percent (since 1945) or as high as 4.4 percent (since 1958). Whatever the influence of the existing administration on any of this, whether it looked like it was doing a wonderful job or a terrible job depended entirely on the base year arbitrarily selected.

Many "trends" reported in the media or proclaimed in politics likewise depend entirely on which year has been chosen as the beginning of the trend. Crime in the United States has been going up if you measure from 1960 to the present, but down if you measure from 1990 to the present. The degree of income inequality was about the same in 1939 and 1999 but, in the latter year, you could have said that income inequality had increased from the 1980s onward because there were fluctuations in between the years in which it was about the same. At the end of 2003, an investment in a Standard & Poor's 500 mutual fund would have earned nearly a 10.5 percent annual rate of return (since 1963) or nearly a zero percent rate of return (since 1998). It all depended on the base year chosen.

Trends outside economics can be tricky to interpret as well. It has been claimed that automobile fatality rates have declined since the federal government began imposing various safety regulations. This is true—but it is also true that automobile fatality rates were declining for decades before the federal government imposed any safety regulations. Is the continuation of a trend that existed long before a given policy was begun proof of the effectiveness of that policy?

National output data, like many other statistics, fluctuate over time. That makes it possible to say that the trends are going up or down, depending on which point in these fluctuations you choose as the base year from which to begin counting. Even in the absence of deliberate manipulation of trend data, honest confusion can lead to false conclusions. One of the first things taught in introductory statistics is that correlation is not causation. Unfortunately, it may also be one of the first things forgotten.

In some countries, especially in the Third World, so much economic activity takes place "off the books" that official data on national output miss much—if not most—of the goods and services produced in the economy. In all countries, work done domestically and not paid for in wages and salary— cooking food, raising children, cleaning the home—goes uncounted. This inaccuracy does not directly affect trends over time if the same percentage of economic activity goes uncounted in one era as in another. In reality, however, domestic economic activities have undergone major changes over time in many countries and vary greatly from one society to another at a given time.

For example, as more women have entered the work force, many of the domestic chores formerly performed by wives and mothers without generating any income statistics are now performed for money by child care centers, home cleaning services and restaurants or pizza-delivery companies. Because money now formally changes hands in the marketplace, rather than informally between husband and wife in the home, today's statistics count as output things that did not get counted before. This means that national output trends reflect not only real increases in the goods and service being produced, but also an increased counting of things that were not counted before, even though they existed before.

The longer the time period being considered, the more the shifting of economic activities from the home to the marketplace makes the statistics not comparable. In centuries past, it was common for a family's food to be grown in its own garden or on its own farm, and this food was often preserved in jars by the family rather than being bought from stores where it was preserved in cans. In 1791, Alexander Hamilton's *Report on Manufactures* stated that four fifths of the clothing worn by the American people was homemade. In pioneering times in America, or in some Third World countries today, the home itself might have been constructed by the family, perhaps with the help of friends and neighbors. As these and other economic activities moved from the family to the marketplace, the money paid for them made them part of official statistics. This makes it harder to know how much of the statistical trends in output over time represents real increases in totals and how much of these trends represents differences in how much has been recorded or has gone unrecorded.

Just as national output statistics can overstate increases over time, they can also understate these increases. In very poor Third World countries, increasing prosperity can look statistically like stagnation. One of the ravages of extreme poverty is a high infant mortality rate, as well as health risks to others from inadequate food, shelter, and medical services. As Third World countries rise economically, one of the first consequences of higher income per capita is that more infants, small children, and frail old people are able to survive, now that they can afford better nutrition and medical care. This is particularly likely at the lower end of the income scale. But, with more poor people now surviving, both absolutely and relative to the more prosperous classes, a higher percentage of the country's population now consists of these poor people. Statistically, the averaging in of more poor people can understate the country's average rise in real income or can even make the average income decline statistically, even if every individual in the country has higher incomes than in the past.[2]

---

[2] Imagine a Third World country with 100 million people, one-fourth of whom average $1,000 a year in per capita income, another fourth average $2,000, another fourth $4,000 and the top fourth $5,000. Now imagine that (1) *everyone's* income rises by 20 percent and (2) the two poorest classes double in size as a result of reduced mortality rates among those most vulnerable to malnutrition and inadequate medical care, while the two top classes remain the same size. If you work out the arithmetic, you will see that per capita income for the country as a whole remains the same, even though every individual's income has risen by one fifth. Obviously, if the income had risen by less than 20 percent, per capita income would have *fallen*, even though each individual's income rose.

Chapter 16

MONEY AND THE
BANKING SYSTEM

Any commodity to be called "money" must be generally acceptable in exchange, and any commodity generally acceptable in exchange should be called money.

Irving Fischer

Money is of interest to most people but why should banking be of interest to anyone who is not a banker? Both money and banking play crucial roles in promoting the production of goods and services, on which everyone's standard of living depends, and they are crucial factors in the ability of the economy as a whole to maintain full employment of its people and resources. While money is not wealth—otherwise the government could make us all twice as rich by simply printing twice as much money—a well-designed and well-maintained monetary system facilitates the production and distribution of wealth.

The banking system plays a vital role in that process because of the vast amounts of real resources—raw materials, machines, labor—whose allocation is affected by the huge sums of money which pass through the banking system. The assets of American banks passed the $10 trillion mark in 2004. One way to visualize such a vast sum is that a trillion seconds ago, no one on this planet could read or write. Neither the Roman Empire nor the ancient Chinese dynasties had yet been formed and our ancestors lived in caves.

THE ROLE OF MONEY

Many economies in the distant past functioned without money. People simply bartered their products and labor with one another. But these have usually been small, uncomplicated economies, with relatively few things to trade, because most people provided themselves with food, shelter and clothing, while trading with others for a limited range of implements, amenities or luxuries. Barter is awkward. If you produce chairs and want some apples, you certainly are not likely to trade one chair for one apple, and you may not want enough apples to add up to the value of a chair. But if chairs and apples can both be exchanged for something that can be subdivided into very small units, then more trades can take place, benefitting both chair-makers and apple-growers, as well as everyone else. All that people have to do is to agree on what will be used as an intermediary means of exchange and that means of exchange becomes money.

Some societies have used sea shells as money, others have used gold or silver, and still others have used special pieces of paper printed by their governments. In colonial America, where hard currency was in short supply, warehouse receipts for tobacco circulated as money. In the early colonial era in British West Africa, bottles and cases of gin were sometimes used as money, often passing from hand to hand for years without being consumed. In a prisoner-of-war camp during the Second World War, cigarettes from Red Cross packages were used as money among the prisoners, producing economic phenomena long associated with money, such as interest rates and Gresham's Law.[1] During the early, desperate and economically chaotic days of the Soviet Union, "goods such as flour, grain, and salt gradually assumed the role of money," according to two Soviet economists who studied that era, and "salt or baked bread could be used to buy virtually anything a person might need."

What made all these different things money was that people would accept them in payment for the goods and services which actually

---

[1] Gresham's Law is that bad money drives good money out of circulation. In the P.O.W. camp, the least popular brands of cigarettes circulated as money, while the most popular brands were smoked.

constituted real wealth. Money is equivalent to wealth for an individual only because other individuals will supply the real goods and services desired in exchange for that money. But, from the standpoint of the national economy as a whole, money is not wealth. It is just a way to transfer wealth or to give people incentives to produce wealth.

While money facilitates the production of real wealth—greases the wheels, as it were—this is not to say that its role is inconsequential. Wheels work much better when they are greased. When a monetary system breaks down for one reason or another, and people are forced to resort to barter, the clumsiness of that method quickly becomes apparent to all. In 2002, for example, the monetary system in Argentina broke down, leading to a decline in economic activity and a resort to barter clubs called *trueque*:

> This week, the bartering club pooled its resources to "buy" 220 pounds of bread from a local baker in exchange for half a ton of firewood the club had acquired in previous trades—the baker used the wood to fire his oven. . . .The affluent neighborhood of Palermo hosts a swanky *trueque* at which antique china might be traded for cuts of prime Argentine beef.

Although money itself is not wealth, an absence of a well functioning monetary system can cause losses of real wealth, when transactions are reduced to the crude level of barter.

Usually everyone seems to want money, but there have been particular times in particular countries when no one wanted money, because they considered it worthless. In reality, it was the fact that no one would accept money that made it worthless. When you can't buy anything with money, it becomes just useless pieces of paper or useless metal disks. In France during the 1790s, a desperate government passed a law prescribing the death penalty for anyone who refused to sell in exchange for money. What all this suggests is that the mere fact that the government prints money does not mean that it will in fact function as money. We therefore need to understand how money functions, if only to avoid reaching the point where it malfunctions. Two of its most important malfunctions are inflation and deflation.

Inflation

Inflation is a general rise in prices. The national price level rises for the same reason that prices of particular goods and services rise—namely, that there is more demanded than supplied at a given price. When people have more money, they tend to spend more. Without a corresponding increase in the volume of output, the prices of existing output simply rise, because the quantity demanded exceeds the quantity supplied at current prices and people bid against each other during the shortage.

Whatever the money consists of—sea shells, gold, or whatever—more of it in the national economy means higher prices. This relationship between the total amount of money and the general price level has been seen for centuries. When Alexander the Great began spending the captured treasures of the Persians, prices rose in Greece. Similarly, when the Spaniards removed vast amounts of gold from their colonies in the Western Hemisphere, price levels rose not only in Spain, but across Europe, because the Spaniards used much of their wealth to buy imports from other European countries. Sending their gold to those countries to pay for these purchases added to the total money supply across the continent.

None of this is hard to understand. Complications and confusion come in when we start thinking about such mystical and fallacious things as the "intrinsic value" of money or believe that gold somehow "backs up" our money or in some mysterious way gives it value.

For much of history, gold has been used as money by many countries. Sometimes the gold was used directly in coins or (for large purchases) in nuggets, gold bars or other forms. Even more convenient for carrying around were pieces of paper money printed by the government that were redeemable in gold whenever you wanted it redeemed. It was not only more convenient to carry around paper money, it was also safer than carrying large sums of money as metal that jingled in your pockets or was conspicuous in bags, attracting the attention of criminals.

The big problem with money created by the government is that those who run the government always face the temptation to create more money and spend it. Whether among ancient kings or modern politicians, this has happened again and again over the centuries, leading to inflation and many economic and social problems that flow from inflation. For this reason, many countries have preferred using gold, silver, or some other material that is inherently limited in supply, as money. It is a way of depriving governments of the power to expand the money supply to inflationary levels.

Gold has long been considered ideal for this purpose, since the supply of gold in the world usually cannot be increased rapidly. When paper money is convertible into gold whenever the individual chooses to do so, then the money is said to be "backed up" by gold. This expression is misleading only if we imagine that the value of the gold is somehow transferred to the paper money, when in fact the gold simply limits the amount of paper money that can be issued.

The American dollar was once redeemable in gold on demand, but that was ended back in 1933. Since then, the United States has simply had paper money, limited in supply only by what officials thought they could or could not get away with politically. To give some idea of the cumulative effects of inflation, a one-hundred-dollar bill would buy less in 1998 than a twenty-dollar bill bought in the 1960s. Among other things, this means that people who saved money in the 1960s had four-fifths of its value silently stolen from them over the next three decades. Sobering as such inflation may be in the United States, it pales alongside levels of inflation reached in some other countries. "Double-digit inflation" during a given year in the United States creates political alarms, but various countries in Latin America and Eastern Europe have had periods when the annual rate of inflation was in four digits.

Since money is whatever we accept as money in payment for real goods and services, there are a variety of other things that function in a way very similar to the official money issued by the government. Credit cards, debit cards, and checks are obvious examples. Mere promises may also function as money, serving to acquire real goods and services, when the person who makes the promises is highly trusted. IOUs from reliable merchants were once passed from hand to hand as money. As noted in Chapter 5, more purchases were made in 2003 by credit cards or debit cards than by cash. What this means is that aggregate demand is created not only by the money issued by the government but also by credits originating in a variety of other sources. What this also means is that a liquidation of credits, for whatever reason, reduces aggregate demand, just as if the official money supply had contracted.

Some banks used to issue their own currency, which had no legal standing, but which was nevertheless widely accepted in payment when the particular bank was regarded as sufficiently reliable and willing to redeem their currency in gold. In those times and places where bankers had more credibility than government officials, bank notes might be preferred to the official money printed by the government. Sometimes money issued by some other country is preferred to money issued by one's own. Beginning in the late tenth century, Chinese money was preferred to Japanese money in Japan. In twentieth century Bolivia, most of the savings accounts were in dollars in 1985, during a period of runaway inflation of the Bolivian peso.

Gold continues to be preferred to many national currencies, even though gold earns no interest, while money in the bank does. The fluctuating price of gold reflects not only the changing demands for it for making jewelry— the source of about 80 percent of the demand for gold—or in some industrial uses but also, and more fundamentally, these fluctuations reflect the degree of worry about the possibility of inflation that could erode the purchasing power of official currencies. That is why a major political or military crisis can send the price of gold shooting up, as people dump their holdings of the currencies that might be affected and begin bidding against each other to buy gold, as a more reliable way to hold their existing wealth, even if it does not earn any interest or dividends. For example, when the World Trade Center in New York was destroyed on September 11, 2001, the price of gold rose from about $270 an ounce to nearly $290 in one day. Later, during the second war with Iraq, the price of gold rose above $400 an ounce, as people worried about what the economic impact of that war would be. During the oil price crisis of 2005, with the stock market falling, the price of gold rose to $475 an ounce, its highest level in more than seventeen years.

Conversely, long periods of prosperity with price stability are likely to see the price of gold falling, as people move their wealth out of gold and into other financial assets that earn interest or dividends and can therefore increase their wealth. The great unspoken fear behind the demand for gold is the fear of inflation. Nor is this fear irrational, given how often governments of all types—from monarchies to democracies to dictatorships—have resorted to inflation, as a means of getting more wealth without having to directly confront the public with higher taxes.

Raising tax rates has always created political dangers to those who hold political power. Political careers can be destroyed when the voting public turns against those who raised their tax rates. Sometimes public reaction to higher taxes can range all the way up to armed revolts, such as those that led to the American war of independence from Britain. In addition to adverse political reactions to higher taxes, there can be adverse economic reactions. As tax rates reach ever higher levels, particular economic activities may be abandoned by those who do not find the net rate of return on these activities, after taxes, to be enough to justify their efforts. Thus many people abandoned agriculture and moved to the cities during the declining era of the Roman Empire, adding to the number of people needing to be taken care of by the government, at the very time when the food supply was declining because of those who had stopped farming.

In order to avoid the political dangers that raising tax rates can create, governments around the world have for thousands of years resorted to inflation instead. As John Maynard Keynes observed:

> There is no record of a prolonged war or a great social upheaval which has not been accompanied by a change in the legal tender, but an almost unbroken chronicle in every country which has a history, back to the earliest dawn of economic record, of a progressive deterioration in the real value of the successive legal tenders which have represented money.

If fighting a major war requires half the country's annual output, then rather than raise tax rates to 50 percent of everyone's earnings in order to pay for it, the government may choose instead to create more money for itself and spend that money buying war materiel. With half the country's resources being used to produce military equipment and supplies, civilian goods will become more scarce just as money becomes more plentiful. This changed ratio of money to civilian goods will lead to inflation as more money is bid for fewer goods and prices rise as a result.

Not all inflation is caused by war, though inflation has often accompanied military conflicts. Even in peacetime, governments have found many things to spend money on, including luxurious living by kings or dictators and numerous showy projects that have been common in both democratic and undemocratic governments. To pay for such things, using the government's power to create more money has often been considered easier and safer than raising tax rates. Put differently, inflation is in effect a hidden tax. The money that people have saved is robbed of part of its purchasing power, which is quietly transferred to the government that issues new money.

In the modern era of paper money, increasing the money supply is a relatively simple matter of turning on the printing presses. However, long before there were printing presses, governments were able to create more money by the simple process of reducing the amount of gold or silver in coins of a given denomination. Thus a French franc or a British pound might begin by containing a certain amount of precious metal, but coins later issued by the French or British government would contain less and less of those metals, enabling these governments to issue more money from a given supply of gold and silver. Since the new coins had the same legal value as the old, the purchasing power of them all declined as coins became more abundant.

More sophisticated methods of increasing the quantity of money have been used in countries with government-controlled central banks, but the net result is still the same: An increase in the amount of money, without a corresponding increase in the supply of real goods, means that prices rise—which is to say, inflation. Conversely, when output increased during Britain's industrial revolution in the nineteenth century, its prices declined because the country's money supply did not increase correspondingly.

Doubling the money supply while the amount of goods remains the same may more than double the price level, as the speed with which the money circulates increases when people lose confidence in its retaining its value. During the drastic decline in the value of the Russian ruble in 1998, a Moscow correspondent reported: "Many are hurrying to spend their shrinking rubles as fast as possible while the currency still has some value."

Something very similar happened in Russia during the First World War and in the years immediately after the revolutions of 1917. By 1921, the amount of currency issued by the Russian government was hundreds of times greater than the currency in circulation on the eve of the war in 1913—and the price level rose to *thousands* of times higher than in 1913. When the money circulates faster, the effect on prices is the same as if there were more money in circulation. When both things happen on a large scale simultaneously, the result is runaway inflation. During the last, crisis-ridden year of the Soviet Union in 1991, the value of the ruble fell so low that Russians used it for wallpaper and toilet paper, both of which were in short supply.

Perhaps the most famous inflation of the twentieth century occurred in Germany during the 1920s, when 40 marks were worth one dollar in July 1920 but it took more than 4 trillion marks to be worth one dollar by November 1923. People discovered that their life's savings were not enough to buy a pack of cigarettes. The German government had, in effect, stolen virtually everything they owned by the simple process of keeping more than 1,700 printing presses running day and night, printing money. Some have blamed the economic chaos and bitter disillusionment of this era for setting the stage for the rise of Adolf Hitler and the Nazis. During this runaway inflation, Hitler coined the telling phrase, "starving billionaires," for there were Germans with a billion marks that would not buy enough food to feed themselves.

The rate of inflation is often measured by changes in the consumer price index. Like other indexes, the consumer price index is only an approximation because the prices of different things change differently. For example, when consumer prices in the United States rose over the previous 12 months by 3.4 percent in March 2006, these changes ranged from a rise of 17.3 percent for energy to 4.1 percent for medical care and an actual decline of 1.2 percent in the prices of apparel.

Deflation

While inflation has been a problem that is centuries old, at particular times and places deflation has also created problems, some of them devastating.

From 1873 through 1896, price levels declined by 22 percent in Britain, and 32 percent in the United States. These and other industrial nations were on the gold standard and output was growing faster than the world's gold supply. While the prices of current output and inputs were declining, debts specified in money terms remained the same—in effect, making mortgages and other debts more of a burden in real purchasing power terms. This problem for debtors became a problem for creditors as well when the debtors could no longer pay and simply defaulted. Farmers were especially hard hit by declining price levels because agricultural produce declined especially sharply in price, while the things that farmers bought did not decline as much and mortgages and other farm debts required the same money as before.

An even more disastrous deflation occurred in twentieth-century America. As noted at the beginning of Chapter 15, the money supply in the United States declined by one-third from 1929 to 1933, making it impossible for Americans to buy as many goods and services as before *at the old prices*. Prices did come down—the Sears catalog for 1931 had many prices lower than they had been a decade earlier —but some prices could not change because there were legal contracts involved.

Mortgages on homes, farms, stores, and office buildings all specified monthly mortgage payments in specific money amounts. These terms might have been quite reasonable and easy to meet when the total amount of money in the economy was substantially larger, but now it was the same as if these payments had been arbitrarily raised—as in fact they were raised in real purchasing power terms. Many home-owners, farmers and businesses simply could not pay after the national money supply contracted—and therefore they lost the places that housed them. People with leases faced very similar problems, as it became increasingly difficult to come up with the money to pay the rent. The vast amounts of goods and services purchased on credit by businesses and individuals alike produced debts that were now harder to pay off than when the credit was extended in an economy with a larger money supply.

Those whose wages and salaries were specified in contracts—whether unionized workers or professional baseball players—were now legally entitled to more real purchasing power than when these contracts were originally signed. So were government employees, whose salary scales were fixed by law. But, while deflation benefitted members of these particular groups *if they kept their jobs*, the difficulty of paying them meant that many would lose their jobs. Similarly, banks that owned the mortgages which many people were struggling to pay were benefitted by receiving mortgage payments worth more purchasing power than before—*if they received the payments at all*. But so many people were unable to pay their debts that many banks began to fail. More than 9,000 banks suspended operations over a four year period from 1930 through 1933. Other creditors likewise lost money when debtors simply could not pay them.

Just as inflation tends to be made worse by the fact that people spend a depreciating currency faster than usual, in order to buy something with it before it loses still more value, so a deflation tends to be made worse by the fact that people hold on to money longer, especially during a depression, with widespread unemployment making everyone's job or business insecure. Not only was there less money in circulation during the downturn in the economy from 1929 to 1933, what money there was circulated more slowly, which further reduced demand for goods and services—which in turn reduced demand for the labor to produce them, creating mass unemployment.

Theoretically, the government could have increased the money supply to bring the price level back up to where it had been before. The Federal Reserve System had been set up, nearly 20 years earlier during the Woodrow Wilson administration, to deal with changes in the nation's money supply. President Wilson explained that the Federal Reserve "provides a currency which expands as it is needed and contracts when it is not needed" and that "the power to direct this system of credits is put into the hands of a public board of disinterested officers of the Government itself" to avoid control by bankers or other special interests. However, what a government can do theoretically is not necessarily the same as what it is likely to do politically or what its leaders understand intellectually.

Economists of both the left and the right, looking back on the Great Depression of the 1930s, have seen the Federal Reserve System's monetary policies during that period as confused and counterproductive. Milton Friedman called the people who ran the Federal Reserve System in those years "inept" and John Kenneth Galbraith called them a group with "startling incompetence." For example, the Federal Reserve raised the interest rate in 1931, as the downturn in the economy was nearing the bottom, with businesses failing and banks collapsing by the thousands all across the country, along with massive unemployment. Today, any student in Economics 1 who answered an exam question by saying that the way to get out of a depression is to raise the interest rate would be risking a zero for that answer, since higher interest rates reduce the amount of credit and therefore further reduce aggregate demand at a time when more demand is needed.

Nor were the presidents who were in office during the Great Depression any more economically sophisticated. Both Republican President Herbert Hoover and his Democratic successor, Franklin D. Roosevelt, thought that wage rates should not be reduced, so this way of adjusting to deflation was discouraged by the federal government—for both humanitarian and political reasons. The theory was that maintaining wage rates in money terms meant maintaining purchasing power, so as to prevent further declines in sales, output and employment. Unfortunately, this policy works only so long as people keep their jobs—and higher wage rates under given conditions, especially deflation, mean lower employment. Therefore higher real wage rates per hour did not translate into higher aggregate earnings, on which higher aggregate demand depends. Joseph A. Schumpeter, a leading economist of that era, saw resistance to downward adjustments in money wages as making the Great Depression worse. Writing in 1931, he said:

> The depression has not been brought about by the rate of wages, but having been brought about by other factors, is much intensified by this factor.

Both the Hoover administration and the Roosevelt administration applied the same reasoning—or lack of reasoning—to agriculture that they had applied to labor: The prices of farm products were to be kept up in order to maintain the purchasing power of farmers. President Hoover decided that the federal government should "give indirect support to prices which had seriously declined" in agriculture. President Roosevelt later institutionalized this policy in agricultural price support programs which led to mass destructions of food at a time of widespread hunger. In short, misconceptions of economics were bipartisan. Nor were such misconceptions confined to the United States. Writing in 1931, John Maynard Keynes said of the British government's monetary policies that the arguments being made for those policies "could not survive ten minutes' rational discussion."

Monetary policy is just one of many areas in which it is not enough that the government could do things to make a situation better. What matters is what government is in fact likely to do, which can in many cases make the situation worse.

It is not only during national and international catastrophes, such as the Great Depression of the 1930s, that deflation can become a serious problem. During the heyday of the gold standard in the nineteenth and early twentieth centuries, whenever the production of goods and services grew faster than the gold supply, prices tended to decline, just as prices tend to rise when the money supply grows faster than the supply of the things that money buys. The average price level in the United States, for example, was lower at the end of the nineteenth century than at the beginning. As in other cases of deflation—that is, an increase in the purchasing power of money—this made mortgages, leases, contracts, and other legal obligations payable in money grow in real value. In short, debtors in effect owed more—in real purchasing power—than they had agreed to pay when they took on these obligations.

So long as everyone's income remains the same, the real value of that income rises with the value of their legal obligations, making these obligations no harder to meet. However, deflation—like inflation—tends to affect different segments of the population differently. In the United States, for example, the prices of what farmers sold tended to fall faster than the prices of what they bought:

> The price of wheat, which had hovered around a dollar a bushel for decades, closed out 1892 under ninety cents, 1893 around seventy-five cents, 1894 barely sixty cents. In the dead of the winter of 1895-1896, the price went below fifty cents a bushel.

Farmers' mortgage payments remained where they had always been in money terms, therefore growing in real terms during deflation, and now had to be paid out of farm incomes that were half or less of what they had been when these mortgages were taken out. This was the background for William Jennings Bryan's campaign for the presidency in 1896, based on a demand to end the gold standard, and climaxed by his dramatic speech saying "you shall not crucify mankind upon a cross of gold." At a time when more people lived in the country than in the cities and towns, he was narrowly defeated by William McKinley. What really eased the political pressures to end the gold standard was the discovery of new gold deposits in South Africa, Australia, and Alaska. These in turn led to rising prices for the first time in twenty years, including the prices of farm produce, which rose especially rapidly.

With the deflationary dangers of the gold standard now past, not only was the political polarization over the issue eased in the United States, more countries around the world went onto the gold standard at the end of the nineteenth century and the beginning of the twentieth century. However, the gold standard does not prevent either inflation or deflation, though it restricts the ability of politicians to manipulate the money supply and thereby keeps both within narrower limits. Just as the growth of output faster than the growth of the gold supply has caused a general fall in the average price level, so discoveries of large gold deposits—as in nineteenth century California, South Africa, and the Yukon—have caused prices to rise to inflationary levels.

THE BANKING SYSTEM

Many of us may think of banks as places where we take our paychecks or have our pay sent electronically, but the role of banks in the economy is much wider and more profound. In a complex modern economy, businesses achieve economies of scale—which is to say, lower prices that raise living standards—by operating on a huge scale requiring far more labor, machinery, electricity and other resources than even rich individuals are able to afford. Most giant corporations are not owned by a few rich people but by vast numbers of people of more modest incomes who buy their stocks. This is just one way in which enormous sums of wealth are collected in individually small amounts, from people who do not know each other, and are turned over to be used by other people who are also strangers to them. Various kinds of financial intermediaries to whom people have entrusted their money—banks, pension funds, brokerage houses—make such transfers feasible by using their expertise to evaluate investment risks and earnings prospects in a way that most of the individuals supplying the money are unable to do.

What the owners of this money evaluate is the riskiness and earnings prospects of the financial institutions themselves. Individuals decide whether to put their money into an insured savings account, into a pension plan, or into a mutual fund or with commodity speculators, while these financial intermediaries in turn evaluate the riskiness and earnings prospects of those to whom they transfer this money. The banking system enables millions of people to spend money belonging to millions of other people, not only for investments in businesses but also for consumer purchases. For example, the leading credit card company, Visa, forms a network in which 14,000 banks and other financial institutions provide the money to pay for purchases made by more than 100 million credit card users in the United States who buy goods from 5.7 million merchants.

The importance of financial intermediaries to the economy as a whole can be seen by looking at places where there are not enough sufficiently knowledgeable, experienced, and trustworthy intermediaries to enable strangers to turn vast sums of money over to other strangers. Such countries are often poor, even when they are rich in natural resources. Financial intermediaries can facilitate turning these natural resources into goods and services, homes and businesses—in short, wealth.

Although money is not wealth, it facilitates the production and transfer of wealth. The real wealth—the tangible things—that people are entitled to withdraw from a nation's output is instead redirected toward others through banks and other financial institutions, using money as the means of transfer. Thus wood that could have been used to build furniture, if consumers had chosen to spend their money on that, is instead redirected toward creating paper for printing magazines when those consumers put their money in the bank and the banks lend it to magazine publishers. These transfers take place not only between individuals and businesses but also among different generations of individuals.

We have already noted, in Chapter 14, one of the most important roles of banks is serving as intermediaries to transfer savings from some people to others who want to borrow. Not only does this happen across generations, as discussed there, it happens also when money is lent to contemporary individuals and organizations of all sorts. A student just emerging from dental school seldom has enough cash on hand to buy all the equipment and supplies needed to get started as a dentist. Almost no one has enough cash on hand to buy a house and many must buy a car with installment payments. Typically, the seller of a home or an automobile receives the full price immediately, not from the buyer, but from some financial institution which the buyer must repay in installments.

Modern banks, however, do more than simply transfer cash. Such transfers do not change the total demand in the economy but simply change who demands what. The total demand for all goods and services combined is not changed by such transactions, important as these transactions are for other purposes. What the banking system does, over and beyond what other financial intermediaries do, is affect the total demand in the economy as a whole. The banking system creates credits which, in effect, add to the money supply through what is called "fractional reserve banking." A brief history of how this practice arose may make the process clearer.

Fractional Reserve Banking

Goldsmiths have for centuries had to have some safe place to store the precious metal that they use to make jewelry and other items. Once they had established a vault or other secure storage place, other people often stored their own gold with the goldsmith, rather than take on the cost of creating their own secure storage facilities. In other words, there were economies of scale in storing gold in a vault or other stronghold, so goldsmiths ended up storing other people's gold, as well as their own.

Naturally, the goldsmiths gave out receipts entitling the owners to reclaim their gold whenever they wished to. Since these receipts were redeemable in gold, they were in effect "as good as gold" and circulated as if they were money, buying goods and services as they were passed on from one person to another. From experience, goldsmiths learned that they seldom had to redeem all the gold that was stored with them at any given time. If a goldsmith felt confident that he would never have to redeem more than one-third of the gold that he held for other people at any given time, then he could lend out the other two-thirds and earn interest on it. Since the receipts for gold and two-thirds of the gold itself were both in circulation at the same time, the goldsmith was, in effect, adding to the total money supply.

In this way, there arose two of the major features of modern banking—(1) holding only a fraction of the reserves needed to cover deposits and (2) adding to the total money supply. Since all the depositors are not going to want their money at one time, the bank lends most of it to other people, in order to earn interest on those loans. Some of this interest they share with the depositors by paying interest on their bank accounts. Again, with the depositors writing checks on their accounts while part of the money in those accounts is also circulating as loans to other people, the banking system is in effect adding to the national money supply, over and above the money printed by the government. Since some of these bank credits are re-deposited in other banks, additional rounds of expansion of the money supply follow, so that the total amount of bank credits in the economy has tended to exceed all the hard cash issued by the government.

One of the reasons this system worked was that the whole banking system has never been called upon to actually supply cash to cover all the checks written by depositors. Instead, if the Acme Bank receives a million dollars worth of checks from its depositors, who received these checks from people whose accounts are with the Zebra Bank, the Acme bank does not ask the Zebra Bank for the million dollars. Instead, the Acme Bank balances these checks off against whatever checks were written by its own depositors and ended up in the hands of the Zebra Bank. For example, if Acme bank depositors had written a total of $1,200,000 worth of checks to businesses and individuals who then deposited those checks in the Zebra Bank, then the Acme Bank would just pay the difference. This way, only $200,000 is needed to settle more than two million dollars' worth of checks that had been written on accounts in the two banks.

Both banks could keep just a fraction of their deposits in cash because all the checks written on all the banks required just a fraction of the total amounts on those checks to settle the differences between banks. Since all depositors would not want their money in cash at the same time, a relatively small amount of hard cash would permit a much larger amount of credits created by the banking system to function as money in the economy, expanding the aggregate demand beyond the money issued by the government.

This system, called "fractional reserve banking," worked fine in normal times. But it was very vulnerable when many depositors wanted hard cash at the same time. While most depositors are not going to ask for their money at the same time under normal conditions, there are special situations where more depositors will ask for their money than the bank can supply from the cash it has kept on hand. Usually, this would be when the depositors fear that they will not be able to get their money back. At one time, a bank robbery could cause depositors to fear that the bank would have to close and therefore they would all run to the bank at the same time, trying to withdraw their money before the bank collapsed. If the bank had only one-third as much money available as the total depositors were entitled to and one-half of the depositors asked for their money, then the bank ran out of money and collapsed, with the remaining depositors losing everything.

The money taken by the bank robbers was often far less damaging than the run on the bank that followed.

The bank may be perfectly sound in the sense of having enough assets to cover its liabilities, but these assets cannot be instantly sold to get money to pay off the depositors. A building owned by a bank is unlikely to find a buyer instantly when the bank's depositors start lining up at the tellers' windows, asking for their money. Nor can a bank instantly collect all the money due them on 30-year mortgages. Such assets are not considered to be "liquid" because they cannot be readily turned into cash.

More than time is involved when evaluating the liquidity of assets. You can always sell a diamond for a dime—and pretty quickly. It is the degree to which an asset can be converted to money without losing its value that makes it liquid or not. American Express traveler's checks are liquid because they can be converted to money at their face value at any American Express office. A Treasury bond that is due to mature next month is almost as liquid, but not quite, even though you may be able to sell it as quickly as you can cash a traveler's check, but no one will pay the full face value of that Treasury bond today.

Because a bank's assets cannot all be liquidated at a moment's notice, anything that could set off a run on a bank could cause that bank to collapse. Not only would many depositors lose their savings, the nation's total money supply could suddenly decline, if this happened to enough banks at the same time. After all, part of the monetary demand consists of credits created by the banking system during the process of lending out money. When that credit disappears, there is no longer enough demand to buy everything that was being produced—at least not at the prices that had been set when the money supply was larger. This is what happened during the Great Depression of the 1930s, when thousands of banks in the United States collapsed and the total money supply of the country contracted by one-third.

In order to prevent a repetition of this catastrophe, the Federal Deposit Insurance Corporation was created, guaranteeing that the government would reimburse depositors whose money was in an insured bank when it collapsed. Now there was no longer a reason for depositors to start a run on a bank, so very few banks collapsed, and as a result there was less likelihood of a sudden and disastrous reduction of the nation's total supply of money and credit.

While the Federal Deposit Insurance Corporation is a sort of firewall to prevent bank failures from spreading throughout the system, a more fine-tuned way of trying to control the national supply of money and credit is through the Federal Reserve System. The Federal Reserve is a central bank run by the government to control all the private banks. It has the power to tell the banks what fraction of their deposits must be kept in reserve, with only the remainder being allowed to be lent out. It also lends money to the banks, which the banks can then re-lend to the general public. By setting the interest rate on the money that it lends to the banks, the Federal Reserve System indirectly controls the interest rate that the banks will charge the general public. All of this has the net effect of allowing the Federal Reserve to control the total amount of money and credit in the economy as a whole, to one degree or another, thereby controlling indirectly the aggregate demand for the nation's goods and services.

Because of the powerful leverage of the Federal Reserve System, public statements by the chairman of the Federal Reserve Board are scrutinized by bankers and investors for clues as to whether "the Fed" is likely to tighten the money supply or ease up. An unguarded statement by the chairman of the Federal Reserve Board, or a statement that is misconstrued by financiers, can set off a panic in Wall Street that causes stock prices to plummet. Or, if the Federal Reserve Board chairman sounds upbeat, stock prices may soar—to unsustainable levels that will ruin many people when the prices come back down. Given such drastic repercussions, which can affect financial markets around the world, Federal Reserve Board chairmen over the years have learned to speak in highly guarded and Delphic terms that often leave listeners puzzled as to what they really mean. What *BusinessWeek* magazine said of Federal Reserve chairman Alan Greenspan could have been said of many of his predecessors in that position: "Wall Street and Washington expend megawatts of energy trying to decipher the delphic pronouncements of Alan Greenspan." In 2004, the following news item appeared in the business section of the *San Francisco Chronicle:*

Alan Greenspan sneezed Wednesday, and Wall Street caught a chill.
The Federal Reserve chairman and his colleagues on the central bank's
policy-making committee left short-term interest costs unchanged, but
issued a statement that didn't repeat the mantra of recent meetings about
keeping rates low for "a considerable period."
Stunned traders took the omission as a signal to unload stocks and
bonds.

The Dow Jones average, Nasdaq, and the Standard & Poor's index all
dropped sharply, as did yields on treasury bonds—all because of what was
not said.

In assessing the role of the Federal Reserve, as well as any other organs of
government, a sharp distinction must be made between their stated goals
and their actual performance or effect. The Federal Reserve System was
established in 1914 as a result of fears of such economic consequences as
deflation and bank failures. Yet the worst deflation and the worst bank
failures in the country's history occurred after the Federal Reserve was
established. The financial crisis of 1907, which helped spur the creation of
the Federal Reserve System, was dwarfed by the financial crises associated
with the stock market crash of 1929 and the Great Depression of the 1930s.

Requirements for a Banking System

Like so many other things, banking looks easy from the outside—simply
take in deposits and lend much of it out, earning interest in the process and
sharing some of that interest with the depositors to keep them putting their
money into the banks. Yet we do not want to repeat the mistake that Lenin
made in grossly under-estimating the complexity of business in general.

At the beginning of the twenty-first century, some post-Communist
nations were having great difficulties creating a banking system that could
operate in a free market. In Albania and in the Czech Republic, for
example, banks were able to receive deposits but were stymied by the
problem of how to lend out the money to private businesses in a way that
would bring returns on their investment. The London magazine *The
Economist* reported that "the legal infrastructure is so weak" in Albania that
the head of a bank there "is afraid to make any loans." Here we see again the
problem of property rights discussed in Chapter 14. Even though another

Albanian bank made loans, it found the collateral it acquired from a defaulting borrower was "impossible to sell." An Albanian bank with 83 percent of the country's deposits made no loans at all, but bought government securities instead, earning a low but dependable rate of return. What this means for the country's economy as a whole, *The Economist* reported, is that "capital-hungry enterprises are robbed of a source of finance."

In the post-Communist Czech Republic, lending was more generous—and losses much larger. Here the government stepped in to cover losses and the banks shifted their assets into government securities, as in Albania. As with Britain several centuries earlier, foreigners have been brought in to run financial institutions that the people of the country were having great difficulty running. Whether such problems will sort themselves out over time—and how much time?—as private enterprises acquire track records and private bankers acquire more experience, while the legal system adapts to a market economy after the long decades of a Communist economic and political regime, is obviously a question for the Czechs and the Albanians. However, their experience again illustrates the fact that one of the best ways of understanding and appreciating an economic function is by seeing what happens when that function does not exist or malfunctions.

In India, a very different problem exists. While the country's rate of saving, as a percent of its economy's output, is much higher than that in the United States, its people are so distrustful of banks that individuals' holdings of gold are the highest in the world. From the standpoint of the country, this means that a substantial part of its wealth does not get used to finance investment.

Chapter 17

GOVERNMENT
FUNCTIONS

You know, doing what is right is easy. The problem is knowing what is right.

President Lyndon B. Johnson

A modern market economy cannot exist in a vacuum. Market transactions take place within a framework of rules and require someone with the authority to enforce those rules. Government not only enforces its own rules but also enforces contracts and other agreements and understandings among the numerous parties transacting with one another in the economy. Sometimes government also sets standards, defining what is a pound, a mile, or a bushel. In order to support itself, government must also collect taxes, which in turn influence economic decision-making by those affected by those taxes.

Beyond these basic functions, which virtually everyone can agree on, governments can play more expansive roles, all the way up to directly owning and operating all the farms and industries in a nation. Controversies have raged around the world, for more than a century, on the role that government should play in the economy. For much of the twentieth century, those who favored a larger role for government were clearly in the ascendancy, whether in democratic or undemocratic countries. The Soviet Union, China, and others in the Communist bloc of nations were at one extreme, but democratic countries like Britain, India, and France also had their governments take over ownership of various industries and tightly control the decisions made in other industries that were allowed to remain privately owned. Wide sections of the political, intellectual and even business communities have often been in favor of this expansive role of government.

During the 1980s, however, the tide began to turn the other way, toward reducing the role of government. This happened first in Britain and the United States, and then such trends spread rapidly through the democratic countries and even Communist China began to let markets operate ever more freely. The collapse of Communism in the Soviet bloc led to market economies emerging in Eastern Europe as well. As a 1998 study put it:

> All around the globe, socialists are embracing capitalism, governments are selling off companies they had previously nationalized, and countries are seeking to entice back multinational corporations that they had expelled just two decades earlier.

Experience—often bitter experience—had more to do with such changes than any new theory or analysis.

Despite the wide range of functions which governments can engage in, and have engaged in, here we can examine the basic functions of government that virtually everyone can agree on and explain why those functions are important for the allocation of scarce resources which have alternative uses.

The most basic function of government is to provide a framework of law and order, within which the people can engage in whatever economic and other activities they choose, making such mutual accommodations and agreements among themselves as they see fit. There are also certain activities which generate significant costs or benefits that extend beyond those individuals who engage in those activities. Here government can take account of such costs and benefits when the marketplace does not.

The individuals who work for government in various capacities tend to respond to the incentives facing them, just as people do in corporations, in families, and in other human institutions and activities. Government is neither a monolith nor simply the public interest personified. To understand what it does, its incentives and constraints must be taken into account, just as the incentives and constraints of the marketplace must be for those who engage in market transactions.

LAW AND ORDER

Where government restricts its economic role to that of an enforcer of laws and contracts, some people say that such a policy amounts to "doing nothing" as far as the economy is concerned. However, what is called "nothing" has often taken centuries to achieve—namely, a reliable framework of laws, within which economic activity can flourish, and without which even vast amounts of rich natural resources may fail to be developed into a corresponding level of output and resulting prosperity.

Corruption

Like the role of prices, the role of a reliable framework of laws may be easier to understand by observing what happens in times and places where such a framework does not exist. Countries whose governments are ineffectual, arbitrary, or corrupt can remain poor despite an abundance of natural resources, because neither foreign nor domestic entrepreneurs want to risk the kinds of large investments which are required to develop natural resources into finished products that raise the general standard of living. A classic example is the African nation of Congo, rich in minerals but poor in every other way. Here is the scene encountered at the airport in its capital city of Kinshasa:

> Kinshasa is one of the world's poorest cities, so unsafe for arriving crews that they get shuttled elsewhere for overnight stays. Taxiing down the scarred tarmac feels like driving over railroad ties. Managers charge extra to turn on the runway lights at night, and departing passengers can encounter several layers of bribes before boarding.

Bolivia is another Third World country where law and order have broken down:

> The media are full of revelations about police links to drug trafficking and stolen vehicles, nepotism in the force, and the charging of illegal fees for services. Officers on meagre salaries have been found to live in mansions.

Whatever the merits or demerits of particular laws, someone must administer those laws—and how efficiently or how honestly that is done can make a huge economic difference. The phrase "the law's delay" goes back at least as far as Shakespeare's time. Such delay imposes costs on those whose investments are idled, whose shipments are held up, and whose ability to plan their economic activities is crippled by red tape and slow-moving bureaucrats. Moreover, bureaucrats' ability to create delay often means an opportunity for them to collect bribes to speed things up—all of which adds up to higher costs of doing business. That in turn means higher prices to consumers, and correspondingly lower standards of living for the country as a whole.

The costs of corruption are not limited to the bribes collected, since these are internal transfers, rather than net reductions of national wealth in themselves. Because scarce resources have alternative uses, the real costs are the foregone alternatives—delayed or aborted economic activity, the enterprises that are *not* started, the investments that are *not* made, the expansion of output and employment that does *not* take place in a thoroughly corrupt society, as well as the loss of skilled, educated, and entrepreneurial people who leave the country. As *The Economist* magazine put it: "For sound economic reasons, foreign investors and international aid agencies are increasingly taking the level of bribery and corruption into account in their investment and lending." A study by the World Bank concluded that "across countries there is strong evidence that higher levels of corruption are associated with lower growth and lower levels of per capita income." The three countries ranked most corrupt were Haiti, Bangladesh, and Nigeria—all poverty stricken.

During czarist Russia's industrialization in the late nineteenth and early twentieth centuries, one of the country's biggest handicaps was the widespread corruption in the general population, in addition to the corruption that was rampant within the Russian government. Foreign firms which hired Russian workers and even Russian executives made it a point *not* to hire Russian accountants. This corruption continued under the Communists and has become an international scandal in the post-Communist era. One study pointed out that the stock of a Russian oil company sold for about one percent of what the stock of a similar oil company would sell for in the United States because "the market expects that Russian oil companies will be systematically looted by insiders." Nor is this corruption confined to the industrial or commercial sector. According to a report from *The Chronicle of Higher Education*'s Moscow correspondent:

> It costs between $10,000 and $15,000 in bribes merely to gain acceptance into well-regarded institutions of higher learning in Moscow, the daily newspaper *Izvestia* has reported. . .At Astrakhan State Technical University, about 700 miles south of Moscow, three professors were arrested after allegedly inducing students to pay cash to ensure good grades on exams. . . . Over all, Russian students and their parents annually spend at least $2 billion—and possibly up to $5 billion—in such "unofficial" educational outlays, the deputy prime minister, Valentina Matviyenko, said last year in an interview.

Corruption can of course take many forms besides the direct bribe. It can, for example, take the form of appointing politicians or their relatives to a company's board of directors, in expectation of receiving more favorable treatment from the government. This practice varies from country to country, like more overt corruption. As *The Economist* put it, "politically linked firms are most common in countries famous for high levels of corruption." Russia led the way in this practice, in which firms with 80 percent of the country's market capitalization were linked to public officials. The comparable figure for the United States was less than 10 percent, partly due to American laws restricting this practice.

It is not just corruption but also sheer bureaucracy which can stifle economic activity. Even one of India's most spectacularly successful industrialists, Aditya Birla, found himself forced to look to other countries in which to expand his investments, because of India's slow-moving bureaucrats:

> With all his successes, there were heartbreaks galore. One of them was the Mangalore refinery, which Delhi's bureaucrats took eleven years to clear—a record even by the standards of the Indian bureaucracy.

While both of us were waiting for a court to open up at the Bombay Gymkhana one day, I asked Aditya Birla what had led him to invest abroad. He had no choice, he said, in his deep, unaffected voice. There were too many obstacles in India. To begin with, he needed a license, which the government would not give because the Birlas were classified as "a large house" under the MRTP [Monopolies and Restrictive Trade Practices] Act. Even if he did get one miraculously, the government would decide where he should invest, what technology he must use, what was to be the size of his plant, how it was to be financed—even the size and structure of his public issue. Then he would have to battle the bureaucracy to get licenses for the import of capital goods and raw materials. After that, he faced dozens of clearances at the state level— for power, land, sales tax, excise, labor, among others. "All this takes years, and frankly, I get exhausted just thinking about it."

This head of 37 companies with combined sales in the billions of dollars—someone capable of creating many much-needed jobs in India—ended up producing fiber in Thailand, which was converted to yarn in his factory in Indonesia, after which this yarn was exported to Belgium, where it was woven into carpets—which were then exported to Canada. All the jobs, incomes, auxiliary business opportunities, and taxes from which India could have benefited were lost because of the country's own bureaucracies.

The Framework of Laws

For fostering economic activities and the prosperity resulting from them, laws must be reliable, above all. If the application of the law varies with the whims of kings or dictators, with changes in democratically elected governments, or with the caprices or corruption of appointed officials, then the risks surrounding investments rise, and consequently the amount of investing is likely to be much less than purely economic considerations would produce in a market economy under a reliable framework of laws.

One of the major advantages that enabled nineteenth-century Britain to become the first industrialized nation was the dependability of its laws. Not only could Britons feel confident when investing in their country's economy, without fear that their earnings would be confiscated, or dissipated in bribes, or that the contracts they made would be changed or voided for political reasons, so could foreigners doing business in Britain or making investments there. For centuries, the reputation of British law for dependability and impartiality attracted investments and entrepreneurs from continental Europe, as well as skilled immigrants and refugees, who helped create whole new industries in Britain. In short, both the physical capital and the human capital of foreigners contributed to the development of the British economy from the medieval era, when it was one of the more backward economies in Western Europe, to a later era, when it became the most advanced economy in the world, setting the stage for Britain's industrial revolution that led the world into the industrial age.

In other parts of the world as well, a framework of dependable laws has encouraged both domestic and foreign investment, as well as attracting immigrants with skills lacking locally. In Southeast Asia, for example, the imposition of European laws under the colonial regimes of the eighteenth and nineteenth centuries replaced the powers of local rulers and tribes. Under these new frameworks of laws—often uniform across larger geographical areas than before, as well as being more dependable at a given place—a massive immigration from China and a substantial immigration from India brought in people whose skills and entrepreneurship created whole new industries and transformed the economies of countries throughout the region.

European investors also sent capital to Southeast Asia, financing many of the giant ventures in mining and shipping that were often beyond the resources of the Chinese and Indian immigrants, as well as beyond the resources of the indigenous peoples. In colonial Malaya, for example, the tin mines and rubber plantations which provided much of that country's export earnings were financed by European capital and worked by laborers from China and India, while most local commerce and industry were in the hands of the Chinese, leaving the indigenous Malays largely spectators at the modern development of their own economy.

While impartiality is a desirable quality in laws, even laws which are discriminatory can still promote economic development, if the nature of the discrimination is spelled out in advance, rather than taking the form of unpredictably biased and corrupt decisions by judges, juries, and officials. The Chinese and Indians who settled in the European colonial empires of

Southeast Asia never had the same legal rights as Europeans there, nor the same rights as the indigenous population. Yet whatever rights they did have could be relied upon and therefore served as a foundation for the creation of Chinese and Indian businesses throughout the region.

Similarly in the Ottoman Empire, Christians and Jews did not have the same rights as Muslims. Yet, during the flourishing centuries of that empire, the rights which Christians and Jews did have were sufficiently dependable to enable them to prosper in commerce, industry, and banking to a greater extent than the Muslim majority. Moreover, their economic activities contributed to the prosperity of the Ottoman Empire as a whole. Similar stories could be told of the Lebanese minority in colonial West Africa or Indians in colonial Fiji, as well as other minority groups in other countries who prospered under laws that were dependable, even if not impartial.

Dependability is not simply a matter of the government's own treatment of people. It must also prevent some people from interfering with other people, so that criminals and mobs do not make economic life risky and thereby stifle the economic development required for prosperity. Governments differ in the effectiveness with which they can enforce their laws in general, and even a given government may be able to enforce its laws more effectively in some places than in others. For centuries during the Middle Ages, the borderlands between English and Scottish kingdoms were not effectively controlled by either country and so remained lawless and economically backward. Mountainous regions have often been difficult to police, whether in the Balkans, the Appalachian region of the United States, or elsewhere. Such places have likewise tended to lag in economic development and to attract few outsiders and little outside capital.

Today, high-crime neighborhoods and neighborhoods subject to higher than normal rates of vandalism or riots similarly suffer economically from a lack of law and order. Some businesses simply will not locate there. Those that do may be less efficient or less pleasant than businesses in other neighborhoods, where such substandard businesses would be unable to compete. The costs of additional security devices inside and outside of stores, as well as security guards in some places, all add to the costs of doing business and are reflected in the higher prices of goods and services purchased by people in high-crime areas, even though most people in such areas are not criminals and can ill-afford the extra costs created by those who are.

Property Rights

One of the most misunderstood aspects of law and order are property rights. While these rights are cherished as personal benefits by those fortunate enough to own a substantial amount of property, what matters from the standpoint of economics is how property rights affect the allocation of scarce resources which have alternative uses. Property rights need to be assessed in terms of their economic effects on the well-being of the population at large, not just property owners. These effects are ultimately an empirical question which cannot be settled on the basis of assumptions or rhetoric.

What is different with and without property rights? One small but telling example was the experience of a delegation of American farmers who visited the Soviet Union. They were appalled at the way various agricultural produce was shipped, carelessly packed and with spoiled fruit or vegetables left to spread the spoilage to other fruits and vegetables in the same sacks or boxes. Coming from a country where individuals owned agricultural produce as their private property, American farmers had no experience with such gross carelessness and waste, which would have caused somebody to lose much money needlessly in the United States, and perhaps go bankrupt. In the Soviet Union, the loss was even more painful, since the country often had trouble feeding itself, but there were no property rights to convey these losses directly to the produce handlers and shippers who caused it.

In a country without property rights, or with the food being owned "by the people," there was no given individual with sufficient incentives to ensure that this food did not spoil needlessly before it reached the consumers. Those who handled the food in transit were paid salaries, which were fixed independently of how well they did or did not safeguard the food. In theory at least, closer monitoring of produce handlers could have reduced the spoilage. But monitoring is not free. The human resources which go into monitoring are themselves among the scarce resources which have alternative uses. Moreover, monitoring raises the further question: Who will monitor the monitors? The Soviets tried to deal with this problem by having Communist Party members honeycombed throughout the society to report on derelictions of duty and violations of law. However, the widespread corruption and inefficiency found even under Stalinist totalitarianism suggest the limitations of official monitoring, as compared to automatic self-monitoring by property owners.

No monitor has to stand over an American farmer and tell him to take the rotten peaches out of a basket before they spoil the others, because those peaches are his private property and he is not about to lose money if he doesn't have to. *Property rights create self-monitoring*, which tends to be both more effective and less costly than third party monitoring. Most Americans do not own any agricultural land or crops, but they have more and better food available at lower prices than in countries where there are no property rights in agricultural land or its produce, and where much food can spoil needlessly as a result.

The only animals threatened with extinction are animals not owned by anybody. Colonel Sanders was not about to let chickens become extinct. Nor will McDonald's stand idly by and let cows become extinct. Likewise, it is inanimate things not owned by anybody—air and water, for example— which are polluted. In centuries past, sheep were allowed to graze on unowned land—"the commons," as it was called—with the net result that land on the commons was so heavily grazed that it had little left but patchy ground and the shepherds had hungry and scrawny sheep. But privately owned land adjacent to the commons was usually in far better condition. Similar neglect of unowned land occurred in the Soviet Union. According to Soviet economists, "forested areas that are cut down are not reseeded," though it would be financial suicide for a lumbering company to let that happen on their own property in a capitalist economy.

All these things, in different ways, illustrate the value of private property rights *to the society as a whole*, including people who own no private property, but who benefit from the greater economic efficiency that property rights create, which translates into a higher standard of living for the population at large.

Despite a tendency to think of property rights as special privileges for the rich, many property rights are actually more valuable to people who are not rich—and such property rights have often been infringed or violated for the benefit of the rich. Although the average rich person, by definition, has more money than the average person who is not rich, in the aggregate the non-rich population often has far more money. This means, among other things, that many properties owned by the rich would be bid away from them by the greater purchasing power of the non-rich, if unrestricted property rights prevailed in a free market. Thus land occupied by mansions located on huge estates would pass through the market to entrepreneurs who would build smaller and more numerous homes or apartment buildings—all for the use of people with more modest incomes, but with more money in the aggregate.

Someone once said, "It doesn't matter whether you are rich or poor, so long as you have money." This was meant as a joke but it has very serious implications. In a free market, the money of ordinary people is just as good as the money of the rich—and in the aggregate, there is often more of it. The individually less affluent need not directly bid against the more affluent. Entrepreneurs or their companies, using their own money or money borrowed from banks and other financial institutions, can acquire mansions and estates, and replace them with middle-class homes and apartment buildings for people of modest incomes. This would of course change these communities in ways the rich may not like, however much others might like to live in the resulting newly developed communities.

Wealthy people have often forestalled such transfers of property by getting laws passed to *restrict* property rights in a variety of ways. For example, various affluent communities in California, Virginia, and other places have required land to be sold only in lots of one acre or more per house, thereby pricing such land and homes beyond the reach of most people and thus neutralizing the greater aggregate purchasing power of less affluent people. Zoning boards, "open space" laws, historical preservation agencies and other organizations and devices have also been used to severely limit the sale of private property for use in ways not approved by those who wish to keep things the way they are in their communities. By infringing or negating property rights, affluent and wealthy property owners are able to keep out people of average or low incomes and, at the same time, increase the value of their own property by ensuring its growing scarcity relative to increasing employment in the area.

While strict adherence to property rights would allow landlords to evict tenants from their apartments at will, the economic incentives are for them to do just the opposite—that is, to try to keep their apartments as fully rented and as continuously occupied as possible, so long as the tenants pay their rent and behave themselves. Only when rent control or other restrictions on their property rights are enacted are landlords likely to do otherwise. Under rent control and tenants' rights laws, landlords have been known to try to harass tenants into leaving, whether in New York or in Hong Kong.

Under stringent rent control and tenants' rights laws in Hong Kong, landlords were known to sneak into their own buildings late at night to vandalize the premises, in order to make them less attractive or even unlivable, so that tenants would move out and the empty building could then be torn down legally, to be replaced by something more lucrative as commercial or industrial property. This of course was by no means the purpose or intention of those who had passed rent control laws in Hong Kong. But it illustrates again the importance of making a distinction between intentions and effects—and not just as regards property rights laws. In short, incentives matter and property rights need to be assessed economically in terms of the incentives created by their existence, their modifications, or their elimination.

The powerful incentives created by a profit-and-loss economy depend on the profits being private property. When government-owned enterprises in the Soviet Union made profits, those profits were not their private property but belonged to "the people"—or, in more mundane terms, could be taken by the government for whatever purposes higher officials chose to spend them on. Soviet economists Shmelev and Popov pointed out and lamented the adverse effects of this on incentives:

But what justifies confiscating the larger part—sometimes 90-95 percent—of enterprises' profits, as is being done in many sectors of the economy today? What political or economic right—ultimately what human right—do ministries have to do that? Once again we are taking away from those who work well in order to keep afloat those who do nothing. How can we possibly talk about independence, initiative, rewards for efficiency, quality, and technical progress?

Of course, the country's leaders could continue to *talk* about such things, but destroying the incentives which exist under property rights meant that there was a reduced chance of achieving these goals. Because of an absence of property rights, those who ran enterprises that made profits "can't buy or build anything with the money they have" which represent "just figures in a bank account with no real value whatever without permission from above" to use that money. In other words, success did not automatically lead to expansions of successful enterprises nor failure to the contraction of unsuccessful ones, as it does in a market economy.

Social Order

Order includes more than laws and the government apparatus that administers laws. It also includes the honesty, reliability and cooperativeness of the people themselves. Honesty and reliability can vary greatly between one country and another. As a knowledgeable observer put it: "While it is unimaginable to do business in China without paying bribes, to offer one in Japan is the greatest of faux pas." When wallets with money in them were deliberately left in public places as an experiment, the percentage of those wallets returned with the money untouched varied greatly from place to place: in Denmark, nearly all of these wallets were returned. In New York, where United Nations representatives have diplomatic immunity from local law, diplomats from various Middle East countries let numerous parking tickets go unpaid—246 by Kuwaiti diplomats—while not one diplomat from Denmark, Japan, or Israel had any unpaid parking tickets.

Honesty and reliability can also vary widely among particular groups within a given country, and that also has economic repercussions. Some insular groups rely upon their own internal social controls for doing business with fellow group members whom they can trust. One such group are the

Marwaris of India, whose business networks were established in the nineteenth century and extended beyond India to China and Central Asia, and who "transacted vast sums merely on the merchant's word." But "doing business among strangers," as *The Economist* magazine puts it, is not "easy" in India. Yet business transactions among strangers are an essential part of a successful modern mass economy, which requires cooperation—including the pooling of vast financial resources from far more people than can possibly know each other personally. As for the general level of reliability among strangers in India, *The Economist* reported:

> If you withdraw 10,000 rupees from a bank, it will probably come in a brick of 100-rupee notes, held together by industrial-strength staples that you struggle to prise open. They are there to stop someone from surreptitiously removing a few notes. On trains, announcements may advise you to crush your empty mineral-water bottles lest someone refill them with tap water and sell them as new. . . . Any sort of business that requires confidence in the judicial system is best left alone.

Where neither the honesty of the general population nor the integrity of the legal system can be relied upon, economic activities are inhibited, if not stifled. At the same time, groups whose members can rely on each other, such as the Marwaris, have a great advantage in competition with others, in being able to secure mutual cooperation in economic activities which extend over distance and time—activities that would be far more risky for others in such societies and still more so for foreigners.

Like the Marwaris in India, Hasidic Jews in New York's diamond district often give consignments of jewels to one another and share the sales proceeds on the basis of verbal agreements among themselves. The extreme social isolation of the Hasidic community from the larger society, and even from other Jews, makes it very costly for anyone who grows up in that community to disgrace his family and lose his own standing, as well as his own economic and social relationships, by cheating on an agreement with a fellow Hasidim.

It is much the same story halfway around the world, where the overseas Chinese minority in various Southeast Asian countries make verbal agreements among themselves, without the sanction of the local legal system. Given the unreliability and corruption of some of these post-colonial legal systems, the ability of the Chinese to rely on their own social and economic arrangements gives them an economic advantage over their indigenous competitors who lack an equally reliable and inexpensive way of making transactions or pooling their money. The costs of doing business are thus less for the Chinese than for Malay, Indonesian or other businesses in the region, giving the Chinese competitive advantages.

What economics professor William Easterly of New York University has aptly called "the radius of trust" extends for very different distances among different groups and nations. For some, it extends no further than the family:

> Malagasy grain traders carry out inspections of each lot of grain in person because they don't trust employees. One third of the traders say they don't hire more workers because of fear of theft by them. This limits the grain traders' firm size, cutting short a trader's potential success. In many countries, companies tend to be family enterprises because family members are the only ones felt trustworthy. So the size of the company is then limited by the size of the family.

Even in the same country, the radius of trust can extend very different distances. Although businesses in some American communities must incur the extra expense of heavy grates for protection from theft and vandalism while closed, and security guards for protection while open, businesses in other American communities have no such expenses and are therefore able to operate profitably while charging lower prices. Rental car companies can park their cars in lots without fences or guards in some communities, while in other places it would be financial suicide to do so. But, in those places where car thefts from unguarded lots are rare, such rare losses may cost less than paying guards and maintaining fences would cost, so that rental car agencies—and other businesses—can flourish as they operate at lower costs in such communities. Those communities also flourish economically, as a result of attracting enterprises and investments that create jobs and pay local taxes.

In short, honesty is more than a moral principle. It is also a major economic factor. While government can do little to create honesty directly, in various ways it can indirectly either support or undermine the traditions on which honest conduct is based. This it can do by what it teaches in its schools, by the examples set by public officials, or by the laws that it passes. These laws can create incentives toward either moral or immoral conduct. Where laws create a situation where the only way to avoid ruinous losses is by violating the law, the government is in effect reducing public respect for laws in general, as well as rewarding specific dishonest behavior.

Advocates of rent control, for example, often point to examples of dishonest behavior among landlords to demonstrate an apparent need for both rent control itself and for related tenants' rights legislation. However, rent control laws can widen the difference between the value of a given apartment building to honest owners and dishonest owners. Where the costs of legally mandated services—heat, maintenance, hot water—are high enough to equal or exceed the amount of rent permitted under the law, the value of a building to an honest landlord can become zero or even negative. Yet, to a landlord who is willing to violate the law and save money by neglecting required services, or who accepts bribes from prospective tenants during a housing shortage under rent control, the building may still have some value.

Where something has different values to different people, it tends to move through the marketplace to its most valued use, which is where the bids will be highest. In this case, dishonest landlords can easily bid apartment buildings away from honest landlords, some of whom may be relieved to escape the bind that rent control puts them in. Landlords willing to resort to arson may find the building most valuable of all, if they can sell the site for commercial or industrial use after burning the building down, thereby getting rid of both tenants and rent control. As one study found:

> In New York City, landlord arsons became so common in some areas that the city responded with special welfare allowances. For a while, burned-out tenants were moved to the top of the list for coveted public housing. That gave *tenants* an incentive to burn down their buildings. They did, often moving television sets and furniture out onto the sidewalk before starting the fire.

Those who create incentives toward widespread dishonesty by promoting laws which make honest behavior financially impossible are often among the most indignant at the dishonesty—and the least likely to regard themselves as in any way responsible for it. Arson is just one of the forms of dishonesty promoted by rent control laws. Shrewd and unscrupulous landlords have made virtually a science out of milking a rent-controlled building by neglecting maintenance and repairs, defaulting on mortgage payments, falling behind in the payment of taxes, and then finally letting the building become the property of the city by default, while they move on to repeat the same destructive process with other rent-controlled buildings.

Without rent control, the incentives facing landlords are directly the opposite—that is, to maintain the quality of the property, in order to attract tenants, and to safeguard it against fire and other sources of dangers to the survival of the building, which is a valuable piece of property to them in a free market. In short, complaints against landlords' behavior by rent control advocates can be valid, even though few of those advocates see any connection between rent control and a declining moral quality in people who become landlords. When honest landlords stand to lose money under rent control, while dishonest landlords can still make a profit, it is virtually inevitable that the property will pass from the former to the latter.

Rent control laws are just one of a number of severe restrictions which can make honest behavior too costly for many people, and which therefore promote widespread dishonesty. It is common in Third World countries for much—sometimes most—economic activity to take place "off the books," which is to say illegally, because oppressive levels of bureaucracy and red tape make legal operation too costly for most people to afford. In the African nation of Cameroon, for example, setting up a small business has required paying official fees (not counting bribes) that amount to far more money than the average person in Cameroon makes in a year. The legal system imposes similarly high costs on other economic activities:

> To buy or sell property costs nearly a fifth of the property's value. To get the courts to enforce an unpaid invoice takes nearly two years, costs over a third of the invoice's value, and requires fifty-eight separate procedures.

These ridiculous regulations are good news for the bureaucrats who enforce them. Every procedure is an opportunity to extract a bribe.

When laws and policies make honesty increasingly costly, then government is, in effect, promoting dishonesty. Such dishonesty can then extend beyond the particular laws and policies in question to a more general habit of disobeying laws, to the detriment of the whole economy and society. As a Russian mother said:

> Now my children tell me I raised them the wrong way. All that honesty and fairness, no one needs it now. If you are honest you are a fool.

To the extent that such attitudes are widespread in any given country, the consequences are economic as well as social.

Despite all the countries which have seen their economic growth rates rise sharply when they went from government-controlled economies to free market economies, Russia saw its output and its standard of living fall precipitously after the dissolution of the Soviet Union and the turning of state-owned property into property owned by former communist leaders turned capitalists. Rampant corruption can negate the benefits of markets, as it negates the benefits of a rich endowment of natural resources and a highly educated population.

While a market economy operates better in a country where honesty is more widespread, it is also true that free markets tend to punish dishonesty. An American investigative journalist who began his career by exposing various kinds of frauds that businesses commit against consumers found this pattern:

> I did hundreds of stories on such scams but over the years, I came to realize that in the private sector, the cheaters seldom get very rich. It's not because "consumer fraud investigators" catch them and stop them; most fraud never even gets on the government's radar screens. The cheaters get punished by the market. They make money for a while, but then people wise up and stop buying.
> There are exceptions. In a multi-trillion-dollar economy with tens of thousands of businesses, there will always be some successful cheaters and Enron-like scams; but the longer I did consumer reporting, the harder it was for us to find serious rip-offs worthy of national television.

Where a government bureaucracy is both small and honest, as in nineteenth-century Britain, it has few negative effects on the economy and, if the relatively few services it performs are useful, its net effect can be positive. However, when a government bureaucracy is both large and pervasive in its powers, the stifling effect on the economy of endless red tape and bureaucratic delays can be mitigated by a certain amount of corruption, such as bribes to get needless bureaucratic obstacles removed and delayed processes speeded up. The beneficial effects of honesty, like the beneficial effects of clean air and clean water, are not absolute and categorical, but incremental. Given large and stifling bureaucracies, an incorruptible one may be worse in its effects than one whose most harmful restrictions can be mitigated with bribes. On the other hand, a thoroughly corrupt bureaucracy tends to inhibit economic activity because, in effect, there are no known laws to depend on when engaging in planning or investment.

EXTERNAL COSTS AND BENEFITS

Economic decisions made through the marketplace are not always better than decisions that governments can make. Much depends on whether those market transactions accurately reflect both the costs and the benefits which result. Under some conditions, they do not.

When someone buys a table or a tractor, the question as to whether it is worth what it cost is answered by the actions of the purchaser who made the decision to buy it. However, when an electric utility company buys coal to burn to generate electricity, a significant part of the cost of the electricity-generating process is paid by people who breathe the smoke that results from the burning of the coal and whose homes and cars are dirtied by the soot. Cleaning, repainting and medical costs paid by these people are not taken into account in the marketplace, because these people do not participate in the transactions between the coal producer and the utility company.

Such costs are called "external costs" by economists because such costs fall outside the parties to the transaction which creates these costs. External costs are therefore not taken into account in the marketplace, even when these are very substantial costs, which can extend beyond monetary losses to include bad health and premature death. While there are many decisions that can be made more efficiently through the marketplace than by government, this is one of those decisions that can be made more efficiently by government than by the marketplace. Clean air laws can reduce harmful emissions by legislation and regulations. Clean water laws and laws against disposing of toxic wastes where they will harm people can likewise force decisions to be made in ways that take into account the external costs that would otherwise be ignored by those transacting in the marketplace.

By the same token, there may be transactions that would be *beneficial* to people who are not party to the decision-making, and whose interests are therefore not taken into account. The benefits of mud flaps on cars and trucks may be apparent to anyone who has ever driven in a rainstorm behind a car or truck that was throwing so much water or mud onto his windshield as to dangerously obscure vision. Even if everyone agrees that the benefits of mud flaps greatly exceed their costs, there is no feasible way of buying these benefits in a free market, since you receive no benefits from the mud flaps that you buy and put on your own car, but only from mud flaps that other people buy and put on their cars and trucks. These are "external benefits." Here again, it is possible to obtain collectively through government what cannot be obtained individually through the marketplace, simply by having laws passed requiring all cars and trucks to have mud flaps on them.

Some benefits are indivisible. Either everybody gets these benefits or nobody gets them. Military defense is one example. If military defense had to be purchased individually through the marketplace, then those who felt threatened by foreign powers could pay for guns, troops, cannon and all the other means of military deterrence and self-defense, while those who saw no dangers could refuse to spend their money on such things. However, the level of military security would be the same for both, since supporters and non-supporters of military forces are intermixed in the same society and exposed to the same dangers from enemy action.

Given the indivisibility of the benefits, even some citizens who fully appreciate the military dangers, and who consider the costs of meeting those dangers to be fully justified by the benefits, might still feel no need to spend their own money for military purposes, since their individual contribution would have no serious effect on their own individual security, which would depend primarily on how much others contributed. In such a situation, it is entirely possible to end up with inadequate military defense, even if everyone understands the cost of effective defense and considers the benefits worth it.

By collectivizing this decision and having it made by government, an end result can be achieved that is more in keeping with what most people want than if those people were allowed to decide individually what to do. Even among free market advocates, few would suggest that each individual should buy military defense in the marketplace. In short, there are things that government can do more efficiently than individuals because external costs or external benefits make individual decisions, based on individual interests, a less effective way of weighing costs and benefits to the whole society.

While external costs and benefits are not automatically taken into account in the marketplace, this is not to say that there may not be some imaginative ways in which they can be. In Britain, for example, ponds or lakes are often privately owned, and these owners have every incentive to keep them from becoming polluted, since a clean body of water is more attractive to fishermen or boaters who pay for its use. Similarly with shopping malls: Although maintaining clean, attractive malls with benches, rest rooms and security personnel costs money that the mall owners do not collect from the shoppers, a mall with such things attracts more customers, and so the rents charged the individual storeowners can be higher because a location in such malls is more valuable than a location in a mall without such amenities.

While there are some decisions which can be made more efficiently by individuals and other decisions which can be made more efficiently through collective action, that collective action need not be that of a national or even a local government but can be that of individuals spontaneously organizing themselves to deal with external costs or external benefits. For example, back during the pioneering days in the American west, when cattle grazed on the open plains that were not owned by anyone, there was the same danger that more animals would be allowed to graze than the land would support, as with sheep on the commons, since no given owner had an incentive to restrict the number of his own animals that were allowed to graze. However, in the American west during the pioneering era, owners of cattle organized themselves into cattlemen's associations that created rules for themselves and in one way or another kept newcomers out, in effect turning the plains into collectively owned land with collectively determined rules, sometimes enforced by collectively hired gunmen.

Modern trade associations can sometimes make collective decisions for an industry more efficiently than individual business owners could, especially when there are externalities of the sort used to justify government intervention in market economies. Such associations can promote the sharing of information and the standardization of products and procedures, benefitting both themselves and their customers.

In short, while externalities are a serious consideration in determining the role of government, they do not simply provide a blanket justification or a magic word which automatically allows economics to be ignored and politically attractive goals to be pursued without further ado. Both the incentives of the market and the incentives of politics must be weighed when choosing between them on any particular issue.

INCENTIVES AND CONSTRAINTS

Government is of course inseparable from politics, especially in a democratic country, so a distinction must be made and kept in mind between what a government *can* do to make things better than they would be in a free market and what it is in fact *likely* to do under the influence of political incentives and constraints. The distinction between what the government can do and what it is likely to do can be lost when we think of the government as simply an agent of society or even as one integral performer. In reality, the many individuals and agencies within a national government have their own separate interests, incentives, and agendas, to which they may respond far more often than they respond to either the public interest or to the policy agendas set by political leaders. Even in a totalitarian state such as the Soviet Union, different branches and departments of government had different interests that they pursued, despite whatever disadvantages this might have for the economy or the society. For example, industrial enterprises in different ministries avoided relying on each other for equipment or supplies, if at all possible. Thus an enterprise located in Vladivostok might order equipment or supplies that it needed from another enterprise under the same ministry located in Minsk, thousands of miles away, rather than depend on getting what it needed from another enterprise located nearby in Vladivostok that was under the control of a different ministry. Thus materials might be needlessly shipped thousands of miles eastward on the overburdened Soviet railroads, while the same kinds of materials were also being shipped westward on the same railroads by another enterprise under a different ministry.

Such economically wasteful cross-hauling was one of many inefficient allocations of scarce resources due to the political reality that government is not a monolith, even in a totalitarian society. In democratic societies, where innumerable interest groups are free to organize and influence different branches and agencies of government, there is even less reason to expect that the government will follow one coherent policy, much less a policy that would be followed by an ideal government representing the public interest. In the United States, some government agencies have been trying to restrict smoking while other government agencies have been subsidizing the growing of tobacco. Senator Daniel Patrick Moynihan once referred to "the warring principalities that are known as the federal government."

Under popularly elected government, the political incentives are to do what is popular, even if the consequences are worse than the consequences of doing nothing, or doing something that is less popular. As an example of what virtually everyone now agrees was a mistaken policy, the Nixon administration in 1971 created the first peacetime nationwide wage controls and price controls in the history of the United States. Among those at the meeting where this fateful decision was made was internationally renowned economist Arthur F. Burns, who argued strenuously against the policy being considered—and was over-ruled. Nor were the other people present economically illiterate. The president himself had long resisted the idea of wage and price controls and had publicly rejected the idea just eleven days before doing an about-face and accepting it. Inflation had created mounting pressures from the public and the media to "do something."

With a presidential election due the following year, the administration could not afford to be seen as doing nothing while inflation raged out of control. However, even aside from such political concerns, the participants in this meeting were "exhilarated by all the great decisions they had made" that day, according to one account. Some advisers later recalled that "more time was spent discussing the timing of the speech than how the economic program would work." There was particular concern that, if his speech were broadcast in prime time, it would cause cancellation of the very popular television program *Bonanza*, leading to public resentments. Here is what happened:

> Nixon's speech—despite the preemption of *Bonanza*—was a great hit. The public felt that the government was coming to its defense against the price gougers. . . During the next evening's newscasts, 90 percent of the coverage was devoted to Nixon's new policy. The coverage was favorable. And the Dow Jones Industrial Average registered a 32.9-point gain—the largest one-day increase up to then.

In short, the controls were a complete success politically. As for their economic consequences:

> Ranchers stopped shipping their cattle to the market, farmers drowned their chickens, and consumers emptied the shelves of supermarkets.

In short, artificially low prices led to supplies being reduced while the quantity demanded by consumers increased. For example, more American cattle began to be exported, mostly to Canada, instead of being sold in the price-controlled U.S. market. Thus price controls produced essentially the same results under the Nixon administration as they had produced in the Roman Empire under Diocletian, in Russia under the Communists, in Ghana under Nkrumah, and in numerous other times and places where such policies had been tried before. Nor was this particular policy unique politically in how it was conceived and carried out. Veteran economic adviser Herbert Stein observed, 25 years after the Nixon administration meeting at which he had been present, "failure to look ahead is extremely common in government policy making."

Another way of saying the same thing is that political time horizons tend to be much shorter than economic time horizons. Before the full negative economic consequences of the wage and price control policies became widely apparent, Nixon had been re-elected with a landslide victory at the polls. There is no "present value" factor to force political decision-makers to take into account the long-run consequences of their current decisions. One of the important fields neglected as a result of the short political time horizon is education. As a writer in India put it, "No one bothers about education because results take a long time to come." This is not peculiar to India. With fundamental educational reform being both difficult and requiring years to show end results in a better educated population entering adulthood, it is politically much more expedient for elected officials to demonstrate immediate "concern" for education by voting to spend increasing amounts of the taxpayers' money on it, even if that leads only to more expensive incompetence in more showy buildings.

The constraints within which government policy-making operates are as important as the incentives. Important and beneficial as a framework of rules of law may be, what that also means is that many matters must be dealt with categorically, rather than incrementally as in a market economy. The application of categorical laws prevents the enormous powers of government from being applied at the discretion or whim of individual functionaries, which would invite both corruption and arbitrary oppression. Since there are many things which require discretionary incremental adjustments, as noted in Chapter 4, for these things categorical laws can be difficult to apply or can produce counterproductive results. For example, while prevention of air pollution and water pollution are widely recognized as legitimate functions of government, which can achieve more economically efficient results in this regard than those of the free market, doing so through categorical laws can create major problems.

Despite the political appeal of categorical phrases like "clean water" and "clean air," there are in fact no such things, never have been, and perhaps never will be. Moreover, there are diminishing returns in removing impurities from water or air. A study of environmental risk regulation cited a former administrator of the Environmental Protection Agency on this:

> A former EPA administrator put the problem succinctly when he noted that about 95 percent of the toxic material could be removed from waste sites in a few months, but years are spent trying to remove the last little bit. Removing that last little bit can involve limited technological choice, high cost, devotion of considerable agency resources, large legal fees, and endless argument.

Reducing truly dangerous amounts of impurities from water or air may be done at costs that most people would agree were quite reasonable. But, as higher and higher standards of purity are prescribed by government, in order to eliminate ever more minute traces of ever more remote or more questionable dangers, the costs escalate out of proportion to the benefits. But, even if removing 98 percent of a given impurity costs twice as much as eliminating 97 percent, and removing 99 percent costs ten times as much, the political appeal of categorical phrases like "clean water" may be just as potent when the water is already 99.9 percent pure as when it was dangerously polluted.

Depending on what the particular impurity is, minute traces may or may not pose a serious danger. But political controversies over impurities in the water are unlikely to be settled at a scientific level when passions can be whipped up in the name of non-existent "clean water." No matter how pure the water becomes, someone can always demand the removal of more impurities. And, unless the public understands the logical and economic implications of what is being said, that demand can become politically irresistible, since no public official wants to be known as being opposed to clean water.

It is not even certain that reducing extremely small amounts of substances that are harmful in larger amounts reduces risks at all. Even arsenic in the water—in extremely minute traces—has been found to have health benefits. An old saying declares: "It is the dose that makes the poison." Similar research findings apply to many substances, including saccharin and alcohol. Although high doses of saccharin have been shown to increase the rate of cancer in laboratory rats, very low doses seem to *reduce* the rate of cancer in these rats. Although a large intake of alcohol shortens people's lifespan, very modest amounts of alcohol—like one glass of wine or beer per day—tend to reduce life-threatening conditions like hypertension. If there is some threshold amount of a particular substance required before it becomes harmful, that makes it questionable whether spending vast amounts of money to try to remove that last fraction of one percent from the air or water is necessarily going to make the public safer by even a minute amount.

The same principle applies in many other contexts, where minute traces of impurities can produce major political and legal battles—and consume millions of tax dollars with little or no net effect on the health or safety of the public. For example, one legal battle raged for a decade over the impurities in a New Hampshire toxic waste site, where these wastes were so diluted that children could have eaten some of the dirt there for 70 days a year without any significant harm—if there had been any children living or playing there, which there were not. As a result of spending more than nine million dollars, the level of impurities was reduced to the point where children could have safely eaten the dirt there 245 days a year. Moreover, without anything being done at all, both parties to the litigation agreed that more than half the volatile impurities would have evaporated by the year 2000. Yet hypothetical dangers to hypothetical children kept the issue going and money being spent.

With environmental safety, as with other kinds of safety, some forms of safety in one respect create dangers in other respects. California, for example, required a certain additive to be put into all gasoline sold in that state, in order to reduce the air pollution from automobile exhaust fumes. However, this new additive tended to leak from filling station storage tanks and automobile gas tanks, polluting the ground water in the first case and leading to more automobile fires in the second. Similarly, government-mandated air bags in automobiles, introduced to save lives in car crashes, have themselves killed small children.

These are all matters of incremental trade-offs to find an optimal amount and kind of safety, in a world where being categorically safe is as impossible as achieving 100 percent clean air or clean water. Incremental trade-offs are made all the time in individual market transactions, but it can be politically suicidal to oppose demands for more clean air, clean water or automobile safety. Therefore saying that the government *can* improve over the results of individual transactions in a free market is not the same as saying that it *will* in fact do so. Among the greatest external costs imposed in a society can be those imposed politically by legislators and officials who pay no costs whatever, while imposing billions of dollars in costs on others, in order to respond to political pressures from advocates of particular interests or ideologies.

In the United States, government regulations are estimated to cost about $4,400 per employee in large businesses and about $7,000 per employee in small businesses. Among other things, this suggests that the existence of numerous government regulations tends to give competitive advantages to big business, since there are apparently economies of scale in complying with these regulations. While government regulations may be defended by those who create them by referring to the benefits which such regulations provide, the economically relevant question is whether such benefits are worth the more than $840 billion in aggregate costs that they impose. In the marketplace, whoever creates $840 billion in costs would have to be sure to create more than $840 billion in benefits that customers will pay for. Otherwise that producer would risk bankruptcy. In the government, there are seldom any incentives or constraints to force such comparisons.

Just as we must keep in mind a sharp distinction between the goals of a particular policy and the actual consequences of that policy, so we must keep in mind a sharp distinction between the purpose for which a particular law was created and the purposes for which that law can be used. For example, President Franklin D. Roosevelt took the United States off the gold standard in 1933 under presidential powers created by laws passed during the First World War to prevent trading with enemy nations. Though that war had been over for more than a dozen years and the United States no longer had any enemy nations, the power was still there to be used for wholly different purposes.

Powers do not expire when the crises that created them have passed. Nor does the repeal of old laws have a high priority among legislators. Still less are institutions likely to close up on their own when the circumstances that caused them to be created no longer exist.

Chapter 18

GOVERNMENT FINANCE

Wall Street yawned when the deficit projections soared.
Michael Boskin

Like individuals, businesses, and other organizations, governments must have resources in order to continue to exist. In centuries past, governments could take these resources directly in the form of a share of the crops, livestock or other tangible assets of the population but, in modern industrial and commercial societies, governments take a share of the national output in the form of money. The financial activities of government affect the economy both by changing the incentives facing members of the general population and by directing the government's own spending into channels that the money might not have taken if left in the hands of those who earned it. Heavily taxed activities, products, localities, industries, or individuals tend to be inhibited from growing or may even decline absolutely, at least within the jurisdictions in which taxes are unusually high. Heavy taxes provide incentives to move elsewhere and the conversion of money that would otherwise have gone into consumption and investment into money to be dispensed by political authorities can change what is bought by that money and therefore what will be produced in the future.

The particular manner in which government acquires money also has repercussions on the national economy and even on international economic activities. The government receives money not only in the form of taxes but also in the form of revenues from sales of the bonds it issues, the prices it charges for some goods and services it provides, and from the sale of assets that the government owns, such as land, office furniture, or surplus military gear. Taxes and bond sales are usually the largest sources of money for the national government, the bonds being essentially claims on future tax revenues.

The choice between financing government activities with tax revenues or revenues from the sale of bonds—going into debt—has further repercussions on the economy at large. Charges for goods and services range from municipal transit fares and fees for using municipal golf courses to charges for entering national parks or cutting timber on federal land. These charges are seldom what they would be if the same goods or services were sold in a free market—and therefore seldom have the same effect on the allocation of scarce resources which have alternative uses. In short, these transactions are not simply transfers of money but, more fundamentally, affect the efficiency with which the economy operates.

In addition to charges for current sales of goods and services, there are also sales of government-owned assets. For example, during the pioneering era of American history, the federal government sold to the public vast amounts of land that it had acquired in various ways from the indigenous population or from foreign governments such as those of France, Spain, Mexico and Russia. In centuries past, governments often also sold monopoly rights to engage in various economic activities, including privateering on the high seas that would otherwise be called piracy without governmental sanction. During the late twentieth century, many national governments around the world that had taken over various industrial and commercial enterprises began selling them to private investors in order to have a more market-directed economy. A government may also simply print money and spend it, as many governments have done at various periods of history. However, the disastrous consequences of the resulting inflation have made this too risky politically for most governments to rely on this as a common practice.

Just as the sources of government revenues are varied, so government spending takes many forms and the choices of where and how to spend the government's money also have economic repercussions. Some spending is for things to be used during the current year—the pay of civilian and military personnel, electricity, paper, and other supplies required by the vast array of government institutions—and some spending is for things to be used both currently and in the future, such as highways, bridges, and hydroelectric dams. Although government spending is often all lumped together in media and political discussions, the particular kind of spending is often related to the particular kind of way that money is raised to pay for it. For example, taxes may be considered an appropriate way for current taxpayers to pay for current spending but issuing government bonds may be considered more appropriate to have future generations help pay for things being created for their future use or benefit, such as highways, dams, national parks or—in the case of cities—subways or buses.

As in many other areas of economics, the facts are relatively straightforward but the words used to describe the facts can lead to complications and misunderstandings. Some of the words used in discussing the financial operations of the government—"balanced budget," "deficit," "surplus," "national debt"— need to be plainly defined in order to avoid misunderstandings or even hysteria.

How much of government's spending is financed by tax revenues and how much by revenue from the sale of bonds determines whether it is operating with a deficit or a surplus in its budget. If all current government spending is paid for with money received in taxes, then the budget is said to be balanced. If current tax receipts exceed current spending there is said to be a budget surplus. If tax revenues do not cover all of the government's spending, some of which is covered by revenues from the sale of bonds, then the government is said to be operating at a deficit. The accumulation of these deficits over time adds up to the government's debt or what is called "the national debt." If this term really meant what it said, the national debt would include all the debts in the nation, including those of consumers and businesses. But in practice "national debt" means the debt owed by the national government.

TAXATION

"Death and taxes" have long been regarded as inescapable realities. But which of the various ways in which taxes can be collected is actually used makes a difference in the way individuals, enterprises, and the national economy as a whole respond. For example, when tax rates are raised 10 percent, it may be assumed by some that tax revenues will also rise by 10 percent. But in fact more people may move out of the heavily taxed jurisdiction, or buy less of the heavily taxed commodity, so that the revenues received can be disappointingly far below what was estimated. The state of Alaska discovered this when it passed a law greatly increasing its tax rates on cigarettes:

> The tax was to go into effect October 1, 1997. Smokers struck back by buying an astounding 175 million more cigarettes than usual in the three months before the tax deadline. Richard Watts of the Great Alaska Tobacco Company told the local papers that some smokers even bought sixty-carton cases—at $1,200 each—rather than pay the tax. As for Alaska's Department of Revenue, it saw its revenue estimates go up in smoke: collections slowed 60 percent following the infamous increase date.

In New York, where the city and state taxes add up to the highest taxes on cigarettes in the country, per capita sales of legally taxed cigarettes have been declining for years, as a large black market has developed. In the four months following another increase in the tax rate on cigarettes, sales of taxed cigarettes fell 50 percent below the same period the previous year.

Conversely, when the federal tax rate on capital gains was lowered from 28 percent to 20 percent in 1997, it was assumed that revenues from the capital gains tax would fall below the $54 billion collected in 1996 and the $209 billion projected to be collected over the next four years, before the tax rate was cut. Instead, tax revenues *rose* after the capital gains tax rate was cut: $372 billion were collected in capital gains taxes over the next four years. People adjusted their behavior to a more favorable outlook for investments by increasing their investments, so that the new 20 percent tax rate on the returns from these increased investments amounted to more total revenue than that produced by the old 28 percent tax rate on a total amount of investment that was not as large.

Instead of keeping their money in tax-exempt municipal bonds, for example, investors could now find it more advantageous to invest in producing real goods and services with a higher rate of return, now that lower tax rates enabled them to keep more of their gains. It was much the same story halfway around the world in India:

> Lower income taxes brought greater compliance and more revenues for the treasury. Direct taxes in 1995-96 accounted for 29 percent of revenues, compared to 19 percent in 1990-91.

None of this should be surprising. Many a business has become more profitable by charging lower prices, thereby increasing sales and earning higher total profits at a lower rate of profit per sale. Taxes are the prices charged by governments and sometimes they too can collect more total revenue at a lower tax rate. Government budgets, including both taxes and expenditures, are not records of what has already happened. They are plans or predictions about what is going to happen. No one really knows what is going to happen, so everything depends on how projections about the future are made. In the United States, the Congressional Budget Office projects tax receipts without fully taking into account how tax rates tend to change economic behavior—and how changed economic behavior then changes tax receipts. For example, the Congressional Budget Office advised Congress that raising the capital gains tax rate from 20 percent to 28 percent in 1986 would increase the revenue received from that tax—but in fact the revenues from this tax fell. Conversely, cuts in the capital gains tax rate in 1978, 1997, and 2003 all led to increased revenues from that tax.

Undaunted, the Congressional Budget Office estimated that an extension of a temporary reduction in the capital gains tax to 15 percent would cost the Treasury $20 billion in lost revenues—even though this temporary tax cut had already resulted in tens of billions of dollars in increased revenues. Many in the media reason the way the Congressional Budget Office reasons—and are caught by surprise when tax revenues do not follow these beliefs. "An unexpectedly steep rise in tax revenues from corporations and the wealthy is driving down the projected budget deficit this year," the *New York Times* reported in 2006.

Neither the Congressional Budget Office nor anyone else can predict the consequences of a given tax rate increase or decrease. It is not just that the exact amount of revenue cannot be predicted. Whether revenue will move in one direction or the opposite direction is not a foregone conclusion. The choice is among alternative educated guesses—or, what is worse, mechanically calculating how much revenue will come in if no one's behavior changes in the wake of a tax change. Behavior has changed too often, and too dramatically, to proceed on that assumption.

Although it is common in politics and in the media to refer to government's "raising taxes" or "cutting taxes," this terminology blurs a crucial distinction between tax *rates* and tax *revenues*. The government can change tax rates but the reaction of the public to these changes can result in either a higher or a lower amount of tax revenues being collected, depending on circumstances and responses. Thus references to proposals for a "$500 billion tax cut" or a "$700 billion tax increase" are wholly misleading because all that the government can enact is a change in tax rates, whose actual consequences can be determined only after the fact. While taxes are often thought of as simply transfers of money from the people to the government, their economic consequences include changes in behavior that can affect the whole economy for better or worse.

People react in many different ways to tax rate increases. In the case of the eighteenth-century American colonies, they reacted by rebelling against British rule, prompting Edmund Burke to declare in the British Parliament: "Your tax yields no revenue. It yields only rebellion."

The Incidence of Taxation

Who pays how much of the taxes collected by the government?

This question cannot be answered simply by looking at tax laws or even at a table of estimates based on those laws. As we have already seen, people react to tax changes by changing their own behavior, and different people have different abilities to change their behavior in order to avoid taxes.

While an investor can invest in tax-free bonds at a lower rate of return or in assets that pay a higher rate of return, but are subject to taxes, a factory worker has no such options and finds whatever taxes the government takes already gone by the time he gets his pay check. Various complex financial arrangements can spare wealthy people from having to pay taxes on all their wealth but, since these complex arrangements require lawyers and other professionals to make such arrangements, people of more modest means may not be equally able to escape their tax burden and can even end up paying a higher percentage of their income in taxes than someone who is in a higher income bracket that is officially taxed at a higher rate.

Since income is not the only thing that is taxed, how much total tax any given individual pays depends also on how many other taxes apply and what that individual's situation is. Obviously, taxes on homes or automobiles fall only on those who own them and, while sales taxes fall on whoever buys any of the many items subject to those taxes, different people spend different proportions of their income on consumer goods. Lower income people tend to spend a higher percentage of their income on consumer goods, while higher income people tend to invest more—sometimes most—of their income. The net effect is that sales taxes tend to take a higher percentage of the incomes of low-income people than they take from the incomes of higher-income people. This is called a "regressive" tax, as distinguished from a "progressive" tax that subjects higher incomes to a higher percentage rate of taxation. Social Security taxes are likewise regressive, since they apply only to income up to some fixed level, with income above that level not being subject to taxes. Income taxes, on the other hand, exempt incomes below some fixed level. Given the different rules for different kinds of taxation, figuring out what the total incidence of taxation is for different people is not easy in principle, much less in practice.

Issues and controversies about tax rates often discuss the incidence of taxes on "the rich" or "the poor," when in fact the taxes fall on income rather than wealth. A genuinely rich person, someone with enough money not to have to work at all, may have a very modest income or no income at all during a given year. Moreover, even during years of high incomes and high rates of taxation on that income, this taxation does not touch the rich individual's accumulated wealth. Most of the people described as "rich" in discussions of tax issues are in fact not rich at all but simply people who have reached their peak earnings years, often having worked their way up to that peak after decades of earning much more modest salaries. Progressive income taxes typically hit such people rather than the genuinely rich.

Since each individual pays a mixture of progressive and regressive taxes, as well as taxes that apply to some goods and not to others, it is by no means easy to determine who is actually paying what share of the country's taxes. What is even more difficult is to determine who bears the real burden of those taxes by suffering the consequences of changed economic behavior, even if no money directly changes hands. For example, American employers pay half of the taxes that support Social Security and all of the taxes that pay for unemployment compensation. However, as we have seen in Chapter 9, how high an employer is willing to bid for a worker's services is limited by the amount that will be added to the employer's revenue by hiring that worker or such workers. But an employee whose output adds $50,000 to a company's sales receipts is not worth $50,000 if Social Security taxes, unemployment taxes, and other costs of employment add up to $10,000. In that case, the upper limit to how far an employer would bid would be $40,000, not $50,000.

Even if the worker does not directly pay any of that $10,000, if the pay received by that worker is $10,000 less than it would be otherwise, then the burden of those taxes has fallen on the worker, no matter who sends the money to the government. It is much the same story when taxes are levied on businesses which then raise their prices to the consumer. Depending on the nature of the tax and the competition in the market, the consumers can end up with anywhere from none to all of the burden of those taxes. In short, the official legal incidence of taxation does not necessarily tell who really bears the burden in the end.

Local Taxation

Taxation of course occurs at both the national and the local levels. In the United States, local property taxes supply much of the revenue used by local governments. Like other governmental units, local governments tend to want to maximize the revenues they receive, which in turn maximize the favorable publicity local officials gain from spending money in ways that will increase their chances of re-election. At the same time, raising tax *rates* produces adverse reactions, which can reduce these officials' re-election prospects. One way of raising local tax revenues without raising local tax rates is to replace low-valued property with higher-valued property. This can be done by condemning as "blighted" the housing and businesses in low-income or even moderate-income neighborhoods, acquiring the property through the power of eminent domain and then transferring it to some enterprise that will build a shopping mall, hotels, or casinos, which will generate more tax revenue than the existing home owners and business owners were paying.

The outraged homeowners and business owners, who typically receive far less in compensation than the market value of their demolished property, are usually a sufficiently small percentage of the voting population that local officials can gain votes on net balance—if they calculate accurately. It is often possible to convince others in the media and the public that it is these dispossessed tenants, homeowners, and business owners who are "selfish" in opposing "progress" for the whole community.

The 2005 U.S. Supreme Court decision in *Kelo v. New London* expanded the powers of governments to take property under the powers of eminent domain for "public purposes," extending beyond the Constitution's authorization of taking private property for "public use" such as building military bases, highways, or bridges. This decision confirmed the power already being exercised to transfer private property from one user to another, even if the latter were simply building amusement parks or other recreational facilities. What this means economically, in terms of the allocation of scarce resources which have alternative uses, is that the alternative uses no longer have to be of higher value, since the alternative users no longer have to bid the property away when they can rely on government officials to simply take the property under the power of eminent domain and sell it to them for less than they would have had to pay the existing property owners to transfer the property to them voluntarily.

European countries often use a "value added" tax as a major source of revenues. This tax is imposed on products as they pass through the production process, each enterprise in the chain of production being taxed on whatever value its operations added to the product. The advantage of this kind of tax, from the standpoint of the officials who impose it, is that the total amount that the taxes add to the final price paid by the consumer is not apparent, as it is with a sales tax, for example. In general, the less visible a tax is, the more revenue can be collected without resistance or electoral retribution by the voters. Income taxes, as well as sales taxes, are more visible than value added taxes but where the taxes are withheld before a pay check is issued, it is less visible than it was in the days before payroll withholding, when each taxpayer had to write a check for all the income tax collected by the government.

GOVERNMENT BONDS

Selling government bonds is a way to raise revenue to pay for goods and services whose costs are not covered by tax revenues. It is simply borrowing money to be repaid from future tax revenues. Government bonds can also be a source of confusion under their other name, "the national debt." These bonds, like all bonds, are indeed a debt but the economic significance of a given amount of debt can vary greatly according to the circumstances. That is as true for the government as it is for an individual.

What would be a huge debt for an average factory worker may be insignificant for a millionaire who can easily pay it off at his convenience. Since countries grow economically over time, a debt that would be crushing when the total national income is low may be quite manageable in a later period when national income is much higher. Thus, although the national debt of the United States reached $6 trillion for the first time in 2002, the Gross Domestic Product exceeded $10 trillion that year, so that the debt as a percentage of GDP was lower than it was a decade earlier—and a much lower percentage than it was back in 1946, when the national debt exceeded GDP by 22 percent.

Like other statistical aggregates, the national debt tends to grow over time as population and the national income grow and as inflation causes a given number of dollars to represent smaller amounts of real wealth or real liabilities. This presents political opportunities for critics of whatever party is in power to denounce their running up record-breaking debts to be paid by future generations. Depending on the specific circumstances of a particular country at a particular time, this may be a reason for serious concern or the criticisms may be simply political theater.

National debts must be compared not only to national output or national income but also to the alternatives facing a given nation at a given time. For example, the federal debt of the United States in 1945 was $258 billion at a time when the national income was $182 billion. In other words, the national debt was 41 percent *higher* than the national income, as a result of paying the huge costs of fighting World War II. The costs of *not* fighting the Nazis or imperial Japan were considered to be so much worse that the national debt seemed secondary at the time. Even in peacetime, if a nation's highways and bridges are crumbling from a lack of maintenance and repair, that does not appear in national debt statistics but it is a loss being passed on to the next generation, just as surely as the cost of a national debt would be. If the cost of repairs is worth the benefits, then issuing government bonds to raise the money needed to restore this infrastructure makes sense— and the burden on future generations may be no greater than if the bonds had never been issued, though it takes the form of money owed rather than the form of crumbling and perhaps dangerous infrastructure that may become even more costly to repair in the next generation, due to continued neglect.

Either wartime or peacetime expenditures by the government can be paid for out of tax revenues or out of money received from selling government bonds. Which method makes more economic sense depends in part on whether the money is being spent for a current flow of goods and services, such as electricity or paper for government agencies or food for the military forces, or is instead being spent for adding to an accumulated stock of capital, such as hydroelectric dams or national highways to be used in future years and for future generations. Going into debt to create long-term investments makes as much sense for the government as a private individual's borrowing more than his annual income to buy a house.

By the same token, someone who borrows more than his annual income to pay for lavish entertainment this year is simply living beyond his means and probably heading for big financial trouble. The same principle applies to government expenditures for current benefits, with the costs being passed on to future generations.

What must also be taken into account when assessing a national debt is to whom it is owed. When a government sells all of its bonds to its own citizens, that is very different from selling all or a substantial part of its bonds to people in other countries. The difference is that an internal debt is held by the same population that is responsible for paying the taxes to redeem the principal and pay the interest. "We owe it to ourselves" is a phrase sometimes used to describe this situation. But, when a significant share of the bonds issued by the U.S. government is bought by people in Japan or China, then the bond-holders and the taxpayers are no longer the same population. Future generations of Japanese or Chinese will be able to collect wealth from future generations of Americans. As of 2004, nearly half the federal debt of the United States—44 percent—was held by foreigners.

Even when a national debt is held entirely by citizens of the country that issued the bonds, different individuals hold different shares of the bonds and pay different shares of the taxes. Much also depends on how members of future generations acquire the bonds issued to this generation. If the next generation simply inherits the bonds bought by the current generation, then they inherit both the debt and the wealth required to pay off the debt, so that there is no net burden passed on from one generation to the next. If, however, the older generation sells its bonds to the younger generation—either directly from individual to individual or by cashing in the bonds, which the government pays for by issuing new bonds to new people—then the burden of the debt has been liquidated as far as the older generation is concerned and passed on to the next generation.

Financial arrangements and their complications should not obscure what is happening in terms of real goods and services.

When the United States fought World War II, running up a large national debt did not mean that the Americans alive at that time got something for nothing on credit. The tanks, bombers, and other military equipment and supplies used to fight the war came out of the American economy at that time—at the expense of consumer goods that would otherwise have been produced by American industry. These costs were not paid for by borrowing from people in other countries. American consumers simply consumed a much smaller part of American production.

The war could have been paid for either by raising taxes or by selling bonds. The particular mixture of ways of paying that was chosen did not relieve that generation from having to sacrifice their standard of living to fight the war. The burden of paying for World War II could be passed on to a later generation only in the sense that the World War II generation could in later years be reimbursed for their sacrifice by the sale of the bonds they had bought during the war. In reality, wartime inflation meant that the real purchasing power of the bonds when they were cashed in was not as great as the purchasing power used to buy them during the war. The World War II generation was permanently stuck with the losses this entailed.

In general, the government's choice of acquiring money through the collection of taxes or the sale of government bonds does not relieve the population of its economic burden unless the government sells the bonds to foreigners. Even in that case, however, the population merely postpones the burden. The choice may be more significant politically to the government itself, as it may encounter less resistance when it does not raise taxes to cover all current spending but relies on bond sales to supplement its tax revenues. This convenience for the government is a temptation to use bond sales to cover current expenses instead of reserving such sales to cover spending on long-term projects.

Although government bonds get paid off when they reach their maturity dates, usually new bonds are issued and sold, so that the national debt is turned over rather than being paid off, though at particular periods of history some countries have paid off their national debts completely. This does not mean that selling government bonds is without costs or risks. The cost to the government includes the interest that must be paid on the national debt. The more important cost to the economy is the government's absorption of investment funds that might otherwise have gone into the private sector, where they would have added to productivity and employment. When the national debt reaches a size where investors begin to worry about whether it can continue to be turned over as government bonds mature, without raising interest rates to attract the needed buyers, that can lead to expectations that higher interest rates will inhibit future investment—an expectation that can immediately inhibit current investment. Rising interest rates for government bonds tend to affect other interest rates, which also rise, due to competition for investment funds in the financial markets—and that in turn tends to reduce credit and the aggregate demand on which continuing prosperity depends.

How serious such dangers are depends on the size of the national debt—not absolutely but relative to the nation's income.

Professional financiers and investors know this and so are unlikely to panic even when there is a record-breaking national debt, if that is not a large debt relative to the size of the economy. That is why, despite much political rhetoric about the American government's budget deficit and the growing national debt it created in the early twenty-first century, distinguished economist Michael Boskin could say: "Wall Street yawned when the deficit projections soared." The financiers were vindicated when the size of the deficit in 2005 declined below what it had been in 2004. The *New York Times* reported:

> The big surprise has been in tax revenue, which is running nearly 15 percent higher than in 2004. Corporate tax revenue has soared about 40 percent, after languishing for four years, and individual tax revenue is up as well.

Surprise is in the eye of the beholder. There was nothing unprecedented about rising tax *revenues* without an increase in tax *rates*. Indeed, there have been at various times and places increases in tax revenues following a cut in tax rates.

The 1997 cut in the capital gains tax, already mentioned, was just one example. While cuts in American government's income tax rates in the early 1980s have sometimes been blamed for the increased federal deficits of that decade, the tax revenues collected during every year of the 1980s were higher than the tax revenues collected in any previous year in the country's history. Federal spending simply rose faster than the tax revenues. Two decades earlier, the Kennedy administration's tax cuts likewise led to higher tax revenues. The same thing happened during the nineteenth century when German principalities along the Rhine agreed to reduce the toll rates that they charged for boats traveling on that river through their territories. Although the toll *rates* fell, these lower rates attracted so much more river traffic that the total toll *revenue* increased.

What will actually happen to tax revenues in response to any given reduction in tax rates depends on many factors, including how much the rates are cut and how responsive the public is to the changed incentives. Ultimately that is an empirical question whose answer will be discovered after the fact. However, it is not true, as often asserted in politics and the media, that the only way to reduce a deficit is to raise tax rates or cut spending. In a growing economy, merely keeping spending from increasing faster than the rising tax revenues can reduce the deficit. In some cases, where reducing the tax rate spurs faster economic growth through its effects on changing people's behavior, the deficit can be brought down faster. But the extent to which this is true in given circumstances can only be discovered after the fact.

CHARGES FOR GOODS AND SERVICES

As already noted, both local and national governments charge for providing various goods and services. These charges are often quite different from what they would be in a free market because the incentives facing officials who set these charges are different—and therefore the allocation of scarce resources which have alternative uses is different.

Mass transportation in cities was once provided by private businesses which charged fares that covered both current expenses—fuel, the pay of bus drivers, etc.—and the longer run costs of buying new buses, trolleys, or subway trains to replace those that wore out, as well as providing a rate of return on the capital provided by investors sufficient to keep investors supplying this capital. Over the years, however, many privately owned municipal transit systems became government-owned. Often this was because the fares were regulated by municipal authorities and were not allowed to rise enough to continue to maintain the transit system, especially during periods of inflation. In New York City, for example, the five-cent subway fare remained politically sacred for years, even during periods of high inflation when all other prices were rising, including the prices paid for the equipment, supplies, and labor used to keep the subways running. Clearly, privately owned subway systems were no longer viable under these money-losing conditions and the ownership of these systems passed to the city government. While municipal transit was still losing money, the losses were now being made up out of tax revenues.

Incentives to stop the losses, which would have been imperative in a privately owned business faced with financial extinction, were now much weaker, if not non-existent, in a municipally owned transit system whose losses were automatically covered by the taxpayers. Thus a service could continue to be provided at costs exceeding the benefits for which passengers were willing to pay. Put differently, resources whose value to people elsewhere in the economy was greater were nevertheless being allocated to municipal transit because of subsidies extracted from taxpayers.

Incentives to price government-provided goods and services at lower levels than in a private business are by no means confined to municipal transit. Since lower prices mean more demanded than at higher prices, those who set prices for government-provided goods and services have incentives to assure a sufficient continuing demand for the goods and services they sell and therefore continuing jobs for themselves. Moreover, since lower prices are less likely to provoke political protests and pressures than are higher prices, the jobs of those controlling the sales of government-provided goods and services are easier, more secure, and less stressful when prices are kept below the level that would prevail in a free market.

In situations where the money paid for the goods and services goes into the general treasury, rather than into the coffers of the government agency, there is even less incentive to make the charges cover the costs of providing the goods and services. For example, the fees collected for entering Yosemite, Yellowstone, or other national parks go into the U.S. government's treasury and the costs of maintaining these parks are paid from the treasury, which is to say, from general tax revenues. There is therefore no incentive for officials who run national parks to charge fees that will cover the costs of running those parks. Even where a national park is considered to be overcrowded and its facilities deteriorating from heavy use, there is still no incentive to raise the entry fees when what matters is how much money Congress will authorize to be paid out of general tax revenues. In short, the normal function provided by prices of causing consumers to ration themselves and producers to keep costs below what consumers are willing to pay is non-existent in these situations.

The independence of prices from costs offers political opportunities for elected or appointed officials to cater to particular special interests by offering lower prices to the elderly, for example, with a one-time $10 fee for a pass that entitles the holders to enter any national park free for the rest of their lives, while others may be charged $25 each time they enter any national park. The fact that the elderly usually have higher incomes than the general population may carry less weight than the fact that the elderly are more likely to vote.

Although there are many contexts in which government-provided goods and services are priced below cost, there are other contexts in which these services are provided well above costs. Bridges, for example, are often built with the idea that the tolls collected from a bridge over the years will eventually cover the cost of building it. However, it is not uncommon for the tolls to continue to be collected long after the original cost has been covered several times over. Where the government agency in charge of the bridge is allowed to keep the tolls it collects, there is every incentive to use that money to undertake other projects—that is, to expand the bureaucratic empire controlled by those in charge of the agency. The bridge authority may decide, for example, to initiate or subsidize ferry service across the same waterway spanned by the bridge, in order to meet an "unmet need" of commuters. As already noted in the first chapter, there are always "unmet needs" in any economy and, at a sufficiently low fare on the ferries, there will be people using those ferries—politically demonstrating that "need"—even if what they pay does not come close to covering the cost of the ferry service.

In short, resources will be allocated to the ferry that would never be allocated there if both the bridge and the ferry were independent operations in a free market. More important, ferries will be allocated resources whose value is greater in alternative uses.

Sometimes taxpayer-provided subsidies for some government-provided goods and services are said to be justified because otherwise "the poor" would be unable to obtain these goods and services. Putting aside for the moment the question whether most of "the poor" are a permanent class or simply people transiently in low income brackets (including young people living with middle-class or affluent parents) and accepting for the sake of argument that it is somehow imperative that "the poor" use the particular goods and services in question, subsidizing *everybody* who uses those goods and services in order to help a fraction of the population seems less efficient than directly helping "the poor" with money or vouchers and letting the others pay their own way. The same principle applies when considering cross-subsidies provided, not by the taxpayers, but by excessive charges on some (such as toll bridge users) to subsidize others (such as ferry boat riders). The weakness of the rationale based on subsidizing "the poor" is shown also by how often the same taxpayer subsidies are used to finance things seldom used by "the poor," such as municipal golf courses or symphony orchestras.

In general, government charges for goods and services are not simply a matter of transferring money but of redirecting resources in the economy, usually without much concern for the allocation of those resources in ways that maximize net benefits.

GOVERNMENT EXPENDITURES

The government spends both voluntarily and involuntarily. Officials may voluntarily decide to create a new program or department or may be involuntarily forced by law to pay unemployment insurance when a downturn in the economy causes more people to lose their jobs. Government spending may also go up automatically when farmers produce such a bumper crop that it cannot all be sold at the prices guaranteed under agricultural subsidy laws and so the government is legally obligated to buy the surplus. Unemployment compensation and agricultural subsidies are just two of a whole spectrum of "entitlement" programs whose spending is beyond the control of any given government officials, once these programs have been enacted into law. Although government spending and the annual deficits and accumulated national debts which often result from that spending are often blamed on those officials who happen to be in charge of the government at a given time, much of the spending is not at their discretion but is mandated by law.

Government spending has repercussions on the economy, just as taxation does—and both the spending going out and the tax revenues coming in are to some extent beyond the government's control. When production and employment go down in the economy, the tax revenues collected from businesses and workers tend to go down as well. Meanwhile, unemployment compensation, farm subsidies and other outlays tend to go up. This means that the government is spending more money while receiving less. Therefore, on net balance, government is adding purchasing power to the economy during a downturn, which tends to cushion the decline in output and employment.

Conversely, when production and employment are booming, more tax revenues come in and there are fewer individuals or enterprises receiving government financial help, so the government tends to be removing purchasing power from the economy at a time when there might otherwise be inflation. These institutional arrangements are called "automatic stabilizers," since they counter upward or downward movements in the economy without requiring any given administration to make any decisions.

Sometimes more is claimed for government spending than the reality will support. Many government programs, whether at local or national levels, are often promoted by saying that, in addition to whatever other benefits are claimed, the money will be spent and respent, creating some multiple of the wealth represented by the initial expenditure. In reality, any money— government or private—that is spent will be respent again and again. In so far as the government takes money from one place—from taxpayers or from those who buy government bonds—and transfers it somewhere else, the loss of purchasing power in one place offsets the gain in purchasing power elsewhere. Only if, for some reason, the government is more likely to spend the money than those from whom it was taken were, is there a net increase in spending for the country as a whole. John Maynard Keynes' historic contribution to economics was to spell out the conditions under which this was considered likely but Keynesian economics has been controversial on this and other grounds.

Costs vs. Expenditures

Often, when discussing government policies or programs, the "cost" of those policies or programs is spoken of without specifying whether that means the cost to the government or the cost to the economy. The cost to the government of forbidding homes or businesses to be built in certain areas is only the cost of running the agencies in charge of controlling such things, which can be a very modest cost, especially after knowledge of the policy becomes widespread and few people would consider trying to build in the forbidden areas. But such bans on building can cost the economy billions of dollars. Conversely, it may cost the government large sums of money to build and maintain levees along the banks of a river but, if the government did not spend this money, the people could suffer even bigger losses from floods. When the cost of any given policy is considered, it is important to be very clear as to *whose costs* are being discussed or considered.

One of the objections to building more prisons to lock up more criminals for longer periods of time is that it costs the government a large amount of money per criminal per year to keep them behind bars. Sometimes a comparison is made between the cost of keeping a criminal in prison versus the cost of sending someone to college for the same period of time. However, the relevant alternative to the costs of incarceration are the costs sustained by the public when career criminals are outside of prison. In early twenty-first century Britain, for example, the financial costs of crime have been estimated at £60 billion, while the total costs of prisons were less than

£3 billion. Government officials are of course preoccupied with the prison costs that they have to cover rather than the £60 billion that others must pay.

Benefits vs. Net Benefits

The weighing of costs against benefits, which is part of the allocation of scarce resources which have alternative uses, can be greatly affected by government expenditures.

While there are some goods and services which virtually everyone considers desirable, different people may consider them desirable to different degrees and are correspondingly willing to pay for them to different degrees. If some Product X costs ten dollars but the average person is willing to pay only six dollars for it, then that product will obviously be purchased by only a minority, even if the vast majority regard Product X as desirable to some extent. Such situations provide political opportunities to those holding, or seeking to be elected to, government positions. What is a common situation from an economic standpoint can be redefined politically as a "problem"—namely that most people want something that costs more than they feel like paying for it. The proposed solution to this problem is often that the government should in one way or another make this widely desired product more "affordable" to more people. Price control is likely to reduce the supply, so the viable options are government subsidies for the production of the desired product or government subsidies for the purchase. In either case, the public now pays for the product through both the prices paid directly by the purchasers and the taxes paid by the population at large.

For the price of this particular ten-dollar product to become "affordable"—that is, to cost what people are willing to pay—that price can be no higher than six dollars. Therefore a government subsidy of at least four dollars must make up the difference and taxes or bond sales must provide that additional money. The net result, under these conditions, is that millions of people will be paying ten dollars for something that is worth only six dollars to them. In short, government finance in such cases creates a misallocation of scarce resources which have alternative uses.

A more realistic scenario would be that the costs of running the government program must be added to the costs of production, so that the total cost of the product would rise above the initial ten dollars, making the misallocation of resources greater. Moreover, it is unlikely that the price would be reduced only to that level which the average person was willing to pay, since that would still leave half the population unable to buy the product at a price that they are willing to pay. A more politically likely scenario would be that the price would be reduced below six dollars and the cost rise above ten dollars.

Many government expenditure patterns that would be hard to explain in terms of the costs and benefits to the public are by no means irrational in terms of the incentives and constraints facing the officials responsible for these patterns. It is, for example, not uncommon to find governments spending money on building a sports stadium or a community center at a time when roads, highways, and bridges are neglected. The cost of damage done to cars using roads with potholes may greatly exceed the cost of repairing the potholes, which in turn would be a fraction of the cost of building a shiny new community center or an impressive sports stadium. Such an expenditure pattern is irrational only if government is conceived of as the public interest personified, rather than an organization run by individuals who put themselves first, as people do in many other institutions and activities.

The top priority of an elected official is usually to get re-elected, and that requires a steady stream of favorable publicity to keep one's name before the public in a good light. The opening of any major new facility, whether urgently needed or not, creates such political opportunities by attracting the media to ribbon-cutting ceremonies. Filling potholes, repairing bridges, or updating the equipment at a sewage treatment plant creates no ribbon-cutting ceremonies or occasions for speeches by politicians.

The pattern of government expenditures growing out of such incentives and constraints is not new or limited to particular countries. Adam Smith pointed out a similar pattern back in eighteenth century England:

The proud minister of an ostentatious court may frequently take pleasure in executing a work of splendour and magnificence, such as a great highway, which is frequently seen by the principal nobility, whose applauses not only flatter his vanity, but even contribute to support his interest at court. But to execute a great number of little works, in which nothing that can be done can make any great appearance, or excite the smallest degree of admiration in any traveller, and which, in short, have nothing to recommend them but their extreme utility, is a business which appears in every respect too mean and paultry to merit the attention of so great a magistrate.

GOVERNMENT OBLIGATIONS

In addition to what the government currently spends, it has various legal obligations to make future expenditures. These obligations are specified and quantified in the case of government bonds that must be redeemed for various amounts of money at various future dates. Other obligations are open-ended, such as legal obligations to pay whoever qualifies for unemployment compensation or agricultural subsidies in the future. These obligations are not only open-ended but difficult to estimate, since they depend on things beyond the government's control, such as the level of unemployment and the size of farmers' crops.

Other open-ended obligations that are difficult to estimate are government "guarantees" of loans made by others to private borrowers or to those who lend to foreign governments. These guarantees appear to cost nothing, so long as the loans are repaid —and the fact that these guarantees cost the taxpayers nothing is likely to be trumpeted in the media by the advocates of such guarantees who can point out how businesses and jobs were saved, without any expense to the government. But, at unpredictable times, the loans do not get paid and then huge amounts of the taxpayers' money get spent to cover one of these apparently costless guarantees. When the U.S. government guaranteed the depositors in savings and loan associations that their deposits would be covered by government-guaranteed insurance, this appeared to cost nothing until these savings and loan associations ran up losses in the hundreds of billions of dollars and their depositors were reimbursed by the government after these enterprises collapsed.

Among the largest obligations of many governments are pensions that have been promised to future retirees. These are more predictable, given the size of the aging population and their mortality rates, but the problem here is that very often there is not enough money put aside to cover the promised pensions. This problem is not peculiar to any given country but is widespread among countries around the world, since elected officials benefit by promising pensions to voters but stand to lose votes by raising tax rates high enough to pay what it would cost to redeem those promises. It is easier to leave it to future governments to figure out how to deal with the financial shortfall.

The difference between political incentives and economic incentives is shown by the difference between government-provided pensions and annuities provided by insurance companies. Government programs may be analogized to the activities of insurance companies by referring to these programs as "social insurance," but without in fact having either the same incentives or the same results as private insurance companies selling annuities. The most fundamental difference between private annuities and government pensions is that the former create real wealth by investing premiums, in order to be able to pay pensions later on, while the latter simply use current premiums from the working population to pay current pensions to the retired population.

What this means is that a private annuity invests the premiums that come in—creating factories, apartment buildings, or other tangible assets whose earnings will later enable the annuities to be paid to those whose money was used to create these assets. Government pension plans, such as Social Security in the United States, simply spend the premiums as they are received. Much of this money is used to pay pensions to current retirees, but the rest of the money can be used to finance other government activities, ranging from fighting wars to paying for Congressional junkets. There is no wealth created to be used in the future to pay the pensions of those who are currently paying into the system.

The illusion of investment is maintained by giving the Social Security trust fund government bonds in exchange for the money that is taken from it and spent on current government programs. But these bonds represent no tangible assets. They are simply promises to pay money collected from future taxpayers. The country as a whole is not one dollar richer because these bonds were printed, so there is no analogy with private investments that create tangible wealth. If there were no such bonds, then future taxpayers would have to make up the difference when future Social Security premiums are insufficient to pay pensions to future retirees. That is exactly the same as what will have to happen when there are bonds. Accounting procedures may make it seem that there is an investment when the Social Security system holds government bonds but the economic reality is that neither the government nor anyone else can spend and save the same money.

What has enabled Social Security—and similar government pension plans in other countries—to postpone the day of reckoning is that a relatively small generation in the 1930s was followed by a much larger "baby boom" generation of the 1940s and 1950s, earning much higher incomes and therefore paying larger premiums, from which pensions could easily be paid to the retirees from the previous generation. Not only could the promises made to the 1930s generation be kept, additional benefits could be voted for them, with obvious political advantages to those awarding these additional benefits.

With the passage of time, however, a declining birthrate and an increasing life expectancy reduced the ratio of people paying into the system to people receiving money from the system. Unlike a private annuity, where each generation creates the wealth that will later pay its own pensions, government pension systems pay the pensions of the retired generation from the premiums paid by the currently working generation. That is why private annuities are not jeopardized by changing demographics but government pension plans are.

Government pension plans enable current politicians to make promises which future governments will be expected to keep. These are virtually ideal political conditions for producing generous pension laws and future financial crises resulting from them. Nor are such incentives and results confined to the United States. Countries of the European Union likewise face huge financial liabilities as the size of their retired population continues to grow, not only absolutely but also relative to the size of the working populations whose taxes are paying their pensions. In Brazil, government pensions are already paying out more money than they are taking in, with the deficits being especially large in the pensions for unionized government workers. In other words, the looming financial crisis which American and European governments are dreading and trying to forestall has already struck in Brazil, whose government pensions have been described as "the most generous in the world." According to *The Economist*:

> Civil servants do not merely retire on full salary; they get, in effect, a pay rise because they stop paying contributions into the system. Most women retire from government service at around 50 and men soon afterwards. A soldier's widow inherits his pension, and bequeaths it to her daughters.

Given that Brazil's civil servants are an organized and unionized special interest group, such generosity is understandable politically. The question is whether the voting public in Brazil and elsewhere will understand the economic consequences well enough to be able to avoid the financial crises to which such unfunded generosity can lead—in the name of "social insurance." Such awareness is beginning to dawn on people in some countries. In New Zealand, for example, a poll found that 70 percent of New Zealanders under the age of 45 believe that the pensions they have been promised will not be there for them when they retire.

In one way or another, the day of reckoning seems to be approaching in many countries for programs described as "social insurance" but which were in fact never insurance at all. Such programs not only fail to create wealth, the more generous retirement plans may in fact lessen the rate at which wealth is created, by enabling people to retire while they are still quite capable of working. For example, while 62 percent of the people in the 55 to 64 year old bracket are still working in Japan and 61 percent in the United States, only 41 percent of the people in that age bracket are still working in the countries of the European Union.

Chapter 19

AN OVERVIEW

Demagoguery beats data in making public policy.
Congressman Dick Armey

The basic economic principles involved in discussions of the national economy are not overly complicated but two crucial misconceptions need to be guarded against: (1) the fallacy of composition and (2) assessing economic activity as if it were a zero-sum game, in which what is gained by some is lost by others.

There are also sometimes misconceptions of the nature of government, leading to unrealistic demands being made on it and hasty denunciations of the "stupidity" or "irrationality" of government officials when those demands are not met.

Understanding political functions can be as much of a challenge as understanding economic functions. What is especially challenging is deciding which things should be done through the economic system and which things should be done through the political system. While some decisions are clearly political decisions and others are clearly economic decisions, there are large areas where choices can be made through either process. Both the government and the marketplace can supply housing, transportation, education and many other things. For those decisions that can be made either politically or economically, it is necessary not only to decide which particular outcome would be preferred but also which process offers the best prospect of actually reaching that outcome. This in turn requires understanding how each process works in practice under their respective incentives and constraints.

419

The public can express their desires either through choices made in the voting booth or choices made in the marketplace. However, political choices are offered less often and are usually binding until the next election. Moreover, the political process offers "package deal" choices, where one candidate's whole spectrum of positions on economic, military, environmental, and other issues must be accepted or rejected as a whole in comparison with another candidate's spectrum of positions on the same range of issues. The voter may prefer one candidate's position on some of these issues and another candidate's position on other issues, but no such choice is available on election day. By contrast, consumers make their choices in the marketplace every day and can buy one company's milk and another company's cheese, or ship some packages by Federal Express and other packages by United Parcel Service. Then they can change their minds a day or a week later and make wholly different choices.

As a practical matter, virtually no one puts as much time and close attention into deciding whether to vote for one candidate rather than another as is usually put into deciding whether to buy one house rather than another—or perhaps even one car rather than another. Perhaps more important, the public usually buys finished products in the marketplace but can choose only among competing promises in the political arena. In the marketplace, the strawberries or the house that you are considering buying are right before your eyes when you make your decision, while the policies that a candidate promises to follow must be accepted more or less on faith— and the eventual consequences of those policies still more so. Speculation is just one aspect of a market economy but it is the essence of elections. On the other hand, each voter has the same single vote on election day, whereas consumers have very different amounts of dollars to vote with in the marketplace. However, these dollar differences may even out somewhat over a lifetime, as the same individual moves from one income bracket to another over the years, although the differences are there as of any given time.

The influence of wealth in the marketplace makes many prefer to move decisions into the political arena, on the assumption that this is a more level playing field. However, among the things that wealth buys is more and better education, as well as more leisure time that can be devoted to political activities and the mastering of legal technicalities. All this translates into a disproportionate influence of wealthier people in the political process, while the fact that those who are not rich often have more money in the aggregate than those who are may give ordinary people more weight in the market than in the political or legal arena.

ZERO-SUM THINKING

The notion that what is gained by some must be lost by others is seldom explicitly expressed. Rather, it is implicit in much discussion—and even laws and policies—dealing with labor-management relations, landlord-tenant relations, or the relations among classes or ethnic groups. Zero-sum thinking also dominates much discussion of international trade, as will become painfully clear in Chapter 20.

Minimum wage laws, for example, are often advocated by those who see themselves as taking the side of the workers against their employers, when in fact the employers may end up less harmed by such laws than are the workers themselves, whose unemployment can deprive them of both current income and the human capital that work experience could build up for them and enable them to earn higher incomes in the future. Similarly, rent control often ends up harming both tenants and landlords, though in different ways. Landlords lose immediately but they are unlikely to end up living homeless on the streets, though some tenants may, given that homelessness is particularly prevalent in cities with strong rent control laws.

Individuals who stand in the relationship of employer and employee, or landlord and tenant, would never have entered into such relationships in the first place unless both sides expected to become better off than they would have been if they had not entered into these relationships. In other words, it is not a zero-sum activity. That is why anything which reduces such relationships is likely to be harmful to both parties—a fact often overlooked by those who think in terms of taking sides.

Zero-sum thinking is especially misleading in countries where wealth is growing. Discussions of the relative shares going to different social groups are often illustrated by pie-charts showing who gets how big a slice of the nation's income. But the actual economic well-being of all these groups—their real income per capita—is often far more dependent on how big the whole pie is, rather than how one group's slice compares to another group's slice. As noted in Chapter 9, even when the share of national income going to the lowest fifth of Americans declined, the per capita real income of people in that bottom bracket rose by thousands of dollars.

Those who are preoccupied with relative shares often show little or no interest in the over-all growth of wealth. That is, they not only fail to pay much attention to the statistics on the growth of national wealth, more fundamentally they show little or no interest in which conditions or which policies would enhance the prospects for such growth and which policies might impede that growth. They tend to view economic policies largely, if not solely, in terms of how these policies will affect the internal distribution of income, rather than its over-all size—even though wealth is the only thing that can prevent poverty and the growth of wealth has reduced poverty far more dramatically than changes in the distribution of income have.

Internationally, zero-sum thinking has led some nations to keep out foreign investors, for fear that these investors would carry off part of their national wealth. Similar thinking has led to popular resentments of various immigrant minorities who send money back to their families in the countries from which they came, because this too has been seen as exporting part of the national wealth to another country. Like much zero-sum thinking, this depends on disregarding the *creation* of wealth. Neither investors nor immigrants simply come into a country and share its pre-existing wealth. They create additional wealth. Part of this additional wealth goes to the population of the country to which they have moved and part goes to themselves and their families, wherever these might be located. But the host country population loses nothing on net balance and typically gains.

If the kind of thinking which would lead people to believe otherwise seems primitive or illogical, that is not to say that it has not prevailed among peoples and rulers in many lands. Some poor nations in Asia, Africa, and Latin America have kept out foreign investments that were desperately needed, for fear of losing wealth that the foreigners would carry away. Accusations of exporting the host country's wealth were made against the overseas Chinese in Southeast Asia for generations, while in fact the Chinese were creating whole industries that never existed before in those countries, thereby adding to these countries' total wealth. Zero-sum thinking and a disregard of the creation of wealth have often gone together in countries around the world.

THE FALLACY OF COMPOSITION

Just as the assumption of a zero sum process may be implicit, rather than explicit, so is the assumption that what is true of a part is true of the whole— that is, the fallacy of composition. The fallacy in the fallacy of composition comes from ignoring the *interactions* which prevent what is true of a part from automatically being true of the whole. Because a national economy involves many complex interactions among millions of individuals, businesses and other organizations, what is true for some of them need not be true for the economy as a whole.

Not only may the fates of particular parts of an economy differ from the fate of the economy as a whole, to some extent it is inevitable that parts of the economy suffer from the progress of the whole. How are the new industries and new technologies to get the resources they need, except by taking capital, labor and other factors of production away from other parts of the economy?

Automobiles, trucks, and tractors displaced horses from their historically large role in transportation and farming in twentieth century America, thereby freeing up all the resources required to feed and maintain vast numbers of horses. Workers were also displaced from agriculture as farming methods became more efficient. One of the key factors in the growth of industrial output during the twentieth century was the ever-growing availability of workers displaced from agriculture. How else could modern industries have gotten all the millions of workers needed to fill their factories, except by taking them from the farms?

Those who lament the passing of the family farm often see no connection between that and the greater outpouring of goods and services from industry and commerce which created a rising standard of living for millions of people. Nothing is easier for the media or for politicians than to present "human interest" stories about someone whose family has been farming for generations and who has now been forced out of the kind of life they knew and loved by the impersonal economic forces of the marketplace. What is forgotten is that these "impersonal" forces represent benefits to consumers, who are just as much persons as the producers who have been arbitrarily selected as the focus of attention. The temptation is always there to try to "solve" the problem of those whose plight has been singled out for attention, without regard for the repercussions on others elsewhere.

The constant shifting of resources which has contributed to American prosperity was often thwarted for decades in India, which followed policies that made it virtually impossible to fire workers or to shut down certain enterprises. Such government restrictions and controls contributed to India's poverty—by an amount estimated at hundreds of dollars per capita annually. In a poor country, that is a very serious loss.

An observer of the Indian economy said: "I sometimes wonder how we could have gone so wrong when we had such brilliant economists." The short answer is that power trumps knowledge—and for nearly half a century the supreme power in India was in the hands of people committed to a government-controlled economy. Efforts by economists to point out what was wrong with the policies being followed were essentially exercises in futility. Some of India's top economists, including a Nobel Prize winner, simply left the country.

THE ROLE OF GOVERNMENT

Too often there has been a tendency to regard government as a monolithic decision-maker or as the public interest personified. But different elements within the government respond to different outside constituencies and are often in opposition to one another for that reason, as well as because of jurisdictional frictions among themselves. Many things done by government officials in response to the incentives and constraints of the situations in which they find themselves may be described as "irrational" by observers but are often more rational than the assumption that these officials represent the public interest personified. Politicians like to come to the rescue of particular industries, professions, classes, or racial or ethnic groups, from whom voting or financial support can be expected—and to represent the benefits to these groups as net benefits to the country. Such tendencies are not confined to any given country but can be found in modern democratic states around the world. As a writer in India put it:

> Politicians lack the courage to privatize the huge, loss-making public sector because they are afraid to lose the vote of organized labor. They resist dismantling subsidies for power, fertilizers, and water because they fear the crucial farm vote. They won't touch food subsidies because of the massive poor vote. They will not remove thousands of inspectors in the state governments, who continuously harass private businesses, because they don't want to alienate government servants' vote bank. Meanwhile, these giveaways play havoc with state finances and add to our disgraceful fiscal deficit. Unless the deficit comes under control, the nation will not be more competitive; nor will the growth rate rise further to 8 or 9 percent, which is what is needed to create jobs and improve the chances of the majority of our people to actualize their capabilities in a reasonably short time.

While such problems may be particularly acute in India, they are by no means confined to India. In 2002, the Congress of the United States passed a farm subsidy bill—with bipartisan support—that has been estimated to cost the average American family more than $4,000 over the next decade in inflated food prices. Huge financial problems have been created in Brazil by such generous pensions to government employees that they can retire in better economic condition than when they were working.

One of the pressures on governments in general, and elected governments in particular, is to "do something"—even when there is nothing they can do that is likely to make things better and much that they can do that will make things worse. Economic processes, like other processes, take time but politicians may be unwilling to allow these processes the time to run their course, especially when their political opponents are advocating quick fixes such as wage and price controls during the Nixon administration or restrictions on international trade during the Great Depression of the 1930s.

In the twenty-first century, it is virtually impossible politically for any American government to allow a recession to run its course, as American governments usually did prior to the Great Depression, when both Republican President Herbert Hoover and then Democratic President Franklin D. Roosevelt intervened on an unprecedented scale, with results that some later scholars have blamed for needlessly prolonging that economic disaster far beyond the time that previous depressions took to run their courses.

During periods when many people are experiencing economic distress, it is always popular to revise the bankruptcy laws to rescue debtors from their creditors by giving them more time to pay off their debts or by making it harder for creditors to foreclose on mortgaged property or to take legal action to seize other assets such as wages or bank accounts. These are always popular and are usually successful in achieving their immediate goals. But, as collecting debts becomes more costly, either in terms of direct expenditures or in the time during which money cannot be collected, lenders respond by making loans harder to get or by charging higher interest to cover the new costs of collection, or both.

The incentives facing government enterprises tend to result in very different ways of carrying out their functions, compared to the way things are done in a free market economy. After banks were nationalized in India in 1969, uncollectible debts rose to become 20 percent of all loans outstanding. Efficiency also suffered: An Indian entrepreneur reported that "it takes my wife half an hour to make a deposit or withdraw money from our local branch." Moreover, government ownership and control led to political influence in deciding to whom bank loans were to be made:

> I once chanced to meet the manager of one of the rural branches of a nationalized bank. . . He was a sincere young man, deeply concerned, and he wanted to unburden himself about his day-to-day problems. Neither he nor his staff, he told me, decided who qualified for a loan.

> The local politicians invariably made this decision. The loan takers were invariably cronies of the political bosses and did not intend to repay the money. He was told that such and such a person was to be treated as a "deserving poor." Without exception, they were rich.

The nationalization of banks in India was not simply a matter of transferring ownership of an enterprise to the government. This transfer changed all the incentives and constraints from those of the marketplace to those of politics and bureaucracy. The proclaimed goals, or even the sincere hopes, of those who created this transfer often meant much less than the changed incentives and constraints.

In the United States, political control of banks' investment decisions has been less pervasive but has nevertheless changed the directions that investments have taken from what they would be in a free market. The Community Investment Act, for example, requires banks to put a certain percentage of their investments into communities designated by government as being especially "needing" investments. Since there is no objective measure of "need," this amounts to directing investments to where politicians want those investments to go.

As an entrepreneur in India put it: "Indians have learned from painful experience that the state does not work on behalf of the people. More often than not, it works on behalf of itself." So do people in other walks of life and in other countries around the world. The problem is that this fact is not always recognized when people look to government to right wrongs and fulfill desires to an extent that may not always be possible.

The tragic bungling of economic policy by American presidents of both political parties, as well as by officials of the Federal Reserve System, during the Great Depression of the 1930s has sobering implications for those who regard government as a force to save the economy from the imperfections of the marketplace. Markets are indeed imperfect, as everything human is imperfect. But "market failure" is not a magic phrase that automatically justifies government intervention, because the government can also fail—or can even make things worse.

Whatever the merits or demerits of particular government economic policies, the market alternative is very new as history is measured, and the combination of democracy and a free market still newer and rarer. As an observer in India put it:

> We tend to forget that liberal democracy based on free markets is a relatively new idea in human history. In 1776 there was one liberal democracy—the United States; in 1790 there were 3, including France; in 1848 there were only 5; in 1975 there were still only 31. Today 120 of the world's 200 or so states claim to be democracies, with more than 50 percent of the world's population residing in them (although Freedom House, an American think tank, counts only 86 countries as truly free).

Where there are elected governments, its officials must be concerned about being re-elected—which is to say that mistakes cannot be admitted and reversed as readily as they are in a private business operating in competitive markets. No one likes to admit being mistaken but, under the incentives and constraints of profit and loss, there is often no choice but to reverse course. In politics, however, the costs of being wrong are often paid by the taxpayers, while the costs of admitting mistakes are paid by elected officials. Given these incentives and constraints, the reluctance of government officials to admit mistakes and reverse course is perfectly rational.

For example, when supersonic passenger jet planes were first contemplated, by both private plane manufacturers like Boeing and by the British and French governments who proposed building the Concorde, it became clear early on that the costs of supersonic passenger jets would be so high that there would be little hope of recovering these costs from fares that passengers would be willing to pay. Boeing dropped the whole idea, absorbing the losses of its early efforts as a lesser evil than continuing on and absorbing even bigger losses by completing the project. But the British and French governments, once publicly committed to the idea of the Concorde, continued on instead of admitting that it was a bad idea. The net result was that British and French taxpayers for years subsidized a commercial venture used largely by very affluent passengers because fares on the Concorde were far higher than fares on other jets flying the same routes, even though these very expensive fares still did not cover the costs. Eventually, as Concordes aged, the plane was discontinued because its huge losses were now so widely known that it would have been politically difficult, if not impossible, to get public support for more government spending to replace planes that had never been economically viable. Although we often speak of "the government" as if it were a single thing, it is not only fragmented into differing and contending interests at any given time, its leadership consists of entirely different people over time. Thus those who put an end to the costly Concorde experiment were not the same as those who had launched this experiment in the first place. It is always easier to admit someone else's mistakes.

In a competitive market, by contrast, the costs of mistakes can quickly become so high that there is no choice but to admit one's own mistakes and change course before bankruptcy looms on the horizon. Because the day of reckoning comes earlier in markets than in government, there is not only more pressure to admit mistakes in the private sector, there is more pressure to avoid making mistakes in the first place. When proposals for new ventures are made in these different sectors, proposals made by government officials need only persuade enough people, in order to be successful within the time horizon that matters to those officials. In a competitive market, however, proposals must convince those particular people whose own money is at stake and who therefore have every incentive to marshall the best available expertise before proceeding.

These two processes can produce very different conclusions about the very same proposals. Thus when the proposal for building a tunnel under the English Channel was being considered, the British and French governments projected costs and earnings that made it look like a good investment, at least to enough of the British and French public to make the venture politically viable. Meanwhile, companies running ferry service across the English Channel obviously thought otherwise, for they proceeded to invest in more and bigger ferries, which could have been financial suicide if the tunnel under the channel turned out to be the kind of success that was projected by political officials, leading people to take the underwater route across the channel, instead of ferries.

Only after years of building and more years of operation did the economic outcome of the tunnel project become clear—and the British and

French officials responsible were long gone from the political scene by then. In 2004 *The Economist* reported:

> "Without a doubt, the Channel Tunnel would not have been built if we'd known about these problems," Richard Shirrefs, the chief executive of Eurotunnel, said this week. Too few people are using the ten-year-old undersea link between Britain and France to repay even the interest on its bloated construction costs, which have left Eurotunnel with some [$11.5 billion] in debt. So, just as happened with supersonic Concorde, taxpayers are being asked to bail out another Anglo-French transport fiasco. . . . None of this will come as a surprise to tunnel-sceptics— who, like the Concorde's, were mostly ignored.

While these examples involved the British and French governments, similar incentives and constraints—and similar results—apply to many governments around the world.

PART VI:

THE INTERNATIONAL ECONOMY

Chapter 20

INTERNATIONAL TRADE

*Facts are stubborn things, and whatever may be our
wishes, our inclinations, or the dictates of our passions,
they cannot alter the state of facts and evidence.*

John Adams

When discussing the historic North American Free Trade Agreement of 1993 (NAFTA), the *New York Times* said:

> Abundant evidence is emerging that jobs are shifting across borders too rapidly to declare the United States a job winner or a job loser from the trade agreement.

Posing the issue in these terms committed the central fallacy in many discussions of international trade—assuming that one country must be a "loser" if the other country is a "winner." But international trade is not a zero-sum contest. Both sides must gain or it would make no sense to continue trading. Nor is it necessary for experts or government officials to determine whether both sides are gaining. Most international trade, like most domestic trade, is done by millions of individuals, each of whom can determine whether the item purchased is worth what it cost and is preferable to what is available from others.

As for jobs, before the NAFTA free-trade agreement among the United States, Canada, and Mexico went into effect, there were dire predictions of "a giant sucking sound" as jobs would be sucked out of the United States to Mexico because of Mexico's lower wage rates. In reality, the number of American jobs *increased* after the agreement and the unemployment rate in the United States fell over the next seven years from more than seven percent down to four percent, the lowest level seen in decades. In Canada, the unemployment rate fell from 11 percent to 7 percent over the same seven years.

Why was what happened so radically different from what was predicted? Let's go back to square one. What happens when a given country, in isolation, becomes more prosperous? It tends to buy more because it has more to buy with. And what happens when it buys more? There are more jobs created for workers producing the additional goods and services.

Make that two countries and the principle remains the same. Indeed, make it any number of countries and the principle remains the same. Rising prosperity usually means rising employment.

There is no *fixed* number of jobs that countries must fight over. When countries become more prosperous, they all tend to create more jobs. The only question is whether international trade tends to make countries more prosperous.

Mexico was considered to be the main threat to take jobs away from the United States when trade barriers were lowered. In the post-NAFTA years, jobs did in fact increase by the millions in Mexico—at the same time when jobs were increasing by the millions in the United States. Both countries saw an increase in their international trade, with especially sharp increases in those goods covered by NAFTA.

The basic facts about international trade are not difficult to understand. What is difficult to untangle are all the misconceptions and jargon which so often clutter up the discussion. The great U.S. Supreme Court Justice Oliver Wendell Holmes said, "we need to think things instead of words." Nowhere is that more important than when discussing international trade, where there are so many misleading and emotional words used to describe and confuse things that are not very difficult to understand in themselves.

For example, the terminology used to describe an export surplus as a "favorable" balance of trade and an import surplus as an "unfavorable" balance of trade goes back for centuries. At one time, it was widely believed that importing more than was exported impoverished a nation because the difference between imports and exports had to be paid in gold, and the loss of gold was seen as a loss of national wealth. However, as early as 1776,

Adam Smith's classic *The Wealth of Nations* argued that the real wealth of a nation consists of its goods and services, not its gold supply.

Too many people have yet to grasp the full implications of this, even in the twenty-first century. If the goods and services available to the American people are greater as a result of international trade, then Americans are wealthier, not poorer, regardless of whether there is a "deficit" or a "surplus" in the international balance of trade.

Incidentally, during the Great Depression of the 1930s, the United States had an export surplus—a "favorable" balance of trade—in every year of that disastrous decade. What may be more relevant is that both imports and exports were sharply lower than they had been during the prosperous decade of the 1920s. This reduction in international trade was a result of rising tariff barriers in countries around the world, as nations attempted to save jobs in their own domestic economies, during a period of widespread unemployment, by keeping out international trade.

Such policies have been regarded by many economists as needlessly worsening and prolonging the worldwide depression. The last thing needed when real national income is going down is a policy that makes it go down faster, by denying consumers the benefits of being able to buy what they want at the lowest price available.

Slippery words can make bad news look like good news and vice versa. For example, the much-lamented international trade deficit of the United States narrowed by a record-breaking amount in the spring of 2001, as *BusinessWeek* magazine reported under the headline: "A Shrinking Trade Gap Looks Good Stateside." However, this happened while the stock market was falling, unemployment was rising, corporate profits were down, and the total output of the American economy declined. The supposedly "good" news on international trade was due to reduced imports during shaky economic times. Had the country gone into a deep depression, the international trade balance might have disappeared completely, but fortunately Americans were spared that much "good" news.

Just as the United States had a "favorable" balance of trade in every year of the Great Depression of the 1930s, it became a record-breaking "debtor nation" during the booming prosperity of the 1990s. Obviously, such words

cannot be taken at face value as indicators of the economic well-being of a
country. We will need to examine more closely what such words mean in
context in this chapter and the next.

THE BASIS FOR INTERNATIONAL TRADE

While international trade takes place for the same reason that other
trades take place—because both sides gain—it is necessary to understand
just why both countries gain, especially since there are so many politicians
and journalists who muddy the waters with claims to the contrary.

The reasons why countries gain from international trade are usually
grouped together by economists under three categories: absolute advantage,
comparative advantage, and economies of scale.

Absolute Advantage

It is obvious why Americans buy bananas grown in the Caribbean.
Bananas can be grown much more cheaply in the tropics than in places
where greenhouses and other artificial means of maintaining warmth would
be necessary. In tropical countries, nature provides free the warmth that
people have to provide by costly means in cooler climates, such as that of the
United States.

Therefore it pays Americans to buy bananas grown in the tropics, rather
than grow them at higher costs within the United States.

Sometimes the advantages that one country has over another, or over the
rest of the world, are extreme. Growing coffee, for example, requires a
peculiar combination of climatic conditions—warm but not too hot, nor
with sunlight beating down on the plants directly all day, nor with too much
moisture or too little moisture, and in some kinds of soils but not others.
Putting together these and other requirements for ideal coffee-growing
conditions drastically reduces the number of places that are best suited for
producing coffee. In the early twenty-first century, more than half the
coffee in the entire world was grown in just three countries—Brazil,

Vietnam, and Colombia. This does not mean that other countries were completely unable to grow coffee. It is just that the amount and quality of coffee that most countries could produce would not be worth the resources it would cost, when coffee can be bought from these three countries at a lower cost.

Sometimes the advantage consists of simply being located in the right place or speaking the right language. In India, for example, the time is about 12 hours different from the time in the United States, which means that an American company which wants round-the-clock computer services can engage a computer company in India to have Indian technicians available when it is night in the Unites States and day in India. Since educated people in India speak English and India produces vast numbers of computer science graduates annually, this combination of circumstances gives India a large advantage in competing for computer services in the American market. Similarly, South American countries supply fruits and vegetables that grow in the summer to North American countries when it is winter in the northern hemisphere and summer in the southern hemisphere.

These are all examples of what economists call "absolute advantage"— one country, for any of a number of reasons, can produce some things cheaper or better than another. Those reasons may be due to climate, geography, or the mixture of skills in their respective populations. Whatever the reason may be in each particular case, absolute advantage means that one country can simply produce a given product or service more cheaply or better than another. Foreigners who buy that country's products benefit from the lower costs, while the country itself obviously benefits from the larger market for its products or services, and sometimes from the fact that part of the inputs needed to create the product are free, such as warmth in the tropics or rich nutrients in the soil in various places around the world.

There is another more subtle, but at least equally important, reason for international trade. This is what economists call "comparative advantage."

Comparative Advantage

To illustrate what is meant by comparative advantage, suppose that one country is so efficient that it is capable of producing *anything* more cheaply than a neighboring country. Is there any benefit that the more efficient country can gain from trading with its neighbor?

Yes.

Why? Because being able to produce *anything* more cheaply is not the same as being able to produce *everything* more cheaply. When there are scarce resources which have alternative uses, producing more of one product means producing less of some other product. The question is not simply how much it costs, in either money or resources, to produce chairs or television sets in one country, but how many chairs it costs to produce a television set, when resources are shifted from producing one product to producing the other. If that trade-off is different between two countries, then the country that can get more television sets by foregoing the production of chairs can benefit from trading with the country that gets more chairs by not producing television sets. A numerical example can illustrate this point.

Assume that an average American worker produces 500 chairs a month, while an average Canadian worker produces 450, and that an American worker can produce 200 television sets a month while a Canadian worker produces 100. The tables below illustrate what the output would be under these conditions if both countries produced both products versus each country producing only one of these products. In both tables we assume the same respective outputs per worker and the same total number of workers—500—devoted to producing these products in each country:

PRODUCTS	AMERICAN WORKERS	AMERICAN OUTPUT	CANADIAN WORKERS	CANADIAN OUTPUT
chairs	200	100,000	200	90,000
TV sets	300	60,000	300	30,000

With both countries producing both products, under the conditions specified, their combined output would come to a grand total of 190,000 chairs and 90,000 television sets per month from a grand total of a thousand workers.

What if the two countries specialize, with the United States putting all its chair-producing workers into the production of television sets instead, and Canada doing the reverse? Then *with the very same output per worker* as before in each country, they can now produce a larger grand total of the two products from the same thousand workers:

PRODUCTS	AMERICAN WORKERS	AMERICAN OUTPUT	CANADIAN WORKERS	CANADIAN OUTPUT
chairs	0	0	500	225,000
TV sets	500	100,000	0	0

Without any change in the productivity of workers in either country, the total output is now greater from the same number of workers, that output now being 100,000 television sets instead of 90,000 and 225,000 chairs instead of 190,000. That is because each country now produces where it has a comparative advantage, whether or not it has an absolute advantage. Economists would say that the United States has an "absolute advantage" in producing both products but that Canada has a "comparative advantage" in producing chairs. That is, Canada loses fewer television sets by shifting resources to the production of chairs than the United States would lose by such a shift. Under these conditions, Americans can get more chairs by producing television sets and trading them with Canadians for chairs, instead of by producing their own chairs directly, at the expense of labor and other resources that could have gone into producing something where their advantage was greater. Conversely, Canadians can get more television sets by producing chairs and trading them for American-made television sets.

Only if the United States produced everything more efficiently than Canada *by the same percentage for each product* would there be no gain from trade because there would then be no comparative advantage. Such a situation is virtually impossible to find in the real world. Similar principles apply on a personal level in everyday life. Imagine, for example, that you are an eye surgeon and that you paid your way through college by washing cars. Now that you have a car of your own, should you wash it yourself or should you hire someone else to wash it—even if your previous experience allows you to do the job in less time than the person you hire? Obviously, it makes no sense to you financially, or to society in terms of over-all well-being, for you to be spending your time sudsing down an automobile instead of being in an operating room saving someone's eyesight. In other words, even though you have an "absolute advantage" in both activities, your comparative advantage in treating eye diseases is far greater.

The key to understanding both individual examples and examples from international trade is the basic economic reality of scarcity. The surgeon has only 24 hours in the day, like everyone else. Time that he is spending doing one thing is time taken away from doing something else. The same is true of countries, which do not have an unlimited amount of labor, time, or other resources, and so must do one thing at the cost of not doing something else. That is the very meaning of economic costs—*foregone alternatives*, which apply whether the particular economy is capitalist, socialist, feudal, or whatever—and whether the transactions are domestic or international.

The benefits of comparative advantage are particularly important to poorer countries. Someone put it this way:

> Comparative advantage means there is a place under the free-trade sun for every nation, no matter how poor, because people of every nation can produce some products relatively more efficiently than they produce other products.

Comparative advantage is not just a theory but a very important fact in the history of many nations. It has been more than a century since Great Britain produced enough food to feed its people. Britons have been able to get enough to eat only because the country has concentrated its efforts on producing those things in which it has had a comparative advantage, such as manufacturing, shipping, and financial services—and using the proceeds to buy food from other countries. British consumers ended up better fed and with more manufactured goods than if the country grew enough of its own food to feed itself. Since the real cost of anything that is produced are the other things that could have been produced with the same efforts, it would cost the British too much industry and commerce to transfer enough resources into agriculture to become self-sufficient in food. They are better off getting food from some other country whose comparative advantage is in agriculture, *even if that other country's farmers are not as efficient as British farmers*.

Such a trade-off is not limited to industrialized nations. When cocoa began to be grown on farms in West Africa, which ultimately produced over half of the world's supply, African farmers there reduced the amount of food they grew, in order to earn more money by planting cocoa trees on their lands, instead of food crops. As a result, their earnings enabled them to live off food produced elsewhere. This food included not only meat and vegetables grown in the region, but also imported rice and canned fish and fruit, the latter items being considered to be luxuries at the time.

Economies of Scale

While absolute advantage and comparative advantage are the key reasons for benefits from international trade, they are not the only reasons. Sometimes a particular product requires such huge investment in machinery, in the engineering required to create the machinery and the product, as well as in developing a specialized labor force, that the resulting output can be sold at a low enough price to be competitive only when some enormous amount of output is produced, because of economies of scale, as discussed in Chapter 6.

It has been estimated that the minimum output of automobiles needed to achieve an efficient cost per car is somewhere between 200,000 and 400,000 automobiles per year. Producing in such huge quantities is not a serious problem in a country of the size and wealth of the United States, where each of the big three domestic auto makers—Ford, General Motors, and DaimlerChrysler—has had at least one vehicle with sales of more than 400,000, as did Toyota, while the Ford F-Series pickup truck had more than 800,000 sales. But, in a country with a much smaller population—Australia, for example—there is no way to sell enough cars within the country to be able to develop and produce automobiles from scratch to sell at prices low enough to compete with automobiles produced in much larger quantities in the United States or Japan. The largest number of cars of any given make sold in Australia is only about half of the quantity needed to reap all the cost benefits of economies of scale. While the number of automobiles owned per capita is very similar in Australia and in the United States, there are more than a dozen times as many Americans as there are Australians.

Even those cars which have been manufactured in Australia have been developed in other countries—Toyotas and Mitsubishis from Japan and Ford and General Motors cars from the United States. They are essentially Australian-built Japanese or American cars, which means that companies in Japan and the United States have already paid the huge engineering, research, and other costs of developing these vehicles. But the Australian market is not large enough to achieve sufficient economies of scale to produce original Australian automobiles from scratch at a cost that would enable them to compete in the market with imported cars. Although Australia is a modern prosperous country, with output per person similar to that of Great Britain and higher than that in Canada, its small population limits its total purchasing power to less than one-seventh that of Japan and one-twentieth of that of the United States.

Exports enable some countries to achieve economies of scale that would not be possible from domestic sales alone. Some business enterprises make most of their sales outside their respective countries' borders. For example, Heineken does not have to depend on the small Holland market for its beer sales, since it sells beer in 170 other countries. Nokia sells its phones around the world, not just in its native Finland. The distinguished British magazine *The Economist* sells three times as many copies in the United States as in Britain. Toyota, Honda, and Nissan all earn most of their profits in North America, and Japanese automakers as a whole began in 2006 to manufacture more cars outside of Japan than in Japan itself. Small countries like South Korea and Taiwan depend on international trade to be able to produce many products on a scale far exceeding what can be sold domestically.

In short, international trade is necessary for many countries to achieve economies of scale that will enable them to sell at prices that can compete with the prices of similar products in the world market. For some products requiring huge investments in machinery and research, only a very few large and prosperous countries could reach the levels of output needed to repay all these costs from domestic sales alone. International trade creates greater efficiency by allowing more economies of scale around the world, even in countries whose domestic markets are not large enough to absorb all the output of mass production industries, as well as by taking advantage of each country's absolute or comparative advantages.

As in other cases, we can sometimes understand the benefits of a particular way of doing things by seeing what happens when they are done differently. For many years, India encouraged small businesses and maintained barriers against imports that could compete with them. However, the lifting of import restrictions at the end of the twentieth century and the beginning of the twenty-first century changed all that. As the *Far Eastern Economic Review* put it:

> The nightmare of the Indian toy industry comes in the form of a pint-sized plastic doll. It's made in China, sings a popular Hindi film song, and costs about 100 rupees ($2). Indian parents have snapped it up at markets across the country, leaving local toy companies petrified. Matching the speed, scale and technology involved in the doll's production—resulting in its rock-bottom price—is beyond their abilities. . . .In areas such as toys and shoes, China has developed huge economies of scale while India has kept its producers artificially small.

The economic problems of toy manufacturers in India under free trade are overshadowed by the far more serious problems created by previous import restrictions which forced hundreds of millions of people in a very poor country to pay needlessly inflated prices for a wide range of products because of policies protecting small-scale producers from the competition of larger producers at home and abroad. Fortunately, decades of such policies were finally ended in India in the last decade of the twentieth century.

INTERNATIONAL TRADE RESTRICTIONS

While there are many advantages to international trade for the world as a whole and for countries individually, like all forms of greater economic efficiency, at home or abroad, it displaces less efficient ways of doing things. Just as the advent of the automobile inflicted severe losses on the horse-and-buggy industry and the spread of giant supermarket chains drove many small neighborhood grocery stores out of business, so imports of things in which other countries have a comparative advantage create losses of revenue and jobs in the corresponding domestic industry. Despite offsetting economic gains that typically far outweigh the losses, politically it is almost inevitable that there will be loud calls for government protection from foreign competition through various restrictions against imports. Many of the most long-lived fallacies in economics have grown out of attempts to justify these international trade restrictions. Although Adam Smith refuted most of these fallacies more than two centuries ago, as far as economists are concerned, such fallacies remain politically alive and potent today.

Some people argue, for example, that wealthy countries cannot compete with countries whose wages are much lower. Poorer countries, on the other hand, may say that they must protect their "infant industries" from competition with more developed industrial nations until the local industries acquire the experience and know-how to compete on even terms. In all countries, there are complaints that other nations are not being "fair" in their laws regarding imports and exports. A frequently heard complaint of unfairness, for example, is that some countries "dump" their goods on the international market at artificially low prices, losing money in the short run in order to gain a larger market share that they will later exploit by raising prices after they achieve a monopolistic position.

In the complexities of real life, seldom is any argument right 100 percent of the time or wrong 100 percent of the time. When it comes to arguments for international trade restrictions, however, most of the arguments are fallacious most of the time. Let us examine them one at a time, beginning with the high-wage fallacy.

The High-Wage Fallacy

In a prosperous country such as the United States, a fallacy that sounds very plausible is that American goods cannot compete with goods produced by low-wage workers in poorer countries, some of whom are paid a fraction of what American workers receive. But, plausible as this may sound, both history and economics refute it. Historically, high-wage countries have been exporting to low-wage countries for centuries. The Dutch Republic was a leader in international trade for nearly a century and a half—from the 1590s to the 1740s—while having some of the highest-paid workers in the world. Britain was the world's greatest exporter in the nineteenth century and its wage rates were much higher than the wage rates in many, if not most, of the countries to which it sold its goods.

Conversely, India has had far lower wage rates than those in more industrialized countries like Japan and the United States, but for many years India restricted imports of automobiles and other products made in Japan and the United States because India's domestic producers could not compete in price or quality with such imported products. After an easing of restrictions on international trade, even the leading Indian industrial firm, Tata, has had to be concerned about imports from China, despite the higher wages of Chinese workers compared to workers in India:

> . . .the Tata group set up a special office to educate the different parts of its sprawling business empire on the possible fallout from the removal of import restrictions. Jiban Mukhopadhyay, economic adviser to the group's chairman, heads the operation. In his desk drawer, he keeps a silk tie bought on a trip to China. Managers who attend the company's WTO [World Trade Organization] workshops are asked to guess its price. "It's only 85 rupees," he points out. "A similar tie made in India would cost 400 rupees."

Economically, the key flaw in the high-wage argument is that it confuses wage rates with labor costs—and labor costs with total costs. Wage rates are measured per hour of work. Labor costs are measured per unit of output. Total costs include not only the cost of labor but also the cost of capital, raw materials, transportation, and other things needed to produce output and bring the finished product to market.

When workers in a prosperous country receive wages twice as high as workers in a poorer country and produce three times the output per hour, then it is the high-wage country which has the lower labor costs per unit of output. That is, it is cheaper to get a given amount of work done in the more prosperous country simply because it takes less labor, even though individual workers are paid more for their time. The higher-paid workers may be more efficiently organized and managed, or have far more or better machinery to work with, or work in companies or industries with greater economies of scale. Often transportation costs are lower in the more developed country, so that total costs of delivering the product to market are less.

There are, after all, reasons why one country is more prosperous than another in the first place—and often that reason is that they are more efficient at producing and delivering output, for any of a number of reasons. In short, higher wage rates per unit of time are not the same as higher costs per unit of output. It may not even mean higher labor costs per unit of output—and of course labor costs are not the only costs. An international consulting firm determined that the average labor productivity in the modern sectors in India is 15 percent of labor productivity in the United States. In other words, if you hired an average Indian worker and paid him one-fifth of what you paid an average American worker, it would cost you *more* to get a given amount of work done in India than in the United States. Paying 20 percent of what an American worker makes to someone who produces only 15 percent of what an American worker produces would increase your labor costs.

None of this means that no low-wage country can ever gain jobs at the expense of a high-wage country. Where the difference in productivity is less than the difference in wage rates, as with India's well-trained and English-speaking computer programmers, then much American computer programming will be done in India. All other forms of comparative advantage will also mean a shift of jobs to countries with particular advantages in doing particular things. But this does not imply a *net* loss of jobs in the economy as a whole, any more than other forms of greater efficiency, domestically or internationally, imply a net loss of jobs in the economy. The job losses are quite real to those who suffer them, whether due to domestic or international competition, but restrictions on either domestic or international markets usually cost jobs on net balance because such restrictions reduce the prosperity on which demand for goods and labor depends.

Labor costs are only part of the story. The costs of capital and management are a considerable part of the cost of many products. In some cases, capital costs exceed labor costs, especially in industries with high fixed costs, such as electric utilities and telephone companies, both of which have huge investments in transmission lines that carry their services into millions of homes. A prosperous country usually has a greater abundance of capital and, because of supply and demand, capital tends to be cheaper there than in poorer countries where capital is more scarce and earns a correspondingly higher rate of return.

The history of the beginning of the industrialization of Russia under the czars illustrates how the supply of capital affects the cost of capital. When Russia began a large-scale industrialization program in the 1890s, foreign investors could earn a return of 17.5 percent per year on their investments— until so many invested in Russia that the rate of return declined over the years and fell below 5 percent by 1900. Poorer countries with high capital costs would have difficulty competing with richer countries with lower capital costs, even if they had a real advantage in labor costs, which they often do not.

At any given time, it is undoubtedly true that some industries will be adversely affected by competing imported products, just as they are adversely affected by every other source of cheaper or better products, whether domestic or foreign. These other sources of greater efficiency are at work all the time, forcing industries to modernize, downsize or go out of business. Yet, when this happens because of foreigners, it can be depicted politically as a case of our country versus theirs, when in fact it is the old story of domestic special interests versus consumers.

Saving Jobs

During periods of high unemployment, politicians are especially likely to be under great pressure to come to the rescue of particular industries that are losing money and jobs, by restricting imports that compete with them. One of the most tragic examples of such restrictions occurred during the worldwide depression of the 1930s, when tariff barriers and other restrictions went up around the world. The net result was that world exports in 1933 were only one-third of what they had been in 1929. Just as free trade provides economic benefits to all countries simultaneously, so trade restrictions reduce the efficiency of all countries simultaneously, lowering standards of living, without producing the increased employment that was hoped for.

These trade restrictions around the world were set off by passage of the Hawley-Smoot tariffs in the United States in 1930, which raised American tariffs on imports to record high levels. Other countries retaliated with severe restrictions on their imports of American products. Moreover, the same political pressures at work in the United States were at work elsewhere, since it seems plausible to many people to protect jobs at home by reducing imports from foreign countries. The net result was that severe international trade restrictions set off by the Hawley-Smoot tariffs were applied by many countries to many other countries, not just to the United States. The net economic consequences were quite different from what was expected—but were precisely what had been predicted by more than a thousand economists who signed a public appeal against the tariff increases, directed to Congressman Hawley, Senator Smoot and President Hoover. Among other things, they said:

> America is now facing the problem of unemployment. The proponents of higher tariffs claim that an increase in rates will give work to the idle. This is not true. We cannot increase employment by restricting trade.

These thousand economists—including many leading professors of economics at Harvard, Columbia, and the University of Chicago—accurately predicted "retaliatory" tariffs against American goods by other countries. They also predicted that "the vast majority" of American farmers, who were among the strongest supporters of tariffs, would lose out on net balance, as other countries restricted their imports of American farm products. All these predictions were fulfilled: Unemployment grew worse and farm exports plummeted, along with a general decline in international trade.

At any given time, a protective tariff or other import restriction may provide immediate relief to a particular industry and thus gain the political and financial support of corporations and labor unions in that industry. But, like many political benefits, it comes at the expense of others who may not be as organized, as visible, or as vocal. When the number of jobs in the American steel industry was cut from 340,000 to 125,000 during the decade of the 1980s, that had a devastating impact and was big economic and political news. It also led to a variety of laws and regulations designed to reduce the amount of steel imported into the country to compete with domestically produced steel. Of course, this reduction in supply led to higher steel prices within the United States and therefore higher costs for all other American industries that were manufacturing products made of steel, which range from automobiles to oil rigs.

All these products were now at a disadvantage in competing with similar foreign-made products, both within the United States and in international markets. It has been estimated that the steel tariffs produced $240 million in additional profits to the steel companies and saved 5,000 jobs in the steel industry. At the same time, those American industries that manufacture products made from this artificially more expensive steel have lost an estimated $600 million in profits and 26,000 jobs as a result of the steel tariffs. In other words, both American industry and American workers as a whole were worse off, on net balance, as a result of the import restrictions on steel. Similarly, a study of restrictions on the importation of sugar into the United States indicated that, while it saved jobs in the sugar industry, it cost three times as many jobs in the confection industry, where some

American firms relocated to Canada and Mexico because sugar costs were one-third lower in Mexico and more than 50 percent lower in Canada.

"Infant Industries"

One of the arguments for international trade restrictions that economists have long recognized as valid, in theory at least, is that of protecting "infant industries" *temporarily* until they can develop the skill and experience necessary to compete with long-established foreign competitors. Once this point is reached, the protection (whether tariffs, import quotas, or whatever) can be taken away and the industry allowed to stand or fall in the competition of the marketplace. In practice, however, a new industry in its infancy seldom has enough political muscle—employees' votes, employers' campaign contributions, local governments dependent on their taxes—to get protection from foreign competition.

On the other hand, an old, inefficient industry that has seen better days may well have some political muscle left and obtain enough protectionist legislation or subsidies from the government to preserve itself from extinction at the expense of the consumers, the taxpayers, or both.

National Defense

Even the greatest advocates of free trade are unlikely to want to depend on imports of military equipment and supplies from nations that could turn out at some future time to be enemy nations. Therefore domestic suppliers of munitions and weapons of war have long been supported in one way or another, in order to assure that those suppliers will be available in the event that they are needed to provide whatever is required for national defense.

One of the rare cases in history where a people did depend on potential enemies for military supplies occurred in colonial America, where the indigenous American Indians obtained guns and ammunition from the European settlers. When warfare broke out between them, the Indians could win most of the battles and yet lose the war when they began to run out of bullets, which were available only from the white settlers. Since guns and bullets were products of European civilization, the Indians had no choice but to rely on that source. But countries that do have a choice almost invariably prefer having their own domestic suppliers of the things that are essential to their own national survival. Unfortunately, the term "essential to national defense" can be—and has been—stretched to include products only remotely, tangentially, or fictitiously, related to military necessity. Such products can acquire protection from international competition under a national defense label for purely self-serving reasons. In short, while the argument for international trade restrictions for the sake of national defense can be valid, whether it is or is not valid for a particular industry in a particular country at a particular time depends on the actual circumstances of that industry, that country, and that time.

Different foreign countries can represent different probabilities of being future enemies, so that the dangers of relying on foreign suppliers of military equipment vary with the particular countries involved. In 2004, for example, Canada was the largest foreign recipient of Pentagon contracts— $601 million worth—followed by Britain and Israel, none of these being countries likely to be at war with the United States.

Sometimes it is not the import of physical goods themselves, but the export of technology embodied in goods, which represents a military threat. In the 1990s, bans on selling American products using advanced computer technology were lifted for sales to China, over the objections of U.S. military authorities. The military wished to keep such restrictions because this advanced technology would enable the Chinese military to acquire the ability to more accurately aim nuclear missiles at American cities. It was not economists but politicians who favored lifting such international trade restrictions. Economists have long recognized the national defense exception to free trade as valid where it applies, even though the national defense rationale has been used in many cases where it does not apply.

"Dumping"

A common argument for government protection against a competitor in other countries is that the latter is not competing "fairly" but is instead "dumping" its products on the market at prices below their costs of production. The argument is that this is being done to drive the domestic producers out of business, letting the foreign producer take over the market, after which prices will be raised to monopolistic levels. In response to this argument, governments have passed "anti-dumping" laws, which ban, restrict, or heavily tax the importation of products from foreign companies declared to be guilty of this practice.

Everything in this argument depends on whether or not the foreign producer is in fact selling goods below their costs of production. As already noted in Chapters 6 and 7, determining production cost is not easy in practice, even for a firm operating within the same country as the government agencies that are trying to determine its costs. For government officials in Europe to try to determine the production costs of a company located in Southeast Asia is even more problematical, especially when they are simultaneously investigating many dumping charges involving many other companies scattered around the world. All that is easy is for domestic producers to bring such charges when imports are taking away some of their customers.

Given the uncertainties of determining cost, the path of least resistance for officials ruling on "dumping" charges is to accept such charges. Authorities in the European Union, for example, declared that a producer of mountain bikes in Thailand was exporting these bikes to Europe below their cost of production because he was charging less for the bikes in Europe than such bikes had been selling for in Thailand. However, since there are economies of scale, the Thai producer's costs when selling huge numbers of mountain bikes in Europe were unlikely to be as high as the costs of other producers selling much smaller numbers of mountain bikes within Thailand, where there was far less demand for such a luxury item from a poorer and smaller population. Indeed, this Thai producer's own costs of selling small numbers of mountain bikes in Thailand were likely to be higher per bike than the costs of selling vast numbers of them in large orders to Europe. To sell bikes in Europe for less than bicycle producers charged in Thailand did not necessarily mean selling below the cost of producing bikes for the huge European market.

This situation was not unique. The European Union has applied anti-dumping laws against bed linen from Egypt, antibiotics from India, footwear from China, microwave ovens from Malaysia, and monosodium glutamate from Brazil, among other products from other places. Nor is the European Union unique. The United States has applied anti-dumping laws to steel from Japan, aluminum from Russia, and golf carts from Poland, among other products. Without any serious basis for determining the costs of producing these things, U.S. government agencies rely on "the best information available"—which is often supplied by those American businesses that are trying to keep out competing foreign products.

Whatever the theory behind anti-dumping laws, in practice they are part of the arsenal of protectionism for domestic producers, at the expense of domestic consumers. Moreover, even the theory is not without its problems. Dumping theory is an international version of the theory of "predatory pricing," whose problems are discussed in Chapter 23. Predatory pricing is a charge that is easy to make and hard to either prove or disprove, whether domestically or internationally. Where the political bias is toward accepting the charge, it does not have to be proven.

Kinds of Restrictions

Tariffs are taxes on imports which serve to raise the prices of those imports and thus enable domestic producers to charge higher prices for competing products than they could in the face of cheaper foreign competition. Import quotas likewise restrict foreign companies from competing on even terms with domestic producers. Although tariffs and quotas may have the same economic end results, these effects are not equally obvious to the public. Thus, while a $10 tariff on imported widgets may enable the domestic producers of widgets to charge $10 more than they could otherwise, without losing business to foreign producers, a suitable quota limitation on imported widgets can also drive up the price of widgets by $10 through its effect on supply and demand. In the latter case, however, it is by no means as easy for the voting public to see and quantify the effects. What that can mean politically is that a quota restriction which raises the price of widgets by $15 may be as easy for elected officials to pass as a tariff of $10.

Sometimes this approach is buttressed by claims that this or that foreign country is being "unfair" in its restrictions on imports from the United States. But the sad fact is that virtually all countries impose "unfair" restrictions on imports, usually in response to internal special interests. However, here as elsewhere, choices can only be made among alternatives actually available. Other countries' restrictions deprive both them and us of some of the benefits of international trade. If we do the same in response, it will deprive both of us of still more benefits. If we let them "get away with it," this will minimize the losses on both sides.

Even more effective disguises for international trade restrictions are health and safety rules applied to imports—rules which often go far beyond what is necessary for either health or safety. Mere red tape requirements can also grow to the point where the time needed to comply adds enough costs to be prohibitive, especially for perishable imports. If it takes a week to get your strawberries through customs, you may as well not ship them. All these measures, which have been engaged in by countries around the world, share with import quotas the political advantage that it is hard to quantify precisely their effect on consumer prices, however large that effect may be.

CHANGING CONDITIONS

Over time, comparative advantages change, causing international production centers to shift from country to country. For example, when the computer was a new and exotic product, much of its early development and production took place in the United States. But, after the technological work was done that turned computers into a widely used product that many people knew how to produce, the United States retained its comparative advantage in the development of computer software design, but the machines themselves could now easily be assembled in poorer countries overseas—and were. Even computers sold within the United States under American brand names were often manufactured in Asia. By the early twenty-first century, *The Economist* magazine reported, "Taiwan now makes the vast majority of the world's computer components." This pattern extended beyond the United States and Taiwan, as the *Far Eastern Economic Review* reported: "Asian firms heavily rely on U.S., Japanese, and European firms as the dominant sources of new technology," while the Asian manufacturers make "razor-thin profit margins due to the hefty licensing fees charged by the global brand firms."

The computer software industry in the United States could not have expanded so much and so successfully if most American computer engineers and technicians were tied down with the production of machines that could have been just as easily produced in some other country. Since the same American labor cannot be in two places at one time, it can move to where its comparative advantage is greatest only if the country "loses jobs" where it has no comparative advantage. That is why the United States could have unprecedented levels of prosperity and rapidly growing employment at the very times when media headlines were regularly announcing lay-offs by the tens of thousands in some American industries and by the hundreds of thousands in others.

Regardless of the industry or the country, if a million new and well-paying jobs are created in companies scattered all across the country as a result of international free trade, that carries less weight politically than if half a million jobs are lost in one industry where labor unions and employer associations are able to raise a clamor. When the million new jobs represent a few dozen jobs here and there in innumerable businesses scattered across the nation, there is not enough concentration of economic interest and political clout in any one place to make it worthwhile to mount a comparable counter-campaign. Therefore laws are often passed restricting international trade for the benefit of some concentrated and vocal constituency, even though these restrictions may cause far more losses of jobs nationwide.

The direct transfer of particular jobs to a foreign country—"outsourcing"—arouses much political and media attention, as when American or British telephone-answering jobs are transferred to India, where English-speaking Indians answer calls made to Harrod's department store in London or calls to American computer companies for technical information are answered by software engineers in India. Those who decry the numbers of jobs transferred to another country almost never state whether these are *net* losses of jobs. While many American jobs have been "outsourced" to India and other countries, many other countries "outsource" jobs to the United States. The German company Siemens employs tens of thousands of Americans in the United States and so do Japanese automakers Honda and Toyota, and the total number of Americans employed by foreign multinational companies runs into the millions.

How many jobs are being outsourced in one direction, compared to how many are being outsourced in the other direction, changes with time. During the period from 1977 to 2001 the number of jobs created in the United States by foreign-owned multinational companies grew by 4.7 million, while the number of jobs created in other countries by American-owned multinational companies grew by just 2.8 million. However, during the last decade of that era, more American jobs were sent abroad by American multinational companies than there were jobs created in the United States by foreign multinationals. Not only is the direction of outsourcing volatile and unpredictable, the net difference in numbers of jobs is small compared to the country's total employment. Moreover, such comparisons leave out the jobs created in the economy as a whole as a result of greater efficiency and wealth created by international transactions.

Even a country which is losing jobs on net balance through outsourcing may nevertheless have more jobs than it would have had without outsourcing. That is because the increased wealth from international transactions means increased demand for goods and services in general, including goods and services produced by workers in purely domestic industries.

Chapter 21

INTERNATIONAL
TRANSFERS OF WEALTH

> *Predicting the paths of foreign-exchange markets is a hit-
> and-miss business, even for those who do it for a living.*
> **The Economist**

Transfers of wealth among nations take many forms. Individuals and
businesses in one country may invest directly in the business
enterprises of another country. Citizens of a given country may put their
money in another country's banks, which will in turn make loans to
individuals and enterprises, so that this is indirect foreign investment. Yet
another option is to buy the bonds issued by a foreign government. Forty-
four percent of the publicly held bonds issued by the U.S. government are
held by people in other countries.

In addition to investments of various kinds, there are remittances from
people living in foreign countries sent back to family members in their
countries of origin. In 2003, a survey in Mexico found that at least one-
fourth of its 100 million people received money from family members in the
United States, for a total of more than $14 billion. Nor is this a new
phenomenon or one confined to Mexicans. Emigrants from China and
India sent more than 20 billion dollars back to their respective countries in
2005. Worldwide, remittances transferred more than twice as much money
as all the foreign aid in the world. Back in the 1840s, remittances from Irish
immigrants in America to members of their families in Ireland enabled
many of these family members not only to survive in famine-stricken
Ireland but also to immigrate to the United States. In centuries past,

imperial powers simply transferred vast amounts of wealth from the nations they conquered. Alexander the Great looted the treasures of the conquered Persians. Spain took gold and silver by the ton from the conquered indigenous peoples of the Western Hemisphere and forced some of these indigenous peoples into mines to dig up more. Julius Caesar was one of many Roman conquerors to march in triumph through the eternal city, displaying the riches and slaves he was bringing back from his victories abroad. In more recent times, both prosperous nations and international agencies have transferred part of their wealth to poorer countries under the general heading of "foreign aid."

None of this is very complicated—so long as we remember Justice Oliver Wendell Holmes' admonition to "think things instead of words." When it comes to international trade and international transfers of wealth, the things are relatively straightforward, but the words are often slippery and misleading.

INTERNATIONAL INVESTMENTS

Theoretically, investments might be expected to flow from where capital is abundant to where it is in short supply, much like water seeking its own level. In a perfect world, wealthy nations would invest much of their capital in poorer nations, where capital is more scarce and would therefore offer a higher rate of return. However, in the highly imperfect world that we live in, that is by no means what usually happens. For example, out of a worldwide total of $9 trillion in international bank loans and deposits in 2001, only about $700 billion went to poor countries—*less than eight percent*. Out of $12 trillion in international investment securities, only about $600 billion went to poor countries, only 5 percent. In short, rich countries tend to invest in other rich countries.

There are reasons for this, just as there are reasons why some countries are rich and others poor in the first place. The biggest deterrent to investing in any country is the danger that you will never get your money back. Investors are wary of unstable governments, whose changes of personnel or policies create risks that the conditions under which the investment was made can change—the most drastic change being outright confiscation by the government, or "nationalization" as it is called politically. Widespread corruption is another deterrent to investment, as it is to economic activity in general. Countries high up on the international index of corruption, such as Nigeria or Russia, are unlikely to attract international investments on a scale that their natural resources or other economic potential might justify. Conversely, the top countries in terms of having low levels of corruption are all prosperous countries, mostly European or European-offshoot nations plus Japan and Singapore. As noted in Chapter 17, the level of honesty has serious economic implications.

Even aside from confiscation and corruption, many poorer countries "do not let capital come and go freely," according to *The Economist*. Where capital cannot get out easily, it is less likely to go in, in the first place. It is not these countries' poverty, as such, that deters investments. When Hong Kong was a British colony, it began very poor and yet grew to become an industrial powerhouse, at one time having more international trade than a vast country like India. Massive inflows of capital helped develop Hong Kong, which operated under the security of British laws, had low tax rates, and allowed some of the freest flows of capital and trade anywhere in the world. Likewise, India today remains a very poor country but, since the loosening of government controls over the Indian economy, investment has poured in, especially for the Bangalore region, where a concentrated supply of computer software engineers has attracted investors from California's Silicon Valley, creating in effect the beginnings of a new Silicon Valley in India.

Simple and straightforward as the basic principles of international transfers of wealth may be, words and accounting rules can make it seem more complicated. If Americans buy more Japanese goods than the Japanese buy American goods, then Japan gets American dollars to cover the difference. Since the Japanese are not just going to collect these dollars as souvenirs, they usually turn around and invest them in the American economy. In most cases, the money never leaves the United States. The Japanese simply buy investment goods—Rockefeller Center, for example—

rather than consumer goods. American dollars are worthless to the Japanese if they do not spend them on something. In gross terms, international trade has to balance. But it so happens that the conventions of international accounting count imports and exports in the "balance of trade," but not things which don't move at all, like Rockefeller Center. However, accounting conventions and economic realities can be very different things.

In some years, the best-selling car in America has been a Honda or a Toyota, but no automobile made in Detroit has been the best-selling car in Japan. The net result is that Japanese automakers receive billions of dollars in American money and Japan usually has a net surplus in its trade with the United States. But what do the makers of Hondas and Toyotas do with all that American money? One of the things they do is build factories in the United States, employing thousands of American workers to manufacture their cars closer to their customers, so that Honda and Toyota do not have to pay the cost of shipping cars across the Pacific Ocean. Their American employees have been paid sufficiently high wages that they have repeatedly voted against joining labor unions in secret ballot elections. On July 29, 2002, the ten millionth Toyota was built in the United States. Looking at *things*, rather than words, there is little here to be alarmed about. What alarms people are the words and the accounting rules which produce numbers to fit those words.

A country's total output consists of both goods and services—houses and haircuts, sausages and surgery—but the international trade balance consists only of physical goods that move. The American economy produces more services than goods, so it is not surprising that the United States imports more goods than it exports—and exports more services than it imports. American know-how and American technology are used by other countries around the world and these countries of course pay the U.S. for these services. For example, most of the personal computers in the world run on operating systems created by the Microsoft Corporation. But foreign payments to Microsoft and other American companies for their services are not counted in the international balance of trade, since trade includes only goods, not services.

This is just an accounting convention. Yet the American "balance of trade" is reported in the media as if this partial picture were the whole picture and the emotionally explosive word "deficit" sets off alarms. Yet there is often a substantial surplus earned by the United States from its services, which are of course omitted from the trade balance. In the year 2000, for example, the United States earned $38 billion from royalty and license fees alone, and more than $278 billion from all the services it supplied to other countries. That is more than the Gross Domestic Product of Austria or any of the Scandinavian countries.

The *Wall Street Journal*'s comment on the trade deficit was:

> On the list of economic matters to worry about, "the trade deficit" is about 75th—unless politicians react to it by imposing new trade barriers or devaluing the currency.

With trade deficits, as with many other things, what matters is not the absolute size but the size relative to the size of the economy as a whole. While the United States has the world's largest trade deficit, it also has the world's largest economy. The American trade deficit is 6 percent of the country's Gross Domestic Product—about the same as that of Turkey or Australia and much less than Iceland's 16 percent.

When you count all the money and resources moving in and out of a country for all sorts of reasons, then you are no longer talking about the "balance of trade" but about the "balance of payments"—regardless of whether the payments were made for goods or services. While this is not as misleading as the balance of trade, it is still far from being the whole story, and it has no necessary connection with the health of the economy. Ironically, one of the rare balance of payments surpluses for the United States in the late twentieth century was followed by the 1992 recession. Germany has regularly run export surpluses but at the same time its economy has had slower growth rates and higher unemployment rates than those of the United States. Nigeria has often had years of international trade surpluses and is one of the poorest countries in the world.

This is not to say that countries with trade surpluses or payments surpluses are at an economic disadvantage. It is just that these numbers, by themselves, do not necessarily indicate either the prosperity or the poverty of any economy.

Data on foreign investments can also produce misleading words. According to the accounting rules, when people in other countries invest in the United States, that makes the U.S. a "debtor" to those people, because Americans owe them the money that they sent to the U.S., since it was not sent as a gift. When people in many countries around the world feel more secure putting their money in American banks or investing in American corporations, rather than relying on their own banks and corporations, then vast sums of money from overseas find their way to the United States. Foreigners invested $12 billion in American businesses in 1980 and this rose over the years until they were investing more than $200 billion annually by 1998. By the early twenty-first century, the United States received more than twice as much foreign investment as any other country in the world. As of 2003, foreigners bought $579 billion more assets in the United States than Americans acquired abroad. That exceeds the Gross Domestic Product of many countries. Most of this money (66 percent) comes from Europe and another 15 percent from Canada. Prosperous countries tend to invest in other prosperous countries.

Looked at in terms of *things*, there is nothing wrong with this. By creating more wealth in the United States, such investments created more jobs for American workers and created more goods for American consumers, as well as providing income to foreign investors. Looked at in terms of *words*, however, this was a growing debt to foreigners.

The more prosperous and secure the American economy is, the more foreigners are likely to want to send their money to the United States and the higher the annual American balance of payments "deficits" and accumulated international "debt" rises. Hence it is not at all surprising that the long prosperity of the U.S. economy in the 1990s was accompanied by record levels of international deficits and debts. The United States was where the action was and this was where many foreigners wanted their money to be, in order to get in on the action. By the end of 2001, the United States was approximately $1.3 trillion in debt to foreigners, including international institutions. While this was largely a result of American prosperity, this is not to say that things cannot be different for other countries with different circumstances.

Some other prosperous countries invest more abroad than foreign countries invest in them. France, Britain, and Japan, for example, invest hundreds of billions of dollars more in other countries than other countries invest in them. There is nothing intrinsically wrong with being a creditor nation, any more than there is anything intrinsically wrong with being a debtor nation. Everything depends on the particular circumstances, opportunities, and constraints facing each country. Switzerland, for example, has had a net investment in other countries larger than the Swiss Gross Domestic Product. Vast sums of money come into Switzerland as a major international financial center and, if the Swiss cannot find enough good investment opportunities within their own small country for all this money, it makes perfect sense for them to invest much of the money in other countries.

The point here is that neither international deficits nor surpluses are inevitable consequences of either prosperity or poverty and neither word, by itself, tells much about the condition of a country's economy. The word "debt" covers very different kinds of transactions, some of which may in fact present problems and some of which do not. Every time you deposit a hundred dollars in a bank, that bank goes a hundred dollars deeper into debt, because it is still your money and they owe it to you. Some people might become alarmed if they were told that the bank in which they keep their life's savings was going deeper and deeper into debt every month. But such worries would be completely uncalled for, if the bank's growing debt means only that many other people are depositing their pay checks in that same bank.

On the other hand, if you are simply buying things on credit, then that is a debt that you are expected to pay—and if you run up debts that are beyond your means of repayment, you can be in big trouble. However, a bank is in no trouble if someone deposits millions of dollars in it, even though that means going millions of dollars deeper in debt. On the contrary, the bank officials would probably be delighted to get millions of dollars, from which they can make more loans and earn more interest.

For most of its history, the United States has been a debtor nation—and has likewise had the highest standard of living in the world for most of its history. One of the things that helped develop the American economy and changed the United States from a small agricultural nation to an industrial giant was an inflow of capital from Western Europe in general and from Britain in particular. These vast resources enabled the United States to build canals, factories and transcontinental railroads to tie the country together economically. As of the 1890s, for example, foreign investors owned about one-fifth of the stock of the Baltimore & Ohio Railroad, more than one-third of the stock of the New York Central, more than half the stock of the Pennsylvania Railroad and nearly two-thirds of the stock of the Illinois Central. Even today, when American multinational corporations own vast amounts of assets in other countries, foreigners have owned more assets in the United States than Americans own abroad for well over a decade.

Obviously, foreign investors would never have sent their money to America unless they expected to get it back with interest and dividends. Equally obviously, American entrepreneurs would never have agreed to pay interest and dividends unless they expected these investments to produce big enough returns to cover these payments and still leave a profit for the American enterprises. These investments usually worked out largely as planned, for generations on end. But this meant that the United States was officially a debtor nation for generations on end. Only as a result of lending money to European governments during the First World War did the United States become a creditor nation. Since then, the U.S. has been both, at one time or another. But these have been accounting details, not determinants of American prosperity or economic problems.

While foreign investments played a major role in the development of particular sectors of the American economy, especially in the early development of industry and infrastructure, there is no need to exaggerate its over-all importance, even in the nineteenth century. For the American economy as a whole, it has been estimated that foreign investment financed about 6 percent of all capital formation in the United States in the nineteenth century. Railroads were exceptional and accounted for an absolute majority of foreign investments in the stocks and bonds of

American enterprises. In various other countries, the role of foreign investors has been much greater than in the United States, even though the large American economy has received more foreign investments in absolute amounts. In the early twentieth century, overseas investors owned one-fifth of the Australian economy and one half that of Argentina.

Neither the domestic economy nor the international economy is a zero-sum process, where some must lose what others win. Everyone can win when investments create a growing economy. There is a bigger pie, from which everyone can get bigger slices. The massive infusion of foreign capital contributed to making the United States the world's leading industrial nation by 1913, when Americans produced more than one-third of all the manufactured goods in the world. Despite fears in some countries that foreign investors would carry off much of their national wealth, leaving the local population poorer, there is probably no country in history from which foreigners have carried away more vast amounts of wealth than the United States. By that reasoning, Americans ought to be some of the poorest people in the world, instead of consistently having one of the world's highest standards of living. The reason for that prosperity is that economic transactions are not a zero-sum activity. They create wealth.

In some less fortunate countries, the same words used in accounting—especially "debt"—may have a very different economic reality behind them. For example, when exports will not cover the cost of imports and there is no high-tech know-how to export, the government may borrow money from some other country or from some international agency, in order to cover the difference. These are genuine debts and causes for genuine concern. But the mere fact of a large trade deficit or a large payments deficit does not by itself create a crisis, though political and journalistic rhetoric can turn it into something to alarm the public.

OTHER TRANSFERS

Even in an era of international investments in the trillions of dollars, other kinds of transfers of wealth among nations remain significant. These include remittances, foreign aid, and transfers of human capital in the form of the skills and entrepreneurship of emigrants.

Remittances

Emigrants working in foreign countries often send money back to their families to support them. During the nineteenth and early twentieth centuries, Italian emigrant men were particularly noted for enduring terrible living conditions in various countries around the world, and even skimping on food, in order to send money back to their families in Italy. Most of the people fleeing the famine in Ireland during the 1840s traveled across the Atlantic with their fares paid by remittances from members of their families already living in the United States. The same would be true of Jewish emigrants from Eastern Europe to the United States in later years.

By the late twentieth century, there were so many emigrants working in so many countries abroad, and sending money home, that their remittances exceeded all the foreign aid from all the government agencies in the world combined. Most of Pakistan's international trade deficit was covered by remittances from Pakistanis working abroad and Jordan received more money from Jordanians living in other countries than it did from all its exports.

At one time, overseas Chinese living in Malaysia, Indonesia and other Southeast Asian nations were noted for sending money back to their families in China. Politicians and journalists in these countries often whipped up hostility against the overseas Chinese by claiming that such remittances were impoverishing their countries for the benefit of China. In reality, the Chinese created many of the enterprises—and sometimes whole industries—in these Southeast Asian nations. What they were sending back to China was a fraction of the wealth they had created and added to the wealth of the countries where they were now living.

Similar charges were made against the Lebanese in West Africa, the Indians and Pakistanis in East Africa, and other groups around the world. The underlying fallacy in each case was due to ignoring the wealth created by these groups, so that the countries to which they immigrated had more wealth—not less—as a result of these groups being there. Sometimes the hostility generated against such groups has led to their leaving these countries or being expelled, often followed by economic declines in the countries they left.

Emigrants and Immigrants

People are one of the biggest sources of wealth. Whole industries have been created and economies have been transformed by immigrants.

Historically, it has not been at all unusual for a particular ethnic or immigrant group to create or dominate a whole industry. German immigrants created the leading beer breweries in the United States in the nineteenth century, and most of the leading brands of American beer in the twenty-first century are still produced in breweries created by people of German ancestry. China's most famous beer—Tsingtao—was also created by Germans and there are German breweries in Australia, Brazil, and Argentina. There were no watches manufactured in London until Huguenots fleeing France took watch-making skills with them to England and Switzerland, making both these nations among the leading watch-makers in the world. Conversely, France faced increased competition in a number of industries which it had once dominated, because the Huguenots who had fled persecution in France created competing businesses in surrounding countries.

Among the vital sources of the skills and entrepreneurship behind the rise of first Britain, and later the United States, to the position of the leading industrial and commercial nation in the world were the numerous immigrant groups who settled in these countries, often to escape persecution or destitution in their native lands. The woolen, linen, cotton, silk, paper, and glass industries were revolutionized by foreign workers and foreign entrepreneurs in England, while the Jews and the Lombards developed British financial institutions. The United States, as a country populated overwhelmingly by immigrants, had even more occupations and industries created or dominated by particular immigrant groups. The first pianos built in colonial America were built by Germans—who also pioneered in building pianos in czarist Russia, England, and France—and firms created by Germans continued to produce the leading American pianos, such as Steinway and Schnabel, in the twenty-first century.

Perhaps to an even greater degree, the countries of Latin America have been dependent on immigrants—especially immigrants from countries other than the conquering nations of Spain and Portugal. According to the distinguished French historian Fernand Braudel, it was these immigrants who "created modern Brazil, modern Argentina, modern Chile." Among the foreigners who have owned or directed more than half of particular industries in particular countries have been the Lebanese in West Africa, Greeks in the Ottoman Empire, Germans in Brazil, Indians in Fiji, Britons in Argentina, Belgians in Russia, Chinese in Malaysia, and many others. Nor is this all a thing of the past. Four-fifths of the doughnut shops in California are owned by people of Cambodian ancestry and more than half the doctors in Britain were born outside of Britain.

Throughout history, national economic losses from emigration have been as striking as gains from receiving immigrants. After the Moriscoes were expelled from Spain in the early sixteenth century, a Spanish cleric asked: "Who will make our shoes now?" This was a question that might better have been asked *before* the Moriscoes were expelled, especially since this particular cleric had supported the expulsions. Some countries have exported human capital on a large scale—for example, when their educated young people emigrate because other countries offer better opportunities. *The Economist* reported that more than 60 percent of the graduates in Fiji, Trinidad, Haiti, Jamaica and Guyana went to live in European countries. For Guyana, 83 percent did so.

Although it is not easy to quantify human capital, emigration of educated people on this scale represents a serious loss of national wealth. One of the most striking examples of a country's losses due to those who emigrated was that of Nazi Germany, whose anti-Semitic policies led many Jewish scientists to flee to America, where they played a major role in making the United States the first nation with an atomic bomb. Thus Germany's ally Japan then paid an even bigger price for policies that led to massive Jewish emigration from Nazi-dominated Europe.

It would be misleading, however, to assess the economic impact of immigration solely in terms of its positive contributions. Immigrants have also brought diseases, crime, internal strife, and terrorism. Nor can all immigrants be lumped together. When only two percent of immigrants from Japan to the United States go on welfare, while 46 percent of the immigrants from Laos do, there is no single pattern that applies to all immigrants. There are similar disparities in crime rates and in other both negative and positive factors that immigrants from different countries bring to the United States and to other countries in other parts of the world.

Russia and Nigeria are usually ranked among the most corrupt countries in the world and immigrants from Russia and Nigeria have become notorious for criminal activities in the United States.

Everything depends on which emigrants you are talking about, which countries you are talking about and which periods of history.

Imperialism

Plunder of one nation or people by another has been all too common throughout human history.

Although imperialism is one of the ways in which wealth can be transferred from one country to another, there are also non-economic reasons for imperialism which have caused it to be persisted in, even when it was costing the conquering country money on net balance. Military leaders may want strategic bases, such as the British base at Gibraltar or the American base at Guantanamo Bay in Cuba. Nineteenth century missionaries urged the British government toward acquiring control of various countries in Africa where there was much missionary work going on—such urgings often being opposed by chancellors of the exchequer, who realized that Britain would never get enough money out of these poor countries to repay the costs of establishing and maintaining a colonial regime there.

Some private individuals like Cecil Rhodes might get rich in Africa, but the costs to the British taxpayers exceeded even Rhodes' fabulous fortune. Modern European imperialism in general was much more impressive in terms of the size of the territories controlled than in terms of the economic significance of those territories. When European empires were at their zenith in the early twentieth century, Western Europe was less than 2 percent of the world's land area but it controlled more than another 40 percent in overseas empires. However, most major industrial nations sent only trivial percentages of their exports or investments to their conquered colonies in the Third World and received imports that were similarly trivial compared to what these industrial nations produced themselves or purchased as imports from other industrial countries.

Even at the height of the British Empire in the early twentieth century, the British invested more in the United States than in all of Asia and Africa put together. Quite simply, there is more wealth to be made from rich countries than from poor countries. For similar reasons, throughout most of the twentieth century the United States invested more in Canada than in all of Asia and Africa put together. Only the rise of prosperous Asian industrial nations in the latter part of the twentieth century attracted more American investors to that part of the world. In the early twenty-first century, the United States had several times as much invested in a small country like the Netherlands than in the whole vast continent of Africa, which is larger than all of Europe or North America. Conversely, of all foreign investments in the United States nearly half (49 percent) came from Europe and 41 percent were from Canada.

Perhaps the strongest evidence against the economic significance of colonies in the modern world is that Germany and Japan lost all their colonies and conquered lands as a result of their defeat in the Second World War—and both countries reached unprecedented levels of prosperity thereafter. A need for colonies was a particularly effective political talking point in pre-war Japan, which has had very few natural resources of its own. But, after its dreams of military glory ended with its defeat and devastation, Japan simply bought whatever natural resources it needed from those countries that had them, and prospered doing so.

Imperialism has often caused much suffering among the conquered peoples. But, in the modern industrial world at least, imperialism has seldom been a major source of international transfers of wealth.

While investors have tended to invest in more prosperous nations, making both themselves and these nations wealthier, some people have depicted investments in poor countries as somehow making the latter even poorer. The Marxian concept of "exploitation" was applied internationally in Lenin's book *Imperialism*, where investments by industrial nations in non-industrial countries were treated as being economically equivalent to the looting done by earlier imperialist conquerors. Tragically, however, it is in precisely those less developed countries where little or no foreign investment has taken place that poverty is at its worst. Similarly, those poor countries with less international trade as a percentage of their national economies have usually had lower economic growth rates than poor countries where international trade plays a larger economic role. Indeed, during the decade of the 1990s, the former countries had declining economies, while those more "globalized" countries had growing economies.

Wealthy individuals in poor countries often invest in richer countries, where their money is safer from political upheavals and confiscations. Ironically, poorer countries are thus helping richer industrial nations to become still richer. Meanwhile, under the influence of theories of economic imperialism which depicted international investments as being the equivalent of imperialist looting, governments in many poorer countries pursued policies which discouraged investments from being made there by foreigners. By the late twentieth century, however, the painful economic consequences of such policies had become sufficiently apparent to many people in the Third World that some governments—in Latin America and India, for example—began moving away from such policies, in order to gain some of the benefits received by other countries which had risen from poverty to prosperity with the help of foreign investments.

Economic realities finally broke through ideological beliefs, though generations had suffered needless deprivations before basic economic principles were finally accepted. Once markets in these countries were opened to foreign goods and foreign investments, both poured in. However small the investments of prosperous countries in poor countries might seem in comparison with their investments in other prosperous countries, those investments have loomed large in the Third World. As of 1991 foreign companies owned 27 percent of the businesses in Latin America and, a decade later, owned 39 percent.

Many economic fallacies are due to conceiving of economic activity as a zero-sum contest, in which what is gained by one is lost by another. This in turn is often due to ignoring the fact that wealth is *created* in the course of economic activity. If payments to foreign investors impoverished a nation, then the United States would be one of the most impoverished nations in the world, because foreigners took nearly $270 billion out of the American economy in 2001—which was more than the Gross Domestic Product of Egypt or Malaysia. Since most of this money consisted of earnings from assets that foreigners owned in the United States, Americans had already gotten the benefits of the additional wealth that those assets had helped create, and were simply sharing part of that additional wealth with those abroad who had contributed to creating it.

It is of course possible to obtain foreign technology, machinery, and expertise by paying for these things with export earnings. The poorer a country is, the more that means domestic hardships as the price of economic development. "Let us starve but export," declared a czarist minister—who was very unlikely to do any starving himself. The very same philosophy was employed later, though not announced, during the era of the Soviet Union, when the industrialization of the economy was heavily dependent on foreign imports financed by exports of food and other natural resources. According to two Soviet economists, writing many years later:

> During the first Five-Year Plan, 40 percent of export earnings came from grain shipments. In 1931 one third of the machinery and equipment imported in the world was purchased by the U.S.S.R. Of all the equipment put into operation in Soviet factories during this period, 80 to 85 percent was purchased from the West.

At the time, however, the growth of the state-run Soviet industrial complex was proclaimed a triumph of communism, though in fact it represented an importation of capitalist technology, while skimping on food in the Soviet Union. The alternative of allowing foreign investment was not permitted in a government-run economy founded on a rejection of capitalism.

Foreign Aid

What is called "foreign aid" are transfers of wealth from foreign governmental organizations, including international agencies, to the governments of poorer countries. The term "aid" assumes *a priori* that such transfers will in fact aid the poorer countries' economies to develop. In some cases it does, but in other cases foreign aid simply enables the existing politicians in power to enrich themselves through graft and to dispense largess in politically strategic ways to others who help to keep them in power. Because it is a transfer of wealth to governments, as distinguished from investments in private enterprises, foreign aid has encouraged many countries to set up government-run enterprises that have failed.

Perhaps the most famous foreign aid program was the Marshall Plan, which transferred wealth from the United States to various countries in Western Europe after the end of World War II. It was far more successful than later attempts to imitate it by sending foreign aid to Third World countries. Western Europe's economic distress was caused by the physical devastations of the war. Once the people were fed and the infrastructure rebuilt, Western Europe simply resumed the industrial way of life which they had achieved—indeed, pioneered—before. That was wholly different from trying to create all the industrial skills that were lacking in poorer, non-industrial nations. What needed to be rebuilt in Europe was physical capital. What needed to be created in much of the Third World was more human capital. The latter proved harder to do, just as the vast array of skills needed in a modern economy had taken centuries to create in Europe.

Even massive and highly visible failures and counterproductive results from foreign aid have not stopped its continuation and expansion. The vast sums of money dispensed by foreign aid agencies such as the International Monetary Fund and the World Bank give the officials of these agencies enormous influence on the governments of poorer countries, regardless of the success or failure of the programs they suggest or impose as preconditions for receiving money. In short, there is no economic bottom line constraining aid dispensers to determine which actions, policies, organizations or individuals could survive the weeding out process that takes place through competition in the marketplace.

In addition to the "foreign aid" dispensed by international agencies, there are also direct government-to-government grants of money, shipments of free food, and loans which are made available on terms more lenient than those available in the financial markets and which are periodically "forgiven," allowed to default, or "rolled over" by being repaid from the proceeds of new and larger loans. Thus American government loans to the government of India and British government loans to a number of Third World governments have been simply cancelled, converting these loans into gifts.

Sometimes a richer country takes over a whole poor society and heavily subsidizes it, as the United States did in Micronesia. So much American aid poured in that many Micronesians abandoned economic activities on which they had supported themselves before, such as fishing and farming. If and when Americans decide to end such aid, it is not at all certain that the skills and experience that Micronesians once had will remain widespread enough in later generations to allow them to become self-sufficient again.

Beneficial results of foreign aid are more likely to be publicized by the national or international agencies which finance these ventures, while failures are more likely to be publicized by critics, so the net effect is not immediately obvious. One of the leading development economists of his time, the late Professor Peter Bauer of the London School of Economics, argued that, on the whole, "official aid is more likely to retard development than to promote it." Whether that controversial conclusion is accepted or rejected, what is more fundamental is that terms like "foreign aid" not be allowed to insinuate a result which may or may not turn out to be substantiated by facts and analysis.

Many Third World countries have considerable internal sources of wealth which are not fully utilized for one reason or another—and this wealth often greatly exceeds whatever foreign aid such countries have ever received. In many poorer countries, much—if not most—economic activity takes place "off the books" or in the "underground economy" because the costs of red tape, corruption, and bureaucratic delays required to obtain legal permission to run a business or own a home put legally recognized economic activities beyond the financial reach of much of the population. These people may operate businesses ranging from street vending to factories, or build homes for themselves or others, without having any of this economic activity legally recognized by their governments.

According to *The Economist* magazine, in a typical African nation, only about one person in ten works in a legally recognized enterprise or lives in a house that has legally recognized property rights. In Egypt, for example, an estimated 4.7 million homes have been built illegally. In Peru, the total value of all the real estate that is not legally covered by property rights has been estimated as more than a dozen times larger than all the foreign direct investments ever made in the country in its entire history. Similar situations have been found in India, Haiti, and other Third World countries.

The economic consequences of these legal bottlenecks in many countries can be profound because they prevent many existing enterprises, representing vast amounts of wealth in the aggregate, from developing beyond the small scale in which they start. Many giant American corporations began as very humble enterprises, not very different from those which abound in Third World countries today. Founders of Levi's, Macy's, Saks, and Bloomingdale's all began as peddlers, for example. While such businesses may get started with an individual's own small savings or perhaps with loans from family or friends, eventually their expansion into major corporations usually requires the mobilization of the money of innumerable strangers willing to become investors. But the property rights system which makes this possible has not been as accessible to ordinary people in Third World countries as it has been to ordinary people in the United States.

An American bank that is unwilling to invest in a small business may nevertheless be willing to lend money to its owner in exchange for a mortgage on his home—but the home must first be legally recognized as his property. After the business becomes a major success, other strangers may lend money on its growing assets or invest directly as stockholders. But all of this hinges on a system of dependable and accessible property rights, which is capable of mobilizing far more wealth internally than is ever likely to be transferred from other nations or from international agencies like the World Bank or the International Monetary Fund.

THE INTERNATIONAL
MONETARY SYSTEM

Wealth may be transferred from country to country in the form of goods and services, but by far the greatest transfers are made in the form of money. Just as a stable monetary unit facilitates economic activity within a country, so international economic activity is facilitated when there are stable relationships between one country's currency and another's. It is not simply a question of the ease or difficulty of converting dollars into yen or euros at a given moment. A far more important question is whether an investment made in the United States, Japan, or France today will be repaid a decade or more from now in money of the same purchasing power.

When currencies fluctuate relative to one another, anyone who engages in any international transactions becomes a speculator. Even an American tourist who buys souvenirs in Mexico will have to wait until the credit card bill arrives to discover how much the item they paid 30 pesos for will cost them in U.S. dollars. It can turn out to be either more or less than they thought. Where millions of dollars are invested overseas, the stability of the various currencies is urgently important. It is important not simply to those whose money is directly involved, it is important in maintaining the flows of trade and investment which affect the material well-being of the general public in the countries concerned.

During the era of the gold standard, which began to break down during the First World War and ended during the Great Depression of the 1930s, various nations made their national currencies equivalent to a given amount of gold. An American dollar, for example, could always be exchanged for a fixed amount of gold from the U. S. government. Both Americans and foreigners could exchange their dollars for a given amount of gold. Therefore any foreign investor putting his money into the American economy knew in advance what he could count on getting back if his investment worked out. No doubt that had much to do with the vast amount of capital that poured into the United States from Europe and helped develop it into the leading industrial nation of the world.

Other nations which made their currency redeemable in fixed amounts of gold likewise made their economies safer places for both domestic and foreign investors. Moreover, their currencies were also automatically fixed relative to the dollar and other currencies from other countries that used the gold standard. As Nobel Prizewinning monetary economist Robert Mundell put it, "currencies were just different names for particular weights of gold." During that era, famous financier J. P. Morgan could say, "money is gold, and nothing else." This reduced the risks of buying, selling, or investing in those foreign countries that were on the gold standard, since exchange rate fluctuations were not the threat that they were in transactions with other countries.

The end of the gold standard led to various attempts at stabilizing international currencies against one another. Some nations have made their currencies equivalent to a fixed number of dollars, for example. Various European nations have joined together to create their own international currency, the euro, and the Japanese yen has been another stable currency widely accepted in international financial transactions. At the other extreme have been various South American countries, whose currencies have fluctuated wildly in value, with inflation sometimes reaching double or triple digits.

These monetary fluctuations have had repercussions on such real things as output and employment, since it is difficult to plan and invest when there is much uncertainty about what the money will be worth, even if the investment is successful otherwise. The economic problems of Argentina and Brazil have been particularly striking in view of the fact that both countries are richly endowed with natural resources and have been spared the destruction of wars that so many other countries on other continents suffered in the course of the twentieth century.

With the spread of electronic transfers of money, reactions to any national currency's change in reliability can be virtually instantaneous. Any government that is tempted toward inflation knows that money can flee from their economy literally in a moment. The discipline this imposes is different from that once imposed by a gold standard, but whether it is equally effective will only be known when future economic pressures put the international monetary system to a real test.

As in other areas of economics, it is necessary to be on guard against emotionally loaded words that may confuse more than they clarify. One of the terms widely used in discussing the relative values of various national currencies are "strong" and "weak." Thus, when the euro was first introduced as a monetary unit in the European Union countries, its value fell from $1.18 to 83 cents and it was said to be "weakening" relative to the dollar. Later it rose again, to reach $1.16 in early 2003, and was then said to be "strengthening." Words can be harmless if we understand what they do and don't mean, but misleading if we take their connotations at face value.

One thing that a "strong" currency does not mean is that the economies that use that currency are necessarily better off. Sometimes it means the opposite. A "strong" currency means that the prices of exports from countries that use that currency have risen in price to people in other countries. Thus the rise in value of the euro in 2003 has been blamed by a number of European corporations for falling exports to the United States, as the prices of their products rose in dollars, causing fewer Americans to buy them. Meanwhile, the "weakening" of Britain's pound sterling had opposite effects. *BusinessWeek* magazine reported:

> Britain's hard-pressed manufacturers love a falling pound. So they have warmly welcomed the 11% slide in sterling's exchange rate against the euro over the past year. . . . As the pound weakens against the euro, it makes British goods more competitive on the Continent, which is by far their largest export market. And it boosts corporate profits when earnings from the euro zone are converted into sterling.

Just as a "strong" currency is not always good, it is not always bad either. In the countries that use the euro, businesses that borrow from Americans find the burden of that debt to be less, and therefore easier to repay, when fewer euros are needed to pay back the dollars they owe. When Norway's krone rose in value relative to Sweden's krona, Norwegians living near the border of Sweden crossed over and saved 40 percent buying a load of groceries in Sweden. The point here is simply that words like "strong" and "weak" currencies by themselves tell us little about the economic realities, which have to be looked at directly and specifically, rather than by relying on the emotional connotations of words.

Chapter 22

AN OVERVIEW

Mistrust of free trade is quite sincere.
Frederic Bastiat

F ree trade may have wide support among economists, but its support among the public at large is considerably less. An international poll conducted by *The Economist* magazine found more people in favor of protectionism than of free trade in Britain, France, Italy, Australia, Russia, and the United States. Part of the reason is that the public has no idea how much protectionism costs and how little net benefit it produces. It has been estimated that all the protectionism in the European Union countries put together saves no more than a grand total of 200,000 jobs—at a cost of $43 billion. That works out to about $215,000 a year for each job saved.

In other words, if the European Union permitted 100 percent free international trade, every worker who lost his job as a result of foreign competition could be paid $100,000 a year in compensation and the European Union countries would still come out ahead. Alternatively, the displaced workers could simply go find other jobs. Whatever losses they might encounter in the process do not begin to compare with the staggering costs of keeping them working where they are. That is because the costs are not simply their salaries, but the even larger costs of producing in less efficient ways, using up scarce resources that would be more productive elsewhere. In other words, what the consumers lose greatly exceeds what the workers gain, making the society as a whole worse off.

The costs of protectionism can be measured not only in money but also in the number of jobs lost by industries adversely affected by the protection given to one particular industry. Since there were 160,000 workers in the American steel industry when tariffs were imposed for their protection and 9 million workers in industries using steel, it can hardly be surprising that there were net losses of jobs from these tariffs.

Only part of the problem of getting the general public to understand international trade is due to their not having the facts. Another part of the problem is their not having enough knowledge of economics to withstand the barrage of self-serving arguments put out by many in business, labor, and agriculture, who wish to escape the consequences of having to compete in the marketplace with foreign producers. When American steel producers have higher production costs per ton than their German, Japanese, Brazilian and South Korean rivals, it is easier to ask the U.S. government for protection from foreign competitors than to go through all the painful changes required to reduce their own high costs of production.

Another reason for public support for protectionism is that many economists do not bother to answer either the special interests or those who oppose free trade for ideological reasons, since the arguments of both have essentially been refuted centuries ago and are now regarded in the economics profession as beneath contempt. But this has only allowed vehement and articulate spokesmen to have a more or less free hand to monopolize public opinion, which seldom hears more than one side of the issue. One of the few leading economists to bother answering protectionist arguments has been internationally renowned economist Jagdish Bhagwati, who agreed to a public debate against Ralph Nader. Here was his experience:

> Faced with the critics of free trade, economists have generally reacted with contempt and indifference, refusing to get into the public arena to engage the critics in battle. I was in a public debate with Ralph Nader on the campus of Cornell University a couple of years ago. The debate was in the evening, and in the afternoon I gave a technical talk on free trade to the graduate students of economics. I asked, at its end, how many were going to the debate, and not one hand went up. Why, I asked. The typical reaction was: why waste one's time? As a consequence, of the nearly thousand students who jammed the theater where the debate was held, the vast majority were anti-free traders, all rooting for Mr. Nader.

Because the buzzword "globalization" has been coined to describe the growing importance of international trade and global economic interdependence, many tend to see international trade and international financial transactions as something new—allowing both special interests and ideologues to play on the public's fear of the unknown. However, the term "globalization" also covers more than simple free trade among nations. It includes institutional rules governing the reduction of trade barriers and the movements of money. Among the international organizations involved in creating these rules are the World Bank, the International Monetary Fund, and the World Trade Organization. These rules are legitimate subjects of controversy, though these are not all controversies about free trade, as such. One of the severest critics of the International Monetary Fund, for example, has been Nobel Prizewinning economist Joseph Stiglitz, who favors free trade but attacks the specific rules imposed by the IMF when making loans to poor countries.

THE ROLE OF TRADE

Americans have not had to pay nearly as much attention to international trade as people in other countries, such as Britain or Holland, whose economies have been more dependent on such trade for centuries. Still, American overseas trade has been growing in recent years, not only absolutely but also as a percentage of the U.S. economy. The ratio of the total international trade of the United States—combining exports and imports—to the total output of the American economy was just 8 percent in 1950 but was 26 percent by 2000. Moreover, even in the past, the modest share of international economic transactions in the American economy was nevertheless significant in transforming the United States from a predominantly agricultural nation into a major industrial power.

In addition to the large foreign investments that went into creating leading American railroads in the late nineteenth century, as noted in Chapter 21, even earlier—in the 1820s and 1830s—foreign purchasers of state bonds financed the digging of canals, the construction of urban public works, and the creation of banks in the United States. Later, in the post-Civil War period, foreign investments financed 15 percent of all the net capital formation in the United States from 1869 to 1875. In short, while international trade and international financial transactions have not played as large or as visible a role in the economy of the United States as in the economies of some other countries, that role has not been negligible.

International trade is basically a further extension of the division and specialization of functions that marks every modern economy. There was a time, not many centuries ago, when farm families provided themselves with food, shelter, and even clothing made with their own hands. They grew their own fruits and vegetables, raised their own livestock to provide meat, milked their own cows and even made their own cheese. Homespun clothing was common as well on the American frontier. A remarkable degree of economic self-sufficiency is possible, even at the level of the individual family. But that only raises the question: Why did this way of doing things die out? Why did people begin to purchase all these things from other people who specialized in producing particular goods?

The answer is of course that specialists could produce better products at lower costs. But, so long as family farms were isolated—that is, could receive specialized products only with high transportation costs added—a self-sufficient way of life made sense. But, once the transportation system was able to bring a wheat farmer numerous consumer products at affordable prices, and to carry his wheat to market at lower cost, it made more sense for the family to spend their time growing more wheat, instead of making homespun clothing, because they could buy their clothing with what they earned from selling more wheat, and still have something left over.

Everything depends on whether the time and efforts required to produce their own clothing directly would yield more clothing in the end if that time were put into growing wheat to sell. The same principle applies not only to clothing but to other products as well—and regardless of whether those products are produced within the same national borders or on the other side of the world. That is the basis for international trade. Although this is often described as trade between nations, it is in fact trade between individuals. Each individual decides whether what is bought is worth it, in the light of

other options available. Each Frenchman decides for himself whether he
wants to see a movie made in Hollywood and each person in Singapore
decides whether to buy a camera made in Germany or Japan.

International trade is not a zero-sum contest between nations, but a wide
array of voluntary transactions between individuals living in different
countries, who must all gain if these transactions are to continue.
International trade is just one more way of getting more output from scarce
resources which have alternative uses.

Just as trade restrictions such as the American Hawley-Smoot tariffs of
the 1930s damaged the already ailing U.S. economy during the Great
Depression, the North American Free Trade Agreement of 1993 helped
enhance the prosperity of the 1990s, creating more jobs and reducing
unemployment to record low levels, despite the cries of protectionists that
NAFTA would lead to a massive flight of jobs from America to low-wage
countries elsewhere. The growth of international trade and international
finance over the years is one sign of the benefits it produces. This growth
has generally exceeded the growth of the national economies involved, so
that international transactions have become a larger proportion of all
transactions in the world.

Third World countries and formerly Communist countries which once
severely restricted their international economic transactions have
increasingly opened up their economies to the international market. The
term "globalization" has been used to describe this process of expanded
international commerce and investment, though there has long been much
global economic activity by particular countries and enterprises. The
British, for example, built the first railroads in many countries, from India
to Argentina and from Australia to West Africa. The leading manufacturer
of agricultural machinery in czarist Russia was the American firm
International Harvester. During the colonial era in East Africa,
entrepreneurs from India were so dominant in the economy that rupees
became the common currency in the region. In short, "globalization" is a
new name for an old phenomenon, but one that has become even more
important in recent times.

Globalization undoubtedly harms some businesses and industries and costs some people their jobs. But so do any other ways of creating greater efficiency in the allocation of scarce resources which have alternative uses. Opponents of free trade try to depict it as harmful to the society as a whole, and appeal to a sense of "us" against "them," as if other countries are in some way making Americans worse off by selling them things that they want to buy.

Like anything else that allows goods and services to be produced more cheaply or better, international trade benefits the consumers while reducing profits and employment among those who produce more costly or obsolete products. Protecting the less efficient producer makes no more sense internationally than it does domestically. Whatever jobs are saved in either case do not represent net savings for the economy as a whole, but only the saving of some jobs by sacrificing others, along with sacrificing the consumer. When particular jobs and businesses succumb to more efficient competition, whether domestic or international, resources which have alternative uses can go to those alternative uses and thus add to the national output. Conversely, preventing such transfers saves relatively few jobs at very high costs per job, as in the European Union countries, or saves jobs in one industry at the expense of more jobs lost in other industries, as in the case of the American steel tariffs.

International trade is one way of sharing in the advantages that other countries have in producing particular products. Together with international investments, this is also a way to share in the technology and organizational advances made in other countries, as well as in agricultural produce transplanted from other parts of the world, such as the rubber transplanted to Malaysia and the cocoa transplanted to Ghana—with each of these countries becoming the world's leading producer of their respective transplanted products at one time.

Perhaps the most important international transplants have been human beings. The vast majority of the populations of the Western Hemisphere are the descendants of people transplanted, mostly from Europe, but also from Asia and Africa. With them have come widespread changes in the prevalent technology of the hemisphere, as well as changes in political and other ideas.

Nor has this transfer of "human capital" stopped in later centuries. The 1990 U.S. Census revealed that there were more than two and a half million highly educated people from Third World countries living in the United States, not counting students.

THE ROLE OF INTERNATIONAL INVESTMENT

The transfer of wealth internationally through market transactions allocates the resources of the world in much the same way that such transfers allocate resources domestically. In both cases, it is like water seeking its own level. If investments with a given degree of risk are paying off at a higher rate in Taiwan than in Sweden, then American, British or German capital will flow to Taiwan and not to Sweden, thereby raising the level of productivity in the world as a whole and raising standards of living internationally. Money and the resources it represents become, as it were, citizens of the world.

Such economic benefits are often not welcome politically, however. While comparative advantage and free trade allow all nations to share in the world prosperity promoted by free movements of resources, not all industries within all nations prosper. Those sectors of particular economies that are unable to match the competition in efficiency not only stand to lose money and jobs, they may even be threatened with bankruptcy and extinction. Seldom will they go quietly. Representatives of industries and regions that stand to lose business and jobs because of international competition are almost certain to seek restrictions on imported goods or resources which threaten their particular well-being, however beneficial such international transactions may be to the population as a whole.

International movements of goods and investments also restrict the range of options available to particular governments. As noted in Chapter 16, governments have for centuries transferred wealth from the people to themselves by the simple process of issuing inflationary amounts of money and spending the newly created money for whatever the government wanted to finance. With free international movements of wealth—at instantaneous speeds with computerized financial transactions—money and the resources they represent tend to be transferred out of countries whose governments are conducting such clandestine confiscations.

Other economically counterproductive policies tend likewise to cause domestic wealth to flow out of a country and foreign wealth to stop coming in. Thus it was a matter of concern to India when the private financial rating agency Standard and Poor's downgraded the rating of the country's currency in August 2001 because of what *The Economist* magazine called the "shaky finances" of India's government. Political leaders have far more control when wealth flows into their countries in the form of "foreign aid"— that is, transfers from national or international agencies to governments— rather than as private investments to private individuals or businesses. But receiving wealth from abroad via the marketplace would require satisfying foreign investors that a project was likely to succeed and that the local legal and political system was one they could rely on when time came to take their earnings out or to take their whole investment out if they wished.

Showy projects with only a political pay-off for the government—a sports stadium, a glitzy plaza, or a national airline in a country without enough passengers to enable it to pay for itself—can all be financed by foreign aid, but are unlikely to be financed by international investors risking their own money. Moreover, government officials can be more generous with themselves and their followers and favorites when it comes to appropriating foreign aid money for personal use, including putting it in Swiss banks. Third World countries often have ruins or remnants of failed projects financed by foreign aid, like these in the African nation of Niger:

> The relics of many high-minded, high-tech development projects litter Niger like the dinosaur bones occasionally discovered beneath the shifting sands. Sophisticated irrigation systems that work well with First World maintenance turned into rusted pipes in Niger. The European cows that were supposed to improve milk production keeled over in the heat.

The availability of foreign aid reduces the necessity for a country to restrict its investments to economically viable projects or to reduce its level of corruption. Far more wealth may be available internationally for the economic development of a poor country through private international investors than through foreign aid, and yet that country's government may prefer to receive a smaller amount through foreign aid, since government officials themselves benefit more from this smaller amount than from a larger amount of wealth that would have preconditions which negatively affect these officials' well-being, even if private investment would enhance the economic well-being of their country as a whole. In short, countries with inefficient economies and corrupt governments are far more likely to receive foreign aid than to receive investments from people who are risking their own money. Put differently, the availability of foreign aid reduces the necessity for a country to restrict its investments to economically viable projects or to reduce its level of corruption.

An intermediary form of wealth transfer is an investment from private sources that is guaranteed by their own government, which stands ready to reimburse them with taxpayers' money should their overseas investment prove unprofitable or the profits uncollectible. Thus when the Mexican government was on the verge of defaulting on its loans from American banks in 1986, the American government lent them the money to pay off these banks and other investors. Obviously, if these banks had been forced to take huge losses, they would have become more wary of risky investments in the future and in other countries. As we have seen in other contexts, losses play as important a role in the economy as profits, though they are not nearly as popular. Artificially preventing losses is reducing incentives to allocate resources efficiently.

The periodic "forgiveness" of loans to Third World countries likewise reduces incentives for the governments of these countries to use the loans in ways that contribute to the growth of national wealth, from which the loans could be paid off. The only clear beneficiaries of such "forgiveness," aside from Third World political leaders who escape responsibility, are those people in wealthier donor countries who feel a sense of *noblesse oblige*. But the subsidizing of Third World politicians' financial irresponsibility has heavy costs that fall ultimately on the peoples of the poorer countries.

The sums of money received in foreign aid are dwarfed by the sums of money available for investment internationally in countries with responsible and dependable governments. Moreover, as noted in Chapter 21, vast sources of untapped capital already exist within Third World countries themselves, in the form of economic assets which cannot be turned into financial assets because of the inaccessibility of property rights for most people in those countries. In short, the internal institutions and policies which inhibit international transfers of private investment to poor countries also inhibit the mobilization of investments based on existing assets within those countries.

These assets also include human capital, which may be as under-utilized as the country's physical assets. Many Third World countries contain entrepreneurial minority groups—Chinese minorities in various Southeast Asian countries, Lebanese in West Africa, Indians in East Africa and Fiji—who have been subjected to discriminatory restrictions on their economic activities or have even been expelled or forced out by mob violence or government edicts of expulsion. Painful as the losses suffered by members of these minorities are when forced to leave countries where they were born, the losses suffered by the countries themselves after such groups have left have often been a major factor in the continuing poverty of some Third World nations. For example, whole sectors of the Ugandan economy collapsed after 50,000 Indians and Pakistanis were forced to leave the country in the 1970s.

Indigenous human capital may also leave because the political and institutional climate offers far less opportunity for individuals to advance economically than the opportunities available in some foreign countries. India, for all its poverty, has for centuries been an exporter of entrepreneurs, who have created thriving enterprises from the Caribbean to the South Pacific and from Russia to Africa. Today, computer engineers from India are a major force in America's Silicon Valley and Indians are 10 percent of all anesthesiologists in the United States.

Despite a vision of helpless Third World countries, whose economic rise is possible only through transfers of foreign aid and foreign know-how from more prosperous and more industrially advanced countries, many Third

World nations have within themselves both physical assets and human assets far exceeding any that they are likely to receive from other countries. This is not to say that it would be easy politically to reform the policies and institutions which hold back internal economic development in the Third World. What is easy politically is to accept foreign aid and use it to help keep existing political leaders in power, whether or not the foreign aid confers any significant benefit on the country as a whole.

Enormous amounts of wealth created in "underground" economies in the Third World provide evidence of the entrepreneurship already present in these countries, even if the legal systems in these countries impede this wealth from being mobilized for larger corporate development, such as occurs in Western countries or in some Asian nations such as Japan. Often there have been entrepreneurial minorities in Third World countries who have been responsible for much, if not most, of the development of modern economic sectors in those countries. The Chinese have played this role in Malaysia, Indonesia and other Southeast Asian nations, Indians and Pakistanis did the same in East Africa and the Lebanese in West Africa. In past eras, Armenians played this role in parts of the Russian and Ottoman Empires, and the Jews in much of Eastern Europe.

Without exception, the success of these minorities has been resented and this resentment has in many cases led politically to their persecution or expulsion. In addition to the tragedies inflicted on these minorities, the economic impact of their departures has been a loss to the countries in which they have not been allowed to contribute what they could. Very few Third World countries have been devoid of the human capital—indigenous or otherwise—needed for economic development. West Africa, for example, became the world's leading grower and exporter of cocoa as a result of the planting and growing of this crop by innumerable African small farmers, even though cocoa was not indigenous to Africa.

During the twentieth century, many poor countries spent decades keeping out foreign products, foreign investments, and multinational corporations, for fear of being exploited. This meant that they had to produce for themselves many products that were available at lower prices in the world market, as well as products that could have been produced more cheaply within their own borders by foreign companies using more advanced technology and industrial experience. People in poor countries were thus denied not only the benefits of a greater abundance of goods, but also opportunities to become familiar with more advanced technology and modern organizational practices that would enable them to create and manage such enterprises themselves. An analysis of 2,700 firms in East Asia by the National Bureau of Economic Research concluded that "firms in which foreigners have a substantial ownership share have markedly higher productivity than those that are domestically owned." More productivity means higher standards of living.

The poorer the country, the less could they afford to forego opportunities for a higher standard of living. Eventually, by the late twentieth century, many Third World governments finally realized their mistake, but whole generations had had their economic well-being needlessly sacrificed in the meantime. Partly this change in policy was made because these governments had observed the dramatic economic improvements in once-poor countries like South Korea and Taiwan, which opted to participate heavily in global markets, as compared to the relative stagnation in countries like India and some Latin American nations which did not. However, the history of Western nations in centuries past could have revealed similar lessons.

While Britain was the nation that led the world into the industrial age, nevertheless in earlier pre-industrial centuries, Britain was much like Third World countries today. It exported raw materials such as wool and imported manufactured products from more advanced nations on the continent of Europe. Britain's financial institutions were run by foreigners and whole British industries, such as watch-making and piano-manufacturing, were created by immigrants and expatriates. It was only after centuries of learning from others that Britain was ready to take its place at the head of technological and organizational advances in the world economy. Japan went through a similar phase in the late nineteenth and early twentieth centuries.

PART VII:

SPECIAL ECONOMIC ISSUES

Chapter 23

MYTHS ABOUT MARKETS

*Many a man has cherished for years as his hobby
some vague shadow of an idea, too meaningless to
be positively false.*

Charles Sanders Peirce

Perhaps the biggest myth about markets comes from the name itself. We tend to think of a market as a *thing* when in fact it is *people* engaging in economic transactions among themselves on whatever terms their mutual accommodations lead to. A market in this sense can be contrasted with central planning or government regulation. Too often, however, when a market is conceived of as a thing, it is regarded as an impersonal mechanism, when in fact it is as personal as the people in it. This misconception allows third parties to seek to take away the freedom of individuals to transact with one another on mutually agreeable terms, and to depict this restriction of their freedom as rescuing people from the "dictates" of the impersonal market, when in fact this would be subjecting them to the dictates of third parties.

There are so many myths about markets that only a sample can be presented here. For example, it is common to hear that the same thing is being sold at very different prices by different sellers, apparently contradicting the economics of supply and demand. Usually such statements involve defining things as being "the same" when in fact they are not. Other misconceptions involve the role of brand names, non-profit organizations, and theories of "predatory pricing," as well as the so-called "trickle-down theory." While these are only a small sample of myths about prices and markets, looking at these myths closely may illustrate how easy it is to create a plausible-sounding notion and get it accepted by many otherwise intelligent people, who simply do not bother to scrutinize the logic or the evidence—or even to define the words they use.

One of the reasons for the survival of economic myths is that many professional economists consider such beliefs too superficial or even downright silly to bother to refute them. But superficial and even silly beliefs have sometimes been so widespread as to become the basis for laws and policies with serious and even catastrophic consequences. Leaving myths unchallenged is risky, so scrutinizing silly notions can be a very serious matter.

PRICES

There seem to be almost as many myths about prices as there are prices. Most involve ignoring the role of supply and demand but some involve confusing prices with costs.

The Role of Prices

The very reasons for the existence of prices and the role they play in the economy have been misunderstood. One of the oldest and most consequential of these myths is a notion summarized this way:

> Prices have been compared to tolls levied for private profit or to barriers which, again for private profit, keep the potential stream of commodities from the masses who need them.

Crude as this notion might seem after examining the many economic activities coordinated by prices, it is an idea which has inspired political movements around the world, movements that have in some cases changed the faces of whole nations. These movements—socialist, communist, and other—have been determined to end what they have seen as the gratuitous payment of profits that needlessly add to the prices of goods and correspondingly restrict the standard of living of working people.

Implicit in this vision is the assumption that what entrepreneurs and investors receive as income from the production process exceeds the value of any contribution they may have made to that process. The plausibility of this belief and the conviction that it was true inspired people from many walks of life to dedicate their lives—sometimes risking or even sacrificing their lives—to the cause of ending "exploitation." But their own political success in replacing price-coordinated economies with economies coordinated by collective political decisions took the issue beyond the realm of plausibility and into the realm of empirical evidence. During the course of the twentieth century, that evidence increasingly made it painfully apparent that eliminating price coordination and profits did not raise living standards but tended to make them lower than in countries where prices remained the method of allocating resources.

For decades, and even generations, many nations clung to their original assumption and the policies based on it, despite economic setbacks that were often attributed to short run "growing pains" of a new system or to isolated individual mistakes, rather than to problems inherent in collective decision-making by third parties. However, by the end of the twentieth century, even socialist and communist governments began abandoning government-owned economic enterprises and all but a few die-hard nations had begun allowing prices to function more freely in their economies. A very elementary lesson about prices had been learned at a very high cost to hundreds of millions of human beings.

No one would say that wages were just arbitrary charges added to the prices of goods for the financial benefit of workers, since it is obvious that there would be no production without those workers and that they would not contribute to production unless they were compensated. Yet it took a very long time for the same thing to be realized about those who manage economic enterprises or whose investments pay for the structures and equipment used in such enterprises. Whether the payments received by those who contributed in these ways were unnecessarily large is a question answered by whether those same contributions are available from others at a lower cost. That question is one which those who are doing the paying have every incentive to have answered by hard facts before they pay out hard cash.

Different Prices for the "Same" Thing

Physically identical things are often sold for different prices, usually because of accompanying conditions that are quite different. Goods sold in attractively decorated stores with pleasant, polished and sophisticated sales staffs, as well as easy return policies, are likely to cost more than physically identical products sold in a stark warehouse store with a no-refund policy. Christmas cards can usually be bought for much lower prices on December 26th than on December 24th, even though the cards are physically identical to what they were when they were in great demand before Christmas.

A consumer magazine in northern California compared the total cost of buying the identical set of food items of the same brands in various stores in their area. These total costs ranged from $80 in the least expensive store to $125 in the most expensive. Indeed, they ranged from $98 to $103 at three different Safeway supermarkets. Part of the reason for the variations in price was the variation in the cost of real estate in the different communities—the store with the lowest prices being located in less expensive Fremont and the one with the highest prices being located in San Francisco, which has had the highest real estate prices of any major city in the country. The cost of the land on which the stores sat was different and these costs had to be recovered from the prices charged the stores' customers.

Another reason for price differences is the cost of inventory. The cheapest store had only 49 percent of the items on the shopping list in stock at a given time, while all three Safeway stores had more than three-quarters of the items in stock. In other words, going to different stores meant having different probabilities of finding what you wanted. Cost differences reflected differences in availability, which is to say, differences in the costs of maintaining inventory, even when the particular commodities were physically the same. It also meant differences in the costs measured in the time that a customer would have to spend going from store to store to find all the items on a shopping list.

A later study by the same consumer magazine found that, although a family spending $125 a week for groceries at the highest priced supermarket in the area could save more than $1,800 a year by buying the same items at the lowest price supermarket, both consumers and the magazine's own staff rated the higher priced supermarkets higher in quality—including such things as the freshness of their produce and meat, the speed of checkout lines, and the variety of brands available. For example, one upscale supermarket was rated "superior" in the speed of its checkout line by 90 percent of its customers but one of the low-price warehouse stores received a similar rating from only 12 percent of its customers.

Another way of saying the same thing is that consumers pay in both money and time, and those who value their time are often willing to pay more money in order to save that time and the exasperation of waiting in long lines or having to go from store to store to buy the items on their shopping lists. In short, people shopping at different supermarkets were paying different prices for different things, although superficially these might be called the "same" things. It was much the same story in computer stores, where the Fry's chain averaged lower prices than CompUSA stores in northern California, but the latter were more often rated superior on staff attitudes and atmosphere by customers.[1]

Mistakes or miscalculations may sometimes cause the same thing to be sold for different prices under comparable conditions temporarily, but competition usually makes this a passing phenomenon. When customers go where prices are lower, those whose prices are higher have little choice but to lower their prices, if they are not offering some offsetting advantages along with the same physical product. Where there are permanently

---

[1] A more attentive sales staff is not free, any more than technical competence is free. If an employer needed to hire 100 people and knew that only about half of the applicants were likely to be knowledgeable enough about technology, then the salary offered would have to be enough to attract 200 applicants, from which the most knowledgeable 100 could be hired. However, if the employer also wanted personable and attentive employees, and only about half the technically qualified fit that description, then it would be necessary to offer a still higher salary, one sufficient to attract 400 applicants.

different prices for things that are truly the same, the higher-price seller usually ends up going out of business for lack of customers.

At the heart of all this is competition. But, where competition is lacking, different prices can persist. For example, a General Motors employee who buys medicine through the mail under that company's prescription drug program "is paying far higher prices for some drugs than ordinary individuals can get walking into retail pharmacies," according to the *Wall Street Journal*. But under GM's "mandatory-mail program," its employees and retirees are prevented "from filling any prescriptions at the Walgreen Co. drugstore chain." In short, the absence of competition is the key to persistently different prices for the same thing in this case, as in others.

It is also possible for prices to be different when they seem to be the same. During the early twenty-first century, American automobile manufacturers offered rebates and zero-percent-interest loans to finance the purchases of their cars, in effect lowering the cost of purchasing these cars while maintaining the same official list prices. In Europe, various automobile manufacturers offered such things as two years of free insurance or coupons for hundreds of dollars worth of gasoline, or threw in expensive options like more powerful engines or alloy wheels without additional charges. All of these were in effect price reductions, even though the official list prices remained the same while the companies waited for stronger demand to enable them to be able to actually charge those official prices.

"Reasonable" or "Affordable" Prices

A long-standing staple of political rhetoric has been the attempt to keep the prices of housing, medical care, or other goods and services "reasonable" or "affordable." But to say that prices should be reasonable or affordable is to say that economic realities have to adjust to our budget, or to what we are willing to pay, because we are not going to adjust to the realities. Yet the amount of resources required to manufacture and transport the things we want are wholly independent of what we are willing or able to pay. It is completely unreasonable to expect reasonable prices. Price controls can of course be imposed by government but we have already seen in Chapter 3 what the consequences are. Subsidies can also be used to keep prices down but that does not change the costs of producing goods and services in the slightest. It just means that part of those costs are paid in taxes.

Often related to the notion of reasonable or affordable prices is the idea of keeping "costs" down by various government devices. But prices are not costs. Prices are what pay for costs. Where the costs are not covered by the prices that are allowed to be charged, the supply of the goods or services simply tends to decline in quantity or quality, whether these goods are apartments, medicines, or other things.

The cost of medical care is not reduced in the slightest when the government imposes lower rates of pay for doctors or hospitals. There are still just as many resources required as before to build and equip a hospital or to train a medical student to become a doctor. Countries which impose lower prices on medical treatment have ended up with longer waiting lists to see doctors, less modern equipment in their hospitals and, in the case of Britain, a substantial proportion of their doctors have come from Third World countries with lower quality medical training, because of an inadequate supply of doctors willing to practice medicine in Britain. Costs have not been lowered for the *same* medical care. Lower prices have been paid for lower quality treatment.

The implicit assumption behind much discussion of prices is the notion that prices can be set—and maintained—by an act of will on the part of the seller, so that the seller's reasonableness or greed becomes an important consideration. This assumes away the competition of other sellers of the same goods or services and the consequent effects of supply and demand on prices. In short, it essentially assumes away economics. Nor is this a matter of whether one chooses to be for or against a free market. Karl Marx was certainly not a fan of free market capitalism but he nevertheless pointed out that prices and profit rates were determined in a competitive market "wholly independent of the will of the capitalist."[2]

"Predatory" Pricing

One of the popular myths which has become part of the tradition of anti-trust law is "predatory pricing." According to this theory, a big company that is out to eliminate its smaller competitors and take over their share of the market will lower its prices to a level that dooms the competitor to unsustainable losses and forces it out of business when the smaller company's resources run out. Then, having acquired a monopolistic position, the larger company will raise its prices—not just to the previous level, but to new and higher levels in keeping with its new monopolistic position. Thus, it recoups its losses and enjoys above-normal profits thereafter, at the expense of the consumers.

One of the most remarkable things about this theory is that those who advocate it seldom even attempt to provide any concrete examples of when this ever actually happened. Perhaps even more remarkable, they have not had to do so, even in courts of law, in anti-trust cases. Nobel Prizewinning economist Gary Becker has said: "I do not know of any documented predatory-pricing case."

Both the A & P grocery chain in the 1940s and the Microsoft Corporation in the 1990s were accused of pursuing such a practice in anti-trust cases, but without a single example of this process having gone to completion. Instead, their current low prices (in the case of A & P) or the inclusion of a free Internet browser in Windows software (in the case of Microsoft) have been interpreted as directed toward that end—though not with having actually achieved it. Since it is impossible to prove a negative, the accused company cannot disprove that it was pursuing such a goal, and the issue simply becomes a question of whether those who hear the charge choose to believe it. But this is more than just a theory without evidence. It is something that makes little or no economic sense.

A company that sustains losses by selling below cost to drive out a competitor is following a very risky strategy. The only thing it can be sure of is losing money initially. Whether it will ever recover enough extra

---

2 See Karl Marx, *Capital*, Vol. III, p. 311 (Kerr edition).

profits to make the gamble pay off in the long run is problematical. Whether it can do so and escape the anti-trust laws as well is even more problematical—and anti-trust laws can lead to millions of dollars in fines and/or the dismemberment of the company. But, even if the would-be predator manages somehow to overcome these problems, it is by no means clear that eliminating all existing competitors will mean eliminating competition.

Even when a rival firm has been forced into bankruptcy, its physical equipment and the skills of the people who once made it viable do not vanish into thin air. A new entrepreneur can come along and acquire both— perhaps at low distress sale prices for both the physical equipment and the unemployed workers, enabling the new competitor to have lower costs than the old and hence be a more dangerous competitor.

As an illustration of what can happen, back in 1933 the *Washington Post* went bankrupt, though not because of predatory pricing. In any event, this bankruptcy did not cause the printing presses, the building, or the reporters to disappear. All were acquired by publisher Eugene Meyer, at a price that was less than one-fifth of what he had bid unsuccessfully for the same newspaper just four years earlier. In the decades that followed, under new ownership and management, the *Washington Post* grew to become the largest newspaper in the nation's capital. By the early twenty-first century, the *Washington Post* had one of the five largest circulations in the country.

Bankruptcy can eliminate particular owners and managers, but it does not eliminate competition in the form of new people, who can either take over an existing bankrupt enterprise or start their own new business from scratch in the same industry. Destroying a particular competitor—or even all existing competitors—does not mean destroying competition, which can take the form of new firms being formed. In short "predatory pricing" can be an expensive endeavor, with little prospect of recouping the losses by subsequent monopoly profits. It can hardly be surprising that it remains a theory without concrete examples. What is surprising is how seriously it is taken in anti-trust cases.

BRAND NAMES

Brand names are often thought to be just ways of being able to charge a higher price for the same product by persuading people through advertising that there is a quality difference, when in fact there is no such difference. In other words, some people consider brand names to be useless from the standpoint of the consumer's interests. India's Prime Minister Nehru once asked, "Why do we need nineteen brands of toothpaste?"

In reality, brand names serve a number of purposes from the standpoint of the consumer. Brands are a way of economizing on scarce knowledge, and of forcing producers to compete in both quality and price.

When you drive into a town you have never seen before and want to get some gasoline for your car or to eat a hamburger, you have no direct way of knowing what is in the gasoline that some stranger at the filling station is putting into your tank or what is in the hamburger that another stranger is cooking for you to eat at a roadside stand that you have never seen before. But, if the filling station's sign says Chevron and the restaurant's sign says McDonald's, then you don't worry about it. At worst, if something terrible happens, you can sue a multi-billion-dollar corporation. You know it, the corporation knows it, and the local dealer knows it. That is what reduces the likelihood that something terrible will happen.

On the other hand, imagine if you pull into a no-name filling station in some little town and the stranger there puts something into your tank that messes up your engine or—worse yet—if you eat a no-name hamburger that sends you to the hospital with food poisoning. Your chances of suing the local business owner successfully (perhaps before a jury of his friends and neighbors) may be considerably less. Moreover, even if you should win, the chances of collecting enough money to compensate you for all the trouble you have been put through is more remote than if you were suing a big corporation.

In an increasingly global economy, Europeans and Americans might be very hesitant to buy telecommunications equipment made halfway around the world in South Korea. But, once the Samsung brand acquired a track record, people in Berlin or Chicago would just as soon buy Samsung products as competing products manufactured down the street. Asian companies in general have only in relatively recent history begun investing much time and money in making their brand names widely known, and still they spend less on this than other multinational companies. However, brand names like Toyota, Honda, and Nikon are recognized around the world, and the Cathay Pacific airline and the Shangri-La hotel chain are also becoming better known internationally.

Brand names are not guarantees. But they do reduce the range of uncertainty. If a hotel sign says Hyatt Regency, chances are you will not have to worry about whether the bed sheets in your room were changed since the last person slept there. If the camera you buy is a Nikon, it is unlikely to jam up the first time you wind the film. Even if you stop at a dingy and run-down little store in a strange town, you are not afraid to drink a soda they sell you, if it is a bottle or can of Coca-Cola or Seven Up. Imagine, however, if the owner of this unsavory little place mixed you a soda at his own soda fountain. Would you have the same confidence in drinking it?

Like everything else in the economy, brand names have both benefits and costs. A hotel with a Hyatt Regency sign out front is likely to charge you more for the same size and quality of room, and accompanying service, than you would pay in some comparable, locally-run, independent hotel *if you knew where to look*. Someone who regularly stops in this town on business trips might well find a locally-run hotel that is a better deal. But it is just as rational for you to look for a brand name when passing through for the first time as it is for the regular traveller to go where he knows he can get the same things for less.

Since brand names are a substitute for specific knowledge, how valuable they are depends on how much knowledge you already have about the particular product or service. Someone who is very knowledgeable about photography might be able to safely get a bargain on an off-brand camera or lens, or even a second-hand camera or lens. But that same person might be well advised to stick to well known brands of new stereo equipment, if his knowledge in that field falls far short of his expertise in photography.

Many critics of brand names argue that the main brands "are all alike." Even when that is so, the brand names still perform a valuable function.

The question is not whether Kodak film is better than Fuji film but whether both are better than they would be if they were sold in anonymous boxes that said simply "film," with no brand name—so that neither company had anything to gain from producing a high quality product. With goods in general, all the brands may be better than they would have to be if products were sold under anonymous or generic labels. But, when film is sold with brand names on the boxes, Kodak knows that it will lose millions of dollars in sales if it falls behind Fuji in quality and Fuji knows that it will lose millions if it falls behind Kodak. Brands have not always existed. They came into existence and then survived and spread for a reason. In eighteenth century England, for example, only a few luxury goods, such as Chippendale furniture, were known by their manufacturer's brand name. It was an innovation when Josiah Wedgwood put his name on chinaware that he sold and which ultimately became world famous for its quality and appearance. In the United States, brand names began to flourish around the time of the Civil War.

In nineteenth century America, most food processors did not put brand names on the food that they sold—a situation which allowed adulteration of food to flourish. When Henry Heinz entered this business and sold unadulterated processed food, he identified his products with his name, reaping the benefits of the reputation he established among consumers, which allowed his company to expand rapidly and an array of new processed foods bearing his name to be readily accepted by the public from the outset. In short, the rise of brands promoted better quality by allowing consumers to distinguish and choose, and forcing producers to take responsibility for what they made, reaping rewards when it was good and losing customers when it was not.

Quality standards for hamburgers, milk shakes and French fries were all revolutionized in the 1950s and 1960s by McDonald's, whose methods and machinery were later copied by some of their leading competitors. But the whole industry's standards became higher than before because McDonald's spent millions of dollars researching the growing, storage and processing of potatoes, in addition to making unannounced visits to its potato suppliers, as it did to its suppliers of hamburger meat, in order to ensure that its quality specifications were being followed, while its huge buying power forced dairies to supply a higher quality of milk shake mix that McDonald's demanded. After all this was done, some might say in later years that leading hamburger chains were "all alike," but they were all better because McDonald's could first reap the rewards of having its brand name identified in the public mind with higher quality products than they had previously been used to in hamburger stands.

Even when the various brands of a product are made to the same formula by law, as with aspirin, quality control is promoted when each producer of each bottle of aspirin is identified than when the producer is anonymous. Moreover, the best-known brand has the most to lose if some impurity gets into the aspirin during production and causes anyone injury or death. This is especially important with foods and medicines. If Campbell's soups were identified on the label only as "soup"—or "Tomato Soup," "Clam Chowder," etc., with no brand name on the label—the pressures on all canned soup producers to maintain both safety and quality would be less.

In countries where there are no brand names, or where there is only one producer created or authorized by the government, the quality of the product or service tends to be notoriously low. During the days of the Soviet Union, the country's only airline, Aeroflot, became notorious for bad service and rudeness to passengers. After the dissolution of the Soviet Union, a new privately financed airline began to have great success, in part because its passengers appreciated being treated like human beings for a change. The management of the new airline declared that its employment policy was that it would not hire anyone who had ever worked for Aeroflot. When it came to consumer products, Soviet customers tried to make up for a lack of brands by developing their own methods of trying to figure out where a given product was made. As *The Economist* reported:

> In the old Soviet Union, where all products were supposed to be the same, consumers learnt how to read barcodes as substitutes for brands in order to identify goods that came from reliable factories.

In effect, Soviet consumers created brands where none existed, indicating that brands have value to consumers as well as producers.

THE ROLE OF PROFITS

As we have already seen, confusion about the role of prices often goes with confusion about the role of profits. However, money that is called "profits" has its own special confusions which cause many people to see some fundamental difference between money received by profit-making enterprises and money received by "non-profit" organizations.

Business and the Market

Those who favor government intervention in the economy often depict those who prefer free competition as pro-business apologists. This has been profoundly wrong for at least two centuries. Adam Smith, the eighteenth-century father of free-market economics, was so scathingly critical of businessmen that it would be impossible to find a single favorable reference to them in his 900-page classic, *The Wealth of Nations*.[3] Instead, Smith warned against "the clamour and sophistry of merchants and manufacturers." Any suggestions about laws and policies coming from such people, he said, ought to be "carefully examined, not only with the most scrupulous, but with the most suspicious attention." In the nineteenth century, the next great classical economist in the free-market tradition, David Ricardo, spoke of businessmen as "notoriously ignorant of the most obvious principles" of economics. Knowing how to run a business is not the same as understanding the larger and very different issues involved in knowing how the economy as a whole affects the population as a whole. Skepticism about the business community has remained part of the tradition of free-market economists throughout the twentieth century as well, with Milton Friedman's views being very similar to those of Adam Smith on this point.

Free market competition has often been opposed by the business community, from Adam Smith's time to our own. It was business interests

---

[3] When I taught economics, I used to offer to give an A to any student who could find even a single favorable reference to businessmen in *The Wealth of Nations*. None ever did.

which promoted the pervasive policies of government intervention known as "mercantilism" in the centuries before Smith and others made the case for ending such interventions and establishing free markets. Then, after free market principles had gained wider acceptance in the nineteenth and twentieth centuries, business leaders were of course prepared to invoke those principles for political reasons, whenever it suited their particular purposes of the moment. But business leaders and organizations have proven equally willing to seek government intervention to keep out foreign competition, bail out failing corporations and banks, and receive billions of dollars in agricultural subsidies, ostensibly for the sake of saving family farms, but in reality going disproportionately to large agricultural corporations.

When President Richard Nixon imposed America's first peacetime wage and price controls in 1971, he was publicly praised by the chairman of General Motors, and cooperation with these policies was urged by the National Association of Manufacturers and the U. S. Chamber of Commerce. Businesses themselves have pushed for laws making it harder for outside investors to take over a corporation and replace its management. Business leaders are not wedded to a free market philosophy or any other philosophy. They promote their own self-interest any way they can, like other special interest groups. Economists and others who are in fact supporters of free markets have known that for at least two centuries but many in the media still seem unaware of the facts.

As noted in earlier chapters, the efficient use of scarce resources by the economy as a whole depends on a system that features both profits and losses. Businesses are interested only in the profit half. If they can avoid losses by getting government subsidies, tariffs and other restrictions against imports, or domestic laws that stifle competition in various agricultural products, they will do so. Those who are pro-businesses and those who favor free markets are often on opposite sides.

Non-Profit Organizations

Non-profit organizations must be examined in terms of the incentives and constraints they face, just as other enterprises are. We have seen that the role of profit-seeking businesses is better understood when they are recognized as profit-and-loss businesses, with all the pressures and incentives created by these dual potentialities, which force these enterprises to respond to feedback from those who use their goods or services. By the same token, what are called "non-profit organizations" can be better understood when they are seen as institutions which are insulated, to varying degrees, from a need to respond to feedback from those who use their goods and services.

This does not mean that non-profit organizations have unlimited money or that they do not need to worry about spending more than they take in. It does mean, however, that with whatever money they do have, non-profit organizations are under very little pressure to achieve their institutional goals to the maximum extent possible with the resources at their disposal. Those who supply those resources include the general public, who cannot closely monitor what happens to their donations, and neither can those whose money provided the endowments—$25 billion at Harvard, for example—which help finance non-profit institutions. Much or most of those endowments were left by people who are now dead and so cannot monitor at all.

Non-profit organizations have additional sources of income, including fees from those who use their services, such as visitors to museums and audiences for symphony orchestras. These fees are in fact the main source of the more than half a trillion dollars in revenue received annually by non-profit organizations in the United States. However, these fees do not cover the full costs of the goods and services being supplied. In other words, the recipients are receiving goods and services which cost more to produce than these recipients are paying, and some are receiving them free. Such subsidized beneficiaries cannot exert the same kind of influence or pressure on a non-profit organization that can be exerted by the customers of a profit-and-loss business, since these latter customers are paying the full cost of everything they get—and will continue to do so only when they find what they receive to be worth what it costs them.

A non-profit organization's goods or services may be worth what it costs the recipients—sometimes nothing—without being worth what it cost to produce. In other words, while an enterprise constrained by profit and loss considerations cannot continue to use resources which have a greater value in alternative uses, a non-profit organization can, since it need not recover the full costs of the resources it uses from the recipients of the goods and services it provides. Where non-profit organizations are making grants of money, the recipients of that money are in no position to influence the way the non-profit organization operates, as customers of profit-seeking organizations can and do.

In general, those who run non-profit organizations are in a position vis-a-vis those who use their goods and services very similar to that of a landlord during a shortage of housing: There is a surplus of applicants. Under these conditions, where neither the desires of the current users of the non-profit organization's goods and services nor the original desires of those who supplied their endowments in the past have the kind of leverage that both customers and investors have on a profit-seeking enterprise, those individuals who happen to be in charge of a non-profit institution at a given time can substitute their own goals for the institution's ostensible goals or the goals of their founders.

It has been said, for example, that Henry Ford and John D. Rockefeller would turn over in their graves if they knew what kinds of things are being financed today by the foundations which bear their names. While that is ultimately unknowable, what is known is that Henry Ford II resigned from the board of the Ford Foundation in protest against what the foundation was doing with the money left by his grandfather. More generally, it is now widely recognized how difficult it is to establish a foundation to serve a given purpose and expect it to stick to that purpose after the money has been contributed, and especially after the original donors are dead.

Academic institutions, hospitals and foundations are usually non-profit organizations in the United States. However, non-profit institutions cover a wide range of endeavors and can also engage in activities normally engaged in by profit-seeking enterprises, such as selling Sunkist oranges or publishing *The Smithsonian* magazine. In whatever activities they engage, non-profit organizations are not under the same pressures to get "the most bang for the buck" as are enterprises in which profit and loss determine their survival—which is to say, when the users of their goods and services determine their fate. This affects efficiency, not only in the narrow financial sense, but also in the broader sense of achieving avowed purposes. Colleges and universities, for example, can become disseminators of particular ideological views that happen to be in vogue ("political correctness") and restrictors of alternative views, even though the goals of education might be better served by exposing students to a range of contrasting and contending ideas.

Back in the eighteenth century, Adam Smith pointed out how academics running colleges and universities financed by endowments can run them in self-serving ways, being "very indulgent to one another," so that each academic would "consent that his neighbour may neglect his duty, provided he himself is allowed to neglect his own." Widespread complaints today that professors neglect teaching in favor of research, and sometimes neglect both in favor of leisure or other activities, suggest that the underlying principle has not changed much in more than two hundred years. Tenure guaranteeing lifetime appointments are common in non-profit colleges and universities, but are practically unknown in businesses that must meet the competition of the marketplace, including profit-seeking educational institutions such as the University of Phoenix.

This is only one of the ways in which the employment policies of non-profit organizations have more latitude than those of enterprises which operate in the hope of profit and under the threat of losses. Before World War II, hospitals were among the most racially discriminatory of American employers, even though their avowed purposes would have been better served by hiring the best-qualified doctors, even when those doctors happened to be black or Jewish. Non-profit foundations were also among the most racially discriminatory institutions at that time.

The same was true of the academic world, where the first black professor was not hired at a major university until 1940, not long after the first Jewish professor received tenure at Columbia University, which was already more than 150 years old at the time. Yet there were hundreds of black chemists working for profit-seeking chemical companies, years before they were hired to teach chemistry at non-profit colleges, and both black and Jewish doctors had flourishing private practices long before they could practice medicine in non-profit hospitals.

None of this should suggest that non-profit organizations are oblivious to money. It is just that the purposes for which the money is spent may be quite different from the purposes for which it was donated. Regardless of the purposes for which the money was donated, it is spent at the discretion of people who can use it for their own perks, prejudices, or politics. Non-profit organizations can be very eager to get more money, and some even skirt the boundaries of the law to do so. In 1999, for example, non-profit organizations took in about $500 million from sellers of commercial products who were allowed to say or suggest in their advertisements that some foundation or other non-profit organization was favorable toward those products. Commercial endorsements by these tax-exempt organizations are illegal, but denials that these commercial tie-ins were endorsements have usually kept law enforcement officials at bay.

The American Heart Association, for example, collected $600,000 for allowing its logo to be displayed in advertisements for a pharmaceutical drug. Another non-profit organization, the American Cancer Society, pulled in more than a million dollars the same year for allowing the use of its name and logo in advertisements for commercial products, even though it claims that it does not endorse anything. Looked at from the other side, American Express has paid hundreds of millions of dollars to a variety of non-profit organizations for advertising tie-ins.

The fact that some organizations' income is called profit and other organizations' income is not may suggest to the unwary that there is some fundamental difference between money that is called one thing and money that is called by a different name. It may even suggest that one institution is greedy and the other is not. But many heads of non-profit organizations receive far more money in salary than the average owner of a store or a restaurant receives in profits. It is not uncommon for presidents of leading American universities to receive more than half a million dollars a year in income—and for college football coaches to receive even more. Several musical directors of symphony orchestras receive more than a million dollars a year in salary and two receive more than two million. That is certainly more than most owners of profit-seeking businesses can expect to earn annually.

The performances of non-profit organizations shed light on the role of profit when it comes to efficiency. If those who conceive of profit as simply an unnecessary charge added on to the cost of production of goods and services are correct, then non-profit organizations should be able to produce those goods and services at a lower cost and sell them at a lower price. Over the years, this should lead to non-profit enterprises taking away the customers of profit-seeking enterprises and increasingly replacing them in the economy. Those who believe, for example, that the high prices of some pharmaceutical drugs are due to unconscionably high profits received by the companies producing those drugs, should recognize that the corollary to that belief is that non-profit organizations could develop and produce such medications at lower prices and their competition would either force the existing drug companies to cut prices or the non-profit enterprises would make inroads into the drug companies' share of the market.

Not only have non-profit organizations not taken away the customers of profit-seeking enterprises, increasingly the opposite has happened: Non-profit organizations have seen more and more of their own economic activities taken over by profit-seeking businesses. Colleges and universities are just one example. Over the years, more and more activities once run by non-profit academic institutions themselves—college bookstores, dining halls, and other auxiliary services—have been increasingly turned over to profit-seeking businesses that can do the job cheaper or better or both. As *The Chronicle of Higher Education* reported:

> Follet runs the Stanford Bookstore. Aramark prepares the meals at Yale University. And Barnes & Noble manages the Harvard Coop. The nation's most prestigious universities—and many others in academe— increasingly contract out portions of their campus operations.

According to *The Chronicle of Higher Education*, "Money is the No. 1 reason that colleges contract out an operation." In other words, commercial businesses not only run such services at lower costs, they make enough profit to pay the colleges more than these non-profit organizations could make from the same operations on their own campuses. For example, the University of South Carolina "rarely netted as much as $100,000 per year" from its college bookstore but Barnes & Noble paid them $500,000 a year to run the same bookstore. This implies that Barnes & Noble must have made even more money in order to pay the University of South Carolina more than the university ever made for itself from the same bookstore.

Sometimes the reason many campus operations are more profitable under commercial business management is that profit-seeking enterprises reduce such waste as hiring year-around employees for highly seasonal businesses like college bookstores, where large sales of textbooks are concentrated at the beginning of each academic term. Other reasons include more experience at marketing. At the University of Georgia's bookstore, for example, 70 percent of the books were stored in inventory when the university ran its own bookstore but, after Follet took over, 70 percent of the books were put on display, where they were more likely to be bought.

Despite a tendency in the media to treat non-profit institutions as disinterested sources of information, those non-profit organizations which depend on continuing current donations from the public have incentives to be alarmists, in order to scare more money out of their contributors. For example, one non-profit organization which regularly issues dire warnings about health risks in the environment has admitted to not having a single doctor or scientist on its staff. Other non-profit organizations that are financially dependent on current contributions, as distinguished from large endowments, have similar incentives to alarm their respective constituencies over various social, political, or other issues, and few constraints to confine themselves to accurate or valid bases for these alarms.

"TRICKLE-DOWN" THEORY

There have been many economic theories over the centuries, accompanied by controversies among different schools of economists. But one of the most politically prominent economic theories today is one that has never existed among economists—the "trickle-down" theory.[4]

People who are politically committed to policies of redistributing income and who tend to emphasize the conflicts between business and labor, rather than their mutual interdependence, often accuse those opposed to them of believing that benefits must be given to the wealthy in general or to business in particular, in order that these benefits will eventually "trickle down" to the masses of ordinary people. But no recognized economist of any school of thought has ever had any such theory or made any such proposal. It is a straw man. It cannot be found in even the most voluminous and learned histories of economic theories.

Proposals to reduce taxes on capital gains, for example, are often opposed politically by saying that those who make such proposals believe in a "trickle-down" theory of economics. In reality, economic processes work in the directly opposite way from that depicted by those who imagine that profits first benefit business owners and that benefits only belatedly trickle down to workers.

When an investment is made, whether to build a railroad or to open a new restaurant, the first money is spent hiring people to do the work. Without that, nothing happens. Even when one person decides to operate a store or hamburger stand without employees, that person must first pay somebody to deliver the goods that are going to be sold. Money goes out first to pay expenses and then comes back as profits later—if at all. The high rate of failure of new businesses makes painfully clear that there is nothing inevitable about the money coming back.

Even with successful and well-established businesses, years may elapse between the initial investment and the return of earnings. From the time when an oil company begins spending money to explore for petroleum to the time when the first gasoline resulting from that exploration comes out

---

[4] A writer in India refers to those promoting a change from government planning to a freer market as people who have "blind faith in the 'trickle-down' theory of distributing the benefits of economic growth among different socio-economic groups in the country." But free market economics is not about "distributing"

of a pump at a filling station, a decade may have passed. In the meantime, all sorts of employees have been paid—geologists, engineers, refinery workers, truck drivers. It is only afterwards that profits begin coming in. Only then are there any capital gains to tax. The real effect of a reduction in the capital gains tax is that it opens the prospect of greater *future* net profits and thereby provides incentives to make *current* investments.

Nor is the oil industry unique. No one who begins publishing a newspaper expects to make a profit—or even break even—during the first year or two. But reporters and other members of the newspaper staff expect to be paid every payday, even while the paper shows only red ink on the bottom line. Amazon.com began operating in 1994 but its first profits did not appear until the last quarter of 2001, after the company had lost a total of $2.8 billion over the years. Even a phenomenally successful enterprise like the McDonald's restaurant chain ran up millions of dollars in debts for years before it saw the first dollar of profit. Indeed, it teetered on the brink of bankruptcy more than once in its early years. But the people behind the counter selling hamburgers were paid regularly all that time.

In short, the sequence of payments is directly the opposite of what is assumed by those who talk about a "trickle-down" theory. The workers must be paid first and then the profits flow upward later—if at all.

anything to anybody. It is about letting people earn whatever they can from voluntary transactions with other people. The quote is from *Dalits in Modern India*, edited by S.M. Michael and published in 1999 by Vistaar Publications in New Delhi.

Chapter 24

"NON-ECONOMIC"
VALUES

*Beware the people who moralize about great issues;
moralizing is easier than facing hard facts.*

John Corry

While economics offers many insights, and makes it easier to see through some popular notions that sound good but will not stand up under scrutiny, economics has also acquired the name "the dismal science" because it pours cold water on many otherwise attractive and exciting—but fallacious—notions about how the world can be arranged. One of the last refuges of someone whose pet project or theory has been exposed as economic nonsense is to say: "Economics is all very well, but there are also *non-economic* values to consider." Presumably, these are supposed to be higher and nobler concerns that soar above the level of crass materialism.

Of course there are non-economic values. In fact, there are *only* non-economic values. Economics is not a value in and of itself. It is only a way of weighing one value against another. Economics does not say that you should make the most money possible. Many professors of economics could themselves make more money in private industry. Anyone with a knowledge of firearms could probably make more money working as a hit man for organized crime. But economics does not urge you toward such choices.

Adam Smith, the father of *laissez-faire* economics, gave away substantial sums of his own money to less fortunate people, though he did so with such discretion that this fact was discovered only after his death, when his personal records were examined. Henry Thornton, one of the leading monetary economists of the nineteenth century and a banker by trade, regularly gave away more than half his annual income before he got married and had a family to support—and he continued to give large donations to humanitarian causes afterwards, including the anti-slavery movement.

The first public libraries in New York City were not established by the government but by industrial entrepreneur Andrew Carnegie, who also established the foundation and the university that bear his name. John D. Rockefeller likewise established the foundation that bears his name and the University of Chicago, as well as creating many other philanthropic enterprises. Halfway around the world, the Tata Institute in Mumbai was established by India's leading industrialist, J. R. Tata, as a scholarly enterprise, while another leading entrepreneurial family, the Birlas, established numerous religious and social institutions across India.

The United States, which has come to epitomize capitalism in the eyes of many people around the world, is unique in having hundreds of colleges, hospitals, foundations, libraries, museums and other institutions created by the donations of private individuals, many of these being people who earned money in the marketplace and then devoted much of it—sometimes most of it—to helping others. *BusinessWeek* magazine in 2005 listed numerous entrepreneurs who had donated hundreds of millions of dollars each—and some, billions—to philanthropy. These were not isolated examples. For the American population as a whole, the amount of private charitable donations per person is several times what it is in Europe. The percentage of the country's output that is donated to philanthropic causes is more than three times that in Sweden, France or Japan. The market as a mechanism for the allocation of scarce resources among alternative uses is one thing; what one chooses to do with the resulting wealth is another.

What lofty talk about "non-economic values" often boils down to is that some people do not want their own particular values weighed against anything. If they are for saving Mono Lake or preserving some historic building, then they do not want that weighed against the cost—which is to say, ultimately, against all the other things that might be done instead with the same resources. For such people, there is no point considering how many Third World children could be vaccinated against fatal diseases with the money that is spent saving Mono Lake or preserving a historic building. We should vaccinate those children *and* save Mono Lake *and* preserve the historic building—as well as doing innumerable other good things, according to this way of looking at the world.

To people who think—or rather, react—in this way, economics is at best a nuisance that stands in the way of doing what they have their hearts set on doing. At worst, economics is seen as a needlessly narrow, if not morally warped, way of looking at the world. Such condemnations of economics are due to the fundamental fact that economics is the study of the use of scarce resources which have alternative uses. We might all be happier in a world where there were no such constraints to force us into choices and trade-offs that we would rather not face. But that is not the world that human beings live in—or have ever lived in, during thousands of years of recorded history. Politics has sometimes been called "the art of the possible" but that phrase applies far more accurately to economics. Politics allows people to vote for the impossible, which may be one reason why politicians are often more popular than economists, who keep reminding people that there is no free lunch and that there are no "solutions" but only trade-offs.

In the world that people live in, and are likely to live in for centuries to come, trade-offs are inescapable. Even if we refuse to make a choice, circumstances will make choices for us, as we run out of resources for many important things that we could have had, if only we had taken the trouble to weigh alternatives.

MARKETS AND VALUES

The market is as moral or immoral as the people in it. So is the government. The fact that we call one set of people "the market" when they engage in transactions among themselves and another set of people "society" when they exercise political power over others does not mean that the moral or other imperfections of the first set of people automatically justify having the second set of imperfect people over-ruling their decisions. Like economics, the market is not some separate entity with its own values. It is people making their own individual choices and their mutual accommodations. Moral and social issues arise when markets are looked at in terms of whether market economies promote moral behavior and how they affect greed or fairness among individuals and groups.

Moral Behavior

The idea persists in many places that decisions made through the market are not as moral as decisions made through the political process. Writers for the *San Francisco Chronicle* referred to "how amoral the marketplace can be" when explaining why the water supply owned by the city of Stockton, California, could not be entrusted to private enterprise. "Water is too life-sustaining a commodity to go into the marketplace with," the *Chronicle* quoted the mayor of Stockton as saying. Yet, every day, life-sustaining food is supplied through private enterprises. Moreover, most new life-saving medicines are developed in market economies, notably that of the United States, rather than in government-run economies.

As for privately run water systems, they already exist in Argentina. *The Economist* magazine reported on the results of this privatization:

> Connections to the water and sewerage networks rose, especially among poorer households: most richer households and families in the city centre were already hooked up. . . Before privatisation really got under way, in 1995, child mortality rates were falling at much the same pace in municipalities that eventually privatised and those that did not. After 1995, the fall accelerated in privatising municipalities. . .The fall was concentrated in deaths from infectious and parasitic diseases, the sort

most likely to be affected by water quality and availability. Death from other causes did not decline.

In Britain as well, the privatized water supply in England has meant lower water bills, higher quality drinking water, less leakage, and a sewage disposal system that complies with environmental regulations a higher percentage of the time than those in Scotland, where the government runs the water system. This evidence may be suggestive, rather than conclusive, but those who argue for political control of the water supply seldom see a need for any evidence at all. To many people, empirical consequences often matter less than deeply ingrained beliefs and attitudes. Whether in urgent or less urgent matters, many believe that those with political power are better qualified to make moral decisions than are the private parties directly concerned. Such attitudes are international. An entrepreneur in India reported his experience with a government minister there:

> I had argued that lowering the excise duty would lower consumer prices of shampoos, skin creams, and other toiletries, which in turn would raise their demand. The tax revenues would thus rise, although the tax rate might be lower. Indian women did not need lipsticks and face creams, felt the minister. I replied that all women wanted to look pretty.
> "A face cream won't do anything for an ugly face. These are luxuries of the rich," he said. I protested that even a village girl used a paste of haldi so that she could look pretty.
> "No, it's best to leave a face to nature," he said impatiently.
> "Sir," I pleaded, "how can you decide what she wants? After all, it is her hard-earned money."
> "Yes, and I don't want her wasting it. Let her buy food. I don't want multinational companies getting rich selling face creams to poor Indians."

The idea that third party observers can impose morally better decisions often includes the idea that they can define what are "luxuries of the rich," when it is precisely the progress of free market economies which has turned many luxuries of the rich into common amenities of people in general, including the poor. Within the twentieth century, automobiles, telephones, refrigerators, television sets, air-conditioners, and personal computers all went from being luxuries of the rich to being common items across the spectrum of Americans and among millions of people in many other market economies. The first videocassette recorders sold for $30,000 each before technological progress, trial and error experience, and economies of scale brought the price down within the budget of most Americans. In past centuries, even such things as oranges, sugar, and cocoa were luxuries of the rich in Europe. Not only do third party definitions of what is a luxury of the rich fail to account for such changes, the stifling of free markets by third parties can enable such things to remain exclusive luxuries longer than they would otherwise.

Markets and Greed

Markets are often criticized for permitting or promoting greed. High prices are often blamed on greedy sellers. But "greed" is seldom defined. Virtually everyone would prefer to get a higher price for what he sells and pay a lower price for what he buys. Would you pay a dollar for a newspaper that was available for fifty cents? Or offer to work for half of what an employer was willing to pay you?

Would adding a string of zeros to prices or salaries change the principle or the definition of greed? It is hard to see why it should. But, if everybody is greedy, then the word is virtually meaningless. If it refers to people who desire far more money than most others would aspire to, then the history of most great American fortunes—Ford, Rockefeller, Carnegie, etc.—suggests that the way to amass vast amounts of wealth is to figure out some way to provide goods and services at *lower* prices, not higher prices.

Back in the nineteenth century, Richard Sears was ferociously determined to overtake Montgomery Ward, the world's largest retailer at that time, and worked tirelessly for incredible hours toward that end, sometimes taking business risks that bordered on the reckless. Sears sought out every way of cutting costs, so that he could undercut Ward's prices, and every way of attracting customers away from all his rivals. He did all this, not because he did not have enough money to live on, but because he wanted more—and he wanted his company to be number one. If that is our definition of "greed," then he was greedy. More important, in this case as in many others, it was precisely such greed that led to *lower* prices. That was how Sears overtook Montgomery Ward and replaced it as the leading retailer in the country at the beginning of the twentieth century. In later years, that is how Wal-Mart overtook Sears.

Those who condemn greed may espouse "non-economic values." But lofty talk about "non-economic values" too often amounts to very selfish attempts to have one's own values subsidized by others, obviously at the expense of those other people's values. A typical example of this appeared in a letter to the newspaper trade magazine *Editor & Publisher.* This letter was written by a newspaper columnist who criticized "the annual profit requirements faced by newspapers" due to "the demands of faceless Wall Street financial analysts who seem, from where I sit, insensitive to the vagaries of newspaper journalism."

Despite the rhetorical device of describing some parties to a transaction in less than human terms ("faceless Wall Street analysts"), they are all people and they all have their own interests, which must be mutually reconciled in one way or another, if those who supply the money that enables newspapers to operate are to be willing to continue to do so. Although people who work on Wall Street may control millions of dollars each, this is not all their own personal money by any means. Much of it comes from the savings, or the money paid into pension funds, by millions of other people, many of whom have very modest incomes.

If "the vagaries of newspaper journalism"—however defined—make it difficult to earn as high a return on investments in newspapers or newspaper chains as might be earned elsewhere in the economy, why should workers whose pension funds will be needed to provide for their old age subsidize newspaper chains by accepting a lower rate of return on money invested in such corporations? Since many editors and columnists earn much more money than many of the people whose payments into pension funds supply newspapers with the money to operate, it would seem especially strange to expect people with lower incomes to be subsidizing people with higher incomes—teachers and mechanics, for example, subsidizing editors and reporters.

Why should financial analysts, as the intermediaries handling pension funds and other investments from vast numbers of people, betray those people, who have entrusted their savings to them, by accepting less of a return from newspapers than what is available from other sectors of the economy? If good journalism, however defined, results in lower rates of return on the money invested in newspaper chains, whatever special costs of newspaper publishing are responsible for this can be borne by any of a number of people who benefit from newspapers. Readers can pay higher prices, columnists, editors and reporters can accept lower salaries, or advertisers can pay higher rates, for example.

Why should the sacrifice be forced onto mechanics, nurses, teachers, etc., around the country whose personal savings and pension funds provide the money that newspaper chains acquire by selling corporate stocks and bonds? Why should other sectors of the economy that are willing to pay more for the use of these funds be deprived of such resources for the sake of one particular sector?

The point here is not how to solve the financial problems of the newspaper industry. The point is to show how differently things look when considered from the standpoint of allocating scarce resources which have alternative uses. This fundamental economic reality is obscured by emotional rhetoric that ignores the interests and values of many people by summarizing them via unsympathetic intermediaries such as "insensitive" financial analysts, while competing interests are expressed in idealistic terms, such as journalistic quality. Financial analysts may be as sensitive to the people they are serving as others are to the very different constituencies they represent.

Often what critics of the market want are special dispensations for particular individuals or groups, whether these are newspapers, ethnic groups, or others—without acknowledging that these dispensations will inevitably be at the expense of other individuals or groups, who are either arbitrarily ignored or summarized in impersonal terms as "the market." For example, a *New York Times* reporter writing about the problems of a middle-aged low-income woman said, "if the factory had just let Caroline work day shifts, her problem would have disappeared." But, he lamented: "Wages and hours are set by the marketplace, and you cannot expect magnanimity from the marketplace."

Here again, the inescapable conflict between what one person wants and what another person wants is presented in a way that recognizes only one side of this equation as human. Most people prefer working day shifts to working night shifts but, if Caroline were transferred to the day shift, someone else would have to be transferred to the night shift. As for "magnanimity," what would that mean except forcing someone else to bear this woman's costs?

What is magnanimous about someone who is paying no cost whatsoever —in this case, the *New York Times* reporter—demanding that someone else be saddled with these costs?

Both in the private sector and in the government sector, there are always values that some people think worthy enough that other people should have to pay for them—but not worthy enough that they should have to pay for them themselves. Nowhere is the weighing of some values against other values obscured more often by rhetoric than when discussing government policies. Taxing away what other people have earned, in order to finance one's own moral adventures via social programs, is often depicted as a humanitarian endeavor, while allowing others the same freedom and dignity as oneself, so that they can make their own choices with their own earnings, is considered to be pandering to "greed." Greed for power is no less dangerous than greed for money, and has historically shed far more blood in the process.

Does a free market, as a mechanism for mutual accommodation, facilitate greed as it facilitates the fulfillment of people's other desires? It certainly does not prevent greed, though it does exact a quid pro quo—providing others with something that they want, in order to get them to part with their money voluntarily. A more relevant question, however, is whether other economic systems, including those founded on altruistic and egalitarian principles, actually end up with less greed than an economic system which depends on prices to allocate scarce resources.

Although socialist systems, including the Communist version, began as attempts to apply egalitarian principles, examples of sacrificing the well-being of millions of people for the well-being of those with political power abounded in the Soviet Union and the Communist bloc in general. At the purely economic level, the ruling *nomenklatura* of the U.S.S.R. had separate stores in which only they were eligible to make purchases, as well as other government-supported facilities to which they alone had access. These were of course the best stores, with the most abundant supplies of the commodities most in demand. In addition, the housing, medical care and other facilities open to Communist Party bosses were likewise the best. The rhetoric of equality—egalitarian terms like "comrade" and "people's democracy"—was no match for the reality of greed, especially when that greed could use the power of a totalitarian state, instead of having to supply others' desires in order to earn their money.

Even in a democratic country like India, the era of massive government controls over the economy—lasting for nearly half a century, from independence in 1947 to the beginning of the last decade of the twentieth century—was an era of massive corruption of both high officials and innumerable petty bureaucrats, whose permissions were necessary to do virtually all of the ordinary things that people do at will in a free market economy. Pervasive bribery was only part of that cost. The inefficiencies created by intrusive bureaucratic controls have been estimated to have cost the economy vast amounts of lost production that would have made the average Indian's income hundreds of dollars a year higher. In one of the poorest countries in the world, where malnutrition has been a serious problem for many, such a loss meant far more than whether the average American's annual income was a few hundred dollars more or less.

In short, greed can flourish under very different economic systems. The only real question is: What are its actual consequences under these systems? Where the desire for a fortune can be satisfied by finding ways to lower prices and thereby expand the market for one's output, that is very different from a system where that same desire is more readily fulfilled by imposing political power. In other words, greed is not the product of one particular economic system, but something that all economic, political, and social systems have to cope with in one way or another.

People who deplore greed often show a disdain for wealth. Although a disdain for wealth may be admired, only those who already have a certain amount of wealth can afford to disdain any further pursuit of it. The hungry do not disdain food nor the homeless disdain shelter. Wealth means options and who would want fewer options? More important, from the standpoint of society as a whole, wealth is the only thing that can prevent poverty. Yet many people who claim to be concerned about poverty show remarkably little interest in how wealth is generated or which policies make it harder or easier to create more wealth. It has been precisely the great increase in wealth in modern industrial societies which has brought dramatic reductions in poverty. After China freed its markets and began to industrialize during the last decades of the twentieth century, an estimated one million people per month rose out of poverty. Even where the lowest income brackets have received a smaller share of the national income over time, as in the United States during the same period, the absolute real income of the poorest Americans still rose because total output grew so much.

One of the variations on the theme of greed is that some businesses are guilty of "charging all that the traffic will bear." Often such statements are made, not simply as a moral condemnation, but as a causal explanation of prices that are considered to be "too high" for one reason or another. If widgets have been selling for five dollars apiece for some time and suddenly the price rises to eight dollars, then the explanation that is offered may be that the widget manufacturers are now charging all that the traffic will bear. As a causal explanation, this immediately raises a question: Were they not charging all that the traffic would bear before? Chances are that they were. It is just that the traffic would not bear more than five dollars before and will now bear eight. Therefore what needs to be understood is a causal explanation of what has changed, if widget manufacturers were charging all that the traffic would bear both times.

It is not just businesses that charge all that the traffic will bear. The very people who are making this accusation would seldom agree to work for half of their present salaries—or even three-quarters of their present salaries. They are charging what the traffic will bear for their work. And if someone else offers to pay them twice what they are currently earning, it is very unlikely that they will continue working for their current employer, unless that employer matches the offer.

Strictly speaking, a business is unlikely to charge literally all that the traffic will bear. If General Motors is selling a certain automobile for $25,000, it could probably still sell some to real devotees of that particular car if they doubled the price to $50,000. But, although the traffic would bear a price of $50,000, sales would probably be so reduced that GM would not make as much money as they would by charging $25,000. However, we can take the phrase "charging what the traffic will bear" as a loose expression meaning simply maximizing total profits. What we really need to understand are the implications of saying that higher prices are due to profit maximizing. We also need to understand the consequences of trying to stop it.

To say that the traffic will bear a higher price is to say that the quantity demanded—of electricity, widgets, cameras, or whatever—exceeds the quantity supplied at the current price. Price controls under these conditions virtually guarantee that the shortage will not be corrected. Focusing on the seller's "greed" neither explains what caused the shortage nor offers much prospect of ending it.

Exploitation

A special variation on the theme of "greed" is "exploitation," another emotionally powerful word which is at least as hard to define as greed. Usually those who decry "exploitation" make no serious attempt to define it, so the word is often used simply to condemn either prices that are higher than the observer would like to see or salaries lower than the observer would like to see. There would be no basis for objecting to this word if it were understood by all that it is simply a statement about someone's emotional reactions, rather than being presented as a statement about some fact in the real world. We have seen in Chapter 4 how higher prices charged by stores in low-income neighborhoods have been called "exploitation" when in fact there are many economic factors which account for these higher prices. Similarly, we have seen in Chapter 10 some of the factors behind low pay for Third World workers whom many regard as being "exploited."

The general idea behind "exploitation" theories is that some people are somehow able to receive more than enough money to compensate for their contributions to the production and distribution of output, by either charging more than is necessary to consumers or paying less than is necessary to employees. In some circumstances, this is in fact possible. But we need to examine those circumstances—and to see when such circumstances exist or do not exist in the real world.

As we have seen in earlier chapters, earning a rate of return on investment that is greater than what is required to compensate people for their risks and contributions to output is virtually guaranteed to attract other people who wish to share in this bounty by either investing in existing firms or setting up their own new firms. This in turn virtually guarantees that the above-average rate of return will be driven back down by the increased competition caused by expanded investment and production by either existing or new firms. Only where there is some way to prevent this new competition can the above-average earnings on investment persist.

Governments are among the most common and most effective barriers to the entry of new competition. During the Second World War, the British colonial government in West Africa imposed a wide range of wartime controls over production and trade, as also happened within Britain itself. This was the result, as reported by an economist on the scene in West Africa:

> During the period of trade controls profits were much larger than were necessary to secure the services of the traders. Over this period of great prosperity the effective bar to the entry of new firms reserved the very large profits for those already in the trade.

This was not peculiar to Africa or to the British colonial government there. The Civil Aeronautics Board and the Interstate Commerce Commission in the United States have been among the many government agencies, at both the national and local levels, which have restricted the number of firms or individuals allowed to enter various occupations and industries. In fact, governments around the world have at various times and places restricted what people and how many people would be allowed to engage in particular occupations or establish firms in particular industries. This was even more common in past centuries, when kings often conferred monopolies on particular individuals to engage in the production of salt or wine or many other commodities, sometimes as a matter of generosity to royal favorites and often because the right to a monopoly was purchased for cash.

The purpose or the net effect of barriers to entry has been a persistence of a level of earnings higher than that which would exist under free market competition and higher than necessary to attract the resources required. This could legitimately be considered "exploitation" of the consumers. Moreover, higher earnings than would exist under free market competition do not always or necessarily mean that these earnings are higher than earnings in competitive industries. Sometimes inefficient firms are able to survive under government protection when such firms would not survive in a free market. Therefore even modest rates of returns received by such inefficient firms still represent consumers being forced to pay more money than necessary in a free market, where the efficient firms would produce a larger share of the industry's output while driving the less efficient firms out of business by offering lower prices. While such situations could legitimately be called exploitation—defined as higher prices than necessary to supply the goods or services in question—these are not usually the kinds of situations which provoke that label.

It would also be legitimate to describe as exploitation a situation where people are paid less than the amount necessary to attract a continuing supply of their levels of skills, experience, and talents. These may be either low-paid workers or highly paid professionals.

Where doctors, for example, have already invested huge sums of money in getting an education in expensive medical schools, in addition to an investment in the form of foregone earnings during years of medical training, followed by low pay as interns before becoming fully qualified to practice medicine, the government can at any given time set medical salary scales or pay scales for particular medical treatments which are not sufficient to continue to attract as many people of the same qualifications into the medical profession in the future. In the meantime, however, existing doctors have little choice but to accept what the government authorizes if the government either pays all medical bills or hires all doctors. Seldom will there be alternative professions which existing doctors can enter to earn better pay, because becoming a lawyer or an engineer would require yet another costly investment in education and training. Therefore doctors seldom have realistic alternatives available and are unlikely to become truck drivers or carpenters, just because they would not have gone into the medical profession if they had known in advance what the actual level of compensation would turn out to be.

In the long run, of course, such government exploitation of people already trapped in a given profession tends to lead to fewer young people entering that profession, but that does not prevent exploitation in the short run, which can include decades or the entire working life of existing practitioners. Britain, for example, has had one of the oldest systems of government-paid and government controlled medical care, leading to a situation where it is hard to attract young Britons into the medical profession, so that a substantial proportion of British doctors are from Third World countries where the standards of education and training are not as high as in Britain. Although there has been much decrying of "exploitation" of low-paid workers, in fact it is higher-paid workers whose specialized skills are not readily transferable who are more susceptible to being paid less than would have been necessary to attract them to their field in the first place, if they had known years earlier what the compensation would turn out to be.

Low-paid workers can be exploited in circumstances where they are unable to move, or where the cost of moving would be high, whether because of transportation costs or because they live in government-subsidized housing that they would lose if they moved somewhere else where they would have to pay market prices for a home or an apartment. Slaves can of course be exploited because they cannot leave their occupations. Indentured servants or contract laborers, especially those working overseas, likewise have high costs of moving and so can be exploited in the short run. However, many very low-paid contract workers choose to sign up for another period of work at jobs whose pay and working conditions they already know about from personal experience, clearly indicating that—however low their pay and however bad their working conditions—these are sufficient to attract them into this occupation. Here the explanation is less likely to be exploitation than a lack of better alternatives or the skills to qualify for better alternatives.

Where there is only one employer for a particular kind of labor, then of course that employer can set pay scales which are lower than what is required to attract new people into that occupation. But this is more likely to happen with highly specialized and skilled people, such as astronauts, rather than to unskilled workers, since unskilled workers are employed by a wide variety of businesses, government agencies, and even private individuals. In the era before modern transportation was widespread, local labor markets might be isolated and a given employer might be the only employer available for many local people in particular occupations. But the spread of low-cost transportation has made such situations rarer than in the past.

Once we see that barriers to entry or exit—the latter absolute in the case of slaves or expensive in the case of exit for doctors or for people living in local subsidized housing, for example—then the term exploitation often legitimately applies to people very different from those to whom it is usually applied. It would also apply to businesses which have invested large amounts of fixed and hard to remove capital at a particular location. A company that builds a hydroelectric dam, for example, cannot move that dam elsewhere if the local government doubles or triples its tax rates or requires the company to pay much higher wages to its workers than similar workers receive elsewhere in a free market.

In the long run, fewer businesses tend to invest in places where the political climate produces such results—the exit of many businesses from California being a striking example—but those who have already invested in such places have little recourse but to accept a lower rate of return there.

Whether the term "exploitation" applies or does not apply to a particular situation is not simply a matter of semantics. Different consequences follow when policies are based on a belief that is false instead of beliefs that are true. Imposing price controls to prevent consumers from being "exploited" or minimum wages to prevent workers from being "exploited" can make matters worse for consumers and workers if in fact neither was being exploited. Where a given employer, or a small set of employers operating in collusion, constitute a local monopoly in hiring certain kinds of workers, then that monopoly can pay lower salaries and a government-imposed increase in salary may—within limits—not result in workers losing their jobs, as would tend to happen with an imposed minimum wage in what would otherwise be a free market. But such situations are very rare.

Fairness

A sense of fairness is so widespread that even small children can say, "That's not fair." But seldom do either children or adults offer a clear definition of fairness. There are at least two different definitions of fairness—and they contradict each other in practice. One conception of fairness is that everyone plays by the same rules, is judged by the same standards, and is rewarded according to the same criteria. Another conception of fairness is that everyone has equal prospects of achieving the same goal, whether that goal is winning, surviving, or gaining a given benefit or reward. These different conceptions of fairness sound just similar enough to be confused with one another. This confusion is a political asset, because it allows people with very different views and agendas to all support proposals described as "fair," without realizing that the specifics of what they are supporting may not match their own conception of fairness.

In the United States, various tax policies at both local and national levels have been described as having individuals or organizations pay their "fair share" of taxes, and major federal legislation has had such names as Fair Trade laws and the Fair Labor Standards Act. Many people say that they are for international free trade, provided that it is also "fair trade."

To have everyone play by the same rules and at the same time have everyone have equal prospects of success is possible only if everyone has the same abilities, desires, and priorities. People who don't care about ballet dancing are unlikely to have the same success in this demanding field as those who are dedicated to it, even if they all were born into the world with the same physical endowments and mental capacity. It is much the same story in many other endeavors that have a wide range of prerequisites for success, since the greater the number of prerequisites the less is the likelihood that everyone will have them all to the same degree.

Giants have advantages over midgets in basketball and smaller people have advantages over bigger people when it comes to being a jockey. Whole races of people who live near harbors are more likely to develop seafaring skills than people who live in mountains or deserts.

There is no way to be "fair" to all these people in both senses of the word.

"Ability" in the abstract may be widely distributed but the ability that counts economically as something that people will pay for is the ability to do highly specific things—build a bridge, fly a plane, perform heart surgery, repair a television set, organize a corporation. These kinds of abilities vary enormously among the people in a given country, and geography alone is enough to prevent such abilities from being the same in different parts of the world. How could Polynesians know as much about working with camels as the bedouins of the Sahara know? And how could bedouins know as much about fishing as Polynesians know? Not only do prospects for doing specific things differ at different places, they differ at the same place over time. Farmland in Western Europe was for centuries not as productive as farmland in other places because the kind of implements required to farm such heavy soils had not yet been invented. But after such implements were created and put to use, Western European farms became more productive than other farms that had been superior in earlier times.

Not only have external circumstances been very different from one group to another, so have internal values. Particular groups in various places and times have not bothered to educate girls, thereby throwing away half the talents and potentialities in their own populations. How can that fail to affect how they compare or compete with other groups that can draw on their whole populations for skills and experience? Some societies restrict which individuals are allowed to make important decisions or contributions according to race or social class rather than sex—again, throwing away the talents and potentialities of large numbers of people.

Where only a heredity elite, an ideological elite, or an elite of education are allowed to do important things, how can such a society expect to have

the same economic performance as a society where a poverty-stricken farm
boy like J.C. Penney could revolutionize retailing or a couple of bicycle
mechanics could invent the airplane? At the individual level, when one child
grows up in a home where sports are a regular topic of conversation at the
dinner table and another child grows up in a home where science or
literature are constantly discussed, are these children likely to take the same
or different paths in life? These and many other different influences make
equal achievements virtually impossible among groups, nations, or
individuals. Fairness in that sense has little chance of being realized.

It is of course possible to ignore skills, performance, or achievements and
follow principles along the line of the old socialist maxim: "From each
according to his ability, to each according to his needs." Even in free-market
societies, many people may operate on that principle within their own
families, spending large sums of money on family members who contribute
little or nothing economically, such as those who are incapacitated, or small
children, or older children who require huge expenditures to go to college.
What the consequences would be in applying that same principle in a
society of millions of strangers is another question.

Because there is no precisely defined and widely agreed upon definition of
fairness, what the term has come to mean in economic policy-making is that
those with political power can restrict the options of individuals and
enterprises, in order to produce whatever end result those in power choose to
call "fair." Thus, during the first half of the twentieth century, after the rise of
low-cost American retail chains like A & P in groceries and Woolworth,
Penney and Sears in general merchandise drove many smaller independent
stores out of business, "fair trade laws" were enacted to keep chain stores from
charging low prices that other retailers were unable to match. Some
questioned whether this was fair to consumers but whoever has political power
can define what fairness means. Very often it means some politically imposed
division of benefits and costs between two sets of entities, disregarding the
repercussions of this on others, including consumers.

After many decades of controversy, "fair trade" laws eventually came to be
widely seen as simply laws that kept prices artificially higher, needlessly

raising consumers' cost of living, and these laws were repealed. However, similar notions of fairness reappeared in the twenty-first century, as many objected to the spread of Wal-Mart, Costco and other giant stores, on grounds that the low prices they charged drove many other stores out of business, since these other stores could not survive the competition from huge retail chains with great economies of scale. These "big box" or "monster stores" were considered to represent "unfair" competition.

Much discussion of fairness involves comparing two sets of people and ignoring other people who may be more numerous than both and have far more at stake. Those who are ignored are often consumers, whether the issue is domestic "fair trade" laws or demands that international trade be "fair," so that low-cost foreigners do not undersell higher-cost domestic producers.

When the Fair Labor Standards Act of 1938 established federal minimum wages in the United States, that raised similar questions about what kind of fairness—and to whom. Some questioned whether it was fair to price low-skilled workers and minority workers out of a job, especially at a time of mass unemployment during the Great Depression of the 1930s. So-called "prevailing wage" laws at the local level often prescribe that government construction be performed by workers paid at levels set by labor unions. This means both higher prices paid by the taxpayers and fewer jobs available to lower-skilled workers who become "unemployable" at wage rates that exceed the value of their productivity, even though these workers are perfectly capable of making productive contributions to society if they are not priced out of a job.

Because different conceptions of "fairness" are incompatible with one another, what the term means in practice is that those who hold political power at a given time and place are authorized to pick winners and losers in the economy, at the expense of the consuming public, the taxpayers, and others who may be adversely impacted but who are ignored in the discussion. Limiting the discussion to employers vs. employees, or "monster stores" vs. local merchants, or foreign vs. domestic producers, enables the interests of other groups to be ignored and over-ridden, even if those ignored are more numerous and have more at stake than those on whom attention has been focused.

SAVING LIVES

Perhaps the strongest arguments for "non-economic values" are those involving human lives. Many highly costly laws, policies, or devices designed to safeguard the public from lethal hazards are defended on grounds that "if it saves just one human life" it is worth whatever it costs. Powerful as the moral and emotional appeal of such pronouncements may be, they cannot withstand scrutiny in a world where scarce resources have alternative uses.

One of those alternative uses is saving other human lives in other ways. Few things have saved as many lives as the simple growth of wealth. An earthquake powerful enough to kill a dozen people in California will kill hundreds of people in some less affluent country and thousands in a Third World nation. Greater wealth enables California buildings, bridges, and other structures to be built to withstand far greater stresses than similar structures can withstand in poorer countries. Those injured in an earthquake in California can be rushed far more quickly to far more elaborately equipped hospitals with larger numbers of more highly trained medical personnel. This is just one of innumerable ways in which wealth saves lives.

Natural disasters of all sorts occur in rich and poor countries alike—the United States leads the world in tornadoes, for example—but their consequences are very different. The Swiss Reinsurance Company reported that the biggest financial costs of natural disasters in 2003 were in the United States, Canada, and France. But that same year the biggest costs of natural disasters in human lives were all in Third World countries—Iran, Algeria, India, Bangladesh, and Pakistan. Given the high cost of medical care and of such preventive measures against disease as water treatment plants and sewage disposal systems, Third World countries likewise suffer far more from diseases, including diseases that have been virtually wiped out in affluent countries. The net result is shorter lifespans in poorer countries.

There have been various calculations of how much of a rise in national income saves how many lives. Whatever the correct figure may be—X million dollars to save one life—anything that prevents national income from rising that much has, in effect, cost a life. If some particular safety law, policy, or device costs 5X million dollars, either directly or in its inhibiting effect on economic growth, then it can no longer be said to be worth it "if it saves just one human life" because it does so at the cost of 5 other human lives. There is no escaping trade-offs, so long as resources are scarce and have alternative uses.

More is involved than saving lives in alternative ways. There is also the question of how much life is being saved and at how much cost. Some might say that there is no limit on how much value should be placed on a human life. But, however noble such words may sound, in the real world no one would favor spending half the annual output of the nation to keep one person alive 30 seconds longer. Yet that would be the logical implication of a claim that a life is of infinite value. When we look beyond words to behavior, people do not behave as if they regard even their own lives as being of infinite value. For example, people take life-threatening jobs as test pilots or explosives experts when such jobs pay a high enough salary for them to feel compensated for the risk. They even risk their lives for purely recreational purposes, such as sky-diving, white-water rafting, and skiing.

Using various indicators of the value that people put on their own lives in various countries, a study at the Harvard Law School estimated that the average American puts a value of $7 million on his or her life, while Canadians put a value of $4 million each on their lives and people in Japan put a value of nearly $10 million. Whatever the validity or accuracy of these particular numbers, the general results seem to indicate that people do not in fact behave as if their own lives are of infinite value—and presumably they value their own lives at least as much as they value the lives of other people.

How much it costs to save one life varies with the method used. Vaccinating children against deadly diseases in Third World countries costs very little per child and saves many lives, including decades of life per child.

Meanwhile, a heart transplant on an eighty-year-old man is enormously expensive and can yield only a limited amount of additional life, even if it is completely successful, since the life expectancy of an octogenarian is not very great in any case.

"UNMET NEEDS"

One of the most common—and certainly one of the most profound—misconceptions of economics involves "unmet needs." Politicians, journalists, and academicians are almost continuously pointing out unmet needs in our society that should be supplied by some government program or other. Most of these are things that most of us wish our society had more of.

What is wrong with that? Let us go back to square one. If economics is the study of the use of scarce resources which have alternative uses, then it follows that there will always be unmet needs. Some particular desires can be singled out and met 100 percent, but that only means that other desires will be even more unfulfilled than they are now. Anyone who has driven in most big cities will undoubtedly feel that there is an unmet need for more parking spaces. But, while it is both economically and technologically possible to build cities in such a way as to have a parking space available for anyone who wants one, anywhere in the city, at any hour of the day or night, does it follow that we should do it?

The cost of building vast new underground parking garages, or of tearing down existing buildings to create parking garages above ground, or of designing new cities with fewer buildings and more parking lots, would all be astronomically costly. What other things are we prepared to give up, in order to have this automotive heaven? Fewer hospitals? Less police protection? Fewer fire departments? Are we prepared to put up with even more unmet needs in these areas? Maybe some would give up public libraries in order to have more places to park. But, whatever choices are made and however it is done, there will still be more unmet needs elsewhere, as a result of meeting an unmet need for more parking spaces.

We may differ among ourselves as to what is worth sacrificing in order to have more of something else. The point here is more fundamental: Merely demonstrating an unmet need is not sufficient to say that it should be met—not when resources are scarce and have alternative uses.

In the case of parking spaces, what might appear to be cheaper, when measured only in government expenditures, would be to restrict or forbid the use of private automobiles in cities, adjusting the number of cars to the number of existing parking spaces, instead of vice-versa. Moreover, passing and enforcing such a law would cost a tiny fraction of the cost of greatly expanding the number of parking spaces. But this saving in government expenditures would have to be weighed against the vast private expenditures currently devoted to the purchase, maintenance, and parking of automobiles in cities. Obviously these expenditures would not have been undertaken in the first place if those who pay these prices did not find the benefits to be worth it to them.

To go back to square one again, *costs are foregone opportunities*, not government expenditures. Forcing thousands of people to forego opportunities for which they have willingly paid vast amounts of money is a cost that may far outweigh the savings from not having to build more parking spaces or do the other things necessary to accommodate cars in cities. None of this says that we should have either more parking spaces or fewer parking spaces in cities. What it says is that the way this issue—and many others—is presented makes no sense in a world of scarce resources which have alternative uses. That is a world of trade-offs, not solutions—and whatever trade-off is decided upon will still leave unmet needs.

So long as we respond gullibly to political rhetoric about unmet needs, we will arbitrarily choose to shift resources to whatever the featured unmet need of the day happens to be and away from other things. Then, when another politician—or perhaps even the same politician at a later time—discovers that robbing Peter to pay Paul has left Peter worse off, and now wants to help Peter meet his unmet needs, we will start shifting resources in another direction. In short, we will be like a dog chasing his tail in a circle and getting no closer, no matter how fast he runs.

This is not to say that we have the ideal trade-offs already and should leave them alone. Rather, it says that whatever trade-offs we make or change should be seen from the outset as trade-offs—not meeting unmet needs.

The very word "needs" arbitrarily puts some desires on a higher plane than others, as categorically more important. But, however urgent it may be to have *some* food and some water, for example, in order to sustain life itself, nevertheless—beyond some point—both become not only unnecessary but even counterproductive and dangerous. Widespread obesity among Americans shows that food has already reached that point and anyone who has suffered the ravages of flood (even if it is only a flooded basement) knows that water can reach that point as well. In short, even the most urgent needs remain needs only within a given range. We cannot live half an hour without oxygen, but even oxygen beyond some concentration level can promote the growth of cancer and has been known to make newborn babies blind for life. There is a reason why hospitals do not use oxygen tanks willy-nilly.

In short, nothing is a "need" categorically, regardless of how urgent it may be to have at particular times and places and in particular amounts. Unfortunately, most laws and government policies apply categorically, if only because of the dangers in leaving every official to become a petty despot in interpreting what these laws and policies mean and when they should apply. In this context, calling something a "need" categorically is playing with fire. Many complaints that some basically good government policy has been applied stupidly may fail to address the underlying problem of categorical laws in an incremental world. There may not have been any intelligent way to apply categorically a policy designed to meet desires whose benefits vary incrementally and ultimately cease to be benefits.

By its very nature, as a study of the use of scarce resources which have alternative uses, economics is about incremental trade-offs—not about "needs" or "solutions." That may be why economists have never been as popular as politicians who promise to solve our problems and meet our needs.

In the normal course of events, people who are spending their own money in the marketplace stop buying most things at a point where additional amounts would still have some value—just not enough value to justify paying the price. This presents an opportunity for politicians to offer some of those things at lower—subsidized—prices, perhaps even free. Now, with artificially lower prices, additional units will be worth the price to the consumer. But, since someone has to pay for the subsidies, the average consumer can end up paying more, in taxes and prices combined, than the additional units are worth. In short, consumers in this situation would buy things that they would never have bought if the full cost had been conveyed to them by the price, instead of being concealed by subsidies and financed by taxes.

It has been suggested that the government should provide jobs for the unemployed, doing work "to satisfy pressing social needs." There is no question that there are unemployed people capable of producing output that will have some value to others. But the money needed to employ the unemployed also has some value to others. Here, as in many other cases, the most important decision is: *Who is to decide?* People spending their own money for things that they value or third parties spending money extracted in taxes from the public to meet what these third parties decide—at no cost to themselves—are "pressing social needs"?

Chapter 25

PARTING THOUGHTS

We shall not grow wiser before we learn that much that
we have done was very foolish.

F. A. Hayek

Sometimes the whole is greater than the sum of its parts. In addition to whatever you may have learned in the course of this book about particular things such as prices, investment, or international trade, you may also have acquired a more general skepticism about many of the glittering words and fuzzy phrases that are mass produced by the media, by politicians, and by others.

You may no longer be as ready to believe those who talk about things selling "below their real value" or about how terrible it is for the United States to be "a debtor nation." Statements and statistics about "the rich" and "the poor" may not be uncritically accepted any more. Nor should you find it mysterious that so many places with rent control laws also have housing shortages.

However, no listing of economic fallacies can be complete, because the fertility of the human imagination is virtually unlimited. New fallacies are being conceived, or misconceived, while the old ones are still being refuted. The most that can be hoped for is to reveal some of the more common fallacies and promote both skepticism and an analytical approach that goes beyond the emotional appeals which sustain so many harmful and even dangerous economic fallacies in politics and in the media.

This should include a more careful use and definition of words, so that statements about how countries with high wages cannot compete in international trade with countries which have low wages do not escape scrutiny because of confusing high *wage rates per unit of time* with high *labor costs per unit of output*. Similarly sloppy use of terms often occurs in media and political discussions of taxation. For example, the growing federal deficits of the 1980s in the United States have often been blamed on the "tax cuts" early in that decade. But, although *tax rates per dollar of income* were cut, the *total tax revenues* of the federal government were higher in every year of the 1980s than in any previous year in the history of the country, as a result of incomes growing by more than the tax rates were cut. It was increased spending which led to growing deficits—a fact concealed by sloppy use of the word "taxes," which can refer to either individual tax rates or the total tax revenues of the government.

Many economic fallacies depend upon not thinking beyond the initial consequences of particular policies. Restricting the importation of foreign steel will indeed save jobs in the domestic steel industry, but its repercussions on the prices and sales of other domestic products made with higher-priced domestic steel can easily cost far more jobs than those that were saved.

Much confusion comes from judging economic policies by the goals they proclaim rather than the incentives they create. In wartime, for example, when military forces absorb many resources which would normally go into producing civilian products, there is often an understandable desire to ensure that such basic things as food continue to be available to the civilian population, especially those with low incomes. Thus price controls may be imposed on bread and butter, but not on champagne and caviar. However right this may seem, when you look only at the goal or the initial consequences, the picture changes drastically when you follow the subsequent repercussions.

If the prices of bread and butter are kept lower than they would be if determined by supply and demand in a free market, then producers of bread and butter tend to end up with lower rates of profit than producers of champagne and caviar, who remain free to charge "whatever the traffic will bear," since no one regards these things as essential. However, because all producers compete for labor and other scarce resources, this means that the higher profits from champagne and caviar enable their producers to bid away more resources, at the expense of producers of bread and butter, than they would have been in a free market without price controls. Shifting resources from the production of bread and butter to the production of champagne and caviar is one of the repercussions that escapes notice when we fail to think beyond the initial stage of consequences of economic policies. For similar reasons, rent control tends to shift resources from the production of ordinary housing for ordinary people toward the production of luxury housing for the affluent and wealthy.

The importance of economic principles extends beyond things that most people think of as economics. For example, those who worry about the exhaustion of petroleum, iron ore, or other natural resources often assume that they are discussing the amount of physical stuff in the earth. But that assumption changes radically when you realize that statistics on "known reserves" of these resources may tell us more about costs of exploration, and about the interest rate on the money that finances it, than about how much of the resource remains underground. Nor is the amount of physical stuff in the ground necessarily what matters, without knowing how much of it can be extracted and processed at what costs.

Some communities may decide to restrict how tall local buildings will be allowed to be built, without any thought that this has economic implications which can result in much higher rents being charged.[1] These are just some of a whole range of problems and issues which, on the surface, might not seem like economic matters, but which nevertheless look very different after understanding basic economic principles.

One of the recurring themes in our consideration of various policies and institutions, in a wide range of countries around the world, has been the distinction between the *goals* of these policies and institutions versus the *incentives* they create. The importance of that distinction extends beyond the particular things discussed in this book—and, indeed, beyond economics. Nothing is easier than to proclaim a wonderful goal.

---

[1] When laws prevent the building of ten-story apartment buildings, a five-story apartment building on the same land now has higher costs per apartment because the cost of the land—which can be higher than the cost of the building in some places—has to be recovered in the rent charged to only half as many people.

Legislation "to relieve the distress of the German people" during the Great Depression of the 1930s gave dictatorial powers to Adolf Hitler, leading to World War II, producing more distress and disaster than the German people—and many other peoples—had ever experienced before.

What must be asked about any goal is: What specific things are going to be done in the name of that goal? What does the particular legislation or policy reward and what does it punish? What constraints does it impose? Looking to the future, what are the likely consequences of such incentives and constraints? Looking back at the past, what have been the consequences of similar incentives and constraints in other times and places? As the distinguished British historian Paul Johnson put it:

> The study of history is a powerful antidote to contemporary arrogance. It is humbling to discover how many of our glib assumptions, which seem to us novel and plausible, have been tested before, not once but many times and in innumerable guises; and discovered to be, at great human cost, wholly false.

We have seen some of those great human costs—people going hungry in Russia, despite some of the richest farmland on the continent of Europe, people sleeping on cold sidewalks during winter nights in New York, despite far more boarded-up housing units in the city than it would take to shelter them all.

Some of the economic policies which have led to counterproductive or even catastrophic consequences in various countries and in various periods of history might suggest that there was unbelievable stupidity on the part of those making these decisions—which, in democratic countries, might also imply unbelievable stupidity on the part of those who voted for them. But this is not necessarily so. While the economic analysis required to understand these issues may not be particularly difficult to grasp, one must first stop and think about the issues in an economic framework. When people do not stop and think through certain issues, it does not matter whether those people are geniuses or morons, because the quality of the thinking that they *would have* done is a moot point.

In addition to the role of incentives and constraints, one of our other central themes has been the role of *knowledge*. In free market economies, we have seen giant multi-billion-dollar corporations fall from their pinnacles, some all the way to bankruptcy and extinction, because their knowledge of changing circumstances, and the implications of those changes, lagged behind that of upstart rivals. What is important is not that A & P succumbed to Safeway or Montgomery Ward to Sears, but that knowledge and insights proved decisive in market competition. The public benefitted from that, by getting what it wanted at lower prices, because some business decisions were based on a clearer understanding of the economic realities of the times and circumstances.

In centrally planned economies, we have seen the planners overwhelmed by the task of trying to set literally millions of prices and keep changing those prices in response to innumerable and often unforeseeable changes in circumstances. It was not remarkable that they failed so often. What was remarkable was that anyone had expected them to succeed, given the vast amount of knowledge that would have had to be marshalled and mastered in one place by one set of people to make such an arrangement work. Lenin was only one of many theorists over the centuries who imagined that it would be easy for government officials to run economic activities—and the first to encounter directly the economic and social catastrophes to which that belief led, as he himself admitted.

Given the decisive advantages of knowledge and insight in a market economy, even when this knowledge and insight are in the minds of people born and raised in poverty, such as J. C. Penney or F. W. Woolworth, we can see why market economies have so often outperformed other economies that depend on ideas originating solely within a narrow elite of birth or ideology. While market economies are often thought of as money economies, they are still more so knowledge economies, for money can always be found to back new insights, technologies and organizational methods that work, even when these innovations were created by people initially lacking in money, whether Henry Ford, Thomas Edison, David Packard, Ray Kroc, or others. Capital is always available under capitalism, but knowledge and insights are rare and precious under any economic system.

Knowledge should not be narrowly conceived as the kind of information in which intellectuals and academics specialize. We should not be like the depiction of the famous scholar Benjamin Jowett, master of Balliol College at Oxford, who inspired this verse:

> My name is Benjamin Jowett.
>   If it's knowledge, I know it.
> I am the master of this college,
>   What I don't know isn't knowledge.

In reality, there is much that the intelligentsia do not know that is knowledge vital to the functioning of an economy. It may be easy to disdain the kinds of highly specific mundane knowledge and its implications which are often economically decisive by asking, for example: "How much knowledge does it take to fry a hamburger?" Yet McDonald's did not become a multi-billion-dollar corporation, with thousands of outlets around the world, for no reason—not with so many rivals trying desperately and unsuccessfully to do the same thing, and some of them failing even to make enough money to stay in business. Anyone who studies the history of this franchise chain[2] will be astonished at the amount of detailed knowledge, insights, organizational and technological innovation, financial improvisation, all-out efforts and desperate sacrifices that went into creating an enormous economic success from selling just a few common food products.

Nor was McDonald's unique. All sorts of businesses—from Sears to Intel and from Honda to the Bank of America—had to struggle upward from humble beginnings to ultimately achieve wealth and security. In all these cases, it was the knowledge that was built up over the years—the human capital—which ultimately attracted the financial capital to make ideas become a reality. The other side of this is that, in countries where the mobilization of financial resources is made difficult by deficiencies in property rights laws, those at the bottom have fewer ways of getting the

---

[2] For example, John F. Love, *McDonald's: Behind the Arches.*

capital needed to back their entrepreneurial endeavors. More important, the whole society loses the benefits it could gain from what these stifled entrepreneurs could have contributed to the economic rise of the nation.

Success is only part of the story of a free market economy. Failure is at least as important a part, though few want to talk about it and none want to experience it. When the same resources—whether land, labor, steel, or petroleum—can be used by different firms and different industries to produce different products, the only way for the successful ideas to become realities is to take resources away from other uses that turn out to be unsuccessful, or which have become obsolete after having had their era of success. Economics is not about "win-win" options, but about often painful choices in the allocation of scarce resources which have alternative uses. Success and failure are not isolated good fortunes and misfortunes, but inseparable parts of the same process.

All economies—whether capitalism, socialism, feudalism or whatever—are essentially ways of cooperating in the production and distribution of goods and services, whether this is done efficiently or inefficiently, voluntarily or involuntarily. Naturally, individuals and groups want their own particular contributions to the process to be better rewarded, but their complaints or struggles over this are a sideshow to the main event of complementary efforts which produce the output on which all depend. Yet invidious comparisons and internecine struggles are the stuff of social melodrama, which in turn is the lifeblood of the media and politics, as well as for portions of the intelligentsia.

By portraying cooperative activities as if they were zero-sum contests—whether in employer-employee relations or in international trade or other cooperative endeavors—those with the power to impose their misconceptions on others through words or laws can create a negative-sum contest, in which all are worse off. A young worker who is destitute of both knowledge and money would today find it virtually impossible to purchase the knowledge that was vital to a future career by working long hours for no pay, as many did in times past—including F. W. Woolworth, who by this means rose from poverty to become one of the richest men of his era in retailing.

Those with a zero-sum vision who have seen property rights as mere special privileges for the affluent and the rich have helped erode or destroy such rights, or have made them practically inaccessible to the poor in Third World countries, thereby depriving the poor of one of the mechanisms by which people from backgrounds like theirs have risen to prosperity in other times and places.

However useful economics may be for understanding many issues, it is not as emotionally satisfying as more personal and melodramatic depictions of these issues often found in the media and in politics. Dry empirical questions are seldom as exciting as political crusades or ringing moral pronouncements. But empirical questions are questions that must be asked, if we are truly interested in the well-being of others, rather than in excitement or a sense of moral superiority for ourselves. Perhaps the most important distinction is between what sounds good and what works. The former may be sufficient for purposes of politics or moral preening, but not for the economic advancement of people in general or the poor in particular. For those who are willing to stop and think, basic economics provides some tools for evaluating policies and proposals in terms of their logical implications and empirical consequences.

If this book has contributed to that end, then it has succeeded in its mission.

QUESTIONS

The information required to answer each of
the questions below can be found by reading
the pages listed after each question.

PART I: PRICES AND MARKETS

1. Can there be a growing scarcity without a growing shortage—or a
   growing shortage without a growing scarcity? Explain with examples.
   (see pages 39, 49-50)

2. Can a decision be economic, if there is no money involved? Why or why
   not? (see page 6)

3. Can there be surplus food in a society where people are hungry? Explain
   why or why not. (see pages 56-57)

4. When a chronic shortage ends too suddenly for there to have been any
   significant increase in the output of whatever was in short supply before,
   what has probably happened? Explain. (see pages 41, 52-53)

5. Which of the following are—or are not—affected by price controls that
   limit how high the product's price can go: (a) the quantity supplied, (b)
   the quantity demanded, (c) the quality of the product, (d) a black market
   for the product, (e) the supply of auxiliary services that usually go with
   the product, (f) efficiency in the allocation of resources or (g) the average
   level of honesty among those who sell or rent the product? Explain in
   each case. (see pages 40-41, 43-44, 52-54, 379-381)

6. Building ordinary housing and luxury housing involves using many of the same resources, such as bricks, pipes, and construction labor. How does the allocation of these resources between ordinary housing and luxury housing tend to change after rent control laws are passed? (see page 44)

7. Are prices usually higher or lower in low-income neighborhoods? Why? Include among prices the interest rate on money borrowed and the cost of getting paychecks cashed. If you were considering opening a business in a low-income neighborhood, would you expect to make a higher or a lower rate of profit there than you would receive if you opened the same business in a middle-class or affluent neighborhood? Which kind of business is more likely to locate in each kind of neighborhood—a highly successful supermarket chain or a small independent business run by recent immigrants with a limited knowledge of English? Why would each kind of business tend to locate in one place but not the other? (see pages 65-67)

8. When a government institution or program produces counterproductive results, is that a sign of irrationality on the part of those who run that particular institution or program? Explain with examples. (see pages 69-70, 74, 122)

9. We all consider some things more important than others. Why then can there be a problem when some official government policy establishes "national priorities"? (see pages 80-81)

10. We tend to think of costs as the money we pay for things. But does that mean that there would be no costs in a primitive society that did not yet use money or in a modern cooperative community, where people collectively produce the goods and services they use and do not charge each other for them? (see pages 83-85)

11. Adam Smith had a high opinion of capitalism, despite his low opinion of capitalists. How does this relate to the difference between systemic causation and intentional causation? (see page 64)

12. Why do American manufacturers of computers or television sets tend to have them transported by others while Chinese manufacturers tend to transport them themselves? (see pages 133-134)

13. Because most basic economic principles are relatively straightforward and not difficult to understand, they are often dismissed as too "simplistic" to explain the complexities of the real world. Critique that belief. (see pages 68-69)

14. How can you put a price on music or health? (see pages 83-84)

15. How does rent control affect the quality of housing, the average age of housing, and the number of people per apartment? (see pages 40-41, 43-44, 46)

PART II: INDUSTRY AND COMMERCE

1. What are some of the reasons why some of the biggest and most profitable businesses have declined into obscurity or even bankruptcy? (see pages 92-98, 101-102, 111-112)

2. Why has Toyota manufactured cars with only enough inventory of parts to last a few hours? Why did Soviet industries have nearly enough inventory to last for a year? (see pages 134-135)

3. In some industries, the four or five top firms may make the great majority of the sales in the whole industry. Moreover, that may be true for decades on end. Does this then mean that there is a lack of competition in this industry? (see pages 156-159)

4. How did the movement of population from rural to urban America affect the economics of retail selling in the early twentieth century? How did the later movement of population from urban to suburban America in the second half of the twentieth century affect the economics of department stores and grocery stores? Explain with examples. (see pages 93, 96-97)

5. Why is it that General Motors can make millions of automobiles, without making a single tire to go on them, while Soviet enterprises not only tended to make all their own components, but sometimes even made the bricks for the buildings in which they operated? (see pages 133-134, 136)

6. How did diseconomies of scale in agriculture affect the way tractor drivers plowed fields in the Soviet Union? What if agricultural enterprises had been privately owned and the tractor drivers were plowing their own fields? Would the work have been done differently and would the farm be likely to be as large? Explain why. (see pages 121-122)

7. Any given individual's knowledge is extremely limited, under any economic or political system. How does the effect of this limitation differ in an economy coordinated by prices than in an economy coordinated by central planners? (see pages 95-99, 102-107, 129, 166-172)

8. Advertising, even when it is successful, is often considered to be a benefit only to those who advertise, but of no benefit to consumers, who have to pay the cost of the advertisements in the higher price of the products they buy. Critique this view. (see page 119)

9. What can and should be done for companies lagging behind while the rest of the economy is moving ahead? (see pages 178-180)

10. Why are retired people able to get much lower priced travel rates—on cruise ships, for example—than most other people? (see page 125)

11. Why is the perennial desire to "eliminate the middleman" perennially frustrated? (see pages 129-132)

12. After the A & P grocery chain cut its profit margins on the goods it sold, back in the early twentieth century, its rate of profit on its investment rose well above the national average. Why? (see page 117)

13. Why would luxury hotels be charging lower rates than economy hotels in the same city? (see page 124)

14. What is the difference between the government's protecting competition and protecting competitors? (see page 152)

15. What determines whether a given business can or will pass on to its customers any increases or decreases in its production costs? (see pages 126-128)

PART III: WORK AND PAY

1. What have been some of the economic and social consequences of the substitution of machine power for human strength, as a result of industrialization, and the growing importance of knowledge, skills, and experience in a high-tech economy? (see pages 195-196)

2. Would you expect the average hammer to drive more nails per year in a richer country or a poorer country? Would you expect the average worker to produce more output per hour in a richer country or a poorer country? Explain the reasons in each case. (see pages 203-206)

3. Some studies have attempted to determine how employment has changed in the wake of a minimum wage increase by surveying individual firms before and after the increase to find out how their employment has changed, and then adding up the results. What is the problem with this procedure? (see pages 214-215)

4. How can per capita income be increasing by 50 percent over a period of years, while average family income and average household income remain almost stationary over those same years? (see pages 192-193)

5. When the difference in income between the top and bottom brackets increases, does that necessarily mean that a given set of individuals are falling further behind another given set of individuals? (see pages 193-194)

6. Would a country in transition between a communist economy and a capitalist economy, such as China, tend to have more equality of income or less, compared to an economy that was continuing to be communist or continuing to be capitalist? (see pages 239, 243-244)

7. Although maximum wage laws existed long before minimum wage laws, only the latter are common today. However, in those special cases where there have been maximum wage laws—as under wage and price controls during World War II, for example, what effects would such laws have on the allocation of scarce resources—and on discrimination against minorities and women? (see page 202)

8. Does inequality of income tend to be greater or less in the long run than in the short run? Greater or less than inequalities in consumption? Why do many statistics about "the rich" and "the poor" include people who are neither rich nor poor in reality? (see pages 188-190, 194)

9. A *New York Times* columnist once used per capita income statistics to judge the economic performance of the administration of President

Lyndon Johnson and, in later years, used household income statistics to judge the economic performance of the administration of President Ronald Reagan. Which set of statistics would tend to make the economic progress of the country look better and why? (see pages 192-193)

10. How can differences in the quality of transportation systems or in the level of corruption in different countries affect the value of labor? (see page 187)

11. Why would a South African manufacturer expand production by opening a plant in Poland, when there were large numbers of workers available in South Africa, where the unemployment rate was 26 percent, and where the average output per hour of South African workers was higher than the average output per hour of Polish workers? (see pages 216-217)

12. Since each baseball player hits his own home runs, why would the number of home runs hit by a given batter be affected by the other batters on his team? (see page 186)

13. Give two different definitions of the phrase "income distribution" and explain how they differ from one another. What does this imply about "income redistribution"? (see page 191)

14. Why are wages lower, and working conditions worse, in Third World countries? What are the likely consequences of various possible ways of trying to improve either or both? (see pages 187, 234-236)

15. What are the implications of the fact that most people today reach their peak earnings years at later ages than in generations past—and that these peak earnings are now usually a larger number of times greater than the earnings of beginners than in times past? (see pages 195-196)

PART IV: TIME AND RISK

1. Does it make economic sense for a ninety-year-old man, with no heirs, to plant trees that will take 20 years to grow to maturity and bear fruit? (see page 273)

2. Education has been called an investment in "human capital" but many poor countries that have greatly increased the number of their people who are educated have seen little economic improvement as a result. What are some of the reasons? (see pages 258-261)

3. Why may the statistics on the known reserves of a natural resource provide a misleading picture of how much of that resource there is in the ground? (see pages 275-281)

4. "Insurance principles often conflict with political principles." Explain why, with examples. (see pages 301-303)

5. How does commodity speculation differ from gambling? What is the effect of commodity speculation on output? On the allocation of scarce resources which have alternative uses? (see page 262)

6. Why does it pay an insurance company or a commodity speculator to offer a deal in which they guarantee to pay a given sum of money to someone under given circumstances? And why does it pay for that person to accept the offer? (see pages 262-263)

7. Why would a bus company owned or controlled by the government charge fares too low to replace existing buses as they wear out? What if the executives of a privately owned and privately controlled bus company decided to divert part of the money they received from bus fares toward paying themselves higher salaries, instead of setting aside enough money to replace buses as they wear out? What would happen to the value of the

stock in their company and how would the stockholders be likely to react? (see pages 317-318)

8. Many poor countries have confiscated businesses or land owned by wealthy foreign companies. Why has this seldom made the poor country more prosperous? (see page 320)

9. Can complex international commodity markets have much impact on small farmers in a Third World country? Can those Third World farmers, who are often poor and poorly educated, participate in international commodity markets? (see page 264)

10.Why does it make sense for an individual driver to get insurance on his automobile? Why then doesn't Hertz buy insurance for its automobiles? (see page 297)

11.How can government regulation of insurance companies improve the efficiency of the industry? How can it make the industry less efficient? Explain with examples of both. (see pages 300-302)

12.Businesses that wish to raise money issue both stocks and bonds but individuals who want to raise money usually simply borrow—that is, the equivalent of issuing bonds. In some cases, however, people raise money by granting shares in their future income—the equivalent of issuing stocks. Explain why. (see pages 293-295)

13.What kinds of income are called "unearned income" and why? What have been the consequences when groups that live on "unearned income" have left the country in large numbers, either voluntarily or because of being expelled? (see pages 268-270)

14.How does the interest rate allocate resources among contemporaries and between different present and future uses? (see pages 270-272)

15. Why would a state's bonds be downgraded by a bond-rating agency like Standard & Poor's when that state was paying its bond-holders regularly and had a surplus in its treasury? (see pages 321-322)

PART V: THE NATIONAL ECONOMY

1. "While taxes are often thought of as simply transfers of money from the people to the government, their economic consequences include changes in behavior that can affect the whole economy for better or worse." Explain with examples. (see pages 396-398)

2. Does the presence or absence of property rights make any difference to people who own no property? For example, are tenants affected economically by whether the community in which they rent apartments or houses allows unbridled property rights or reduces those property rights through zoning laws, open space laws, height restrictions on buildings, or rent control laws? Explain how people who own no property are affected. (see pages 374-375)

3. How does the level of honesty or corruption in a country affect the effectiveness of its economy? How do economic policies affect the level of honesty and corruption? (see pages 366-368)

4. During the Great Depression of the 1930s, both Republican President Herbert Hoover and his successor, Democratic President Franklin D. Roosevelt, tried to keep up the prices of goods and labor. What was the economic problem with these policies? (see pages 353-354)

5. During a period of inflation, does money circulate faster or slower—and why? What are the consequences? What do you suppose happens during a period of deflation—and what are the consequences then? (see pages 349-350, 352)

6. During an all-out war, how can a country's military plus civilian consumption add up to more than its output, without borrowing from other countries? (see pages 330-331)

7. What is the fallacy of composition and why is it fallacious? Give examples. (see pages 326-327)

8. "The nationalization of banks in India was not simply a matter of transferring ownership of an enterprise to the government. This transfer changed all the incentives and constraints from those of the marketplace to those of politics and bureaucracy." Explain what consequences followed and why. (see pages 426-427)

9. Those who favor increases in tax rates are often disappointed that the additional revenue turns out to be less than they expected. Conversely, those who fear that cuts in tax rates will substantially reduce the government's revenues have often been surprised to find the government's revenues rising. Explain both phenomena. (see pages 396-398)

10. Even if detailed statistics are available, why is it difficult to compare the national output at the beginning of the twentieth century with the national output at the beginning of the twenty-first century, and say by what percentage it has increased? Why is it hard even to say how much prices for particular goods have increased from one century to another? (see pages 331-333)

11. Why would an Albanian bank, with 83 percent of the country's deposits, refuse to make any loans? And what were the consequences for the Albanian economy? (see pages 362-363)

12. How can the average age of a country's population affect the economic well-being represented by the Gross Domestic Product per capita? (see pages 334-335)

13. Since "money talks" in the marketplace, why would rich people want to shift some decisions out of the marketplace and have these decisions made politically or by courts? (Hint: housing is a classic example.) (see pages 374-375)

14. Distinguished economist Michael Boskin said: "Wall Street yawned when the deficit projections soared." Why were neither Wall Street financiers nor Professor Boskin worried? Under what conditions should they be worried? (see page 406)

15. From time to time there are conflicting estimates of how much of the total taxes are collected from which individuals and organizations. Why is it not easy to tell who is really bearing the burden of taxation? (see pages 398-400)

PART VI: THE INTERNATIONAL ECONOMY

1. If laws restrict the importation of a particular foreign product, in order to protect the jobs of domestic workers who produce that product, how is it possible that this can end up reducing domestic employment? (see pages 449-450)

2. Britain began importing farm products at a time when its own farmers were more efficient than the foreign farmers whose products it was importing. How could this be beneficial to Britain? How did this affect the international allocation of scarce resources which have alternative uses? (see pages 440-441)

3. What are the three most important benefits of international trade? Explain each in terms of its effect on the efficient allocation of scarce resources which have alternative uses. (see pages 435-444)

4. Why might the government of a Third World country prefer to receive a smaller amount of money as foreign aid, rather than a larger amount of money as private investment? (see pages 487-488)

5. What is meant by a "favorable balance of trade"? Why was it considered favorable? Is it also favorable to producing prosperity in the economy? (see pages 434-435)

6. When foreigners annually take more wealth out of the U.S. economy than the Gross Domestic Product of Egypt or Malaysia, how can that fail to make Americans poorer? (see pages 465, 472)

7. What is "dumping" and what are the problems in trying to enforce laws against it? (see pages 451-453)

8. In the absence of restrictions on international trade, would low-wage countries tend to take jobs away from high-wage countries through lower production costs that would allow them to sell at lower prices? Explain. (see pages 445-448)

9. The United States has often been a "debtor nation" owing more to people in other countries than people in other countries owe to Americans, while Switzerland has often been a "creditor nation," to whom others owe more to the Swiss than the Swiss owe to others. What tends to lead to this difference and is it economically beneficial or harmful to Americans or Swiss? (see pages 462-463)

10. What were the causes and effects of a large worldwide decline in international trade in the 1930s compared to the 1920s? (see pages 448-449)

11. Since capital tends to be more scarce in poorer countries, and therefore earns a higher rate of return than in more richer countries, the net flow of capital might be expected to be from the richer to the poorer

countries. Why would the net international movement of capital often be in the opposite direction? (see pages 458-459)

12. Why did the movement of jobs from high-wage countries to low-wage countries that was expected after the North American Free Trade Agreement not happen? (see pages 433-434)

13. Suppose that country *A* outsources more jobs to country *B* than country *B* outsources to country *A*. How could that still lead to more jobs in country *A* than before trading with country *B*? (see page 456)

14. One of the complaints about immigrant minorities like the overseas Chinese in various Southeast Asian countries is that they send money back to relatives in the country from which they came, thereby reducing the wealth of the country in which they are living. What is the flaw in this argument? (see pages 466-467)

15. Why would it be difficult for Australia to develop its own original automobiles, instead of manufacturing cars that are offshoots of Japanese or American cars? (see page 442)

PART VII: SPECIAL ECONOMIC ISSUES

1. Costly safety devices or policies have often been defended on grounds that "if it saves just one life, it is worth it." What is the problem with that reasoning? (see pages 538-540)

2. What are some of the reasons why different prices are charged for things that are physically identical? (see pages 498-500)

3. Some people respond to economic analysis by saying, "But there are also *non-economic* values to consider." Discuss. (see page 518)

4. What is the point of having different brands of the same product if in fact all the brands are of pretty much the same quality and sell for about the same price? What would happen in this situation if laws did away with brands, so that each consumer could only identify what the product was, but not who made it? (see pages 504-507)

5. What is the theory of "predatory prices"? How could a Nobel-Prizewinning economist have failed to see a single example of it? (see pages 502-503)

6. Explain how the presence or absence of the profit motive affects an organization's likelihood of achieving the purpose for which it was created, to the maximum extent possible with the resources at its disposal. (see pages 509-513)

7. What are the problems with the "trickle-down theory"? (see pages 515-517)

8. Critics have claimed that profits exceed the value of the services performed by those who receive those profits. What empirical evidence could be used to test this belief? (see page 514)

9. When fighting a war leads to a diversion of a substantial amount of resources from civilian to military purposes, most people would be more concerned to see that the poor could still get bread than that the rich could still get caviar. Why then not put price controls on bread but not on caviar? (see pages 545-546)

10. Just as it is possible for prices to seem to be different for the same product when they are not, it is also possible for prices to seem to be the same when in fact they are different. Give examples of the latter. (see page 500)

11. Can government-imposed prices for medical care reduce the costs of that care? (see page 501)

12. Nobel Prizewinning economist F. A. Hayek said: "We shall not grow wiser before we learn that much that we have done was very foolish." What do you consider to be the three most foolish policies discussed in this book? Would you have considered those policies foolish before reading *Basic Economics*?

13. What is the difference between being pro-business and being pro-free market? (see pages 508-509)

14. A government official in India said: "I don't want multinational companies getting rich selling face creams to poor Indians." What does that statement imply? (see page 522)

15. What are some of the differences in the incentives and constraints facing non-profit enterprises as compared to profit-seeking enterprises? Explain with examples. (see pages 509-515)

SOURCES

It is neither possible nor necessary to document the source of every statement made in this book. However, there are some key facts which some readers may want to check out or to explore further. Rather than clutter the text with footnotes, in a book intended for the general public, the citations are listed here in an informal way that should nevertheless make it possible to find the original sources.

CHAPTER 1: WHAT IS ECONOMICS?

The epigraph is from page 294 of *Collected Legal Papers* by Oliver Wendell Holmes. Data on the value of natural resources per capita in Japan, Switzerland, Uruguay and Venezuela are from page 27 of *Culture and Prosperity* by John Kay, and data on the incomes in these four countries are from pages 793, 837, 847, and 848 of *The World Almanac, 2006*. The article about middle-class Americans began on the front page of Section 3 of the *New York Times* of August 1, 1999 and was written by Louis Uchitelle. The fact that the Soviet Union produced more steel, but fewer steel products, than the United States is from page 128 of *The Turning Point: Revitalizing the Soviet Economy* by Nikolai Shmelev and Vladimir Popov. Differences between the efficiency of energy use in China and Japan were noted on page 50 of the April 11, 2005 issue of *BusinessWeek* magazine. The statement that Marxist economist Oskar Lange did not differ fundamentally from Milton Friedman on certain basic propositions and procedures can be verified by reading Oskar Lange, "The Scope and Method of Economics," in the *Review of Economic Studies* (1945-1946), pages 19-32, and comparing that with Milton Friedman's essay "The Methodology of Positive Economics" in his book *Essays in Positive*

Economics. The estimates of millions of people rising out of poverty in India and China were from, respectively, p. B1 of the May 5, 2006 issue of the *Wall Street Journal*, in an article titled "Newspaper Nirvana?" and page 3 of *The Undercover Economist* by Tim Harford.

CHAPTER 2: THE ROLE OF PRICES

The epigraph from Will Rogers is from page 193 of *A Will Rogers Treasury*, edited by Bryan B. Sterling and Frances N. Sterling. The quotation about China's imports of food is from page 79 of the May 24, 2004 issue of *Forbes* magazine, in an article titled "Feed Me." The fact that KFC has more sales in China than in the United States is from page 82 of the same article. British Prime Minister Margaret Thatcher's comment about Soviet President Mikhail Gorbachev's lack of knowledge of economics is from page 81 of *Statecraft: Strategies for a Changing World* by Margaret Thatcher. The various quoted statistics and analyses about the Soviet economy in various parts of the chapter are from *The Turning Point: Revitalizing the Soviet Economy* by Soviet economists Nikolai Shmelev and Vladimir Popov, especially pages 129, 130-131, 141, 160, 170, 181, 213. Boris Yeltsin's experience in an American supermarket is described on pages 317 to 318 of *Down with Big Brother* by Michael Dobbs; his reactions are described on page 291 of *The Ideas That Conquered the World* by Michael Mandlebaum and on page 329 of *Yeltsin* by Leon Aron. The quotations about home prices in Phoenix were from page A1 of the June 18, 2006 issue of *The Arizona Republic* in an article titled "How Low Will It Go?" Information on how long homes for sale remained on the market is from pages A1 and A20 of the same article. Information on similar trends nationwide is from an article beginning on the front page of the *Wall Street Journal* of August 23, 2006, titled "Housing Slump Proves Painful for Some Owners and Builders." Information on Ghana and the Ivory Coast is from a book by Robin W. L. Alpine and James Pickett, *Agriculture, Liberalisation and Economic Growth in Ghana and Côte D'Ivoire: 1960-1990*, published in Paris by the Organisation for Economic Co-operation and Development. South Korea's surpassing of India, after starting from a similar economic level, was mentioned on page 222 of *The Commanding Heights* by Daniel Yergin and Joseph Stanislaw. India's relaxation of government controls over its economy was reported on page 13 of the June 2, 2001 issue of *The Economist*. India's average growth rate of 2 percent from 1950 to 1990 was reported on page 279 of *Culture and Prosperity* by John Kay. The quote from Friedrich Engels is from his preface to the first German edition of *The Poverty of Philosophy* by Karl Marx. The comment on the role of prices in connecting the far-flung activities in a market economy is from page 172 of *The Turning Point*. The use of food and electricity in an Israeli kibbutz, before and after prices were charged for them, is discussed on pages 332 and 333 of *Heaven on Earth: The Rise and Fall of Socialism* by Joshua Muravchik. The role of rising oil prices in bringing new oil reserves into production was explained on page A1 of the *Wall Street Journal* of March 27, 2006 in an article titled "As Prices Surge, Oil Giants Turn Sludge Into Gold." The decline in apartment rents across the United States was reported in a news story beginning on page A1 of the November 29, 2003 issue of the *New York Times* titled "Apartment Glut Forces Owners to Cut Rents in Much of U.S." The relationship between housing prices and population changes in upstate New York was described on page 70 of an article titled "Down-and-Out Upstate," in the Autumn 1999 issue of *City Journal*.

CHAPTER 3: PRICE CONTROLS

The epigraph is from page 329 of *The Wisdom of Henry Hazlitt*. The fact that the housing shortage in the United States occurred when there was no change in the ratio of housing to people is from a book titled *Roofs or Ceilings?* by Milton Friedman and George J. Stigler. The book itself has long been out of print, but excerpts from it were included in a collection of writings titled *Rent Control: Costs and Consequences*, edited by Robert Albon. This particular statement occurs on page 16. The facts about rent control in Sweden are from a different article in the same book, "The Rise, Fall and Revival of Swedish Rent Control." The fact that nearly half the rent-controlled apartments in San Francisco had only one tenant is from page 21 of *San Francisco Housing DataBook*, a 2001 study commissioned by the city and produced by consultants called Bay Area Economics. The fact that 48 percent of the households in Manhattan had just one occupant is from page A2 of the September 3, 2005 issue of the *San Francisco Chronicle* under the title "Census: More

Americans Living Alone." Many of the facts about rent control and homelessness in the United States are from *The Excluded Americans* by William Tucker (especially pages 19, 162, 163, 275 and Chapter 19, which discusses various elite celebrities living in rent-controlled apartments). The comment from the *New York Times* is from page 40 of an article by John Tierney in their Sunday magazine section of May 4, 1997, titled "At the Intersection of Supply and Demand." The lack of building in Melbourne under Australian rent control is mentioned on page 125 of *Rent Control: Costs and Consequences*, edited by Robert Albon. The age of rent-controlled housing in San Francisco is from page 56 of *San Francisco Housing DataBook*, cited above. The high vacancy rate in commercial and industrial buildings was discussed on page B6 of the January 7, 2004 issue of the *Wall Street Journal* under the title, "Study Sees Record Industrial Space Vacancies." Facts about the effects of rent control in Britain, France, Germany, and the Netherlands are from *Rent Control in North America and Four European Countries* by Joel F. Brenner and Herbert M. Franklin, pages 4, 9, and 69. The decline of the housing stock under rent control in Washington is cited in an article by Thomas Hazlett in a book titled *Resolving the Housing Crisis*. The decline in London's rental advertisements is from page 11 of the January 24, 1975 issue of *The Times*. The withdrawal of rental units after the imposition of rent control in Toronto was mentioned on page 21 of *Zoning, Rent Control and Affordable Housing* by William Tucker. Data on the number of buildings taken over by the city government in New York can be found on page 99 of *The Homeless* by Christopher Jencks. The fact that building resumed in various Massachusetts communities after the state banned local rent control laws can be found in *Rude Awakenings* by Richard W. White, Jr. The news story illustrating the non-comparability of rents under New York's rent control laws appeared on the front page of the *Wall Street Journal* of March 21, 1994 under the title, "Some Rich and Famous of New York City Bask in Shelter of Rent Law." Information on the benefits of rent control being greater for tenants in luxury housing is from pages 62 and 64 of the Summer 2006 issue of *City Journal* in an article titled "Is There a New York Housing Crisis?" San Francisco's experience under rent control is from a study whose results were reported on page 13 of the *San Francisco Weekly* of January 30, 2002 in an article titled "Legends in Our Own Minds." The paradox of higher rents in rent-controlled cities is from another study by William Tucker, "How Rent Control Drives Out Affordable Housing," *Policy Analysis* paper number 274,

published by the Cato Institute. The data on housing in San Francisco after the 1906 earthquake are on pages 5 and 6 of *Rent Control: Costs and Consequences*, edited by Robert Albon. Information on the amounts of gasoline sold during the 1970s gasoline shortages is from table 8a in Section VII of the September 1984 *Basic Petroleum Data Book*, published by the American Petroleum Institute. See also "Experts Offer a Host of Reasons for Gas Crisis in New York Area," *New York Times*, July 29, 1979, p. 30 and "The Gas Lines of '79," *The Public Interest*, Summer 1980, page 47. Soviet economists' comments on the gasoline shortage in the United States are from page 89 of *The Turning Point* by Nikolai Shmelev and Vladimir Popov. The smuggling of food during the early years of the Soviet Union is mentioned on page 8 of *The Turning Point* by Shmelev and Popov and their discussion of widespread black markets in the later era is on pages 198-199. The postwar meat shortage in the United States under price controls is discussed on pages 58 and 59 of *Prices and Price Controls* published by the Foundation for Economic Education, Inc. The effects of price control on the use of medical care are discussed in detail in Chapter 3 of *Applied Economics* by Thomas Sowell. London's newspaper *The Guardian* reported the story of the British girl who received a breast implant in its November 9, 1998 issue, page 6, under the title, "Girl, 12, to Get Breast Implant." The 10,000 people in Britain who had waited 15 months or more for surgery were reported in *The Economist* magazine of London on page 55 of its April 13, 2002 issue. The British woman whose cancer surgery was postponed until it had to be cancelled because the cancer had become inoperable during the long delays was mentioned in *The Economist* of November 24, 2001, on page 52. Data of the relative waiting times for elective surgery in five English-speaking countries are from page 12 of a study titled *Tackling Excessive Waiting Times for Elective Surgery: A Comparison of Policies in Twelve OECD Countries* by Jeremy Hurst and Luigi Siciliani. The agricultural price support program in general is covered in Chapter 1 of *The Structure of American Industry* by Walter Adams and James Brock. The surpluses of wheat and rice created by India's agricultural price support program were reported on page 63 of the *Far Eastern Economic Review* of December 6, 2001, in an article titled "The Problems of Plenty." The quotation about hunger in India, despite surplus food, is from page A3 of the *New York Times* of December 2, 2002 in a story titled "Poor in India Starve as Surplus Wheat Rots." Data on the costs of European Union agricultural subsidies in general in 2002 are from page 33 of *The Economist* of October 5, 2002, under the title "Scandalous." Information on the effects of price supports in the sugar industry is from a front-page article in the *New York Times* of May 6, 2001 titled "Sugar Rules Defy Free-Trade Logic." The costs of the 2002 American farm subsidy bill were estimated in the August 29, 2002 issue of *National Review* in an article titled "Twisting 'The Facts.'" Inflated prices of lamb, butter, and sugar in the European Union were reported in *The Economist*, June 9, 2001, page 70, in an article titled "Special Report: Agricultural Trade." The statement that every cow in the European Union gets more subsidies per day than most Africans have to live on is from page A13 of the January 7, 2003 issue of the *Wall Street Journal* in a column titled "Fight Poverty, Not Patents." The fact that 85 percent of Mexico's agricultural subsidies go to the top 15 percent of farmers is from page A13 of the *Wall Street Journal* of March 5, 2003. Discussions of the effects of price controls in besieged sixteenth-century Antwerp, as well as the eighteenth-century and nineteenth-century local food shortages in India are from pages 33 and 34 of *Forty Centuries of Wage and Price Controls* by Robert L. Schuettinger and Eamonn F. Butler.

CHAPTER 4: AN OVERVIEW

The epigraph is from pages 292-293 of *Collected Legal Papers* by Oliver Wendell Holmes. The quotes from Frederick Engels and Adam Smith are from, respectively, page 476 of *Selected Correspondence* by Karl Marx and Frederick Engels and page 423 of the Modern Library edition of *The Wealth of Nations* by Adam Smith. The relative costs for security in inner city and suburban shopping malls were discussed on page 251 of *America in Black and White* by Stephan Thernstrom and Abigail Thernstrom. The quote from the Soviet manager about not wanting "to get eight years" is from page 134 of *The Red Executive* by David Granick. Comparisons of bombing and rent control as means of destroying housing appear on pages 422 and 425 of an article by Walter Block titled "Rent Control" in *The Fortune Encyclopedia of Economics*, edited by David Henderson. Former food-exporting countries which became unable to feed themselves are mentioned in innumerable places, including *Modern Times* by Paul Johnson, pages 724-727 of the 1992 edition. The quote that "people brought provisions no more to markets" after the emperor Diocletian's price controls is from page 24 of *Forty Centuries of Wage and Price Controls* by Robert L. Schuettinger and Eamonn F. Butler. The economic problems of the rich "black earth" country of Russia are discussed on page A1 of the October 19, 1998 issue of the *San Francisco Chronicle*, in an article titled "Russian Farmland Withers on the Vine: Politics, Mind-set Keep Nation on a Diet of Imports" and in an article beginning on page A1 of the October 16, 1998 issue of the *Wall Street Journal* titled "Food Lines." California's subsidized water for farmers is discussed on pages A1 and A6 of the May 30, 1991 issue of the *Wall Street Journal* under the title "Big Farmers in West Get Subsidized Water Despite Drought Crisis." The effects of subsidized water to farmers in India were reported on page 14 of *The Economist* of June 2, 2001, under the title, "Grim Reapers."

CHAPTER 5: THE RISE AND FALL OF BUSINESSES

The epigraph is from page 52 of the May 27, 2002 issue of *Fortune* magazine. Information on the number of A & P stores in 1929 is from pages 89 and 90 of the April 14, 2003 issue of *Fortune*. The fact that 36 companies dropped off the list of the *Fortune* 500 in just one year is from page F-21 of the same issue. The quotation about F.A.O. Schwarz's bankruptcy, in the face of competition from Wal-Mart, is from section 4, page 1, of the December 7, 2003 issue of the *New York Times*. The decline of Japan's Mizuho bank was reported on page C1 of the May 8, 2003 issue of the *Wall Street Journal* in a news story titled "Mizuho's Fate May Rest on a Japan Bailout." The changing profitability of Japanese manufacturers of compact disc players was mentioned on page 45 of the *Far Eastern Economic Review* of November 28, 2002, in an article titled "Picturing the Future." Sony's shift from large losses to large profits was discussed on page 63 of the March 1, 2003 issue of *The Economist*, in an article titled "The Complete Home Entertainer?" A similar change in profitability by Lloyd's of London was reported on page C1 of the *Wall Street Journal* of November 17, 2003 in a story titled "The Master of Disaster is Trying to Avoid One." General Motors' turnaround in profitability was discussed on page 52 of the February 10, 2003 issue of *BusinessWeek* in an article titled "Rick Wagoner's Game Plan." U.S. Steel's fall from its long-held position of number one steel producer in the world, and its operating at a loss, were reported on page 42 of the

July 21, 2003 issue of *BusinessWeek*, in an article titled "Up From the Scrap Heap." Boeing's similar fall from its number one position as the world's leading commercial aircraft producer was reported on page 146 of the November 10, 2003 issue of *Fortune* magazine, in an article titled "Lord of the Air." The problems of Airbus were discussed in two front-page articles in the *Wall Street Journal* of July 3, 2006 ("Airbus Problems Lead to Ouster of Key Executives") and July 14, 2006 ("Under Pressure, Airbus Redesigns A Troubled Plane"). The historical sketches of various businesses are based on information from a variety of sources, including innumerable newspaper and magazine articles, as well as books such as *New and Improved: The Story of Mass Marketing in America* written by Richard S. Tedlow, *Brand New: How Entrepreneurs Earned Consumers' Trust from Wedgwood to Dell* by Nancy F. Koehn, *Forbes Greatest Business Stories of All Time* by Daniel Gross and the editors of *Forbes* magazine, *Masters of Enterprise* by H. W. Brands, *Empire Builders* by Burton W. Folsom, Jr., *The First Hundred Years are the Toughest: What We Can Learn from the Century of Competition Between Sears and Wards* by Cecil C. Hoge, Sr., *A & P* by M. A. Adelman, *The Rise and Decline of the Great Atlantic & Pacific Tea Company* by former A & P executive William L. Walsh and *Made in America* by Sam Walton. The declining circulation of New York City newspapers is from a story on page E5 of the *New York Times* of November 18, 1990 titled, "Suburban Sprawl Also Applies to the Circulation of Newspapers." Data on newspapers with daily circulation of a million or more copies is from page ix of *Editor and Publisher Yearbook*, 2005, Part I. The big New York department stores' initial rejection of credit cards is mentioned on page 204 of *The New York Times Century of Business*, edited by Floyd Norris and Christine Bockelmann. The fact that credit card or debit purchases exceeded cash purchases for the first time in 2003 is from page 130 of an article titled "Just One Word: Plastic" in the February 23, 2004 issue of *Fortune* magazine. The fact that some companies made more profit from their own credit cards than from the rest of their business is from page 38 of the March 17, 2003 issue of *Fortune*. On the misallocation of gasoline, see "The Gas Lines of '79," *The Public Interest*, Summer 1980, page 47; "Gas Crisis: Experts Find Mixture of Causes," *New York Times*, June 24, 1979, pp. A1 ff; "U.S. to Allow Shift of Some Gas Stocks to Urban Sections," *New York Times*, June 30, 1979, pp. A1 ff. On the lack of gasoline shortages in the United States during the 1967 Arab oil embargo, see Thomas W. Hazlett, *TV Coverage of the Oil Crises*, pp. 14-15. The dire predictions that ending price controls on oil would cause skyrocketing gasoline prices are quoted in "Snake Oil Salesmen," *Policy Review*, Summer 1986, pp. 74-77, *passim*. On gasoline prices reaching an all-time low, see "Gas is Cheap, But Taxes are Rising," *Consumers' Research*, August 1994, pp. 28-29. The founding of the Bank of Italy is discussed on page 28 of *A.P. Giannini: Banker of America* by Felice A. Bonadio.

CHAPTER 6: THE ROLE OF PROFITS—AND LOSSES

The epigraph is from page 251 of *Give Me a Break* by John Stossel. The report on the competition between Wal-Mart and Kroger's is from page B1 of the *Wall Street Journal* of May 27, 2003, under the title "Price War in Aisle 3." Soviet Premier Leonid Brezhnev's comment that Soviet managers shied away from innovation "as the devil shies away from incense" was quoted on page 437 of a paper by Joseph S. Berliner titled "Prospects for Technological Progress" in a 1976 publication by the Joint Economic Committee of Congress titled *Soviet Economy in a New Perspective*. Information and comments on the Ambassador automobile in India are from *The Economist* of September 11, 1999, under the title, "Free to be Poor" and from page 14 of the December 30, 1997 issue of the London newspaper *The Independent*. The story of the microchip, including Intel's risking its corporate survival for the sake of research, is discussed on pages 247-248, 254, 259-262 of *Forbes Greatest Business Stories of All Time*, edited by Daniel Gross, et al. Advanced Micro Device's billion-dollar losses while trying to gain market share from Intel were reported on pages 66-67 of the March 10, 2003 issue of *BusinessWeek*. The quotation about AMD's Opteron chip is from page 43 of the April 10, 2006 issue of *Forbes* magazine in an article titled "Only the Paranoid Resurge." The rise of AMD's share of chips in personal computers and the decline in Intel's stock in 2006 were reported on pages A1 and A15 of the *Wall Street Journal* of April 28, 2006 in an article titled "Intel Promises Sweeping Overhaul Amid PC Slowdown, Rival's Gains." Announced layoffs of 1,000 Intel managers was reported on page C2 of the *New York Times* of July 14, 2006 in an item titled "Intel to Lay Off Managers." The 57 percent decline in Intel's profits while AMD's profits rose 53 percent was reported on page A11 of the *Wall Street Journal* of July 21, 2006 under the title

"Price War Weighs on AMD's Results." Intel's changing market shares are from page D1 of the July 28, 2006 issue of the *San Francisco Chronicle* in an article titled "Intel Introduces Fastest Microprocessors." The quotation from the dean of the Yale School of Management is from page 26 of the April 11, 2005 issue of *BusinessWeek*. The fact that 120 out of the top 500 companies in America made losses in 2002 was reported on page 199 of the April 14, 2003 issue of *Fortune* magazine under the title "Honey, I Shrunk the Profits." Data on corporate profit rates are from page 7 of the May 2006 issue of the *Survey of Current Business*, in an article titled "Note on the Returns for Domestic Nonfinancial Corporations in 1960-2005." The fact that *Fortune* 500 companies averaged just pennies of profit on each dollar of revenue is from page 197 of the April 14, 2003 issue of *Fortune* under the title "Honey, I Shrunk the Profits." Higher price markups and lower profit rates in ghetto businesses are discussed on page 31 of *The State Against Blacks* by Walter E. Williams. Data on the time required to manufacture a Model T Ford in the early twentieth century, and the fact that the price of this car was cut in half between 1910 and 1916 are from pages 62 and 161 of *Global Capitalism* by Jeffry A. Frieden. Data on economies and diseconomies of scale in the automobile and beer industries are from pages 76, 77, 131 and 145 of *The Structure of American Industry*, 9th edition, by Walter Adams and James Brock. The statistic that the largest manufacturer of automobiles in the United States in the early twentieth century produced just six cars a day is from *The American Car Dealership* by Robert Genat, page 7. Diseconomies of scale in banking are discussed on page 4 of a special supplement section of the May 20, 2006 issue of *The Economist* titled "Thinking Big." Data on the relative costs of airlines are from page C3 of the *New York Times* of April 27, 2002 in a news story that began on page C1 under the title "U.S. Airways Ready to Test Federal Loan Program." The survey of airline quality was published in the May 14, 2001 issue of *BusinessWeek* on page 14. Information on the rising circulation in the McClatchy newspaper chain is from page C1 of the September 19, 2005 issue of the *New York Times* in an article titled "Even a Darling of the Newspaper Industry Is Starting to Sweat a Bit." The quotation from the Indian entrepreneur is from page 266 of *India Unbound* by Gurcharan Das. The fact that Soviet farms were ten times the size of American farms and employed more than ten times as many people is from page 117 of *The Turning Point* by Nikolai Shmelev and Vladimir Popov. Other data and comments on the efficiency of Soviet enterprises are from the same book. The practices of Soviet tractor drivers are discussed on page 184 of *The Age of Delirium: The Decline and Fall of the Soviet Union* by David Satter.   Howard Johnson's pioneering in restaurant franchising is discussed on page 51 of *Fast Food: Roadside Restaurants in the Automobile Age* by John A. Jakle and Keith A. Sculle. A news story about fancy hotels renting rooms for less than the price at more modest hotels was in the *Wall Street Journal* of July 19, 2001, on page B1 under the title, "Deluxe Travel at Discount Prices." A similar story appeared in the same newspaper on August 10, 2001, pages W1 and W9, under the title "Peak Season, Off-Peak Prices." The rebound of prices in 2004, when there were fewer empty hotel rooms, was discussed in a story beginning on page D1 of the July 6, 2004 issue of the *Wall Street Journal* under the title, "Hotels Raise Prices As Travel Picks Up" by Christina Binkley. Discount prices by cruise lines with excess capacity were discussed on pages D1 and D2 of the October 29, 2003 issue of the *Wall Street Journal* under the title, "Luxury Cruises At Discount Prices." The discussions and analysis of middlemen in West Africa are from pages 22 through 27 of *West African Trade* by P.T. Bauer. Gunnar Myrdal's opposite conclusions are from page 89 of his book *Asian Drama*, abridged edition, published in 1972 by Vintage Books. Soviet enterprises' tendency to make things for themselves, rather than get them from specialized producers, is discussed on page 135 of *The Red Executive* by David Granick. Chinese firms that supplied their own transportation services are discussed on pages 28-31 of the *Far Eastern Economic Review* of July 25, 2002 under the title, "The Perils of Delivering the Goods." The huge inventories in the Soviet Union, compared to those in Japan or the United States, were discussed on pages 133 to 137 of *The Turning Point* by Shmelev and Popov. The high levels of inventory carried in some sub-Saharan African regions are discussed on page 14 of *West African Trade* by P.T. Bauer. The inventory practices of the Chrysler division of DaimlerChrylser were reported on page C2 of the March 15, 2003 issue of the *New York Times* under the title, "Uncertain Economy Hinders Highly Precise Supply System." The Soviet official who complained about a lack of tires for their motor vehicles was quoted on page 83 of *The Wisdom of Henry Hazlitt*.

CHAPTER 7: BIG BUSINESS AND GOVERNMENT

The epigraph is from page 171 of *Economic Sophisms* by Frederic Bastiat. The government of India's restrictions on businesses' output were discussed on pages 99, 174 and 175 of *India Unbound* by Gurcharan Das. The differing costs of producing electricity to run a dishwasher at different times are discussed on page 112 of the March 26, 2001 issue of *BusinessWeek*, in a column titled "How to Do Deregulation Right." Riots in India over electricity rates are mentioned on page 46 of an article titled "Impossible India's Improbable Chance" in the book *The World in 2001*, published by the British magazine, *The Economist*. Data on the trucking industry are from pages 435 and 436 of an article titled "Trucking Deregulation" in *The Fortune Encyclopedia of Economics*. Data on airlines are from pages 379, 380 and 381 of an article in the same book by Alfred E. Kahn titled "Airline Deregulation." The decline of air fares after European airlines were deregulated is discussed on pages 44 and 45 of the May 8, 2006 issue of *BusinessWeek* in an article titled "A Closer Continent." The U.S. Supreme Court anti-trust cases referred to included, respectively, *Federal Trade Commission v. Morton Salt Co.* (1948), *Standard Oil Co. v. Federal Trade Commission* (1951), *United States v. Borden Co.* (1962), *Brown Shoe Co. v. United States* (1962), *United States v. Von's Grocery Company* (1966). *United States v. Aluminum Co. of America* (1945) was decided by the 2nd Circuit Court of Appeals. The financial asset restrictions under India's Monopolies and Restrictive Trade Practices Act are discussed on page 169 of *India Unbound* by Gurcharan Das. The division of air and rail traffic between Madrid and Seville was shown on page 267 of *Industries in Europe*, edited by Peter Johnson. Data on the division of Transatlantic passengers between ocean liners and airplanes is from page B4 of the October 2, 2003 issue of the *Wall Street Journal*, in an article beginning on page B1 under the title, "Cunard's Grand Gamble." The city of Munich's switching its computers from using Microsoft Windows to using Linux was reported in *The Times* of London under the headline "Need to Know" by Tom Bawden, Ingrid Mansell and Neelam Verjee (downloaded from the Internet). The shift from petroleum oil to corn oil for making plastics was discussed on page B1 of the *Wall Street Journal* of October 12, 2004 under the title, "One Word of Advice: Now It's Corn." The economic effects of India's Monopolies and Restrictive Trade Practices Act and its repeal in 1991 are discussed in *India Unbound*, pages 159-170, 183-184,

220, 263-264. The discussion of the effect on India's largest company, Tata Industries, is based on information from an article in the February 14, 2005 issue of *Forbes* magazine titled "Tempest in a Teapot," beginning on page 118.

CHAPTER 8: AN OVERVIEW

The epigraph is from page 241 of *The Seven Fat Years* by Robert L. Bartley. *Forbes* magazine's report on Toyota's costs and profits is from page 75 of an article that began on page 72 of the April 14, 2003 issue, under the title "The 'Ooof' Company." The statement that Toyota's profits were greater than those of Detroit's Big Three is from page 10 of the January 29, 2005 issue of *The Economist* under the title "The Quick and the Dead." Data on the hours spent producing a car and the rate of defects are from page 117 of the November 17, 2003 issue of *BusinessWeek*, in an article titled "Can Anything Stop Toyota?" *BusinessWeek's* comment on Wal-Mart is from page 102 of the cover story of its October 6, 2003 issue. The information on the McDonald's restaurant chain is from *Fast Food* by John A. Jakle and Keith Sculle, pages 58 and 146-147, from *McDonald's: Behind the Arches*, revised edition (1995), by John H. Love, Chapters 1-4, and from page 222 of *Masters of Enterprise: From John Jacob Astor and J. P. Morgan to Bill Gates and Oprah Winfrey* by H. W. Brands. Lenin's estimate of how easy it was to run an enterprise was from his book *The State and Revolution,* written on the eve of the Bolshevik revolution. His later change of mind is from "The Fight to Overcome the Fuel Crisis," "The Role and Functions of Trade Unions Under the New Economic Policy," "Five Years of the Russian Revolution and the Prospects of the World Revolution," and "Ninth Congress of the Russian Communist Party (Bolsheviks)," all quoted from the 1951 edition of *Selected Works* by V. I. Lenin, published in Moscow by the Foreign Languages Publishing House. Examples of the kinds of detailed information about hotel services and amenities provided by trade association data can be found in *2001 Lodging Survey: Lodging Services, Facilities, and Trends*, published by the American Hotel & Lodging Association in Washington, D.C. Data on American profits as a percentage of national output (Gross Domestic Product) are from page 65 of *The Economist* of December 8, 2001, under the title "What Doth It Profit?" The quotation about service differences in India is from page 112 of *India Unbound* by

Gurcharan Das and the comment on India's bank tellers is from page 6 of a supplement to *The Economist* of February 22, 1997, titled "A Survey of India: Time to Let Go." The McDonald's practice of making unannounced inspections of the suppliers of their hamburger meat and the potatoes used for French fries is from pages 130 and 131 of *McDonald's* by John F. Love. Kroc's insistence on stringent cleanliness inside, outside and around each restaurant is detailed on pages 142 to 144 and page 147. Henry J. Heinz's competitive advantages from selling unadulterated horseradish are discussed on pages 52 and 53 of *Brand New: How Entrepreneurs Earned Consumers' Trust from Wedgwood to Dell* by Nancy F. Koehn. Woolworth's early travails are recounted in the first three chapters of *Remembering Woolworth's* by Karen Plunkett-Powell. The decline in the number of pay telephones was reported in the May 14, 2001 issue of *BusinessWeek* on page 16. JetBlue Airlines' taking over gates at Kennedy Airport once occupied by Pan American Airways was mentioned on page 12 of the September 2003 issue of *Consumers' Research* magazine under the title, "The Low-Cost Future of Air Travel."

CHAPTER 9: PRODUCTIVITY AND PAY

The epigraph is from page 149 of *The Wisdom of Henry Hazlitt*. Comparisons of labor productivity in Japanese-owned and Chinese-owned cotton mills in China are from page 47 of *The Rise of "The Rest"* by Alice Amsden. Comparisons of American-owned manufacturing firms in Britain and British-owned manufacturing firms were made on page 52 of the October 12, 2002 issue of *The Economist* under the title, "Blame the Bosses." Higher labor productivity in South African firms than in firms in some other countries is mentioned on page 51 of the January 14, 2006 issue of *The Economist* under the title, "Spend More but Wisely." Data on Americans' changing incomes between 1975 and 1991 are from pages 8 and 22 of the 1995 *Annual Report* of the Federal Reserve Bank of Dallas. Earlier studies indicating similar patterns include *Years of Poverty, Years of Plenty* by Greg Duncan et al. Similar changes in individual incomes in continental European countries were reported on page 5 of *Poor Statistics: Getting the Facts Right About Poverty in Australia* by Peter Saunders, published in April 2002 by the Centre for Independent Studies in Sydney, Australia. Similar data on incomes in Britain and New Zealand were reported on pages 32 and 33 of *Poverty and Benefit Dependency* by David Green, published in 2001 by the New Zealand Business Roundtable, and similar data from Canada appeared in an article titled "Time Reveals the Truth about Low Income," which appeared on pages 24-26 of the Summer 2001 issue of *Fraser Forum*, published by the Fraser Institute in Vancouver, Canada. Data on American household incomes in 2001 are from page 16 of Section 4 of the January 12, 2003 issue of the *New York Times* in an article titled "Defining the Rich in the World's Wealthiest Nation," beginning on page 1 of that section. Changes in the composition of the 400 richest Americans are from pages 80 and 81 of the September 30, 2002 issue of *Forbes* magazine in an article titled "The March of the 400." The data showing 64 million people in the top 20 percent of American households and 39 million in the bottom 20 percent are from page 11 of *Income Inequality: How Census Data Misrepresent Income Distribution* by Robert Rector and Rea S. Hederman, published by the Heritage Foundation in Washington. The misleading claim that income quintiles divide the country into five equal parts was made on page 48 of *Economics Explained* by Robert Heilbroner and Lester Thurow. Data on numbers of heads of household working in high-income and low-income households in 2000 are from Table HINC 06 from the *Current Population Survey*, downloaded from the Bureau of the Census web site. The fact that the top 10 percent of American income earners worked less than the bottom 10 percent in the late nineteenth century, and just the reverse in the early twenty-first century is from page 92 of *Saving Capitalism from the Capitalists* by Raghuram Rajan and Luigi Zingales. The fact that household income rose by just 6 percent between 1969 and 1996, while per capita real income rose by 51 percent over that same span is calculated from statistics on pages C-6 and C-33 of the Census Bureau's *Current Population Reports*, P-60-203, whose individual title is *Measuring 50 Years of Economic Change*. The misguided remark from the *Washington Post* is from page 34 of its September 7, 1998 national weekly edition, in an article titled "The Rich Get Richer, and So Do the Old." The fact that 3.5 percent of American households have a net worth of one million dollars or more, and that 80 percent of American millionaires inherited nothing, is from page 3 of *The Millionaire Next Door* by Thomas J. Stanley and William D. Danko. The fact that the real income of those who had been in the bottom 20 percent in 1975 was by 1991 higher than the real income of the average American in 1975 is from page 14 of the 1995 *Annual Report*

of the Federal Reserve Bank of Dallas. The falling income share and rising real
income of households in the bottom 20 percent is documented on page 19 of *Money
Income in the United States: 2001*, which is one of the *Current Population Reports*,
number P60-218, published by the Census.   Comparisons of the incomes and
consumption of the average American and those Americans in the bottom 20
percent of income recipients are from page 17 of *Myths of Rich and Poor* by W.
Michael Cox and Richard Alm. The upward shift in the peak earning years during
the last half of the twentieth century was reported on page 16 of the 1995 *Annual
Report* of the Federal Reserve Bank of Dallas. The number of Americans working
in the Soviet Union is from page 11 of *The Turning Point* by Nikolai Shmelev and
Vladimir Popov. The fact that women who worked continuously earned slightly
more than men who did the same is from page 103 of "The Economic Role of
Women," *The Economic Report of the President, 1973*. The differences between the
earnings of women with and without children are from page 15 of a valuable
compendium of data on women in the economy titled *Women's Figures*, 1999
edition, written by Diana Furchtgott-Roth and Christine Stolba and published by
the American Enterprise Institute. Data on male predominance in work-related
deaths are from the same source, page 33. Comparison of the incomes of black,
white, and Hispanic males of the same age and IQ are from page 323 of *The Bell
Curve* by Richard Herrnstein and Charles Murray. The comparison of the incomes
of Maoris with those of other New Zealanders of comparable age, skill, and literacy
is quoted from pages 43 and 44 of *Poverty and Benefit Dependency* by David Green.
Violations of apartheid laws by employers in South Africa are discussed on pages
152 and 153 of *Capitalism and Apartheid* by Merle Lipton. Violations of these laws
by home builders in Johannesburg are discussed on page 164 of *Apartheid: A History*
by Brian Lapping. Violations of the residential aspects of the apartheid laws are
discussed on pages 112 and 113 of *South Africa's War Against Capitalism* by Walter
E. Williams—a black American economist who himself violated these laws by
living in an area set aside for whites. The round-the-clock use of trucks in mid-
twentieth century West Africa is discussed on pages 14 and 15 of *West African Trade*
by P.T. Bauer. The international sales of used cars from Japan was discussed in a
front page story in the January 8, 2004 issue of the *Wall Street Journal*, under the
title,"How Japan's Second-Hand Cars Make Their Way to Third World." Taxis in
Cameroon were mentioned on page 179 of *The Undercover Economist* by Tim

Harford. Data on the average life of capital equipment in the Soviet Union and in the United States are from pages 145-146 of *The Turning Point* by Nikolai Shmelev and Vladimir Popov.

CHAPTER 10: CONTROLLED LABOR MARKETS

The epigraph is from a column on page A10 of the *Wall Street Journal* of November 25, 2005 titled "Once Upon a Time in America." Data on the unemployment rate in South Africa and the comments on it are from page 49 of the May 28, 2005 issue of *The Economist* under the title "Unions v Jobs" and on page 4 of a special section titled "Survey of South Africa" in an article titled "Chasing the Rainbow" in the April 8, 2006 issue of *The Economist.* The fact that the average American has nine jobs between the ages of 18 and 34 is from page 79 of *Saving Capitalism from the Capitalists* by Raghuram G. Rajan and Luigi Zingales. The European Union countries' lower rates of job creation and higher rates of unemployment than in the United States are documented on page 50 of the June-September 2005 issue of Italy's *Banca Nazionale del Lavoro Quarterly Review* in an article titled "The Economists' 'Manifesto' On Unemployment in the EU Seven Years Later: Which Suggestions Still Hold?" The rioting of French students over a weakening of job security laws was reported on page A18 of the March 14, 2006 issue of the *Wall Street Journal* under the title "Les Misérables." The fact that only two percent of American workers age 25 and over earn minimum wages is from a U.S. Department of Labor publication titled *Characteristics of Minimum Wage Workers: 2004.* The unemployment rate in Switzerland in February 2003 was reported on page 100 of the March 15, 2003 issue of *The Economist.* The data from the *Wall Street Journal* about the unemployment rate in Hong Kong in 1991 was from page C16 of the January 16, 1991 issue. New government-mandated benefits for workers in Hong Kong and the higher unemployment rates after China took control are mentioned on page 45 of *Country Commerce: Hong Kong*, a report released in December 2002 by The Economist Intelligence Unit, based in New York and affiliated with the London magazine, *The Economist.* The record high unemployment rate for Hong Kong in 2003 was reported in the *Wall Street Journal Online* of June 17, 2003. The effect of Europe's government-mandated worker benefits on unemployment was discussed on page 39 of *The Economics of Life* by Gary Becker and Guity Nashat Becker. Comparisons of Canadian minimum wages and unemployment rates with those of the United States are from a monograph titled *Measuring Labour Markets in Canada and the United States: 2003 Edition* by Amela Karabegovic et al, published by the Fraser Institute. The effects of "living wage" laws in various American cities are discussed in the July 2005 issue of *California Economic Policy*, in an article titled "A Decade of Living Wages." Conflicting studies of the employment effects of minimum wages are discussed in an article titled "Employment and the 1990-1991 Minimum-Wage Hike," in the May 1995 issue of the *American Economic Review*. The denial by South African labor unions that high unemployment was due to South Africa's labor laws is from page 49 of the May 28, 2005 issue of *The Economist* in a news item titled "Unions v Jobs." A criticism of a study which claimed to "refute" the "myth" that minimum wages foster increased unemployment was published in the May 1995 issue of the *American Economic Association Papers and Proceedings* under the title, "Employment and the 1990-1991 Minimum-Wage Hike." The effects of informal minimum wages in West Africa are discussed on pages 18 and 19 of *West African Trade*, written by P. T. Bauer of the London School of Economics. A similar situation in South Africa was described on page A3 of the *New York Times* of March 13, 2004, under the title, "Low Labor Standard Leads South Africans to Export Jobs." The fact that South Africa's minimum wage law has led employers to use more capital per worker is from page 51 of the January 14, 2006 issue of *The Economist* in an article titled "Spend More but Wisely." The effect of minimum wages in reducing the employment of workers in general in various countries, and the employment of younger and less skilled workers in particular, is discussed on pages xvi, xvii, 23-24, 33-35, 45 of *What Future for New Zealand's Minimum Wage Law*, based on a study done by ACIL Economics and Policy, Pty. Ltd., and published by the New Zealand Business Roundtable. The views of economists from various countries on the effects on minimum wage laws are mentioned on pages 32-34. Conclusions for the United States are found in *Youth and Minority Unemployment*, written by Walter E. Williams and published by the Hoover Institution. The difference between adult and teenage unemployment in France is shown on a graph on page 11 of a special supplement on France in the November 16, 2002 issue of *The Economist* under the title "A Divided Self: A Survey of France." The unemployment rates for young workers in Belgium and Italy are from page A13 of the January 19, 2005 issue of the *Wall Street Journal* in a column tilted "Shall We Eat Our Young?" The fact that the lowest unemployment rate in more than 20 years for Australia's younger workers was still higher than the highest unemployment rate for the population in general was reported on page 110 of *State of the Nation*, edited by Jennifer Buckingham, and published in Australia by The Centre for Independent Studies. The use of minimum wage laws to promote racial discrimination is discussed on page 14 of *Youth and Minority Unemployment* by Walter Williams, Hoover Institution edition, and on pages 49 and 50 of *The Japanese Canadians* by Charles H. Young and Helen R. Y. Reid. Data on the changing ratio of black unemployment to white unemployment in the wake of minimum wage laws are from page 103 of *Only One Place of Redress* by David E. Bernstein. The effects of minimum wages on the employment of black teenagers are discussed extensively in *Youth and Minority Unemployment* by Walter E. Williams. The collapse of organized attempts of white employers and landowners to hold down the pay of black farmers in the American South after the Civil War, and of Japanese immigrant farmers and farm workers in California a generation later, are covered in *Competition and Coercion: Blacks in the American Economy 1865-1914* by Robert Higgs, especially on pages 47 to 49 and in Robert Higgs, "Landless by Law: Japanese Immigrants in California Agriculture to 1941," *Journal of Economic History*, March 1978, pages 207 to 209. Data on American automobile production and employment are from *Motor Vehicle Facts & Figures: 1997*, published by the American Automobile Manufacturers Association, and from pages 19, 20 and 22 of an article titled "Auto Industry Jobs in the 1980s: A Decade of Transition," which appeared in the U. S. Department of Labor's *Monthly Labor Review* for February 1992. Data on Japanese automobile production was downloaded from the web site of The Japan Automobile Manufacturers Association, Inc. (www.JAMA.org). The quotation from the *New York Times* about unions reining in their demands in the automobile industry is from a front-page article in the September 20, 2003 issue. Data on the decline of unionization is available from many sources, one being an article titled "Labor's Gains Undercut by Lingering Problems," which appeared in *The Detroit News* of July 26, 1999. The amount of hours of labor used per automobile produced by American and Japanese auto makers is from page 69 of the April 21, 2003 issue of *BusinessWeek* magazine in an article beginning on page 68 and titled, "Pick Me as

Your Strike Target! No, Me!" The quotation about the effect of an economic slump in Europe in causing employee benefits to erode is discussed on page A6 of the July 24, 2006 issue of the *Wall Street Journal*, in a news story beginning on the front page under the title, "More Flexibility in Europe's Labor Stokes a Recovery." The comment about child labor laws is from page 42 of *Give Me a Break* by John Stossel. Data on the annual hours worked in France, Japan, and the United States are from page 58 of the October 27, 2003 issue of *BusinessWeek* magazine under the title "Give This Policy the Guillotine." Information on laws mandating paid vacations and paid holidays in France is from an article titled "Working Hard or Hardly Working?" in the November 18, 2004 edition of the *Wall Street Journal Online*. The *New York Times* report about working conditions in Cambodia is from page A19 of the January 14, 2004 issue of that newspaper in a column titled "Inviting All Democrats." Rising wage rates and improving working conditions in China as a result of increasing competition for workers by multinational companies there are from pages 32 and 34 of the March 27, 2006 issue of *BusinessWeek* in an article titled "How Rising Wages are Changing the Game in China."

CHAPTER 11: AN OVERVIEW

The epigraph from Peter Bauer is from page 23 of his book *Equality, the Third World, and Economic Delusion*. International data on poverty and inequality are from pages 69 to 71 of the March 13, 2004 issue of *The Economist* in a feature article titled "More or Less Equal?" Information on China's income inequalities is from "Income Distribution in China: To Each According to His Abilities," *The Economist*, June 2, 2001, pages 39 and 44. Data on regional differences in poverty rates in India are from page 7 of a special section on India in *The Economist* of June 2, 2001. The quotation about the consequences of the transition from communist economies to market economies in Europe is from page 58 of the August 27, 2005 issue of *The Economist* under the title, "Change and Decay." The fact that most Americans living below the official poverty line owned a microwave oven and a videocassette recorder in 1994 is from page 22 of the 1995 *Annual Report* of the Federal Reserve Bank of Dallas. The fact that poor New Zealanders own VCRs, freezers, washing machines, and a vehicle is reported on page 32 of *Poverty and*

Benefit Dependency by David Green, published in 2001 by the New Zealand Business Roundtable. The estimate that a million Chinese per month were rising out of poverty is from page 3 of *The Undercover Economist* by Tim Harford. The stories of the great American fortunes created by Carnegie, Ford, Vanderbilt, etc., are widely available in numerous books but the stories of similar individuals in India are from pages 187-195, 207-210, 246-248 of *India Unbound* by Gurcharan Das. Data on long-term unemployment in various countries are from page A8 of the December 30, 2004 issue of the *Wall Street Journal*, in an editorial titled "That 'Sluggish' Economy." Data on rates of employment in Iceland and France are from international comparisons on page 74 of the September 20, 2003 issue of *The Economist*. Comparisons of labor force participation rates among 55 to 64 year olds in Switzerland and in France are from page 11 of a special supplement to the November 16, 2002 issue of *The Economist*, under the title "A Divided Self: A Survey of France." Child labor in Niger is discussed on page 144 of the December 24, 2005 issue of *The Economist* under the title "Child Labour." The fact that nearly half the billionaires in the world are in the United States is from page 132 of the March 17, 2003 issue of *Forbes* magazine. See also p. 116 of the March 27, 2006 issue of *Forbes* in an article titled "Billionaire Bacchanalia." The information that vast regions of Africa are without a single billionaire is from page 116 of the March 27, 2006 issue of *Forbes* magazine under the title "Billionaire Bacchanalia." Greater wage inequality in the United States than in a number of other countries is shown on page 6 of a monograph titled *Wage Inequality* by Francine D. Blau and Lawrence M. Kahn.

CHAPTER 12: INVESTMENT AND SPECULATION

The Economist magazine's definition of investment is from page 72 of the March 4, 2006 issue, in an article titled "Getting A Grip on Prosperity." The experiences of the Tata and Birla enterprises in India are from page 93 of *India Unbound* by Gurcharan Das. The statement that businesses in India must break laws in order to operate is from page 143 of the same book. The numerous government regulations in India are discussed on page 94. India's freeing up its economy is discussed on page 29 and the rising foreign investment that followed is discussed on page 220.

The fact that different groups within a given society tend to have qualitatively different education can be seen by reading page 63 of *Competing Equalities* by Marc Galanter, page 80 of *The Soviet Middle East* by Alec Nove and J.A. Newth, page 173 of "The Dynamics of Ethnic Inequalities: The Case of Israel," by Sammy Smooha and Yochanan Peres in Volume I of *Studies of Israeli Society*, edited by Ernest Krausz, pages 125 to 145 of *From Independence to Statehood*, edited by Robert B. Goldmann and A. Jeyaratnam Wilson, and chapters 5, 6, and 7 of *No Excuses* by Abigail Thernstrom and Stephan Thernstrom. The spread of international commodity market information in India was described in a story beginning on the front page of the *New York Times* of January 1, 2004 titled "India's Soybean Farmers Join the Global Village." The disastrous speculation in silver by the Hunt brothers is covered on pages 249-250 of *The New York Times Century of Business*, edited by Floyd Norris and Christine Bockelmann. The speculation of Henry Heinz that led to bankruptcy is discussed in *Brand New* by Nancy F. Koehn, page 321. The prediction of *The Economist* magazine that the price of oil was heading downward appeared on page 23 of the March 6, 1999 issue under the title, "The Next Shock?" The ability of Dell computers to operate with only enough inventory to last for five days was reported in the May 14, 2001 issue of *BusinessWeek* on page 38B. The fact that the ratio of inventory to sales hit a record low in the United States during the third quarter of 2003 was reported on page 42 of the October 27, 2003 issue of *BusinessWeek*, in an article beginning on page 40 with the title "Jobs: The Turning Point is Here." The quotation from *The Economist* magazine about interest rates bringing savings and investment into balance is from page 8 of a supplement to its September 24, 2005 issue titled "The Great Thrift Shift." The downgrading of California's state bonds in 2001 was covered in many places, including page A3 of the April 25, 2001 issue of the *Wall Street Journal*. The buying up of future payments due to accident victims in installments by paying a lump sum is discussed in an article beginning on the front page of the *Wall Street Journal* of February 25, 1998 titled "Thriving Industry Buys Insurance Settlements from Injured Plaintiffs." Statistics on the purchase of annuities are from page 65 of *U.S. News & World Report*, October 22, 2001, in an article titled "Betting on A Long Life." Twentieth century energy consumption and the growth of known reserves of various metals are discussed on pages 40 and 41 of an article titled "Natural Resources" in *The Fortune Encyclopedia of Economics*. Statistics on the known reserves of petroleum in various years are from Section II, Table 1 of *Basic Petroleum Data Book*, Vol. XXI, No. 1 (February, 2001), published by the American Petroleum Institute. Information on the proportion of exploratory oil wells which turn out to produce oil and on the percentage of oil extracted from pools of oil are from pages 19 and 20 of a supplement titled "A Survey of Oil" in the April 30, 2005 issue of *The Economist*. Data on the reserves of copper are from pages 12 and 13 of *A Poverty of Reason* by Wilfred Beckerman, published by the Independent Institute. The bet between Julian Simon and Paul Ehrlich was covered in the *New York Times* of December 2, 1990, Section VI, page 52, in an article titled "Betting On The Planet." Estimates of oil reserves in the Athabasca region of Canada are from p. A5 of the October 8, 2005 issue of the *Wall Street Journal* in an article titled "Is the World Running Out of Oil?" The fact that the cost of finding oil had fallen by two-thirds between 1977 and 1998 is based on U. S. Department of Energy statistics quoted on page 42 of *Julian Simon and the Triumph of Energy Sustainability* by Robert L. Bradley, Jr., published in 2000 by the American Legislative Exchange Council.

CHAPTER 13: RISKS AND INSURANCE

The epigraph is from page 174 of *The Americans: The Democratic Experience*, 1973 edition. Comparisons of the interest rates in Mexico, Brazil, and the United States are based on data in a graph on page 68 of the June 29, 2002 issue of *The Economist* in an article titled "Spreading Risk." Short-term interest rates in Hong Kong, Russia, and Turkey were reported on page 98 of the May 3, 2003 issue of *The Economist*. Rates of return on venture capital are from page C1 of the *Wall Street Journal* of April 29, 2002 in a story titled "Venture Firms Face Backlash from Investors." Information on the current value of a dollar invested in gold, stocks, and bonds in 1801 is from an article titled "Now What?" in the September 21, 1998 *Forbes Global Business & Finance*, pages 20-21. Data on real rates of return on stocks and bonds from the 1930s to the end of the twentieth century are from *The Economist*, May 5, 2001, page 7 of a special section titled "Global Equity Markets: The Rise and Fall." The fact that the 400 richest Americans lost $283 billion in one year was reported on pages 80 and 81 of the September 30, 2002 issue of *Forbes* magazine, under the title, "The March of the 400." The fact that more than 50 mutual funds have assets exceeding $10 billion was reported on page R1 of the May 1, 2006 issue of the *Wall Street Journal* in an article titled "When Mutual Funds Don't Want Your Cash." The fact that just over half of the actively managed mutual funds did better than the Standard & Poor's index in 2005 was reported on page 76 of the January 28, 2006 issue of *The Economist.* The discussion of mutual funds draws on two articles from page R1 of the April 9, 2001 issue of the *Wall Street Journal:* "Seven Reasons to Index—and to Avoid Playing Those Favorites" and "Index Funds: 25 Years in Pursuit of the Average." The fact that mutual funds as a whole lost money between early 1998 and early 2003 is from an article titled "Five Years of Feast and Famine" in the *Wall Street Journal* of June 2, 2003, beginning on page R1. The one exception is covered on the same page of the same issue under the title "Survivor: How One Fund Avoids Losses." The information about Yale's offer of student loans to be repaid according to the students' future income is from page 70 of *The Economics of Life* by Gary S. Becker and Guity Nashat Becker. Information on the number of insurance companies in the United States and their assets is from pages 507 and 508 of the Bureau of the Census publication *Statistical Abstract of the United States: 2000.* Data on the percentage of current premium income that is paid out in current claims by Allstate and State Farm insurance companies is from page C10 of the January 2, 2003 issue of the *Wall Street Journal* in an article beginning on page C1 titled "'Colossus' at the Accident Scene." The proportion of life insurance companies' income from premiums and investments is from page 81 of *Life Insurers Fact Book: 2000*, published by the American Council of Life Insurers. The quotation from *The Economist* about premiums not covering the claims on insurance companies is from page 15 of the September 18, 2004 issue, under the title, "The Storms Ahead." The fact that automobile and property insurers in 2004 made their first overall profit from underwriting alone since 1978 was reported on page 46 of the August 29, 2005 issue of *U.S. News & World Report*, in an article titled "Auto Rates Shift into Lower Gear." The evolution of federal deposit insurance in the 1930s and the half-trillion-dollar bailout of the savings & loan industry in the 1980s are both discussed in Chapter 4 of *FDR's Folly* by Jim Powell. Data on varying motor vehicle death rates by age are from page 109 of *The Insurance Information Institute Fact Book 2001.* The quotation from a City Attorney in Oakland who complained that it was unfair to charge people different automobile insurance premiums based on where they lived was from page B1 of the

San Francisco Chronicle of May 30, 2003 under the title "Car Insurance Rates Hit." Differences in prices for the same automobile insurance coverage in different cities were reported on page 47 of the August 29, 2005 issue of *U.S. News & World Report*. Data on differences in automobile insurance premiums between Manhattan and Brooklyn are from page D2 of the January 7, 2004 issue of the *Wall Street Journal*, in an article beginning on page D1 of that issue under the title "Car Premiums are Pushed Up by Rising Fraud." The U.S. Senate's 95-0 vote to forbid insurance companies from using information from genetic tests to determine coverage or premiums was reported on page D11 of the *Wall Street Journal* of October 15, 2003 under the titled "Senate Approves Bill Banning Bias Based on Genetics." The banning of different insurance charges for women and men in France, and attempts to extend the ban to the European Union as a whole, are mentioned on page 70 of the November 15, 2003 issue of *The Economist,* under the title, "The Price of Equality." The quote about the use of FEMA as insurance for an affluent beach community is from page 12 of the June 14-20 issue of *The Washington Post National Weekly Edition* in an article titled "Shoring Up Beach Towns." John Stossel's experience building and insuring an ocean-front house is discussed on pages 136 to 139 of his book *Give Me a Break.* Thousands of repeatedly damaged properties which received government insurance payments over the years that exceeded the total value of those properties are discussed on page A14 of the May 24, 2006 issue of the *Wall Street Journal* under the titled "Taxpayers Get Soaked." The use of global positioning systems by insurance companies looking for their policy-holders in the wake of natural disaster is from a story beginning on the front page of section C of the *New York Times* of September 18, 1999. The title of the story is "Headed for Trouble; Insurers Deploy Legions of Adjusters to Areas Hit by Storm." The contrast between private sector responses and governmental responses to hurricane Katrina was discussed in an editorial titled "Private FEMA" on page A18 of the September 8, 2005 issue of the *Wall Street Journal.* The Indian government's tardiness in responding to a cyclone is discussed on page 535 of Indian economist Barun S. Mitra's article, "Dealing with Natural Disaster: Role of the Market," in the December 2000 issue of *Journal des Economistes et des Etudes Humaines.*

CHAPTER 14: AN OVERVIEW

The epigraph is from a column titled "Economic Profit vs. Accounting Profit" by Robert L. Bartley on page A17 of the *Wall Street Journal* of June 2, 2003. The zero rate of savings by Canadians 30 years old and younger and the negative rate of savings by Americans in the same age bracket are from page 147 of the June-September 2005 issue of the Italian journal *Banca Nazionale del Lavoro Quarterly Review* in an article titled "Modigliani's Life-Cycle Theory of Savings Fifty Years Later." Information on Western-owned banks in Eastern Europe is from a front page story in the *Wall Street Journal* of October 5, 2005, under the title "In Eastern Europe, Western Banks Fuel Growth, Fears." The comment on the negative effects of anticipations of land reform is from page 30 of *Development Without Aid* by Melvyn B. Krauss. The economic consequences of political threats to nationalize the tea plantations in Sri Lanka were discussed on page 832 of Volume II of *Asian Drama: An Inquiry into the Poverty of Nations* by Gunnar Myrdal, first printing published in 1968 by the Pantheon division of Random House. The declining Malaysian currency and stock market after irresponsible statements by its prime minister were mentioned on page 251 of *Thunder from the East* by Nicholas D. Kristof and Sheryl WuDunn, 2001 paperback edition. Hoarding by Russian consumers and business enterprises during the 1991 inflation was discussed on pages 7 and 10 to 11 of *Kapitalizm: Russia's Struggle to Free Its Economy* by Rose Brady. The downgrading of California's state government bonds by Standard & Poor's was reported on the front page of the April 25, 2001 issue of the *San Francisco Chronicle*, under the headline: "S&P Lowers California's Bond Rating" and Moody's downgrading was reported in the *Sacramento Bee* of November 22, 2001, under the title "State's Bond Rating Lowered Again."

CHAPTER 15: NATIONAL OUTPUT

The epigraph is from page 191 of *Our Culture, What's Left of It* by Theodore Dalrymple. The fact that the money supply in the United States declined by more than one-third from 1929 to 1933 is noted on page 352 of *A Monetary History of the United States: 1867-1960* by Milton Friedman and Anna Jacobson Schwartz. The decline in real output from 1929 to 1933 is shown on page 157 of the February 2004 issue of *Survey of Current Business.* Data on unemployment in Germany and the United States during the Great Depression are from page 176 of *Global Capitalism* by Jeffry A. Frieden and page 324 of the 2006 *Economic Report of the President.* The fears of a glutted market expressed by Seymour Harris and Vance Packard are quoted from the latter's book *The Waste Makers,* pages 7 and 19. The accelerated growth of durable equipment owned by both businesses and consumers after the Second World War is documented on page 17 of the April 2000 issue of the *Survey of Current Business.* Data showing the real value of consumer durables between 1945 and 1950 more than doubling are from page 9 of the May 2004 issue of the same publication. The rises and falls in the real prices of various American consumer goods between the years 1900 and 2000 are shown on page 91 of the December 23, 2000 issue of *The Economist.* Data on the increased square footage of new houses between 1983 and 2000 are from page 29 of the November 2001 issue of *Housing Market Statistics,* published by the National Association of Home Builders. Over-estimates of inflation by the consumer price index, and the resulting under-estimates of the average Americans' real income are discussed on page 21 of *Myths of Rich and Poor* by W. Michael Cox and Richard Alm. The median ages of the populations of various countries are from page 20 of the 2006 edition of *Pocket World in Figures,* published by *The Economist* magazine. Differences between the average per capita incomes in Japan and the United States, when measured by official exchange rates rather than by the actual purchasing power of the yen and the dollar, are discussed on page 6 of the third edition of *The Illustrated Guide to the American Economy* by Herbert Stein and Murray Foss. The fact that per capita output in Japan was just three-quarters of the per capita output in the United States is from page 98 of the June 5, 2004 issue of *The Economist,* under the title "GDP per Person." The Gross Domestic Products of Norway and Portugal in 2002 were reported on page 100 of the March 15, 2003 issue of *The Economist.* Keynes' statement is quoted on page 69 of *The Economist* of January 21, 2006. Results of an international opinion survey showing a rough correlation between national prosperity and personal satisfaction were reported on page 58 of the August 27, 2005 issue of *The Economist* under the title "Change and Decay." The list of the five countries with the highest Gross Domestic Product is from page 8 of a special supplementary section on China in the October 2, 2004 issue of *The Economist* and the list of the five countries with the highest Gross Domestic Product per capita is from page 29 of the *Pocket World in Figures: 2006 Edition* published by *The Economist*. Data on the changing degrees of income inequality in the United States are from an article by Goldin and Katz titled "Decreasing (and then Increasing) Inequality in America: A Tale of Two Half-Centuries" in *The Causes and Consequences of Increasing Inequality*, edited by Finis Welch. Data on the rate of return on Standard & Poor's 500 mutual funds are from page C5 of the *New York Times* of January 1, 2004, in a story beginning on page A1. Alexander Hamilton's estimate that four-fifths of the American people's clothing were made in their own homes was cited on page 97 of *The Americans: The Democratic Experience*, 1973 edition, by Daniel J. Boorstin.

CHAPTER 16: MONEY AND THE BANKING SYSTEM

The epigraph by Irving Fischer is from page 2 of his book *Purchasing Power of Money*. The fact that the assets of American banks passed the $10 trillion mark in 2004 is from page 236 of the Spring 2005 issue of the *Federal Reserve Bulletin*, in an article titled "Report on the Condition of the U.S. Banking Industry: Fourth Quarter, 2004." The use of warehouse receipts for tobacco as money in colonial America is mentioned on page 75 of *A History of the American People* by Paul Johnson. The use of gin as currency in British West Africa was mentioned on page 233 of *The Economic Revolution in British West Africa* by Allan McPhee, second edition. The use of cigarettes as money in a prisoner-of-war camp during World War II was described by an economist who was one of those prisoners in an article in the November 1945 issue of *Economica* titled "The Economic Organisation of a P.O.W. Camp." The use of salt and bread as money in the early days of the Soviet Union was mentioned on page 8 of *The Turning Point* by Shmelev and Popov. The quote about Argentineans' resort to barter during the Argentine monetary crisis of 2002 was from page A5 of the *Los Angeles Times* of May 6, 2002, in a story that began on page A1 under the title "Where To Swap Till You Drop." The fact that a hundred-dollar bill in the 1990s had less purchasing power than a twenty-dollar bill in the 1960s is from page 47 of an article titled "Going Underground," in the September 21, 1998 issue of *Forbes Global Business and Finance*. The fact that Chinese money was once preferred to Japanese money in Japan is from page 150 of a book titled *Money*, edited by Jonathan Williams. The fact that most savings accounts in Bolivia were in dollars during that country's runaway inflation is from page 210 of an article titled "Hyperinflation," in *The Fortune Encyclopedia of Economics*, where the German hyperinflation of the 1920s is also discussed on page 208. The estimate that 80 percent of the demand for gold comes from the jewelry industry is from the *Wall Street Journal* of October 8, 2002, in a story titled "Hoarders Drive Up Gold, Despite Slump in Jewelry Sales." The rising price of gold on the day that the World Trade Center in New York was attacked by terrorists was shown on page 69 of *The Economist* of September 15, 2001 and its rise above $400 during the second Iraq war is from page C4 of the August 23, 2004 edition of the *Wall Street Journal*. The rise in the price of gold to a seventeen-year high in 2005 was reported on page C1 of the *Wall Street Journal* of October 11, 2005 in an article titled "Stocks Fall Amid Auto-Sector Woes, With Dow Off 53.55; Gold Price Shines." The quotation from John Maynard Keynes about inflation is from page 86 of the 1952 printing of his *Essays in Persuasion*. The haste of Russians to spend their rubles during that country's inflation was in a news story from the front page of the *Christian Science Monitor* of August 31, 1998 in a story titled "Russians Replay 'Bad Old Days'." Data on the 1921 inflation in the Soviet Union is from page 6 of *The Turning Point* by Nikolai Shmelev and Vladimir Popov. Russians using rubles for wallpaper and toilet paper in 1991 was reported on page 11 of *Kapitalizm: Russia's Struggle to Free Its Economy* by Rose Brady. Information on the exchange rates between dollars and marks, and the number of printing presses in use during the German inflation of the 1920s are from pages 450-451 of *Germany: 1866-1945* by Gordon A. Craig. Hitler's phrase "starving billionaires," used during the German inflation, is mentioned on page 4 of *Wilson's War* by Jim Powell. Internal differences among various goods within the consumer price index were discussed on page A2 of the April 20, 2006 issue of the *Wall Street Journal* in an article titled "Jump in Prices Stirs Rate Concerns." Data on the declining price levels in Britain and the United States from 1873-1896 are from page 8 of *Global Capitalism* by Jeffry A. Frieden. The slowing circulation of money in the United States, along with the declining amount of money, in the years following the stock market crash of 1929 is spelled out on pages 302 to 305 of *A Monetary History of the United States* by Milton Friedman and Anna Jacobson Schwartz. President Woodrow Wilson's statement about the powers and structure of the Federal Reserve System was quoted on page 3 of *A History of the Federal Reserve* by Allan H. Meltzer. The remarkable agreement of both liberal and conservative economists in the United States on the confused and counterproductive monetary policies of the Federal Reserve during the Great Depression of the 1930s can be found by comparing the accounts in *The Great Crash* by John Kenneth Galbraith (especially his comment on page 27 of the 1997 edition) and in *A Monetary History of the United States* by Milton Friedman and Anna J. Schwartz, where this point is discussed on pages 407-419. The upward shift in the Federal Reserve's discount rate in 1931 is shown on page 304 of the latter book and the collapse of thousands of American banks during the Great Depression is mentioned on page 351. The quotation from Schumpeter about the role of wages in the Great Depression is from page 181 of the March 1931 issue of the *American Economic Review*. President Herbert Hoover's use of the federal government to try to prevent agricultural prices from falling is mentioned on pages 50 and 52 of the third volume of his *Memoirs*. John Maynard Keynes' comments on the monetary policy of the British government in 1931 are from page 283 of his *Essays in Persuasion*, 1952 printing. The decline of wheat prices in the 1890s is discussed on page 13 of *Global Capitalism* by Jeffry A. Frieden. The fact that more countries went on the gold standard at the end of the nineteenth century and early twentieth century is noted on pages 16 and 17 of the same book. The number of financial institutions and merchants connected by Visa credit cards was mentioned on page C1 of the July 16, 2005 issue of the *San Francisco Chronicle* in a news story titled "Grocers, Drugstores Sue Visa USA." *BusinessWeek* magazine's comment on Federal Reserve chairman Alan Greenspan was on page 45 of the June 16, 2003 issue. The *San Francisco Chronicle* story about Wall Street reactions to the Federal Reserve's omission of a phrase is from page B1 of the January 29, 2004 issue, under the title "Fed's New Wording Worries Wall Street." The problems of Albanian and Czech banks in the post-Communist era were reported in *The Economist* of April 28, 2001 on pages 77 and 78. The fact that individuals' holdings of gold are largest in India was reported on pages 69-70 of an article titled "Foreseeing the Future" in the March 15, 2003 issue of *The Economist*.

CHAPTER 17: GOVERNMENT FUNCTIONS

The epigraph by President Lyndon B. Johnson is quoted from page 181 of *The Johnson Years: The Difference He Made* by Robert L. Hardesty, published in 1993 by the Lyndon Baines Johnson Library. The comment on the changing role of government in economies around the world is from page 10 of a book that goes into that subject at length—*The Commanding Heights*, written by Daniel Yergin and Joseph Stanislaw. The account of the airport at Kinshasa, Congo, is from page A1 of the April 30, 2002 issue of the *Wall Street Journal*, in a story titled "Kinshasa is Poor, Scary and a Boon For Air France." Police corruption in Bolivia was reported on page 37 of the May 4, 2002 issue of *The Economist* under the title "Policing the Police." The fact that both businesses and international aid agencies are taking the level of bribery and corruption into consideration when deciding where to invest and lend is mentioned on page 65 of the March 2, 2002 issue of *The Economist*. The ranking of corrupt countries is from the *Transparency International Corruption Perceptions Index of 2004*, available on-line at www.transparency.org. The reluctance of foreign companies to use Russian accountants during the czarist era is mentioned on page 187 of *Pioneers for Profit* by John P. McKay. The comment about the looting of Russian oil companies is from page 57 of *Saving Capitalism from the Capitalists* by Raghuram G. Rajan and Luigi Zingales. Bribery in Russian universities was reported in the April 18, 2002 issue of *The Chronicle of Higher Education*, in a story titled "Reports of Bribe-Taking at Russian Universities Have Increased, Authorities Say." The quote and statistic about politically linked enterprises in Russia are from page 63 of the November 1, 2003 issue of *The Economist*. The comments by Aditya Birla on the problems created by India's bureaucracy are from page 183 of *India Unbound* by Gurcharan Das. The comments by Soviet economists on the cutting down of forests without reseeding them are from page 109 of *The Turning Point* by Shmelev and Popov. Their comments about confiscation of the profits of Soviet enterprises are on page 261 and these enterprises' inability to spend these profits is mentioned on page 147. The ingenious devices used by many affluent northern California communities to prevent development are explored in articles in *Land Use and Housing on the San Francisco Peninsula: 1982 Annual*, edited by Thomas M. Hagler and published by the Stanford Environmental Law Society. The comment on bribes in China and Japan is from page 42 of *The Character of Nations* by Angelo

Codevilla. The high percentage of wallets with money in them that were turned in by people in Denmark was mentioned on page 80 of *The White Man's Burden* by William Easterly. Unpaid parking tickets by U.N. diplomats from various countries were discussed on page 11 of the August 13, 2006 *New York Times* in David Brooks' column. The ability of the Marwaris of India to rely on each other's word in business is mentioned on page 143 of *India Unbound* by Gurcharan Das and of Hasidic Jews to do the same in the New York diamond industry is covered in chapter 5 of *Diamond Stories* by Renée Rose Shield. The comment that it is not easy to make transactions among strangers in India and the examples of extraordinary efforts to prevent fraud are from page 9 of a special supplement on India in the June 2, 2001 issue of *The Economist*. The term "the radius of trust" appears on pages 79 and 80 of *The White Man's Burden* by William Easterly and restriction of Malagasy grain trading firms to the level of family enterprises is discussed on page 81 of the same book. The story of how unscrupulous landlords exploit and destroy rent-controlled apartment buildings is told on page 43 of *Zoning, Rent Control and Affordable Housing* by William Tucker and in *The Ecology of Housing Destruction* by Peter D. Salins. The high cost of officially setting up a business in Cameroon is discussed on page 188 of *The Undercover Economist* by Tim Harford. The comment by a Russian mother about her children's view of honesty is from page 3 of *Kapitalizm* by Rose Brady. The quotation about consumer frauds by investigative journalist John Stossel is from page 250 of his book *Give Me a Break*. Examples of private market ways of taking externalities into account are found in an article titled "Public Goods and Externalities" in *The Fortune Encyclopedia of Economics*, edited by David R. Henderson. The story of the genesis and consequences of President Nixon's wage and price controls is told from pages 60 to 64 of *The Commanding Heights* by Daniel Yergin and Joseph Stanislaw and from an essay by Herbert Stein in the *Wall Street Journal* of August 15, 1996, page A12. The comment that educational results "take a long time to come" is from page 313 of *India Unbound* by Gurcharan Das. The mention of a former EPA administrator's conclusions about removing toxic material is from page 11 of *Breaking the Vicious Circle: Toward Effective Risk Regulation* by Stephen Breyer. The beneficial effects of extremely minute traces of arsenic in water were discussed on page 34 of the January 19, 2004 issue of *Insight on the News* under the title, "Can Toxins Lead to Healthier Lives?" by John Pike. The effects of small and large doses of saccharin on cancer in laboratory rats are from an article beginning on page 54 of the June 9, 2003 issue of *Fortune* magazine, titled "A Little Poison Can Be Good for You." The costly cleanup of a toxic waste site in New Hampshire is discussed on pages 11 and 12 of *Breaking the Vicious Circle* by Stephen Breyer. The bad effects of the gasoline additive MTBE on ground water have been discussed in many places, including the *San Francisco Chronicle* of August 19, 2001 in a front page story titled "Congress Not Told of MTBE Dangers." The costs of U.S. government regulations on business are from a study titled "The Impact of Regulatory Costs on Small Firms" published by the Small Business Administration. Franklin D. Roosevelt's use of presidential powers created during the First World War to take the United States off the gold standard is mentioned on page 86 of *The New York Times Century of Business*.

CHAPTER 18: GOVERNMENT FINANCE

The epigraph is from the front page of a November 2004 "Policy Brief" titled "Sense and Nonsense About Federal Deficits and Debt" by Professor Boskin, published by the Stanford Institute for Economic Policy Research. Smokers' responses to higher taxes on cigarettes in Alaska are discussed on page 37 of *The Greedy Hand: How Taxes Drive Americans Crazy and What to Do About It* by Amity Shlaes. Information on reactions to New York's high cigarette tax rate is from a study by the Cato Institute, *Policy Analysis* No. 468 titled "Cigarette Taxes, Black Markets, and Crime: Lessons from New York's 50-Year Losing Battle." Data on increased revenue after a reduction in the capital gains tax are from the *Wall Street Journal* of May 14, 2001 in an article on page A18 titled "Real Relief: A Capital-Gains Tax Cut." The quotation about rising tax revenues after a tax rate cut in India is from page 200 of *India Unbound* by Gurcharan Das. Discussion of rising tax revenues after the capital gains tax rate was cut in the United States in 1978, 1997, and 2003 is from page A14 of the March 2, 2006 issue of the *Wall Street Journal* under the title "Non-Dynamic Duo." The *New York Times*' surprise over a rise in tax revenues after a cut in tax rates was expressed in a front page story titled "Surprising Jump in Tax Revenues Curbs U.S. Deficit" in their July 9, 2006 issue. Data on the national income and national debt of the United States in 2002, 1992, and 1946 are from page 375 of the *Economic Report of the President*, February 2006, published by the U.S. Government Printing Office that year. Data on the national income and national debt of the United States in 1945 are from pages 224 and 1117 of the Census Bureau publication *Historical Statistics of the United States: Colonial Times to 1970.* The statistic that 44 percent of the U.S. government's debt was held by foreigners in 2004 is from page 257 of *Analytical Perspectives: Budget of the United States Government, Fiscal Year 2006* published by the U.S. government in 2005. The *New York Times* story about a declining deficit was on the front page of the July 13, 2005 issue under the title "Sharp Increase in Tax Revenue Will Cut Deficit." Data on the costs of crime and of prisons in Britain are from page 109 of *A Land Fit for Criminals* by David Fraser. Adam Smith's comment on government spending patterns in 18th century England is from page 687 of his classic *The Wealth of Nations*, Modern Library edition. The quotation about Brazil's government workers' pension plan is from page 36 of the April 5, 2003 issue of *The Economist* in an article titled "Lula's Great Pension Battle." The New Zealand poll on the likelihood of receiving government pensions is cited on page 71 of the April-May issue of *Policy Review* in an article titled "Market Reform: Lessons from New Zealand." The discrepancies among the percentages of people aged 55 to 64 who are still working in the United States and Japan versus the European Union countries was reported on page 117 of *The World in 2004*, a publication of *The Economist* magazine.

CHAPTER 19: AN OVERVIEW

The epigraph is from page of 183 of *Armey's Axioms* by Dick Armey. Examples of various policies in India are from *India Unbound* by Gurcharan Das. On page 162, he raised the question of how the country could have gone so wrong when it had such outstanding economists. The quote about favors to special interests by India's government is from page 318 of the same book, and the quote about how new and rare free market democracies are is from page 317. The cost of the 2002 farm bill to the average American family is from the April 29, 2002 issue of *National Review* in an article titled "Twisting 'The Facts'." The argument that government policy worsened, rather than alleviated, the Great Depression can be found in *A Monetary History of the United States* by Milton Friedman and Anna J. Schwartz, pages 407-419, in Paul Johnson's *A History of the American People*, pages 737-760 and in *Out of Work* by Richard K. Vedder and Lowell E. Gallaway, pages 89-97, 137-146. That is the central theme throughout *FDR's Folly* by Jim Powell, where John Maynard Keynes' statements at the time that Roosevelt's policies were hindering recovery are quoted on pages 105, 117-118. The problems of India's nationalized banks are discussed on page 164 of *India Unbound* by Gurcharan Das. The comment that liberal democracy is based on free markets is from page 317 of the same book and the comment that India's government looks out for itself is from page 349. The economic results of the English Channel projects are from page 59 of the February 14, 2004 issue of *The Economist* under the title "Under Water."

CHAPTER 20: INTERNATIONAL TRADE

The epigraph is from pages 121 and 122 of *John Adams: A Biography in His Own Words*, edited by James Bishop Peabody. The comment from the *New York Times* about whether the United States was a "job winner" or a "job loser" from freer trade was from an article titled "Nafta and Jobs," which appeared in the November 14, 1993 issue, page 4 of section 4. The declining unemployment rate in the United States from 1993 to 2000 is shown on page 26 of a special supplement in the June 29, 2002 issue of *The Economist* under the title "Present at the Creation." The declining unemployment rate in Canada was discussed on page 14 of the January 3, 2004 issue of the same magazine in an article titled "Free Trade on Trial," which began on page 13. The increase of jobs in Mexico was reported on page A13 of the *Wall Street Journal* of March 5, 2003 and the simultaneous increase of jobs in the United States was reported on page 364 of *The Economic Report of the President*, February 2002. Justice Holmes' statement, "we need to think things instead of words" is from page 293 of *Collected Legal Papers* by Oliver Wendell Holmes. The American export surpluses during the 1930s and its lower total international trade in that decade compared to the 1920s can be calculated from data on page 864 of the U.S. Bureau of the Census publication, *Historical Statistics of the United States: Colonial Times to 1970*. The record-breaking reduction in the international trade deficit of the United States in the spring of 2001 was reported on page 35 of *BusinessWeek's* May 7, 2001 issue under the title, "A Shrinking Trade Gap Looks

Good Stateside." India's advantages in supplying computer services to American businesses are discussed on pages 57-74 of the March 2003 issue of *Banca Nazionale del Lavoro Quarterly Review* (published in Italy) under the title "Software Exporting: A Developing Country Advantage." The quoted statement about the importance of comparative advantage to poor nations is from page 218 of an article by Daniel T. Griswold titled "International Markets, International Poverty: Globalization and the Poor" in the book *Wealth, Poverty and Human Destiny*, edited by Doug Bandow and David L. Schindler. The West African example of comparative advantage among cocoa farmers is from page 68 of *The Economic Revolution in British West Africa* by Allan McPhee, published originally in 1926 and reprinted in 1971 by Frank Cass & Co., Ltd. The estimate of economies of scale in automobile production is from page 76 of *The Structure of American Industry*, ninth edition, by Walter Adams and James Brock. Pages 97 and 104 of the same book discuss job losses in the American steel industry and the job losses in the U.S. economy as a whole from trying to protect jobs in the steel industry. Statistical estimates are from page 57 of the November 15, 2003 issue of *The Economist*, in an article titled "Sparks Fly over Steel." Data on sales of automobiles and pickup trucks in the United States in 2003 are from page 16 of the Spring 2004 issue of the *J.D. Power Car Guide*. Information on automobile production in Australia is from pages 59 and 81 of *Ward's Automotive Yearbook*, 59th edition, published in 1997. Data on Australian and American populations and purchasing power in Australia are from pages 22, 24, 62, and 102 of *Pocket World in Figures 2001*, published by *The Economist*. Data on sales of *The Economist* in Britain and the United States are from page 9 of the October 30, 2004 issue of that magazine. The fact that Toyota, Honda, and Nissan all earn most of their profits in North America is from page W1 of the October 31, 2002 issue of the *New York Times*, in a news story titled "Slowdown? Don't Tell Toyota Motor." The fact that Japanese carmakers began to produce more cars outside of Japan than inside Japan was reported on page C1 of the *New York Times* of August 1, 2006, in an article titled "Japan Makes More Cars Elsewhere." Information on China's toy exports to India, and on the Tata group's response to other Chinese exports are from pages 48 and 49 of the May 3, 2001 issue of *Far Eastern Economic Review*, in an article titled, "No More Fun and Games." Holland's position as a leading international trade nation from the 1590s to the 1740s was discussed on page 2 of *The Dutch Republic* by Jonathan Israel and the high wages of

Dutch workers were discussed on pages 88-93 of *An Economic and Social History of the Netherlands 1800-1920* by Michael Wintle. Data on labor productivity in India and the United States are from page 65 of the September 8, 2001 issue of *The Economist*, under the title "Unproductive." The declining rates of return on capital invested in czarist Russia as the amount invested increased during its early industrialization are from page 139 of *Pioneers for Profit* by John P. McKay. The fact that world exports in 1933 were one-third of what they were in 1929 is from page 83 of *Against the Dead Hand* by Brink Lindsey. The appeal by more than a thousand American economists against passage of the Hawley-Smoot tariff of 1930 was reported and quoted extensively, beginning on the front page of the May 5, 1930 issue of the *New York Times* under the headline, "1,028 Economists Ask Hoover to Veto Pending Tariff Bill." The economic repercussions of the tariff are reported on pages 43 to 45 of *FDR's Folly* by Jim Powell. American job losses due to restrictions on imported sugar are discussed on page A14 of the March 6, 2006 issue of the *Wall Street Journal*, under the title "Sweet Opportunity." Foreign producers of American military equipment were discussed on page C1 of the September 27, 2005 issue of the *New York Times*, in a column titled "U.S. Weapons, Foreign Flavor." Examples of the application of anti-dumping laws in the European Union are from pages 29 to 32 of *The Race to the Top: The Real Story of Globalization* written by Tomas Larsson. The application of American anti-dumping laws is discussed on pages 173 and 174 of *Globalization and Its Discontents* by Joseph E. Stiglitz. The report that Taiwan produces most of the computer components in the world is from page 15 of a special section of the October 22, 2005 issue of *The Economist* titled "A Market for Ideas." That Asian firms rely on American, Japanese and European firms for new technology was reported on page 31 of the May 2006 issue of the *Far Eastern Economic Review* in an article titled "The Offshoring of Innovation." Data on jobs gained and lost in the United States through outsourcing are from pages 53 and 54 of the March 2004 issue of *Survey of Current Business* in an article titled "A Note on Patterns of Production and Employment by U.S. Multinational Companies."

CHAPTER 21: INTERNATIONAL TRANSFERS OF WEALTH

The epigraph is from page 115 of *The World in 2004*, published by *The Economist*. The statistic that 44 percent of the U.S. government's debt was held by foreigners in 2004 is from page 257 of *Analytical Perspectives: Budget of the United States Government, Fiscal Year 2006* published by the U.S. government in 2005. Data on remittances from the United States to Mexico are from page A14 of the *New York Times* of October 28, 2003, under the title "A Surge in Money Sent Home by Mexicans." Data on worldwide remittances are from page 116 of the November 26, 2005 issue of *The Economist* in an article titled "Remittances." Data on money sent by Irish immigrants in America to members of their families in Ireland in the 1840s is from page 251 of *The Americans*, Volume III, by Daniel Boorstin. Data on international investments are from page 6 of a special section of *The Economist* of May 3, 2003, that section being titled "A Cruel Sea of Capital." The creation of American software companies in Bangalore, India, is discussed on page C3 of the March 20, 2006 issue of the *New York Times* in a news story titled "Is the Next Silicon Valley Taking Root in Bangalore?" The production of the ten millionth Toyota in the United States was reported on page W1 of the October 31, 2002 issue of the *New York Times*, in a story titled "Slowdown? Don't Tell Toyota Motor." Data on payments earned by the United States from royalty and license fees from other countries are from page 77 of the December 2001 issue of *Survey of Current Business*. Data on payments earned for all services supplied to other countries are from page 49 of the November 2001 issue of the same publication. The comment on the trade deficit is from page A12 of the February 1, 2005 issue of the *Wall Street Journal*. The comparison of the trade deficit of the United States with that of other countries is from page 19 of the April 8, 2006 issue of *The Economist* in an article titled "Still Waiting for the Big One." The fact that a balance of payments surplus preceded the 1992 recession is from page D-20 of the December 1999 issue of the *Survey of Current Business*. Germany's export surpluses, slower growth rates, and higher unemployment rates than the United States are mentioned on page A12 of the January 10, 2005 issue of the *Wall Street Journal* under the title, "The German Disease." The fact that the United States received more than twice as much foreign investment as any other country was reported on page 91 of *The World in 2004*, a publication by the British magazine *The Economist*. Data on foreign acquisitions of assets in the United States are from page 59 of the April 2004 issue of *Survey of Current Business.* The fact that 66 percent of foreign investments in the United States came from Europe was reported on page 33 of the June 2006 issue of the *Survey of Current Business* in an article titled "Foreign Direct Investment in the United States." The $1.3 trillion total international debt of the United States at the end of 2001 was reported on page 14 of the July 2002 issue of *Survey of Current Business.* The fact that France, Britain, and Japan have large net foreign investments was reported on page 89 of the July 1, 2006 issue of *The Economist,* under the title "Foreign Direct Investment" and the foreign investments of Switzerland were reported on page 99 of the December 7, 2002 issue. Data on foreign ownership of American railroads in the nineteenth century are from page 195 of *The History of Foreign Investment in the United States to 1914,* written by Mira Wilkins. Information on the over-all amount of foreign investment in nineteenth-century America, and on the railroads' majority share of foreign investment in American stocks and bonds are from pages 463 and 466 of "U. S. Foreign Financial Relations in the Twentieth Century" by Barry Eichengreen in *The Cambridge Economic History of the United States,* Volume III: *The Twentieth Century,* edited by Stanley L. Engerman and Robert E. Gallman. The fact that foreign investors in the early twentieth century owned one-fifth of the Australian economy and one-half of the Argentine economy was reported on page 20 of *Global Capitalism* by Jeffry A. Frieden. Information on Americans producing more than one-third of all the manufactured goods in the world in 1913 is from page 142 of *The History of Foreign Investment in the United States to 1914,* cited above. Page 38 of Myron Weiner's 1995 book, *The Global Migration Crisis* is the source of the statement that remittances from citizens living abroad exceed all the foreign aid from all the government agencies in the world. The role of foreigners in various British industries and in finance is discussed on page 69 of *Alien Immigrants to England* by W. Cunningham and on pages 325-340 of *The Persecution of Huguenots and French Economic Development: 1680-1720* by Warren C. Scoville. The statement by Fernand Braudel that immigrants created modern Brazil, Argentina, and Chile is from page 440 of his book *A History of Civilizations.* The economic role of the Lebanese in Africa is discussed on page 309 of "The Lebanese in West Africa," by R. Bayly Winder, which appeared in Vol. IV, No. 3 (April 1962) of *Comparative Studies in Society and History.* The economic role of the Greeks in the Ottoman Empire is discussed on pages 262-263 and 266 of "The Transformation of the Economic Position of the *Millets* in the Nineteenth Century," by Charles Issawi, which appeared in Volume I (*The Central Lands*) of *Christians and Jews in the Ottoman Empire: The Functioning of a Plural Society*, edited by Benjamin Braudel and Bernard Lewis. The economic role of the Germans in Brazil is discussed in Chapter 2 of *Migrations and Cultures* by Thomas Sowell and the role of the Chinese in Malaysia and the Indians in Fiji are discussed in Chapters 5 and 7 of the same book. The role of the British in Argentina is discussed throughout *British-Owned Railways in Argentina: Their Effect on the Growth of Economic Nationalism, 1854-1948* by Winthrop R. Wright. The role of the Belgians in Russia is discussed on page 35 of *Pioneers for Profit* by John P. McKay. Cambodian ownership of most doughnut shops in California is discussed in a front page story in the February 22, 1995 issue of the *Wall Street Journal* under the title "How Cambodians Came to Control California Doughnuts." The fact that most doctors in Britain are foreign was reported in the October 25, 1998 issue of the British newspaper *The Independent*. The Spanish cleric who supported expulsion of the Moriscoes was quoted on page 795 of *The Mediterranean and the Mediterranean World in the Age of Philip II*, Vol. II by Fernand Braudel, 1973 English translation. Data on the emigration of educated people from various countries is from page 94 of the April 2, 2005 issue of *The Economist*. Differences in the percentage of immigrants on welfare are from page 126 of *The Debate in the United States over Immigration*, edited by Peter Duignan and Lewis H. Gann. The percentage of the world's land inhabited by Western Europeans and the additional percentage controlled by them in their overseas colonies is from page 87 of *The Dynamics of Global Dominance* by David B. Abernethy. Data on American investments in the Netherlands and in Africa in 2001 are from page 20 of the February 2003 issue of *Survey of Current Business* and data on foreign earnings from assets owned in the United States in 2001 are from page 10 of the same issue. Data on the sources of foreign investment in the United States are from page 31 of the June 2005 issue of *Survey of Current Business* in an article titled "Foreign Direct Investment in the United States." The positive growth rates of poor countries that are more "globalized" and the negative growth rates of those that are not are from *The Economist* of December 8, 2001, under the title "Going Global." The percentage of Latin American businesses owned by multinational companies in 1991 and 2001 is from page 97 of *The World in 2004*. The fact that foreigners took nearly $270 billion out of the American economy in 2001 is based on data on page 10 of the February 2003 issue of the *Survey of Current Business*. The quotation from two Soviet economists on the USSR's importation of capitalist technology is from page 49 of *The Turning Point* by Shmelev and Popov. P. T. Bauer's comment on foreign aid is from page 102 of his book *Equality, the Third World and Economic Delusion*. The estimate that only one person in ten works in a legally recognized enterprise in a typical African nation is from an article titled "Poverty and Property Rights," on pages 20 to 22 of the March 31, 2001 issue of *The Economist*. The estimate of the number of illegally built homes in Egypt is from page 20 of *The Mystery of Capital* by Hernando de Soto and the value of the illegally produced wealth in Peru is from pages 33 and 34. Peddlers who became founders of major companies like Levi Strauss, Macy's, etc. are discussed in Chapter 6 of my *Migrations and Cultures*, where further specific citations of sources can be found in the end notes. Robert Mundell's comment on the era of the gold standard is from his lecture at the Central Bank of Uruguay in May 2002 and J. P. Morgan's comment on gold was quoted on page 41 of *The New York Times Century of Business*. The varying exchange rates between the dollar and the euro have been discussed in many places, including two news stories beginning on page C1 of the *New York Times* of May 20, 2003 and an article in the May 19, 2003 issue of *BusinessWeek* magazine titled "Beware the Super Euro." The quotation about the effect of Britain's pound sterling "weakening" against the Euro is from page 52 of the May 19, 2003 issue of *BusinessWeek* magazine, under the title "The Wonderful Falling Pound." The effect of the "strong" Norwegian krone on purchases of groceries from Sweden was reported on page 42 of the August 31, 2002 issue of *The Economist*, under the title "Have Car-Boot, Will Travel."

CHAPTER 22: AN OVERVIEW

The epigraph is from page 3 of *Economic Sophisms* by Frederic Bastiat, reprinted in 1997 by the Foundation for Economic Education, Inc. The public opinion poll on protectionism and free trade was mentioned on page 56 of *The Race to the Top: The Real Story of Globalization*, written by Tomas Larsson. The estimated costs of protectionism in the European Union countries are from page 62 of the same book. The statistics on the number of steel workers and the number of workers in steel-using industries are from page 229 of *Saving Capitalism from the Capitalists* by Rajan and Zingales. The respective costs of producing steel in the United States, Germany, Japan, Brazil, and South Korea were published on page 61 of *The Economist* of March 9, 2002. Professor Jagdish Bhagwati's experience debating at Cornell is from pages 8 and 9 of his book *Free Trade Today*. Joseph Stiglitz's criticisms of the International Monetary Fund are found, among other places, in his book *Globalization and Its Discontents*. Data on the increasing role of international trade in the American economy is from page 76 of *Saving Capitalism from the Capitalists* by Rajan and Zingales. Information on the role of foreign investments in the economic development of the United States is from "U. S. Foreign Financial Relations in the Twentieth Century," by Barry Eichengreen in *The Cambridge Economic History of the United States*, Vol. III: *The Twentieth Century*, edited by Stanley L. Engerman and Robert E. Gallman. Standard and Poor's downgrading the rating of India's currency was reported in the August 11, 2001 issue of *The Economist*, in an article titled "Slaves of the State." The report on failed development projects in Niger is from a front page story in the May 10, 2002 issue of the *Wall Street Journal*, under the title "The Radio Offers Africans Rare Aid in Tune With Needs." The role of entrepreneurs and professionals from India in other countries is explored in Chapter 7 of *Migrations and Cultures* by Thomas Sowell. The National Bureau of Economic Research study showing that East Asian firms with substantial foreign ownership had higher productivity than domestically-owned firms is titled "Global Links Raise Asian Countries' Productivity" from the August 2002 edition of the *NBER Digest*.

CHAPTER 23: MYTHS ABOUT MARKETS

The epigraph is from page 35 of *Essays in the Philosophy of Science* by Charles Sanders Peirce, in an article originally published in *Popular Science* magazine in 1878. The quotation about prices as barriers to consumption was Joseph Schumpeter's characterization of popular notions and appeared on page 118 of *Essays of J. A. Schumpeter*, edited by R. V. Clemence. Information on prices at various California grocery stores is from page 47 of the Winter/Spring 2001 issue of *Bay Area Consumers' Checkbook* and from the Fall 2003/Winter 2004 issue of the same magazine. Comparisons of prices and service at computer stores are from pages 75, 77 and 78 of the Spring/Summer 2004 issue of *Checkbook*. The higher prices charged through the General Motors employee benefits plan were discussed in the February 15, 2005 issue of the *Wall Street Journal* in a story beginning on page B1 under the title "Generic Drugs by Mail Can Be a Raw Deal" by Barbara Martinez. The quote from Gary Becker that he did not know of any documented example of predatory pricing is from page 163 of *The Economics of Life* by Gary S. Becker and Guity Nashat Becker. The quote from India's Prime Minister Nehru about the number of brands of toothpaste is from page 153 of *India Unbound* by Gurcharan Das. Josiah Wedgwood's pioneering in the use of brand names on consumer products was discussed on page 33 of *Brand New* by Nancy F. Koehn and Henry Heinz's pioneering in the use of brand names for processed foods on pages 59 and 60. The role of McDonald's in pioneering higher standards for French fries, hamburgers and milk shakes is from Chapter 6 of the revised 1995 edition of *McDonald's: Behind the Arches* by John F. Love. The fact that Soviet consumers had used bar codes to identify the makers of various products is from page 7 of a special section on consumers (titled "Crowned at Last: A Survey of Consumer Power") in the April 2, 2005 issue of *The Economist*. The adverse comments about businessmen from Adam Smith are from the Modern Library edition of *The Wealth of Nations*, pages 128 and 250. The quote from David Ricardo is from page 123 of Volume III of *The Works and Correspondence of David Ricardo*, edited by Piero Sraffa and published by Cambridge University Press. The fact that the bulk of agricultural subsidies go to big corporations, rather than to family farmers, can be verified from many sources, including *The Structure of American Industry* by Walter Adams and James Brock, 9th edition, page 29. Business support for President Nixon's wage and price controls is mentioned on page 149 of *The Suicidal Corporation* by Paul Weaver. Harvard's endowment of $25 billion was reported on page 33 of the Almanac section of *The Chronicle of Higher Education*, Vol. 53, No 1. Information on fees charged by non-profit organizations is from an interview with Peter Drucker that was published in the March/April 1999 issue of *Philanthropy* on page 11. Adam Smith's comments on the self-indulgences of professors are from page 718 of his classic *The Wealth of Nations*, Modern Library edition. Pre-World War II discrimination against blacks and Jews by non-profit organizations is discussed on pages 695 and 705 of "Through the Back Door: Academic Racism and the Negro

Scholar in Historical Perspective" in the Summer 1971 issue of *Daedalus*, on page 480 of *American Democracy* by Harold J. Laski and on page 323 of *An American Dilemma* by Gunnar Myrdal. The controversial practice of non-profit organizations selling the right to use their logos to commercial businesses is discussed in a *New York Times* story beginning on page A1 of their May 3, 1999 issue under the title, "Marketing Tied to Charities Draws Scrutiny From States." The salaries of symphony orchestras' musical directors were revealed on the front page of Section 2 of the July 4, 2004 issue of the *New York Times* under the title "The Plight of the White-Tie Worker." The outsourcing of college and university operations to commercial businesses was discussed in articles beginning on the first page of Section B of the January 28, 2005 issue of *The Chronicle of Higher Education.* The non-profit organization whose admission to not having a doctor or scientist on its staff was discussed in a January 2004 publication of the Capital Research Center titled "The Environmental Working Group: Peddlers of Fear" by Bonner R. Cohen. The McDonald's chain's early brushes with bankruptcy are discussed on pages 175–181, and 199 of *McDonald's: Behind the Arches* by John F. Love.

CHAPTER 24: "NON-ECONOMIC" VALUES

The epigraph is from page 131 of *My Times: Adventures in the News Trade* by John Corry. *BusinessWeek*'s survey of philanthropic entrepreneurs appeared in the November 28, 2005 issue, beginning on page 59. The fact that Americans make larger donations per capita to charitable causes than Europeans is from page 78 of the March 13, 2004 issue of *The Economist.* That Americans also donate more than three times as high a percentage of the country's output to philanthropic causes than do the Swedes, the French or the Japanese is mentioned in the February 25, 2006 issue of *The Economist*, on page 4 of a special section titled "The Business of Giving." The comment that the marketplace was "amoral" and the mayor of Stockton's comment that "life-sustaining" water could not be entrusted to private enterprise are from page 11 of the February 9, 2003 issue of the *San Francisco Chronicle Magazine* in an article titled "Water Profit on Tap?" The report on the privatization of the municipal water supply in Argentina is from page 68 of the March 22, 2003 issue of *The Economist* under the title "Raise a Glass." Comparisons of the private water system in England with the government-owned water system in Scotland are from page 56 of the May 31, 2003 issue of *The Economist*, under the title "Frozen Taps." The exchange between an official in India and an Indian entrepreneur trying to get him to reduce excise taxes is from page 234 of *India Unbound* by Gurcharan Das. The fact that videocassette recorders initially sold for $30,000 each is from page 139 of *Culture and Prosperity* by John Kay. The complaint that newspapers have to meet profit requirements determined by "faceless Wall Street analysts" is from a letter to the editor of *Editor & Publisher* magazine, published on page 4 of the October 8, 2001 issue. The *New York Times* reporter's statement that "you cannot expect magnanimity from the marketplace" is from page 27 of the January 18, 2004 issue of the *New York Times Magazine*, in an article titled, "A Poor Cousin of the Middle Class." The rise of an estimated million people per month out of poverty in China was reported on page 3 of *The Undercover Economist* by Tim Harford. Price controls in West Africa were discussed on page 33 of *West African Trade* by Peter Bauer. Data on the financial costs of natural disasters and their costs in human lives in various countries are from page 116 of the March 20, 2004 issue of *The Economist*. Estimates of the value that people put on their lives, and of the costs of saving lives in various ways, are both from page 7 of a special supplement titled "Living Dangerously" in *The Economist* of January 24, 2004. The suggestion that the government should provide jobs for the unemployed doing work "to satisfy pressing social needs" appeared on page 4 of Section 3 of the February 12, 2006 issue of the *New York Times* in an article titled, "Chasing Full Employment."

CHAPTER 25: PARTING THOUGHTS

The epigraph is from page 239 of *The Road to Serfdom* by F.A. Hayek, 1972 edition. The quotation from Paul Johnson is from page 138 of *The Quotable Paul Johnson* published in 1994 by Farrar, Straus and Giroux.

INDEX